English Composition and Grammar

BENCHMARK EDITION

John E. Warriner

Third Course

 Harcourt Brace Jovanovich, Publishers

Orlando   San Diego   Chicago   Dallas

THE SERIES:

English Composition and Grammar: Introductory Course
English Composition and Grammar: First Course
English Composition and Grammar: Second Course
English Composition and Grammar: Third Course
English Composition and Grammar: Fourth Course
English Composition and Grammar: Fifth Course
English Composition and Grammar: Complete Course

Annotated Teacher's Edition and Teacher's Resource Book for each above title

CORRELATED SERIES:

English Workshop: Introductory Course
English Workshop: First Course
English Workshop: Second Course
English Workshop: Third Course
English Workshop: Fourth Course
English Workshop: Fifth Course
English Workshop: Review Course

Composition: Models and Exercises, First Course
Composition: Models and Exercises, Second Course
Composition: Models and Exercises, Third Course
Composition: Models and Exercises, Fourth Course
Composition: Models and Exercises, Fifth Course
Advanced Composition: A Book of Models for Writing, Complete Course

Vocabulary Workshop: Introductory Course
Vocabulary Workshop: First Course
Vocabulary Workshop: Second Course
Vocabulary Workshop: Third Course
Vocabulary Workshop: Fourth Course
Vocabulary Workshop: Fifth Course
Vocabulary Workshop: Complete Course

John E. Warriner taught English for thirty-two years in junior and senior high schools and in college. He is chief author of the *English Composition and Grammar* series, coauthor of the *English Workshop* series, general editor of the *Composition: Models and Exercises* series, and editor of *Short Stories: Characters in Conflict.* His coauthors have all been active in English education.

To the Student

The title of this textbook is *English Composition and Grammar*. Let's consider briefly the meaning of the two words *composition* and *grammar*.

The word *composition* means "putting together." When you speak and write, you are thinking and putting words together to express your ideas. You compose sentences in this way, and you compose essays and stories by grouping sentences.

Much in this book will help you to speak better, but another important purpose of this book is to help you to write better. Unlike speaking, which you learned before you went to school, writing is something that you learned in school, where you first encountered the need for it. To learn how to write, you must study and practice. Written sentences must be more carefully composed than spoken ones. Writing requires more careful organization than informal speaking. You are not aware of paragraphs and paragraph structure when you carry on a conversation, but you must understand the structure of a paragraph if you are to write clearly. Writing requires other skills—punctuation, capitalization, and spelling, for example.

Grammar is a description of the way a language works. It explains many things. For example, grammar tells us the order in which sentence parts must be arranged. It explains the work done by the various kinds of words—the work done by a noun is different from the work done by a verb. It explains how words change their form according to the way they are used. Grammar is useful because it enables us to make statements about how to use our language. These statements we usually call rules.

The grammar rule that the normal order of an English sentence is subject-verb-object may not seem very important to us, because English is our native tongue and we naturally use this order without thinking. But the rule would be very helpful to people who are learning English as a second language. However, the rule that subjects and verbs "agree" (when the subject is plural, the verb is plural), and the rule that some pronouns (I, he, she, we, they) are used as subjects while others (me, him, her, us, them) are used as objects are helpful rules even for native speakers of English.

Such rules could not be understood—in fact, they could not be formed—without the vocabulary of grammar. Grammar, then, helps us to state how English is used and how we should use it.

With the aid of the grammar explained in this book, the rules of composition, and the practice exercises provided, you will be able to improve your English.

J.W.

CONTENTS

2. Writing Paragraphs   42
STRUCTURE AND DEVELOPMENT

5. Writing Persuasive Compositions 155

LETTERS TO THE EDITOR, PERSUASIVE
COMPOSITIONS

Picture the Possibilities: IDEAS FOR WRITING IW1

Part Two: COMPOSITION: Writing and Revising Sentences

---

10. Writing Complete Sentences 301
SENTENCE FRAGMENTS AND RUN-ON SENTENCES

11. Writing Effective Sentences 313
SENTENCE COMBINING AND REVISING

Part Three: Tools for Writing and Revising

GRAMMAR

12. The Parts of Speech 341
THE WORK THAT WORDS DO

USAGE

17. The Correct Use of Verbs 495
PRINCIPAL PARTS, REGULAR AND IRREGULAR VERBS

18. The Correct Use of Pronouns 518
NOMINATIVE AND OBJECTIVE USES

19. The Correct Use of Modifiers 539
COMPARISON AND PLACEMENT

20. A Glossary of Usage 557
COMMON USAGE PROBLEMS

MECHANICS

Part Four: RESOURCES FOR WRITING AND STUDYING

Part Five: SPEAKING AND LISTENING

PART ONE

COMPOSITION:
The Writing Process

CHAPTER 1

Writing and Thinking

THE WRITING PROCESS

Writing is more than putting words on paper; it is a *process,* or series of stages. In this chapter you will learn and practice the stages of the writing process and the critical thinking skills needed for making decisions at each stage.

THE WRITING PROCESS

PREWRITING—Identifying your purpose and audience; choosing a subject; considering attitude and tone; limiting the subject; and gathering and ordering information

WRITING A FIRST DRAFT—Expressing your ideas in sentences and paragraphs

EVALUATING—Making judgments about the content, organization, and style of a draft

REVISING—Improving the content, organization, and style

PROOFREADING—Checking the revised version to correct errors in grammar, usage, and mechanics

WRITING THE FINAL VERSION—Preparing a final version and proofreading it

PREWRITING

Prewriting is all the thinking and planning you do in order to be able to express your ideas in sentences and paragraphs. You may take notes or make an outline at this stage, but basically you are preparing to write. Most prewriting takes place before you write your first draft. Occasionally, however, you will find yourself returning to this stage even when you are in other stages of the writing process.

During the prewriting stage you need to make several important decisions: *Why am I writing?* (purpose) *For whom am I writing?* (audience) *What will I write about?* (subject) *What will I say?* (content) *How will I say it?* (language). Understanding and making sound decisions about each of these questions will help you produce strong writing.

IDENTIFYING PURPOSE AND AUDIENCE

1a. Determine your purpose for writing.

Most writing has one of four basic purposes: to tell a story (a letter to a friend about your surprise party), to explain or to inform (a recipe for a special rice and vegetable dish), to describe (a composition describing a city of the future), or to persuade (a letter to the editor urging readers to clean up vacant lots in the neighborhood).

A piece of writing may have more than one purpose, but you can usually identify the main one. A movie review, for example, may describe the film's setting and characters and tell part of the story. Its main purpose, however, is to give information about the quality of the movie.

Not all writing fits precisely into one of the four basic categories. Keeping a diary, for example, is usually a means of self-expression. Most of the writing you will do in school and in the business world, however, will have one of the four basic purposes.

Before You Write. Consider your purpose for writing. Is it

- To tell a story? A composition about the day you learned to dive
- To explain or to inform? An essay-question answer explaining kinetic energy
- To describe? A composition describing a city of the future
- To persuade? A poster encouraging students to join a club

EXERCISE 1. Identifying Purposes for Writing. Identify the purpose or purposes you would have in writing about each of the following topics.

1. Why students should be required to pass a competency exam before graduating from high school
2. What happened when you went for your first job interview
3. The benefits of swimming
4. What your school halls are like between classes
5. Why your school should have a dress code

1b. Identify the audience for whom you are writing.

You always write for some reader or readers—an audience. Both the ideas you include and the language you use in your writing are affected not only by your purpose but also by this intended audience. Audiences vary widely—in age and background, in knowledge and interests, and in opinions and feelings. Your audience may be yourself (in a journal), a close friend or relative (in a personal letter), acquaintances (in a report on your school's fund-raising efforts), or strangers (in a letter to the editor of a newspaper). Your teacher may specify a particular audience for a classroom assignment, or you may be expected to assume that your teacher and classmates are your audience.

Before You Write. Ask yourself the following questions about your audience:

- What does the audience already know about the topic?
- What does the audience want or need to know about the topic?
- What language is appropriate for this audience: simple words and sentences, or complex ones?
- Does the audience have any strong opinions or feelings about the topic? What are they? Could these views affect how you write about your topic?

EXERCISE 2. Identifying Purpose and Audience. List at least five different pieces of writing that you have read during the past two weeks. (You might include, for example, news items in a magazine, a sports column in a newspaper, or a set of instructions for playing a game.) Identify the main purpose and the intended audience of each piece of writing.

CRITICAL THINKING:
Analyzing Purpose and Audience

When you analyze, you divide a whole into its parts to see how the parts are related. Analyzing purpose and audience helps you make decisions about the content and language for your writing.

To understand how purpose affects the content you include, consider a paragraph about starting a freshwater aquarium. If your purpose is to inform, you might provide specific details on the equipment needed and the steps involved.

EXAMPLE   To start a freshwater aquarium, spread a layer of natural or colored gravel on the bottom of a glass tank, and fill the tank with tap water. You will need to add special chemicals so that the fish will not be killed by the chlorine in tap water. A chemical filter may be placed inside the tank or hung from the back of the tank. Because fish become agitated in bare, undecorated tanks, you should add real or artificial rocks and plants for decoration.

If, however, your purpose is to tell a story, you might provide specific details that would interest and amuse your audience.

EXAMPLE   Last winter my sister and I began saving our money to buy a freshwater aquarium. Every Saturday we'd go to the pet store and choose the fish we'd take home when we had enough money. Agreeing on which fish we'd buy wasn't hard, but we couldn't agree on what to name them. My sister liked everyday "people" names, like Michael, Angela, and Edward, but I preferred romantic, fantastic names, like Periambra and Loassha. We argued so much about what to name future fish that we finally decided not to buy an aquarium. We spent the money we'd saved for it on cassette tapes instead.

These two examples also show how your audience affects the language you choose. The first paragraph, written for an audience unknown to the writer, uses fairly formal language. The second paragraph was written for an audience made up of the writer's friends; it uses informal language.

EXERCISE 3. Analyzing the Audience for a Paragraph. The following paragraph about predicting earthquakes was written for *Smithsonian* magazine. Do you think the readers of this magazine are children, teen-agers, or adults? What special knowledge does the writer assume they have? Does the writer seem to think they have a special interest in science? Use specific details from the paragraph to explain your answers.

The scientists face not only virtually impossible technical problems—they cannot afford to instrument all of the earth's fault systems with creepmeters, tiltmeters, and level lines—but knotty ethical issues as well, for the consequences of an erroneous prediction could be serious indeed. One bad prediction could cause unnecessary pandemonium; a series of them could produce the same effect as the boy who cried "Wolf!"

EXERCISE 4. Analyzing Audiences for a Particular Topic and Purpose. Read the following information about a persuasive paper. Then answer in writing the four questions about the paper's audiences.

Topic: Why a proposed rock concert to be held in a city park should be approved

Purpose: To persuade

Audiences: (a) Homeowners from the area next to the park, (b) your friends, (c) members of the city council, and (d) members of a symphony orchestra

1. Which audience would probably be most familiar with the topic? Least familiar?
2. For which audiences would terms need to be defined? Which terms should be defined for these audiences?
3. Which audiences would need background information? What would this information be?
4. Which audiences might have strong feelings in favor of the topic? Against the topic? What might these feelings be?

CHOOSING A SUBJECT

1c. Use your own or others' experiences to choose a subject to write about.

Your Own Experiences

Many of your own experiences can provide you with subjects to write about. Even subjects that are part of everyone's experiences may seem unique and special if they are described effectively in writing.

People you have known: Look at a friend or relative as though you had never seen that person before.

Trips and vacations: Remember someone special you met, some unusual incident, some ordinary place that impressed you—one person, one town, one motel, etc.

Hobbies and skills: Tell what the hobby means to you, what you know about your hobby, or what suggestions you would give someone else about it.

Ideas and information: Tell what you think, and use facts you know to support your thoughts.

Something you have owned: Remember a pet, a hat, a book, or something seemingly useless; show why it was special.

The Experiences of Others

You do not always have to write about things you know first-hand. You can use outside sources to expand your experiences. Look for subjects in the experiences of other people.

Talk to people.   About their views, the way they got started in their careers, their special experiences

Look around.   For out-of-the-ordinary places in your neighborhood, community, or a nearby city

Read.   About anything that interests you, interesting expressions or quotations, points you disagree with

EXERCISE 5. Choosing Subjects for Writing.   Answer the following questions in writing. Then look back at your answers and circle five subjects you are interested in writing about.

1. What three famous people would you most like to meet? Why?
2. If you could live at any other time (past or future) and in any other place, when and where would you live?
3. What are the subjects or activities that you are an expert on? Which ones would you like to learn more about?

4. If you had a thousand dollars, how would you spend it?
5. What careers strike you as being exciting or interesting? Why?

EXERCISE 6. Writing About an Experience. Do any one of the following activities that interests you. Write about the activity and share it with your class.

1. Describe the oldest or most unusual building in your neighborhood or in your town.
2. Ask the oldest resident in your neighborhood or town what the area used to be like and how that person came to live there.
3. Interview an artist, musician, or skilled worker. Ask how that person got started and what advice he or she would give to a young person interested in the same kind of work.
4. What exciting moments does one of your school's coaches remember? What are this coach's hopes for the future?
5. Read any five consecutive issues of a weekly news magazine published in the year you were born. What picture do they give of American life in those days?

1d. Choose a subject that is appropriate for your audience.

The subject you choose should be appropriate to the age, background, and interests of your audience. Your classmates, for example, would have little interest in Social Security, while an explanation of how to skateboard would probably not appeal to older adults.

EXERCISE 7. Choosing a Subject Appropriate for an Audience. Decide whether each subject is appropriate for the audience indicated. Be prepared to explain your answers.

1. How to find out about college financial aid—seventh-graders
2. How to choose a day-care center—parents of young children
3. The need for calcium—readers of a local newspaper

4. The bombing of Pearl Harbor—an American history class
5. Pollution in local wells—area homeowners

1e. Consider your attitude toward the subject and the tone you want to express.

Once you have chosen a subject, decide on the attitude you will take toward it. A writer's attitude can make even an ordinary subject appealing. Many good writers, for example, take the attitude that seemingly commonplace people, objects, and events are interesting if they are looked at more closely or from a different angle than usual. Your attitude, or feeling about your subject, will be reflected in the *tone* of your writing.

Tone is revealed by the language a writer chooses. The following paragraph, for example, is about an ordinary subject— the writer's dog Kelly. What is Jean Kerr's attitude toward Kelly? How does her attitude help make Kelly seem special? How does her language reveal her attitude?

> I never meant to say anything about this, but the fact is that I have never met a dog that didn't have it in for me. You take Kelly, for example. He's a wire-haired fox terrier and he's had us for three years now. I wouldn't say that he was terribly handsome, but he does have a very nice smile. What he doesn't have is any sense of fitness. All the other dogs in the neighborhood spend their afternoons yapping at each other's heels or chasing cats. Kelly spends his whole day, every day, chasing swans on the millpond. I don't actually worry because he will never catch one. For one thing he can't swim. Instead of settling for a simple dog paddle like everybody else, he has to show off and try some complicated overhand stroke, with the result that he always sinks and has to be fished out. Naturally, people talk and I never take him for a walk that somebody doesn't point him out and say, "There's that crazy dog that chases swans."
>
> JEAN KERR

Your tone, or expressed attitude, should be appropriate to your topic and purpose. Tone may be serious or humorous, formal or informal, personal or impersonal. In the paragraph about Kelly, for example, the writer's humorous tone is appropriate to her topic, Kelly, and to her purpose, to tell an amusing story.

LIMITING THE SUBJECT

1f. Limit your subject so that it can be covered adequately in the form of writing you choose.

In this book, the word *subject* refers to a broad area of knowledge; the word *topic* refers to a limited subject—one that can serve as the basis for a particular form of writing, such as a paragraph or a composition. "Baseball," for example, is a subject; "Jackie Robinson's impact on major-league baseball" is a limited subject, or a topic.

In general, the broader the topic, the longer the writing. A topic for a paragraph, for example, must be limited enough so that it can be covered adequately in several sentences. A topic for a composition must be limited enough so that it can be covered adequately in several paragraphs.

EXERCISE 8. Recognizing Subjects and Topics.   Study the following list. Place each item into the category that you think most suitable: (a) subjects, (b) topics suitably limited for a paragraph, (c) topics suitably limited for a composition of five or more paragraphs. Label each item *a, b,* or *c.* Be prepared to explain your choices.

1. Benefits of playing video games
2. Safety precautions for swimmers
3. Five dangerous diets
4. Why all students should take home economics
5. Interesting people
6. The most annoying commercial on TV
7. Classrooms I have known
8. Characteristics of an outstanding school marching band

9. The Summer Olympics
10. Development of the mechanical heart

CRITICAL THINKING:
Analyzing a Subject

Dividing a subject into its smaller parts can help you find topics for writing. Depending on the particular subject, you can analyze it on the basis of such divisions as time periods, examples, features, places, uses, and causes.

EXAMPLES   1. Subject divided into time periods
            Subject: Television
            Topics: TV's early years
                        TV in the 1980's
                        TV in the future
         2. Subject divided into examples
            Subject: Computer voices
            Topics: Computer voices for directory
                        assistance
                        Computer voices at check-out
                        counters
                        Computer voices to alert car drivers
         3. Subject divided into features
            Subject: Pueblo Indians
            Topics: Pueblo Indian government
                        Pueblo Indian history
                        Pueblo Indian art

   Sometimes the topics you find in this way will be suitably limited for the form in which you are writing. At other times, however, you will need to divide the topics themselves into smaller parts. In the following diagram, notice how the topics become progressively more limited. The three topics at the bottom—"traditional pottery," "contemporary pottery," and "Maria Martinez"—are all limited enough for a composition. A further division, "the black-on-black pottery of Maria Martinez," is limited enough for a paragraph.

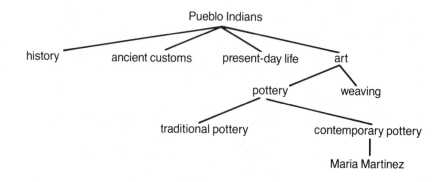

EXERCISE 9. Analyzing Subjects to Find Topics. From the following list of subjects, choose the five that most interest you. Analyze each subject by dividing it into at least three smaller parts. Be prepared to explain the basis on which you made each division (time periods, features, uses, etc.).

1. Space travel
2. Medical research
3. Ancient civilizations
4. The American Revolution
5. Cars
6. Sports
7. Movies
8. Art
9. Fads
10. Music

EXERCISE 10. Analyzing a Subject to Find Topics for Paragraphs. Choose one of the subjects that you analyzed for Exercise 9. Could each of the topics you listed be covered adequately in a paragraph of several sentences? If not, divide the topics further to find at least three topics that could be covered in a paragraph. Show your work in the form of a diagram like the one at the top of this page.

GATHERING INFORMATION

1g. Gather information according to your purpose.

Your purpose for writing determines the kind of information you need to gather. To describe the masses of people who jam

Chicago's Lincoln Park on the Fourth of July, for example, you would collect details that would help your readers picture the crowd—sights, sounds, and smells. To explain how lasers are used in modern surgery, on the other hand, you would look for facts about and examples of laser surgery.

The following techniques will help you realize what you already know about a topic as well as what you need to find out about it.

Direct and Indirect Observation

(1) Use your powers of observation.

All writing is based on observation, either direct or indirect. *Direct observation* involves firsthand experiences through the senses: sight, hearing, taste, touch, and smell. Specific sensory language enables readers to re-create the writer's sense impressions in their own minds.

One student, for example, decided to describe the scene outside his front door. Concentrating on noticing sights, sounds, smells, and textures that he had never noticed before, he made the following list of specific sensory details:

the swoosh of traffic from a nearby expressway
the banging noises and rancid smells of a passing garbage truck
a neighbor's window box with a single red geranium with brown-edged leaves drooping over the side
a tired-looking young woman carrying a crying child and pulling a shopping cart
warm, humid air; smoky, overcast sky

Indirect observation involves looking at, listening to, or reading about someone else's experiences. One student, for example, asked her aunt, a computer programmer, some questions about how she had gotten started in her job. The student used the answers to write a paper about the training and skills needed to become a computer programmer.

CRITICAL THINKING:
Observing Specific Details

Observation means carefully noting the specific details that make up an experience. For example, you may have seen cartoons that challenge you to find missing or inaccurate details in a scene—perhaps one of a room with people in it. At first glance, most people see nothing wrong with the picture. Only after observing the picture closely do they notice the three legs on a chair, the woman with one sleeve on her coat, and an upside-down moustache on one of the men.

When you observe, pay attention to as many specific details as possible. Sharpening your powers of observation will prove useful as you gather information for writing.

EXERCISE 11. Testing Your Powers of Observation. Answer the following questions without looking around the room or around the school.

1. Is there a bulletin board in the classroom? If so, what is it made of? What items are on it?
2. Is there overhead lighting in the room? If so, where? What do the fixtures look like?
3. How many students in the room are males? Females?
4. What do the cleaning materials used in the school smell like? Where and when can you smell them?
5. How many times during the school day do bells ring? How is the fire alarm different from the end-of-period bell?

A Writer's Journal

(2) Keep a writer's journal.

A writer's journal is an excellent source of ideas for public writing. In it, you can write about anything that interests, amuses, or puzzles you.

Before You Write. Keep a journal in which you record the following subjects:

- Things that you experience or observe
- Your reactions to people and events
- Observations on how people behave
- Things that make you glad, angry, or sad
- Brilliant ideas
- Opinions about music, movies, TV, or books
- Questions to which you would like to find the answers
- Quotations or sayings that you think are true
- Things that you value

When you keep a journal, you can look back through it for topics to write about and for specific details to include. As you read the following excerpt from a journal, notice the specific details that the writer includes and think about how they might be used as a source for writing.

Evenings were spent mainly on the back porches where screen doors slammed in the darkness with those really very special summertime sounds. And, sometimes, when Chicago nights got too steamy, the whole family got into the car and went to the park and slept out in the open on blankets. Those were, of course, the best times of all because the grownups were invariably reminded of having been children in the South and told the best stories then. And it was also cool and sweet to be on the grass and there was usually the scent of freshly cut lemons or melons in the air. Daddy would lie on his back, as fathers must, and explain about how men thought the stars above us came to be and how far away they were.

I never did learn to believe that anything could be as far away as *that*. Especially the stars . . .

LORRAINE HANSBERRY

The writer could use the details and information in this journal entry in many ways. If she merely wanted to describe those summer evenings, she could use many of the sensory details—

sights, sounds, feelings—that are already there. She could also use the entry as a starting point for something else, perhaps an explanation of how air conditioning has changed America or a fictional account of a storyteller in a city park. In any case, the journal entry is a good source of material for writing.

EXERCISE 12. Analyzing a Journal Entry. Read the following journal entry, and answer the questions that follow it.

> Mom's birthday last night. Grandpa, Uncle Buzzy, Aunt Sue came for dinner. I baked a cheesecake. We sat around the dining room table for a long time—laughing and talking. Grandpa told stories about when he first came to America. In New York City in 1918, he lived with his cousin's family. His cousin's husband got Grandpa a job in a clothing factory. Worked six days a week from 7:30 a.m. to 7 p.m. Wow—I wonder when workers started working from 9 to 5.

1. List the details the writer included that make the journal entry a source of ideas for writing.
2. List at least five additional specific details the writer might have included.
3. On the basis of this journal entry and the specific details you listed, suggest four limited topics the writer might use: two for a paragraph and two for a brief composition.

EXERCISE 13. Writing Journal Entries. Begin to keep a writer's journal. Every day this week, write an entry in a separate notebook, which will become your writer's journal.

Brainstorming and Clustering

(3) Use brainstorming and clustering.

Brainstorming and clustering are techniques that stimulate a free flow of thinking. To **brainstorm,** find a place where you can concentrate and follow these steps:

1. Write any subject at the top of a sheet of paper.
2. Jot down any ideas that come to mind.

3. Do not stop to evaluate, or judge, what you write.
4. Keep going until you run out of ideas.

Only when you have finished brainstorming should you stop to evaluate what you have listed. Decide which of the items might be possible topics for writing and then circle them. The circled topics may make you think of other ideas.

Here are some brainstorming notes on "video games."

my favorite games	newest video games
video arcades	competition
family tournaments	improved concentration
highest scores	develop eye-hand
dangers of playing	coordination
video games	

Clustering (or making connections) produces a diagram instead of a list. To **cluster,** begin by writing a subject in the center of a piece of paper and drawing a circle around it. Concentrate on the circled subject, and write around it whatever related ideas come to mind. As one idea leads to another, draw a line and add another circle.

One student's cluster diagram looked like this:

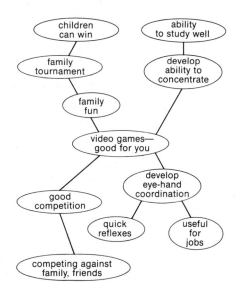

EXERCISE 14. Using Brainstorming or Clustering. Choose one of the topics you found for Exercise 10, or choose another topic. Use brainstorming or clustering to gather information about the topic.

Asking Questions

(4) Use questioning strategies.

Six basic questions called the *5 W-How?* questions can help you gather information about your topic: *Who? What? Where? When? Why?* and *How?* Although not all of the questions apply to every topic, they can help you think of others to ask.

EXAMPLE   *Topic:* Why video games are good for you
                        Who? My family, my friends, and I
                        What? Playing video games
                        Where? At home and in video arcades
                        When? During free time
                        Why? Because it's fun, develops concentration and eye-hand coordination, a good way for families to share time

EXERCISE 15. Using the *5 W-How?* Questions. Use the *5 W-How?* questions to gather information about one of the following topics or a topic of your own. Write the questions that you ask as well as the answers to the questions. (You may need to do some research to find the answers.) Some of the *5 W-How?* questions may not apply to your topic.

1. Advantages of cassette tapes over records
2. Early life of a famous musical performer
3. Types of bicycle races available in the community
4. An ideal camping weekend
5. My oldest relative

Another questioning method is to consider your topic from three different points of view. This technique is based on ideas in *Rhetoric: Discovery and Change,* by Richard E. Young,

Alton L. Becker, and Kenneth E. Pike (New York: Harcourt Brace Jovanovich, 1971).

1. *What is it?*

For the first point of view, you focus on the topic itself. If your topic is a place, person, or object, you may ask questions that will bring out information about what it looks like, what it does, and how it is different from others of its kind.

EXAMPLE   *Topic:* The street where I live [What is the name of the street? Where is it? What does it look like? Is it a busy street or a quiet street? How is it different from other streets?]

2. *How does it change or vary?*

For the second point of view, you focus on how the topic changes in time. Questions for this point of view help bring out information about the topic's history and its future.

EXAMPLE   *Topic:* The street where I live [How has the street changed? What did it look like fifty years ago? Twenty years ago? Five years ago? How will the street change in the future? What will the street look like in ten years? In a hundred years?]

3. *What are its relationships?*

For the third point of view, you focus on how the topic's various aspects, or parts, are related to each other and to the topic as a whole.

EXAMPLE   *Topic:* The street where I live [How does the street relate to the other streets in town? Who uses the street—local residents, business traffic, trucks? How important is this street to our town? How does it affect the lives of the people who live there?]

EXERCISE 16. Using the Point-of-View Questions.   Using the three different points of view, gather information about two of the following topics. Write all of the questions that you think of as well as your answers. Remember that the three points of view can be summarized by the questions *What is it? How does it change or vary?* and *What are its relationships?*

1. A specific community (neighborhood, town, or city)
2. A school club or organization
3. A specific building
4. A person you know well
5. A body of water

CLASSIFYING AND ORDERING INFORMATION

1h. Classify and arrange your ideas and information.

Once you have gathered and listed details on your topic, the next step is to *classify,* or group, them. This group will, in effect, become an informal outline of your topic.

> *Before You Write.* Use the following questions to classify your information.
>
> - Are any of the items similar in some way? What do they have in common? What larger heading would explain how they are related?
> - Do some of the items seem more important than others? Which are the most important (or main) ideas?
> - Which items seem to be subdivisions (examples, parts, etc.) of the main ideas? If you have not listed any of these subdivisions, what do you think they might be?

CRITICAL THINKING:
Classifying Information

When you classify, you identify details that are similar in some way, and you group them together under a heading that explains what they have in common. Here is how one writer grouped information on the topic "Requirements for obtaining a driver's license."

EXAMPLE   Written test
    Tests knowledge of road signs, laws, and safety
    measures
    Based on material in driving instruction manual
   Vision test
   Driving test
    Demonstrate ability to drive safely
    Demonstrate ability to make right and left turns
    Demonstrate ability to parallel-park
   Age requirements
    Age requirements vary in different states
     In this state, age 18 for driver's license
     In this state, age 16 for learner's permit
   Payment of fee for four-year license

EXERCISE 17. Classifying Information.   Classify the items on the following list under these two main headings:

Dangers of exposure to the sun
How to protect yourself against skin cancer

 Sunscreen to be used during exposure to sun
 Avoid exposure 10:00 A.M.–3:00 P.M.—ultraviolet rays strongest
 Very fair skin, maximum protection (SPF 8–14) or ultra protection (SPF 15 +) sunscreen
 Damage to skin (wrinkling and drying of skin)
 Increases chances of skin cancer
 Fair skin, extra protection (SPF 6–7) sunscreen
 Light to medium skin, minimal protection (SPF 2–3) sunscreen
 Dark brown or black skin, minimal protection (SPF 2–3) sunscreen
 Any mole or other spot on skin that is getting darker or larger or itches—see doctor right away

Your next step is to arrange your ideas in the order in which you will discuss them. Often, the order will depend on your purpose. For example, to explain how to assemble the parts of a model airplane, you would follow chronological (time) order. To persuade your audience to join a club, you might arrange your ideas with the most important reason last.

If your purpose or the ideas themselves do not suggest an order, choose an arrangement that you think will be clear to your audience. You will learn more about the different types of order in Chapter 2.

REVIEW EXERCISE A. Following the Steps for Prewriting.
Prepare to write a paragraph on a topic of your choice:

1. Decide on your purpose and audience.
2. Choose a subject, and limit it to a topic that can be covered adequately in a single paragraph.
3. Determine your attitude and tone.
4. Gather information, using at least one of the techniques on pages 15–21, and make a list of specific details to include in your paragraph.
5. Classify the details and arrange them in order.

WRITING A FIRST DRAFT

This stage in the writing process is sometimes called *drafting*. By this stage, you will have a clear notion of your audience and purpose. You will also have gathered much of your information and made some early decisions about how to arrange it.

WRITING A FIRST DRAFT

1i. Write a first draft, keeping your audience and purpose in mind.

As you write your first draft, keep in mind your purpose and audience. With your notes in front of you, try to express your ideas as clearly as possible. Some writers find it helpful to say each idea aloud in a sentence and then simply write the sentence. Remember that this draft is not your final version; you will revise your writing at least once.

CRITICAL THINKING:
Synthesizing Ideas for Your Writing

Synthesizing is putting together separate parts, or elements, to create a new whole. All writing involves synthesis, for writers put words and ideas together in new ways to create letters, paragraphs, compositions, poems, stories, and plays.

As you write your first draft, you will be rethinking all of your earlier decisions. You may decide that a term you earlier thought would be clear needs to be defined. You may even decide that your topic is not suitable for your audience or that you do not have enough information to make your writing interesting and specific. In these instances you will need to back up in the writing process to the point where you made the unworkable decision.

When You Write.   As you write your first draft

- Use your prewriting plans to guide your writing.
- Write freely, focusing on what you are saying.
- Consider including new ideas you discover about your topic **as** you write your first draft.
- Do not let correcting errors in grammar, usage, and mechanics stand in the way of your writing.

REVIEW EXERCISE B. Writing a First Draft.   Use the following details to write a first draft of a paragraph explaining an exhibit at the zoo to an audience of ninth-grade students. Begin your paragraph with the topic sentence given. Arrange the information in an order you think is effective. (You do not have to use all of the details.) As you write, try to express the ideas clearly. Be sure to define terms appropriately for the audience.

Topic Sentence: For three days last week, record crowds came to the zoo to stare at a new exhibit—*Homo sapiens urbanus.*

Details:
Homo sapiens urbanus = Urban Man
Played by Spanish mime named Albert Vidal; mime = actor who communicates without words
Vidal—38 years old; played Urban Man in zoos in Spain, Italy, Germany, and Switzerland
Dressed in business suit and tie
Paid $10,000 for 72 hours; many protested fee
Slept, ate, drank, watched TV, read newspapers, communicated (without words) with zoo visitors
Vidal in special exhibit area next to Galapagos turtle
No cage, no fence—yet protected from the crowds
Attendance at zoo more than doubled during three-day exhibit

EXERCISE 18. Writing a First Draft. Using the prewriting notes you developed for Review Exercise A (page 24), write a first draft of a paragraph. You may want to refer to the Guidelines for Evaluating Paragraphs (page 76) for some extra help before you begin. Be sure to keep your audience and purpose in mind as you write your draft.

EVALUATING

Any draft, even one written by a professional writer, has some weaknesses that can be corrected or improved. As a result, all writers—including you—must be able to evaluate what they have written. They must be able to separate the strengths that should be saved from the weaknesses that should be corrected.

EVALUATING YOUR WRITING

1j. Evaluate your first draft.

Evaluation is the process of making judgments, of assessing what has been done and deciding what works and what does not work. Even though you may do some evaluating while you are writing, evaluation is often easier and more effective once you have finished the first draft. Many of the problems that might block your creativity if you thought about them while you were writing can be easily addressed at this stage.

Evaluating your writing requires several rereadings of your first draft. With these rereadings, you try to pull back from what you have written, reading it as though you were a member of the audience who has never seen the paper before.

When You Evaluate. Use the following techniques to view your draft from a different perspective:

- Set your draft aside for a while and come back to evaluate it when it is not so fresh in your mind.
- Read your draft aloud, listening for missing details, missing words, or points of confusion. Try to "hear" what you have said.
- Ask a classmate or someone else you know to read your draft and look for strengths and weaknesses. (Professional writers almost always have a friend or an editor who reads and evaluates what they have written.)

For the purpose of evaluation, every paper can be divided into three aspects: *content, organization,* and *style.* Rather than trying to judge everything at once, most writers and editors find that they are more successful when they examine only one of these aspects at a time.

Content	What have you said?
Organization	How have you arranged your ideas?
Style	How have you used words and sentences?

The following Guidelines for Evaluating can be used with almost any form of writing. Use them as a checklist when you reread your draft in order to identify any problems that you should address. Then use the symbols on page 41 to mark the problems you discover, so you can locate them easily when you are ready to make improvements.

GUIDELINES FOR EVALUATING

Content

Purpose
1. Do the ideas and information included in the paper help to explain, to describe, to persuade, or to tell the story?

Audience
2. Will the audience find the paper interesting? Are unfamiliar terms explained and necessary background information supplied to help the audience understand?

Topic Development
3. Are enough information and details provided to help the audience understand the topic? Does all of the information "belong" in this paper?

Organization

Order
4. Are the ideas arranged in a way that will be clear to the reader? Is the pattern of organization appropriate for the paper?

Transitions
5. Are the ideas smoothly joined by connecting words and phrases? Are the relationships between sentences obvious, rather than confusing and unclear?

Style

Tone
6. Does the paper sound serious or light enough for the audience to accept what is said? Does the tone seem suitable for the purpose of the paper?

Sentence Structure
7. Do the sentences vary in length to avoid monotony? Do the sentences begin in different ways and follow different patterns?

Word Choice
8. Does the writing contain precise, specific words? Do the words make the meaning clear rather than general and fuzzy?

CRITICAL THINKING:
Evaluating Content, Organization, and Style

When you *evaluate,* you make judgments about your writing. Good judgments are made on the basis of carefully developed *criteria,* or standards. When you evaluate your first draft, you judge the effectiveness of the content, organization, and style on the basis of whether it helps you achieve your purpose and reach your audience. The guidelines on page 28, and those in the other composition chapters of this book, state the criteria for revising specific forms and kinds of writing.

EXERCISE 19. Evaluating a First Draft. Read the following draft and use the evaluation guidelines on page 28 to evaluate it. Number your paper as the guidelines are numbered—1 to 8. As you judge the paper, write *yes* beside the appropriate number if the guideline is met. Write *no* beside the number if the guideline is not met.

Topic: Discovery of penicillin
Purpose: To inform
Audience: Students in ninth-grade science class

Alexander Fleming, a British scientist, discovered something very strange one day in 1928. Fleming was working in his laboratory, growing cultures of bacteria in petri dishes. He had been working night and day for several weeks. He noticed that a bit of mold that had fallen into one of the cultures had destroyed all of the bacteria in the vicinity of the mold and that no new bacteria had reappeared on this site. Taking some of the mold from this culture, Fleming distributed it in a series of other cultures in order to validate these results. Fleming repeated the experiments many times. Fleming found that the mold always eradicated the bacteria. Fleming worked patiently to extract whatever it was in the mold that was destroying the bacteria. That substance is the medicine penicillin, an antibiotic, isometric compound whose formula is $C_9H_{11}N_2O_4SR$. Today penicillin is manufactured synthetically and also made from filtrates of certain molds, such as *Penicillium notatum* and *Penicillium chrysogen*. Fleming was one fantastic scientist!

EXERCISE 20. Evaluating a First Draft. Use the Guidelines for Evaluating on page 28 to evaluate the first draft that you wrote for Exercise 18 or another piece of writing. Reread your draft several times. As you reread it, keep your audience and purpose in mind and think about content, organization, and style. You may want to exchange papers with another student and use the evaluation guidelines to evaluate the other student's paper. When you return the draft, attach a paper on which you indicate which guidelines were met and which ones were not met.

REVISING

When you evaluate, you identify problems with your paper. When you revise, you make changes to improve your paper or to correct mistakes. Some writers write the first draft with little or no stopping to look back at what they have written. Others are constantly evaluating and revising, even as they write. Whatever approach you use, you will still need to find ways to improve what you have written.

REVISING YOUR WRITING

1k. Revise your first draft.

After you have stepped back and looked at your paper to locate any problems, you still have to find a way to improve it. Most of the problems that occur in writing can be corrected with one of these four basic techniques—adding, cutting, replacing, or reordering.

When You Revise. Use the following techniques to make changes:

TECHNIQUE	EXAMPLE
● *Add* Add new information, new details, new examples, new sentences, or new words.	Sequoya invented symbols for all the sounds in the *Cherokee* ⌃language.
● *Cut* Take out information, details, examples, sentences, or words.	On his last voyage to the New World, Columbus tried to find a passage ~~to the Pacific~~ through Central America.
● *Replace* Take unnecessary or unimportant information, details, examples, sentences, or words out and put something more relevant in.	The mistakes of James Buchanan, *President of the United States* ~~the Secretary of State~~ from ~~1845~~ *1856* to ~~1849~~ *1860*, all but ensured the election of Abraham Lincoln in 1860.
● *Reorder* Move information, details, examples, sentences, or words to another position.	In 1872 Thomas Edison received the first patent on an electric typewriter. Typewriters were not widely used in offices until the 1950's. However, the modern electric typewriter was not developed until the 1920's. ⓣ

These techniques can be used to solve problems with content, with organization, and with style. Notice how the techniques are used to revise the following paragraph.

Topic: Regulations for Olympic archery competition
Purpose: To explain
Audience: General young adult

Olympic archery competition takes place

over a four-day period. ~~This competition~~ is   replace

and

strictly regulated. Each archer shoots a total

of 288 arrows. Because different competitors   add

aluminum

use the same target, the arrows are color-

coded ~~in order to tell whose shots are whose~~.   replace *easily.*

so that officials can determine the score

Arrows may travel at speeds up to one hun-

dred and fifty miles an hour. ~~There are com-~~   cut

~~petitions for both men and women.~~ Archers   reorder

shoot a total of 72 arrows from each of four

different distances (90, 70, 50, and 30 meters   ⓣ.

for the men; 70, 60, 50, and 30 for the women).

Each archer shoots for six hours a day and

has ~~to make three shots within two and a half~~   replace

a strict time limit.

~~minutes.~~ The colored targets contain ten dif-

ferent colored rings. The bull's eye in the   add

An arrow that hits

center ~~is gold colored and~~ is worth 10 points.   cut

The outer ring of the target is worth 1 point.

The following chart shows how the revision techniques can
be combined with the evaluation guidelines (page 28) to solve
problems in any draft. In the other composition chapters, you
will find charts that show how the revision techniques can be
used with each form and kind of writing.

REVISING A DRAFT

PROBLEM	TECHNIQUE	REVISION
Content The ideas and information do not help to explain, describe, persuade, or tell the story.	Add/Cut	Add explanations, descriptive details, arguments, or narrative details. Check for ideas unrelated to the purpose and cut them.
The reader will not find the paper interesting.	Add/Replace/ Cut	Add examples, anecdotes, dialogue, or additional details. Replace details that are unrelated to the audience's interests or background.
Unfamiliar terms have not been explained.	Add/Replace	Add definitions or explanations. Replace unfamiliar terms with familiar ones.
There are not enough details and information, examples, etc. to help the audience understand what is being said.	Add	Add more details, facts, examples, etc. to support the topic.
Some of the information does not "belong" in the paper. It does not help the reader understand what the paper is about.	Cut	Cut sentences or parts of sentences that do not relate directly to what is being said.
Organization The reader will find the arrangement of ideas unclear.	Reorder	Check the order of details in your plan. Move the ideas or details to make the meaning clear.
The connections between the ideas in different sentences are not clear.	Add	Add words that will help link ideas: *this, when, then, first, these,* etc.

PROBLEM	TECHNIQUE	REVISION
Style The tone is not suitable for the audience and the purpose.	Replace	To create a lighter tone, replace formal words with less formal words (slang, contractions, etc.). To create a more serious tone, replace slang and contractions with standard vocabulary.
The sentences are monotonous.	Replace/ Reorder	Combine sentences by joining them with *and, but, for,* or *or;* by making one subordinate to the other; or by making one a modifying phrase. Change the word order so that sentences do not all begin in the same way.
The words are dull and vague. They do not make the meaning clear.	Replace	Replace words that stand for a group of things or a general idea with words that are precise and exact.

EXERCISE 21. Revising a First Draft. In Exercise 19, you evaluated the draft of a paragraph about the discovery of penicillin. Using that evaluation, revise the paragraph. Begin by identifying the strategy to be used—add, cut, reorder, or replace—to improve the specific weakness. Then, use that strategy to make the improvement.

EXAMPLE   Evaluation   An unfamiliar term is not explained.
                Strategy   *Add* a definition for technical words.
                Revision   Taking some of the mold from this culture, Fleming distributed it in a series of other cultures in order to validate, *or confirm,* these results.

EXERCISE 22. Revising Your First Draft. Using the evaluation of your first draft from Exercise 20, write a revision. Use the four revision strategies to make any needed improvements in content, organization, and style.

PROOFREADING

The stage in the writing process following revision is called *proofreading*. In the proofreading stage, you carefully reread your revised draft. Your purpose in this reading, however, is different from your purpose in previous readings. This time you look for and correct mistakes in grammar, usage, and mechanics (spelling, capitalization, and punctuation).

PROOFREADING YOUR WRITING

1l. Proofread your writing.

Good proofreaders have identified some techniques that will help you spot inaccuracies in your writing.

1. Putting your revised draft away for a day or two before proofreading helps you spot mistakes more easily.
2. Covering the lines below the one you are proofreading with a sheet of paper allows you to concentrate on each word and punctuation mark.

The Guidelines for Proofreading on page 36 apply to all forms and kinds of writing. You will also find the Symbols for Revising and Proofreading on page 41 helpful.

CRITICAL THINKING:
Applying the Standards of Written English

The purpose of proofreading is to apply the standards of written

English to your writing. These standards, which are summarized in the proofreading guidelines below, are the rules that are generally used in books, magazines, and newspapers. The main reason for applying these standards is to prevent your reader from becoming confused or, even worse, from simply refusing to read further.

EXERCISE 23. Applying the Standards of Written English. Proofread the following paragraph. Copy the paragraph, applying the standards of written English.

> When I was six my faverite aunt painted a picture for me. I still remember Aunt Cele sitting at the table in her sunny, yellow kitchen while I told her what I wanted her to put in the painting. The tiny painting which hangs above my desk today shows a two-story red brick house surrounded by a white picket fence the house sits in the middle of a grassy field with no other houses in sight. Each of the ten windows have a set of stiff white curtains, and two windows are decorated with bunchs of daffodils A little girl stands in the front yard, facing the house with it's red door and brass handle. The girls arms are full of yellow flowers.

EXERCISE 24. Proofreading a Revised Draft. Proofread the draft you revised for Exercise 22 or another paper you have revised. Use the following Guidelines for Proofreading.

GUIDELINES FOR PROOFREADING

1. Is every sentence a complete sentence, not a fragment or run-on? (pages 301–12)
2. Does every sentence end with a punctuation mark? Are other punctuation marks used correctly? (pages 594–681)
3. Does every sentence begin with a capital letter? Are all proper nouns and appropriate proper adjectives capitalized? (pages 575–93)
4. Does every verb agree in number with its subject? (pages 474–89)
5. Are verb forms and tenses used correctly? (pages 495–517)
6. Are subject and object forms of personal pronouns used correctly? (pages 520–30)

7. Does every pronoun agree with its antecedent in number and in gender? Are pronoun references clear? (pages 489–93)
8. Are frequently confused words (such as *lie* and *lay*, *fewer* and *less*) used correctly? (pages 510–15)
9. Are all words spelled correctly? (pages 682–708)
10. Is the paper neat and free from obvious corrections? (pages 37–38)

WRITING THE FINAL VERSION

Correct Manuscript Form

1m. Write the final version, following correct manuscript form.

The last step in the writing process is to prepare a clean copy of your revised and proofread draft. This will be the final version of your manuscript. (A *manuscript* is any word-processed, type-written, or handwritten paper, as distinguished from a document printed on a printing press.) Although there is no single correct way to prepare a manuscript, the following standards are commonly accepted.

1. Use lined composition paper or, if you type, $8\frac{1}{2} \times 11$–inch white paper.
2. Write on only one side of a sheet of paper.
3. Write in blue, black, or blue-black ink, or typewrite. If you type, double-space the lines.
4. Leave a margin of about two inches at the top of a page and margins of about one inch at the sides and the bottom. The left-hand margin must be straight; the right-hand margin should be as straight as possible.
5. Indent the first line of each paragraph about one-half inch.
6. Follow your teacher's instructions for placing your name, the class, the date, and the title on the manuscript.
7. If the paper is more than one page long, number the pages

after the first one. Place the number in the upper right-hand corner, about one-half inch from the top.

8. Write legibly and neatly. If you are using unlined paper, try to keep the lines straight. If you are typing, do not strike over letters or cross out words. If you have to erase, do it neatly.

9. Before handing in your final version, proofread it carefully to make certain that you have recopied accurately.

1n. Learn the rules for using abbreviations.

In most of your writing, you should spell out words rather than abbreviate them. A few abbreviations, however, are commonly used.

The following abbreviations are acceptable when they are used along with a name: *Mr., Mrs., Ms., Dr., Jr.,* and *Sr.* If they do not accompany a name, spell out the words instead of using the abbreviations.

EXAMPLES   **Mr.** Casey   **Dr.** Macmillan
                Mrs. Murphy   George C. White, **Sr.**
                I have an appointment with our family **doctor.**
                Sally Wu is organizing the picnic that the **junior** class is giving for the **seniors.**

The abbreviations A.M. (*ante meridiem*—"before noon"), P.M. (*post meridiem*—"after noon"), A.D. (*Anno Domini*—"in the year of the Lord"), and B.C. (before Christ) are acceptable when they are used with numbers.

EXAMPLES   The party is scheduled to begin at 7:30 P.M.
                Octavian (63 B.C.–A.D 14) is now known as Augustus Caesar. [Notice that the abbreviation A.D. precedes the number, and B.C. follows it.]

Abbreviations for organizations are acceptable if they are generally known.

EXAMPLES   My father gave up his weekly swim at the **YMCA** to attend the **PTA** meeting.
                I am reading a book about the **FBI;** Margaret plans

a report on a booklet published by the **UN.** [Abbreviations for government agencies are usually written without periods.]

1o. Learn the rules for writing numbers.

Numbers of more than two words should be written in numerals, not words. If, however, you are writing several numbers, some of them one word and some more than one, write them all the same way. Always spell out a number that begins a sentence.

EXAMPLES   Agnes has sold **257** magazine subscriptions.
Mother has canned **thirty-seven** quarts of peaches.
I have only **five** days in which to write **seven** reports.
There are **563** students in the freshman class, **327** in the sophomore class, **143** in the junior class, and **98** in the senior class.
One thousand five hundred band members attended the annual State Contest Festival.

Write out numbers like *seventh, fifty-third,* and so on. If they are used with a month, however, it is customary to use numerals only.

EXAMPLES   My brother graduated **second** [not 2nd] in his class at the Naval Academy.
School closes on **June 6** [or the sixth of June; not June 6th].

1p. Learn the rules for dividing words at the end of a line.

Sometimes you do not have room to write all of a long word at the end of a line. It may look better to start the word on the next line; however, if doing so would leave a very uneven right-hand margin, you should divide the word, using a hyphen after the first part. Learn the rules for dividing words (see Chapter 26). Remember that you should try to avoid dividing words if possible. Usually a slightly irregular margin looks better than a hyphenated word.

EXERCISE 25. Writing the Final Version. Write the final version of the paper you proofread for Exercise 24. Follow correct manuscript form as given in this chapter or as provided by your teacher. Proofread the final version carefully.

CHAPTER 1 WRITING REVIEW

Applying the Writing Process. As directed by your teacher, use the writing process to write a paragraph on a topic of your choice. Follow these steps as you plan, write, evaluate, and revise your paragraph:

1. Identify your purpose and audience.
2. Choose a subject.
3. Consider your attitude toward the subject.
4. Limit your subject to a suitable topic.
5. Gather information about the topic.
6. Classify and arrange your ideas and information.
7. Write a first draft, keeping your audience and purpose in mind.
8. Evaluate what you have written, looking for strengths and weaknesses.
9. Revise your draft to eliminate the weaknesses.
10. Proofread the final draft, looking for errors in mechanics and usage.
11. Follow standard manuscript form as you write a clean final version.

REVISING AND PROOFREADING SYMBOLS

Symbol	Example	Meaning of Symbol
≡	Fifty-first street	Capitalize a lowercase letter.
/	Jerry's Aunt	Lowercase a capital letter.
∧	differ$_e$nt	Change a letter.
∧	the capital ^{of} Ohio	Insert a missing word, letter, or punctuation mark.
⌐—	beside the ^{lake} river	Replace a word.
℘	Where's the the key?	Leave out a word, letter, or punctuation mark.
ℐ	an invisib⌢le guest	Leave out and close up.
⌒	a close friend ship	Close up space.
∿	thier	Change the order of letters.
(tr,)	Avoid having too many corrections of your paper on the final version.	Transfer the circled words. (Write tr in nearby margin.)
¶	¶ "Hi," he smiled.	Begin a new paragraph.
⊙	Stay well⊙	Add a period.
∧	Of course, you may be wrong.	Add a comma.
#	ice#hockey	Add a space.
⊙	one of the following⊙	Add a colon.
;	Maria Simmons, M.D. ; Jim Fiorello, Ph.D.	Add a semicolon.
=	a great=grandmother	Add a hyphen.
∨	Pauls car	Add an apostrophe.
(Stet)	On the fifteenth of July	Keep the crossed-out material. (Write stet in nearby margin.)

CHAPTER 2

Writing Paragraphs

STRUCTURE AND DEVELOPMENT

A paragraph is a group of closely related sentences. It may be long or short, a section of a longer piece of writing or complete in itself. In any case, it should clearly develop a single main point about one topic. It should stick to that point.

In this chapter you will learn about the structure and characteristics of effective paragraphs. You will also learn to use the writing process to develop your own effective paragraphs.

THE STRUCTURE OF A PARAGRAPH

THE MAIN IDEA

2a. A *paragraph* is a series of sentences that presents and develops one main idea about a topic.

Together, the sentences in a paragraph make one main idea clear. This main idea is often stated in a single sentence.

In the following paragraph, the topic is air pollution. The main idea, that burning causes this health hazard, is stated in the first sentence: the other sentences give details (specific information) that develop or support that idea.

Air pollution, a health hazard in many   main idea
American cities, occurs every time something
burns. Gasoline burned in automobiles ac-   detail 1
counts for half the pollution in the air. Oil   detail 2
burned in furnaces to heat factories and
homes is another major pollution source.
Burning garbage in incinerators and city   detail 3
dumps is a third cause of filthy air. The in-   conclusion
dustrial world could not live without fire, yet
its polluting effects continually endanger
lives.

THE TOPIC SENTENCE

2b. The *topic sentence* states the one main idea of a paragraph.

In the paragraph about air pollution, the topic sentence is the
first sentence. This sentence controls the whole paragraph: all
of the other sentences develop the idea it expresses.

    The topic sentence often comes at the beginning of a para-
graph. It may, however, appear elsewhere. In the following
paragraph, for example, the details come first; the topic sentence
concludes the paragraph.

    In the summer, hosts of big red-and-yellow grasshoppers,
with heads shaped like horses, will descend and eat holes in
all the softer leaves. Walking sticks fly like boomerangs.
Shining brown leaf-shaped palmetto bugs scurry like cockroaches. Spiders like tiny crabs hang in stout webs. The
birds snap at small moths and butterflies of every kind. A
blue racer, the snake that moves across the cleared sand like
a whiplash, will with one flick destroy the smooth, careful
cup of the ant lion in the hot sand. The whole world of the
pines and of the rocks hums and glistens and stings with life.
                           MARJORY STONEMAN DOUGLAS

Until you have had more experience in writing paragraphs, plan to make your topic sentence the first sentence. This will help you develop skill in clearly presenting and supporting a main idea.[1]

EXERCISE 1. Identifying Topic Sentences. Identify the topic sentence in each of the following paragraphs. Be prepared to discuss how the other sentences develop the main idea.

1. Wiping the sweat from his brow, it seemed to Kunta that his people were always enduring one hardship or another—something uncomfortable or difficult, or frightening, or threatening to life itself. He thought about the burning, hot days and the cold nights that followed them. And he thought about the rains that would come next, turning the village into a mudhole and finally submerging the walking paths until the people had to travel in their canoes from place to place where usually they walked. They needed the rain as much as they needed the sun, but there always seemed to be too much or too little.

    ALEX HALEY

2. Nature photography requires but two things: a reasonable level of photographic skill and a lively sensitivity to the natural world. Assuming that you are already possessed of an interest in nature—why else would you be inspired to photograph it?—the necessary photographic equipment and skills can be acquired with little money and lots of practice. Nature photography is not some secret specialty requiring gimmicks and arcane tricks. Chances are you can do a lot with the camera and accessories you already own if your eyes and your heart are in the right place.

    PATRICIA MAYE

3. A crude basket for large objects can be made in seconds from a palm leaf. Butt and tip are removed, and two cuts,

---

[1] In your reading, you will notice that not all paragraphs have topic sentences. Narrative paragraphs (those that tell a story) and descriptive paragraphs (those that describe) often have no topic sentences.

six inches apart, are made in the midrib. The leaf is bent at the notches, and the leaflets are twisted together on both sides of the basket. At the top of each side, the leaflets are gathered into a six-strand braid. The twist must be tight, as this is all that holds the leaflets.

GEORGE B. STEVENSON

SUPPORTING SENTENCES

2c. Other sentences in the paragraph give specific information that supports the main idea stated in the topic sentence.

In an effective paragraph, the main idea in the topic sentence is supported by three or more details in the rest of the paragraph. A paragraph with only one or two supporting details is said to have *weak development;* it simply does not give enough information to make the main idea clear.

WEAK   Computers come in all sizes. The largest computers, called mainframes, can fill one whole floor or department in an office building. Personal computers are small enough to sit on top of a desk.

STRONG   Computers come in all sizes—from gigantic to tiny. The largest computers, called mainframes, can be used by twenty or thirty people at the same time. Frequently they occupy an entire floor or department in an office building. Minicomputers are smaller than mainframes, but a minicomputer will easily fill a small office. The personal computers advertised on television are often called microcomputers. A microcomputer can be set up on a desk or table and is used by one person at a time. Journalists and engineers often carry portable microcomputers when they travel. These weigh about twenty to thirty pounds and have their own carrying cases. Recently, computers no larger than a pocket calculator have appeared in stores. These handheld computers can weigh as little as three pounds.

EXERCISE 2. Revising a Weak Paragraph. The following paragraph has weak development. Study the paragraph and the questions that follow it. Using your answers to the questions, revise the paragraph so that it has enough information to support the main idea in the topic sentence. Write your revised paragraph on a separate piece of paper.

> The neighborhood grocery store of today is, in fact, a vast warehouse of assorted goods and services. Customers can buy many products there that were once available only in hardware and department stores. In addition, shoppers can take advantage of the many services the store offers.

1. How large is the store? Does it cover a city block? With the size of what other building can you compare its size?
2. How else is the store like a warehouse? For example, are the aisles long and narrow?
3. What products does the grocery store sell that were once sold only in hardware stores? Electrical wiring? Light bulbs?
4. What are some specific products that were once sold only in department stores? For example, can you buy clothes in the neighborhood grocery store? What kinds of clothes?
5. What services are offered in the grocery store? Film developing? Appliance repair? Check cashing?

THE CLINCHER SENTENCE

2d. A *clincher*, or *concluding*, sentence may be used to summarize or restate the main idea.

In some paragraphs, especially long ones, a concluding sentence restates the main idea or summarizes the information given. A clincher sentence may also emphasize an important point or suggest a course of action. What is the purpose of the clincher sentence in the following paragraph?

> Finally, *avoid* the false economy of riding around on near-bald tires—to get the last sixteenth of an inch of wear from

them. If you are one of these "economizers," note this warning by the Tire Industry Safety Council: "A bald or near-bald tire is far more likely to skid on a wet road than one with an adequate amount of tread; *and* a tire with less than $\frac{1}{16}$ inch of tread is eighteen times more likely to blow out or be punctured than one with more than this amount of tread." Among the new federal safety regulations covering tires is a requirement that manufacturers include wear indicators which show as smooth, narrow bands across the tread so you can tell when only $\frac{1}{16}$ inch of tread remains. Look for this indicator as your tires wear down. After it appears, *you are risking your life*.

SYLVIA PORTER

The concluding sentence emphasizes an important point: that driving on a worn tire can cause a fatal accident.

Here are some other possible clincher sentences for this paragraph:

RESTATES MAIN IDEA   You will have to buy a new tire eventually; don't try to save money by driving on a dangerously worn tire.

SUMMARIZES   The appearance of a wear indicator is a signal that your tire is no longer safe.

SUGGESTS ACTION   If you want to stay alive, replace your tire as soon as a wear indicator appears.

EXERCISE 3. Writing Clincher Sentences. For each of the following paragraphs, write a clincher sentence. Try writing several different concluding sentences for each paragraph, and then choose the one you think is most effective.

1.   At Fort Dix, New Jersey, a herd of army goats has an official assignment: to eat the grass in a twenty-acre tract. The herd of goats (eleven nannies, twelve billies, and six kids) feeds at will on an overgrown, fenced-in tract around the army base's water treatment plant. Base officials predict that the goats will save them as much as $2,500 a year in labor and fuel costs.

2.   If you watch television, you may have noticed the increasing use of computer graphics, those colorful visual images that look like animated cartoons. Computer graphics are used not only in news programs but also in reports on special events such as the Olympics, Presidential elections, and space probes. Each network has its own computer graphics staff made up of artists and engineers. As many as fifty computer graphics experts use several million-dollar machines, including one that has more than five thousand color variations, to produce the striking visuals.

3.   Like many kinds of jargon (work-related terms), the vocabulary of computer technology includes familiar words that have new meanings. *Hardware,* for example, doesn't refer to pliers, wrenches, and screwdrivers. In computer terminology *hardware* is the machine itself—the terminal, display screen, keyboard, printer, and other machine accessories. A computer *program* is not the kind of program handed out at a play. It is the list of instructions that tells a computer what to do. *Memory* used to refer only to the human capacity to remember; today *memory* often refers to a computer's physical capacity to store information.

UNITY

2e. Every sentence in a paragraph should be directly related to the main idea.

A paragraph in which all of the sentences are directly related to the main idea has *unity.* Any sentence that does not relate to the main idea as it is expressed in the topic sentence should be omitted. Such sentences make the writer's ideas difficult to follow.

   As you read the following paragraph, look for the one sentence that is not related to the topic sentence.

   I never know what to do with my hands when I am in an awkward situation. For instance, when I am making an oral report, sometimes I self-consciously clasp my hands behind me so that they won't show. At other times, I hide them in my pockets and start jingling coins noisily. A good speaker does not have distracting mannerisms—such as saying "uh" at every pause, pacing back and forth, or looking out the window instead of at the audience. I can understand why Napoleon, the emperor of France, kept one hand safely buried inside his coat.

The sentence that destroys the paragraph's unity begins "A good speaker does not have . . . ." This sentence has nothing to do with the main idea of the paragraph (that the writer, when in a difficult situation, does not know what to do with his hands); therefore, it should be removed.

The best way to achieve a unified paragraph is to check each sentence against the topic sentence, both as you write and as you evaluate what you have written.

EXERCISE 4. Identifying Sentences That Destroy Unity. Read each of the following paragraphs carefully. On your paper, write the number of each paragraph. If a paragraph is unified, write *U* after its number. If it is not, write the sentence(s) you think should be omitted.

1.   The woods of any region are filled with edible plants, but don't go gathering wild plants for food unless you know what you're doing. In Appalachia, for example, you can make a delicious salad from dandelion leaves and other wild plants, such as shepherd's purse, peppergrass, curly dock, poke shoots, and wild onion, but be careful not to add too much sheep sorrel. Although it is rich in vitamin C, sheep sorrel has a high content of poisonous oxalic acid. If you look carefully in the Appalachian woods, you can find edible wild strawberries. Wild rhubarb leaves cannot be eaten raw, although the stalks are delicious when cooked. Personally, I like the combination of cooked rhubarb and strawberries.

2.   Many people worry about the effects of television on the young. According to studies, some children spend more time watching television than they spend in school. Because of this extensive passive viewing, children may not develop the

habit of reading and the ability to entertain themselves. No one worries much about radio programs, although radios can be very noisy. People also wonder about the effects of television commercials. In one year an average child will see twenty-five thousand television commercials, all planned and written by adults to make a child want things that the children in the commercial possess.

3. No one is quite sure of the origin of the scoring method used in tennis, but we do know how the word *love* (meaning "zero") got into the game. Early French tennis players chalked up scores on a blackboard, using the egg-shaped numeral zero (0) to indicate "no score." Gradually, the French came to refer to zero as *l'oeuf,* which means "the egg" and is pronounced something like "luf." When the English took up tennis, the French word for zero, *l'oeuf,* in time became the English *love.*

4. The word *phobia,* meaning "an extreme and persistent fear of an object or situation," combines with Greek and Latin roots to give a name to just about every fear imaginable. Some of the most common phobias are *acrophobia,* fear of heights, and *astraphobia,* fear of storms, lightning, and thunder. *Claustrophobia,* fear of enclosed places, makes its victims panic on elevators, subways, and buses. Many people have *iatrophobia,* fear of doctors, or *apiphobia,* fear of bees, while some suffer from *ailurophobia,* fear of cats. More serious phobias include *monophobia,* fear of being alone, and *decidophobia,* fear of making decisions. My sister Eileen has a terrible time deciding what to wear each day.

COHERENCE

2f. The ideas in a paragraph should be arranged in a logical order and clearly connected.

A paragraph in which the ideas are easy to follow has *coherence.* In a coherent paragraph, information is presented in an orderly way, and the relationship between the ideas is clear.

Logical Order

The word *logical* here means "reasonable" or "orderly." When ideas are presented in a logical order, the reader can easily follow the ideas from one sentence to the next. Three types of logical order that may be used in a paragraph are chronological order, spatial order, and order of importance.

Chronological Order

(1) Ideas may be arranged in chronological order.

It is natural to arrange the events in a story or incident in the order in which they happened—*chronological order.* Chronological order is also used to explain a process, with the steps in the process arranged in the order in which they must be carried out.

Cooking up a spicy Italian sauce for spaghetti is not difficult. The *first* step is to brown four strips of bacon in a large frying pan. *When* the bacon begins to turn brown, add one pound of ground beef and salt and pepper to taste. Stir the meat to brown it on all sides. *As soon as* the hamburger loses its bright red color, add one chopped onion and one chopped green pepper. *After* the meat is thoroughly browned, pour off the grease and add three cans of tomato paste, three cans of tomato sauce, and one tablespoon of Worcestershire sauce. You may also add one small can of chopped mushrooms from which you have drained the liquid. *Finally,* allow the sauce to simmer for at least an hour before serving.

Notice how the italicized words in the paragraph clarify the order of the steps. Such words are called *transitional expressions;* they show the relationship between ideas. The following words and phrases are often used as transitional expressions in paragraphs arranged in chronological order. (On pages 58–59, you will learn more about transitional expressions.)

after	as soon as	at last
after that	at first	at the same time
before	finally	now
before long	first (second, third, etc.)	soon
earlier	next	then

EXERCISE 5. Arranging Ideas in Chronological Order. Arrange sentences 1–6 in chronological order. Then write the paragraph, beginning with the topic sentence given.

Topic sentence: The process by which glass is made involves three basic steps.

1. Then the liquid glass is cooled.
2. First, the raw materials are mixed together in huge batches.
3. In the process of cooling, it is shaped by one of four methods: blowing, pressing, drawing, or casting.
4. These materials include large quantities of sand and small amounts of soda, lime, and other ingredients.
5. This mixture of raw materials is heated in a furnace until it becomes a syrupy mass.
6. One of the other ingredients is cullet, recycled broken glass.

EXERCISE 6. Writing a Paragraph Using Chronological Order. Use the following information to write a first draft of a paragraph in which the details are arranged in chronological order. When you evaluate your writing, check to see whether adding one or more transitional expressions would improve the clarity of the paragraph.

Topic sentence: The discovery of gold attracted so many new settlers to California that less than two years later California was admitted to the Union as a state.
Details:
December 1848—President Polk confirms discovery of gold in California
September 1850—California admitted as thirty-first state
January 1848—gold nuggets found by James W. Marshall, building a sawmill for John A. Sutter—on branch of American

River, near present-day Sacramento
By end of 1849—approximately 100,000 new settlers; called
"forty-niners"
1849—News of gold attracts people from all over world
1848—population of California before gold rush—26,000

Spatial Order

(2) Ideas may be arranged in spatial order.

If your purpose is to describe, you may want to use *spatial order* to show where objects are in relation to one another. The order that you choose (from left to right, from near to far, from top to bottom, from bottom to top, and so on) depends partly on what you are describing and partly on the impression you want to create. For example, if you wished to emphasize the great height of a skyscraper, you might begin by describing specific details at street level (or even below ground) and then move the "reader's eye" gradually upward, stage by stage, to the top of the building.

Which spatial arrangement does the following description from *The New Yorker* magazine use? What impression does this arrangement create?

It's ten-thirty in the morning at Columbus Avenue and Ninety-fourth Street. The arm of the traffic light casts a diagonal shadow across the pavement which almost touches the manhole cover near the center of the intersection. White lines painted on the black asphalt mark off the crosswalks, and in one of them two women shepherd a group of small children across the street, the children going in twos, holding hands and chattering. A man pushes an empty hand truck out of a drugstore. Two teen-agers stroll along; they, too, are holding hands. They are both dressed in white trousers and white shirts. The girl has several dozen tiny blond braids into which colored beads have been woven. She shakes her head, obviously enjoying the clicks that the beads make, and they both laugh. "Say you're sorry," the boy says. A maroon van with Chinese characters on the side goes through the intersection. On the four corners, apartment buildings rise as much as twenty-five stories into the hazy blue sky. There are six visible clouds, soft and yellow-white. Above the clouds, the sky, very high up, dissolves into a deep blue, and higher still, into blue-black, and, still higher, into black, in a zone populated by manmade objects, satellites sending signals to earth and observing the earth and the heavens. Beyond is the endless black in which the other planets of our solar system move, and, beyond them, widely scattered stars. One of the stars is Vega, and one of the satellites has recently sent down signals indicating that moving around this star is what might be another solar system.

The following words and phrases help to clarify locations in paragraphs in using spatial order.

above	before	in a corner	outside
across	behind	in back of	over
against	below	in front of	to the side of
ahead	beside	inside	toward
alongside	between	in the middle	under
around	beyond	on	underneath

EXERCISE 7. Analyzing a Paragraph Written in Spatial Order. Read the following paragraph, and then list the words and phrases that indicate spatial order. Draw a diagram that shows where the numbered objects are in relation to one another.

The ¹farmhouse stood in the middle of a very large ²yard, and the yard was fenced on three sides with rails and on the rear side with high ³palings. Against these stood the ⁴smoke house; beyond the palings was the ⁵orchard; beyond the orchard were the ⁶tobacco fields. The front yard was entered over a ⁷stile made of sawed-off logs of graduated heights; I do not remember any gate. In a corner of the front yard were a dozen lofty ⁸hickory trees and a dozen ⁹black walnuts, and in the nutting season riches were to be gathered there.

MARK TWAIN

Order of Importance

(3) Ideas may be arranged in order of importance.

In paragraphs that give information or persuade, details are often arranged according to the order of importance. An expository paragraph may begin with the least important or striking details and build up to the most important ones. A persuasive paragraph might save the most convincing reason until last.

In the first of the following paragraphs, the order is from least important to most important; in the second, taken from the textbook *Rise of the American Nation,* the order is reversed. The topic sentences are underlined in red; the supporting ideas are numbered, with *1* being the most important.

The world is running very quickly out of oil, and once it is gone, there is no more. [3]In the United States we have already discovered and have already consumed more than half the producible oil that was created by nature over hundreds of millions of years. [2]We have done this in fifty years, a brief interval since this country was founded, and a mere blip of time in the recorded history of mankind. [1]In fifty years we have used over half of all there ever was, and at the rate we are going, we'll finish off the rest very quickly.

OWEN PHILLIPS

During the postwar period the interest in traditional spectator sports rose markedly. [1]Baseball remained the most popular professional game, with an average yearly attendance of between 9 and 10 million at major-league games. Babe Ruth replaced Ty Cobb as the idol of fans and in 1927 astounded the baseball world by hitting a record number of sixty home runs. [2]College football drew some 30,000,000 spectators in the same year. Red Grange, a halfback for the University of Illinois, became a national hero and won a movie contract. [3]Prizefighting continued to enjoy tremendous popularity, and in 1927 ardent boxing fans spent $2,658,660 to see the famous Dempsey-Tunney match. [4]Professional golf and tennis matches also increased their audiences during the 1920's.

CRITICAL THINKING:
Evaluating the Importance of Ideas

To tell which one of a list of reasons or details is most important, you use the critical thinking skill of evaluating, or judging. You consider how important or convincing each idea would be to your audience. Which of the following reasons do you think the audience of school board members would find most convincing?

Purpose: To persuade
Audience: Members of the local school board
Topic sentence: Passing a driver's education course should be a requirement for graduating from high school.
Reasons:
  a. Studies show that high-school students who pass a driver's education course are involved in fewer traffic accidents than those who do not take such a course.
  b. The driver's education teachers could also serve as homeroom teachers; therefore, the homerooms could be smaller.
  c. New drivers would have a better chance of passing the driving test the first time.

For school board members, the most important reason would be *a*.

EXERCISE 8. Evaluating the Importance of Ideas. Two audiences are listed for each of the following numbered items. Which reason would be most important for each audience? Be prepared to explain your choices.

1. *Audience:* City council members
   Audience: Members of a dog-owners' association
   Topic sentence: All dog owners living within the city limits should be required to walk their dogs on leashes.
   Reasons:
     a. Prevents dogs from being hit by cars
     b. Prevents dogs from fighting each other
     c. Prevents dogs from running away and getting lost

2. *Audience:*   Members of a bicycle racing club
   Audience: Emergency-room doctors
   Topic sentence: All bicyclists should be required to wear protective helmets when bicycling.
   Reasons:
      a. Makes cyclist more aware of possibilities of serious injury and thus tends to increase bicycle safety
      b. Makes cyclist more visible to motorists
      c. Helps prevent skull fractures, most common cause of death in cycling accidents

EXERCISE 9. Choosing a Logical Order for Developing a Topic.   Number your paper 1–10. Indicate the kind of order you would use for each of the following topics by writing *C* (chronological), *S* (spatial), or *I* (importance) after the corresponding number.

1. The double play in baseball
2. My newly decorated room
3. Ways to make yourself unpopular
4. Drawing a map
5. Why homework (should, should not) be abolished
6. My plans for the future
7. A good place for a campsite
8. Washing my dog
9. The duties of the class secretary
10. Locating a book in the library

Direct References

The most natural way to achieve coherence in a paragraph is by using direct references. *Direct references* link sentences by referring the reader to a noun or an idea mentioned earlier.

(1) Use a pronoun that refers to a noun or to an idea in a preceding sentence.

EXAMPLE   Eva spent Saturday cleaning out the garage. **This** did not seem to **her** to be a proper use of the holiday, but **it** had to be done.
[*This* and *it* refer to *cleaning out the garage; her* refers to *Eva*.]

(2) Repeat a key word from a preceding sentence.

EXAMPLE   None of us recognized the young **actor** who played the part of Tony. The **actor** could sing and dance well but apparently had never become famous.

(3) Use a demonstrative adjective with a repeated noun.

EXAMPLE   My personal library includes several rather valuable books. **These books** were a gift from my grandmother.

(4) Use a word or phrase that means the same thing as a word or phrase in a preceding sentence.

EXAMPLE   The runaway engine sped down the inclined track. On and on the **mighty monster** raced as we watched in horror, overcome by the unharnessed power of the **giant machine.** [Both *mighty monster* and *giant machine* refer to *runaway engine*.]

Transitional Expressions

Transitional expressions are words or phrases that make transitions from one idea to another by showing the relationship between the ideas. Such expressions must be chosen carefully, for each one indicates a particular kind of relationship.

EXAMPLES   Angela has always had difficulty with her backhand. Since she has been taking lessons, **however,** her backhand is stronger and more accurate.

I am planning to work full time this summer and to take at least one evening class. **Therefore,** I won't be able to go on the camping trip.

Transitional Expressions

To link similar ideas

again	for example	likewise
also	for instance	moreover
and	furthermore	of course
another	in addition	similarly
besides	in a like manner	too

To link ideas that are dissimilar or apparently contradictory

although	however	on the other hand
as if	in spite of	otherwise
but	instead	provided that
conversely	nevertheless	still
even if	on the contrary	yet

To indicate cause, purpose, or result

as	for	so
as a result	for this reason	then
because	hence	therefore
consequently	since	thus

To indicate time or position

above	before	here
across	beyond	meanwhile
afterward	eventually	nest
around	finally	presently
at once	first	thereafter

Transitional expressions are not required in every sentence. A paragraph in which all the sentences are linked by means of such expressions sounds artificial. Direct references are needed more frequently and should be used whenever possible.

EXERCISE 10. Analyzing a Paragraph for Coherence. In the following paragraph, transitional expressions and direct references are italicized. Study these words and be prepared to explain what ideas each word or phrase connects and how it connects them. The lines are numbered for your convenience.

1. The American Wheelmen and other bicycle groups are
2. attempting to promote the bicycle as one solution to the

3. problem of too many automobiles and too little gasoline.
4. *They* have some interesting facts to back up *their idea. For*
5. *example,* a recent national transportation study shows that
6. 62.4 percent of all automobile trips average less than five
7. miles. *This* is a distance that under reasonably good con-
8. ditions can be covered by bicycle in about twenty minutes.
9. In the United States last year, *these short trips* used up
10. approximately thirteen billion gallons of gasoline. The bi-
11. cycle, *unlike the car,* doesn't pollute and doesn't cause
12. traffic jams. *Furthermore, it* does provide, *in addition to*
13. transportation, a healthful kind of physical exercise.

REVIEW EXERCISE A. Structuring a Paragraph. Choose a "how- to" topic. You may choose a serious topic or a humorous one. When you have selected your topic, plan your paragraph: gather supporting information; eliminate any information that might destroy the paragraph's unity; arrange the information in a logical order; and write an effective topic sentence. Then write a first draft of your paragraph.

THE DEVELOPMENT OF A PARAGRAPH

You have seen how a paragraph is structured. Now you will learn how the stages of the writing process apply to the paragraph form.

PREWRITING

CHOOSING AND LIMITING A SUBJECT

2g. Choose a subject and limit it to find a suitable topic.

Usually, the broader, or more general, a subject is, the more space is required to cover it adequately. Although paragraphs vary in length, most are from 100 to 150 words long. Thus, a general subject must be limited to a topic that can be covered clearly and precisely in the space available in a paragraph.

One way to limit a general subject is to divide it into its smaller, more specific parts. If the smaller parts are still too broad, subdivide them into their smaller parts.

TOO BROAD Birds of North America [Covers more than 1700 species of birds and more than 9,000,000 square miles.]

TOO BROAD Birds of Ohio [Area and species still too great.]

TOO BROAD Hummingbirds [Includes too many aspects: habitat, nesting and feeding habits, physical appearance.]

LIMITED The humming sound produced by the wing movement of the hummingbird [One unique feature of one family of bird.]

Using the *5 W-How?* questions can also help you find a suitably limited topic. (See pages 12–14 for more information on limiting subjects.)

EXAMPLE *General subject:* Gas ballooning
    5 W-How? questions:
     Who has flown gas balloons?
     How do gas balloons work? *How* are they constructed?
     What are gas balloons?
     Where were gas balloons first flown?
     When were they first flown?

Before You Write. Use techniques you have already learned (see Chapter 1) to limit a subject to a topic suitable for a paragraph:

- Divide and subdivide the subject according to time periods, examples, features, places, uses, or causes.
- Use the *5 W-How?* questions to divide and subdivide the subject into its smaller, more specific parts.
- Use clustering to divide and subdivide the subject.

EXERCISE 11. Choosing and Limiting Subjects. Select a subject that interests you. Use the *5 W-How?* questions to divide and subdivide the subject until you have three topics limited enough for a paragraph. Be ready to explain why each topic is suitable for a paragraph.

CONSIDERING PURPOSE

2h. Determine your purpose for writing.

Most writing has one main purpose: to explain or inform, to persuade, to tell a story, or to describe. Your purpose for writing affects both your tone—your manner of expression—and the details you include in your paragraph. Determining what your purpose is helps you decide what your attitude toward the topic is and what kind of details you will gather. (See pages 4–5 for more information on purpose.)

EXAMPLES
Purpose: To inform
Limited topic: How gas balloons work
Details: Balloon rises as sandbags discarded
Balloon descends as gas released from it
Helium often used as the lifting gas
Passengers in basketlike compartment under balloon

Purpose: To describe
Limited topic: My flight in a gas balloon
Details: Striped red, white, and blue balloon against pale sky
Quiet as balloon escapes traffic noises
Sense of freedom as balloon stays aloft
Hiss of gas being released as balloon descends

EXERCISE 12. Classifying Details by Purpose. Following is a list of details about whales. On your paper, write the headings *To Persuade, To Inform,* and *To Describe.* Under each heading, write the details you would use to develop a paragraph written for that purpose. Some details may be placed under more than one purpose.

Not fish but mammals—give birth to live young
Streamlined body resembling fish
Blue, bowhead, humpback, and right whale species—threatened with extinction
Surfaces to breathe—can go long time without surfacing
Powerful tail fins
Baleen whales—no teeth; thin mouth plates strain out food
Toothed whales—eat fish, squid, cuttlefish
Movement to stop all commercial whaling until whales plentiful enough to be hunted again
Smooth, rubbery skin; no hair
Poor eyesight, no sense of smell
Proposal—boycott products of countries continuing whaling
International Whaling Commission—limits hunting and prohibits killing certain kinds of whales
Blue whale largest animal that ever lived (up to 100 feet long, 150 tons)

CONSIDERING AUDIENCE

2i. Consider how your audience will affect your writing.

Your teacher may specify a particular audience for your paragraph; if not, consider your teacher and classmates your audience. Keep in mind that your audience affects your writing in the following ways:

1. *The topic you choose.* [Will your audience be more interested in a description of the first gas balloon flight or in an explanation of how balloons fly?]

2. *The details you include.* [For an audience without specialized knowledge, you might explain difficult concepts by comparing them to something in the audience's experience. For example, you might compare lowering a gas balloon by releasing helium to deflating a small balloon by releasing air.]

3. *The language you use.* [You would use shorter, simpler sentences and simpler vocabulary for a very young audience than

for an adult audience. For example, few six-year-olds would know the terms *ballast* and *dirigible* or understand a sentence such as "Because they used dangerously combustible hydrogen, gas balloons, in the initial stages of their development, were not for the timid."]

Before You Write. To consider how your audience will affect your writing, ask yourself:

- What topic will my audience find most interesting?
- What details about this topic will my audience find most interesting?
- What level of language will my audience be able to understand?

EXERCISE 13. Analyzing a Paragraph for Purpose and Audience. Read the following paragraph. Then answer questions 1–5.

The number of calories used daily by each person also varies. Large persons burn more fuel than small ones because they have a greater body surface giving out heat. People in cold countries use more calories than people in hot lands because they lose body heat faster to the surrounding air. And people who do hard physical work require food yielding more calories than those who do less strenuous work. Most adults require from 2,000 to 3,500 calories each day. A lively teen-age boy can easily put away food yielding 4,000 calories a day. A sedentary person may require only about 15 calories per pound of body weight daily. An athlete, lumberjack or soldier may need 24 calories per pound—60 percent more.

L. SPRAGUE DE CAMP

1. What is the purpose of the paragraph?
2. What audience do you think the paragraph was intended for?
3. State the main idea of the paragraph in your own words. Write the sentence from the paragraph that comes closest to stating this main idea.

4. Write the words in the paragraph, if any, that you think are difficult words. Using a dictionary, write easier words or phrases with which you could replace these words.
5. Are the sentences in the paragraph mostly very short or very long?

GATHERING INFORMATION

2j. Gather information about your limited topic.

As you gather information, record your ideas on sheets of paper or note cards. Save your notes to use as you organize and draft your paragraph.

The information you gather should answer the basic questions your audience may have. One way to be certain that you have included this information is to ask yourself the *5 W-How?* questions. Some questions will be more useful than others for a particular topic. (See pages 14–23 for more suggestions.)

EXAMPLE   *Limited topic:* The world's largest computer
            Questions: *What* is the world's largest computer?
                           What does it look like? *What* is its function?
                           When was this computer developed?
                           Where is this computer located?
                           Who developed it?
                           How is it different from other computers?

If you cannot answer a question that would reveal important information about your topic, find the answer. Look in books and articles, or interview someone who knows your topic well.

EXERCISE 14. Developing Questions to Use in Gathering Information. Choose three of the following limited topics. Write all the questions you can think of that will help you gather information about each topic.

1. Discovery of anesthesia
2. Recent stars admitted to Basketball Hall of Fame
3. Making a kaleidoscope
4. Emily Dickinson's life as a recluse
5. The "I Have a Dream" speech of Martin Luther King, Jr.

EXERCISE 15. Gathering Information.   Gather information about one of the topics you chose for Exercise 14 or another limited topic. Save the information you gather.

DEVELOPING A WORKING PLAN

2k. Develop a working plan for your paragraph.

A *working plan* for a paragraph consists of a topic sentence and a list of supporting details arranged in a logical order.

Writing an Effective Topic Sentence

An effective topic sentence states the main idea of the paragraph, suggests the writer's purpose, and arouses the reader's interest. When you write a topic sentence, keep the following four suggestions in mind.

(1) A topic sentence should be neither too broad nor too limited.

Think of the topic sentence as an umbrella that must "cover" all of the other sentences in the paragraph. A topic sentence is too broad if it states an idea that cannot be fully developed in one paragraph. It is too limited if it states a fact that needs no further development or if it covers only some of the information in the other sentences.

TOO BROAD   Water is an important natural resource. [Paragraph could not develop this idea completely; books could be written about water as an important natural resource.]

TOO LIMITED Water is made up of two atoms of hydrogen and one atom of oxygen. [Topic sentence states a fact that needs no further development.]

TOO LIMITED Desalination is the process by which sea water is made drinkable. [Paragraph goes on to describe problems in a desalination plant; topic sentence gives no indication of those problems; it indicates only part of the content of the paragraph.]

EFFECTIVE Water is a chemical compound that can occur in three different states: liquid, gas, and solid. [Paragraph can develop this main idea with information about each of the three states; topic sentence would cover all information.]

(2) A topic sentence should suggest the writer's purpose.

Your reader should be able to tell from your topic sentence what kind of paragraph (narrative, descriptive, expository, or persuasive) will follow. Avoid, however, direct explanations of purpose, such as "In this paragraph I am going to explain . . ."

WEAK In this paragraph I am going to try to persuade you to join the North Central Soccer League.

IMPROVED When you become part of the North Central Soccer League, you will receive at least four benefits.

WEAK I am going to tell you about a funny thing that happened to Michelle and me.

IMPROVED Last Saturday Michelle and I set out to spend the day shopping but instead ended up organizing the lost-and-found department in the bus station.

Be especially careful when using a topic sentence that asks a question. If your purpose is to inform, you can begin your paragraph with a question and then provide specific information that answers the question. If your purpose is to persuade, however, the topic sentence must clearly state your opinion.

WEAK Should high-school students be required to take four years of English?

IMPROVED All high-school students should be required to take four years of English for three important reasons.

(3) A topic sentence should state the main idea of the paragraph directly and precisely.

Wording your topic sentence clearly and directly helps you focus your main idea. It tells your reader precisely what the paragraph is about.

> WEAK   Bicycling can lead to problems.
>
> WEAK   Some people wish they'd never seen a bicycle.
>
> IMPROVED   Whenever you get on your bicycle, keep these three basic rules in mind if you want to reach your destination safely.

(4) A topic sentence should arouse the reader's interest.

Whenever possible, the topic sentence should introduce the topic in a forceful and lively way. Colorful details and a different "twist" will make the audience want to read on.

> WEAK   The Manx cat is unusual.
>
> IMPROVED   Looking more like a rabbit than a cat, the tailless Manx cat is an object of curiosity.

A topic sentence can be made more interesting in the following ways:

Unusual comparison: Learning to read music is like learning to read a foreign language.

Unexpected statement: If you can read this sentence, you can learn to read music.

Strong verbs and vivid modifiers: You have already trained your mind to extract meaning from the spiky, curved symbols we call letters; you can conquer musical notes, too.

Before You Write.   In developing your topic sentence:

- Check to see that it is neither too broad nor too limited.
- Indicate your purpose.
- State your main idea directly and precisely.
- Try to arouse the interest of your audience.

EXERCISE 16. Choosing Topic Sentences. Three topic sentences are given for each of the following paragraphs. Write the one you think would be most effective as the first sentence in the paragraph. Be ready to explain your choices.

1.   The old-fashioned dogcatcher, for example, is now known as an "animal control expert." Workers who empty garbage cans are classified as "sanitation engineers." Truant officers, those determined people who check up on students who are not in school, are now called "special investigative unit officers." If you need help in a library, don't look for a librarian; look instead for the "media specialist."

   a. Today's jobs require more training than they once did.
   b. As jobs change, language changes.
   c. For good examples of euphemisms (words that seem less offensive than those they replace), consider job titles.

2.   The process of making fuel from these natural plants and plant material is called *biomass conversion.* Such synthetic fuels, or *synfuels,* are not yet being commercially produced because synfuel made from seaweed or any other plant material is much more expensive than gasoline. When the world's supply of natural gas and oil comes close to depletion, however, synfuels made from plants may be our major source of energy.

   a. Plants are a potential source of energy.
   b. Liquid fuel made from oil shale, gas made from coal, and alcohol made from plants are synthetic fuels of the future.
   c. Instead of filling up your gas tank with gasoline, someday you may be filling it with synthetic fuels made from seaweed, water hyacinths, cattails, or even recycled garbage.

3.   In ancient Greece and Rome, spectators cheered on players of *harpaston* and *harpastrum,* both similar in some ways to football as we know it today. In Italy throughout the Middle Ages, fans and players continued to enjoy a game called *calcio,* which is still played in the area around Florence, Italy. The game of football that developed in England during the Middle Ages was so unruly that on two occasions

royal edicts were issued to ban the game. It was so popular, however, that the masses would not obey the edicts, and the football-like game continued until the nineteenth century, when rugby and soccer replaced it in England.

a. The history of football is interesting.
b. The game of football has a long history.
c. For more than three thousand years, games similar to modern football have been popular with fans.

EXERCISE 17. Improving Topic Sentences. Revise each of the following topic sentences, adding any information you need to make it effective.

1. Dancing is my favorite pastime.
2. A sombrero is a type of hat.
3. Computers can be fun to use.
4. I plan to discuss some ways that teen-agers can earn money.
5. Our school can be improved.

EXERCISE 18. Writing Topic Sentences. For each of the following lists of details, write an effective topic sentence.

1. *Details:* Fall line—place where Appalachian rivers drop to coastal plains; many waterfalls along fall line
   Industrial cities built near waterfalls
   Pawtucket, Rhode Island, waterfall city; first cotton mill in 1790, powered by a waterfall
   Niagara Falls—most spectacular U.S. waterfall; city produces many kinds of manufactured goods
2. *Details:* Must be easily inflated by parachutist
   Material must be light in weight, fold to small size
   Must permit slow, balanced descent
   Harness for parachutists must be easily detachable
3. *Details:* "The Star-Spangled Banner," American national anthem, written by Francis Scott Key—young lawyer from Washington, trying to get the release of Maryland doctor captured by British during War of 1812

Key on board a British ship during night of September 13–14, 1814, while British attacked Fort McHenry in Baltimore, Maryland
Key relieved to see American flag still over fort at dawn—wrote poem on way to shore
Verses set to music of popular English tune

CRITICAL THINKING:
Forming a Generalization

A *generalization* is a general conclusion about a group of people, events, objects, places, or ideas. To be *valid* (well-grounded on evidence), a generalization must be based on a fairly large number of facts or unbiased observations. A valid generalization suggests that additional facts or observations about the group will also probably support the conclusion.

EXAMPLES   More traffic accidents are caused by men between the ages of eighteen and twenty-five than are caused by women of the same age.

Lobbyists play an important role in determining what new legislation is passed by the state legislature.

Runners who "overtrain" (run more than twenty miles a day) are more likely to injure their legs, knees, and feet than runners who run fifteen to twenty miles a week.

Often, the topic sentence of a paragraph states a generalization. The other sentences provide evidence—facts, examples, or reasons—to support the generalization. Consider, for example, the following generalization made in the topic sentence on page 44.

EXAMPLE   Nature photography requires but two things: a reasonable level of photographic skill and a lively sensitivity to the natural world. (The writer concludes that nature photography requires only these two things and that it will probably continue to require only these two things.)

When you state a generalization in a topic sentence, remember that your conclusion must be based on adequate, unbiased evidence. You cannot make a valid generalization based on just one or two facts or observations.

EXERCISE 19. Identifying Generalizations. In paragraphs you find in outside reading, identify at least five topic sentences that state generalizations. Be prepared to explain your choices.

EXERCISE 20. Writing a Generalization. Study the following table. Then write a generalization that could serve as the topic sentence of a paragraph.

Annual consumption of meat per person in the United States
(in pounds)

	1960	1970	1982
beef	85.0	117.9	104.4
veal	6.1	2.9	2.0
lamb	4.8	1.6	1.7
pork	77.7	60.3	62.7
chicken	27.8	46.7	52.9

Choosing Supporting Details

Review the information you collected for Exercise 15, and arrange it in a logical order (see pages 51–55). If any of the information does not relate directly to the main idea stated in your topic sentence, discard it. If, on the other hand, you cannot find enough details to support your main idea, you will need to develop a different aspect of your topic or select a new topic.

CRITICAL THINKING:
Deciding Which Details Support a Main Idea

Before you begin writing your paragraph, you must decide which details support your main idea and which ones do not. You will rethink your decisions later, as you write and evaluate your paragraph.

To make these decisions, you use the critical thinking skill of analysis. You examine each detail to see how it relates to the main idea in your topic sentence and to the other details in the paragraph. Your goal is to produce a unified, coherent paragraph—one in which all of the sentences are directly related to the main idea and to each other.

EXAMPLE

Topic sentence: Washington, the only state in the United States named for a President, was almost called Columbia.

Possible Details:
a. Many early attempts to name states for three Presidents (Jackson, Jefferson, and Washington) failed.
b. Four state capitals now named for Presidents: Lincoln, Nebraska; Jackson, Mississippi; Madison, Wisconsin; Jefferson City, Missouri
c. In 1853 new territory formed in Northwest—to be called Territory of Columbia
d. 1853—As part of law forming territory, Representative Richard H. Stanton of Kentucky suggested that Territory of Columbia be renamed Territory of Washington
e. Also proposed that someday a state from that territory be named Washington—Stanton proposal passed
f. Washington became forty-second state in 1889

Details *a* and *b* do not directly relate to the paragraph's main idea: how Washington State got its name. These two details should not be included in the paragraph.

Before You Write. Use the following questions to determine which details support your main idea.

● Does this detail contribute to the main idea as it is stated in the topic sentence?
● Will the detail help readers understand the main idea rather than confuse or distract them?
● How does the detail function within the paragraph—is it an example? A fact? A reason?

EXERCISE 21. Analyzing Details for a Paragraph. Decide which of the following details support the main idea in the topic sentence given, and write them on a separate sheet of paper. Be prepared to explain your choices.

Topic sentence: Of all the scenery in the Southwest, the mesas are the strangest and most picturesque.

Possible details:

Mesa—"table" in Spanish; tall, flat-topped hills; two or more sides steeply perpendicular

Often deep red or yellow

Television commercial with car on top of remote mesa

Most famous mesas—Mesa Verde in Colorado, Enchanted Mesa in New Mexico

Mesa Verde National Park—three hundred ancient cliff dwellings built by ancestors of Pueblo Indians

Other cliff dwellings in New Mexico, Arizona, Utah

Origin of mesas: hard rock on top kept mesa from eroding; surrounding land eroded

CHOOSING A TITLE

2l. Choose a title that reflects your purpose and topic.

A catchy title can help attract the interest of your audience. The title you choose should identify both your topic and your purpose. If your topic is "Frankenstein," for example, you might use the title "Frankenstein: Medical Student, Not Monster," for a paragraph explaining that the monster is often mistakenly called by the name of its creator. For a paragraph relating an incident that took place when you watched the movie version of the story at home alone, however, you might use the title "Frankenstein and I: Alone Together." Keep in mind as you choose a title that you will have the chance to improve it later.

REVIEW EXERCISE B. Developing a Working Plan. Develop a working plan for the topic on which you gathered information for Exercise 15. Include a title for your paragraph.

WRITING

WRITING A FIRST DRAFT

2m. Write the first draft of your paragraph.

Your draft is your first attempt to express ideas about your topic in sentences. Writing is a creative process, so new ideas might occur to you as you write. Feel free to include them in your draft. You should focus on *what* to say rather than *how* to say it. Remember that you will have time later to evaluate and improve your writing.

> **When You Write.** As you draft your paragraph:
> - Use your working plan as a guide.
> - Write freely, adding related ideas as you think of them.
> - Keep your purpose and audience in mind.
> - Focus on the ideas you are including rather than on grammar, usage, and mechanics.

EXERCISE 22. Writing a First Draft. Using the working plan you prepared for Review Exercise B, write the first draft of your paragraph.

EVALUATING

EVALUATING YOUR PARAGRAPH

2n. Evaluate the first draft of your paragraph.

To evaluate, or judge, your paragraph, reread it carefully several times, looking for strengths and weaknesses in the content, organization, and style (word choice and sentence structure).

If you can, put your paragraph aside for a short time before you evaluate it. When you see it again, you will be more likely to notice areas that need to be improved. If your teacher approves, you may also ask a classmate to evaluate your paragraph.

You will find the following Guidelines for Evaluating Paragraphs helpful for judging any paragraph you write. In Chapter 3 you will find specific guidelines for evaluating different types of paragraphs (expository, persuasive, descriptive, and narrative). You may also want to refer to the general Guidelines for Evaluating in Chapter 1.

GUIDELINES FOR EVALUATING PARAGRAPHS

Topic Sentence	1. Does the topic sentence identify the topic and state the main idea clearly? Does it indicate the purpose of the paragraph?
Topic Development	2. Are enough details given to develop the main idea fully?
Concluding Sentence	3. Does the clincher sentence, if there is one, provide a strong ending for the paragraph?
Unity	4. Is each sentence directly related to the main idea in the topic sentence?
Order	5. Are the ideas arranged so they will be clear to the audience? Is the order of ideas suitable for the purpose?
Relationships Between Ideas	6. Do the ideas flow smoothly from one sentence to the next? Are the ideas clearly linked?
Word Choice	7. Will the audience understand the words used? Are technical terms and difficult words defined or explained?

EXERCISE 23. Evaluating the First Draft of a Paragraph.
Read the following first draft of a paragraph. Then use the Guidelines for Evaluating Paragraphs on this page to evaluate

it. Answer each question on the guidelines in writing, numbering your answers to match the numbers on the guidelines. Be prepared to discuss your answers.

Dieters are often taken in by products that promise them fast and easy weight loss. One such device is a belt that melts away fat. A small object fits into the ear and is supposed to make the dieter want to eat less. Writers of one book recommend eating ice cream for six weeks. Manufacturers of a special "vanishing" cream claim to melt away fatty tissue. My friend Sean can eat anything and not gain weight.

EXERCISE 24. Evaluating Your Paragraph. Use the Guidelines for Evaluating Paragraphs on page 76 to judge the first draft you wrote for Exercise 22. Answer each question on the guidelines in writing. You may also want to refer to the appropriate guidelines for evaluating a specific type of paragraph in Chapter 3.

REVISING

When you evaluate your writing, you identify aspects, or parts, that need to be improved in order to make your writing effective. Making changes that improve your writing is *revising*.

REVISING YOUR PARAGRAPH

2o. Revise your paragraph to improve the content, style, and organization.

As with other forms of writing, you can use four basic techniques to improve a paragraph: *adding, cutting, reordering,* and *replacing*. The following chart shows how you can apply these four techniques to the paragraph form.

REVISING PARAGRAPHS

PROBLEM	TECHNIQUE	REVISION
The paragraph does not have a topic sentence.	Add	Add a sentence to the paragraph that identifies the topic and clearly states the main idea.
The topic sentence is too broad.	Cut/Replace	Remove words, phrases, or clauses that do not keep to one main idea. Replace topic sentence with one that is suitably limited.
The topic sentence is too narrow.	Add	Add words, a phrase, or a clause that will make the sentence cover all the information in the paragraph.
The paragraph does not include enough information to make the main idea clear.	Add	Add facts, statistics, examples, concrete or sensory details, incidents, or reasons.
The paragraph includes material that does not directly relate to the main idea.	Cut	Remove the material.
The paragraph trails off or ends abruptly.	Add	Add a concluding sentence that restates the main idea of the paragraph, summarizes the details in the paragraph, emphasizes an important point, or suggests a course of action.
The ideas are not arranged in a logical order.	Reorder	Rearrange the sentences to make the order of ideas clear.

PROBLEM	TECHNIQUE	REVISION
The ideas do not flow smoothly from one sentence to the next.	Add/Replace	Add direct references and transitional expressions to link sentences. Substitute transitional expressions for those that do not clearly show how ideas are related.
The language is too difficult for the audience.	Add/Replace	Add definitions and explanations of terms. Substitute easier words for difficult ones.

EXERCISE 25. Analyzing a Writer's Revisions. Study the following revised draft carefully. Then answer the questions that follow the paragraph.

> _and books_
>
> Dieters are often taken in by products␣that *add*
>
> promise them fast and easy weight loss. One
> _(supposedly)_ _(while the dieter sleeps)_ _(Another is)_
> such device is a belt that␣melts away fat. A *add*
> _that_
> small object␣fits into the ear and is supposed *add*
> _decrease_ _'s appetite_
> to ␣make the dieter␣want to eat less. Writers *replace*
> _diet_ _only_
> of one␣book recommend eating␣ice cream for *add*
> _while_
> six weeks␣Manufacturers of a special "van- *add*
> _that it_ _'s_
> ishing" cream claim␣to melt␣away fatty tissue. *replace*
>
> ~~My friend Sean can eat anything and not gain~~ *cut*
> ~~weight.~~

1. Why did the writer add the words *and books* to the topic sentence?
2. What specific information did the writer add to the paragraph?

3. How did the writer improve the coherence of the paragraph?
4. How did the writer improve the word choice and sentence structure?
5. Why did the writer remove the last sentence?

EXERCISE 26. Revising Your Paragraph. Using your answers for Exercise 24, revise the paragraph you wrote for Exercise 22.

PROOFREADING AND PREPARING A FINAL COPY

PROOFREADING YOUR PARAGRAPH AND PREPARING A FINAL COPY

2p. Proofread your revised paragraph, make a final copy, and proofread again.

Once your paragraph meets the criteria in the Guidelines for Evaluating Paragraphs, proofread it carefully, using the Guidelines for Proofreading on page 36. Then recopy the paragraph in correct manuscript form (see pages 37–39), and proofread it again to make sure that you have copied correctly.

EXERCISE 27. Proofreading Your Paragraph and Preparing a Final Copy. Use the Guidelines for Proofreading on page 36 to proofread your revised paragraph. After recopying your paragraph in correct manuscript form, proofread it carefully again.

CHAPTER 2 WRITING REVIEW

Writing an Effective Paragraph. For this assignment your teacher may provide a topic; you may be directed to choose your own topic; or you may limit one of the following subjects to find a topic:

Magazines	Neighbors
Popular myths about snakes	My childhood
Learning a sport	Seasons
Observing people	Pet owners
Machines in the home	A view from the top

PREWRITING Be sure that your topic is limited enough for a paragraph. After you have decided on your purpose and audience and gathered information, prepare a working plan by writing a topic sentence and listing supporting details in a logical order.

WRITING As you write, follow your working plan. Remember to keep your purpose and audience in mind as you put your ideas into sentences.

EVALUATING AND REVISING Use the Guidelines for Evaluating Paragraphs on page 76 to judge your writing. You may also want to use the appropriate evaluation guidelines in Chapter 3 for the specific type of paragraph you have written. Refer to the chart on pages 78–79 as you revise your paragraph.

PROOFREADING AND PREPARING A FINAL COPY Proofread your revised paragraph, using the Guidelines for Proofreading on page 36. Then prepare a final copy and proofread it as well.

Writing Four Types of Paragraphs

PARAGRAPHS FOR DIFFERENT PURPOSES

Most paragraphs can be classified into four types, depending on the writer's main purpose:

TYPE OF PARAGRAPH	PURPOSE	EXAMPLE
Expository	To explain or inform	A paragraph explaining how Father's Day began
Persuasive	To persuade	A paragraph persuading students to take their fathers to dinner on Father's Day
Descriptive	To describe	A paragraph describing a meal on Father's Day
Narrative	To tell a story	A paragraph relating an incident that happened on Father's Day

This chapter discusses the methods of developing these four types of paragraphs. Each method uses a different kind of *detail* (item of information). The methods you use for a particular paragraph will depend on your specific purpose and audience.

THE EXPOSITORY PARAGRAPH

The purpose of *exposition* is to explain or inform. Exposition has several uses: (1) to give directions; (2) to present information about a person, place, event, or object; (3) to explain how to make or do something; or (4) to define a term.

Developing Expository Paragraphs

3a. Develop an expository paragraph with specific details of a procedure.

Paragraphs that give directions and those that explain how to make or do something present details that show how to carry out the procedure. Often the concluding sentence of the paragraph identifies the outcome or results to be expected.

In a paragraph giving directions, the details are items such as the names of streets, buildings, and other landmarks; distances; and directional words. (The topic sentences in the model paragraphs in this chapter are underlined in red.)

My house is easily reached from Kennedy High School. As you leave the parking lot, turn left onto Route 27. Go three miles north to Tram Road, where you will see a blinking yellow light. Turn right at the light, and go one-half mile east on Tram. Then turn right again, onto Circle Drive. My house is the third one on the left, number 2814.

In a *process paragraph,* one that explains how to make or do something, the details are the supplies and equipment needed and the specific actions to be carried out.

There are six easy ways to clean shelled mollusks—freezing, boiling, preserving, salting, rotting out, or bleaching out. Freezing is the most modern method, adopted within the last twenty years, because there are few homes, hotels, and motels that do not have facilities for freezing packets of food. Fill a plastic bag with your mollusks and place the bag, tied shut, in the lower part of the refrigerator for a couple of hours. Then place it in the freezer for two or three days.

When you are thawing the contents, put the bag back in the lower part for half a day and then in a cold water soak. This process is done gradually to prevent fine cracks from developing in the enamel of large, glossy shells. When completely thawed, usually over a period of twenty-four hours, most meats of univalves[1] will come out completely by pulling on them in an unwinding, corkscrew fashion, using a fork or bent safety pin. Save the operculum[2] with each shell.

R. TUCKER ABBOTT

Notice that in both model paragraphs, the steps are arranged in chronological (time) order. This order enables the audience to duplicate the procedure. (See pages 51–52 for more information on chronological order.)

EXERCISE 1. Writing a Paragraph Using Details of a Procedure.
Write an expository paragraph developed with details of a procedure. Your teacher may provide a topic, or you may use a topic of your own.

PREWRITING Gather information by carrying out the procedure yourself and making notes on the details involved. Then arrange the steps in chronological order, and write a topic sentence that identifies your topic and indicates your purpose.

WRITING Write your first draft quickly, shaping your notes into sentences and adding transitions where they are needed. As you write, keep in mind that your audience is probably not as familiar with the procedure as you are.

EVALUATING AND REVISING Ask yourself: Have I included every detail my audience would need in order to carry out the procedure? Have I arranged the steps in chronological order? Then use the Guidelines for Evaluating Expository Paragraphs on page 93 to judge your paragraph, and revise your writing.

PROOFREADING AND MAKING A FINAL COPY Use the Guidelines for Proofreading on page 36. Then make a final copy and proofread again.

[1] *univalves:* mollusks having a one-piece shell.
[2] *operculum:* the horny plate serving to close the shell when the animal is retracted.

3b. Develop an expository paragraph with facts and statistics.

A *fact* is a piece of information that can be proved to be true, such as the fact that water is made up of hydrogen and oxygen. Historical events and dates are also facts. A *statistic* is a numerical fact that has been carefully checked and recorded.

Facts and statistics are useful for developing paragraphs that give information. In the following paragraph, for example, the writer uses facts to give information about an American athlete. The facts are numbered in red.

> Babe Didrikson Zaharias, who lived from 1914 to 1956, was a remarkable athlete. [1]During a twenty-three-year period, she won more medals and set more records in more sports than any other athlete, male or female. [2]As a teenager, she won prizes in basketball, track and field, lifesaving, and figure skating. [3]In the 1932 Olympics, she took three gold medals, setting world records in the javelin throw, eighty-meter hurdles, and high jump. [4]In the 1940's, she won every available golf title, including the World Open and the National Open. [5]Only eight male golfers could drive a ball farther than Babe. [6]She could throw a baseball more than three hundred feet. [7]She was even an expert diver and lacrosse player.

EXERCISE 2. Writing a Paragraph Using Facts and Statistics. Write an expository paragraph developed with facts and statistics. Your teacher may provide a topic, or you may use a topic of your own.

PREWRITING   To gather accurate facts and statistics, use reliable reference works such as those listed in Chapter 28. Keep your readers in mind as you select details to include: too much information may confuse or bore them. Arrange the material in an order that your audience can follow. Then write a topic sentence that states your main idea and indicates your purpose.

WRITING   As you write your first draft, evaluate your choice of details once again. Also keep in mind that you may need to define or explain certain terms for your audience.

EVALUATING AND REVISING Ask yourself: Does every fact and statistic support the main idea in my topic sentence? Have I included neither too many details nor too few? Then, using the Guidelines for Evaluating Expository Paragraphs on page 93, revise your paragraph.

PROOFREADING AND MAKING A FINAL COPY After making sure that you copied the information from your notes correctly, use the Guidelines for Proofreading on page 36 to proofread your paragraph. Proofread again after recopying your paper.

3c. Develop an expository paragraph with examples.

An *example* is an item or instance that is typical of others of the same kind. Using examples with which your audience is familiar enables you to explain an unfamiliar topic concisely.

Sometimes a single example is enough to make your main idea clear. To explain how mammals feed their young, for example, you could discuss how one type of mammal, such as the horse, feeds its offspring. Since this aspect of the horse's behavior is typical of the behavior of mammals, you would not need to discuss other types of mammals.

In other cases, two or more examples may be required. Paragraphs of definition, for instance, often use several examples to explain an unfamiliar term, as the following paragraph does. The examples are numbered in red.

Connotation is the emotional meaning associated with a word. Words acquire their connotations by the ways and circumstances in which they are used. [1]The word *springtime*, for example, literally means that season of the year between the vernal equinox and the summer solstice, but the word usually makes most people think of such things as youth, rebirth, and romance. [2]The word *shroud* literally means a cloth used for burial purposes, or anything that covers or protects. However, most people associate the word *shroud* with death, gloom, darkness, and other unpleasant things. [3]Advertisers are especially sensitive to the connotations of words; for example, a clothing store would probably not be called "Cheap Clothes" but rather "Budget Boutique."

EXERCISE 3. Writing a Paragraph Using Examples. Write an expository paragraph developed with examples. Your teacher may provide a topic, or you may use a topic of your own.

PREWRITING To gather information, first determine which aspect of your topic can best be explained through the use of examples. Keep in mind that the examples you select should be ones that are familiar to your audience. Arrange the material in an order that will be easy for your audience to follow, and write a topic sentence that states your main idea.

WRITING As you draft your paragraph, evaluate once again the examples you have selected, keeping in mind both your purpose and your audience. Remember that you will have another opportunity to consider both the examples and their arrangement when you evaluate your paper.

EVALUATING AND REVISING Ask yourself: Does every example help clarify my main idea? Would another example be more appropriate for my audience? Then, using the Guidelines for Evaluating Expository Paragraphs on page 93, revise your writing.

PROOFREADING AND MAKING A FINAL COPY Use the Guidelines for Proofreading on page 36 to proofread your paragraph. Then recopy your paragraph and proofread once again.

3d. Develop an expository paragraph with details of an incident.

Relating an *incident,* or brief story, is like using an extended example to explain your point. For an incident, the details are ones that answer the *5 W-How?* questions: *Who? What? When? Where? Why?* and *How?*

Paragraphs giving information about people or events often use incidents to clarify a general idea about a situation or a character trait. The incident in the following paragraph, for example, shows Olympic boxer Mark Breland's adaptability.

A little more than two years ago Breland proved that his ability to learn and adapt extends outside the ring. A casting

director from Paramount saw his photograph in the newspaper and was struck by his stark good looks. She offered
him a role in the *The Lords of Discipline,* and he accepted
with the alacrity of any eighteen-year-old discovered by Hol-
lywood. In the film Breland plays Pearce, the first black cadet
at a southern military academy that is unofficially bent on
continuing as an all-white institution. Pearce is subjected to
brutal hazing and then torture at the hands of his fellow
cadets. The role of a strong, silent man-child who resolutely
takes what the world dishes out and still triumphs was a
familiar one to Breland after his youth in Bedford-Stuyves-
ant. Although the film role did not demand a broad range
of emotion, he performed with dignity and little self-
consciousness.

G. A. TAUBES

**EXERCISE 4. Writing a Paragraph Using Details of an In-
cident.** Write an expository paragraph developed with details
of an incident. Your teacher may provide a topic, or you may
use a topic of your own.

PREWRITING Using one or more of the techniques described
on pages 14–21, collect possible incidents to use. Then select
one incident, and use the *5 W-How?* questions to gather details.
Arrange the events of the incident in chronological order and
write a topic sentence that makes a general statement about
what the incident illustrates about the topic.

WRITING As you write your first draft, include all of the
significant details, but avoid getting bogged down in details that
do not help make the point stated in your topic sentence. Remember that your audience will be relying on your selection
and arrangement of details to help them understand your main
idea.

EVALUATING AND REVISING Ask yourself: Does the incident
simply and clearly illustrate my main idea? Have I arranged the
events of the incident in the order in which they took place?
Then, using the Guidelines for Evaluating Expository Paragraphs on page 93, revise your paragraph.

PROOFREADING AND MAKING A FINAL COPY After using the Guidelines for Proofreading on page 36 to proofread your paragraph, make a final copy and proofread it as well.

3e. Develop an expository paragraph with details of comparison, contrast, or both.

A *comparison* makes clear how two or more topics are similar; a *contrast* shows how they are different. Used separately or together, these methods of development help an audience understand an unfamiliar topic by drawing on their knowledge of a familiar one. For a science class, for example, you could present information about whales by comparing them with and contrasting them to fish, as the following paragraph does.

> Whales have the same basic shape as fish, but they differ from fish in many ways. The most visible difference is the tail. Fish have vertical (up and down) tail fins, but whales have sideways tail fins. Fish breathe by means of gills, which absorb dissolved oxygen from water. Whales, on the other hand, have lungs and must come to the surface from time to time to breathe. But they can hold their breath for long periods. One kind of whale, the sperm whale, can hold its breath up to 75 minutes.
>
> WORLD BOOK ENCYCLOPEDIA

The paragraph about whales is an example of the *alternating* or *point-by-point method* of organizing details of comparison and contrast. The writer first presents a detail about fish and then one about whales, then another one about fish, and so on. An alternative arrangement is the *block method,* which first presents all the information about one topic and then all the information about another topic.

EXERCISE 5. Writing a Paragraph Using Details of Comparison and Contrast. Write an expository paragraph developed with details of comparison, contrast, or both. Your teacher may provide a topic, or you may use a topic of your own.

PREWRITING Begin by selecting a comparison topic your audience knows enough about to use as a point of reference for understanding your topic. Next, make two lists of details, one labeled "similarities" and the other "differences." Thinking again about your audience, decide whether to use details of comparison, details of contrast, or both. Then decide whether you will use the point-by-point or the block method of organization; arrange the material accordingly; and write a topic sentence that sets forth your main idea.

WRITING With your organized list of details and your topic sentence in front of you, write your first draft. As you shape your notes into sentences, keep in mind that you may need to define or explain certain terms.

EVALUATING AND REVISING Ask yourself: Will my audience be able to understand my topic by drawing on knowledge they already possess? Will the method of organization I have used be easy for my audience to follow? Then, using the Guidelines for Evaluating Expository Paragraphs on page 93, revise your paragraph.

PROOFREADING AND MAKING A FINAL COPY First use the Guidelines for Proofreading on page 36 to proofread your paragraph. Then make a final copy of your paragraph and proofread it.

Before You Write. To develop an expository paragraph:

- Identify details, facts and statistics, examples, incidents, or similarities and differences that explain your topic.
- Arrange the information in the order that best suits your topic.
- Write a topic sentence that identifies the topic and your purpose for writing about it.

Writing Specific Kinds of Expository Paragraphs

The following sets of guidelines summarize important points about writing four kinds of expository paragraphs.

Process Paragraphs

1. Be sure you understand the process thoroughly.

2. Ask yourself what someone unfamiliar with the process would need to know in order to be able to carry it out.

3. List all the supplies and equipment needed, including exact amounts required.

4. List all the steps involved in the process, and arrange them in chronological order.

5. Write a topic sentence that identifies the process.

6. As you write your first draft, define or explain unfamiliar terms and use transitions to indicate the sequence of steps. In your concluding sentence, identify the expected outcome or results.

7. To evaluate your writing, carry out the process as you have explained it; then determine where you should add, cut, reorder, or replace details.

EXERCISE 6. Writing a Process Paragraph. Using the preceding guidelines, write a paragraph explaining how to make or do something. Use a topic of your own.

Paragraphs Defining a Term

1. First place the term in the general class of which it is a member. A wristwatch, for example, is a member of the general class *timepieces*.

2. If the term names a *concrete* object, one you can perceive with your senses, list the physical properties (size, shape, texture, and so on) that set it apart from all other members of its class. If the term is an *abstract* noun—one that names a quality, a characteristic, or an idea—gather examples that illustrate its meaning.

3. Arrange the details or examples in an order that will be easy for your audience to follow.

4. Write a topic sentence that identifies the term and places it in its general class.

5. As you draft your paragraph, use appropriate transitions to link sentences, and keep your audience in mind.

6. To evaluate your paragraph, consider whether you have included sufficient details or examples and whether each one truly distinguishes the term from all other members of its class.

EXERCISE 7. Writing a Paragraph Defining a Term. Using a topic of your own and following the guidelines above, write a paragraph defining a term.

Paragraphs Giving Directions

1. Be sure you know how to get to the place you are writing about.

2. Ask yourself what someone unfamiliar with the route would need to know.

3. Jotting down street names, landmarks, and other details, mentally follow the route you intend to explain.

4. Arrange the details in the order in which the audience would encounter them.

5. Write a topic sentence that makes clear *from* where and *to* where you are giving directions.

6. As you draft your paragraph, visualize the route in your mind, and remember to add appropriate transitions where they are needed.

7. To evaluate your draft, mentally follow your directions to determine where you should add, cut, reorder, or replace details.

EXERCISE 8. Writing a Paragraph Giving Directions. Following the guidelines above, write a paragraph giving directions. Use a topic of your own.

Paragraphs Giving Information About a Topic

1. Evaluate your topic carefully to make sure that it is limited enough for a paragraph.

2. Gather details on the topic, and decide which method or combination of methods you will use to develop the paragraph.

3. Arrange the details in an order that will present the information clearly.

4. Write a topic sentence that identifies your topic and presents your main idea.

5. As you write your first draft, define or explain any terms that may be unfamiliar to your audience.

6. In evaluating your draft, check your selection and arrangement of details as well as your word choice, sentence structure, and tone.

EXERCISE 9. Writing a Paragraph Giving Information About a Topic. Using the guidelines above, write a paragraph giving information about a topic of your own choice.

Evaluating and Revising Expository Paragraphs

Use the following guidelines to evaluate expository paragraphs. Then refer to the chart on revising paragraphs on page 78 to make the changes necessary to improve your writing.

GUIDELINES FOR EVALUATING EXPOSITORY PARAGRAPHS

Topic Sentence	1. Does the topic sentence identify the topic and make clear that the purpose of the paragraph is to explain or give information?
Topic Development	2. Does the method of development (or combination of methods) suit the main idea and the audience? Are enough details given to make the main idea clear? Is the information accurate?
Conclusion	3. Does the clincher sentence, if there is one, provide a strong ending for the paragraph?
Unity	4. Is each sentence directly related to the main idea in the topic sentence?
Order	5. Are the ideas arranged in an order that will be easy for the audience to follow?
Relationships Between Ideas	6. Do the ideas flow smoothly from one sentence to the next? Are they clearly linked with direct references and appropriate transitional expressions (such as *first, then, finally,* and *therefore*)?

Word Choice   7. Is the language clear, specific, and "right" for the audience? Are technical terms and difficult words defined or explained?

REVIEW EXERCISE A. Writing an Expository Paragraph.
Write a paragraph corresponding to any of the following kinds of expository paragraphs. Your teacher may provide topics, or you may use one of the topics listed or one of your own.

After deciding which kind of paragraph you will write, select a topic, determine your audience, and review the appropriate set of guidelines from those on pages 93–113. Then plan your paragraph: gather information; choose a method of development; arrange the material in a logical order; and write a topic sentence that states your main idea. Once you have completed your first draft, use the Guidelines for Evaluating Expository Paragraphs on page 93 to judge it. Then revise your draft, referring to the revising chart on page 78, and use the Guidelines for Proofreading on page 36 to improve and correct your writing.

1. *A paragraph explaining how to make or do something:* how to make a jack o'lantern; how to sew a button on a shirt
2. *A paragraph giving directions:* how to reach your favorite recreational facility from school
3. *A paragraph defining a term:* define *isthmus* or *melodrama*
4. *A paragraph giving information about a person, place, event, or object:* a favorite relative; the oldest building in your community; your community's Fourth of July celebration; your favorite personal possession

THE PERSUASIVE PARAGRAPH

The purpose of a persuasive paragraph is to convince the audience to agree with an opinion or, sometimes, to perform a specific action. In order to accomplish this purpose, the writer creates an *argument*, which is a logically sound discussion of the issue.

Developing Persuasive Paragraphs

3f. Develop a persuasive paragraph with reasons.

The topic sentence of a persuasive paragraph states the writer's opinion; the supporting sentences present *reasons,* statements that explain the opinion. Each reason is, in turn, supported by details such as facts, statistics, or examples.

Distinguishing Between Facts and Opinions

The topic for a persuasive paragraph should be a debatable issue, a matter on which different conclusions could be reached. The topic sentence for a persuasive paragraph, sometimes called the *position statement,* states the writer's opinion on the issue. Factual statements, which are not debatable, are not suitable topic sentences for persuasive paragraphs. (See pages 772–73.)

FACT   Many students wear shorts to school.

OPINION   Every student should be allowed to wear whatever he or she wants to wear to school.

EXERCISE 10. Distinguishing Between Facts and Opinions.   Number your paper 1–10. Write *O* if the statement is an opinion; write *F* if it is a fact.

1. The color green is made by mixing yellow and blue.
2. Green is the best color for walls and carpeting.
3. New Mexico became a state in 1912.
4. Jim Thorpe (1888–1953) was America's greatest athlete.
5. Every high-school student should be required to take a CPR (cardiopulmonary resuscitation) course.
6. Nan Konig is the best candidate for student-body president.
7. Poodles make the best pets.
8. An adult gorilla can weigh as much as 500 pounds.
9. A *million* is one thousand thousands.
10. Twelve inches of rain have fallen in the last three days.

To be effective, the topic sentence of a persuasive paragraph should be direct and precise. Notice how each of the following improved sentences clearly states an opinion.

WEAK	School officials have been discussing a dress code.
IMPROVED	Our school should adopt a dress code prohibiting shorts, halters, and other distracting clothing.

WEAK	Vandalism in the schools is a serious problem.
WEAK	Can you think of ways to stop vandalism to school buildings and equipment?
IMPROVED	To eliminate school vandalism, patrols should be formed of students found guilty of vandalism.

Before You Write. In choosing a topic and writing a topic sentence for a persuasive paragraph:

- Make sure that the topic is a debatable issue, not a statement of fact.
- State your opinion on the issue directly and precisely.

EXERCISE 11. Identifying and Writing Effective Topic Sentences. Some of the following topic sentences are effective ones for a persuasive paragraph; others are not. If a topic sentence is effective, write *E* after its number. If it is not, revise it so that it is direct and precise.

1. Every student planning to graduate from high school should be required to take a one-semester public-speaking course.
2. Emily Dickinson was America's greatest poet.
3. Every neighborhood in this community should form an association that would meet monthly.
4. Bus and subway fares are too high.
5. Students should be taught to appreciate music.

Building an Argument

An effective persuasive paragraph answers the audience's *Why?* questions: Why should we agree with you? Why should we do what you want us to do? To answer these questions, you provide *reasons,* statements that clearly explain your opinion. Usually, at least three reasons are required to develop an opinion. Reasons that are vague, that are not related to the topic sentence, or that simply restate the opinion, should be eliminated.

Each reason should be supported with accurate details. For instance, examples of successful programs in other cities for hiring handicapped persons would strengthen the argument for organizing a program in your city to hire handicapped persons.

Responding to arguments against your opinion also strengthens your argument. It shows that you have researched the issue carefully and that you can refute other opposing views.

The reasons in a persuasive paragraph are usually arranged in order of importance, with the most important reason given last so that it will linger in the reader's mind. Sometimes the most important reason is given first in order to catch the reader's attention immediately. Whichever arrangement you use, each reason should lead smoothly and directly to the next one.

The tone of a persuasive paragraph should be serious and unemotional, in order to give the audience the impression that the argument is fair and reasonable.

Before You Write. To develop a persuasive paragraph:

- Provide at least three reasons that explain your opinion.
- Support each reason with details (facts, examples, etc.).
- If possible, respond to arguments against your opinion.
- Arrange the reasons and their supporting details in order of importance, from least important to most important.
- Plan to use a serious, unemotional tone.

EXERCISE 12. Evaluating and Arranging Reasons Used to Support an Opinion. Consider the following topic sentence and list of supporting reasons for a persuasive paragraph. Decide which reasons you would include if you were writing the paragraph, and arrange the reasons in an effective order.

Topic sentence: All members of a family should take turns doing all of the household jobs.

1. People who live alone do all of these things.
2. By taking turns, everyone would learn these important skills.
3. One person would not have to do all the work.
4. Doing everything is too much work for one person, especially one who also works outside the home.
5. Some people like cooking best; others prefer cleaning.
6. Even children as young as six can do certain chores.
7. Young people would get a realistic idea of the responsibilities involved in maintaining a household.
8. Everyone would have a feeling of mutual respect and caring.
9. Cookbooks have easy recipes.
10. That's how we do it at our house.

Avoiding Emotional Appeals and Fallacies

An *emotional appeal* is one that attempts to stir the feelings of the audience. Emotional appeals are widely used in advertisements and political speeches, but they are generally inappropriate in persuasive writing. Your argument should be based strictly on logical appeals.

1. *Loaded words.* Words to which most people attach strong feelings, either positive ones or negative ones, are called *loaded words.* They tend to prejudice the reader for or against something. Words like *flag, patriotism,* and *family* are examples of loaded words that have positive associations. (See Chapter 9, pages 291–94, for information about the positive and negative connotations of words.)

2. *Bandwagon appeal.* This appeal suggests that "everyone else" is doing something and that unless the reader "jumps on the bandwagon"—joins everyone else—he or she will be isolated and alone.

EXAMPLE   Don't be the only person without a yearbook. Order your copy today—before it's too late.

3. *Testimonial.* Used primarily in advertising, this device shows or quotes a famous person endorsing a product. Often

the person, whose success is in a completely unrelated field, has no expert knowledge of the product. This is different from citing an authority, someone who is truly an expert in the field being discussed.

EXAMPLE   Sheila D., the famous movie star, stays slim because she starts each day with Super Cereal.

4. *Plain folks appeal.* Advertisements using this appeal show ordinary-looking people using a product. Political candidates use this appeal when they stress their humble origins.

EXAMPLE   Product X is the kind of bread the good folks in your hometown used to bake for themselves.

5. *Snob appeal.* The opposite of plain folks appeal, snob appeal suggests that acting in a certain way or buying a specific product will bring about a glamorous way of life.

EXAMPLE   Be among the discerning few who appreciate the fine taste of Goormay Mayonnaise.

Fallacies are errors in reasoning. Although they seem logical on the surface, they do not stand up under close examination.

1. *Hasty generalization.* A *generalization* is a general conclusion about an entire group, such as "Women live longer than men." To be valid (well grounded), a generalization must be based on a fairly large number of facts or objective observations. A *hasty generalization* is one that is based on inadequate or biased evidence. The conclusion that flying is extremely dangerous because airplanes occasionally crash is an example of a hasty generalization.

2. *Stereotype.* A stereotype is an unfounded, usually negative generalization: "Teenagers are irresponsible" or "Athletes aren't too bright."

3. *Circular reasoning.* In this fallacy, a statement that is simply a rewording of an opinion is offered as a reason.

EXAMPLE   Moses Johnson is the best candidate for class president because he would make the best president.

4. *Cause/effect*. The fact that one event follows another (even immediately afterward) does not necessarily mean that the first event caused the second one. For example, just because a fight broke out after a pep rally had been canceled does not prove that the cancellation caused the fight.

5. *Only-cause*. Suggesting that a complicated problem has a simple solution is using the only-cause fallacy. Complicated situations have more than a single cause.

EXAMPLE   Juvenile delinquency would disappear completely if we only had more after-school recreation centers.

EXERCISE 13. Identifying Emotional Appeals and Fallacies.   Read the following paragraph carefully. Then identify the emotional appeals and fallacies it contains.

The mandatory seat-belt law is an abomination. What the state is saying is: "We know what is best for you. Let us save your life." Seat belts do save lives. Once again, that is not the issue. It is also true that exercise and a proper diet probably extend life expectancy. Perhaps the state should make it mandatory to run a mile a day, have smokers give up cigarettes, and call for increased vegetable and fruit consumption. I'm exaggerating, of course, but the principle is the same. Are the people of New York intelligent enough to look out for their own interest in safety and health, or do they need coercion from the state? Our legislators, by a surprising majority, seem to believe the latter.

MICHAEL BARRY

Writing a Clincher Sentence

In a persuasive paragraph, a clincher sentence performs one of two functions.

(1) A clincher sentence may summarize the writer's argument.

CLINCHER SENTENCE   For all of these reasons, I believe that a school dress code should be adopted.

(2) A clincher sentence may specify a course of action.

CLINCHER SENTENCE Therefore, I urge you to write your state senator and ask him or her to support the proposed bill to alter the course of Hawk River.

Evaluating and Revising Persuasive Paragraphs

Use the following guidelines to evaluate your persuasive paragraph. Then refer to the chart on revising paragraphs on page 78 to make the changes necessary to improve your work.

GUIDELINES FOR EVALUATING PERSUASIVE PARAGRAPHS

Topic Sentence	1. Is the topic a debatable issue? Does the topic sentence state an opinion directly and precisely?
Topic Development	2. Are at least three reasons given to explain the opinion in the topic sentence? Is each reason supported by accurate details?
Conclusion	3. Does the clincher sentence either summarize the argument or specify a course of action?
Unity	4. Is each sentence directly related to the opinion in the topic sentence?
Order	5. Are the reasons arranged from least important to most important?
Relationships Between Ideas	6. Is the line of reasoning obvious and easy to follow?
Word Choice	7. Have emotional appeals and fallacies been left out?
Tone	8. Is the tone consistently serious and unemotional?

REVIEW EXERCISE B. Writing a Persuasive Paragraph. Write a persuasive paragraph on a debatable issue. Your teacher may provide a topic, or you may choose a topic of your own.

PREWRITING First gather information; you may need to research the issue by observations, interviews, or the use of library sources. Arrange the material (reasons and supporting details) in order of importance, and then write a topic sentence that states your opinion directly and precisely.

WRITING As you write your first draft, remember to avoid using emotional appeals and fallacies. Conclude your paragraph with a clincher sentence that sums up your argument or suggests a course of action.

EVALUATING AND REVISING Ask yourself: Have I stated my opinion clearly? Have I built a strong argument for my position? Then use the guidelines above to judge your draft and revise it, referring to the revising chart on the preceding page.

PROOFREADING AND MAKING A FINAL COPY Use the Guidelines for Proofreading on pages 36–37 to correct your paragraph. Then make a final copy and proofread it.

THE DESCRIPTIVE PARAGRAPH

A descriptive paragraph creates a picture in words. It may present an *objective* picture, one that attempts to reproduce exactly what the writer has observed, or a *subjective* picture, one that appeals to the reader's emotions. The details are usually arranged in spatial order, to show where the parts of the topic are in relation to one another.

Developing Descriptive Paragraphs

3g. Develop a descriptive paragraph with precise concrete and sensory details.

Concrete details are things you can see or touch. *Sensory details* are words that appeal to the senses (sight, hearing, taste, touch, and smell). In order to create a vivid picture, you must use precise details, ones that *show* the reader exactly what you have observed.

Effective descriptive details are precise nouns and verbs: *watercolor* or *etching* rather than *picture; scampered* or *slithered* rather than *moved.* Adverbs and adjectives can make nouns and verbs even more precise: a *delicate watercolor; slithered menacingly*. Notice how Richard Dunlop uses precise details to describe a city in the following paragraph:

> In their hotel room the men could hear roosters crowing every morning. At night jackals yelped right in the heart of the city. In this land of fiery curry, of a plain or fancy dosa[1] for breakfast, where the sweet lemon was sweeter than an orange, and oranges tended to be flavorless, the young Americans found they had a lot of readjusting to do. Pedestrians and cows as gentle as kittens strolled in and out of the rush of bikes, rickshaws, auto-rickshaws, trucks, autos, and chemical-burning buses spewing their showers of burning coals behind them. In the heat of the day men dragged their bedlike charpoys out onto the sidewalks and stretched out to nap with the expectation that the breeze from passing vehicles would keep them a trifle cooler. Bears danced for the entertainment of the crowds, flute playing fakirs[2] charmed cobras, and, incredibly, in the open place in front of the Red Fort, built long ago by the Mogul emperors, a holy man actually levitated in broad daylight.
>
> RICHARD DUNLOP

In order to use descriptive details effectively, you must be able to recognize the difference between a general word like *seasoning* and a precise one like *curry*. You must also be able to observe your topic closely. Questions such as the following ones will help you gather precise concrete and sensory details.

Gathering Information About a Person

How old is the person?	five years old
What does the person look like?	thin, freckled, twinkling brown eyes, curly blond hair in ringlets, impish smile
What was the person wearing?	rumpled khaki shorts, blue shirt with ice-cream stains, dirty sneakers

[1] *dosa:* a dish made of rice and lentils.
[2] *fakirs:* beggars.

When and where did I see this person?	at the mall, when I picked him up after he had fallen on the escalator
How did the person move?	stumbled over my feet as he ran up the escalator
How did other people react?	scowled, lifted their eyebrows, chuckled softly

Gathering Information About a Place

Sight

What does this place look like? What is the first thing I notice when I look at it? How big is it? Are there any people here? What do they look like?	dim, ugly, beautiful, vibrant, gigantic, etc.

Smell

Do I notice any pleasant odors? Any unpleasant ones? Does the place have different odors at different times? What do the odors remind me of?	pungent, dank, acrid, fragrant, etc.

Taste

Is anything here edible? What does it taste like? Does it taste like anything else I know?	bitter, sour, spicy, rich, rancid, burnt, sweet, etc.

Hearing

Do I hear any sounds? Are they loud or soft? What do they sound like?	clang, roar, purr, hum, clunk, etc.

Touch

What textures can I feel? Are they soft, rough, or smooth? Do they feel cool or warm?	greasy, heavy, squishy, wet, chilly, fluffy, etc.

Gathering Information About an Object

Sight

What shape is the object? Do I have to turn it around or walk around it to see all of its parts? What do I notice most when I look at it?

immense, octagonal, dark, etc.

Smell

Does it have any odor? Does it smell like anything else I know?

stale, fragrant, oily, etc.

Taste

Is it edible? Does it taste like anthying else I know? Does it leave an aftertaste?

bitter, tangy, juicy, sour, rich, spicy, etc.

Hearing

Does it make any sounds? What do the sounds remind me of?

smack, bang, roar, shriek, whir, etc.

Touch

What does it feel like? Does it have sharp or rounded edges? Is it smooth or rough?

damp, dry, gritty, dusty, smooth, scratchy, etc.

EXERCISE 14. Gathering Sensory Details. For each of the following topics, write at least three details appealing to the senses. Be sure to use each of the senses at least once.

EXAMPLE   1. Bracelet
   1. *Sparkling in the sunlight*

1. A baseball glove
2. Chewing gum
3. An intersection
4. A locker room
5. A fur rug

6. Icicles
7. A fire in a fireplace
8. Barbecued chicken
9. A baby
10. A hospital emergency room

Creating a Main Impression

A descriptive paragraph may create a single main impression of a topic. In the following paragraph, for example, the topic sentence gives the writer's main impression of the way she saw the animals—as silhouettes. Each supporting detail that she includes helps reinforce that impression. Notice that unlike the excerpt on page 103, which uses details that appeal to all the senses, this paragraph concentrates on only one sense—that of sight.

On the bare hills one begins to see unfamiliar silhouettes of animals against the sky. Giraffe first—slanting geometric lines, bending over bushes—like tipsy cranes on the horizon; the peaked humpbacks of gnu on a ridge; the high shoulders of hartebeest sloping down triangularly to hindquarters; the rounded buttocks of zebra; the delicately horned heads of gazelle, and feathery bushes that become ostrich when they raise long necks.

ANNE MORROW LINDBERGH

CRITICAL THINKING:
Synthesizing Ideas to Create a Main Impression

Synthesis is the bringing together of separate elements to form a new whole. You use this critical thinking skill when you select and combine details to create a main impression in a descriptive paragraph.

Before You Write. To create a main impression in a descriptive paragraph:

- Use variations of the *5 W-How?* questions to gather precise concrete and sensory details.
- Select only those details that will contribute to presenting a single main impression of the topic.
- Write a topic sentence that gives your main impression of the topic.

EXERCISE 15. Creating a Main Impression. Write a paragraph describing a season of the year in your community for people who live in another part of the country.

PREWRITING   Use brainstorming or clustering, or read through your writer's journal to collect concrete and sensory details to use. If you are planning to describe the current season, you can also use observation. Try to collect details that will appeal to each of the senses. Then review the material, and decide what main impression you want to create. Select from your list only those details that will reinforce that impression, and arrange them in an order that your audience can follow. Then write a topic sentence that states your main impression.

WRITING   As you write your first draft, add any related details you think of. Remember to use precise language to create a vivid picture for your readers.

EVALUATING AND REVISING   Ask yourself: Have I included only details that reinforce the main impression? Have I used precise language to create a vivid picture? Then, using the Guidelines for Evaluating Descriptive Paragraphs below and referring to the revising chart on pages 78–79, revise your writing.

PROOFREADING AND MAKING A FINAL COPY   Using the Guidelines for Proofreading on page 36, proofread your work. Then make a final copy of your paragraph and proofread that also.

Evaluating and Revising Descriptive Paragraphs

Use the following guidelines to evaluate your descriptive paragraph. Then refer to the chart on revising paragraphs on pages 78–79 to make the changes needed to improve your writing.

GUIDELINES FOR EVALUATING DESCRIPTIVE PARAGRAPHS

Topic Sentence	1. Does the topic sentence identify the topic? If the description is subjective, does the topic sentence present the main impression?

Topic Development	2. Are enough concrete and sensory details included to create a vivid picture of the topic?
Unity	3. Do the details used in the description support the main impression identified in the topic sentence?
Order	4. Are the details arranged in spatial order or in another easy-to-follow order?
Relationships Between Ideas	5. Do the ideas flow smoothly from one sentence to the next? Are direct references and transitional expressions used to show where the parts of the topic are in relation to one another?
Word Choice	6. Is the language precise rather than general? Do the details *show* the reader the topic instead of telling about it?

EXERCISE 16. Evaluating and Revising a Descriptive Paragraph. Use the guidelines above to evaluate the following paragraph for content, organization, and style. Then revise the paragraph.

Our kitchen is comfortable and practical. The floor is vinyl. The ceiling has a good light. The cabinets and countertops are made of Formica. There is a rug on the floor. There are stools to sit on. We have a stove to use when we cook. Inside the refrigerator and cabinets, you can find things to eat. The kitchen is not too big, just the right size to move around in.

REVIEW EXERCISE C. Writing an Objective Description. Write a paragraph describing one of the following topics for someone who has never seen the object, or select another object to describe.

Topics: A photograph or painting; a bacon-lettuce-and-tomato sandwich; a cactus; a car

PREWRITING Examine the object closely, using the questions on pages 103–05 to collect concrete and sensory details. Keep a notebook and pen or pencil nearby so that you can jot down the details you observe. Then arrange the details in a logical order, and write a topic sentence that identifies the object.

WRITING As you draft your paragraph, remember that you are trying to describe the object objectively for someone who has never seen it. Use precise language to make your description as exact as possible.

EVALUATING AND REVISING Ask yourself: Have I included enough details to create a clear picture of the object in my readers' minds? Is each detail described in precise language? Then, using the Guidelines for Evaluating Descriptive Paragraphs on page 107 and referring to the chart on page 78, revise your writing.

PROOFREADING AND MAKING A FINAL COPY Use the Guidelines for Proofreading on page 36 to correct your writing. Then make a final copy and proofread again.

THE NARRATIVE PARAGRAPH

The purpose of a narrative paragraph is to tell a story. The story may be based on real events or on imaginary ones. It may simply entertain, or it may illustrate a general idea.

Developing Narrative Paragraphs

3h. Develop a narrative paragraph with details of an incident.

An *incident* is a brief story, one that takes place in no more than a few hours—often in just a few minutes. The details of the incident are arranged in chronological order. They answer the question *What happened?*

Using Narrative Details

To be effective, a narrative paragraph must *show* what happens, not just tell about it. *Narrative details* are precise nouns, verbs, and modifiers that help the audience picture the actions of an incident. One way to gather such details is to use the *5 W-How?* questions. Notice how the narrative details in the following paragraph clearly show *what happened*.

The ray came down with a thunderous splash and drove forward again. The flexible net followed every movement, impeding it hardly at all. The man weighed a hundred seventy-five pounds, and he was braced for the shock, and he had the desperate strength that comes from looking into the blank eyes of death. It was useless. His arm straightened out with a jerk that seemed to dislocate his shoulder; his feet shot out from under him; his head went under again. Now at last he knew how the fish must feel when the line tightens and drags him toward the alien element that is his doom. Now he knew.

ARTHUR GORDON

EXERCISE 17. Gathering Narrative Details. Using the 5 *W-How?* questions, make up narrative details that would help your classmates picture the actions of the following incident.

It was almost time for band practice and I had forgotten my flute. I went home to get it. My room looked different. Everything was straight and neat. My flute wasn't where I had left it. I looked everywhere. By the time I finally found where my mother had put it, I was late for practice.

Illustrating a General Idea

In some narrative paragraphs, like the one at the top of this page, the first sentence simply sets the action in motion. In others, it functions as a topic sentence by stating a general idea, which the incident illustrates. In the following model, for example, the writer begins with a general statement about what the girls learned from the stories the adults told; the incident she relates illustrates that general idea.

When we Chinese girls listened to the adults talking-story, we learned that we failed if we grew up to be but wives or slaves. We could be heroines, swordswomen. Even if she had to rage across all China, a swordswoman got even with anybody who hurt her family. Perhaps women were once so dangerous that they had to have their feet bound. It was a woman who invented white crane boxing only two hundred years ago. She was already an expert pole fighter, daughter of a teacher trained at the Shao-lin temple, where there lived an order of fighting monks. She was combing her hair one morning when a white crane alighted outside her window. She teased it with her pole, which it pushed aside with a soft brush of its wing. Amazed, she dashed outside and tried to knock the crane off its perch. It snapped her pole in two. Recognizing the presence of great power, she asked the spirit of the white crane if it would teach her to fight. It answered with a cry that white crane boxers imitate today. Later the bird returned as an old man, and he guided her boxing for many years. Thus she gave the world a new martial art.

MAXINE HONG KINGSTON

Before You Write. To develop a narrative paragraph:

- Select an incident that takes place within a few hours.
- Use the *5 W-How?* questions to gather details of the incident.
- Arrange the details in chronological order.
- If the paragraph is intended to illustrate a general idea, write a topic sentence that states the idea clearly.

EXERCISE 18. Writing a Narrative Paragraph. Write a paragraph using the details of an incident to illustrate a general idea for the readers of your school newspaper. You may use one of the following general ideas or develop one of your own.

1. If you expect trouble, you may get it.
2. Beauty is not always skin deep.
3. As Alexander Pope wrote, "Fools rush in where angels fear to tread."
4. To do well in life, a person must have self-discipline.
5. Ignorance is not bliss.

   PREWRITING Brainstorm or read through your writer's journal to find an incident you can use to illustrate a general idea, perhaps one about a lesson you learned the hard way. You may instead choose to make up an incident. In either case, gather details that will answer the *5 W-How?* questions. Then decide whether you will use a serious tone or a humorous one, and arrange the events of the incident in chronological order. Before you write your first draft, write a topic sentence stating the general idea that the incident illustrates.

WRITING As you write, keep in mind that your specific purpose in this paragraph is to illustrate a general idea. Use precise language that will help your audience picture the actions of the incident, and try to keep the tone consistent.

EVALUATING AND REVISING Ask yourself: Does the incident I have used clearly illustrate the general idea in my topic sentence? Have I included all of the details of the incident that are necessary to illustrate my main idea? Then, using the Guidelines for Evaluating Narrative Paragraphs below and referring to the chart on page 78, revise your writing.

PROOFREADING AND MAKING A FINAL COPY Use the Guidelines for Proofreading on page 36 to proofread your paragraph. Then make a final copy and proofread that, too.

Evaluating and Revising Narrative Paragraphs

Use the following guidelines to evaluate your narrative paragraph. Then refer to the chart on revising paragraphs on page 78 to make changes needed to improve your writing.

GUIDELINES FOR EVALUATING NARRATIVE PARAGRAPHS

Topic Sentence	1. Does the first sentence set the action in motion or state a general idea?
Topic Development	2. Are enough details included so that the audience will be able to picture the incident and understand what happened?
Unity	3. Have repetitive and unrelated details been left out?

Order   4. Are the actions arranged in the order in which they took place?

Relationships Between Ideas   5. Do the ideas flow smoothly from one sentence to the next? Are ideas clearly linked?

Word Choice   6. Are precise nouns, verbs, and modifiers used to help the audience picture the action?

EXERCISE 19. Evaluating and Revising a Narrative Paragraph. Using the guidelines above, evaluate the following narrative paragraph. Then revise the paragraph.

Gretchen had never been superstitious before the cat crossed her path. She fell over the shoes lying beside her bed. A bus went past her and splashed water. She was helping her father carry out the garbage and it fell all over the sidewalk. She spilled food onto the floor of the school cafeteria. She sometimes wonders about that cat. She fell over the shoes getting into bed.

REVIEW EXERCISE D. Writing a Narrative Paragraph. Write a narrative paragraph for your classmates telling about an entertaining incident that happened to you.

PREWRITING   Use brainstorming, read through your writer's journal, or talk with other members of your family to find a humorous or dramatic incident you would like to share with your classmates. Those techniques can also help you collect narrative details, as can using the *5 W-How?* questions. Arrange the details in chronological order before you begin writing.

WRITING   Begin with a sentence that sets the action in motion; you might, for example, tell how the incident came about. As you write, keep in mind that your specific purpose is to entertain your audience. Include all of the essential details, but try not to get sidetracked with unrelated ones.

EVALUATING AND REVISING   Ask yourself: Will the incident entertain my audience? Have I kept to details that will help the audience picture the action? Then, using the Guidelines for

Evaluating Narrative Paragraphs above and the revising chart on page 78, revise your paragraph.

PROOFREADING AND MAKING A FINAL COPY   Using the Guidelines for Proofreading on page 36, make a final copy and proofread that as well.

CHAPTER 3 WRITING REVIEW

Writing Different Types of Paragraphs.   Write a paragraph of one of the four kinds you have studied in this chapter. (Your teacher may specify the type of paragraph you are to write.) As you plan and develop the paragraph, use your knowledge of the writing process. To judge your writing, refer to the guidelines in this chapter for evaluating the type of paragraph in question. Then revise your paragraph and use the Guidelines for Proofreading on page 36 to correct it. Finally, recopy your paragraph and proofread once again.

CHAPTER 4

Writing Expository Compositions

COMPOSITIONS THAT INFORM OR EXPLAIN

A composition is a group of closely related paragraphs. Together, the paragraphs present and develop a single topic.

The purpose of the expository composition, like that of the expository paragraph, is to inform or explain. In this chapter you will learn to use the steps of the writing process to write compositions that (1) give information about a person, a place, an event, or an object; (2) explain how to make or do something; or (3) explain an opinion.

PREWRITING

SEARCHING FOR SUBJECTS

4a. Search for subjects.

Sometimes your teacher will give you a specific limited topic for an expository composition. At other times, you will be expected to find a suitable topic of your own. When you must find a topic, begin by exploring your experiences for possible subjects.

Listing Your Experiences

Your experiences include not only the things you have seen and done but also those you have heard or read about. One student searching for subjects for an expository composition made the following list of experiences:

> went wilderness camping last summer
> helped parents plant a vegetable garden
> visited Niagara Falls with neighbors
> learned from Aunt Elizabeth how to make bread
> helped get advertisers for the school paper
> saw all films in the *Star Wars* series
> read several articles about the space shuttle
> talked to an Australian teen-ager

Before You Write. To find possible subjects, ask yourself:

- What interests me the most? Why?
- What knowledge do I have through my hobbies, sports participation, reading, or interviewing?
- What have I experienced firsthand? What experiences have I heard about, read about, or seen?

EXERCISE 1. Listing Your Experiences. List at least ten experiences you have had in the past year. (*Hint:* Begin each item as in the list above, using words such as *went, visited,* and *helped.*)

Using a Writer's Journal

In a writer's journal, you record your experiences, opinions, and feelings. You can read your journal to find possible subjects for writing. For example, one student's journal entries about his family's move to another city yielded these subjects:

packing for a cross-country move
moving from a large house to a small apartment
how teen-agers can contribute to a family move
the advantages of moving to a new place
coping with a new environment

EXERCISE 2. Using a Writer's Journal. For three to five days, keep a writer's journal you can share. You may also select several entries from a journal you already keep. Using these entries as a source, list at least five possible subjects for an expository composition.

Using Brainstorming

Brainstorming is another technique you can use in your search for subjects. In brainstorming, the goal is to list as many ideas as possible without stopping to judge them. For example, one student developed the following list of possible subjects by brainstorming answers to the question "What do I know how to make or do?"

clean seashells I've collected
play the clarinet
surf
manage my free time
make submarine sandwiches
play word games
make models of prehistoric animals
arrange weekend jobs
go wilderness camping

EXERCISE 3. Using Brainstorming. At the top of a sheet of paper, write *What do I know how to make or do?* Then brainstorm to find at least ten possible subjects for an expository composition.

SELECTING AND LIMITING SUBJECTS

4b. Select and limit your subject.

With several subjects to choose from, you are ready to select one subject and to limit it to a manageable size.

Selecting a Subject

To select a subject, review the subjects you discovered through listing experiences, using a writer's journal, and brainstorming. The subject you choose should be one you understand well enough to explain to someone else.

> ***Before You Write.*** Use the following questions to select one subject to write about. The subjects in brackets show how the student who made the list on page 117 answered each question.
>
> - What subject am I interested enough in to want to explain to someone else? [playing word games, surfing, wilderness camping, playing the clarinet]
> - What subject do I know enough about to explain to someone else? [making submarine sandwiches, cleaning seashells, wilderness camping]
> - What subject do I have enough experience with to explain to someone else? [wilderness camping, cleaning seashells, arranging weekend jobs]

Notice that two subjects from page 117 do not appear as answers: "managing free time" and "making models of prehistoric animals." In answering the questions, the student realized that she did not have enough knowledge, interest, or experience to explain those subjects. Also notice that some subjects appear as answers to only one question. Usually, subjects that you understand well enough to explain to someone else will appear in at least two of the three answers.

EXERCISE 4. Selecting a Subject. Review the subjects you discovered for Exercises 1–3. Then use the questions on page 118 to select one subject for an expository composition.

Limiting a Subject

A subject is a broad area, one that has too many parts to explain clearly and precisely in the five to eight paragraphs of a short composition. The subject "wilderness camping," for example, includes such parts as skills needed, places to camp, and equipment required. To find a topic, or limited subject, that you can explain clearly and precisely in several paragraphs, you begin by dividing your subject into its parts.

CRITICAL THINKING:
Analyzing a Broad Subject

To limit a subject, you analyze it by dividing it into its smaller, more specific parts. Analyzing your subject enables you to find a topic that is limited enough for a short composition.

Depending on the subject, you can analyze it on the basis of one or more divisions: examples, features, causes, time periods, places, skills, and uses. For example, to limit "wilderness camping" for a *process composition,* one that explains how to make or do something, you could analyze the subject on the basis of places and skills:

WILDERNESS CAMPING

Places to Camp	*Skills Needed for Camping*
desert	selecting equipment
mountains	building shelters
seashore	selecting food supplies
national parks	knowing how to survive

For some subjects, you may need to continue the analysis. For example, "survival skills needed for wilderness camping" is still too broad for a composition. This topic can, in turn, be divided into its smaller parts, such as "how to survive in the mountains" or "how to survive when you are lost."

Once you have found several specific topics, select one to write about by thinking again about your knowledge, interests, and experiences. For example, the student who analyzed the subject "wilderness camping" decided that the topic that best suited her knowledge, interests, and experience was "how to survive when you are lost."

Before You Write. To limit your subject, use one or more of the following questions:

- What are *examples* of the subject?
- What are *features* of the subject?
- What are *causes* of the subject?
- What *time periods* does the subject cover?
- What *places* does the subject include?
- What *skills* does the subject require?
- What are *uses* for the subject?

Then, to select one topic to write about, use this question:

- Which topic best suits my knowledge, interests, and experience?

EXERCISE 5. Analyzing Subjects to Find Limited Topics. Choose three of the following subjects. Then use the questions above to analyze each subject to find five limited topics for an expository composition. You may have to divide a subject more than once in order to find topics that are limited enough.

1. Friends
2. Community problems
3. Athletes
4. Computers
5. Explorers
6. School rules
7. Baby-sitting
8. Shopping
9. Music
10. Movies

EXERCISE 6. Developing Your Own Limited Topics. Analyze the subject you selected in Exercise 4 or another subject to find three limited topics, one for each kind of expository composition: (1) one that explains how to make or do something, (2) one that gives information, and (3) one that explains an opinion.

EXAMPLE   *Subject:* Photography
Limited topics:
(1) Process: How to develop film
(2) Information: Equipment for color photography
(3) Opinion: Why I like taking pictures

CONSIDERING PURPOSE, AUDIENCE, AND TONE

4c. Evaluate your topic: consider purpose, audience, and tone.

Before you proceed with the writing process, take time to evaluate the limited topic you have selected.

CRITICAL THINKING:
Evaluating a Topic

To evaluate something, you judge it by applying criteria, or standards. When you write, you evaluate your limited topic in terms of your *purpose* for writing, your *audience*, and the *tone* you want to convey.

Considering Purpose

The purpose of an expository composition is to inform or to explain within the limits of several paragraphs. For example, in a short composition you would not have enough space to explain clearly and precisely all of the parts of the topic "bicycle repair." A more limited topic, such as "how to repair brakes on ten-speed bicycles," would be better suited to the purpose of a short composition.

Before You Write. To evaluate your topic in terms of purpose, ask yourself this question:

● Is my topic limited enough to explain clearly and precisely in several paragraphs?

EXERCISE 7. Evaluating Topics According to Purpose.
Number your paper 1–10. After each number, write *L* if the topic is limited enough to explain clearly and precisely in a composition. Write *NL* if it is not limited enough.

1. Planning foreign travel
2. Good movies
3. Making date muffins
4. How thunderstorms form
5. Why I prefer reading to watching television
6. School activities
7. Steps in photosynthesis
8. Preparing dinner
9. The benefits of my hobby
10. How oxygen enters the blood

Considering Audience

Since the needs and interests of different audiences vary widely, you must keep your audience in mind as you evaluate your topic. For example, suppose you are writing about wilderness survival for classmates who are experienced campers. For them, you might limit the topic to "advanced techniques in mapping an unfamiliar course." For students unfamiliar with camping, you might limit the topic to "how to survive when you are lost."

Before You Write. Use the following questions to evaluate your topic in terms of your audience. Your answers will also give you information you can use as you write your composition.

- For whom am I writing?
- What information about this topic will interest my audience?
- What does my audience already know about this topic?
- What does my audience want or need to know about it?
- What will my audience be able to understand about it?

EXERCISE 8. Evaluating Topics According to Audience.
Following are topics and audiences for expository compositions. Discuss which audience each topic *best* fits.

1. Building birdhouses for fun and profit
   a. First-graders in a reading class
   b. Craft-club members
   c. Hardware store owners
2. Enjoyable G-rated movies for teen-agers
   a. An advanced class in foreign film study
   b. Parents of elementary-school children
   c. Readers of your high-school newspaper
3. Rigging sails for recreational sailing
   a. Crew members for *America*'s Cup racing sloops
   b. An intermediate sailing class
   c. Powerboat owners
4. Hannibal's journey with elephants across the Alps in 218 B.C.
   a. Students of ancient history
   b. Travelers planning skiing vacations in the Alps
   c. Circus-animal trainers

Considering Tone

The tone of a composition reflects the writer's point of view or attitude toward the topic. That tone may be personal or impersonal, formal or informal, serious or humorous. Your attitude toward your topic is revealed through the language you use. For example, in the topic "how to survive when you are lost in the wilderness," the words *how to* and *you* convey a personal, informal tone. The same topic reworded to convey an impersonal, formal tone might read "skills required for surviving in uninhabited terrain."

> *Before You Write.* Think about your attitude toward the topic.
>
> • What is my attitude—personal or impersonal, formal or informal, serious or humorous?
> • Does the statement of my topic reflect my attitude?

EXERCISE 9. Identifying and Revising the Tone of Topics.
Identify the tone of each of the following topics. Then revise each topic to convey a different tone.

EXAMPLE   Local activities for teen-agers—*impersonal*
          How you can become active in your community—personal

1. Dangerous expeditions by Arctic explorers
2. Raising bunnies for profit
3. The ever-so-serious life and times of Paul Bunyan
4. Three decisions that changed the world
5. Why being grounded is an inconvenience

REVIEW EXERCISE A. Evaluating Your Own Topic.   Use the questions on pages 121 and 122 to evaluate one of the limited topics you found for Exercise 6 or another limited topic.

GATHERING INFORMATION

4d. Gather information on your topic.

In Chapter 1 you studied several techniques for gathering information on a topic. You can also use these techniques for an expository composition.

   Listing, or *brainstorming,* allows you to discover what you already know about a familiar topic. When you do not know your topic well, the questioning techniques may be more helpful. For compositions giving information about a topic, you can use the three *point-of-view questions* and the *5 W-How?* questions. For compositions explaining opinions, you can develop *questions about the topic,* such as: What do I think about it? What is its value? What is it good for? Other *questions about the topic* are useful for compositions explaining how to make or do something: What are its parts? How is it made or done? How is it put together?

   The student who decided to write on "how to survive when you are lost" used brainstorming to gather the following information.

mark location
essential backpacking
  equipment
look for signs of water
stay dry and warm
prevent starvation
stay put to be found
prevent dehydration
build fire
obtain food and water
prevent hypothermia
seek shelter
ration supplies
conserve energy
eat insects, birds, fish,
  frogs, small animals

eat edible berries, plants,
  seeds
make signals
smoke from fire
blasts on whistle
collect rainwater on leaves
  and in water pockets
caves
overhangs
trees
avoid panic
let rescuers find you
seek lush vegetation
follow streams to bottoms of
  hills
avoid contaminated water

EXERCISE 10. Gathering Information on a Topic. Select one topic from the following list, and gather information on it. If your teacher agrees, you and a classmate may compare and discuss the information you gather.

1. Why summer (fall, winter, or spring) is my favorite season
2. How to organize a school-sponsored car wash
3. Our community's annual Fourth of July celebration
4. How to assemble a saltwater aquarium
5. Our community's best-known historical figure

EXERCISE 11. Gathering Information on Your Own Topic. Gather information on the topic you evaluated for Review Exercise A or on another limited topic.

CLASSIFYING AND ARRANGING IDEAS

4e. Classify and arrange your ideas.

To use the information you gather as the basis for a composition, you must first organize it. In doing so, you will be developing a plan for your composition.

CRITICAL THINKING:
Classifying Ideas and Details

The first step in organizing your ideas and details is to classify them. To do this, you identify and group together items that treat the same aspect, or part, of the topic. Then you give each group a heading that shows how the items are related. For example, the ideas and details from the list on page 125 can be classified into the following three groups.

GROUP 1: *To Stay Dry and Warm*
> prevent hypothermia, seek shelter, build fire, conserve energy, caves, overhangs, trees

GROUP 2: *To Obtain Food and Water*
> prevent dehydration and starvation, eat insects, eat edible berries, ration supplies, collect rainwater on leaves and in water pockets, look for signs of water, avoid contaminated water, seek lush vegetation, follow streams to bottoms of hills

GROUP 3: *To Be Found*
> stay put, make signals, smoke from fire, blasts on whistle, avoid panic, mark location, let rescuers find you

Notice that some ideas from the original list have been omitted. "Essential backpacking equipment," for example, does not fit into any of the three groups because it is not closely connected to the other ideas and details. Similarly, you may not use all of the information you gather on your topic.

> *Before You Write.* Use the following questions to classify the information you have gathered:
> - Which items treat the same part of the topic?
> - What headings show how the items in each group are related?

EXERCISE 12. Classifying Ideas and Details. Classify the ideas and details you gathered for Exercise 10.

Arranging Ideas

Each of your groups of ideas can be the basis of one paragraph of your composition. In order to present the information clearly, you must decide on a logical order for the groups.

Your specific purpose may suggest a logical order to use. For example, to explain how to assemble the parts of a bicycle, you would use *chronological,* or *sequential, order* to show the order of the steps. To explain your opinion of a school policy, you might arrange your reasons in *order of importance:* from most important to least important or the opposite. To explain how to assemble a shadow box, you might use *spatial order:* from top to bottom or from inside to outside.

When arranging ideas, it is sometimes important to decide whether the ideas in one group are necessary for understanding those in another group. For example, the information about survival skills can be arranged with the ideas about the primary objective—being found—first, followed by those on staying warm and obtaining food and water.

For more information on arranging ideas, see pages 50–55 of Chapter 2.

Before You Write. To arrange your ideas in a logical order, use the following questions:

- Does my specific purpose suggest the use of chronological order, spatial order, or order of importance?
- Will my audience need to understand certain ideas before they will be able to understand other ideas?

EXERCISE 13. Arranging Ideas and Details. Arrange the groups of ideas and details you classified for Exercise 12.

EXERCISE 14. Classifying and Arranging Ideas and Details on Your Own Topic. Classify and then arrange the ideas and details you gathered for Exercise 11.

Developing a Topic Outline

By grouping and arranging your ideas, you are developing an informal plan for your composition. You can also prepare a *formal,* or *topic, outline,* which has a specific format.

A topic outline is one in which the items are words or phrases, not complete sentences. It shows the relative importance of the ideas as well as their order. The main headings are the most important ideas, and the subheadings are the supporting ideas and details.

A topic outline should include a title and a statement of purpose. Be sure that the title clearly indicates your topic and is interesting. Notice how the following topic outline adheres to the rules for outline form.

Topic Outline

Title: Surviving in the Wilderness
Purpose: To explain how to survive when you are lost

   I. How to be found   main topic
    A. Avoiding panic
    B. Marking your location
    C. Staying put   subtopics
    D. Letting rescuers find you
    E. Making signals
       1. Giving smoke signals   further divisions of
       2. Making blasts on whistle subtopics
  II. How to stay dry and warm
    A. Preventing hypothermia
    B. Seeking shelter
       1. Using caves   note use of words or phrases,
       2. Using overhangs   not sentences, throughout out-
       3. Using trees   line
    C. Building fire
    D. Conserving energy
 III. How to obtain food and water
    A. Rationing supplies
    B. Preventing starvation
       1. Eating berries, plants, seeds

2. Eating insects, birds, fish,
   frogs, small mammals
C. Preventing dehydration
   1. Collecting rainwater on leaves
      and in water pockets
   2. Digging to reach water table
   3. Looking for signs of water
      a. Seeking lush vegetation at
         bases of cliffs
      b. Following streams to bottoms
         of hills
D. Avoiding contaminated water

Using Outline Form

Observe the following rules when you prepare a topic outline.

(1) Place the title and the purpose above the outline. These are not numbered or lettered parts of the outline.

(2) Use Roman numerals for the main topics. Subtopics are given capital letters, then Arabic numerals, then small letters, then Arabic numerals in parentheses, and then small letters in parentheses. Study the following outline form:

Correct Outline Form

I. main topic
  A. ⎫
  B. ⎬ subtopics of I
    1. ⎫
    2. ⎬ subtopics of B
      a. ⎫
      b. ⎬ subtopics of 2
        (1) ⎫
        (2) ⎬ subtopics of b
          (a) ⎫
          (b) ⎬ subtopics of (2)
II.
  A. etc.

(3) Each number or letter in an outline must have a topic.

Each number or letter must stand on its own line. Never, for example, write fig *1A* or *A1* in an outline.

(4) When subtopics are included in an outline, there must be more than one subtopic under a topic.

Since you cannot divide something into fewer than two parts, you cannot divide a topic into fewer than two subtopics. If you find yourself with a single subtopic, revise the topic above it to include the subtopic.

INCORRECT   F. How to be found
            1. Being found by rescuers
CORRECT   F. Letting rescuers find you

(5) A subtopic must be closely related to the topic under which it is placed.

UNRELATED   D. Making signals
            1. Making smoke signals
            2. Avoiding panic [not related to topic]

(6) Indent subtopics so that all letters or numbers of the same kind are lined up directly under one another.

(7) Begin each topic and subtopic with a capital letter.

Since topics and subtopics are not sentences, they should not be followed by periods.

(8) Do not include the terms *Introduction, Body,* and *Conclusion* in the outline.

These terms are not topics that you intend to discuss; they should not be listed in your outline.

EXERCISE 15. Preparing a Topic Outline. On your paper, write the following title, purpose, and main headings, leaving several blank lines between the headings. Then write each item on the list under the heading to which it is related. Add numbers and letters to form a topic outline.

Title: My Kind of Town
Purpose: To explain why I like my hometown
Main Headings: Location
               School
               Entertainment facilities
               People

Unsorted List:

friendly	well-trained teachers
near a large city	in the mountains
charitable	modern classrooms
superior library	recreation center
parks	well-balanced curriculum
on a river	theaters

EXERCISE 16. Preparing a Topic Outline. The following list includes ideas and details on the topic "facts about the moon" as well as four items that can serve as main headings for an outline. First, classify and arrange the ideas and details under the main headings. Then write them as a topic outline, using the form on pages 128–29. Add an appropriate title and a specific purpose.

Ideas and details:

Only celestial body visited by human beings
Shortest distance from the earth: 221,456 miles
The moon-earth connection
One-sixth the earth's gravity
The moon's gravity
Twelve men on moon in Apollo program
The lunar surface
Greatest distance from the earth: 252,711 miles
Surface hotter and colder than earth's surface
Highest temperature: 260° F
Average distance from the earth: 238,857 miles
The earth's only natural satellite

32,000 major craters visible from the earth
The earth's nearest celestial neighbor
Too weak to catch and keep an atmosphere
First moon landing by *Apollo 11* on July 20, 1969
Earth orbit every 29½ days
Consequently, no weather on the moon
Oldest soil on surface about 4.6 billion years old
Lowest temperature: −400° F

EXERCISE 17. Preparing Your Own Topic Outline. Prepare a topic outline for the ideas and details you classified and arranged for Exercise 14. Use the form on pages 128–29.

WRITING A THESIS STATEMENT

4f. Write a thesis statement.

In a paragraph, the topic sentence states the one main idea. The sentence that states the one main idea in a composition is called the *thesis statement.*

The thesis statement indicates the purpose of the composition and makes clear what aspects of the topic the writer will discuss. It tells the audience what the composition will be about, and it reminds the writer to keep to the main idea throughout the composition.

For example, using the topic outline on pages 128–29, the writer developed the following thesis statement: *For a lost camper, wilderness survival depends on knowing how to be found, staying dry and warm, and obtaining food and water.*

Notice how the thesis statement includes each main idea in the outline. It also makes the purpose of the composition clear, and it does so briefly, directly, and specifically.

> *Before You Write.* In developing a thesis statement, keep these points in mind:
>
> ● Indicate the purpose of your composition.
> ● Make clear what main ideas you will discuss.

EXERCISE 18. Evaluating Thesis Statements. Decide which of the following thesis statements would be most suitable for a composition based on the topic outline you prepared for Exercise 16.

1. The moon is a fascinating celestial body.
2. Lunar exploration has provided detailed knowledge about the gravity and surface of Earth's nearest celestial neighbor.
3. The moon is Earth's nearest neighbor and is the only celestial body ever visited by human beings.

EXERCISE 19. Writing a Thesis Statement. Using the following topic outline, write a thesis statement.

Title: The Language of Baseball
Purpose: To give information on baseball slang

   I. Equipment
      A. Bats
      B. Balls
  II. Pitches
      A. Fast balls
      B. Curve balls
 III. Plays
      A. Strikeouts
      B. Line drives
         1. Foul balls
         2. Fair balls
      C. Home runs

REVIEW EXERCISE B. Writing Your Own Thesis Statement. Using your informal plan or topic outline as a guide, write a thesis statement for your composition.

WRITING

4g. Write the parts of your composition: the introduction, the body, and the conclusion.

An expository composition has three main parts: an introduction, a body, and a conclusion. Each part has a specific function.

Writing the Introduction

(1) The introduction should arouse the reader's interest and present the thesis statement.

The introduction should make the reader want to read further. It should also establish the tone of the composition. The thesis statement, either as originally written or in a revised form, is often the last sentence in the introduction.

Following are five ways to write the introduction of an expository composition. Notice how each type of introduction catches the attention of the audience and presents the thesis statement. (Each thesis statement is underlined in red.)

1. *Begin with an anecdote or example.* When you are writing for an audience unfamiliar with your topic, a brief anecdote or example can vividly and quickly reveal aspects of your topic.

> In the early 1940's a Chinese sailor survived on a raft in the Atlantic Ocean for 133 days. I thought about his still-unsurpassed feat last summer as I sat alone in a pine forest deep in a national park. My backpacking friends had gone ahead to explore a nearby ridge, and within moments I could no longer hear their voices. Strange thoughts crept into my mind. What if we were separated? What if I became lost in the woods? <u>I realized that my survival, like the sailor's, would depend on my skill at being found, staying dry and warm, and obtaining food and water.</u>

2. *Begin with a question.* A question that requires more than a simple yes or no answer encourages the reader to read on to find an answer.

> What skills enable a hiker or camper to survive being lost in the wilderness? <u>My own experience suggests that knowing how to be found, how to stay dry and warm, and how to obtain food and water can get a lost camper or hiker out of the woods alive.</u>

3. *Begin with a direct statement of the topic.* In a short composition, especially on a topic in which reader interest is already strong, you may begin simply by stating your thesis.

There is no need to fear being lost in the wilderness. Survival can be more than just a stroke of good luck for hikers and campers who know how to be found, how to stay dry and warm, and how to obtain food and water.

4. *Begin with a statement that contradicts your thesis and counter it in your thesis statement.* This technique arouses interest by taking the audience by surprise.

To survive being lost in the wilderness seems impossible. By knowing how to be found, how to stay dry and warm, and how to obtain food and water, however, a lost camper or hiker can survive this frightening experience.

5. *Begin with general background information.* This method can be especially useful when your audience is not familiar with your topic.

Each year increasing numbers of hikers and campers enjoy our national parks and wilderness areas. Being lost is always a possibility for those who enter the wilderness, but it does not have to end in disaster. For a lost camper, survival depends on knowing how to be found, how to stay dry and warm, and how to obtain food and water.

When You Write. In writing your introduction:

- Catch the interest of the audience.
- Present your thesis statement.
- Establish the tone of the composition.

EXERCISE 20. Writing Introductory Paragraphs. Select one of the following thesis statements. Then write two different types of introductions for it, referring to the models above and on the previous page. Be sure to include the thesis statement in each introduction.

1. Building a birdhouse involves gathering the necessary materials, assembling the parts, and adding the finishing touches.
2. With its memorable characters, exciting special effects, and action-packed plot, the *Star Wars* saga is my favorite science-fiction film series.
3. Our school's student leaders have started several fund-raising projects to support the intramural program.
4. To establish a neighborhood odd-job service, you should conduct a survey of your neighbors' needs, decide what jobs will be your specialties, and determine your fees.
5. The typical curriculum at our school consists of a mix of academic and nonacademic subjects.

EXERCISE 21. Writing Your Own Introductory Paragraph.
Write an introduction for your own composition, using the thesis statement and topic outline you have developed.

Writing the Body

(2) The body should state and develop the main points in the outline.

The body of a composition consists of several paragraphs, each of which should support one part of the thesis statement. As a general rule, you should write a separate paragraph for each point in your thesis statement. For example, the thesis statement for the composition on how to survive when you are lost includes three main points: how to be found, how to stay dry and warm, and how to obtain food and water. Each of these points should be developed in a separate paragraph.

The body of each of the other kinds of expository compositions can be developed in much the same way. For instance, in the body of a composition that explains an opinion, each paragraph should present one reason supporting the opinion. In the body of a composition that gives information, each paragraph should develop one aspect of the topic.

As you write the body, be sure to use your topic outline, which lists your main points and supporting details. Include a topic sentence in each paragraph, and support it by using one of the methods of paragraph development. (See Chapter 3.) The body paragraphs may or may not end with clincher sentences.

Two additional elements to consider as you draft the body of your composition are *emphasis* and *coherence*.

(2a) Emphasize your most important ideas.

In any composition, some ideas are more important than others. You can emphasize your most important ideas in three ways.

1. *Direct statement*. Phrases like *the most important reason* and *the major step in preparation* identify the ideas that should receive the greatest emphasis.

2. *Emphasis by position*. Ordinarily, the strongest positions in the body are the first and last parts. In compositions explaining opinions, for example, it is usually wise to begin and end strongly, putting your weakest reasons in the middle.

3. *Emphasis by proportion*. The more important the idea, the more space you will want to devote to it. Keep in mind, however, that it is the idea itself, not the number of subtopics it has in the outline, that determines its importance.

EXERCISE 22. Discussing Emphasis. In a magazine or newspaper, find an expository article and bring it to class. Be prepared to discuss how the writer achieves emphasis in the article.

(2b) Connect your ideas to achieve coherence.

A coherent composition is one in which the flow of ideas is logical and therefore easy to follow. One way to achieve coherence is to arrange your ideas to show how they are related, as you did when you prepared your topic outline. By following this outline as you draft the body, you present your ideas in a logical order.

Another way to achieve coherence is to use *transitions* to join ideas within and between paragraphs. Two kinds of transitions are *transitional expressions* and *direct references*.

Since transitional expressions indicate the relationship between ideas, you must be careful to use those that are appropriate. For example, compositions that follow chronological order use words such as *first* (*second, third,* etc.), *next, then,* and *finally.* Compositions that use order of importance rely on expressions such as *above all, moreover,* and *furthermore.*

Direct references refer the reader to something mentioned in a previous sentence or paragraph. One form of direct reference is the use of words such as *this, those, other,* and *another.* A second form is the repetition of key words or ideas.

(For further help with using transitional expressions and direct references, see pages 57–59 of Chapter 2.)

When You Write.   In writing the body of your composition:

- Use your topic outline as a guide.
- Write a separate paragraph for each point in your thesis statement.
- Include in each paragraph a topic sentence developed by means of one of the methods of paragraph development.
- Emphasize your most important ideas.
- Use transitions to join ideas within and between paragraphs.

EXERCISE 23. Connecting Paragraphs with Transitions.
The following paragraphs make up the body of a composition on "why reading is important." Revise the first sentence in both the second and third paragraphs by adding a transitional expression or a direct reference to connect the ideas between the paragraphs.

Reading is an essential skill in all areas of life. Every school subject, from English to math, requires the ability to read. Nearly every job, skilled or unskilled, requires some reading, whether it be following the directions on a container of floor wax or interpreting the Constitution of the United States. Most spare-time activities, from finding a number in a telephone book to buying tickets to Disney World, also require reading skills.

Reading can be a limitless source of pleasure. Through the written word, readers can travel to faraway places and to places that exist only in the writer's imagination. They can meet people who lived centuries ago as well as characters who have never existed and never will. They can witness historical or fictional events that changed—or might have changed, or may someday change—the world.

Reading is a completely portable pastime. It can take place on a crowded subway car or on a deserted beach, in a tree-shaded hammock on a sweltering day or under layers of blankets on a freezing one. It can fill uninterrupted hours or be fitted into brief moments between other activities.

EXERCISE 24. Writing the Body of Your Own Composition. Using your own topic outline and thesis statement as guides, write the body of your composition.

Writing the Conclusion

(3) The conclusion should clinch the main points made in the body of the composition.

As the last paragraph of the composition, the conclusion leaves a final impression on the audience. That impression should reinforce the main idea presented in the thesis statement, thus giving the composition a sense of completeness.

To write the conclusion, think about the main idea in your thesis statement, and ask yourself, "What do I want my audience to remember most about this topic?" For example, a composition that explains an opinion can conclude by summarizing the reasons given or by restating the opinion without repeating it word for word. The following conclusion restates the writer's opinion that Leonardo da Vinci was an extraordinary man.

No one can explain him. "Genius" does scant justice to the phenomenal range and originality of his work. There is no name, from all history, to place alongside his. Put most simply, Leonardo da Vinci remains the most gifted human being who ever lived.

LEO ROSTEN

A process composition, which explains how to make or do something, usually ends by focusing on the outcome of the process. The following conclusion discusses how a lantern made from a candle and a tin can can be safely used.

This make-do device can be safely set on a table or other flat surface or be carried by its wooden handle. You can also use it to light a tent or similar shelter by suspending the lantern in front of your abode's door. *It's best not to use any open flame inside a tent.* The shiny back (ex-bottom) of the can will serve admirably as a reflector, while the mouth of the lantern will act as a sort of barrel that allows you to aim the illumination. And if you keep its back pointed into the wind, this little light will shine even in a storm.

THE MOTHER EARTH NEWS HOUSEHOLD & HOMESTEAD
ALMANAC FOR 1985

A composition that gives information can end by restating the aspects of the topic discussed in the composition. In the following conclusion, the writer restates his main idea: that bird migration, despite extensive study, remains mysterious.

Despite the certainty of their yearly sweeps across the world, the interaction between migrants and the cues that guide them is still elusive. It will probably be some time before anyone knows exactly how birds—some weighing no more than a teacup—complete their seasonal feats.

PATRICK COOKE

When You Write. To write your conclusion:

- Reinforce the main idea presented in your thesis statement.

EXERCISE 25. Evaluating a Conclusion. In a magazine or newspaper, find an expository article and bring it to class. Explain why the conclusion does or does not provide an effective ending to the article.

EXERCISE 26. Writing the Conclusion for Your Own Composition. Write the conclusion for your composition.

Studying a Sample Composition

As you read the following expository composition, notice how the introduction, body, and conclusion work together to present and develop the main idea in the thesis statement.

SURVIVING IN THE WILDERNESS

Each year increasing numbers of hikers and campers enjoy our national parks and wilderness areas. While being lost is always a possibility for those who enter the wilderness, it does not have to end in disaster. For a lost camper, wilderness survival depends on knowing how to be found, how to stay dry and warm, and how to obtain food and water. | introduction

thesis statement

Knowing how to be found is very important for a lost camper. If you think you are lost, begin by stopping immediately and remaining calm. Check to see if you have just temporarily lost sight of your trail. You can do this by marking your location and taking short walks in several directions, returning each time to your starting point. If you do not find the trail, it is absolutely essential for you to stay in one place so that rescuers can find you. You can also aid rescue efforts by signaling. If you can, give smoke signals from a damp fire or whistle blasts in sets of three, | topic sentence/main topic I: how to be found

body

the universal distress signal, to indicate your location. If you hear voices in the distance, shout but do not move; let your voice guide rescuers to your location. Despite these efforts, however, you may not be found right away and may have to spend the night in the wilderness. Be sure to prepare for this possibility long before night falls.

In preparing for the night, your aim should be to keep dry and warm. Even in the summertime, hikers and campers risk hypothermia, a condition in which body temperature rapidly drops below normal. To prevent hypothermia, stay dry—also an important step toward staying warm—by seeking shelter. If you have a tent, set it up to protect both you and your equipment from a sudden downpour. If you have no sleeping gear, seek shelter in your surroundings. Caves, rock overhangs, and low-lying tree branches can be safe, dry places that offer protection from the wind and rain. Of course, if you know how and have the necessary supplies, you should build a fire. Another way to stay warm is to avoid wasting energy. Try not to rush about aimlessly. By not becoming chilled and exhausted, you can also avoid the potential dangers of injury, confusion, and panic.

Just as important as staying dry and warm is obtaining food and water. When you realize that you are lost and cannot predict when you will be found, you should ration your food and water supplies. When you run out of food, you do not risk starvation. Remember

[margin notes]

topic sentence/main topic II: how to stay dry, warm; also includes direct reference to previous sentence

direct reference

direct reference

topic sentence/main topic III: how to obtain food and water; also includes a direct reference and shows order of importance that the wilderness is full of edible plants, berries, and seeds. Eat what you know is safe and avoid what you are uncertain of, such as wild mushrooms. You may also have to overcome squeamishness in the interest of staying alive. You can catch and cook insects, birds, fish, frogs, and small mammals. Water is <u>even more important than food,</u> for you must prevent dehydration, or loss of body fluids, at all costs. To obtain water, collect rainwater on leaves and in water pockets, and dig into the soil to reach the water table. Also look for signs of water, such as lush vegetation at the bases of cliffs or streams at the bottoms of hills. Without water-testing equipment, you will have difficulty determining if water is contaminated; a general guide is to avoid water holes with no vegetation growing around them. If you can build a fire, you can also boil water for drinking. Above all, remember that by calmly using what is available, you need not starve or die of thirst.

direct reference

Being lost in the wilderness does not have to be a tragic experience. By using the resources immediately available to you, you can keep yourself alive until help reaches you—without injury, exhaustion, confusion, or panic. It is all a matter of using your good sense and skills for the most important purpose: to stay alive.

conclusion

reinforces thesis statement

EXERCISE 27. Studying an Expository Composition. Answer each of the following questions about the sample composition. You may refer to the explanations on pages 134–40.

1. On pages 134–35 you read five different types of introductions. Which type is used in this composition? Do you think one of the other four introductions would have been more effective? Why or why not?
2. Select any one of the paragraphs in the body. What method of paragraph development does it use? Do you think the paragraph contains enough supporting details to make the topic sentence clear? Why or why not?
3. Which paragraphs in the body contain clincher sentences? How effective is each one?
4. How does the writer achieve coherence in the composition? Emphasis?
5. What final impression does the conclusion leave on you? How does the conclusion reinforce the thesis statement?

REVIEW EXERCISE C. Writing a Process Composition. Write a composition explaining how to make or do something. You may select a topic from the following list or use a topic of your own. Refer to the Guidelines for Writing a Process Composition on pages 152–53.

1. How to plant a backyard vegetable garden
2. How to prepare three kinds of nutritious beverages
3. How to audition for a community theater production
4. How to plan a picnic
5. How to choose a personal computer

REVIEW EXERCISE D. Writing a Composition Giving Information About a Topic. Write a composition giving information about a person, place, event, or object. Select one of the following topics, or use a topic of your own. Refer to the Guidelines for Writing a Composition Giving Information on pages 153–54.

1. My three most outstanding accomplishments
2. Opportunities for weekend jobs in my neighborhood
3. My family's most prized possessions
4. Four fund-raising projects for my favorite school activity
5. Community activities for artistic teen-agers

REVIEW EXERCISE E. Writing a Composition Explaining an Opinion. Write a composition in which you explain an opinion. You may use one of the following topics or one of your own. Refer to the Guidelines for Writing a Composition Explaining an Opinion on page 154.

1. Why I value my privacy
2. Why doing nothing is sometimes worthwhile
3. Why teen-agers make great baby sitters
4. Why sports do (or do not) build a young person's character
5. Why Latin is worth studying

EVALUATING

During the prewriting and drafting stages of the writing process, you focused on developing a topic and on deciding how to write about it. With a first draft completed, you are now ready to evaluate, or judge, what you have written.

EVALUATING YOUR WRITING

4h. Evaluate the content, organization, and style of your draft.

When you evaluate a draft, your aim is to locate its strengths and weaknesses. You need to decide what changes would improve your draft. In doing this, your work as a writer changes. Now you must see your draft from a different perspective. That is, you must become a reader of your own writing, judging how well you have explained the topic to your audience.

You should evaluate three aspects of your draft: its *content* (what you say about your topic), its *organization* (how ideas are arranged), and its *style* (how you use language to explain your topic). The following Guidelines for Evaluating Expository Compositions present standards for judging these aspects of your draft. The guidelines will help you discover what you should change in order to achieve your purpose: to explain your topic clearly and thoroughly to your particular audience. Read each guideline question and answer each honestly. When you answer no, you have located a place in your draft where you need to make changes. You should also refer to the general evaluation guidelines found in Chapter 1 (page 28).

GUIDELINES FOR EVALUATING EXPOSITORY COMPOSITIONS

Purpose	1. Does the introduction tell the audience what the composition will be about? Does it attract the audience's attention?
Paragraph Unity	2. Does each paragraph in the body discuss only one main idea about the topic?
Thesis Development	3. Are enough points included to help the audience understand what the paper is about? (For a short paper, are there at least two supporting points?)
Conclusion	4. Is it obvious that the paper has ended? (The audience should not be left hanging.)
Coherence	5. Does the paper have a clear organizational pattern? Is the pattern logical? Does it suit the topic?
Coherence	6. Are ideas clearly related, both within and between paragraphs? Do words like *this, those, another, first,* and *finally* link ideas?
Emphasis	7. Can the audience easily identify the most important idea in the composition?
Word Choice	8. Will the audience understand the language used in the composition? Are technical terms and unusual words defined or explained?

EXERCISE 28. Applying the Guidelines for Evaluating Expository Compositions. Following is a draft of the second paragraph in the sample composition (pages 141–43). Read the draft and reread the Guidelines for Evaluating Expository Compositions. Then answer each question that follows. Be prepared to explain your answers.

Knowing how to be found is very important for a lost camper. If you think you are lost, initiate action by stopping immediately and remaining calm. Check to see if you have just temporarily lost sight of your trail. To check to see if this is the case, start by marking your location and taking short walks in several directions, returning each time to your starting point. You can also aid rescue efforts by signaling. If you bomb out, it is absolutely essential for you to stay in one place so that rescuers can find you. If you can, give smoke signals from a damp fire which you may have learned how to do at summer camp or whistle blasts in sets of three to indicate your location. If you hear voices in the distance, shout, but do not move; let your voice guide rescuers to your location. You may not be found right away and may have to spend the night in the wilderness. Be sure to prepare for this possibility long before night falls. Just thinking about staying in the woods overnight gives some people the creeps.

1. What is the main idea of the paragraph? What points support it?
2. Does the draft include any ideas that do not explain the main idea? If so, what are they?
3. What organizational pattern does the draft follow? Are there any ideas that seem to be out of order?
4. The writer's audience is high-school students who are beginning campers. Is the language of the draft appropriate for this audience? Why or why not?
5. What specific problems do you think the writer ought to remedy in this draft? Give at least one reason for each change you suggest.

EXERCISE 29. Evaluating Your Own Composition. Judge your own draft by answering each of the questions in the Guidelines for Evaluating Expository Compositions. Mark places in your draft where you should make changes, and keep this draft for later use. You may also want to exchange papers with a classmate to evaluate each other's work.

REVISING

By evaluating your draft, you locate problems, or items you should change. Using this information, you should then revise your draft, making the changes that will improve it.

REVISING YOUR WRITING

4i. Revise your draft, making changes to improve the content, organization, and style of your composition.

You can use four techniques to revise any piece of writing: you can *cut,* or omit, words, phrases, and sentences; you can *add* ideas and details; you can *reorder,* or rearrange, words, sentences, and paragraphs; and you can *replace* one thing with another. The following chart suggests how you can use these techniques to revise expository compositions.

REVISING EXPOSITORY COMPOSITIONS		
PROBLEM	**TECHNIQUE**	**REVISION**
The introduction is dull.	Add	Begin with an anecdote or example, a direct statement, a contradictory statement, or some background information.
The introduction has a weak thesis statement or none at all.	Add	Include a sentence that clearly states what the composition is about.
A paragraph discusses more than one main idea.	Cut/Add	Remove details that do not discuss one main idea. Make a new paragraph with these details, or add them to an existing paragraph that discusses the same idea.

PROBLEM	TECHNIQUE	REVISION
There is not enough support for the main idea of the composition.	Add	Add at least one more paragraph to support the main idea. (It should include a topic sentence that is backed up with facts, details, statistics, examples, incidents, or reasons.)
The composition does not end obviously.	Add	Add ideas and details that emphasize the main idea without repeating it word for word.
The order of ideas doesn't make sense.	Reorder	Find the sentence or paragraph where the composition becomes unclear; move it so the order of ideas is clear.
It is not clear how ideas are related.	Add	Add words that help to link ideas, such as *these, other, first, second, then,* or *thus.*
It is not clear which idea is the most important.	Add/Reorder	Show which point is the most important by (1) stating it in a sentence, (2) adding information about it, or (3) placing it at the beginning or at the end of the body of the composition.
Some of the words are not familiar to the audience.	Add/Replace	Add definitions and explanations. Replace technical terms or unusual vocabulary with familiar words.

Following is a revised draft of the second paragraph in the sample composition (pages 141–43). As you study the paragraph, refer to the notes in the margin. They indicate what revision strategies the writer used.

1   Knowing how to be found is very im-

2   portant for a lost camper. If you think you

3   are lost, ~~initiate action~~ *begin* by stopping imme-   replace

4   diately and remaining calm. Check to see

5   if you have just temporarily lost sight of

6   your trail. ~~To check to see if this is the~~ *You can do this*   replace

7   ~~case, start~~ by marking your location and

8   taking short walks in several directions, *(returning each time to your starting point)*   add

9   You can also aid rescue efforts by signal-   reorder

10   ing. If you ~~bomb out,~~ *do not find the trail,* it is absolutely essen-   replace

11   tial for you to stay in one place so that

12   rescuers can find you. If you can, give

13   smoke signals from a damp fire ~~which you~~   cut

14   ~~may have learned how to do at summer~~   cut

15   ~~camp~~ or whistle blasts in sets of three, *the universal distress signal,* to   add

16   indicate your location. If you hear voices

17   in the distance, shout but do not move; let

18   your voice guide rescuers to your location.

19   *Despite these efforts, however,* You may not be found right away and may   add

20   have to spend the night in the wilderness.

21   Be sure to prepare for this possibility long

22   before night falls. ~~Just thinking about stay-~~   cut

23   ~~ing in the woods overnight gives some peo-~~

24   ~~ple the creeps.~~

EXERCISE 30. Evaluating a Revised Paragraph. Answer each of the following questions by referring to the preceding paragraph.

1. The writer replaced words or phrases in lines 3, 6, and 10. Why do you think the writer made each change?
2. The writer added three phrases to the paragraph (lines 8, 15, and 19). How do these changes help the reader?
3. Why do you think the writer cut the clause in lines 13–15 and the sentence in lines 22–24?
4. Why do you think the writer moved the sentence in lines 9–10?
5. Does the revision correct any of the problems you located in Exercise 28? Do you think the revised version is better than the first draft? Why or why not?

EXERCISE 31. Revising Your Own Composition. Use the revising chart on pages 148–49 to decide what strategies you should use to revise your composition. Then make the necessary changes. For further help on sentence combining and revising, refer to Chapter 11. You may also want to exchange papers with a classmate.

PROOFREADING

4j. Proofread your composition.

Mistakes in capitalization, spelling, punctuation, grammar, or usage may confuse or distract your readers. By checking to make sure that your writing is correct, you make it more effective. Use the Guidelines for Proofreading on pages 36–37 to proofread any expository composition you write.

EXERCISE 32. Proofreading Your Expository Composition. Proofread your expository composition, using the Symbols for Revising and Proofreading on page 41. If your teacher agrees, you may also exchange compositions with a classmate to double-check each other's proofreading.

WRITING THE FINAL VERSION

4k. Prepare your final copy.

After you proofread your revised draft, you are ready to prepare the final copy of your composition. As you do so, be sure to follow correct manuscript form (see Chapter 1) or your teacher's specific instructions. Before you give your paper to your audience, proofread again.

REVIEW EXERCISE F. Preparing Your Final Copy. Prepare a final copy of any expository composition you have written and revised in this chapter. Be sure to proofread again after you have recopied your composition.

CHAPTER 4 WRITING REVIEW

Writing an Expository Composition. Using your knowledge of the writing process, write one of the following expository compositions. As you develop your composition, refer to the appropriate Guidelines on the next three pages.

1. A composition explaining how to make or do something
2. A composition giving information about a person, place, event, or object
3. A composition explaining an opinion

Guidelines for Writing a Process Composition

PREWRITING Select a process you understand thoroughly. To gather information, first determine all materials, supplies, or tools needed, including exact amounts required. Then ask yourself what someone unfamiliar with the process would need to know in order to carry it out. As you jot down your ideas, determine whether any terms will need to be defined or explained. Next, list all the necessary steps and arrange them in chronological order. Double-check your list to be sure that you have not left out any steps and that they are in the correct order. Prepare an informal plan or a topic outline; then write a thesis statement that identifies the process and indicates your purpose.

WRITING Write an introductory paragraph that will catch the interest of your audience, being sure to include your thesis statement. Follow your topic outline or informal plan as you write the body, devoting one paragraph to each main heading. Use appropriate transitions to show the sequence of the steps, and emphasize your most important points by means of direct statement, position, or proportion. In your conclusion, make clear the expected outcome of the process.

EVALUATING, REVISING, AND PROOFREADING Check your explanation by following your instructions *exactly* to determine where you need to add, omit, change, or rearrange details. Also, make sure that you have clearly defined or explained all technical terms for your audience. Then proofread your paper carefully and prepare a final copy.

Guidelines for Writing a Composition Giving Information

PREWRITING Limit your topic to include only those aspects you can make clear in the space available. Depending on your topic and audience, gather concrete or sensory details, facts, statistics, examples, or incidents. You will need to find not only *enough* information but the *right kind* for your purpose. For a composition on your community's recreational facilities, for example, the kinds of facilities and their locations, services, and hours of operation would be appropriate; an incident that you witnessed at the community swimming pool would not. Organize the information so that it will be easy for your audience to follow, and prepare an informal plan or topic outline. Use this outline or plan to draft your thesis statement.

WRITING Incorporate your thesis statement into an introductory paragraph that will catch the interest of your audience. As you draft the body of your composition, follow your outline, connecting ideas within and between paragraphs with transitions and emphasizing your most important ideas. In your conclusion, reinforce your thesis statement by summarizing the main points in the body.

EVALUATING, REVISING, AND PROOFREADING As you reread your composition, determine whether you have included enough information of the right kind. Evaluate the arrangement of the ideas, and make sure that your word choice is appropriate for your audience 'and accurately reflects your attitude toward the topic. Proofread your revised draft; then prepare a final copy.

Guidelines for Writing a Composition Explaining an Opinion

PREWRITING Select as a topic a personal belief or preference. For example, "astronomy is a fascinating hobby" is an opinion you can explain but "Earth is the third planet from the sun" is a fact that requires no further explanation. Next, list as many reasons as you can think of to explain your opinion, using the *5 W-How?* questions to find specific details such as facts and examples to support each reason. Then, keeping your audience in mind, select the strongest reasons and most vivid details to use, classify them, and arrange them in order of importance. Prepare an informal plan or topic outline, and write a thesis statement that clearly sets forth your opinion.

WRITING Write an introductory paragraph that identifies your topic, suggests your purpose, and includes your thesis statement. In drafting the body, follow your outline, using one reason as the topic sentence of each paragraph and supporting it with specific details. As you write, use appropriate transitions to connect ideas within and between paragraphs, and use direct statement, position, or proportion to emphasize your most important ideas. Reemphasize your opinion in the conclusion by summarizing your reasons or by restating the opinion.

EVALUATING, REVISING, AND PROOFREADING With your audience and purpose in mind, review each of your reasons and its supporting details. Think again about the arrangement of the ideas, and evaluate your word choice to make sure it is appropriate for your topic, purpose, and audience. Then proofread your paper carefully, and prepare a final copy.

CHAPTER 5

Writing Persuasive Compositions

LETTERS TO THE EDITOR, PERSUASIVE COMPOSITIONS

The purpose of persuasion is to convince an audience to agree with an opinion and, sometimes, to perform an action. In this chapter you will use the writing process with two forms of persuasion: letters to the editor and persuasive compositions.

WRITING A LETTER TO THE EDITOR

Letters to the editor appear on the editorial pages of newspapers and in special columns in magazines. Such letters should be brief and direct. To be effective, though, they must present sufficient reasons and evidence to be convincing.

PREWRITING

Choosing a Topic and Considering Audience and Tone

5a. Choose a debatable topic, and consider audience and tone.

The *topic* for a letter to the editor should be a debatable issue, one on which people can reach different conclusions. Often, letters to the editor comment on a story, photograph, or editorial that appeared in the publication. (Occasionally, a letter to the editor is written simply to praise or to criticize a person or an organization. The purpose of such a letter is to inform the public of the person's or the group's accomplishments or shortcomings rather than to persuade.)

The *audience* for a letter to the editor of a local newspaper is the general public—people of all ages, with a wide variety of backgrounds. For a special-interest publication, such as one on woodworking or black history, the audience is people who share that interest. Who is the audience for a letter to the editor of your school newspaper?

The *tone* of a letter to the editor should usually be serious and unemotional. Using a reasonable tone helps convince the reader that you are being fair and logical.

Before You Write. In choosing a topic, ask yourself:

- Is the topic a debatable issue?
- Will the topic interest the audience?
- Can I write about the topic using a serious tone?

EXERCISE 1. Analyzing a Letter to the Editor. Read the following letter to the editor and then answer the questions.

To the Editor:

I was utterly flabbergasted by the *Bulletin*'s August 3 editorial, in which you irresponsibly stated that the UFO's (unidentified flying objects) sighted in the Upstate Mountains the week before could be alien spacecraft. The truth is that all UFO sightings have logical, scientific explanations.

In his book *UFO's Explained*, researcher Philip Klass also concludes, after examining the available evidence, that UFO sightings can be explained as inaccurate or misinformed observations, as natural phenomena, or as hoaxes. He has shown that "basically honest and intelligent persons who are suddenly exposed to a brief, unexpected event, especially one that involves an unfamiliar object, may be grossly inaccurate in trying to describe precisely what they have seen." I personally know experienced astronomers who, despite years of nighttime viewing, occasionally mistake the planet Venus or airplane landing lights for UFO's. As a licensed pilot, I know how easy it would be to create a hoax by flying planes in formation at night—with navigation lights off and landing lights on. From the ground such a formation would look like a great ring of lights—a UFO.

We all know that the tourist trade is down in the Upstate Mountains. The UFO report and the *Bulletin*'s editorial may just be part of a clever scheme to attract gullible city folk to the area to bolster the local economy.

LESLIE GRIFFIN

1. What is the writer's opinion about UFO sightings in the Upstate Mountains? Where does she state that opinion?
2. Identify three pieces of evidence the writer uses to support her opinion. What types of evidence (facts, examples, statistics, personal experiences, quotations from experts) does she give? How convincing do you think this evidence is?
3. Who is the writer's intended audience? How do you think she might change the letter for each of these audiences?
   a. A group of astronomers
   b. A group of third-graders
   c. A group of people who have reported UFO sightings
4. What is the tone of the letter (serious, humorous, angry, suspicious)? Which words or phrases create this tone? What, for example, is the effect of the expression *utterly flabbergasted*? What other loaded words can you identify?
5. What conclusion does the writer draw from the evidence?

EXERCISE 2. Analyzing Letters to the Editor.   Find two letters to the editor, one in a school or local newspaper and one in a special-interest publication. Cut them out and bring them to class. Be prepared to read the letters aloud and answer the following questions.

1. What is the purpose of the letter?
2. What is the topic of the letter?
3. Who is the audience for the letter?
4. What is the tone of the letter?

EXERCISE 3. Choosing a Topic. Choose a debatable issue to use as the topic of a letter to the editor of a local newspaper. You may use one of the topics your class identified for Exercise 2 or another debatable issue.

Writing a Position Statement

5b. Write a position statement that expresses your opinion clearly and concisely.

Like the topic sentence in a persuasive paragraph, the position statement in a letter to the editor should express your opinion clearly and concisely. For a letter on the issue of wearing seat belts, for example, one student wrote this position statement:

EXAMPLE   The state legislature should pass a law requiring all motorists to wear seat belts.

In many cases, you will need to research the issue in order to come up with an appropriately specific position statement. A position statement that is too general or that merely states a personal preference is not suitable for a letter to the editor.

TOO GENERAL	Something should be done about homeless people in our city.
SUITABLE	The city should restore abandoned buildings and convert them into shelters for homeless people.
PERSONAL PREFERENCE	I do not like the smell of tobacco smoke.
SUITABLE	Smoking should be banned in public places.

Before You Write. To decide what your position is, ask yourself:

- What different conclusions can people draw on the issue?
- Which conclusion do I favor?
- What action do I think should be taken?

EXERCISE 4. Identifying and Writing Position Statements. Identify the position statements in the two letters you found for Exercise 2. If one or both of the letters do not contain position statements, write suitable ones and decide where to place them in the letters. If both of the letters already have position statements, write statements that take the opposite points of view.

EXERCISE 5. Writing a Position Statement. Write a position statement for the topic you chose for Exercise 3 or for another suitable topic.

Building an Argument

5c. Formulate reasons and gather evidence to support your opinion, and outline your argument.

An *argument* is a logical discussion of an issue. To build an effective argument, first use brainstorming, reading, or interviewing to formulate at least three *reasons,* statements that explain your opinion. Then use those techniques to gather *evidence* (facts, statistics, examples, incidents, or quotations from experts) to support each reason. Keep in mind that evidence should come from a reliable source or, if it comes from personal observation, should be based on a number of experiences—not just one. In general, a variety of different kinds of evidence is more convincing than only one kind.

To outline your argument, write your position statement and then list below it the reasons that back it up. For each reason, list the supporting evidence you have found.

CRITICAL THINKING:
Evaluating Reasons

To evaluate, or judge, the effectiveness of an argument, you need to consider several factors: (1) the number of reasons offered to support the position statement; (2) whether the reasons *directly* support the position statement and are appropriate for the audience; (3) the amount and type of evidence given to back up the reasons; and (4) the reliability of the evidence.

Which of the following seven reasons directly support the position statement? Which reasons would be most effective for the general public?

EXAMPLE

Position statement: The city should increase its highway tolls from fifty cents to one dollar.

Reasons: a. Money from the increase could be used to build new roads and repair old ones, thus, shifting the burden from the general public to those who actually use the roads.
  b. Some cities charge more than one dollar.
  c. Toll takers would not have to make change as often.
  d. Increasing the toll would encourage the use of car pools and public transportation, thus improving traffic conditions.
  e. Money from the increase could be used to provide pay raises for toll takers.
  f. Fewer cars on the road would mean a decrease in air pollution.
  g. Until three years ago the toll was thirty cents.

Reasons *a, d,* and *f* directly support the position statement and are appropriate for the general public. Reason *b* is too vague to be convincing. Reasons *c* and *g* are precisely stated, but they do not directly support the position statement. Reason *e* might help convince an audience of toll takers and their families, but it would not help convince the general public.

Before You Write. Review your list of reasons, asking yourself:

- Do I have at least three sound reasons?
- Do my reasons *directly* support the position statement?
- Are my reasons appropriate for the audience?
- Are my reasons backed up by reliable, specific evidence?

EXERCISE 6. Evaluating Reasons Given to Support a Position Statement. For each numbered item, study the position statement and list of reasons. Then choose the reasons that you think would most effectively support the position statement. Be prepared to explain your choices.

1. *Position statement:* School hours should be extended in order to add another period to the school day.
   a. Students could have a double lunch period.
   b. Students could choose another elective.
   c. Students could use the time for advanced or remedial work.
   d. Students' scores on nationally standardized tests have been falling.
   e. Students could participate in extracurricular activities during school hours.
   f. Students could take more academic classes, such as English, math, science, and history.

2. *Position statement:* Main Street should *not* be made into a one-way street.
   a. It is wide enough to accommodate two lanes of two-way traffic plus parking at the curb lanes.
   b. Drivers are used to traffic the way it is and would be confused.
   c. Bus routes would have to be changed.
   d. The city would have to pay for new One-Way traffic signs for every intersection.

    e. Statistics show that fewer accidents occur on one-way streets than on two-way streets.

    f. Statistics show that traffic moves faster on one-way streets than on two-way streets.

3. *Position statement:* High-school students who are taking social studies courses should be required to read a local newspaper every day.

    a. They could find out what stores are having sales.

    b. They could be informed about important local and national events that directly affect their lives.

    c. They could find out about important world events that affect their lives.

    d. They could learn about the history of American government.

    e. They could discuss columnists' views on current issues.

    f. The local newspaper offers reduced rates to students.

EXERCISE 7. Gathering Information and Outlining Your Argument. Formulate reasons and gather evidence to support the position statement you wrote for Exercise 5. (You may instead gather information to support a position statement on another topic.) Then outline your argument by writing each of your reasons and listing the evidence (statistics, other facts, examples, quotations) you will use to support it.

WRITING

Writing the First Draft of Your Letter

5d. Use business letter form, and follow the guidelines provided by the publication to which you are writing.

When you write a letter to the editor, use business letter form (see Chapter 8). Also, follow the publication's guidelines, which you will find in the section where letters to the editor are printed. Here, for example, is one such notice.

Guide for Letter Writers

The Herald welcomes your views on any public issue. Letters must bear the writer's signature and printed or typed name, full address, and telephone number. Send them to: The Readers' Forum; The Miami Herald; 1 Herald Plaza; Miami, FL 33101.

We routinely condense letters and we correct errors of fact, spelling, and punctuation. Because our mail far exceeds our space for letters, we publish only original letters addressed to us. We do not publish poetry, open letters, or copies of letters sent elsewhere. And, to ensure diversity, we limit each writer to one published letter every thirty days.

When You Write. In writing your letter:

- Begin with your position statement, or make it the last sentence of the first paragraph.
- Refer to your outline of reasons.
- Think about the order of your reasons. (You may want to save for last your strongest reason and evidence.)
- Keep your tone serious and unemotional.
- Try a clincher, or concluding, sentence that restates your opinion, summarizes your reasons, or suggests a specific course of action.
- Follow business letter form and the guidelines provided by the publication.

EXERCISE 8. Writing a Letter to the Editor. Write a letter to the editor of your local newspaper, using the outline you prepared for Exercise 7. (You may instead select a new topic for this exercise.) Follow these steps to develop your first draft:

1. Write a position statement that expresses your opinion clearly.

2. Then gather information and outline your argument, choosing the reasons and evidence that you think will be most convincing to your audience.
3. With your position statement and the outline of your argument in front of you, write the first draft of your letter to the editor.
4. Consider ending your letter with a concluding sentence that restates your opinion, summarizes your argument, or suggests a course of action.

EVALUATING AND REVISING

Evaluating Your Letter

5e. Evaluate the first draft of your letter.

Use the following guidelines to evaluate the first draft of your letter to the editor.

GUIDELINES FOR EVALUATING LETTERS TO THE EDITOR

Position Statement	1. Does the position statement express a clear, specific opinion about a debatable issue?
Argument Development	2. Do at least three reasons directly support the position statement? Is each reason directly supported by evidence, such as facts, statistics, examples, or quotations?
Coherence	3. Are the ideas arranged in an order that will help convince the reader to support the position?
Tone	4. Is the tone of the letter serious and reasonable?
Style	5. Is the letter brief and to the point? Have vague or unnecessary details been left out?

Revising Your Letter

5f. Revise the first draft of your letter.

Use the following techniques to revise the first draft of your letter to the editor.

REVISING LETTERS TO THE EDITOR		
PROBLEM	**TECHNIQUE**	**REVISION**
The main opinion is not clear.	Add	Begin with a position statement. Add a suggested course of action to the position.
The argument is not convincing.	Add/Replace	Add reasons, backed up by evidence (there should be at least three reasons). Replace weak reasons with ones that are more convincing to the audience.
Some evidence is not convincing or reliable.	Replace	Replace weak evidence with reliable evidence of interest to the audience. Replace a reason that lacks sound evidence.
The argument is hard to follow.	Reorder/Add	Rearrange the reasons from least to most important. Add words that show how ideas are related (such as *first, then,* and *finally*).
The tone is not serious	Replace	Replace loaded, informal, or slang words with unemotional, logical ones.

PROBLEM	TECHNIQUE	REVISION
The letter is wordy or rambling.	Cut	Remove unrelated reasons or evidence, unneeded words, and flowery expressions.

EXERCISE 9. Evaluating and Revising a Letter to the Editor. Evaluate and revise the following first draft. Make sure that it begins with a clearly stated opinion and ends with a strong concluding sentence. You may omit any information that you think weakens the argument and add information to strengthen it.

Dear Editor,

Standards for participation in high-school athletics and other extracurricular activities vary in different schools in this city. It used to be that a student could fail two classes and earn as low as a .66 grade point average and still be allowed to play football and take part in other activities. Now in some schools a student must have at least a 1.0 grade point average (which is a D average). In others it's a 1.5 (C-) and sometimes its a 2.0 (C). Requirements about how many courses a student must pass are also a whole lot different. Anywhere from three out of five subjects to all of them. In some cases a student can play football but if he moves and transfers to a nearby high school, he can't. Some coaches put pressure on teachers to pass their best athletes, and sometimes students who have problems with grades take easy courses like weight lifting and shop.

State Senator Jack Gordon says that the coaches need to take the grade point average seriously. All students can learn academic subjects and if they need extra tutoring, their coaches should see that they get it. Senator Gordon believes that anyone who can learn complicated football plays can learn to pass school subjects with at least a 2.0 average.

Last year throughout the country 122 football players were

benched because they did not meet grade point average requirements.

EXERCISE 10. Evaluating and Revising Your Letter to the Editor. Evaluate and revise the letter you wrote for Exercise 8. Use the Guidelines for Evaluating Letters to the Editor on page 164 and the revising techniques on page 165.

PROOFREADING AND MAKING A FINAL COPY

Proofreading Your Letter and Making a Final Copy

5g. Proofread your letter and make a final copy.

Since your letter may be the only contact you have with the people who read it, you will want to make sure that it represents you well. A letter containing errors in grammar, usage, or mechanics indicates that the writer is uninterested or careless—or both.

EXERCISE 11. Proofreading a Letter to the Editor. Proofread the letter you evaluated and revised for Exercise 9. Use the Guidelines for Proofreading on page 36 and the standard practices for business letters on pages 256–60. Then make a final copy of the letter and proofread it for copying errors.

EXERCISE 12. Proofreading Your Letter to the Editor. Use the Guidelines for Proofreading (page 36) and the business letter standards (pages 256–60) to check the letter you evaluated and revised for Exercise 10. Proofread your letter again after making a final copy of it.

REVIEW EXERCISE. Writing a Letter to the Editor. Write a letter to the editor of your school or local newspaper. Choose a problem that you think needs correcting in your school or in your community. Decide how you think the problem should be solved, and use this idea as the basis for your position statement. Then gather information (reasons and evidence) and outline your argument. Be sure to evaluate, revise, and proofread your letter before you send it.

WRITING A PERSUASIVE COMPOSITION

Usually, a persuasive composition has at least five paragraphs. The introductory paragraph arouses the reader's interest and sets forth the position statement; it may also include background information. The body consists of three or more paragraphs, each of which presents one reason and its backup evidence to support the position statement. The concluding paragraph "clinches" the writer's argument.

PREWRITING

Choosing a Topic

5h. Choose a debatable topic.

Any of the topics that you used or considered in the section on persuasive paragraphs in Chapter 3 may be dealt with in a persuasive composition. The longer form will give you more room in which to introduce your opinion, develop a strong argument, and present a forceful conclusion.

Keep in mind that the topic you select must be one about which people have varying opinions; that is, it must be debatable.

NOT SUITABLE The public education system needs to be improved.

SUITABLE The public education system would be improved if teachers were given salary adjustments to make teaching a well-paid profession.

EXERCISE 13. Choosing a Topic. Choose a topic for a persuasive composition, referring to the topics suggested in this chapter or in the section "The Persuasive Paragraph" in Chapter 3.

Considering Audience and Tone

5i. Consider your audience and tone.

A persuasive composition may be written for many different audiences. You may write to convince a group of parents to become active in the Band Parents' Association, for example, or to convince members of the city council to grant permission for the band to use the civic center for a fund-raising concert. Your particular audience will determine the background information you provide, the reasons and evidence you include, and the language you use.

In general, a serious and formal tone is appropriate for a persuasive composition, which deals with an important issue. An informal or humorous tone may offend your audience, and shifts in tone may confuse them about your attitude.

Writing a Position Statement

5j. Write a position statement that expresses your opinion clearly and directly.

You may need to research the issue you have selected as a topic before you can decide what your opinion on it is. Once you have decided what your opinion is, you should write a position statement that clearly expresses your viewpoint. Like the thesis statement in an expository composition, the position statement focuses attention on your debatable topic. This will help you as you plan and draft your essay, and it will help your audience as they read your finished essay. Remember, too, that you may revise your position statement later, after you have done more research to formulate reasons and gather evidence.

Before You Write. Keep in mind that a position statement must be

- an opinion, not a fact

  NOT SUITABLE   The United States has fifty states.
  SUITABLE   Puerto Rico should be admitted to the United States as its fifty-first state.

- an opinion about an important issue, not merely a personal preference

  NOT SUITABLE   My car is the best model on the road today.
  SUITABLE   The federal government should use import quotas to limit the number of foreign cars sold.

EXERCISE 14. Evaluating Position Statements. Decide which of the following statements are appropriate for a persuasive composition. Write *S* for those that are suitable and *NS* for those that are not. Revise or replace the ones that are not suitable.

1. Every student in this school should be required to carry a photo identification card during school hours.
2. Schools should offer more interesting courses.
3. The federal government should increase its funding for research to find cures for cancer.
4. More drivers should wear seat belts.
5. It is healthier to participate in a sport than to be a spectator.
6. People should be required to fly American flags outside their homes on national holidays.
7. Elderly, frail people should be cared for in their homes or in a family member's home instead of in nursing homes.
8. Most people do not eat enough fruits and vegetables.
9. Divorce has a profound impact on young children.
10. It is difficult to be alone on a holiday.

EXERCISE 15. Writing a Position Statement. Write a position statement expressing your opinion on the topic you chose for Exercise 13.

Building an Argument

5k. Formulate reasons and gather evidence to support your opinion, and outline your argument.

Research your topic to be sure you have at least three reasons to support your opinion. Your study will also help you locate supporting evidence.

> *Before You Write.* To formulate reasons and gather evidence:
>
> - Use techniques such as brainstorming, clustering, observation, and the *5 W-How?* questions for familiar topics.
> - Use library sources such as magazines for topics less familiar to you. (Use the *Readers' Guide to Periodical Literature* to find magazine articles.)

Take notes as you look for facts, statistics, examples, and quotations to use as evidence. You may also want to take notes on reasons and evidence that support the opposing point of view, so that you can respond to possible objections.

Once you are satisfied that you know enough about the issue, outline your argument—your reasons and evidence. Usually, each reason in a persuasive composition is developed in a separate paragraph. The reason serves as the topic sentence of the paragraph, and the evidence is expressed in two or more sentences that provide clarifying information and specific evidence to support the reason.

Following is the outline for an argument on the issue of the selection of judges. Notice that the outline includes the position statement as well as the reasons and evidence.

EXAMPLE

Position statement: Judges should not be elected or removed from office by popular vote. Instead, their appointment and their term of office should be regulated by the governor and by a panel of lawyers and other citizens.

Reason 1: The voting public is not qualified to tell who would make the best judge.

    a. Lawyers are much better able to evaluate candidates for judge.

    b. Most voters do not bother to find out about candidates—there are too many candidates and the ballots are too confusing.

Reason 2: Opponents: Elections are necessary to remove incompetent or unethical judges from office.

    a. A procedure already exists for removing such judges (Judicial Qualifications System); this has nothing to do with elections.

    b. A panel of experts is better able than the public to decide when judges should be removed from office.

Reason 3: Judgeships can be "bought" by candidates who spend most on campaigns.

    a. Candidates who spend a lot of money may not be well qualified, but the media make their names familiar to voters.

    b. Judges should be selected on the basis of their qualifications, not on the basis of the money they can raise.

EXERCISE 16. Gathering Information and Outlining Your Argument. Using your position statement from Exercise 15 or another suitable position statement, gather information for a persuasive composition; then, outline your argument. Use at least three reasons to support your position statement, and include supporting evidence for each reason.

CRITICAL THINKING:
Evaluating an Argument

In order to write an effective persuasive composition, you must be able to evaluate, or judge, whether an argument is convincing. In part, you do this when you make up your mind about which side of an issue you are on.

The following chart gives a position statement and outlines two opposing arguments. In the Pro ("for") column are five reasons to support the position statement; in the Con ("against") column are five reasons against the position statement. Study both arguments carefully and then answer the questions in Exercise 17.

Position statement: Experiments on animals done for medical research purposes should be stopped immediately.

PRO	CON
a. Animals have feelings, just as humans do. Cruel experiments cause them to suffer.	a. Ninety-five percent of all medical research done on animals is done on rats, mice, and other rodents. Even experiments perceived as "cruel" are done for a good cause—the saving of human lives.
b. Animal research cannot yield exact information about the body.	b. Animal research does yield information from which we can theorize about the effects of certain substances on human beings.
c. Researchers should use advanced technology to do alternate forms of research, such as tissue cultures, mechanical models, and genetic engineering.	c. Such alternate forms of research yield information only about specific groups of cells; we need to know what happens to the whole animal.

d. Eliminating cruelty to research animals by stopping animal experiments is worth any delay in finding a cure for human diseases.

e. Medical research should concentrate on preventing diseases rather than finding cures for diseases.

d. Stopping animal research will slow down progress in our finding a cure for cancer and other diseases. We cannot experiment with human beings.

e. Certain serious diseases, such as diabetes and kidney disease, do not seem to be preventable.

EXERCISE 17. Evaluating an Argument. Refer to the chart above as you answer the following questions.

1. Which position do you favor—Pro or Con? Why?
2. For the position that you favor, which reason do you think is the strongest? The weakest? Why?
3. Look closely at the reasons for both sides. Which ones would you say are facts? Which are opinions?
4. Are the reasons on each side separate and distinct, or is the same reason repeated in different words? Are any of the reasons merely restatements of the opinion in the position statement? If so, which ones?
5. What additional reasons can you think of for either side?
6. If you were writing a persuasive composition based on this topic, which three reasons would you use? In what order would you arrange them?
7. How could you find evidence to support each of the reasons for the position that you favor?

WRITING

Writing the First Draft of Your Composition

5l. Write a first draft based on your outline.

A persuasive composition has three main parts: the *introductory paragraph,* the *body,* and the *concluding paragraph.*

The *introductory paragraph* should catch the reader's ïnterest, identify the topic, and indicate the writer's opinion. The position statement usually appears at the end of the introductory paragraph. If background information such as a brief history of the issue or definitions of terms is necessary for your audience, you may include it in the introductory paragraph or place it in a separate paragraph between the introduction and the body.

The *body* consists of reasons and evidence that support the position statement. In general, you should devote one paragraph to each reason and its evidence. You will probably want to arrange your reasons in order of importance, with the most important (or strongest) reason coming just before the concluding paragraph.

In the *concluding paragraph,* you summarize your argument by restating your opinion and reasons, without the evidence. You may also draw a conclusion from the evidence or suggest a specific course of action.

EXERCISE 18. Writing a Persuasive Composition. Write the first draft of your composition, using the outline you prepared for Exercise 16 as a guide. You may instead select a new topic for this exercise.

PREWRITING If necessary, research the issue so that you can decide what your position is. Then write a preliminary position statement and gather information to support it. Also consider whether you want to respond to opposing arguments. Arrange the reasons in order of importance, with the most important reason last, keeping in mind the needs and interests of your audience.

WRITING Include your position statement in an introductory paragraph that will arouse the reader's interest. Develop each reason in a separate paragraph, supporting it with evidence. In your concluding paragraph, summarize your argument; you may also want to suggest that a specific course of action be taken.

EVALUATING

Evaluating Your Composition

5m. Evaluate the content, organization, and style of your first draft.

Read your first draft carefully three times, so that you can concentrate on one aspect at a time. Use the following guidelines to decide where your draft needs improvement.

GUIDELINES FOR EVALUATING PERSUASIVE COMPOSITIONS

Position Statement	1. Does the position statement express a specific opinion about a serious, debatable issue? Is it in the introductory paragraph?
Argument Development	2. Is the position statement directly supported by at least three reasons? Are the reasons clearly related to the issue? Is each reason the main idea of a separate paragraph?
Evidence	3. Is each reason supported by evidence? Is the evidence appropriate for the audience?
Background Information	4. Does the first draft include essential background information?
Conclusion	5. Does the concluding paragraph summarize or emphasize the argument?
Coherence	6. Are the reasons arranged in an effective order? Are the ideas clearly linked?
Tone	7. Is a serious tone used throughout the composition?

The following first draft was written from the outline on page 172. Notice that the writer has changed the order of the reasons and has added some information. As you read this composition, keep in mind that it is a first draft, not a revised and polished version.

For months before every election, candidates can be seen scrambling for votes. You've seen them—shaking hands, smiling endlessly, kissing babies, plastering their posters across the community. Judges, too, who should be above any kind of politics, are forced to beg for votes the same as any other candidate for political office. <u>Judges should be removed from this political scene; they should be appointed, not elected.</u>

introductory paragraph

position statement

In this state, judges for the Court of Appeals are already appointed by the governor from a list of candidates proposed by a nominating committee. This committee consists of lawyers and nonlawyers, who look over the credentials and records of the individuals interested in becoming judges. The panel then offers the names of three people to the governor, who appoints one of them as judge. Every six years the names of appointed judges appear on the ballot for the people to cast a simple yes-or-no vote: yes, keep the judge; no, get someone else.

background information

People who say that judges must be elected use the argument that the election procedure is necessary in order for the public to vote out of office judges who turn out to be incompetent or unethical. That's ridiculous. Certainly we need to remove such judges from office, but elections aren't the only way. The Judicial Qualifications System already exists. There is a standing statewide committee of lawyers who can investi-

reason 1—refutes opposing argument (con)

(pro)

gate a judge charged with doing something bad or stupid and recommend to the governor that the judge be fired.

Elections of judges are a mistake because the general public is not able or qualified to decide who would make a good judge. There are so many candidates, and ballots are so confusing that voters generally mark ballots without any knowledge of who the judicial candidates actually are, or they simply leave these ballots blank. Lawyers, who know the judicial system well, are much better able to evaluate candidates for judge.

reason 2

Thomas Jefferson, who wrote the Declaration of Independence, believed that judges should not be elected. He believed that judges should be appointed and "should hold estates for life in their offices or, in other words, their commissions should be during good behavior." How shocked Thomas Jefferson would be to see today's judges campaigning for votes.

reason 3—quotes authority

When judges are forced to run for election, judgeships can be "bought" by those candidates who raise the most money for their campaigns. Big bucks can make a candidate's name familiar—from radio and television ads, posters, bumper stickers, campaign buttons. All this media hype costs a lot of money. Alas, it is not always the best-qualified candidate who raises the most money for a campaign. Judges should be se-

reason 4

lected on the basis of their qualifications,
not on the amount of money they can raise
for a campaign.

The legislature must do whatever needs
to be done to remove judges from politics.
A Constitutional amendment should be proposed by the legislature and passed by the
voters to make judges for all state, county,
and local judgeships appointed—not elected.

concluding
paragraph

restated
position
statement

EXERCISE 19. Evaluating a First Draft. Answer the following questions by referring to the first draft above.

1. How effective is the introductory paragraph? Which sentence
   is the position statement? How effective is it?
2. Is the background information essential, or should it be omitted?
3. How effectively are the reasons arranged? (*Hint:* Which do
   you think is more important—reason 2 or reason 3?)
4. Is enough evidence given to back up each reason? (*Hint:*
   Consider reason 3.)
5. How effective is the concluding paragraph? How could it be
   improved? (*Hint:* What could the writer ask the reader to
   do?)
6. How consistent is the writer's tone? Do any words or phrases
   need changing? If so, which ones?
7. How effective is the argument as a whole? Should any of the
   reasons be omitted? If so, which ones? (*Hint:* Is reason 3 a
   strong reason?)

EXERCISE 20. Evaluating Your First Draft. Evaluate the
first draft you wrote for Exercise 18, using the guidelines on
page 176.

REVISING

Revising Your Composition

5n. **Revise your first draft to improve its content, organization, and style.**

After you evaluate your first draft, you should make changes that will improve it. Remember the four revising techniques you can use: *cut,* or omit, words, phrases, or sentences; *add* words or ideas; *reorder,* or rearrange, words, sentences, or paragraphs; and *replace* words or ideas. The following chart suggests how you can use these techniques based on your evaluation of a first draft.

REVISING PERSUASIVE COMPOSITIONS		
PROBLEM	**TECHNIQUE**	**REVISION**
The position statement is weak.	Replace/Add	In the introductory paragraph, replace the position statement with one that clearly states whether you are "pro" or "con" on a debatable issue. Propose a specific action that may help resolve the debate.
There are not enough reasons to convince the audience.	Add	Include at least three reasons and evidence for them, based on more research, if needed. Write a separate paragraph for each reason.
A reason or some evidence does not fit the argument or the audience.	Cut/Replace	Remove or replace unrelated or inappropriate ideas.
The argument is lost in background information.	Cut/Reorder	Remove ideas that are not essential to the argument. Place essential background in the introductory paragraph or in a separate paragraph between the introduction and the body.

PROBLEM	TECHNIQUE	REVISION
The argument is not convincing.	Reorder/Add	Move the strongest reasons and evidence toward the end, before the conclusion. Add or reorder the ideas in the last paragraph to emphasize the logic of the argument.
Ideas do not flow or clearly relate to each other.	Add/Replace	Add or change words to help link ideas. (See page 57–59.)
The tone is informal or too emotional.	Replace/Cut	Replace informal words such as contractions and slang with more formal ones. Remove emotional words or phrases, or replace them with serious, fair-sounding ones.

EXERCISE 21. Analyzing a Writer's Revisions.   Study the following revision of the third paragraph in the composition on pages 177–78. Then answer the questions.

People who ~~say~~ *maintain* that judges must be elected .... replace

~~use the argument that~~ *say* the election *^* ~~procedure~~ .... replace/cut

~~is~~ *are* necessary ~~in order for~~ *so that* the public ~~to~~ *can* vote .... replace

out of office judges who ~~turn out to be~~ *are* incom- .... replace

petent or unethical. ~~That's ridiculous!~~ Cer- .... cut

tainly we need to remove such judges from

office, but elections ~~aren't~~ *are not* the only way. ~~The~~ *We already have a procedure for removing such judges from office.* .... replace

Judicial Qualifications System ~~already exists.~~ .... cut

~~There~~ *This Committee has the power to* is a standing statewide committee *made up* of .... cut/add

lawyers, ~~who can~~ investigate a judge charged .... replace

with~~being unethical or incompetent~~ can
with~~doing something bad or stupid~~ and~~rec-~~   replace/add

ommend to the governor that the judge be
removed from office.
~~fired~~.   replace

1. Why did the writer remove the second sentence? Why did the writer replace the contraction *aren't* in the third sentence with the words *are not*? How do these changes affect the tone of the paragraph?
2. Why did the writer add the sentence that begins "We already have a procedure . . ." ?
3. Find two sentences that the writer combined. What is the effect of combining these sentences?
4. Find one sentence that the writer made into two sentences. What is the effect of this change?
5. Why did the writer replace the expression *something bad or stupid* in the last sentence? Why did the writer replace the word *fired* in that sentence?

EXERCISE 22. Revising Your Composition. Revise the first draft you evaluated for Exercise 20, using the chart on page 180.

PROOFREADING AND MAKING A FINAL COPY

Proofreading Your Composition and Making a Final Copy

5o. Proofread your revised composition and make a final copy.

To proofread your revised version, reread it carefully several times, using the Guidelines for Proofreading on page 36 to check your grammar, word use, spelling, punctuation, and capitalization. Check in a dictionary the spelling of any word about which you are not sure. If you are in doubt about a point of usage, punctuation, or capitalization, use the Index of this book to find the appropriate rule and example.

After you have proofread your composition, make a final copy on a separate sheet of paper, following correct manuscript form (see pages 37–38) or your teacher's directions. Then proofread you composition again to make sure that you have copied it correctly.

EXERCISE 23. Proofreading Your Composition. Proofread the composition you revised for Exercise 22. Then make a final copy and proofread it again.

CHAPTER 5 WRITING REVIEW

Writing Persuasion. Look through recent magazines and newspapers to find debatable issues that interest you. Choose one issue to use as the topic for a letter to the editor or a persuasive composition. Follow the steps detailed in this chapter: Consider your audience and tone; write a position statement; formulate reasons and gather evidence; outline your argument; write a first draft; evaluate and revise your writing; proofread and make a final copy.

CHAPTER 6

Writing Stories

NARRATIVES, CHARACTER SKETCHES, AND DESCRIPTIONS

Essentially, all *narratives,* or stories, are concerned with *what happened.* Certain elements are common to all forms of narrative writing, from short stories to television shows. In this chapter you will learn to use the writing process to combine these elements into effective narratives of your own.

THE ELEMENTS OF NARRATIVE WRITING

The essential elements of narrative writing are *setting, characters,* and *plot* (a sequence of events consisting of *conflict, action, climax,* and *outcome*).

The Setting

Every story happens *somewhere at some time.* Together, the place and time make up the *setting* of the story. In factual accounts, the *when* and *where* are clearly stated, but in a story they may instead be revealed through details. In many of O. Henry's best-known stories, for example, certain details make it clear that the setting is New York City in the early 1900's, even though the city and the decade are not named.

The Characters

Every story has at least one leading character, called the *protagonist*. Often, another character, called the *antagonist,* opposes the plans or wishes of the main character. There may also be other characters, of major or minor importance.

To understand these concepts better, assume that you are creating a story in which the protagonist is a high-school girl. (The other characters will appear later.)

The Conflict

A group of characters placed in a setting does not make a story; something has to *happen.* Usually what happens centers on a *conflict,* or *problem,* the main character faces. The conflict may be physical or nonphysical, within the character, or with someone or something else. The conflict in your story might be this: The high-school girl is doing poorly in her work; she wants to drop out of school, but her parents object. (Now you have added two antagonists.)

The Action

The conflict sets events in motion; now *action* begins to take place. The action consists of a series of related events, usually arranged chronologically. For example, the girl decides to run away. She withdraws her savings from the bank and takes a bus to New York City. When she becomes lost, she is questioned and taken into custody by a police officer, who notifies her parents.

The Climax

The action arising out of the conflict leads to the *climax,* the point of greatest interest or emotional intensity. For example, the girl's parents drive to the police station in New York. Seeing them, the girl hesitates before rushing toward them. The parents smile and hug her.

The Outcome

After the climax has been reached, the conflict is resolved, or worked out. The *resolution* is the outcome of the story. For example, on the drive home, the girl and her parents have a long talk. She decides to go on with school; they agree to find a way to get her help with her studies.

PREWRITING

CHOOSING A SUBJECT

6a. Search for subjects for a short story.

Begin planning a short story by searching your own experience for possible story ideas. Keep in mind that your experience includes more than what has happened to you alone. It includes what you have seen and heard and felt and thought and believed. It also includes what has happened to people you know.

You can find possible subjects by brainstorming (see pages 18–19), interviewing, or reading. Your mother, for example, might remember the time you got lost in the woods or stories about your great-grandparents' immigration to the United States. Perhaps you have a journal entry about helping a new student overcome the fear of a new school.

In a story, you do not have to stick to the facts as they are. Writers change names, places, characters; they may use only one small part of what actually happened. This is where their imagination comes in—not in creating something out of nothing, but in creating something imagined out of something real.

EXERCISE 1. Finding Subjects. Ask yourself the following questions. Then use your answers to list five possible subjects for a short story.

1. Who is the most interesting person I have ever met? What has he or she done that is so interesting to me?

2. What is the most interesting thing I have ever done? What happened?
3. What is the most exciting thing that has ever happened to me? What happened?
4. Do I know anyone who has overcome a problem—a health problem, a fear, or a conflict with someone? How did the person overcome the problem?
5. What historical figure do I find interesting (a President, a scientist, a civil rights leader, etc.)? What did the person do that was so interesting?

LIMITING THE SUBJECT

6b. Limit the subject to a situation involving a conflict that takes place in a brief period of time.

A subject for a short story should be limited to a situation involving a conflict that can be resolved in a few pages. For example, your great-grandparents' struggles when they immigrated to this country may have lasted many years. If you limited the subject to a situation in which they faced a single conflict—such as their first encounter with a dishonest landlord—you could include specific details of the conflict in a few pages.

Before You Write. Choose one of the four basic types of conflict for your story:

- Conflict within the character's own mind (a conflict centered on a decision or a fear)
- Conflict between two or more characters (a physical conflict such as a boxing match, or a nonphysical competition such as an election)
- Conflict between the character and nature (a conflict with an animal, or a natural event such as a flood.)
- Conflict between the character and society (a conflict with the rules or laws of society or government)

EXERCISE 2. Limiting Subjects. For each of the following situations, make up two conflicts limited enough for a short story.

EXAMPLE   1. Situation: A river floods a town.
   a. *Conflict: A teen-ager tries to rescue her younger brother.*
   b. *Conflict: A man is stranded in his stalled car.*

1. Situation: A woman takes flying lessons.
2. Situation: A family moves to a new town.
3. Situation: A family adopts a child.
4. Situation: A principal suspends publication of a high-school paper.
5. Situation: A building inspector condemns a hotel.

EXERCISE 3. Selecting and Limiting Subjects. Select three of the subjects you developed for Exercise 1. Limit each subject to identify two situations and conflicts suitable for a short story. Follow the example in Exercise 2.

EVALUATING FOR PURPOSE, AUDIENCE, AND TONE

6c. Evaluate the situation and conflict: Consider purpose, audience, and tone.

The *purpose* of a short story is to entertain. (Some stories, such as fables, are also meant to teach a lesson.) A story does not have to be amusing to be entertaining; a good mystery or science fiction story may not be at all humorous, but it certainly keeps the reader interested. You should keep this purpose in mind.

The *audience* for your short story may be your teacher, your classmates, your family, your friends, or the readers of a magazine. Consider the experience and knowledge of your audience. For example, if you plan to write about a mad computer scientist, will your audience need to know any computer terminology?

The details and language of a short story create a *tone* that reflects the writer's attitude. Consider your attitude toward your characters and the events. Do you admire one character and despise another? As you determine the tone you will create, keep in mind that although nearly any tone can be used for any situation, you do not want to offend your audience.

As you read the following models, compare the tone, the attitude the writers take toward the characters and the events.

1   My father is a priest; I am the son of a priest. I have been in the Dead Places near us, with my father—at first, I was afraid. When my father went into the house to search for the metal, I stood by the door and my heart felt small and weak. It was a dead man's house, a spirit house. It did not have the smell of man, though there were old bones in a corner. But it is not fitting that a priest's son should show fear. I looked at the bones in the shadow and kept my voice still.

STEPHEN VINCENT BENÉT

2   The sun wasn't quite up yet, but there was enough light so's I could see the whole front of the First Bank of Sheep-shank, Colorado, laying out in the road right across from me and half the roof caved off sideways and some black smoke still puffing up out of the inside, and then I seen two men come stumbling and coughing out of the wreckage, carrying a heavy pair of joined saddlebags and twisting their ankle amongst the busted planks and generally acting like they'd just as soon get going someplace else. One had lost his hat, and they was both trying to wipe their eyes with their sleeve, but they kept jerking each other off balance, what with starting and stopping and both hanging onto them saddlebags and taking time to swear at this, that, and each other.

DAVID WAGONER

Both models present serious situations: a visit to "Dead Places" and an explosion in a bank. The tone of the first model is serious, whereas the tone of the second one is humorous. Benét is concerned about what the Dead Places mean for the people in the story. Wagoner, on the other hand, is making fun of the situation. How do the writers' choices of details and words reflect their attitudes?

Before You Write. Evaluate the situation and conflict you have chosen by asking yourself:

- *Purpose:* Will the situation and conflict keep my readers interested?
- *Audience:* Will my readers understand this situation and conflict? What special terms should I explain? What background information should I provide?
- *Tone:* How do you want your audience to feel about the events and characters in your story?

EXERCISE 4. Considering Purpose, Audience, and Tone. Select one of the conflicts you identified for Exercises 2 and 3. Then answer the questions that follow.

1. Can I achieve my purpose, to tell an entertaining story, with this conflict?
2. Who will my audience be? How old are they? Will they understand the conflict and find it interesting?
3. What is my attitude toward the events and the characters? Will I establish a solemn tone? A mysterious, angry, or humorous tone?

GATHERING INFORMATION

6d. Gather information for your story.

Once you have selected and limited a situation, begin gathering information—details about the characters, the setting, and the action. You can gather these details by using some of the same techniques you used to search for a subject, such as brainstorming, reading, interviewing, and observing. You can also use the *5 W-How?* questions and other questioning techniques.

Asking the 5 W-How? Questions

Whether you are reading, observing, or interviewing, you will find some form of the *5 W-How?* questions useful for gathering information for your story.

- *Who?* Who is the central character? Who is responsible for the action? Who are the other important characters?
- *What?* What is the situation at the beginning of the story? What is the conflict that has to be resolved? What happens to the central character?
- *When?* When does the story take place? When does the action begin? When does it end?
- *Where?* Where does the action take place?
- *Why?* Why do the characters become involved in the conflict?
- *How?* How does the main character become involved in the conflict? How is the conflict resolved?

EXERCISE 5. Using the 5 W-How Questions to Brainstorm.
Using the conflict you chose for Exercise 4 or another conflict, ask yourself the *5 W-How?* questions and brainstorm for answers. Write out your answers.

Asking Questions About Character and Setting

The following questions can help you gather details about characters and setting. Although you may not use all of the information you gather, you will collect details from which to choose.

A CHARACTER

Questions	*Sample Answers*
• What does the character look like? Does he or she have any outstanding or unusual characteristics? How does he or she dress, walk, and talk?	Medium height and build; very curly brown hair; physically strong; also has strength of character; dresses in uniform; has a strong, youthful stride; speaks gently unless angry

- How does the character behave? How does he or she treat other people or animals? Why does the character behave as he or she does? What does he or she do for a living?

  Takes command of the situation; is gentle with people who need help; is firm with criminals; recalls a childhood experience when a police officer helped her; works as a police sergeant

- What do other people think of the character? What has the character done to make other people feel this way? How do other people react to the character?

  Co-workers respect her; parents and husband are proud of her; most people think she is good and kind; criminals think she is tough; most people seem to feel comfortable with her

- What does this character want out of life? What does he or she feel deeply about? What secrets does this character have?

  Loves music and hopes someday to be a famous musician; spends some off-duty evenings playing jazz piano in a hotel

A SETTING

Questions

Sample Answers

- What do I see when I look at the setting? Is it comfortable and attractive? Is it harsh?

  Steep cliffs, sharp rocks, patches of snow; looks cold and difficult

- What smells or sounds do I associate with the setting? What is my physical reaction to the setting? What tastes or textures do I associate with it?

  Smell dampness of rocks; hear the wind whistling around the cliffs; cold fingers and feet, sore muscles; cold, sharp rocks

- What day is it? How much time elapses between the beginning of the story and the end? Is the time of day important? Is the year important?

  Tuesday; three hours; 3:00 P.M., only three hours before dark; the year does not matter

- What season is it? What is the weather? What does it feel like? | Early spring; cold, about 37 degrees; combined with the wind makes flesh raw

EXERCISE 6. Gathering Information About a Character. Select one of the characters you identified for the *Who?* question in Exercise 5 or one of the following characters. Gather information about the character by using the questions on pages 191–92. Be prepared to discuss the character in class.

1. The first female quarterback of a high-school football team
2. A Vietnam War veteran
3. A high-school student who can program computers
4. A young child who accurately predicts the future
5. A notorious pirate

EXERCISE 7. Gathering Information About a Setting. Use the setting you identified in Exercise 5 or one of the following settings. Gather information about the setting by using the questions on pages 192–93. Be prepared to discuss the setting in class.

1. A desert
2. A shopping mall
3. A city street
4. A supposedly haunted mansion
5. A beach

CHOOSING A POINT OF VIEW

6e. Decide on the point of view you will use.

A story can be told from at least two points of view: *first person* or *third person*. A story that begins "*I* shivered with fear as *I* heard the wind howling around *our* house" is an example of the first-person, or *I*, point of view. In this point of view, the *narrator*, the character through whom the writer tells the story, is involved in the events, usually as the main character but sometimes merely as an observer. In either case, a writer who uses the first-person point of view can logically include only those events and details that the narrator experienced, saw, or heard about. The advantage of using the first-person point of view is that the audience tends to identify with the narrator and thus feels closer to the action.

A story that begins "Mario Cabrera and his sister shivered with fear as *they* heard the wind howling around *their* house" is an example of the third-person point of view. In this point of view, the writer can be *omniscient,* or all-knowing. The advantage of using the third-person omniscient point of view is that the writer can reveal the thoughts and actions of all the characters.

Before You Write. Decide on a point of view by asking yourself:

- What roles have I assigned to the characters?
- Is the story based on something that actually happened to me? (If so, will first-person point of view be easier to use?)
- Do I plan to show what two or more of the characters do and think? (If so, the third-person omniscient point of view will be appropriate.)

EXERCISE 8. Changing Point of View. The following paragraphs use the third-person point of view. Rewrite the paragraphs, changing the point of view to first person and making the King the narrator. Some sentences may have to be changed to fit the new point of view.

The King accepted the proposal and drove toward the church. He had been traveling for hours through dark forest regions, but here it looked more cheerful, with fairly large meadows and villages, and with the Dal River gliding on light and pretty, between thick rows of alder bushes.

But the King had ill luck to this extent: the bell ringer took up the recessional chant just as the King was stepping from the coach on the church knoll and the people were coming out from the service. But when they came walking past him, the King remained standing, with one foot in the wagon and the other on the footstep. He did not move from the spot—only stared at them. They were the finest lot of folk he had ever seen. All the men were above the average height, with intelligent and earnest faces, and the women were dignified and stately, with an air of Sabbath peace about them.

SELMA LAGERLÖF

PLANNING YOUR SHORT STORY

6f. Prepare a story plan.

A story plan is an outline of the essential elements of narrative writing. To prepare your plan, organize your answers to the 5 *W-How?* questions under the following six headings:

1. *Setting*—*When?* and *Where?* questions. Note the time and place specifically. This does not mean, however, that you must begin your story by describing the setting.
2. *Characters*—*Who?* question. Name each character. Then briefly note his or her role in the story.
3. *Conflict* (the problem)—*Why?* and *How?* questions. Note the main character's problem. Then describe his or her situation as the story opens.
4. *Action* (what happens)—*What?* question. Write a brief summary of the major events in the story.
5. *Climax* (the turning point)—*What?* question. Indicate the point to which the action leads, the point of highest suspense.
6. *Outcome* (the resolution)—*What?* and *How?* questions. Indicate how the conflict is resolved at the end of the story.

EXERCISE 9. Preparing a Story Plan.   Prepare a story plan using your answers for Exercise 5 or one of the following situations. Include all six parts of the plan shown above.

1. Mistaking an animal (squirrel, cat, raccoon) for an intruder
2. Canoeing through white water rapids

3. A meeting between long-lost relatives
4. Fighting a grass fire
5. Discovering that a close friend is dishonest

WRITING

AROUSING INTEREST

6g. Try to arouse the reader's interest from the very beginning.

Some people will not read beyond the beginning of a story if they do not find it interesting. Opening with a startling statement or beginning with a clue to the conflict can capture the reader's interest quickly. Notice how the following story openings use surprise, curiosity, or suspense to arouse interest.

1   They would not let him alone.

They would never let him alone. He realized that that was part of the plot against him—never to leave him in peace, never to give him a chance to mull over the lies they had told him, time enough to pick out the flaws and to figure out the truth for himself.

ROBERT A. HEINLEIN

Creates suspense with the unknown "They" and "him." Creates mystery by mentioning a plot.

2   The day had been one of those unbearable ones, when every sound had set her teeth on edge like chalk creaking on a blackboard, when every word her father or mother said to her or did not say to her seemed an intentional injustice. And of course it would happen, as the end to such a day, that just as the sun went down back of the mountain

Surprises the reader with the discovery that something about an otherwise tedious day is unusual: ". . . Rollie was not around."

and the long twilight began, she noticed that Rollie was not around.

DOROTHY CANFIELD

3 The gorge bent. The walls fell suddenly away, and we came out on the edge of a bleak, boulder-strewn valley. . . . *And there it was*.

    Osborn saw it first. He had been leading the column, threading his way slowly among the huge rock masses of the gorge's mouth. Then he came to the first flat bare place and stopped. He neither pointed nor cried out, but every man behind him knew instantly what it was. The long file sprang taut, like a jerked rope. As swiftly as we could, but in complete silence, we came out one by one into the open space where Osborn stood, and we raised our eyes with his.

JAMES RAMSEY ULLMAN

Creates curiosity with "And there it was."

Builds suspense by witholding identity of "it."

    As you open your story, try to create enough interest to keep the reader's attention. Whether you begin by describing a character, the setting, or an event, try to create a mood or atmosphere and make the situation and the conflict apparent early.

    Before writing, review your story plan. If you have difficulty getting started, just start. Once you get going or when you revise the story, you may have an idea for a better beginning.

EXERCISE 10. Writing a Story Beginning. Write a beginning for the story you planned in Exercise 9.

USING DIALOGUE

6h. Use dialogue to advance the action and to reveal personality.

When people talk, they reveal a great deal about themselves: their education, their attitudes, and their background. To seem real, your characters should talk the way they would in real life.

If your characters are high-school students in an informal situation, for example, they will use colloquial language and, perhaps, slang. If they are adults in a formal situation, the conversation will be quite different. Characters for whom English is a second language may occasionally use words or expressions in their native language.

Before you attempt to write dialogue, spend some time listening carefully to the way people talk. Notice their facial expressions and gestures also.

When You Write. To make your characters "come alive," keep in mind the following features of natural dialogue:

- *The words and attitudes should fit the character.* Make all characters sound like themselves. A six-year-old should not sound like a high-school sophomore.
- *Be as brief as possible.* Most people talk in just a few sentences or words. Even then, they are often interrupted by an impatient listener.
- *Use contractions.* People often use *I'm, we're, don't, who's* instead of *I am, we are, do not,* or *who is.*
- *Limit your dialogue to remarks that advance the action or reveal personality.* Much of real-life conversation is little more than polite or friendly chatter. If you included this "chitchat," your story would lose its focus and become boring.

As you read the following model, notice how the writer uses the features of natural dialogue.

She went toward her. "Hello, Jeanne."

The other, not recognizing her, showed astonishment at being spoken to so familiarly by this common person. She stammered, "But . . . madame . . . I don't recognize . . . You must be mistaken."

advances action; shows how much Mathilde has changed

"No, I'm Mathilde Loisel."

Her friend gave a cry, "Oh, my poor Mathilde, how you've changed!"

"Yes, I've had a hard time since last seeing you. And plenty of misfortunes—and all on account of you!" *(advances action; in real life, Mathilde might have identified the misfortunes)*

"Of me . . . How do you mean?"

"Do you remember that diamond necklace you loaned me to wear to the dance at the Ministry?" *(advances action; gets right to the necklace)*

"Yes, but what about it?"

"Well, I lost it."

"You lost it! But you returned it."

"I brought you another just like it. And we've been paying for it for ten years now. You can imagine that wasn't easy for us who had nothing. Well, it's over now, and I am glad of it." *(advances action; does not repeat details of how it was lost (given earlier); shows Mathilde's honesty)*

Mme. Forestier stopped short. "You mean to say you bought a diamond necklace to replace mine?"

"Yes. You never noticed, then? They were quite alike."

And she smiled with proud and simple joy. *(shows Mathilde's pride in her own honesty)*

Mme. Forestier, quite overcome, clasped her by the hands. "Oh, my poor Mathilde. But mine was only paste.[1] Why, at most it was worth only five hundred francs!" *(shows Jeanne's compassion; advances action; creates dramatic ending)*

GUY DE MAUPASSANT

EXERCISE 11. Writing Dialogue. Using one of the following situations or a situation of your own choice, write a brief dia-

---

[1] *paste:* a brilliant glass used in making artificial gems.

logue. Remember that dialogue should advance the action or reveal personality.

1. A spaceship from earth has just landed on another planet. Two creatures are arguing about the meaning of the spaceship's arrival.
2. Two teen-age girls are climbing a mountain. One falls and sprains her ankle. They disagree about what to do next.
3. Two boys are being punished for disrupting a class. One of the boys tries to persuade the other to talk to the teacher about the punishment.

EXERCISE 12. Writing Dialogue.   Write a brief dialogue between two of the characters from the plan you prepared for Exercise 9. To check how realistic your dialogue sounds, ask a friend or classmate to read it aloud. You can also make a tape recording as you read your dialogue aloud; then, listen to your recording.

CRITICAL THINKING:
Evaluating Dialogue

When you make a judgment, you are using the critical thinking skill of *evaluation*. To evaluate the conversations of the characters in your story, you use a set of criteria, or standards, based on the features of natural dialogue.

EXERCISE 13. Evaluating Dialogue.   Using the following set of standards, evaluate the dialogue you wrote for Exercise 11 or 12. Number your paper 1–4. After the appropriate number, write "yes" if your dialogue meets the standard and "no" if it does not. Try to develop a fair and objective evaluation.

1. The words and attitudes are appropriate for the characters.
2. The comments of the characters are brief.
3. The dialogue either advances the action or reveals personality.
4. The characters use contractions as real people would.

WRITING CHARACTER SKETCHES AND DESCRIPTIONS OF SETTING

6i. Use descriptions to present characters and setting.

A story with no description at all would be flat and colorless. Although lengthy descriptive passages are only rarely found in modern writing, bits of vivid description throughout a story help the reader visualize both the characters and the setting.

Describing a Character

Dialogue is not the only way to reveal character. You can also describe physical characteristics and personality traits.

To describe a character's appearance, use words that appeal to the senses—precise, colorful nouns, verbs, and modifiers—and sharp, interest-arousing details. Notice how McCullers uses such techniques to describe a woman.

> She was a tall, straight woman with a pale and haggard face. Her eyes were deeply shadowed and she wore her dark, ragged hair pushed back from her forehead. She had large, delicate hands, which were very grubby.
>
> CARSON McCULLERS

An effective description of a character usually includes more than just physical details. It also includes details that reveal personality and prepare the reader for the character's reactions to the events of the story. Such a description is often called a *character sketch*.

To reveal personality, first decide what the character's dominant personality trait is—the character is *generous* or *stingy* or *religious* or *cruel*—and then choose details that show that trait. Also show what motivates the character—the experiences and emotions that cause the character's behavior.

A character sketch may consist of one or more paragraphs, and it may include incidents and background information (exposition) as well as descriptive details. Notice how the following excerpt from a short story combines all of these elements to reveal a dominant personality trait.

Shawn Kelvin, a blithe[1] young lad of twenty, went to the States to seek his fortune. And fifteen years thereafter he returned to his native Kerry, his blitheness sobered and his youth dried to the core, and whether he had made his fortune or whether he had not, no one could be knowing for certain. For he was a quiet man, not given to talking about himself and the things he had done. A quiet man, under middle size, with strong shoulders and deep-set blue eyes below brows darker than his dark hair—that was Shawn Kelvin. One shoulder had a trick of hunching slightly higher than the other, and some folks said that came from a habit he had of shielding his eyes in the glare of an open-hearth furnace[2] in a place called Pittsburgh, while others said it used to be a way he had of guarding his chin that time he was a sort of sparring-partner punching bag at a boxing camp.

Shawn Kelvin came home and found that he was the last of the Kelvins, and that the farm of his forefathers had added its few acres to the ranch of Big Liam O'Grady, of Moyvalla. Shawn took no action to recover his land, though O'Grady had got it meanly. He had had enough of fighting, and all he wanted now was peace. He quietly went among the old and kindly friends and quietly looked about him for the place and peace he wanted; and when the time came, quietly produced the money for a neat, handy, small farm on the first warm shoulder of Knockanore Hill below the rolling curves of heather. It was not a big place but it was in good heart, and it got all the sun that was going; and best of all, it suited Shawn to the tiptop notch of contentment for it held the peace that tuned to his quietness, and it commanded the widest view in all Ireland—vale and mountain and the lifting green plain of the Atlantic Sea.

MAURICE WALSH

In the first paragraph, Walsh gives information about Kelvin's background and describes his physical characteristics. The second paragraph relates an incident, his purchase of a farm.

[1] *blithe:* lighthearted.
[2] *open-hearth furnace:* a type of furnace used in making steel.

Together, the two paragraphs reveal one dominant personality trait: Shawn Kelvin is *a quiet man*.

When You Write. To develop a believable character sketch:

- Describe the character's appearance with details and words that appeal to the senses.
- Reveal personality by deciding on a dominant personality trait; then, include details, incidents, and background information that help explain the character's behavior.

EXERCISE 14. Writing a Physical Description of a Character. Write a paragraph describing a person's physical characteristics. Use your notes from Exercise 6, or select another character and use the questions on pages 191–92 to gather information.

EXERCISE 15. Writing a Character Sketch. Write a character sketch of one or more paragraphs. Use the material you gathered for Exercise 6, or select another character. If you choose a new character, use the questions on pages 191–92 to gather information. (If appropriate, you may also include the description you wrote for Exercise 14.)

PREWRITING First decide on a dominant personality trait. Next, organize your information into two groups: physical details and details related to personality. Select physical details that relate to the character's dominant personality trait. Decide whether you will provide background information, relate an incident, or both.

WRITING As you write, remember the trait you want to reveal. Bring the character to life with vivid physical description, background information, an incident, or all three elements.

EVALUATING AND REVISING Ask yourself: Is the character believable? Have I provided enough details to reveal the character? Do all of the details contribute to a clear impression of the character's personality? Does one idea logically follow another? Do any incidents illustrate the character's dominant personality trait? Ask a classmate: After reading the sketch, can you picture the character? Do you know what the dominant personality trait is?

PROOFREADING AND MAKING A FINAL COPY Use the Guidelines for Proofreading on page 36 to check your work. Then make a final copy and proofread it.

Describing a Setting

In describing the setting of your story, try to create an appropriate atmosphere or mood for the development of the action. Use precise details and words that appeal to the senses to help the audience picture the scene.

Weather is often used to create a mood and prepare the reader for the events in the story. The following model is from the beginning of a short story called "The Fall of the House of Usher." Notice how Poe uses not only the weather but also the season and the scenery to establish a gloomy mood.

> During the whole of a dull, dark, and soundless day in the autumn of the year, when the clouds hung oppressively low in the heavens, I had been passing alone, on horseback, through a singularly dreary tract of country, and at length found myself, as the shades of evening drew on, within view of the melancholy House of Usher.
>
> EDGAR ALLAN POE

EXERCISE 16. Writing a Description of a Setting. Write a one- or two-paragraph description of the setting for your short story. Use the answers from Exercises 7 and 9, or select a new situation and conflict, writing a story plan and using the setting from that plan.

DEVELOPING THE PLOT

6j. Develop the plot of your short story.

Plot consists of *conflict, action, climax,* and *outcome*—four of the six basic elements of narrative writing. As you develop the plot of your story, remember that the climax (the moment of highest emotional intensity) should come near the end of the story. The curtain goes up on the dancer's first recital; the boxer staggers to his feet and throws another punch; the firefighter enters the burning building.

Build suspense and interest to the climax, and then quickly resolve the conflict. The dancer has overcome her stage fright; the boxer has won the match; the firefighter has rescued the children; the class president has convinced the school board to change the rule.

EXERCISE 17. Discussing the Use of Narrative Elements.
Read the following story. Then discuss with your classmates how the writer uses the essential elements of narration—setting, characters, conflict, action, climax, and outcome—to create and hold the reader's interest.

CEMETERY PATH

Ivan was a timid little man—so timid that the villagers called him "Pigeon" or mocked him with the title "Ivan the Terrible." Every night Ivan stopped in at the saloon which was on the edge of the village cemetery. Ivan never crossed the cemetery to get to his lonely shack on the other side. The path through the cemetery would save him many minutes, but he had never taken it—not even in the full light of the moon.

Late one winter's night, when bitter wind and snow beat against the saloon, the customers took up the familiar mockery.

Ivan's sickly protest only fed their taunts, and they jeered cruelly when the young Cossack[1] lieutenant flung his horrid challenge at him.

"You are a pigeon, Ivan. You'll walk all around the cemetery in this cold—but you dare not cross the cemetery."

Ivan murmured, "The cemetery is nothing to cross, Lieutenant. It is nothing but earth, like all the other earth."

The lieutenant cried, "A challenge, then! Cross the cem-

[1] *Cossack:* Russian cavalryman.

etery tonight, Ivan, and I will give you five rubles[2]—five gold rubles!''

Perhaps it was the vodka. Perhaps it was the temptation of the five gold rubles. No one ever knew why Ivan, moistening his lips, said suddenly: ''Yes, lieutenant, I'll cross the cemetery!''

The saloon echoed with their disbelief. The lieutenant winked to the men and unbuckled his sword. ''Here, Ivan. When you get to the center of the cemetery, in front of the biggest tomb, stick the sword into the ground. In the morning we shall go there. And if the sword is in the ground—five gold rubles to you!''

Ivan took the sword. The men drank a toast: ''To Ivan the Terrible!'' They roared with laughter.

The wind howled around Ivan as he closed the door of the saloon behind him. The cold was knife-sharp. He buttoned his long coat and crossed the dirt road. He could hear the lieutenant's voice, louder than the rest, yelling after him, ''Five rubles, pigeon! If you live!''

Ivan pushed the cemetery gate open. He walked fast. ''Earth, just earth . . . like any other earth.'' But the darkness was a massive dread. ''Five gold rubles . . .'' The wind was cruel, and the sword was like ice in his hands. Ivan shivered under the long, thick coat and broke into a limping run.

He recognized the large tomb. He must have sobbed— that was drowned in the wind. And he kneeled, cold and terrified, and drove the sword into the hard ground. With his fist, he beat it down to the hilt. It was done. The cemetery . . . the challenge . . . five gold rubles.

Ivan started to rise from his knees. But he could not move. Something held him. Something gripped him in an unyielding hold. Ivan tugged and lurched and pulled—gasping in his panic, shaken by a monstrous fear. But something held Ivan. He cried out in terror, then made senseless gurgling noises.

They found Ivan, next morning, on the ground in front of the tomb that was in the center of the cemetery. His face

---

[2] *ruble:* the basic unit of money in Russia.

was not that of a frozen man's, but of a man killed by some nameless horror. And the lieutenant's sword was in the ground where Ivan had pounded it—through the dragging folds of his long coat.

SATURDAY REVIEW

EXERCISE 18. Establishing Conflict.   Review your story plan (Exercise 9). Then write one or two paragraphs establishing the conflict or problem facing your main character. Include the character's thoughts about the conflict. You may instead choose a new situation and conflict and prepare a new story plan.

ACHIEVING COHERENCE

Arranging Events in Chronological Order

6k. Arrange the events of your story in chronological order.

Since a story relates a series of events that take place in time, the natural order of arrangement is chronological. Think now about how much time your story will cover. Do not try to cover too much time, and remember that the time does not have to be minute-by-minute. "Cemetery Path," for example, begins late one night and ends the next morning. All of the paragraphs except the last one take place during the late-night hours. Then, in a single *leap in time,* the last paragraph tells what happens the following morning. The writer does not include details about the rest of the night because they are not important to the story.

EXERCISE 19. Arranging Events in Chronological Order. Review the "Action" section of the story plan you made for Exercise 9. Using chronological order, list all the events that will take place in your story. If an event is not important to the story, consider omitting it and using a leap in time instead.

EXERCISE 20. Evaluating the Use of Chronological Order. Exchange papers from Exercise 19 with a classmate, and evaluate each other's use of chronological order.

Connecting Ideas

6l. Use transitional expressions and direct references to connect ideas within and between paragraphs.

Transitional expressions and direct references help your reader follow your ideas and understand how they are related.

Transitional Expressions

If you have arranged events in chronological order, you will need to add only a few time-signaling transitional expressions (see pages 58–59). When you use other types of transitional expressions, be sure that they accurately indicate the relationship you intend to show.

Direct References

Direct references (see pages 57–58) usually sound less artificial than transitional expressions. Notice the direct references in the following paragraph from "Cemetery Path."

> *He* recognized the large tomb. *He* must have sobbed— *that* was drowned in the *wind*. And *he* kneeled, *cold* and terrified, and drove the *sword* into the hard *ground*. With *his* fist, he beat *it* down to the *hilt*. It was done.
> The *cemetery* . . . the *challenge* . . . *five gold rubles.*

The pronouns *he* and *his* link Ivan with the action. The repetition of the key words *wind, cold, sword, hilt, cemetery,* and *challenge* links the action in the paragraph with earlier events.

EXERCISE 21. Using Transitional Expressions and Direct References. Write one or two paragraphs developing one of the events you listed for Exercise 19. Judge whether the order of events is clear, and add transitional expressions and direct references as needed to improve coherence. Finally, underline all the transitional expressions and direct references you used.

WRITING A FIRST DRAFT

6m. Write a first draft of your short story.

You have selected and limited a subject, chosen a conflict, and made a story plan. You have written descriptions and dialogue. You have also thought about your point of view, the climax, the outcome, and the organization of details. You are now ready to write a first draft of your story.

Before you begin writing, reread your story plan and the descriptions and dialogue you have written. Think again about your purpose, your audience, and your tone. Then, as you draft your story, let your thoughts flow quickly, keeping in mind that you will have time to improve and correct your writing later.

EXERCISE 22. Writing a First Draft.   Using the story plan you developed for Exercise 9, write a short story. As you write, remember to follow chronological order and to connect your ideas clearly.

EVALUATING

EVALUATING YOUR SHORT STORY

6n. Evaluate your story for content, organization, and style.

No matter how carefully you have planned your story, you will always see new possibilities once you begin writing. Evaluating gives you the chance to review your draft. Other readers—classmates, friends, teachers—can also help you find areas for improvement. Use the following guidelines to evaluate your draft.

GUIDELINES FOR EVALUATING SHORT STORIES

Plot Development	1. Does the beginning draw the reader into the story? Does it clearly present a situation and a conflict?
Plot Development	2. Do all the events and details directly relate to the story? Does the action move rapidly toward the climax? Does the story have a believable ending?
Coherence	3. Are events clearly arranged in chronological order? Are words used to make this order clear?
Setting	4. Does the setting help create the right mood or atmosphere?
Character Development	5. Do the characters sound and act "real"? Are the characters' main personality traits clear? Are the characters vividly described?
Dialogue	6. Does the dialogue reflect how real people sound? Is it appropriate for the characters?
Point of View	7. Is the point of view consistent? Does the narrator know something he or she could not logically know?
Verb Tense	8. Is the verb tense consistent? Do you stick to past or present tense?
Paragraphing	9. Does a new paragraph begin each time the speaker changes? Does a new paragraph signal a sudden shift in place or time?

EXERCISE 23. Evaluating Your Short Story. Judge your draft by applying each of the Guidelines for Evaluating Short Stories. Mark places in your draft where you should make changes, and keep this draft for later use. Exchanging papers with a classmate or reading your short story to a small group may also help you evaluate your story.

REVISING

REVISING YOUR WRITING

6o. Revise your short story draft, making changes to improve its content, organization, and style.

You can use four techniques to revise any piece of writing: you can *cut,* or omit, words, phrases, and sentences; you can *add* ideas and details; you can *reorder,* or rearrange, words, sentences, and paragraphs; and you can *replace* one thing with another. The following chart suggests how you can use these techniques to revise your short story.

REVISING SHORT STORIES

PROBLEM	TECHNIQUE	REVISION
The beginning is dull.	Add/Cut	Add a description of a character, the setting, or an event. Add an opening dialogue. Cut details and words that do not set up the situation and conflict.
The situation and conflict aren't clear.	Add	Add details that explain or describe the situation and conflict.
Some of the action fails to center on the conflict.	Cut	Remove any events that do not relate to the major conflict.
The action moves too slowly.	Cut/Add	Cut descriptive details that slow down the story. Add words or phrases that push the action forward (see pages 204–05).
The ending doesn't seem possible.	Replace	Substitute another ending that is a logical result of events in the story.
The order of events is jumbled and confused.	Reorder/Add	Rearrange events in chronological order. Add words that show the order of events (see pages 207–08).

PROBLEM	TECHNIQUE	REVISION
The setting doesn't contribute to the mood, and descriptions seem lifeless.	Add/Cut	Add precise words and sensory details to make the setting vivid. (Refer to a dictionary or thesaurus.) Cut details that do not contribute to the dominant mood.
The main character's dominant personality trait isn't clear.	Add	Add physical details, incidents, and background information that show this trait.
Characters don't seem like real people.	Add/Cut	Add details, incidents, and dialogue that show characters acting like real people. Cut details and dialogue that do not relate to how people really behave.
The dialogue doesn't sound "real."	Cut/Replace	Cut sentence length. Cut words that a character could not logically know. Cut "chitchat" that doesn't push the action along. Substitute contractions, informal expressions, and slang for formal words that seem unrealistic.
The point of view shifts.	Cut	Cut information that the narrator can't logically know.
The verb tense changes.	Replace	Replace past tense with present tense or vice versa.
Paragraphing is confusing.	Reorder	Make a new paragraph each time the speaker changes and when the time or place shifts.

EXERCISE 24. Analyzing a Writer's Revisions. Read the following draft of a short story, and analyze the writer's revisions (in red). (The notes in the margin show the revision techniques the writer used.) Then answer the questions that follow the story.

On a crisp, clear day

∧ In August, a plane flew my friend Franklin and   add

two-week

me into Canada and left us for a ∧ vacation. ~~There~~   add/cut

a cabin,

~~was a cabin and~~ we had ∧ food and fishing gear, but   cut/add

there was not another human being within 30 miles.

For the   three days,

∧ ~~At~~ first ∧ we fished and swam during the daylight   replace

hours and slept peacefully during the night. This

enjoyable schedule was ruined the night something

tried to get in the cabin.

That something

∧ ~~It~~ was a black bear, which was attracted by the   replace

smell of   *On the third night*

∧ food in our cabin. ∧ We took turns clanging pans   add/reorder

together to scare him away. We kept him out by

the first night

barricading the door. He tried to get through the   add

the second night

window, and we kept him out by shoving the bureau   add

but

in front of it. He still managed to claw a small hole   add

through the door. ~~One afternoon I surprised Franklin~~   cut

~~by catching a three-pound trout.~~

flopped

After four nights without sleep, Franklin ~~sat~~   replace

has to

down on a chair in the cabin and said, "This ~~must~~   replace

have

stop. Let us call the park service and tell them ~~to~~   replace

send a plane for us."

I hesitated. "Maybe he will give up and go away   replace

after another night or two," I pointed out.

"Maybe, ~~the bear will~~ get through the door   replace

tonight," Franklin yelled.   replace

"You are right," I said. "I will use the   replace

radio to call the park service."

Since the park service couldn't send a

plane ~~right away~~, we ~~stayed~~ one more ~~day.~~ replace

When morning finally came, the park service

plane landed in a nearby field and rescued us

from our vacation.

1. Why did the writer add several words and phrases?
2. Where did the writer add transitions to indicate a change in time?
3. Why did the writer change the placement of one sentence?
4. Why did the writer make some changes in the dialogue?
5. Why did the writer remove one entire sentence?

EXERCISE 25. Revising Your Short Story. Using the revising chart on pages 211–12, revise the short story you wrote for Exercise 22.

PROOFREADING

PROOFREADING YOUR SHORT STORY

6p. Proofread your short story.

No matter how informal or even humorous your short story is, errors such as an incorrect spelling or a missing end mark can confuse your audience. Be especially careful with the punctuation of dialogue. Remember that direct quotations must be enclosed in quotation marks and that each change of speaker must be signaled by a new paragraph. For a review of the use of other marks of punctuation with quotation marks, see Chapter 24.

EXERCISE 26. Proofreading Your Short Story.   Proofread the short story you revised for Exercise 25, using the guidelines on page 36.

WRITING THE FINAL VERSION

WRITING THE FINAL VERSION

6q. Prepare your final copy.

Since your paper will not be neat after you have revised and made corrections, you need to write or type a final copy. Be sure to proofread your final version to make sure that you have copied correctly.

EXERCISE 27. Preparing Your Final Copy.   Prepare a final copy of your short story, following the standards for correct manuscript form on pages 37–38.

CHAPTER 6 WRITING REVIEW 1

Writing a Short Story Using First-Person Point of View. Write a story based completely on your imagination or on something that actually happened to someone you know. Use the point of view of a first-person narrator who is the main character in the story, and establish a light, humorous tone. If your teacher does not specify an audience, choose one of the following ones: (1) adult readers of an outdoor recreation magazine; (2) teen-age readers of a science fiction or fantasy magazine; or (3) readers of a teen magazine.

PREWRITING To search for possible subjects, try to recall interesting experiences you have heard or read about. Read the local newspaper for a few days, looking for possible story ideas, and ask your parents and other relatives to recall experiences they have had. Select one experience; then, limit it to a situation that involves a brief conflict you can develop within the space of a short story. Gather details to develop the characters, the setting, and the plot. Then prepare a story plan, arranging the events chronologically.

WRITING Review your notes and story plan just before you begin to write. If you have trouble writing an interesting opening, save the beginning for later. Follow your story plan, and try to keep the events in chronological order. If you include dialogue, remember to have the characters talk the way they would in real life.

EVALUATING AND REVISING Ask yourself: Is my story appropriate for my audience? Will they find it entertaining and humorous? Is the point of view consistent? Use the Guidelines for Evaluating Short Stories on page 210 and the revising chart on pages 211–12.

PROOFREADING AND MAKING A FINAL COPY After you have completed your revision, use the Guidelines for Proofreading on page 36 to check your work. Then make a final copy and proofread it once again.

CHAPTER 6 WRITING REVIEW 2

Writing a Short Story Using Third-Person Point of View. Write a story about a conflict between a person and nature. You may use one of the following situations, or select another experience and limit it to a situation that involves a conflict. Use the point of view of a third-person narrator, and establish a serious tone. If your teacher does not specify an audience, select one of the following ones: (1) readers of your school paper or magazine or (2) readers of your local newspaper's Sunday magazine or features section.

Situations:
1. A teen-ager becomes lost during a snowstorm
2. A volcanic eruption threatens a community
3. An amateur sailor gets caught in a storm on a lake
4. A fire breaks out in the house where a teen-ager is baby-sitting
5. A hot-air balloonist encounters a fierce storm

PREWRITING Choose a situation and a conflict and decide what you want the outcome to be. By brainstorming, interviewing other people, or reading about similar events, gather details to develop the characters, the setting, and the plot. Focus especially on your main character and the setting. Then prepare a story plan, and arrange the events in chronological order.

WRITING Reread your story plan before you start writing, keeping your audience, purpose, and tone in mind. Remember that a third-person omniscient narrator can know what any of the characters are thinking and feeling. Try to build suspense as your main character approaches the climax of the story. Then create a realistic resolution of the conflict.

EVALUATING AND REVISING Ask yourself: Is my story appropriate for my audience? Have I established and maintained a serious tone? Is the point of view consistent? Use the Guidelines for Evaluating Short Stories on page 210 and the revising chart on pages 211–12.

PROOFREADING AND MAKING A FINAL COPY Use the Guidelines for Proofreading on page 36 to check your paper. Then prepare a final copy and proofread again.

CHAPTER 7

Writing Summaries and Reports

WRITING FROM OUTSIDE SOURCES

Many compositions you write are based on personal experiences and opinions; others, such as summaries and reports, are based on knowledge from outside sources. This chapter will guide you in writing three kinds of compositions: (1) the *summary,* (2) the *report,* and (3) the *book report.*

Many of the exercises in this chapter require knowledge of the library; therefore, study Chapter 28 before you study this chapter.

WRITING A SUMMARY

A *summary* is a brief composition that gives the most important points of a longer work. In almost all of your classes, you may be asked to write summaries of articles from magazines, encyclopedias, or books. To write a summary, you must first read the original work carefully, deciding which points are most important. Then you must write the summary in your own words, being careful not to omit important information or to add any ideas of your own.

PREWRITING

Reading the Article

7a. Read the article carefully.

Read the article at least twice. The first time, skim the article, reading it quickly and noting its overall organization and most important points. The second time, read the article more carefully, looking for supporting as well as main ideas. Read the introductory paragraph slowly and thoughtfully, since the whole point of the article is often expressed there in a general way. Read the final paragraph in this manner also; it often sums up the article's main ideas.

CRITICAL THINKING:
Analyzing Relationships Among Ideas

An important critical thinking skill in writing a summary is analyzing ideas to determine their relationships. You must distinguish between the main ideas and the supporting ideas, or details.

To begin analyzing relationships among ideas, identify the general topic of the article. The *topic* is the most general statement that you can make when asked, "What is this article about?" Next, locate the *main ideas,* the most important points the author makes about the topic. Finally, identify *supporting ideas,* or *details,* which may *describe, explain, exemplify,* or *support* main ideas.

EXAMPLE

HYPNOSIS

Some areas of psychology attract both real   topic (as indicated
scientists and unqualified people. Hypnosis is   by title)
one of these areas. Hypnosis is not a major

field of interest to most psychologists. But it is an accepted area of scientific study.

What is hypnosis? Hypnosis is an unusual state of consciousness that has some features in common with sleep. Perhaps you can remember what you feel like when you are about to fall asleep or about to wake up. You are aware of what is going on around you. And you find it difficult to fall either into a deep sleep or to wake up completely. People who have been hypnotized sometimes report that the experience is similar to going to sleep.

first part of main idea statement (as indicated by subtitle)
details that explain main idea

Hypnosis is not the same as sleep, however. People who are hypnotized are usually very open to suggestion. They understand what is said to them and are able to carry out simple directions. People in normal sleep, on the other hand, are usually open to little, if any, suggestion. And generally they are not aware of what is going on around them.

second part of main idea statement
details that explain main idea

ENGLE/SNELLGROVE

Before You Write. Reread the hypnosis article, and ask yourself the following questions:

- What is the general topic of the article? (*Hint:* The title often states the topic, and the first and last paragraphs often introduce and sum up the general topic.)
- What are the most important ideas about this topic? (*Hint:* Subtitles or headings often identify main ideas.)
- What supporting details describe or explain main ideas?
- What details are examples or reasons that support main ideas?

EXERCISE 1. Identifying Main Ideas and Supporting Ideas, or Details. Following are the first three paragraphs from the second section of the hypnosis article. (The section is subtitled "How is hypnosis produced?") The word *subject* in these paragraphs refers to the person being hypnotized. Read the paragraphs and then answer the questions following them.

> *How is hypnosis produced?* There is no certain formula to follow in producing a state of hypnosis. Some psychologists use one technique; some use another.
>
> One instrument used to hypnotize someone is a flashing light. The light flashes at a specific rate per minute, while the subject stares steadily at it. It tends to make the subject more relaxed and sleepy and therefore more open to being hypnotized. The presence of the flashing light also gives the subject something to focus on.
>
> Other methods for producing hypnosis include the use of sounds or objects, such as a pencil, to which subjects direct their attention. Still other methods involve no mechanical aid of any kind. They rely on the spoken word, encouraging the subject to concentrate on a specific thought.

1. What is the main idea of this section?
2. What are four supporting ideas, or details, in these paragraphs?
3. Which of the supporting ideas is itself supported by details that explain how something is done?

Taking Notes

7b. Take accurate notes using your own words, your own abbreviations.

An important part of taking notes is to record information about the article to be summarized. In doing so, follow the MLA (Modern Language Association of America) guidelines for preparing bibliography cards. (See pages 233–34 of this chapter.)

> ***Before You Write.*** When you take notes for a summary, remember to
>
> - Use a dictionary to look up unfamiliar words or phrases.
> - Identify your source correctly.
> - Follow the pattern of organization used in the article.
> - Put ideas into your own words, instead of copying.
> - Use words or phrases, rather than sentences, and use abbreviations.
> - If you use a direct quotation, copy the writer's exact words, enclose them in quotation marks, and give the page number on which the quotation appears.

EXAMPLE

In your own words:

> Hypnosis — state like going
>   to sleep
> Diff. — hypnosis subjects
>   respond to suggestions

Using a quotation:

> "Hypnosis is an unusual state of
> consciousness that has some
> features in common with
> sleep."   page 27
>   Diff. — hypnosis subjects
> respond to suggestions.

CRITICAL THINKING:
Evaluating the Importance of Ideas

A summary includes all the main ideas in an article, as well as the most important supporting details. To evaluate the importance of details, think of topic, main idea, and supporting details as occupying different levels on a branching, or tree, diagram. At the top of the diagram is the topic. The main ideas, branching from the topic, are on the second level. The third level consists of details about the main ideas. A fourth level includes details about third-level details, and so on. (Note that you have now arranged topic, main ideas, and supporting details in *descending order,* from the most general to the most specific.)

The following example is based on the first and second sections of the hypnosis article, on pages 219 and 220.

Tree Diagram

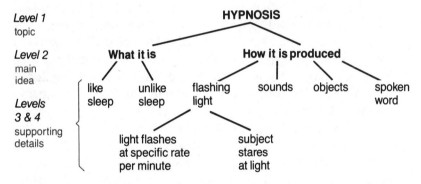

In writing a summary your goal is to cover only the most important points. As details become more and more specific, as they occupy lower and lower levels, they become less important to understanding the main points in the article.

EXAMPLE

HOW IS HYPNOSIS PRODUCED?

No one procedure is used by psychologists to produce hypnosis (main idea—second level). One procedure is to use a flashing light (supporting detail—third level).

Others are to use sounds (supporting detail—third level), objects (supporting detail—third level), or just the spoken word (supporting detail—third level).

EXERCISE 2. Evaluating the Importance of Ideas. Read twice the following article on the significance of beards throughout history. The first time, skim the article to identify the main ideas. Then reread the article, noting supporting as well as main ideas. Finally, make a tree diagram including the topic, the main ideas, and the supporting details.

BEARDS THROUGHOUT HISTORY

One of the earliest symbols of *machismo,* the beard has had its ups and downs through the centuries, being sometimes "in" and sometimes "out." But from Zeus and Adam through King Arthur and Charlemagne and on to the antiestablishment youth of this century, beards have always been serious business.

The Mohammedan swears by the beard of the Prophet, while the most shattering curse a primitive Bedouin can utter is, "May God pluck your beard!" To "beard" a man—to touch, much less pull at, his beard—was in early times a bold and daring insult. In 1185 England's future King John, on a visit to Ireland, infuriated native chieftains by tugging on their flowing beards.

Beards were status symbols, emblems of royalty, in the 2nd millennium B.C. Beards shaped from metal were tied with ribbons or straps to the chins of kings—and queens. In ancient Egypt and Babylonia, men of stature used curling irons, tongs, and dyes on their whiskers and, at festival time, dusted them with perfumed starch and gold. The kings of Persia went even further, plaiting golden threads into their sacred beards.

Beardlessness, as well, has added to history's footnotes. Alexander the Great, having seen that an opponent could seize a soldier by his beard and lop his head off, ordered his troops to shave. In the 12th century the small son of Saladin, sultan of Egypt and Syria, wept in terror at the unaccustomed sight of the Crusaders' envoys' bare chins. It took

Queen Elizabeth I to exploit the beard for tax money: anyone with a two-week growth paid the price. The lowest rate, for those of the bottom social rank, was 3 shillings 4 pence a year. Eras in which beards have been "in" have alternated with those in which they have been "out." The French, under the bearded Francis I, followed the leader. But a century later, under the bare-chinned Louis XIII, they shaved.

In the United States the first 15 presidents, Washington through Buchanan, were clean-shaven, only to have Lincoln introduce the beard to the White House. Since then only four presidents have had real beards—Grant, Hayes, Garfield, and Benjamin Harrison—and none since Taft has sported any facial hair.

EXERCISE 3. Taking Notes on an Article. Using the tree diagram you made in Exercise 2, take notes on the beard article. Use your own words. Include quotations from the article.

Considering Purpose and Audience

7c. Adjust your writing to your purpose and audience.

The purpose for writing a summary is to convey, in briefer form, the main ideas of a longer work. How you communicate these ideas, however, depends upon the audience for whom you write. Ask yourself the same questions about the audience for a summary that you would for any other piece of writing. How old are they? What kind of knowledge do they have about the topic? What kind of background information do they need? Thinking carefully about your audience will help you determine appropriate vocabulary as well as sentence length and complexity.

EXAMPLE

Original: A WAY WITH WATER

The rhythm of an elephant's day is set largely by its watering routine. An adult needs about 30 gallons of water a day. When water is abundant there is no problem. But during droughts elephants resort to an intriguing technique:

digging wells. In a dried-up riverbed they scoop out holes with their forefeet until they reach water. After waiting patiently for the sand to settle, they drink in order of seniority—calves last. Elephants spray water over their ears to stay cool. So vital is this to their survival that in extreme drought conditions elephants have been known to put their trunks deep inside their own throats, sucking out water with which to cool themselves.[1]

Summary for an audience of your classmates:

The basic pattern of an elephant's day is mostly determined by the thirty gallons of water it needs for drinking and for staying cool. During droughts, elephants will often find water by digging wells and sometimes even by sticking their trunks down into their own throats.

Summary for an audience of six-year-old children:

Elephants need a great deal of water. They need this water to drink and to stay cool. When the earth is very dry, they may dig wells with their feet. They may even stick their trunks down into their own throats to get water.

EXERCISE 4. Writing Summaries for Different Audiences. Use the *Readers' Guide to Periodical Literature* to find a short article on any subject. On a note card or piece of paper, write the following information about the article: (1) the author's name, (2) the title of the article, (3) the name and date of the magazine, (4) the page numbers on which the article is found. (See pages 233–34.) Then write two summaries of the article, one for an audience of your classmates, the other for an audience of six-year-old children.

PREWRITING List, in outline form, the main ideas in the article. For each main idea, give at least two supporting details.

EVALUATING AND REVISING When you have completed your summary, check it against the Guidelines for Evaluating Sum-

---

[1] From *Wild, Wild World of Animals/ELEPHANTS & OTHER LAND GIANTS*. Reprinted by permission of Time-Life Books Inc.

maries on page 228. Exchange summaries with a classmate. What information did you include for each audience? Discuss whether this information should have been included.

WRITING

Writing the Summary

7d. Write the summary, making it one-fourth to one-third the length of the article.

Put aside the article, and use your notes to write the summary. Don't begin with "This article is about . . ."; instead, begin directly: "Capital punishment, which is the death penalty for crime, has existed as long as there have been laws and courts. . . ."

> **When You Write.** As you write your summary, remember to
>
> - State ideas clearly and briefly.
> - Present ideas in the same order used in the original article.
> - Include all important ideas but do not add ideas not in the article.
> - Keep your summary to one-fourth or one-third the length of the original article.

EXERCISE 5. Reading, Taking Notes, and Writing a Summary. Use the *Readers' Guide* to find a magazine or newspaper article on a subject of your choice. On a note card, record the author's name, the title of the article, the name and date of the magazine or newspaper, and the page numbers of the article. Read the article twice, first skimming it to note the main ideas and then reading it more carefully to look for supporting as well as main ideas. As a prewriting activity, prepare a tree diagram similar to the one on page 223. Take notes in your own words, with one or two quotations. Write a summary based on your notes.

EVALUATING AND REVISING

Evaluating and Revising the Summary

7e. Compare your summary with the article.

Summaries, like other kinds of writing, benefit from evaluation and revision. If possible, put your first draft away for a day or two so that you see it more objectively. Skim once more the article you summarized, this time comparing your summary with it. Use the following guidelines to evaluate your summary; then revise it by referring to the chart on pages 148–49.

GUIDELINES FOR EVALUATING SUMMARIES

Topic	1. Does the summary identify the topic of the article?
Main Ideas	2. Does the summary include the article's main ideas?
Supporting Details	3. Does the summary include important supporting details?
Order	4. Does the summary present points in the order in which they are given in the original work?
Paraphrasing	5. Is the summary written in the writer's words, not those of the original work? Are quotations included correctly?
Length	6. Is the summary one-fourth to one-third the length of the article?

REVIEW EXERCISE A. Writing Summaries in Other Subjects. Select a three- or four-paragraph passage from your social studies, science, or other textbook. Read the selection, take notes, and write a summary. To evaluate the importance of ideas, prepare a four-level tree diagram before you write.

A REPORT BASED ON SEVERAL SOURCES

The *research report,* also called the *library paper,* requires the use of library sources. The research report is likely to be five hundred words or more, factual, and based on information derived from three or more sources. In report writing, the purpose is to inform or to explain and the tone is formal.

PREWRITING

Choosing Your Subject

At times you may be assigned a specific subject to investigate. If you are given a choice of subject, however, much depends on how you choose. The wrong subject can result in additional work for you and an inferior report.

7f. Choose a subject for which sufficient material is readily available.

Don't make trouble for yourself by selecting a subject not discussed in the books and periodicals in your school library. Subjects on which you are likely to find little or no information in your library include those in the following categories:

  a. Subjects too recent in development (a new kind of camera invented just last month)
  b. Subjects too limited in scope (automobile production during the past few months)
  c. Subjects too technical in content (the use of iambic meter in the poetry of Robert Frost)

After you have chosen a tentative subject that is of interest to you, check the card catalog (books) and the *Readers' Guide* (magazines) in your library to make sure that there are enough references at hand.

Getting An Overview

7g. Get a broad perspective of your subject.

Begin your research by getting an overview—a broad perspective of your subject. Reading general articles about your subject, such as those found in encyclopedias, will help. You can also look through the card catalog and the *Readers' Guide* to find books and articles about your subject. Another helpful method is to skim information found on covers of books about your subject and to scan their tables of contents.

Developing a Limited Topic

7h. Narrow your subject to a sufficiently limited topic.

A five-hundred-word report will be effective only if it deals with a topic limited enough to discuss in detail. (See pages 119–20 for more information on limiting a subject.) To determine whether your topic is sufficiently limited, consider the length of your report and how much detail you can include.

Suppose, for example, that you enjoy reading accounts of great explorations, such as those to other planets and in the depths of the oceans. Would "exploration" be a good topic for a short report? No, for you would be covering a great deal of time—from the beginning of civilization to the present—and a great deal of space—from outer space to the oceans. Therefore, you decide to limit this broad subject. Notice how each example below is more specific than the one it follows.

Exploration (broad subject)
Exploring shipwrecks on the oceans' bottoms (a specific type of exploration)
Recent developments in exploring shipwrecks (a specific time period)
Recent explorations of the *Titanic* (a specific shipwreck in a specific time period)

EXERCISE 6. Developing Limited Topics from Broad Subjects. For each of the following broad subjects, develop a limited topic suitable for a five-hundred-word paper.

1. Computers
2. Physical fitness
3. Horror movies
4. Music
5. Space exploration

EXERCISE 7. Choosing a Limited Topic. Choose a limited topic for your own research report. You may use a topic you developed for Exercise 6, or you may develop another limited topic of your own.

Determining Your Purpose and Audience

7i. Develop a purpose statement to guide your report.

A *purpose statement* is exactly what the name implies—a straightforward statement of what you plan to accomplish in your paper. Although the statement will not appear in your paper, it can help guide your research. Keep your audience in mind as you draft your purpose statement, and make your purpose statement as specific as possible.

EXAMPLES

I plan to discuss the peacemaking activities of several Americans and to explain how each one struggled against a particular form of violence.

I plan to explain how air conditioning was developed and how it drastically affected the American economy and the life styles of the American people.

I plan to explain why the story of the *Titanic* continues to fascinate explorers and how the wreck of the *Titanic* has been recently explored.

Before you complete your research, you might decide to change your purpose statement. For example, you might realize that the topic of American peacemakers is too broad. In the meantime, however, the purpose statement can help make your search for information more efficient.

EXERCISE 8. Writing a Purpose Statement for a Report.
Using the overview of your topic as a basis, write a specific purpose statement for your report. Be sure that your purpose statement is specific.

Locating Source Materials

7j. Find specific information that will help you develop your topic.

To find specific information about your topic, use the card catalog and the *Readers' Guide* and refer to general articles in encyclopedias. These sources will include specific books and magazine articles on your topic. As you discover sources, note that one source can be invaluable in leading you to other sources. (In this way, at least, research is somewhat like a treasure hunt, with one source leading to another.) If in this first hunt for sources you do not find at least three good references, it would be wise (with your teacher's permission) to change your topic.

Before You Write. To locate specific sources with information about your topic:

- Note the titles of books and magazine articles listed at the end of general articles in encyclopedias and look for these sources.
- Check all possible subject headings in the card catalog and *Readers' Guide*. Sources with information on the *Titanic*, for example, might be listed under *Shipwrecks, Oceanliners,* or *Steamships*.
- When you locate one source, check the bibliography (a list of books and articles the author used) to identify other possible sources.
- Check the index and table of contents in books to find how much information they include on your topic.
- Ask the librarian for assistance.

EXERCISE 9. Using Library Resources to Gain an Over-view of a Topic. Use your library resources to gain an overview of the topic you selected in Exercise 7. As you research, refer to your purpose statement.

Developing a Working Bibliography

7k. Compile a list of your sources as a working bibliography.

A *working bibliography* is a list of sources (usually on a set of note cards) that you use as you begin your research. The best method is to put information about each source—each book or magazine—on a separate note card, called a *bibliography card.*

Different kinds of sources require slightly different bibliography cards. Recording information correctly and carefully on your bibliography cards will make your work easier when you prepare a bibliography for the final draft. (See pages 244–45 for more information about bibliography entries.)

Bibliography card for a book: Record the following information in the order shown with the punctuation indicated.

1. The author's name (last name first with a comma between the last and first names), followed by a period
2. The title of the book (underlined), followed by a period
3. The place of publication, followed by a colon
4. The name of the publishing company, followed by a comma, and the year of publication, followed by a period

Bibliography card for a newspaper or magazine article: Record the following information in the order shown, punctuated as indicated.

1. If given, the name of the author (last name first), followed by a period
2. The title of the article (in quotation marks), followed by a period
3. The name of the magazine or newspaper (underlined)
4. The date of publication, followed by a colon
5. The section number (newspapers only) and page numbers of the article followed by period

The word *page* and its abbreviation are not used. If the article begins on one page and is continued later in the magazine, put a comma between the page numbers. A hyphen between page numbers means the article appears on all the pages between the numbers. Note, too, that months of the year—except May, June, and July—are abbreviated.

Study the sample bibliography cards below. Note that each has a circled number in the upper right-hand corner. As you prepare each bibliography card, number them in this way. Later, when you take notes, you can put this number on the note card instead of writing out the full title of the source.

EXAMPLES

An article:

Murphy, Joy Waldron. "It Was Sad When the Great Ship Went Down." *Smithsonian* Aug. 1986: 57-67.

②

number assigned to this source

A book:

Lord, Walter. *A Night to Remember.* New York: Holt, Rinehart and Winston, 1955.

③

number assigned to this source

Before You Write. When you prepare a working bibliography, be sure to

- Check that you recorded all necessary information (author, title, date of publication, etc.) about the source.
- Check that you have used punctuation correctly.
- Assign a number to each source.

EXERCISE 10. Preparing a Working Bibliography. Prepare bibliography cards for each of the sources you have located. If you do not have note cards, write *Working Bibliography* at the top of a sheet of paper and list your sources on the paper.

Drafting an Outline

7l. Develop a preliminary outline.

In making your preliminary outline, you will rely on the general information about your topic that you gained from the overview. (To review outlining, see Chapter 4, pages 128–30.) You may also find it helpful to read one of your sources first, especially if much of the information is new to you. The following outline shows the form the preliminary outline should take. In this outline, topics are indicated by Roman numerals, subtopics by capital letters.

EXPLORING THE *TITANIC*

I. Sinking of the *Titanic*
II. Discovery of the *Titanic*'s location
   A. Long search for location
   B. Discovery in 1985
III. Exploration of the *Titanic*
   A. Role of undersea robot
   B. Knowledge about *Titanic* gained
   C. Tests of undersea robots made
IV. Future of the *Titanic*

    Notice that in this preliminary outline, the writer is making early decisions about how the material will be organized. Since the writer intends to describe the stages of the exploration as they occurred, most details will be arranged chronologically.

EXERCISE 11. Developing a Preliminary Outline. Develop a preliminary outline on the topic you chose in Exercise 7 and used for your bibliography in Exercise 9. Check Chapter 4 (pages 129–30) for proper outline form.

Taking Notes

7m. Take notes on your sources. Use a separate note card for each topic and for each source.

Taking notes for a research report is much like taking notes for a summary (see pages 221–22). First, read quickly over your source material. Then, reread the material, this time more slowly and carefully, taking notes as you read. For the most part, your notes should be written in your own words. If a quotation seems appropriate, remember to use quotation marks.

All your notes should relate to a topic or subtopic from your preliminary outline. In the upper left-hand corner of each card, write the topic or subtopic from your preliminary outline with which the note card deals. Since you assigned a number to each source on your bibliography cards, you can identify sources on your note cards by writing the corresponding number in the upper right-hand corner of the card.

When you begin to take notes on a different topic or subtopic, use a new note card. Also, change cards each time you begin to take notes from a different source, even if on the same topic. Thus, notes from a single magazine article covering several of your outline topics might use up several cards. Preparing note cards in this manner allows you to arrange and rearrange them until you find a suitable order.

Study the following sample note cards. The numbers at the sides indicate the various entries that will appear on your note cards:

1. Outline topic or subtopic
2. Source (identified by number)
3. Direct quotation
4. Page numbers on which information was found

On the second sample card, the writer includes a direct quotation. Notice that an ellipsis (. . .) is used to show that some words have been omitted from the author's original statement.

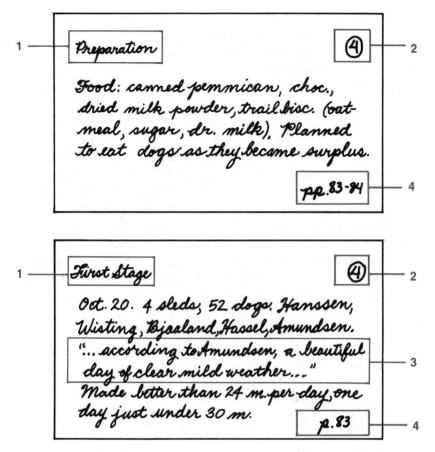

Preparation ④

Food: canned pemmican, choc.,
dried milk powder, trail bisc. (oat-
meal, sugar, dr. milk). Planned
to eat dogs as they became surplus.

pp. 83-84

First Stage ④

Oct. 20. 4 sleds; 52 dogs. Hanssen,
Wisting, Bjaaland, Hassel, Amundsen.
"... according to Amundsen, a beautiful
day of clear mild weather..."
Made better than 24 m. per day, one
day just under 30 m.

p. 83

EXERCISE 12. Taking Notes. Take notes on the sources that you have found. (You should have found at least three.) Be certain that each note relates to a topic or a subtopic of your preliminary outline. Use a separate note card for each topic or subtopic and for each source. Follow the format illustrated by the sample note cards above to prepare your own cards.

Evaluating and Revising the Preliminary Outline

7n. Use your new information to evaluate and revise the preliminary outline.

When you prepared your preliminary outline, you had only a

general understanding of your topic. As you read and took notes, your knowledge of the topic changed. Perhaps you discovered important new information; perhaps you found little information about a point you wanted to develop. As a result of your research, you should revise your preliminary outline.

Begin by sorting your note cards into groups, putting closely related ideas together. For example, if you were writing on explorations of the *Titanic*, you might put notes about the use of an undersea robot in one group and notes about the night the ship sank in another group. Next, decide on a heading for each group (use of the undersea robot *Jason Jr.*, the sinking of the *Titanic*) and determine in what order each group should be covered. Finally, compare these headings with those in your preliminary outline, and make any necessary changes so that your final outline will be an accurate guide as you write your first draft. Compare the following revised outline with the preliminary outline on page 235.

EXPLORING THE *TITANIC*

I. First voyage of the *Titanic*
II. Sinking of the *Titanic*
    A. Collision with iceberg
    B. Flooding of ship
    C. Loading of lifeboats
III. Discovery of *Titanic*'s location
    A. Long search for location
    B. Discovery by Dr. Robert Ballard
IV. Exploration of the *Titanic*
    A. Role of undersea robot *Jason, Jr.*
        1. Descent into ship's interior
        2. Photographs from ship's interior
    B. Knowledge gained about *Titanic*
    C. Test of undersea robots
        1. Exploring ocean depths
        2. Rescuing lost submarines
V. Future of *Titanic*
    A. Efforts to raise *Titanic*
    B. Leaving *Titanic* in ocean

Before You Write. As you revise your preliminary outline, ask yourself these questions:

- What headings or subheadings should be omitted, changed, or added to my outline?
- Is correct outline form used to indicate smaller and smaller divisions of the topic? See pages 129–30.
- Are all subtopics under a heading closely related to that particular heading? (For help in organizing ideas, see pages 125–27.)
- Are topics and subtopics arranged in a logical order that will be easy for readers to follow?

EXERCISE 13. Revising a Preliminary Outline. Revise your preliminary outline. Be prepared to explain what changes you have made and why you have made them.

WRITING

Writing the First Draft

7o. Using your revised outline as a guide, write the first draft of your research report.

Go through your note cards, discarding those that are no longer needed and rearranging the remaining ones so that they conform to your revised outline. All cards dealing with the same outline topic, regardless of the source from which they come, should be placed together.

Referring to your cards for facts and information, begin to write your first draft, following the same order as your outline and the note cards. Each topic in your outline may become a separate paragraph, or even two paragraphs, in your paper. Notice, for example, that the first main topic in the sample outline on page 238 is "First voyage of the *Titanic*." In the sample research report, which begins on page 245, that topic has been developed in the first paragraph. The second main topic of the outline, "Sinking of the *Titanic*," has been developed in two paragraphs.

In writing your first draft, there are two important points you should keep in mind.

(1) Use your own words.

Again, be sure not to use the exact wording of your sources without giving credit. If you do so, you are committing *plagiarism*. This not only is dishonest but also diminishes the value of your paper as an original work. If you take notes in your own words, you will not be likely to plagiarize as you write your first draft.

(2) Acknowledge sources when you use an author's ideas or when you quote.

When you use an author's ideas that are not simply general information such as you would find in an encyclopedia, you must acknowledge the source from which the information comes. If you decide to use a word-for-word quotation, enclose it in quotation marks, as you learned to do in a summary. Then identify the source of the quotation.

There are three places where information about sources can be given: (1) in parentheses right after the ideas or quotation, (2) in a footnote at the bottom of the page, or (3) in a list with all the other sources on a page at the end of the paper. Your teacher will tell you how much identifying information is required and where it should be given.

Recently, the MLA (Modern Language Association of America) has simplified the procedure for acknowledging the sources used within a paper. According to the *MLA Handbook,* you insert in parentheses following the author's ideas or the quotation just enough information for your readers to identify the source: often, the last name of the author and the numbers of the pages from which you took the information. In the bibliography at the end of your paper you will list complete information about your sources. In the following example, notice that neither the words *page* and *pages* nor the abbreviations *p*. and *pp*. are used. Notice also that there is no comma between the author's name and the page number(s).

> In great confusion, the lifeboats were filled and lowered into the freezing water. Looking desperately back at the rapidly sinking *Titanic*, the survivors could hear the music being played by the ship's heroic band in an attempt to calm passengers and crew who could not get into the lifeboats. For a while, survivors could still see the ship, "brilliantly lit from stern to stern . . . like a sagging birthday cake" (Lord 76).

Turning to your *bibliography*, or list of works cited, readers can quickly tell that your reference is to page 76 of the book *A Night to Remember* by Walter Lord and that the book was published in New York in 1955 by Holt, Rinehart and Winston.

Depending on the sources you use, the following MLA guidelines on documenting source material within a paper will also be helpful.

1. If two or more authors have the same last name, give both the first and last names of the author in the parentheses. Again, do not use the words *page, pages,* or their abbreviations, and do not place a comma between the author's name and the page number: (Mavis Smith 84).

2. If more than one work by the same author is used, give the title or a shortened version of it after the author's last name. In this case, notice that a comma comes between the author's last name and the title: (Cohen, *Mysterious Places* 3).

3. If two authors wrote one work, give both last names, separated by *and*. If there are more than two names, you may either give each of the last names with the final one separated by *and,* or you may use the first author's last name followed by *et al.* (Latin, meaning "and others"): (Johnson and Smith 64); (Vasquez et al. 99).

4. If a source does not give an author, use the title or a shortened form of it: ("Exploring the *Titanic*" 43).

The sample research report on pages 245–49 uses the MLA format for documentation. The Modern Language Association of America is a highly regarded scholarly organization, but there are other acceptable formats for preparing reports. Your teacher may prefer that you use one of these other formats.

EXERCISE 14. Writing a First Draft. Write your first draft, inserting within parentheses information about your sources. Follow the MLA format described in this chapter unless your teacher asks you to do otherwise. Before you begin writing, study the sample research report on pages 245–49.

EVALUATING AND REVISING

Evaluating the First Draft

7p. Evaluate the first draft for content, organization, and style.

An effective research paper has many of the same characteristics as any effective composition. For example, the paper should begin with an interesting introductory paragraph and should end with an effective concluding paragraph. Sufficient details should be provided to develop each topic, and this material should be arranged in a logical order. Linking expressions should be used to make transitions between paragraphs, sentences, and ideas. If necessary, review the material on writing compositions in Chapter 4. Study carefully the following Guidelines for Evaluating Research Reports.

GUIDELINES FOR EVALUATING RESEARCH REPORTS

Introduction   1. Is the main idea of the paper clearly stated in an effective introductory paragraph?

Topic Development	2. Are there enough details to develop each topic so that it is clear and interesting?
Conclusion	3. Does a concluding paragraph effectively draw the paper to a close?
Relationship Between Ideas	4. Are transitions used to show how ideas (within and between paragraphs) are related?
Documentation	5. Is the paper written in your own words, with proper acknowledgment given for direct quotations and use of someone else's ideas?
Sources	6. Have three or more sources been used?
Format	7. Is a correct research paper format followed, either that of the MLA or one of your teacher's choosing?

Revising the First Draft

7q. Revise the first draft to improve content, organization, and style.

After you have evaluated your report, you are ready to make changes to improve it. Writers use four basic techniques to revise their work; they add, reorder, cut, or replace words and sentences. The technique you use will depend on the problem you want to correct. For example, if your report does not adequately develop one of the topics in your outline, you may need to add more information and details. If one paragraph or section of the report seems disorganized and difficult to follow, you may need to rearrange details or omit an unrelated idea. Use the chart on page 148 to select a technique to solve a specific problem.

EXERCISE 15. Evaluating and Revising a First Draft. Evaluate your first draft. Before you begin, study the sample research report on pages 245–49. Also, refer to the Guidelines for Evaluating Research Reports. When you have decided what needs improvement, revise your first draft, referring to the chart on page 148.

Preparing the Final Draft

7r. Proofread and prepare a copy of your revised draft.

Once you have completed your revision, proofread the paper, checking punctuation, spelling, capitalization, usage, and grammar. Then, make a final copy of your report, using the manuscript form that your teacher recommends. Proofread it again.

EXERCISE 16. Preparing a Final Draft. Prepare a copy of your revised draft for submission to your teacher.

Preparing a Final Bibliography

7s. Prepare a list of works cited.

In your final bibliography, which should be listed on a separate page, list only those sources from which you actually used information. Unless your teacher suggests otherwise, use the following MLA guidelines to prepare a bibliography, also called "Works Cited."

For Books:
    1. Alphabetize entries by the last name of the author, followed by the first name. If there are two or more authors, enter the first author's last name and first name, followed by a comma. Then write the other authors' names in the regular order (first name, last name), with the word *and* preceding the final name given.
    2. Follow the author's name with a period and two spaces.
    3. Write the title of the book (underlined), followed by a period and two spaces.
    4. Write the city in which the book was published (if more than one city is listed, use only the first city). Follow the name of the city with a colon and one space. Then write the name of the publishing company, followed by a comma, a space, and the date of publication. End the entire entry with a period.
    5. Begin each entry so that it is even with the left margin of your paper. If the entry is longer than one line, indent the remaining lines of the entry five spaces.

EXAMPLE   Lord, Walter. <u>A Night to Remember</u>. New York:
Holt, Rinehart and Winston, 1955.

For Newspaper or Magazine Articles:
1. Follow the same guidelines for listing authors of articles that you would for books.
2. Following the author's name, write the name of the article (in quotation marks). Place a period inside the closing quotation marks. Skip two spaces. Then write and underline the title of the magazine or book from which the article comes.
3. Skip one space after the publication's title. Give the date of publication, followed by a colon, a space, and the page numbers of the article. End the entry with a period.

EXAMPLE   Murphy, Joy Waldron. "It Was Sad When the Great
Ship Went Down." <u>Smithsonian</u> Aug. 1986: 56–
57.

EXERCISE 17. Writing a Final Bibliography.   Write *Bibliography* or *Works Cited* on the last page of your report or at the top of a separate sheet of paper. Unless you are directed otherwise, use the MLA guidelines explained in this section. List the sources from which you used information for your paper. Before you begin, study the sample bibliography on page 249 of this chapter.

Sample Research Report:

EXPLORING THE *TITANIC*

On April 10, 1912, the world's most lux-   begins with interest-
urious cruise liner sailed from a port in south-   ing, specific details
ern England, bound for New York City on its   about the *Titanic*
first voyage. Eleven stories high and four blocks long, the *Titanic* was also the largest ship ever built. In those days a North Atlantic crossing was a dangerous undertaking. "Fierce gales and menacing icebergs" made shipping hazardous (<u>Joy Waldron</u>

<u>Murphy</u> 60). In fact, for several days, ships in the area had reported seeing icebergs. Captain E. J. Smith, however, continued on course. He believed that the *Titanic*, with its double hull and sixteen watertight compartments, was also the safest ship afloat.

The night of April 14 was clear, calm, and bitterly cold. Suddenly, at 11:40 P.M., a tremor passed through the ship. The *Titanic* had struck an iceberg. <u>Shortly thereafter</u>, water began flooding into the ship, filling engine rooms and passenger cabins. In the radio room, the international call of distress, CQD, was sent time and time again, along with the ship's position. Making a careful survey of the damage, Captain Smith and his officers found the first five compartments flooded. They knew that with these compartments gone, the ship was doomed (Lord 35–36).

Quickly, Captain Smith ordered the lifeboats lowered and all ladies on deck. (Because the *Titanic* carried lifeboats for only 1,178 of the more than 2,000 passengers and crew members, only women and children were allowed in them.) In great confusion, the lifeboats were filled and lowered into the freezing water. Looking desperately back at the rapidly sinking *Titanic,* the survivors could hear the music being played by the ship's heroic band in an attempt to calm the passengers and crew who could not get into lifeboats. For a while, they could still see the ship, "brilliantly lit from stern to

source—two authors with same last name appear in bibliography

chronological sequence of events

transition

source

time sequence continues (Note that paper reflects revised outline.)

stern . . . like a sagging birthday cake" (<u>Lord</u>   source
<u>76</u>). Less than three hours after it was struck,
the *Titanic* slipped beneath the icy waters of
the north Atlantic, taking with it some 1,500
passengers and crew members.

    The *Titanic* <u>now</u> lies on the ocean's bot-   transition
tom, some 12,500 feet beneath the surface.
Fascinated with the liner's story, explorers
have for decades searched for the exact location of the ship. But it was not until September 1985 that an expedition led by marine
biologist Dr. Robert Ballard found the wreckage of the *Titanic* lying 850 miles off the coast
of Massachusetts. Photographs taken by an
underwater device showed that the ship had
broken in two and that the forward half lay
upright on the ocean floor, surrounded by a
large field of debris (<u>Jamie Murphy 48–49</u>).   source

    In July 1986, Dr. Ballard, with an expe-
dition from the Woods Hole Oceanographic
Institution, revisited the *Titanic*. <u>This time</u>,   transition
the mother ship, *Atlantis II*, carried with it a
manned undersea craft, *Alvin*, a submersible
capable of surviving the intense pressure of
water at 12,500 feet. *Alvin*, with a three-man
crew, descended to the wreckage, and then
released an undersea robot, *Jason, Jr.* The
robot, carrying underwater cameras, was attached to the *Alvin* by a 250–foot tether that
carried commands from the pilot of the *Alvin*
and television pictures back to the *Alvin*.   repetition of name

    Winding its way around obstacles to pre-   *Jason, Jr.*, provides
vent entangling its tether, *Jason, Jr., or J. J.,*   transition to new
    paragraph

as the robot is called, went inside the *Titanic,* descending four levels down the ship's grand staircase, sending back photographs from the wreckage. Through videotapes, scientists saw such remains as a still-intact chandelier hanging ghostlike in the water, brass fittings, a porcelain doll's head, a shoe, and even an unbroken coffee cup. As the scientists watched the videotapes coming back from *Alvin* and *Jason, Jr.,* they remarked, "Views of the railings where doomed passengers and crew members stood evoked images of the moonless night 74 years ago when the great ship slipped beneath the waves" (Jamie Murphy 48).   *source*

Scientists have already learned much from this first exploration of the *Titanic.* The original explanation for the sinking of the ship was that the iceberg had struck a long gash in its hull; now scientists believe that the ships' plates (sheets of metal covering the ship) simply buckled in, causing the ship to break up as it sank (Jamie Murphy 48). Other scientists plan to visit the *Titanic* soon to explore the ship's interior with wide-ranging robots. In addition, the expeditions have served as tests for undersea robots. Scientists believe that such devices will enable them to explore the oceans' depths and perhaps even perform such tasks as rescuing lost submarines.   *transition / transition / source / transition*

The future of the *Titanic* is uncertain. For decades, plans for raising the wreckage of the great ship have been proposed, and some sci-   *chronological sequence* entists are now trying to raise money for the project. Other scientists, while continuing to explore the *Titanic*, wish to see it remain at the bottom of the ocean. Members of the Explorers Club of New York plan to place a brass plaque on the deck of the sunken ship, reading, "Any who come hereafter leave undisturbed this ship and her contents as a memorial to deep water exploration" (Sullivan 6). But perhaps the most personal reflection of what should happen to the wreck of the *Titanic* was offered by a woman who, at the age of twelve, was a survivor of the disaster. Says Mrs. Blanchard, "It's the graveyard of 1,500 people. I believe they should rest in peace" (Joy Waldron Murphy 67).

concludes with interesting, specific details

source

source

Works Cited

Gleick, James. "Video Robot Probing Ship Is Navy Tool." *New York Times* 16 July 1986: 6.

Lord, Walter. *A Night to Remember*. New York: Holt, Rinehart and Winston, 1955.

Murphy, Jamie. "Down into the Deep." *Time* 11 Aug. 1986: 48–54.

Murphy, Joy Waldron. "It Was Sad When the Great Ship Went Down." *Smithsonian* Aug. 1986: 57–67.

Sullivan, Walter. "Undersea Robot Gets a Look Inside Still Luxurious *Titanic*." *New York Times* 16 July 1986: 1, 6.

REVIEW EXERCISE B. Analyzing the Research Reports of Others. Exchange the final draft of your research report with one or more classmates. On a separate sheet of paper, answer the following questions about each report. Be prepared to support your answers with specific details from your classmates' reports.

1. State in your own words the purpose statement for the report. Does the report fulfill this purpose?

2. Is the topic developed with specific details throughout the report? What are some of these specific details?
3. Are ideas presented in a logical order? What transitions are used to show this order?
4. Are there at least three sources? Are they correctly acknowledged in parentheses following ideas or quotations from them?
5. Is the form of the bibliography correct? Do the sources for the report appear current and reliable?

WRITING A BOOK REPORT ON A NOVEL

A *book report* is an expository composition in which you explain your understanding and evaluation of a book. In your English classes, you will often be asked to write a book report on a novel, which will require you to use many of the thinking and writing skills you have learned for other forms of writing. In planning and writing a report on a novel, you should include the following steps. Like the steps you followed in writing a summary, some of these overlap.

PREWRITING

Determining Audience and Purpose

7t. Determine the audience and purpose of your book report.

As you begin to plan your book report, consider your audience and purpose. If you are writing a report to be read only by your teacher, your purpose will probably be to demonstrate how well you understood the novel and how thoughtfully you evaluated it. If, on the other hand, your report will be read by your peers, your purpose might be to encourage (or discourage) their reading the novel. Your audience and your purpose will affect your choice of book (if you are free to make a selection), the details you will be alert to as you read, and the way you will use these details in the report.

Reading the Novel and Taking Notes

7u. Read the novel carefully with your book report in mind. Take notes as you read.

Read the book carefully, noticing the settings and moods that the author creates, the characters and how they are developed, the plot, the author's tone, and the dominant theme (or themes) of the novel.

To be sure that you remember details, take notes as you read. Although you may wait until you have finished the book, an effective approach is to write notes after reading each chapter or some other division of the book. Your notes should include title (underlined), author, setting(s), characters, events in the plot, and statements of theme. Your teacher may require that your book report include discussion or evaluation of certain literary elements that you have studied in literature classes. If so, include these kinds of details in your notes.

> *Before You Write.* As you take notes for your book report, ask yourself the following questions:
>
> • Who is the audience for this report?
> • What is the purpose of the report? To show how well I understand the book? To interest others in reading the book?
> • What opinions about the book will I include in this report?
> • What incidents, statements, or other details from the book can I use to support my opinions?

Developing a Working Plan

7v. Using your notes, develop a working plan for writing your book report.

Follow the steps that you use in writing any longer composition. With your audience and purpose in mind, determine the main idea that your report will develop. State this idea clearly as your thesis. List details from your notes that will support and illustrate your thesis. Arrange your details in an appropriate order.

WRITING

Writing a First Draft

7w. Using your working plan, write a first draft of your book report.

You have completed the prewriting for your report. Now you are ready to draft a first version. As you write this first draft, three things are important: (1) keep your audience in mind, (2) keep your purpose in mind, (3) follow the details and order of your working plan.

EVALUATING AND REVISING

Evaluating and Revising a First Draft

7x. Evaluate and revise your first draft, taking care to include more than simple plot summary.

An important aspect of evaluating your book report is checking to see that you have written more than a plot summary. A good report reveals enough of the plot to give the audience a general idea of the story. However, a book report has a purpose beyond this—for example, to encourage others to read the book, to analyze the theme, or to evaluate the style.

Use the following guidelines to evaluate your book report. Then revise the draft, referring to the chart on page 148. When

Writing a Book Report on a Novel > 253

7
w-x

you are satisfied with your revised draft, prepare a final copy. Always proofread the final version.

GUIDELINES FOR EVALUATING BOOK REPORTS ON NOVELS

Purpose	1. Does the report have a clear purpose that suits the intended audience?
Plot Details	2. Is there sufficient information about the plot to acquaint the reader with the novel?
Development	3. Does the report go beyond plot summary to fulfill a specific purpose? Is this purpose well developed with specific details that are logically ordered?

EXERCISE 18. Planning and Writing a Book Report on a Novel. Using a novel assigned by your teacher or one of your own choosing, follow the steps for planning and writing a book report on a novel. Before you begin, study the following sample book report. Before you revise your first draft, refer to the Guidelines for Evaluating Book Reports on Novels. Proofread your final version.

Sample Book Report:

Charles Dickens certainly knew how to snare a reader's attention and hold it to the very end of his novel. In *A Tale of Two Cities*, Dickens created a masterful story by combining unforgettable characters with suspenseful action. As if this were not enough, he included one more element, the romance of heroic love. Readers who like any or all of these qualitites will be absorbed in reading *A Tale of Two Cities*.

main idea

first point of development

second point of development purpose of report

The story takes place in England and France in the eighteenth century. It opens with a mysterious episode of a man's being

paragraph acquaints reader with plot

"recalled to life." That early event draws the reader into mystery, espionage, the cruelties of war and imprisonment, the joys of friendship and love. The plot weaves back and forth among different generations of people, all of whom are caught in some way in the drama of the French Revolution. The novel ends somewhat the way it began, with another episode of a man's being "recalled to life."

One of these characters whose life is part of the Revolution is a woman named Madame Defarge. She is the wife of a wineshop keeper. At first she puzzles the reader. Each time she is present in the story, she is sitting behind the counter in the wineshop, observing everything, saying little, and always knitting. As the plot unfolds, the reader begins to fear Madame Defarge; she is cruel and without pity. By the end of the novel her personal history is revealed; the causes of her cruelty are terrible. Many readers end up feeling deeply sorry for her. Whether one's response is fear or pity, no reader forgets Madame Defarge or her knitting.

an unforgettable character

why readers remember her

There are many levels of love in the novel. In many instances the love demands heroism. To save his daughter's happiness, Dr. Manette courageously goes back into his fearsome past. Lucie braves the frenzy of maddened revolutionaries to stand each day where her prisoner husband might get a glimpse of her and their little girl. It is Sydney Carton, though, whose love reaches astound-

heroic love

example 1

example 2

example 3

ing heroism. He speaks his love just once in the story, but the message of his love is the most often quoted line from this moving novel.

Charles Dickens fills the imagination and memory of his readers. They are caught in the movement of the Revolution. They see, hear, and feel with the characters. They never forget the love with which the novel reaches its bittersweet ending.

restatement of main idea of paper

CHAPTER 7 WRITING REVIEW

Writing a Summary and a Book Report. For this exercise, either use a novel you have already read and remember well or select a new novel. First, write a summary of the novel, using the Guidelines for Evaluating Summaries that appear on page 228 of this chapter. Then, write a book report on the novel, using the Guidelines for Evaluating Book Reports on Novels on page 253 of this chapter. (The purpose of the book report is to interest your classmates in reading the novel.) Be prepared to discuss the differences between your summary and your book report. What information did you include in the summary that you did not include in the book report? What ideas did you discuss in the book report that you did not put in the summary?

CHAPTER 8

Writing Business Letters and Completing Forms

FORM AND CONTENT

Although the telephone satisfies many business needs, on certain occasions a letter is more effective. There are also occasions when filling out a form is required. In this chapter you will learn the standard practices used in writing business letters and the general procedures used in completing forms.

PREWRITING

APPEARANCE AND FORM

Whether your purpose is to order merchandise, to make a request, or to express dissatisfaction with a product or a service, your letter should be short and to the point, and your tone should be courteous.

Stationery and Appearance

8a. Use appropriate stationery.

Use white, unlined 8½ x 11–inch paper for your letter. Many firms make photostatic copies of the letters they receive, and white paper photographs best.

8b. Make your business letters attractive and easy to read.

A neatly typed letter is more legible and therefore more quickly read than a handwritten one. If you write the letter by hand, use ink (preferably blue, blue-black, or black) rather than pencil, and always use your best handwriting.

Leave fairly wide margins, usually about 1 inch, on both sides, the top, and the bottom of the page. These margins should all be approximately equal in width. However, when a letter is very short, the top and bottom margins will be larger. If the letter will not fit on one sheet of paper, carry over at least two sentences onto the next sheet. Never write on the back of a page.

Form

8c. Learn the proper form for the six parts of a business letter.

The parts of a business letter are the *heading, inside address, salutation, body, closing,* and *signature.* The parts are labeled in the following illustration, which shows *semiblock form.*

In semiblock form, the first line of each paragraph is indented; and the heading, closing, and signature are begun just to the right of the middle of the page. (The *pure block form,* or *block form,* in which the first lines of paragraphs are not indented and the heading, closing, and signature are flush with the left margin, is also acceptable for business letters.)

Notice the spacing between the parts of the following letter. The entire letter is centered on the page, with approximately equal margins at the top and at the bottom and with equal margins on both sides. If you type your business letters, double-space after the inside address, after the salutation, between paragraphs, and after the last line of the last paragraph.

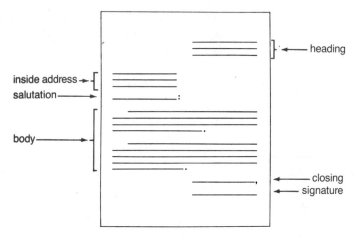

Form of a Business Letter

The Heading

Put your *complete* address and the *full* date in the upper right-hand corner of the page, beginning no less than one inch from the top. The heading usually consists of three lines, two for the address and one for the date. Insert a comma between the city and the two-letter state code (see page 277) or state name but not between the state and the ZIP code. Also insert a comma between the day of the month and the year.

EXAMPLE   685 Lawton Street
Dayton, OH 45411
October 9, 1989

The Inside Address

Place the inside address several spaces (at least four if you are typing) below the heading, flush with the left-hand margin. It should include the full name and address of the company to which you are writing. If you are writing to a specific person in a firm, use the person's full name and title. Insert a comma between the two if they are on the same line. If the name and title are too long to look attractive on one line, put the title on the next line.

EXAMPLES Ajax Auto Supply
6890 Clifton Road
Dayton, OH 45412

Ms. Ann King, President
American Humane Society
P.O. Box 1266
Denver, CO 80201

Circulation Department
Field and Stream
1515 Broadway
New York, NY 10036

Dr. William N. Kirkpatrick
Assistant Director
Defense Research Laboratory
The University of Texas
Austin, TX 78712

The Salutation

The salutation is your greeting to the reader. It is placed two spaces below the inside address and flush with the left-hand margin; it is followed by a colon.

If you are writing to a group or a company, you may use an impersonal salutation (*Customer Service, Editors*) or the traditional salutation (*Gentlemen*). When such salutations are used, it is understood that the group may be composed of both men and women.

If you are writing to an individual within the firm, the correct salutation is *Dear Mr.* _____ (*Mrs., Ms.,* or *Miss*). If you know a person's professional title (*Dr., Professor,* etc.), use it instead of *Mr., Mrs.,* etc. The abbreviation of a title before a person's name is followed by a period.

EXAMPLES Gentlemen: Circulation Department:
Dear Sir: Dear Dr. Patrick:
Dear Madam: Dear Ms. King:

The Body

The body is your message. Begin the body two spaces below the salutation. Be sure to divide your letter into fairly short paragraphs, clearly indenting the first line of each paragraph if you are using semiblock style. If your letter is very short (seven lines or less), you may double-space the entire body. For a longer letter, however, single-space the paragraphs and double-space between them.

Do not end your letter with phrases such as "Hoping to hear from you soon, I am," or "Thanking you in advance, I am." End the body of your letter with a complete sentence and a *period*. Then begin your closing.

The Closing

Place the closing two spaces below the last line of the body and just to the right of the center of the page. Try not to let it trail into the right-hand margin.

Appropriate closings for business letters are limited. *Very truly yours, Yours truly,* and *Yours very truly* are the ones most frequently used. *Sincerely yours* and *Yours sincerely* are also appropriate. Only the first word of the closing is capitalized; the closing is followed by a comma.

EXAMPLES   Very truly yours,
                   Yours sincerely,

The Signature

A signature should always be handwritten. If your letter is typewritten, type your name flush with the first letter of the closing and far enough (usually four spaces) below it to allow room for your signature above it.

Sign your full name. Do *not* put *Miss, Ms.,* or *Mrs.* before your name. A woman may indicate her marital status by writing *Miss* or *Mrs.* in parentheses before her signature. Unless a woman includes such a title in her signature, the receiver of the letter may feel free to use *Ms.* in a letter of reply.

EXAMPLES   (Miss) Mary Jane Fiske   Sue Glucken

303 Clayton Street
Huntington, West Virginia 25703
February 10, 1988

Executive Secretary
Chamber of Commerce
Mystic, Connecticut   06355

Dear Sir:

    I am writing a report on whaling in old New England
and would appreciate your sending me any pamphlets and
pictures you have about Mystic Seaport.

    I would especially like pictures of the town itself,
as well as information on early whaling ships and
equipment. Any maps you have of Mystic Seaport and of
early sailing routes would be useful, too.

          Very truly yours,

Theodore Jonas

          Theodore Jonas

A Business Letter

EXERCISE 1. Arranging the Parts of a Business Letter.
After studying the proper form for the six parts of a business
letter, close your book and write each part in its proper place
on a sheet of paper. Use your own address in the heading. Draw
twelve lines to represent the body, dividing them into two paragraphs. Be careful about spacing and about correct punctuation
of the heading, salutation, and closing. In the margins of your
paper, label each part of the letter. You may use either pure
block or semiblock style, but be consistent.

EXERCISE 2. Writing a Business Letter. Write a business letter using the following information. Be sure to use the proper form and include all necessary punctuation.

1. *Heading:* 2420 Nicholson Drive, Portland, Oregon 97221, November 12, 1989
2. *Inside Address:* Mr. James E. Clark, Business Manager, Allison's Greeting Card Company, P.O. Box 3452, Los Angeles, California 90035
3. *Salutation:* Dear Mr. Clark
4. *Body:* As the secretary of my ninth grade class, I am writing to find out more about the offer you are advertising in local newspapers. My class is considering selling your Christmas cards to raise money for the "Toys for Tots" campaign. Please send me information about the kinds of cards you have, the price range, and the percentage of profit we can make on each box sold.
5. *Closing:* Very truly yours
6. *Signature:* Charles Evans

WRITING

TYPES OF BUSINESS LETTERS

Different types of business letters have different purposes. By learning about the features of each type, you can write each kind effectively.

Request Letters

8d. Make letters of request simple and clear.

A letter of request asks for information. It is a good idea to state your request in your first sentence. The other sentences can give further details. The letter on page 261 and in Exercise 2 are examples of the request letter.

EXERCISE 3. Writing a Request Letter. Write to any place of business (a department store, a publishing firm, a motor company, a sporting goods store, etc.), requesting information about a particular product. Ask for circulars describing the merchandise and listing the prices. (Do not mail the letter unless you are seriously interested in the product.)

EXERCISE 4. Writing a Request Letter. Your school's winter dance committee wants to give a souvenir to everyone who attends. Write to a novelty company asking for information about its products.

EXERCISE 5. Writing a Request Letter. Find an advertisement in one of your favorite magazines for a firm that interests you, and write a letter of request. A flour manufacturer, for example, may give away a recipe book. A travel bureau may offer free pamphlets or posters. Some companies may provide information that will help you in making reports. (Do not mail the letter unless you really need the information and cannot find it in a library.)

Order Letters

8e. Make order letters complete and accurate.

Although order blanks and "clip-and-mail" coupons are becoming more common, sometimes you need to write a letter to order merchandise.

When writing an order letter, list the items one below the other, with complete information (style, size, price, catalog number, or trade name) about each item. Put the prices at the far right, flush with the right-hand margin, and line them up so that the column of figures will be easy to add. Unless you know that the firm pays for shipping, list the cost of shipping separately, and include it in the total. Also be sure to state how you are paying for the order—by check or money order.

R.F.D. 2
Cedar Falls, Iowa 50613
April 30, 1988

Ajax Auto Supply
6890 Clifton Road
Dayton, Ohio 45410

Gentlemen:

Will you please send me the following merchandise
as advertised in your spring catalog:

1 pr. swimming fins, Cat. No. S20, adjustable
straps, heavy-duty $19.00

2 skull caps, Cat. No. B261, one blue (size 7)
and one red (size 6 1/2), at $3.25 each   6.50

1 bicycle mirror, Cat. No. M45, small (4 by 2),
chrome-trimmed   4.75
                                                      $30.25

I enclose a money order for $34.00 to cover the
cost of the order and the postal charge of $3.75.

Yours very truly,

Angela Green

Angela Green

An Order Letter

EXERCISE 6. Writing an Order Letter.

Write an order letter to Academy Novelty Company, P.O. Box 3975, Los Angeles, California 90064, for the following merchandise: two green Wizard shirts, one size 14 and the other size $15\frac{1}{2}$, at $9.98 each; one OO-GA whistle, at $1.49; six yellow Bond pencils, with the name "Skippy" printed in gold, at $.25 each; and one set of six Canton steak knives with white handles, at $15.95. You are adding $2.80 for postage and handling and enclosing a money order to cover the total cost.

Adjustment Letters

8f. Make adjustment letters specific and courteous.

An adjustment letter is one that you write after an error has been made. You should feel free to write to a company if you are dissatisfied with its product.

```
                              R.F.D. 2
                              Cedar Falls, Iowa  50613
                              May 5, 1988




        Ajax Auto Supply
        6890 Clifton Road
        Dayton, Ohio   45410

        Gentlemen:

             In my letter of April 30, I ordered a pair of
        heavy-duty swimming fins with adjustable straps.
        Advertised on page 26 of your spring catalog, these
        fins are numbered S20.  This morning, however,
        I received a yellow inflatable sea serpent, which I
        am returning to you by parcel post.  I'll appreciate
        your exchanging the sea serpent for the fins.


                              Yours truly,

                              Angela Green

                              Angela Green
```

An Adjustment Letter

The only way for you, as a consumer, to be sure that the quality of the products you buy remains high is to express any dissatisfaction directly to the manufacturer. Occasionally, an individual product in a line of normally high-quality goods is defective. If you write, the manufacturer will usually replace the item for you and apologize for your inconvenience.

In your letter, be sure to mention specifics—how much you paid, exactly why you were unhappy with the product, and what you wish the manufacturer to do about it. By all means be courteous. Your adjustment letter should not include curt remarks like "Can't you read? Why didn't you send me what I ordered?" or "I'll never buy another thing from your store." Always be polite as you explain what happened and as you ask for an adjustment, but insist that some action be taken.

Also, be prompt about pointing out a mistake. Don't wait two or three weeks before you exchange an article or complain about not receiving something that you ordered.

EXERCISE 7. Writing an Adjustment Letter. Suppose that the Academy Novelty Company (see Exercise 6) failed to send you the six pencils that you ordered. It has been four days now since you received the package, and you still have had no word from the company about the missing pencils or a refund of your money. Write an adjustment letter.

THE ENVELOPE

8g. Fold your letter to fit your envelope.

There are two sizes of standard business envelopes, both of which are acceptable: $6\frac{1}{2} \times 3\frac{1}{2}$ inches and $9\frac{1}{2} \times 4\frac{1}{2}$ inches. You should fold your business letter (on the standard $8\frac{1}{2} \times 11$–inch sheet) to fit the size of the envelope you are using.

For the larger envelope, first fold the bottom third of the page up. Then fold the top of the page down to about a half inch from the bottom, so that it will be easy to open. Place the letter in the envelope with the open end up.

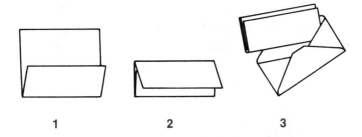

For the smaller envelope, first fold the bottom of the page up to within a quarter of an inch of the top. Then fold the right side over a third of the way. Finally, fold the left side over, leaving about a fourth of an inch so that the letter can be opened easily.

If your letter is more than one page long, it is better to use the larger envelope.

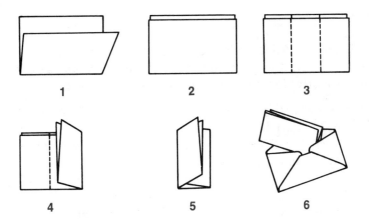

8h. Address your envelope correctly.

The envelope for a business letter is addressed in block form. Your name and address appear in the upper left-hand corner, without a title such as "Miss" or "Mr." Always use a title before the name of the person to whom you are writing, however. Use abbreviations only for titles and states.

Place the name and address of the person to whom you are writing on the lower half of the envelope. They should be identical to the inside name and address.

```
Theodore Jonas
303 Clayton Street
Huntington, WV 25703



                      Executive Secretary
                      Chamber of Commerce
                      Mystic, CT 06355
```

EXERCISE 8. Addressing Envelopes. Draw two envelopes on your paper; then use the following information to address them correctly. (You will not use every word given.)

1. *Sender:* Ms. Ginny D'Espies, Point Pleasant, New Jersey, 08472, 1851 Riviera Parkway
   Receiver: Mr. Robert Cleveland, 1112 Rose Boulevard, Utah 84112, Salt Lake City
2. *Sender:* Mr. Thomas Flanders, New York City, 81 Waverly Place, New York, ZIP code 10013
   Receiver: Department of Parks and Recreation, Commissioner, Grand Rapids, Michigan ZIP code 49506, 336 East High Street

EXERCISE 9. Addressing an Envelope. Address an envelope for the letter that you wrote for Exercise 3. Be sure that your return address is accurate and that the address on the envelope matches the inside address in your letter. Fold your letter and place it in the envelope; do not seal the envelope.

TYPES OF FORMS

Learning to complete printed forms correctly is important, because businesses, institutions, and government agencies use them to collect information. Read the directions carefully and follow them precisely to fill out forms accurately and completely. Be sure your writing is legible by typing the information or by printing in black or blue-black ink.

Change-of-Address Order

8i. Learn how to complete a change-of-address order to have mail forwarded.

To be sure your mail is delivered when you move, you need to complete a *change-of-address order,* available at your post office. This form instructs the postal service to forward your mail from your old address to your new address. It is important to complete the form accurately so that postal employees can read and understand your instructions.

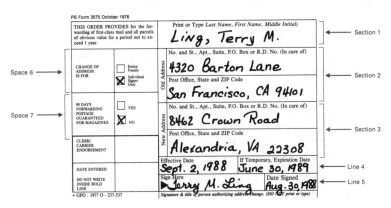

Change of Address Form

In section 1, type or print your name. Notice that your last name is followed by your first name and middle initial. Write your old address in section 2 and your new address in section

3. On these lines, the term "Post Office" refers to your city. The ZIP code shows the correct station if your city has more than one post office. In section 4, write the date you want the change to begin. If your new address is temporary, write the date you will return as the expiration date. If the change is permanent, leave this space blank. In section 5, sign the form and write the date. In section 6, indicate whether the change of address applies only to you or to the entire family. For example, if you were going to camp for the summer, you would mark the box "Individual Signer Only." In section 7, indicate whether you will pay postage for forwarding magazines. The remaining two sections will be completed by post office personnel.

Mail-Order Forms

8j. Fill out mail-order forms completely and accurately.

Many companies send out mail-order catalogs so that you can purchase merchandise and have it delivered directly to your home. To use this service, you must fill out a mail-order form. By filling it out completely and accurately, you will avoid unnecessary disappointments. Take time to read the directions carefully so you understand what information is needed. Then give the information by printing it legibly or by typing it. Although each company has its own form, the example on page 271 shows the general pattern of mail-order forms.

In section 1, write your name, address, and telephone number. Complete section 2 if you would like the package to be delivered to a work address or to a neighbor. Include the name of the person to be contacted upon delivery. Section 3 asks for information about each item in your order: item name and number, color, size, name or initials, quantity, and price. The total cost of merchandise, the shipping charges, and any required state sales tax are written in section 4. The total of all three is the cost of your order. In section 5, indicate your method of payment: check, money order, or credit card. Credit card purchases require additional information.

CHESTNUT HILL, INC.

P.O. 8942

Oak Brook, Illinois 60522–0942

Fill in name and address in space below.

NAME _Tracy L. Stevens_

STREET ADDRESS _284 Southbury_   APT# _____

CITY/STATE _Roberts, NC_   ZIP _28772_

HOME PHONE: (_704_) _566-5397_

① →

Fill in here if you want order sent to where you work
or to another address

First Name	Initial	Last	
Address			
City	State	Zip	
Daytime Phone	Area Code	Number	

② →

PACKING & DELIVERY

For Orders Totaling	Include
Up to $15.99	$2.95
$16.00-30.99	$3.95
$31.00-40.99	$4.95
$41.00-50.99	$5.95
$51.00-75.99	$7.50
$76.00-100.99	$8.25
$101.00-150.99	$12.00
Over $151.00	$15.00

③ →

Name of item	Item number	No.	Color Name	Size	Name, initials	Qty.	Price each		Total price	
Cotton Sweater	04 2683		red	M	TLS	1	30	00	30	00
Locker Bag	72 3696		navy			2	3	50	7	00
Exercise mat	08 7835		tan			1	15	00	15	00
Sweat Pants	08 9097		gray	14		1	17	00	17	00

Total for merchandise	$69	00
Total delivery charge see delivery chart	7	50
Handling charge	$ 1	00
Add sales tax to orders sent to GA, IL, NC, NV, PA	4	14
TOTAL AMOUNT	$81	64

METHOD OF PAYMENT (No C.O.D.'s or Cash)

CHECK or MONEY ORDER FOR $ ___ 81 64

CREDIT CARDS

☐ Visa ☐ Mastercard

⑤

We also accept ☐ American Express ☐ Diner's Club/Carte Blance

④

CREDIT CARD NUMBER:

Expiration Date _____ Signature _____
(Required for charge orders only)

PLEASE DO NOT WRITE IN THIS SPACE					
PP	OT	BL	ST	MC	D

56A

Mail-Order Form

EXERCISE 10. Completing Forms. Locate a mail-order catalog and select several items to order. Complete the mail-order form in the catalog. Do not mail the form.

EVALUATING AND REVISING

Clarity and appearance are especially important in a business letter or form. Careful evaluation can make each more effective. With your evaluation completed, you can make the changes needed to improve your draft.

EVALUATING YOUR WRITING

8k. Evaluate your business letter or form.

The draft of a business letter or form, like any other writing, should be evaluated to determine what changes would improve it. Before the final copy is prepared, the draft should be read several times to locate strengths and weaknesses in its form and appearance, its content, its organization, and its style. Use the following guidelines to evaluate your business letter or form.

GUIDELINES FOR EVALUATING BUSINESS LETTERS AND FORMS

Appearance	1. Is the letter neat and attractive? Is each part of the letter correctly placed? Is the form legible?
Form of the Letter	2. Does the heading give the complete address and the full date? Do commas separate the city from the state and the day of the month from the year?
	3. Is the inside address complete, accurate, and properly spaced?
	4. Is the salutation appropriate and followed by a colon?

5. Is pure block or semiblock form used consistently?
6. Is the closing appropriate? Does it begin with a capital letter and end with a comma?

Development   7. Is the purpose stated in the first sentence? Are enough details included to explain the kind of information, service, or adjustment wanted? Are details arranged in a logical order?

Tone   8. Is the tone courteous?

Envelope   9. Is block style used? Is the address accurate, complete, well placed, and identical to the inside address? Is the return address complete?

Information   10. Is the form complete and accurate? Is all required information supplied?

REVISING YOUR WRITING

8l. Revise your business letter or form to improve its form and appearance, its content, its organization, and its style.

Most of the problems in business letters and forms can be corrected by using four techniques: cutting, adding, replacing, and reordering. The following chart shows how to use these techniques to revise your business letter or form.

REVISING BUSINESS LETTERS AND FORMS

PROBLEM	TECHNIQUE	REVISION
The heading or inside address is incomplete or incorrect.	Add/Replace	Add details, such as the date or street address. Replace incorrect information.
The salutation or the closing doesn't sound right.	Replace	Use the impersonal or traditional forms, such as *Dear Madam* or *Sincerely yours.*

PROBLEM	TECHNIQUE	REVISION
The form is not consistent.	Replace	Use either block or semi-block form throughout.
The signature form is incorrect.	Cut/Add/Reorder	Omit a title, or place it in parentheses. Align the signature with the closing.
The purpose is unclear.	Add	Add an introductory sentence that states the purpose. Add details that explain what kind of information, service, or adjustment is needed.
Not enough details are included.	Add	Add pertinent details, such as the date the items were returned or the order number.
The order of ideas doesn't make sense.	Reorder	Rearrange sentences in a logical order.
The letter is not polite.	Cut	Omit discourteous remarks.
The addresses inside the letter and on the envelope do not match.	Replace	Substitute the correct information.
The form doesn't include enough information.	Add	Add information to complete each item on the form.

EXERCISE 11. Evaluating and Revising a Business Letter.
Read the following draft of a business letter and an envelope.
Evaluate each by applying the guidelines on page 272. Then
revise the letter and envelope by referring to the chart on pages
273–74.

Karen Boyd
211 Pine Street
Broadalbin, New York
November 23

Customer Service
Images, Inc.
3224 Saxon Avenue
Ellenwood, Georgia   30049-0270

Dear Sir,

Several weeks ago I returned some things I ordered
from your company. The package was insured. I still
have not heard from you. What's the matter with this
company? Why don't you send me a refund or different
merchandise?

The package was sent parcel post. If you did
not receive it, let me know immediately.

Yours Truly,

Karen Boyd

Miss Karen Boyd

Karen Boyd
211 Pine Street
Broadalbin, NY   12025

Images, Inc.
3224 Saxon Avenue
Ellenwood, GA   30049

PROOFREADING AND MAKING A FINAL COPY

After you revise a business letter or form, you should proofread it carefully before you prepare a final copy.

PROOFREADING AND MAKING A FINAL COPY

8m. Proofread your business letter or form and make a final copy.

Since appearance is important in business letters and forms, you should proofread carefully. Pay particular attention to spelling and to capitalization and punctuation in the parts of your letter. Refer to the Guidelines for Proofreading on page 36, and prepare a neat and legible final copy. Proofread once again before you send your business letter or form.

EXERCISE 12. Completing a Business Letter. Select any business letter you have written in this chapter. Evaluate it, using the guidelines on page 272. Then revise it, referring to the chart on page 273. Proofread and make a final copy. Also prepare an envelope. Do not seal the envelope or mail the letter.

☞ **NOTE** The United States Postal Service recommends the use of two-letter codes for states, the District of Columbia, and Puerto Rico, and the use of nine-digit ZIP codes for particular addresses.

EXAMPLE   Ms. Mary Suarez
19 Battle Creek Drive
Wichita, KS 67208–1313

The two-letter code is in capital letters and is never followed by
a period. Refer to the following list for two-letter codes.

Alabama AL	Montana MT
Alaska AK	Nebraska NE
Arizona AZ	Nevada NV
Arkansas AR	New Hampshire NH
California CA	New Jersey NJ
Colorado CO	New Mexico NM
Connecticut CT	New York NY
Delaware DE	North Carolina NC
District of Columbia DC	North Dakota ND
Florida FL	Ohio OH
Georgia GA	Oklahoma OK
Hawaii HI	Oregon OR
Idaho ID	Pennsylvania PA
Illinois IL	Puerto Rico PR
Indiana IN	Rhode Island RI
Iowa IA	South Carolina SC
Kansas KS	South Dakota SD
Kentucky KY	Tennessee TN
Louisiana LA	Texas TX
Maine ME	Utah UT
Maryland MD	Vermont VT
Massachusetts MA	Virginia VA
Michigan MI	Washington WA
Minnesota MN	West Virginia WV
Mississippi MS	Wisconsin WI
Missouri MO	Wyoming WY

CHAPTER 8 WRITING REVIEW

Writing a Business Letter.   Choose one of the following assignments. Write a complete draft of the letter; then revise it,
using the Guidelines for Evaluating Business Letters and Forms

on page 272 and referring to the revising chart on page 273. Address an envelope, and fold your letter to fit it. Do not seal the envelope or mail the letter.

1. Write to the Commissioner of Patents, Department of Commerce, Washington, D.C. 20025, asking for information regarding recent patents of interest to hunters. Request a copy of Patent 3,065,821 and mention that you are enclosing twenty-five cents to cover the cost.
2. Write to the Bureau of Information, *Popular Mechanics,* 224 West 57th Street, New York, New York 10019. Ask for the free "Where-to-Find-It List" for the current month.
3. Write to the Forest Service, U.S. Department of Agriculture, Washington, D.C. 20250. Ask for information about America's national forests.

CHAPTER 9

Making Writing Clear and Interesting

ENGLISH: ORIGINS, MEANINGS, USES

Writers develop a deep respect for words. They know that whether their writing is interesting or uninteresting, clear or unclear, depends largely on the words they choose.

One of the best ways to improve your writing is to cultivate an interest in words. In this chapter you will trace the history of your language; you will explore word origins, meanings, and uses.

THE HISTORY OF ENGLISH

The passage shown here is written in the earliest form of the English language.

> "Hwaet, we Gar-Dena   in geardagum
> þeodcyninga   þrym gefrunon,
> Hu þa æþelingas   ellen fremedon!
> Oft Scyld Scefing   sceaþena þreatum
> Monegum mægþum   meodosetla ofteah,
> Egsode eorlas,   syþþan ærest wearð
> Feasceaft funden;   he þæs frofre gebad,
> Weox under wolcnum,   weorðmyndum þah,
> Oð þæt him æghwylc   þara ymbsittendra
> Ofer hronrade   hyran scolde,
> Gomban gyldan;   þæt wæs god cyning!"

This form, called *Anglo-Saxon* or *Old English,* traces its origins back more than 1,500 years to the country now called England. There, beginning in about A.D. 449, three groups of Germanic peoples—the Angles, the Saxons, and the Jutes—settled in three separate parts of England. At first, each of the groups used its own dialect of a Germanic language. Gradually, however, as the three groups began to intermix, the dialects blended with each other. These groups of people are known today as *Anglo-Saxons;* the language that resulted from the blending of their dialects is *Old English.*

Obviously, to become the familiar English you are now reading, Old English underwent many changes. The changes—in vocabulary, pronunciation, and syntax (how words are arranged in sentences)—were partly the result of the English people's mingling with people of other languages. Among the languages that influenced English most heavily during the early part of its history were Latin, French, Greek, German, and Scandinavian. When trade and commerce became more widespread in the fifteenth century, Dutch, Italian, Russian, and Spanish influences began to be felt. Still later, as the British colonists settled in North America, American English slowly emerged. Essentially a development of seventeenth-century British English, it was influenced by the native Indian languages and by the languages of people from Africa, Europe, and every other continent in the world.

The history of the English language is divided into three periods: Old English, Middle English, and Modern English. By the beginning of each of these periods, the language had changed enough to be recognized as a separate form. Because English is a living language, spoken and written by millions of people, it continues to change. Partly, the continuing change is the result of high-speed communication among the peoples of the world. Developments in science and technology, such as advances in computers and in the space program, also affect the language, contributing to it such new words or new uses of old words as *input, disk drive, byte,* and *countdown.* Indeed, it is possible that the English your descendants will use five hundred years from now would be unrecognizable to you.

EXERCISE 1. Exploring the History of the English Language. As your teacher directs, use your school library to find more information on one of the following English language periods. In your research, look for answers to such questions as the following ones: (a) In what specific ways did the language change during the period? (b) What were some causes of these changes? (c) What people were important in the history of the language during this period?

1. Old English 450–1100
2. Middle English 1100–1500
3. Modern English 1500–today

EXERCISE 2. Writing a Dialogue in "Future English." Consider what you know about words that have come into use recently (such as computer terms and space terms). Think about how language reflects changes in attitude. Words such as *fireman, policeman, stewardess* are being replaced with *firefighter, police officer, and flight attendant.* Imagine how English might read and sound fifty years from now. Then, using that English, write a dialogue that might take place between two friends as they discuss the news of the day.

THE VARIETIES OF ENGLISH

Standard to Nonstandard English

Standard English is the most widely used form of English; it is generally used in newspapers and magazines, on television and radio, and in business and professional conversations and correspondence.

Standard English is characterized by the kinds of features described in the Usage part of this textbook. These features include the following conventions:

1. A verb agrees with its subject in number.
2. Subjects joined by *and* take a plural verb.
3. Use the comparative degree to compare two things; use the superlative degree to compare more than two.

4. The subject of a verb is in the nominative case.
5. *Good* is an adjective; *well* is an adverb.

Nonstandard English is characterized by features that do not conform to conventions like the ones listed above.

EXAMPLES   1. The children go to the playground at recess. (*Standard*)
The children goes to the playground at recess. (*Nonstandard*)
2. That dog and cat fight all the time. (*Standard*)
That dog and cat fights all the time. (*Nonstandard*)
3. She's the friendliest person I've ever met. (*Standard*)
She's the friendlier person I've ever met. (*Nonstandard*)
4. He and I have jobs after school. (*Standard*)
Him and me have jobs after school. (*Nonstandard*)
5. The band played well. (*Standard*)
The band played good. (*Nonstandard*)

EXERCISE 3. Revising Sentences Written in Nonstandard English.   Each of the following sentences has a usage that varies from standard English. Chapter numbers in parentheses indicate where in the Usage part of this textbook the feature is explained. After referring to the discussion of the feature, rewrite the sentence so that it conforms to standard English.

1. Jason don't want to go to the movie with us. (Chapter 16)
2. Either of the two students are qualified for the job. (Chapter 16)
3. There's many reasons that I won't have my term paper ready on time. (Chapter 16)
4. Did you know that one of these questions are supposed to be on the test? (Chapter 16)
5. Not until you've brung some proof of your age can you apply for a driver's license. (Chapter 17)

6. Us chickens have decided to draw straws to determine which one has to face the fox. (Chapter 18)
7. I was surprised at how good the children did in weaving class. (Chapter 19)
8. We would of gone boating if the ocean hadn't been so rough. (Chapter 20)
9. The musicians look like they're having a good time. (Chapter 20)
10. I took my dog to obedience school because I didn't have no success trying to train him by myself. (Chapter 20)

Formal to Informal English—Levels of Usage

Language, like clothes, varies from the very formal to the very informal; also like clothes, language offers a range of choices. Think of formal to informal English as two ends of another language ruler, with most uses of English falling somewhere in between the two ends. The choices available on this new language ruler are often called *levels of usage*. However, because no one use of English is on a higher (in the sense of "better") or lower (in the sense of "worse") level than any other use of English, the term "levels of usage" is somewhat misleading.

The level of usage chosen by an effective writer depends on the audience and on the situation. Very formal English is most often used for a large, general audience on very formal occasions. Very informal English is most often used in speaking (this kind of language is often called *conversational English*) and in very casual situations.

Although you seldom have occasion to use the most formal English, you do need to consider levels of usage when you speak or write. If you were speaking to a class of fourth-graders, you would naturally use different words from those you would use when speaking to a meeting of the Parent-Teachers Association, although you might be saying about the same thing to both groups.

The following features describe very formal and very informal English. Remember, though, that few uses of language are absolutely formal or absolutely informal.

Very Formal:
   More often used in writing than in speaking
   More often used for formal occasions such as weddings
   Likely to have long and complex sentences
   Likely to have extensive and specific vocabulary
   Likely to sound formal, unlike spoken language
   Unlikely to have colloquialisms, jargon, or slang
   Unlikely to have sentence tags such as *You know* or *Well*

Very Informal:
   More often used in speaking than in writing
   More often used in casual settings such as conversations
   with friends
   Likely to have shorter and less complex sentences
   Likely to sound natural, like spoken language
   Likely to have colloquialisms, jargon, or slang
   Likely to have sentence tags such as *You know* or *Well*

EXERCISE 4. Classifying Language as Formal or Informal.
In your opinion, where does each of the following selections
fall on the formal/informal language ruler? What features char-
acterize each selection as formal or informal? Be prepared to
give reasons for your answers.

1. From a *Chicago Tribune Magazine* article, a first-person
   account of a day in the life of a professional mover.

   The driving is the easiest part of my job. The cars stay
   out of my way. But ice is terrible, just terrible. Driving on
   ice is like sitting on a time bomb and knowing that somebody
   lit the fuse but not knowing how long it is. The truck weighs
   anywhere from 50,000 to 60,000 pounds, depending on the
   weight of the load. And it's 48 feet long—as long as the law
   allows. There's no way in the world I'm going to be able to
   stop quickly on ice. So I keep my distance, and I look for
   the shallowest ditch.

2. From a *New Yorker* article, "A Reporter at Large (Pakistan)," by Richard Reeves. (Chitral is a small village in north-
   western Pakistan.)

In the winter, people huddled together in hay for warmth at night. Even in the summer, food was short—my wife and I were told one morning that we had just eaten the last egg in Chitral—and in the winter there would be no meat or fresh fruit or vegetables. Chronic malnutrition and the fact that the aquamarine water was used for sanitation and for the irrigation of manure-fertilized fields had made these valleys part of the world where measles and pneumonia were still fatal diseases. Until I spent time in those parts, I had had the vague impression that native populations were somehow immune to problems associated with bad water.

THREE USES OF ENGLISH

Three uses of language—slang, colloquialism, and jargon—are usually found only in informal English. Most dictionaries show such uses with a label, sometimes in brackets and sometimes abbreviated.

EXAMPLE

drag (drag) *v.* **dragged, drag·ging** *v.t.* **1.** To pull along by main force; haul. **2.** To sweep or search the bottom of, as with a net or grapnel; dredge. **3.** To catch or recover, as with a grapnel or net. **4.** To draw along heavily and wearily. **5.** To harrow (land). **6.** To continue tediously; protract: often with *on* or *out*. **7.** To introduce (an irrelevant subject or matter) into a discussion, argument, etc.: usually with *in*. — *v.i.* **8.** To be pulled or hauled along; trail to or as to the ground. **9.** To move heavily or slowly. **10.** To lag behind. **11.** To pass slowly. **12.** To use a grapnel, drag, or dredge. **13.** To cause a feeling of clutching or tugging: Worry *dragged* at him. — **to drag one's feet** *U.S. Informal* To act or work with deliberate slowness. — *n.* **1.** The act of dragging. **2.** The amount of resistance encountered in dragging: a heavy *drag* on the left wheel. **3.** A slow, heavy, usually impeded motion or movement **4.** Something that slows down movement, as a clog on a wheel. **5.** Something heavy that is dragged. **6.** A contrivance, as a dragnet, for dragging through water to find or bring up something. **7.** Anything that hinders; an impediment. **8.** A stagecoach, usually drawn by four horses, with seats inside and on the top. **9.** The scent or trail left by a fox. **10.** An artificial scent used in hunting. **11.** A drag hunt (which see). **12.** *Aeron.* That component of the total forces exerted upon an aircraft in flight that is opposite to the direction of motion and parallel to the relative wind. **13.** *U.S. Slang* Influence that brings special favors; pull. **14.** *Slang* A puff on a cigarette, cigar, or pipe. **15.** *U.S. Slang* One who or that which is tedious, boring, or colorless. **16.** *U.S. Slang* A drag race (which see). [ME *draggen*, prob. < OE *dragan*; infl. in form by ON *draga*. Akin to DRAW.]

DRAG (*n.*, *def.* 8)

In this entry, the word *drag* when used as a noun has sixteen definitions. The last four of these are slang uses. The italicized abbreviation *Aeron.* in definition 12 indicates that the word has a special meaning in aeronautics.

Slang

Slang consists of new words, or old words used in new ways, that seem clever and colorful and that show that the user is up-to-date. It is most often found in the speech of young and somewhat isolated groups, such as students and military recruits. High-school students are especially fond of slang and ingenious at inventing it.

Most slang words live a short life; slang from the 1970's would seem old-fashioned today. Sometimes, however, a slang word becomes so widely used that it becomes a more lasting part of the language. The following words, when used with the given meanings, are all marked *slang* in *Webster's New World Dictionary*.

> *bummer:* a depressing experience
> *cool:* having a dispassionate or detached attitude
> *cop out:* to quit, abandon, renege
> *hassle:* to annoy, harass
> *hang-up:* an emotional problem
> *vibes:* emotional reactions
> *weirdo:* a bizarre or strange person

Although slang is sometimes effective in informal speech, it is usually not effective in writing because it is too general. To write that a book you have just read is "cool" or "far-out," for example, will not help your reader understand its good points. When you write the book's review, take the time to choose words that are more specific and thus more informative than slang.

EXERCISE 5. Replacing Slang with More Formal English.

The italicized words and phrases in the following sentences are, or have been, used as slang. Rewrite each of the sentences, replacing slang usages with more formal words and sentences.

(Use your dictionary if you need help.) Which words and phrases are still in use today?

1. "Bought another *coffin nail,* huh? Haven't you heard about the Surgeon General's report?"
2. She didn't buy the camera because she thought it was *hot.*
3. If I can't get my parents to *cough up* the money, I won't be able to have my bike repaired.
4. "No, I won't go to the dance with him! He's a *nerd!*"
5. The county commissioner was on trial for allegedly accepting a *kickback* from several contractors who do business with the county.

Colloquialisms

Colloquialisms are words and phrases usually found only in informal speech and writing. Writers sometimes use colloquialisms in order to capture the sounds of spoken English. Colloquialisms are much more widespread than slang and less likely to mark the user as a member of a distinct group. Also, while much slang consists of single words, colloquialisms are typically phrases or sentences. The colloquialisms in the following examples are italicized.

EXAMPLES   I may have made a mistake, but you don't have to *fly off the handle* about it.
The bride's parents are usually expected to *foot the bill* for the wedding.
The judge, who had been convicted of accepting bribes, swore that he *had been framed.*

EXERCISE 6. Replacing Colloquial Words and Phrases.
Each of the following phrases has one or more colloquial uses. For each phrase, write an original sentence showing its colloquial use. (You may need to reword the phrases slightly.) Then write a second sentence in which you "translate" the colloquialism into more formal English. If you need help, use a dictionary that labels colloquialisms.

1. lead with one's chin
2. let up on
3. for free
4. lock, stock, and barrel
5. call it a day

EXERCISE 7. Finding Slang or Colloquial Meanings. Each of the following words has either a slang or a colloquial usage. In a dictionary that labels such uses, look up each word. Then write the word and its slang or colloquial meaning. If the word is used as part of a phrase, write the entire phrase. (Note that many of the words may be used as more than one part of speech.)

1. limb   6. buzz
2. pickle   7. chicken
3. pain   8. fit
4. line   9. jaw
5. bounce   10. loop

Jargon

Jargon consists of words and phrases used in a particular sport or field of study or by members of a particular profession or occupation. Often, jargon assigns a specialized meaning to a word already in widespread use. The general public uses the word *pan,* for example to mean a container for cooking or washing. In television and movie production, however, the word is given a special meaning—"to move a camera across a wide angle"—and thus becomes jargon.

A single word may be used as jargon by two or more groups, with each group giving it a different meaning. A familiar word may appear unfamiliar when used by different people.

EXAMPLE   Lead (as a noun):
           Card players—the act of playing first
           Electricians—a wire that carries current
           Journalists—the opening paragraph of a news story
           Printers—space between lines of type

Many dictionaries indicate specialized uses of a word by listing the area in which it is used and the meaning it has in that area.

EXAMPLE

> **dig·it** (dij′it)   *n.* **1.** A finger or toe.   **2.** Any one of the ten Arabic numeral symbols, 0 to 9: so named from counting upon the fingers.   **3.** An old measure of length, equal to the breadth of a finger, or about three fourths of an inch.   **4.** The twelfth part of the diameter of the sun or moon.   **5.** *Electronics* One of a set of characters by which, singly or in combination, a digital computer processes required information. [< L *digitus* finger]

In this entry, five definitions are given for the noun *digit*. The word *Electronics* in italics for definition 5 indicates that the definition is special to that field. The word *Electronics* is a usage label, telling what the word means when used as jargon.

Jargon can be an effective way for members of a particular group to communicate, because it reduces many words to just one or two. When it is used inappropriately, however, jargon can be unclear or misleading. Generally, jargon should not be used when members of an audience do not belong to the same profession or occupation as the speaker or writer.

EXERCISE 8. Defining Words with Specialized Uses.   Each of the following words or phrases has a specialized use. Using an appropriate source, find the meaning of the term as it is used in the occupation, profession, or sport indicated.

1. *lift*—golf
2. *noise*—electronics
3. *property*—motion pictures, theater, and television
4. *dingbat*—printing
5. *love*—tennis
6. *snake*—plumbing
7. *mole*—espionage
8. *nickleback*—football
9. *platform*—politics
10. *terminal*—electronic data processing

REVIEW EXERCISE A. Classifying Levels of Language.

The following passage is from the beginning of a short story written by Toni Cade Bambara. The speaker is a young girl. In your opinion, where does this usage of English fall on the standard/nonstandard language ruler? Does the speaker use any colloquialisms, jargon, or slang? If so, what are they? What features in this selection are characteristic of formal or informal English? Think about these questions and be prepared to explain your answers.

My cousin Joanne has not been allowed to hang out with me for some time because she went and told Aunt Hazel that I scare her to death whenever she sleeps over at our house or I spend the weekend at hers. The truth is I sometimes like to tell stories about blood-thirsty vampires or ugly monsters that lurk in clothes closets or giant beetles that eat their way through the shower curtain, like I used to do at camp to entertain the kids in my bunk. But Joanne always cries and that makes the stories even weirder, like background music her crying. And too—I'm not going to lie about it—I get spookier on purpose until all the little crybabies are stuffing themselves under their pillows and throwing their sneakers at me and making such a racket that Mary the counselor has to come in and shine her flashlight around the bunkhouse. I play like I'm asleep. The rest of them are too busy blubbering and finding their way out from under the blankets to tell Mary that it's me. Besides, once they get a load of her standing against the moonlight in that long white robe of hers looking like a ghost, they just start up again and pretty soon the whole camp is awake. Anyway, that's what I do for fun. So Joanne hasn't been around. And this year I'll have to go to the circus by myself and to camp without her. My mother said on the phone to Aunt Hazel—"Good, keep Jo over there and maybe Harriet'll behave herself if she's got no one to show off to." For all the years my mother's known me, she still doesn't understand that my behaving has got nothing to do with who I hang out with. A private thing between me and me or maybe between me and the Fly family since they were the ones that first got me to sit through monster movies and withstand all the terror I could take.

SEMANTICS: THE MEANING OF WORDS

Since English is a living language, it changes as the world of its users changes. *Semantics* is the study of the meanings of words and the changes in those meanings.

Idioms

Words change in the combinations they form and the meanings they acquire. In any language, certain words and phrases cannot be explained grammatically or translated literally (word-for-word). These are *idioms,* words or combinations of words that are unique to a language. Idioms develop when the usual meanings of words are bypassed for some reason and other meanings are created to meet a specific purpose. Idioms enrich a language, making it distinct from all other languages.

Many English idioms involve the use of a particular preposition with a word; changing the preposition changes the whole meaning of the idiom. You might say: The senior *talked to* the ninth-graders. The senior *talked down to* the ninth-graders. The senior *talked up* the ninth-grade sports banquet. In each case the meaning is quite different. Notice also that the idiom in the third example would be difficult to explain grammatically.

Some idioms are combinations of words that mean something different from the literal meaning. For example, what do you mean when you say that you *lost your temper*? What happened when your father *ran across some old school friends*?

Meanings of Words: Denotations and Connotations

As you know, a word may have many different meanings. The noun *ring,* for example, has such varied meanings as "a band worn around a finger," "a roped-off area for boxing," and "a telephone call." These direct, plainly expressed meanings of a word are called *denotations*. In addition to their denotations, many words have *connotations*. These are meanings suggested by or associated with the word.

The words *statesman* or *stateswoman* and *politician,* for example, may have the same denotation—one who is engaged in government or politics. Their connotations are different, however. By referring to an elected government official as a statesman or stateswoman, you honor him or her. By referring to the same person as a politician, you may be insulting him or her because the word *politician* has an unfavorable connotation for some people. To them, it suggests a person who is more concerned with his or her own interests than with the needs of the people represented.

Usually the connotations of a word stir people's feelings, and they react to the word emotionally. Although the words *capitalist* and *capitalism* have clear, technical denotations, for example, they might arouse strong negative feelings in some countries whose industries are controlled by the state. Similarly, the words *dictator* and *dictatorship* might arouse negative feelings in democratic societies.

Using words with strong connotations is not in itself inappropriate; connotations are a vital part of life and, therefore, of language. What may be inappropriate is a writer's or speaker's reason for using them. In reading and listening, and in using words yourself, be aware of both the denotations and connotations of words.

EXERCISE 9. Classifying Words According to Their Connotations. The words in each group following have similar denotations but vastly different connotations. List the words in each group in descending order according to the favorableness of their connotations; that is, put the word with the most favorable connotation first and the word with the most unfavorable connotation last. Opinions will differ.

1. thin, skinny, gawky, slender, lanky
2. defeat, edge out, swamp, beat, overrun

3. conceited, vain, arrogant, cocky, self-confident
4. informer, stool pigeon, tattletale, spy, undercover agent
5. tight, thrifty, stingy, frugal, economical

As you may have discovered, the connotations of words may affect different people differently. Some words, such as *motherhood, friendship, freedom, home, peace,* will have favorable connotations for almost everyone; other words will cause widely varying reactions. People's reactions to various words are determined by their experience and knowledge. Your reaction to *Nazi* will be negative because of your knowledge of history. Your reaction to *Yankee* probably depends on whether you were born in the South or in New England.

EXERCISE 10. Analyzing the Connotations of Words. Read the following list of words and give your immediate reaction to each: negative, affirmative, or neutral. Be prepared to explain in class the reasons for your reactions. Ask your parents for their reactions to the words.

1. snake	8. millionaire	15. soup
2. dentist	9. student	16. beach
3. chocolate	10. breakfast	17. pig
4. labor union	11. cheap	18. skinny
5. Republican	12. soap opera	19. media
6. Democrat	13. salesman	20. gossip
7. welfare	14. new	

EXERCISE 11. Analyzing the Connotations of Words. Distinguish between the connotations of the words in each of the following pairs. The denotative meanings of the paired words are similar. Their connotative meanings may prove to be quite different.

1. dog, cur	6. used, secondhand
2. idealist, dreamer	7. graveyard, memorial park
3. rare, half-cooked	8. job, chore
4. determined, obstinate	9. cook, chef
5. fastidious, fussy	10. boat, yacht

Loaded Words

Closely related to the fact that words may have strong connotations is a writer's deliberate use of words that will prejudice
the reader for or against something. Words that tend to prejudice
the reader for or against something are called *loaded words*.

EXERCISE 12. Analyzing Loaded Words. Both of the following descriptions of the same candidate contain loaded words.
Read the two descriptions; the first is loaded against the candidate, and the second is in his favor. Make a list of the loaded
words and expressions in the first selection; then, after each,
write the corresponding loaded word from the second selection.

1

After suffering a major defeat in last week's presidential
primary, Senator Blank addressed a mere handful of people
last night at the Civic Center. Looking drained and feverish,
the senator threatened to continue his futile bid for the nomination. His voice rose hysterically as he ended his speech
with these foolhardy words: "I intend to beat Governor Blab
next week right here in his home state."

2

After suffering a temporary setback in last week's presidential primary, Senator Blank addressed a small but spirited
audience last night at the Civic Center. Looking tired but
fiercely determined, the senator vowed to come from behind
and win the nomination. His voice shook with emotion as
he ended his speech with these courageous words: "I intend
to beat Governor Blab next week right here in his home
state."

Tired Words

A "tired" word is one that has been used so much and so
carelessly that it has lost much of its meaning and its effectiveness. Tired words like *nice, swell, wonderful,* and *great* are
common in conversation; they are not, however, exact enough

to be effective in writing. When a friend asks you what kind of time you had at a party, you may use any one of those words to convey the idea that you enjoyed the party. If you were writing a book report, however, you would be telling your reader little if you simply characterized the book as nice or swell or wonderful.

Another name for a tired word or a tired expression is *cliché* (kle-sha'). Clichés may be single words or expressions of more than one word. Among the most common clichés are tired comparisons: busy as a bee, clear as crystal, quick as a flash, white as a sheet, fat as a pig, straight as an arrow, thin as a rail. Not all clichés are comparisons: few and far between, accidents will happen, gala occasion, last but not least.

Good writers avoid clichés in any form—tired words, tired comparisons, or other tired expressions.

EXERCISE 13. Identifying Tired Words and Clichés. Prepare a list of five tired words, five tired comparisons, and five tired expressions that are not comparisons. Do not include in your list any of the words or expressions previously used as examples. Compare your list with those of your classmates. By combining lists, you should have a large collection of expressions to avoid when you write.

REVIEW EXERCISE B. Analyzing the Uses and Effects of Language. As your teacher directs, complete one of the following projects.

1. Use several reference sources available in your school or local library. Read the entries on *semantics*. Write a clear explanation of the term with several good examples. Present your explanation orally to your class.
2. Read a speech noted for its effect on the thoughts and feelings of those who listened to it. Analyze how the speaker's word choice contributed to the effect of the speech. Be prepared to read the speech to your class and to present your analysis. You might look at some of the "fireside chats" of President Franklin Roosevelt, the speeches of Winston Churchill during

World War II, or the speech given by Martin Luther King, Jr., at the Washington Monument in 1963.

3. Read several advertisements in your Sunday newspaper. Make a list of words and phrases that you think the ad writer chose because of their likely effect on readers. Select five words or phrases from your list. Write an explanation of the way each of these might affect a potential buyer.

THE WRITER'S CHOICE OF WORDS

Appropriate Words for Your Purpose and Audience

When you write, you must make a great many decisions. You must decide which word will best say what you want to say. You must decide also which word (words) will best suit your purpose and your audience. In choosing words, keep in mind their connotations as well as their denotations. Choose words that are appropriate for the situation—formal or informal—and that are specific rather than general. Avoid slang, tired words, and clichés. The more time you spend on word choice, the more effective your writing will be.

Always keep your purpose and audience in mind, and avoid extremes. Using an artificially high-toned vocabulary may annoy your reader, who will realize that you are putting on airs. For an oral report on a recent school play, for example, it would be inappropriate for your purpose and audience to write, "The audience manifested nothing but disdain for the inferiority of script and ineptness of thespian performance." On the other hand, you should not use language as informal as slang in serious compositions. In your oral report it would be inappropriate to write, "The plot was stupid; the whole thing was a flop."

EXERCISE 14. Evaluating Language Choices in Terms of Audience and Purpose. The following paragraph is from a classroom assignment for a book report. Is the language appropriate for the audience and purpose? If not, what changes should the writer make? Be prepared to explain your answer.

Maigret's Rival by Georges Simenon is a mystery story that takes place in France. A friend invites Maigret, a former police inspector, to a jerkwater town. There are some nasty rumors flying around town, and Maigret is supposed to keep a lid on them. Meanwhile one of Maigret's old buddies turns up—Cavre, who had been given the boot from the police force. Cavre gets the townspeople all worked up against Maigret, and they start to smell a rat regarding Maigret's visit. Naturally, since this is a murder mystery, it turns out that there is a stiff involved. I can't tell you any more without lousing up the story for you, so read it for yourselves. You'll get a big kick out of it.

CHAPTER 9 WRITING REVIEW

Applying Your Knowledge of Effective Word Choice. The following paper was written for an oral report on animal care in pet shops. Study the word choices. List all the words you consider inappropriate. Next to each, write a word or word group that is more specific, more effective, more appropriate for the intended purpose and audience. Then, as your teacher directs, revise the paper.

While gawking around in a pet store, did you ever feel real down when you saw all those cooped-up birds? Well I hate to bust your bubbles, but those pampered pets have it made. First and foremost, they're not being hassled by any predators. As far as Polly is concerned, that tooth-and-claw jungle scene is too hairy for words—in fact, it's for the birds.

Second, Polly gets all the eats it wants. I don't mean slim pickin's, either, but the cream of the crop—seeds, veggies, nuts, vitamins, the works. It's small wonder that caged birds have the laid-back look. They're living on easy street. And if they get daily exercise, their life is a bed of roses.

Last but not least, a caged bird is safe from all those

weird tropical diseases it can get in the wild. There's never any need for Polly to get its feathers ruffled worrying about jungle rot or creeping crud or any of that jazz. If by a stroke of fate Polly does get its snoot stopped up with the sniffles, there are scads of vets who have hung out their shingles, all set to get Polly back into the pink of health.

To put it in a nutshell, a pet bird gets tender loving care and a free ride on the gravy train instead of a raw deal from nature. And when a pet bird returns its owner's affection, you know it's not feeling down-in-the-mouth. So before all you bleeding hearts get steamed up about birds' rights, just cool your jets. Remember, a well-treated pet bird is really flying high!

PICTURE T H E POSSIBILITIES:

IDEAS FOR WRITING

Pictures have the power to prompt the memory, stir the emotions, and spark the imagination. In this section you will learn how to use pictures as a powerful source of ideas for writing.

Probing the Picture

At first glance, this picture might make you wonder how the soccer game came out—in other words, *What happened?* In order to answer that question, you could develop the elements of a **narrative** (character, setting, and so on) by asking the *5 W-How?* questions as follows: *What* is the conflict? *Who* are the main characters? *When* and *where* does the action take place? Your answers to these and other questions would give you the raw material for your story plan.

Another way to approach the picture would be to think of it as a starting point for **persuasive** writing. The heart of persuasive writing is a debatable issue. To find possible issues, you could focus on the principal elements of the picture. Here, for example, you might focus on the girls and the soccer ball. Thinking about these two elements in combination, you could brainstorm to develop a list of debatable issues such as *Should girls be allowed to play contact sports? Should girls' soccer become an interscholastic sport? Should boys and girls play on the same team? Should boys' and girls' teams compete against one another?*

Writing Activities

Using the steps of the writing process, complete one of the following activities.
- Prepare a story plan and write a story about the picture.
- Write a letter to the editor of your school paper on one of the issues mentioned above or on another issue the picture suggests.

Probing the Picture

For this picture, the obvious approach would be to write a **description.** To create a main impression, you could focus on the strongest elements of the picture: the repetition of pattern and the contrasting areas of light and shadow. You could instead imagine yourself in the bicycle shop and gather concrete and sensory details by asking yourself questions such as *What odors do I smell in this part of the shop? How do the spokes of the wheels feel when I touch them? What do I hear when I accidentally bump into one of the racks that support the wheels?* Thus the picture both provides certain details and, if you imagine yourself in the scene, suggests others.

A second way to use the picture would be to make "bicycle wheels" the topic of an **expository** paragraph or composition. To gather information, you could use the *point-of-view questions,* developing questions such as *What are the parts of a bicycle wheel? How are they assembled? Is the same metal used for the rim and the spokes? When and where were bicycles with equal-size wheels first made?* Once you had found answers to your questions, you could decide whether to explain or to give information and then determine your main idea.

Writing Activities

Using the steps of the writing process, complete one of the following activities.

- Use the picture to write a descriptive paragraph that creates a main impression.
- Write an expository paragraph on the topic "bicycle wheels."

Probing the Picture

This picture could serve as the basis for an **expository** paragraph defining the term *icicle.* After identifying the general class to which icicles belong, you could brainstorm to develop a list of questions whose answers would help you explain the distinguishing characteristics of icicles. You might consider questions such as *What is the structure of an icicle? Do all icicles have the same structure? Under what conditions (temperature, wind speed, humidity) do icicles form? Why do almost all icicles take the form of stalactites rather than that of stalagmites?*

You might instead see **narrative** possibilities in this picture. For example, you could use the scene as the setting for a story in which the conflict is between the main character and nature (the weather). Using the *5 W-How?* questions would help you develop the other elements of a narrative. For example, *who* is the main character? *Where* is he or she—inside the house looking out, or approaching (or passing) the house? *What* month, day, and time of day is it? As part of your story, you could include a character sketch, using the details of an incident and physical details to reveal the main character's dominant personality trait.

Writing Activities

Using the steps in the writing process, complete one of the following activities.

- Write an expository paragraph defining the term *icicle.*
- Use the picture to write a story in which the conflict is between the main character and nature.

Probing Pictures to Discover Ideas for Writing

The following questions will help you use any picture to discover ideas for writing.

1. What about this picture most interests me? What specific idea does it suggest?
2. For what purpose could I use this idea?
3. What are the strongest elements of the picture? How could I combine those elements to achieve my purpose?
4. Would using the 5 *W-How?* questions help me gather information to use?
5. What might have happened just before or just after the picture was taken? What might the person(s) have said?
6. What main impression do I get from this picture?
7. What concrete and sensory details do I observe as I examine the picture? What details do I imagine when I think of myself as being in the scene?
8. Could I explain how to make or do what the picture shows?
9. Could I give information about what the picture shows by telling who or what the subject is, what its history is, or how it is related to others of its kind?
10. What debatable issues does the combination of elements in the picture suggest to me?

On Your Own

Using any of the pictures you have not written about, write a paper for your classmates. You may choose the form (paragraph, composition, letter to the editor, story) and the purpose (to tell a story, to describe, to explain or give information, or to persuade). Follow the steps of the writing process as you prepare your paper.

PART TWO

COMPOSITION:
Writing and Revising
Sentences

CHAPTER 10

Writing Complete Sentences

SENTENCE FRAGMENTS AND RUN-ON SENTENCES

You already have sentence sense regarding spoken language. When you are speaking, your voice rises and falls naturally to indicate the beginning and the end of a sentence.

You can develop sentence sense in writing by "listening" to the sentences you write. If you practice "listening" to the exercise sentences in this chapter, you will learn to avoid the two common errors of writing discussed here: the *fragment* and the *run-on sentence*.

THE SENTENCE FRAGMENT

10a. A *fragment* is a separated sentence part that does not express a complete thought.

A fragment is usually an additional idea that has been incorrectly cut off from the sentence in which it belongs.

EXAMPLES Scratching noises on the cabin porch indicated that I had a visitor. *Probably a raccoon or a wildcat.*

As we ran toward the bus, it drove off. *Leaving Nan and me standing helplessly on the corner.*

In the first example above, *Probably a raccoon or a wildcat* is a fragment cut off from the preceding sentence. It does not make sense by itself. In the second example, *Leaving Nan and me standing helplessly on the corner* is also a fragment; without a subject and verb, it does not express a complete thought. These fragments should be joined to the preceding sentences.

EXAMPLES   Scratching noises on the cabin porch indicated that I had a visitor, **probably a raccoon or a wildcat.**
As we ran toward the bus, it drove off, **leaving Nan and me standing helplessly on the corner**.

Sometimes a fragment should be corrected by being placed at the beginning or within the sentence from which it was separated.

FRAGMENT   Hubert works slowly and deliberately on the mound. *Taking plenty of time between pitches.*
CORRECTED   **Taking plenty of time between pitches,** Hubert works slowly and deliberately on the mound.

FRAGMENT   We talked with Mrs. Jackson in her office. *The principal of the school.*
CORRECTED   We talked with Mrs. Jackson, **the principal of the school,** in her office.

EXERCISE 1. Identifying Fragments and Sentences. How good is your "sentence sense"? Find out by deciding whether or not each group of words is a sentence. Number your paper 1–10. After the proper number, write *F* for fragment or *S* for sentence.

1. Thumbing through the first few pages of *The Way to Rainy Mountain* by N. Scott Momaday.
2. To warn motorists of the ice forming on bridges.
3. On the other side of the mountain is a beautiful valley.
4. Can you prove that statement?
5. After rehearsal we got together and memorized our lines.

6. Leroy, playing defensive end for the Lions.
7. Singing is Martina Arroyo's profession.
8. An old two-story house with spacious rooms, designed to accommodate a large family of a dozen or more.
9. In the spring, when the warm sun shines upon the fresh green beauty of the earth and when red tulips wave in the March winds.
10. Even though she had to support her mother and three younger sisters with her earnings as a stockbroker.

EXERCISE 2. Identifying Fragments and Sentences. Number your paper 1–10. If a numbered item contains a fragment, write *F* after its number. If it contains only sentences, write *S* for sentences.

1. A few Eskimos live on the Barren Grounds. A remote area of northern Canada.
2. A flycatcher has a forked tail almost a foot long. In flight this bird looks like something from outer space.
3. Four of us were standing on the corner. Waiting for the five o'clock bus to Riverside Skating Arena in the mall.
4. The sports editor interviewed Mrs. Franklin. She is the new history teacher and coach of the swim team.
5. I wrote to an office in Tallahassee, Florida. To get some information for my report on environmental protection laws.
6. I cast my plug about twenty yards from where I was standing. I waited for a long silver bass to strike the bait.
7. We tried to do an especially good job on our first day at work. Hoping to earn a generous tip from customers.
8. In Wyoming we traveled through Cody, a city named for W. F. Cody. Who is better known as "Buffalo Bill" Cody.
9. P. T. Barnum was a legendary American figure. He was a showman who is best known for his circus, *The Greatest Show on Earth.*
10. Yesterday at the ice-cream parlor I ordered a "shipwreck." A banana split without the banana.

Common Types of Sentence Fragments

10b. A subordinate clause must not be written as a sentence.

A subordinate clause always depends on an independent clause to complete its meaning. Notice that the subordinate clause fragment below does not express a complete thought.

Although Bertha receives a large allowance

The clause has a verb, *receives,* and a subject, *Bertha.* Because of the word *although,* however, the thought is not complete. Like all fragments, this one may be corrected by being placed in a sentence—that is, by being attached to an independent clause.

Although Bertha receives a large allowance, she often seems miserly.
Bertha often seems miserly although she receives a large allowance.

Relative pronouns (the pronouns *which, that, who, whom, whose*) and subordinating conjunctions (see the list on page 324) introduce subordinate clauses. These little words are very important; they can change a complete thought to a fragment.

SENTENCE   Claude told the truth.
FRAGMENTS   **Unless** Claude told the truth
That Claude told the truth
Claude, **who** told the truth

EXERCISE 3. Revising by Correcting Subordinate Clause Fragments. Most of the following items contain subordinate clauses that are punctuated as sentences. Correct these fragments by making them a part of the sentence in the item. You may have to leave out or add words. When you are revising, be particularly careful to avoid misplaced modifiers. If an item is correct, write a *C* after the appropriate number.

1. Next week we are going to Williamsburg. Which is a historic city in Virginia.

2. Although it was nothing more than a small village in the seventeenth century. Williamsburg was the scene of several important events in the eighteenth century.

3. Though many of the buildings in Williamsburg today are not the original ones, they are exact likenesses. The town's only major industry is restoration.

4. What I want most to see is the Public Gaol. Which once housed fifteen of Blackbeard's pirates, thirteen of whom were hanged.

5. Completed in 1720, the Governor's Palace was later the official residence of the first two governors of the state. Who were Patrick Henry and Thomas Jefferson.

6. The Raleigh Tavern, which was the center of many heated political discussions. It was the inn in which both George Washington and Thomas Jefferson frequently dined.

7. The tools that were used for trade in the eighteenth century. These have been re-created in various craft shops in the town.

8. In Virginia we will see my sister. She is a student at the College of William and Mary.

9. William and Mary is the second oldest college in the United States. Which is located in Williamsburg.

10. Because we want to see the White House. We may stop in Washington, D.C., on the way home.

10c. A verbal phrase must not be written as a sentence.

Verbals are forms of verbs that are used as other parts of speech. Present participles and gerunds are verbals ending in -*ing* (*coming, working, being, laughing*). Past particles usually end in -*d*, -*ed*, -*t*, -*n*, or -*en* (*looked, slept, broken*). Infinitives usually consist of *to* plus the verb (*to go, to play*).

A verbal phrase is a phrase containing a verbal. By itself, a verbal phrase is a fragment: it cannot express a complete thought.

FRAGMENTS   Spilling juice all over the floor
             Poised on her toes
             Saying goodbye
             To approve his son's marriage

Like subordinate clauses, verbals depend upon independent clauses to make their meaning complete.

SENTENCES   Spilling juice all over the floor, I dashed back to the television.
             A ballet dancer, poised on her toes, waited for the cue.
             Carl and Shirley parted quickly without even saying goodbye.
             Mr. Yen was happy to approve his son's marriage.

EXERCISE 4. Revising by Correcting Verbal Phrase Fragments. Correct the ten fragments in the following paragraph by attaching them logically to independent clauses. Remember to change the punctuation as necessary.

Many stories and songs have been written about Lorelei. The name of a huge rock which juts from the Rhine River in Germany. According to one song the rock is inhabited by a woman. Blessed with supernatural powers. Glittering in the sunlight. Her gold jewelry catches the attention of a sailor. Passing in a sailboat. By singing a magical song. She casts a spell on the sailor. Forcing him to stare up at her. As a result he never sees the dangerous obstacles in the water. The jagged rocks which can tear into a ship's hull. Deprived of his senses. The sailor runs his boat upon the rocks. Then, still caught within the woman's spell. He follows his boat to a watery death. Many ships have sunk near Lorelei. Destroyed by the power of this magical woman.

EXERCISE 5. Using Verbal Phrases in Sentences. All of the following verbal phrases are written incorrectly as sentences. Use each in a complete sentence.

1. Pushing her way forward.
2. Disturbed by a nagging conscience.
3. To mutter to himself and to the typewriter.
4. After sharpening four red pencils.
5. Before getting a new pair of boots.

REVIEW EXERCISE A. Identifying and Correcting Fragments. Some of the following groups of words are sentences; others are subordinate clauses or verbal phrases incorrectly written as sentences. Number your paper 1–10. Place *S* after the corresponding number of each complete sentence. Write *F* after the corresponding number of each fragment. Be prepared to tell how you would correct each fragment by making it a part of a related sentence.

1. In the bloodstream are red blood cells.
2. Which are carriers of oxygen.
3. Provided by the lungs.
4. Every day new red blood cells are born.
5. As old ones wear out.
6. There are also white cells in the bloodstream.
7. These white cells destroy harmful germs.
8. Too many white cells in the bloodstream may indicate a serious infection.
9. When they are needed to fight hordes of germs.
10. The body manufactures a great number of white cells.

10d. An appositive phrase must not be written as a sentence.

An appositive is a word which means the same thing as the noun or pronoun it follows. (See Chapter 14.) An appositive phrase, made up of the appositive and its modifiers, does not contain the basic parts of a sentence. By itself it is a fragment.

FRAGMENT   The reaper was invented by Cyrus McCormick. *A famous farmer of Virginia.*

SENTENCE   The reaper was invented by Cyrus McCormick, **a famous farmer of Virginia.**

EXERCISE 6. Correcting Appositive Fragments. Some of the following items are correctly written and punctuated. Some contain appositive phrases that have been incorrectly written as complete sentences. On your paper write *C* if an item is correct. Rewrite and punctuate correctly each incorrect item. Number your answers 1–10.

EXAMPLES   1. In English class we are studying types of humor. My teacher is Ms. Blevins.
          1. *C*
          2. We have learned two new literary terms. Indirect satire and irony.
          2. *We have learned two new literary terms, indirect satire and irony.*

1. Ms. Blevins gave us an interesting assignment, a composition dealing with an ironical situation.
2. In his paper Roy Welch described what recently happened to Mrs. Myer. Roy's next-door neighbor.
3. A detective with wide experience. Mrs. Myer gave a lecture to the Civic Club.
4. She is an interesting speaker. The stories she tells are fascinating.
5. In her lecture she gave advice on one topic. Methods of outwitting pickpockets.
6. The Civic Club audience listened intently because they had heard stories about citizens who had had their pockets picked.
7. An ironic thing happened the very next Saturday. The day of the big game.
8. Mrs. Myer went to the game. She had arranged to meet at the ticket booth several invited friends.
9. She had a great deal of money. Approximately seventy dollars in her wallet.
10. When she reached for her wallet, she discovered to her dismay that her purse had been picked by somebody in the crowd.

10e. Avoid other sentence fragments.

On this page is a list of other common types of fragments. Although you do not need to learn the names of these, you should be able to recognize them as incomplete ideas so that you can avoid writing them as sentence fragments in your compositions.

1. *Prepositional phrases:* The annual athletic awards were presented. After the last game of the season.

2. *Compound parts of a sentence:* On July 4 Donna packed everything for our picnic. But forgot paper plates.

3. *Parts of a comparison:* The dinner tempts me. As much as a cage tempts a sparrow.

4. *Items in a series:* All her essays are written in the same fine style. Clear, concise, and interesting.

Each fragment should be attached to a complete sentence. Sentence 1, for example, may be rewritten as follows:

After the last game of the season, the annual athletic awards were presented.

The annual athletic awards were presented **after the last game of the season.**

REVIEW EXERCISE B. Revising by Correcting Sentence Fragments.
Revise each of the following items so that the fragment is eliminated.

1. The woman skipped briskly down the sidewalk in front of me. Like a child playing hopscotch on a summer afternoon.

2. When the parakeet hid under the chair, Sue gently broomed it out. And eventually returned it to its cage.

3. The people of Grand Rapids, Michigan, manufacture many products. Such as chemicals, furniture, and tools.

4. Acorns are eaten not only by squirrels. But also by pigs.

5. Before going to sleep, I like to eat something. Especially ham sandwiches and cold chicken.

6. This all-purpose cleanser brightens pots and pans. Including copper-bottomed skillets.

7. I don't know how to cook vegetables. To keep them from tasting flat.
8. On Saturdays I not only help around the house. But also work in the yard.
9. Louise bought herself a ruling pen. After deciding to learn mechanical drawing.
10. I learned many things at camp. Such as how to dive.

THE RUN-ON SENTENCE

Sometimes writers don't recognize where a sentence ends, and they keep on going into the next sentence. They use a comma or no mark of punctuation at all instead of a period after a sentence. They permit the sentence to "run on" into the next.

10f. A *run-on sentence* **consists of two or more sentences separated only by a comma or by no mark of punctuation.**

Every sentence should begin with a capital letter and should be followed by an end mark: period, question mark, or exclamation point. Sentences should never be run together without punctuation.

> RUN-ON Where are Riff and Raff those cats won't come when I call them.
>
> CORRECTED Where are Riff and Raff? Those cats won't come when I call them.

The comma should never take the place of an end mark.

> RUN-ON Last year we spent our vacation at a resort, this summer we plan to go camping.
>
> CORRECTED Last year we spent our vacation at a resort. This summer we plan to go camping.

Revising Run-on Sentences

In the previous example, the run-on sentence was revised by making two separate sentences. Notice, however, that the sentences are closely related. (Writers usually do not run unrelated sentences together.)

Instead of punctuating it as two sentences, you may prefer to revise a run-on sentence by making a compound sentence. If you do, use either a comma and a coordinating conjunction (*and, but, or*) or a semicolon and no conjunction between the two independent clauses.

EXAMPLES Last year we spent our vacation in Pennsylvania, **but** this summer we plan to drive through the Southwest.

Last year we spent our vacation in Pennsylvania; this summer we plan to drive through the Southwest.

Occasionally a run-on sentence may be revised by expressing one of the parts in a subordinate clause.

EXAMPLE Although we spent our vacation in Pennsylvania last year, this summer we plan to drive through the Southwest.

EXERCISE 7. Revising Run-on Sentences. You will find the following passages hard to read because run-on sentences always interfere with the clear expression of ideas. Exercise your sentence sense to decide where each sentence should end. Write your corrected version after the corresponding number.

EXAMPLE 1. We were eating breakfast, Dad made a dramatic gesture and knocked over the sugar bowl. I choked on my milk my grandmother chuckled so hard that the table shook.

    1. *While we were eating breakfast, Dad made a dramatic gesture and knocked over the sugar bowl. I choked on my milk, and my grandmother chuckled so hard that the table shook.*

1. The inventor of the typewriter probably thought that he was doing the world a favor, it's too bad that he didn't consider the effect of his invention on me, in fact, typewriting lessons are making a nervous wreck out of me.

2. Why must all the letters of the alphabet be in such confusion on the keyboard why must typewriters in school have black tabs covering the jumbled letters why must my typewriter play hopscotch when I rest my thumb on the long bar?
3. It is fun to grow ornamental peppers, if you have one plant, you can start a forest of them because each pod has scores of seeds, each seed is a potential plant in the spring tiny white and purple blossoms appear.
4. These blossoms slowly transform themselves into green pods later the green turns to purple then it changes to yellow and orange finally it turns bright red, since each pod is at a different growth stage, the plant looks like a Christmas tree.
5. After graduating from college, my mother took graduate courses in environmental studies at night, worked part-time as a reporter during the day, and helped fight fires as a volunteer on Saturdays, since she was very concerned with the condition of the environment she enjoyed her activities.

REVIEW EXERCISE C. Revising Paragraphs to Eliminate Run-ons and Sentence Fragments. Revise the following paragraph, eliminating all fragments and run-ons.

For many centuries scientists knew very little about the blood, in the early seventeenth century William Harvey's theory of blood circulation started a kind of revolution in medicine. One hundred and fifty years later Edward Jenner found out that a person who had had cowpox was immune to smallpox, this discovery helped Jenner find a good way to fight smallpox, by vaccination. Thus preventing the disease rather than attempting to treat it. In the nineteenth century Louis Pasteur proved that germs cause disease, he also discovered several methods of killing germs including pasteurization, a process named after him. Though Florence Nightingale was not a scientist, she was dedicated to the nursing profession, after studying the latest nursing techniques, she traveled to the Crimea, there she helped wounded soldiers. Often working nineteen hours a day. Modern medicine is greatly indebted to these pioneers.

CHAPTER 11

Writing Effective Sentences
SENTENCE COMBINING AND REVISING

You can add interest to your compositions by varying the way you construct sentences. If too many of your sentences are short and choppy or long and stringy, your style becomes monotonous and makes the most interesting topic seem dull. Avoid monotony of style by learning to combine sentences and to vary sentences effectively.

SENTENCE COMBINING

Short sentences are often effective in a composition, but a long series of short sentences is a sign of an immature style. Notice how the short, choppy sentences in the following paragraph sound childish and make the paragraph difficult to read.

> In my hands money doesn't last long. My aunt sent me ten dollars. It was a birthday present. I held onto the money for about ten minutes. My brother demanded repayment. I had borrowed two dollars from him a week before. Marcia and Jennie are my best friends. They had treated me to lunch a long time ago. They suddenly suggested that I return the favor. My mother's birthday is next week. I am almost broke.

Maybe I can make something for her, like a cake. It won't cost me any money.

The next paragraph shows several of these short, choppy sentences combined into longer sentences.

> In my hands money doesn't last long. When my aunt sent me ten dollars as a birthday present, I held onto the money for about ten minutes. My brother demanded repayment of the two dollars I had borrowed from him a week before. Marcia and Jennie, my best friends, who had treated me to lunch a long time ago, suddenly suggested that I return the favor. My mother's birthday is next week. Since I am almost broke, maybe I can make something for her that won't cost me any money, like a cake.

Combining short, related sentences into longer sentences is valuable practice for improving your writing style. The following rules offer several ways to combine sentences.

11a. Combine short, related sentences by inserting adjectives, adverbs, or prepositional phrases.

TWO SENTENCES	Pearl S. Buck was an American writer. She was a great writer.
ONE SENTENCE	Pearl S. Buck was a great American writer. [The adjective *great* in the second sentence is inserted into the first sentence.]
TWO SENTENCES	She wrote about the Chinese way of life. She was compassionate.
ONE SENTENCE	She wrote compassionately about the Chinese way of life. [The adjective *compassionate* in the second sentence has been changed into the adverb *compassionately* and inserted into the first sentence.]
TWO SENTENCES	Pearl S. Buck won the Pulitzer Prize. She won the Pulitzer Prize for her novel *The Good Earth*.
ONE SENTENCE	Pearl S. Buck won the Pulitzer Prize for her novel *The Good Earth*. [The second sentence,

> *She won the Pulitzer Prize for her novel* The Good Earth, has been reduced to the prepositional phrase, *for her novel* The Good Earth, and inserted into the first sentence.]

Notice in the last example that the sentences could have been combined in another way: *For her novel* The Good Earth, *Pearl S. Buck won the Pulitzer Prize.* (See Chapters 12 and 14 for more information on adjectives, adverbs, and prepositional phrases.)

EXERCISE 1. Combining Sentences by Inserting Adjectives, Adverbs, or Prepositional Phrases. Combine each group of short, related sentences into one sentence. There may be more than one way to combine the sentences.

EXAMPLE   1. The nurses waited.
　　　　　　　They waited for the doctors to come.
　　　　　　　They were calm.
　　　　　1. *The nurses calmly waited for the doctors to come.*

1. Doctors huddle over the patient.
   They are in the emergency room.
   The patient is badly injured.
2. One doctor checks for a heartbeat.
   He checks immediately.
   He checks with his stethoscope.
3. Another doctor peers into the patient's eyes.
   The eyes look glassy.
   The doctor uses a special light.
4. The eyes act as windows.
   They are windows into the body.
   They are windows for doctors.
5. Doctors detect clues to disorders.
   They look through the eyes.
   The disorders are medical.
6. Problems show up in the eyes.
   They are problems of the circulatory system.
   They usually show up.

7. Therefore doctors check the eyes.
   The check is routine.
   They check in any emergency.
8. After the examination, the patient is moved.
   The examination is brief.
   The patient is moved to another room.
9. When surgery begins, the patient is given blood.
   The surgery is an emergency.
   It begins in less than an hour.
   The blood is given in large amounts.
10. The patient recovers from surgery.
    The recovery is quick.
    The recovery is fortunate.

11b. Combine closely related sentences by using participial phrases.

A participial phrase (see page 429) is a group of related words that contains a participle and that acts as an adjective, modifying a noun or a pronoun. In the following sentences, all the words in boldfaced type are part of a participial phrase.

EXAMPLES **Beginning a stamp collection,** I found ten valuable stamps in less than a week.
Begun by concerned citizens, the ecology patrol was a neighborhood success.

Two closely related sentences can be combined by making one sentence a participial phrase.

TWO SENTENCES The batter was hit by the pitch.
He stood too close to the plate.
ONE SENTENCE Standing too close to the plate, the batter was hit by the pitch.

To avoid confusing the reader, a participial phrase must be placed close to the noun or pronoun it modifies.

MISPLACED The batter went to first hit by the pitch.
IMPROVED Hit by the pitch, the batter went to first.

> ☞ **NOTE**   Use a comma after a participial phrase that begins a sentence.

EXAMPLE   Leaning perilously over the guardrail, Janet shouted her name and waited for the echo.

EXERCISE 2. Combining Sentences by Using Participial Phrases.

Combine each of the following groups of sentences into one sentence by using a participial phrase. There may be more than one correct way to combine the sentences. Add commas where they are necessary.

EXAMPLE   1. Lisa bought a bicycle.
           We saw her.
        1. *We saw Lisa buying a bicycle.*

1. Ursula Le Guin spoke about science fiction.
   We listened to her.
2. Rita was pleased by the invitation.
   She accepted it immediately.
3. I applauded wildly at the end of the play.
   I rose from my seat.
4. The raccoon escaped from its cage.
   It chewed through metal bars.
5. We were encouraged by Ida's success.
   We decided to try trout fishing.
6. She read the news over the radio this morning.
   She spoke with an excited voice.
7. Mozart wrote musical compositions at the age of five.
   He astounded his family.
8. I spilled ink onto my best pair of jeans.
   I had leaned over my desk.
9. The moped weaved between parked cars.
   It barely missed a small child.
10. A team of scientists entered the pyramid's secret chamber.
    They sought pottery and other relics.

11c. Combine short, related sentences by using appositive phrases.

Appositive phrases (see page 441) are useful for explaining or identifying nouns or pronouns. The following sentence contains an appositive phrase in boldfaced type.

EXAMPLE   Inez Mexia, **a famous botanist,** explored the jungles of Brazil.

Two related sentences can be combined by using an appositive phrase.

TWO SENTENCES   Dr. Stone is my teacher at medical school.
She is the author of several books.

ONE SENTENCE   Dr. Stone, the author of several books, is my teacher at medical school.

EXERCISE 3. Combining Sentences by Using Appositive Phrases.   Combine each group of sentences by using an appositive phrase. Place the phrase next to the noun or pronoun it explains or modifies. Put commas at the beginning and end of each appositive phrase to set it off from the rest of the sentence.

EXAMPLE   1. Maggie L. Walker is honored at the Mary McLeod Bethune Museum.
She was one of the first woman bank presidents in our country.

1. *Maggie L. Walker, one of the first woman bank presidents in our country, is honored at the Mary McLeod Bethune Museum.*

1. Brenda Washington gave her report on Tuesday.
Tuesday was the last day of classes.
2. The race car belonging to Janet Guthrie was in the parking lot.
Janet Guthrie was a driver at the Indianapolis 500.
3. Soccer is gaining fans in the United States.
It is the most popular sport in the world.
4. As an explorer, Roald Amundsen was bold and courageous.
He became the first person to reach the South Pole by land.

5. *Roots* is the story of seven generations of one man's family.
   The book is an important contribution to American studies.
6. The Mayan kingdom covered most of Central America.
   The Mayan kingdom was a loose federation of cities.
7. Mystery Hill poses a riddle for archaeologists.
   It is a group of large stone buildings in New Hampshire.
8. Witchcraft is often associated with the site's past.
   Witchcraft is another name for sorcery.
9. Ellen Goodman's newspaper column won the Pulitzer Prize.
   It is the highest award given to journalists.
10. My cousin broke his ankle during a ski-jumping competition.
    He is an inexperienced skier.

11d. Combine short, related sentences by using compound subjects and verbs.

The subjects in a compound subject, like the verbs in a compound verb, are joined by conjunctions such as *and, but,* or *or* and by correlative conjunctions such as *neither—nor, either—or,* and *both—and* (see pages 389–90).

EXAMPLES   **Both** Nancy Lopez **and** Tracy Austin began their sports careers at a young age.
              The soldiers **neither** ate **nor** rested during the long march.

To combine short sentences by using a compound subject, look for sentences with the same verb but different subjects.

TWO SENTENCES   Maria wrote a long story about family life.
                 Leonard wrote one, too.

ONE SENTENCE   Maria and Leonard wrote long stories about family life.

To combine sentences by using a compound verb, look for sentences with the same subject but different verbs.

TWO SENTENCES   The yellow blossoms appear in late April.
                 They last until the middle of May.

ONE SENTENCE   The yellow blos̲s̲oms a̲ppear in late April and
last until the middle of May.

A combined sentence may have both a compound subject and
a compound verb.

THREE SENTENCES   The secr̲etary t̲yped the letter.
The treas̲urer a̲lso t̲yped letters.
They both a̲ddressed envelopes.

ONE SENTENCE   The secr̲etary and the treas̲urer t̲yped
letters and addressed envelopes.

EXERCISE 4. Combining Sentences by Using Compound Subjects and Compound Verbs.
Combine the following groups of sentences into one sentence by using compound subjects and verbs. There may be more than one correct way to combine the sentences. In the combined sentences, be sure the subjects and verbs agree in number.

EXAMPLE   1. A slight rise in temperature will not be noticed.
A slight drop in temperature will not be noticed
either.

1. *Neither a slight rise nor a slight drop in
temperature will be noticed.*

1. The lifeguard was not able to see the stranded swimmer.
The sunbathers on the beach also could not see the swimmer.
2. What Jeremy said was important.
How he said it was also important.
3. The guard had turned away.
He did not notice the general approaching.
4. Mary Lou Retton finished her gymnastics routine.
She awaited the results from the judges.
5. While I was there, I did not glimpse any of the birds.
I did not hear any of the birds either.

11e. Combine short, related sentences by writing a compound sentence.

A compound sentence (see page 463) is really two or more simple sentences joined together by one of the conjunctions *and, but, or, for, nor, so,* or *yet.*

EXAMPLE   The sandbags were piled high along the river, **yet** the flood waters crashed through the fortifications with ease.

When writing a compound sentence, be sure the ideas you connect are related and equal in importance.

UNRELATED IDEAS   The helicopter safely rescued the mountain climbers.
The mountain was in California.

RELATED IDEAS   The helicopter safely rescued the mountain climbers.
Their perilous adventure was over.

UNEQUAL IDEAS   The national census is taken every ten years.
I was interviewed by a census taker.

EQUAL IDEAS   The national census is taken every ten years.
The results are tabulated by computer.

☞ **NOTE**   Use a comma before *and, but, or, nor, for, so,* and *yet* when they join independent clauses.

EXERCISE 5. Revising by Combining Sentences into a Compound Sentence.   Most of the following items consist of two or more closely related ideas. Combine these ideas into a single compound sentence, using *and, but, or, for, nor,* or *yet.* A few items contain unrelated or unequal ideas. In such cases, write *U* after the appropriate number on your paper.

1. Rainfall is scarce in desert regions.
   Some plants and wildlife can thrive in this arid climate.
2. A desert may receive no rain for several years.
   Then torrents of rain may fall in a few hours.

3. Desert plants cannot store this sudden flood of water.
   The desert soil cannot absorb it.
4. The rainfall quickly erodes the desert landscape.
   Deserts have highly varied landscapes.
5. After a rainfall, colorful flowers bloom in the desert.
   These plants live only a short time.
6. During dry periods, desert plants are widely scattered.
   Many of them store large amounts of water in their leaves, roots, or stems.
7. The stem of the barrel cactus bulges with water after a rainfall.
   The plant depends on this private water supply for its life.
8. Desert animals include many kinds of insects, spiders, reptiles, birds, and mammals.
   The camel is one example of a desert animal.
9. Desert conditions have not changed for thousands of years.
   The size of deserts has grown considerably in recent centuries.
10. Trees have been planted to prevent desert expansion.
    Destructive winds still cover fertile land with desert soil.

When combining equal ideas, you use a compound sentence. When combining unequal ideas, however, you should use a complex sentence.

11f. Combine short, choppy sentences into a complex sentence. Put one idea into a subordinate clause.

A complex sentence (see page 464) has an independent clause and at least one subordinate clause. ￼

(1) Use an adjective clause to combine sentences.

An adjective clause (see pages 452–53) is a subordinate clause that, like an adjective, modifies a noun or a pronoun. In the following example, the adjective clause is in boldfaced type.

EXAMPLE Eight of the planets **that orbit the sun** are named after Roman gods.

Adjective clauses begin with one of the relative pronouns—
who, whom, whose, which, or *that.* When two sentences are
closely related, they may be combined by using an adjective
clause.

TWO SENTENCES The belladonna plant is also called deadly
nightshade.
Brad brought this plant into the house.

ONE SENTENCE The belladonna plant that Brad brought into
the house is also called deadly nightshade.

**EXERCISE 6. Combining Sentences by Using Adjective
Clauses.** Combine each of the following groups of sentences
into one sentence by putting one of the ideas into an adjective
clause. In the combined sentence the adjective clause should be
placed as close as possible to the word it modifies.

EXAMPLES 1. He does not have "a right to his own opinion."
He knows nothing about the topic.
1. *He who knows nothing about the topic does not
have "a right to his own opinion."*
2. The test covered yesterday's assignment.
I did well on it.
2. *I did well on the test that covered yesterday's
assignment.*

1. The student enjoys practical jokes.
She put pepper on my popcorn.
2. The player stole second base.
He was covered with dust.
3. The horse once belonged to my grandmother.
It has a broken leg.
4. The dress is too large for me.
It may fit Marian.
5. Manuel drove the new red station wagon.
The car led the parade.
6. I liked the sketches by the artist.
She lives next door.

7. I stumbled over the shovel.
   It was lying on the sidewalk.
8. My parents paid over a hundred dollars for a chair.
   It was once owned by the first governor of the state.
9. At the zoo a monkey lost its temper.
   It began throwing rocks at us.
10. The tall man coaches our football team.
    I introduced him to you at the picnic.

(2) Use an adverb clause to combine sentences.

An adverb clause (see pages 455–56) is a subordinate clause that, like an adverb, modifies a verb, adjective, or adverb.

EXAMPLE   **After she had seen the terrible effects of slavery,**
            Harriet Beecher Stowe wrote *Uncle Tom's Cabin.*

Adverb clauses, like adverbs, may tell *when, how, where, to what extent,* or *under what condition* an action is done. An adverb clause begins with a subordinating conjunction. Study the following list:

Common Subordinating Conjunctions

after	before	than	whenever
although	if	unless	where
as	since	until	wherever
because	so that	when	while

When you combine two short sentences by turning one of them into an adverb clause, be careful to choose the correct subordinating conjunction. Because a subordinating conjunction shows the relationship between clauses, a poorly chosen conjunction will show a false or meaningless relationship. For example, a number of subordinating conjunctions could be used to join the two sentences in the following example, but not all of them would show a relationship that makes sense.

TWO SENTENCES   The alarm rings.
                  I leap out of bed.

FALSE RELATIONSHIP   Until the alarm rings, I leap out of bed.

CLEAR   When the alarm rings, I leap out of bed.

☞ **NOTE** A comma sets off an introductory adverb clause.

EXERCISE 7. Combining Sentences by Using an Adverb Clause.

Combine each of the following groups of sentences into a single complex sentence by changing the sentence in italics into an adverb clause. Refer to the list of subordinating conjunctions on page 324. Add commas where they are necessary.

EXAMPLE   1. *I can begin my sketch.*
I must sharpen all my pencils.

1. *Before I can begin my sketch, I must sharpen all my pencils.*

1. *I visit the city.*
I like to see a play.
2. I found my glasses.
I had looked for them all morning.
3. Michael hasn't spoken with Jeannie.
She made the soccer team.
4. *We were at the movies.*
Someone ran into our parked car.
5. *Rachel filled out the job application carefully.*
She was interviewed immediately.
6. *Carlos canceled his subscription.*
He still receives the magazine by mail.
7. Vicky collects shells.
She can find them.
8. *The weather turned cold.*
The pond froze.
9. You must register.
You will be able to vote.

10. I learn something new.
    I open this dictionary.

REVIEW EXERCISE A. Revising by Combining Sentences.
Combine each of the following groups of sentences into one
sentence by using various sentence-combining techniques. Add
commas where they are necessary. There may be more than one
way to combine the sentences.

EXAMPLE 1. Cora climbed up the hillside.
             She edged forward quietly and stealthily.
             She moved toward the spot.
             She had seen the gorilla there.
          1. *Climbing up the hillside, Cora quietly and steal-*
             thily edged toward the spot where she had seen
             the gorilla.

1. The door swung open.
   We wheeled around.
   We saw Mr. Cates.
   He lumbered into the room.
2. We saw Hilda.
   She was taking photographs.
   She was by the lake.
   She had her camera focused on a flock of geese.
3. My dog grew impatient.
   He yowled at me.
   He wanted to go for a walk.
   It was not yet time.
4. Doctors use a stethoscope.
   With it they listen to the heart.
   They also listen to the lungs.
5. Hilary looked calmly over at the jury.
   She picked up the letter.
   She said the letter could prove her client's innocence.

(3) Use a noun clause to combine sentences.

A noun clause is a subordinate clause used as a noun.

Noun clauses (see pages 458–59) are usually introduced by *that,
how, what, whatever, who, whoever, whom,* or *whomever.*

EXAMPLE   The scientists agreed **that the sun offered a huge
supply of energy.**

Two sentences can combine with a noun clause.

TWO SENTENCES   Something puzzles me.
I don't know how the burglar broke the lock.

ONE SENTENCE   How the burglar broke the lock puzzles me.

**EXERCISE 8. Combining Sentences by Using a Noun
Clause.**   Combine each of the following groups of sentences
by turning the italicized sentence into a noun clause.

1. *The road to Palo Alto was closed for repairs.*
Pedro did not know this fact.
2. *He told us.*
It was not what we expected to hear.
3. *The boat somehow capsized in calm water.*
The mystery remains.
4. *There was a time to keep quiet.*
The soldier knew.
5. *Someone wore my coat.*
Someone will pay the dry-cleaning bill.

REVIEW EXERCISE B. Revising by Combining Sentences.
Combine each of the following groups of sentences into one
smooth, clear sentence by using the sentence-combining techniques you have learned. Do not change the meaning of the
sentences you combine. Add commas where they are necessary.

1. My hobby is photography.
I took an unusual picture.
It is a picture of the stars.
In this picture, the stars are long white streaks.

2. I worked hours to get this effect.
   I propped the camera in my backyard.
   Then I set the time exposure.
   Hours later, I closed the shutter.
3. My sister graduated from high school last year.
   She has started college.
   She is taking science courses.
   She wants to enter medical school.
4. The bicycling road trip was scheduled for September.
   It has been postponed.
   The newspaper reported the postponement.
   The trip will be rescheduled soon.
5. Wendy was running in the marathon this afternoon.
   She passed two people wearing roller skates.
   They were also entered in the race.
   They were probably disqualified.

REVIEW EXERCISE C. Revising a Paragraph by Combining Sentences. Revise and rewrite the paragraph by combining sentences to create clear, varied sentences. Be careful not to change the meaning of the original paragraph. Add commas where they are necessary.

> The North Pole is one of the most remote areas on the earth. The South Pole is too. They are different from one another. The difference is dramatic. The North Pole is covered by an ocean. The South Pole is within a frozen land. The polar region in the North is inhabited. It has been the home of Eskimo peoples for millennia. The Antarctic is still largely uninhabited. It was an unknown region until two centuries ago. The climate of Antarctica is harsh. It is many degrees colder than the Arctic.

REVIEW EXERCISE D. Revising a Paragraph by Combining Sentences. Revise and rewrite the following paragraph to eliminate choppy sentences. Be careful not to change the meaning of the original paragraph. Add commas where they are necessary.

American voters do not vote directly for the President. This is according to the Constitution. They vote for people called electors. These people cast the official vote for the President. Electors' names may appear on ballots. Then again, they may not appear on the ballots. The ballots are presented to voters on Election Day. Election Day is in November. Electors gather in each state capital. They gather early in December. Their votes are sent to the U.S. Senate. They are sent immediately. The votes are counted. This is official. One of the candidates is declared President. It is the candidate who receives a majority of electoral votes.

AVOIDING STRINGY SENTENCES

An occasional long sentence is good; it characterizes a mature style, and it adds both smoothness and variety to your compositions. Stringy sentences, however, in which main clauses are monotonously strung together with *and, but, for, or, nor,* should be avoided. To correct the stringy sentences in your compositions, use subordinating conjunctions (see page 324), compound verbs, and verbals.

STRINGY   Cleveland caught the pass, and he ran twenty-two yards, and so he made a first down.

BETTER   **After** he had caught the pass, Cleveland ran twenty-two yards, **making** a first down.

STRINGY   Marc went to the board, and he drew a map, but his directions were still not clear to the class.

BETTER   **Although** Marc went to the board and drew a map, his directions were still not clear to the class.

Sometimes it is better to break a long, stringy sentence into two or more sentences.

STRINGY   I read the assignment, and then I began making notes on cards, for I wanted to memorize the main points in the lesson, but the bell rang, and I was not through, and so I had to carry my heavy book home.

BETTER   **After reading the assignment,** I began making notes on cards **so that** I could memorize the main points in the lesson. **Since I was not through when the bell rang,** I had to carry my heavy book home.

EXERCISE 9. Revising Stringy Sentences.   Revise the following stringy sentences by using subordinating conjunctions, compound verbs, and verbals. Some of the very long sentences should be made into two or more sentences.

1. An accident occurred at the busy intersection, and several persons were injured, and then the police decided to put up a traffic light.
2. Small children may swallow a dozen aspirins, or they may wander out into the street, for they are too young to think for themselves, and adults must make decisions for them.
3. Fever is usually the first sign of measles, and the eyes soon grow red, or the eyelids swell, and later the sneezing and coughing make a person think that it's merely a cold.
4. The trouble with New Year's resolutions is that they are always broken, for people make too many of them, or they hope for impossible reform, and they often try to become perfect all at once.
5. We are all creatures of habit, and bad habits are hard to break, but a person can make one resolution a year, and can concentrate on that one aim, and then is able to keep it.

VARYING SENTENCE BEGINNINGS

Although sentences which have the subject first may be grammatically correct, too many of them in one paragraph are monotonous. To avoid this common cause of dullness in writing, vary the beginnings of your sentences.

11g. Vary the beginnings of your sentences.

Read the following paragraph, an example of monotonous writing in which every sentence begins with the subject.

I have now found a solution to my crying problems when I peel strong onions. I read a magazine article entitled "Onions Without Tears." Seven persons, according to this article, once tested ways to peel onions without weeping. These guinea pigs, after making various experiments, discarded two popular but useless theories. Chewing buttered bread did not stop tears. Keeping an ice cube inside one's closed mouth did not help, either. The testers found other ways of helping to avoid watery eyes. The first one was keeping a bread slice between the teeth. Another way was using an electric fan to blow away onion fumes. All experimenters, however, agreed that there are only two really effective ways to peel an onion without crying. You can shut your nose with the same kind of clip that swimmers sometimes use. You can talk or sing to keep your mouth open. I may try my own method. I will get a songbook and a swimmer's noseclip and give them to a friend. I will then ask my friend to peel the onions.

As you see, too many subject-first sentences in the paragraph lessen the effectiveness of the ideas presented. Notice the varied beginnings of sentences in a revision of the same paragraph.

Now I have found a solution to my crying problems when I peel strong onions. According to a magazine article entitled "Onions Without Tears," seven persons once tested ways to slice onions without weeping. *After making various experiments,* these guinea pigs discarded two popular but useless theories. *Neither* chewing buttered bread *nor* keeping an ice cube inside one's closed mouth helped to stop tears. The testers found other ways of helping to avoid watery eyes: by keeping a bread slice between the teeth, or by using an electric fan to blow away onion fumes. However, all the experimenters agreed that there are only two really effective ways to peel an onion without crying: shutting your nose and keeping your mouth open. *First,* to shut your nose, you can use a swimmer's noseclip. *Second,* to keep your mouth open, you can talk or sing. *Although I may try these ways,* I will first try my own method. I will give a friend a songbook and a swimmer's noseclip and ask my friend to peel the onions.

As this paragraph shows, there are many ways to begin sentences. Instead of putting the subject first in every sentence, you can vary your style by starting with a modifying word, phrase, or clause.

(1) You may begin sentences with single-word modifiers.

Learn to use adjectives, adverbs, and participles at the beginnings of sentences.

ADJECTIVES **Angry,** the umpire turned his back.
     Dark and **empty,** the house looked very different from the way I remembered it.
     Informal and **friendly,** she put everyone at ease.

ADVERBS **Soon** her cold glances reached the freezing point.
    Unfortunately, Aunt Eloise did not preheat the oven.

PARTICIPLES **Sighing,** Adam shoved the spinach aside.
     Delighted, the squirrel grabbed the nut and bounded away to bury it.

EXERCISE 10. Revising Sentences by Using Introductory Single-Word Modifiers. The following sentences, all of which begin with the subject, contain a modifier that can be placed at the beginning of the sentence. Revise each sentence, placing the modifier at the beginning of the sentence.

1. The league leaders, unbeaten and untied, expected little trouble from our team.
2. My dog, wet and dirty, jumped onto the couch.
3. Mrs. Bermudez' fingers impatiently drummed on the desk.
4. The ghost appeared to Hamlet again.
5. Wilbur, stumbling, bumped into a passer-by.

EXERCISE 11. Writing Sentences That Begin with Single-Word Modifiers. Use the following modifiers to begin sentences of your own.

1. often	4. bewildered
2. hurriedly	5. hungry and cold
3. whispering	

(2) You may begin sentences with phrases.

Another good way to achieve sentence variety is to place prepositional, participial, or infinitive phrases at the beginning of sentences.

PREPOSITIONAL PHRASES **On the other side of the island,** there is a fine natural harbor.
Behind Helga and me stood Mr. Soames, the night guard.

PARTICIPIAL PHRASES **Blowing in the breeze,** the laundry was a mixture of bright colors.
Turned to stone by Zeus, Niobe continued to shed tears.

INFINITIVE PHRASES **To be polite,** I chuckled at her jokes.
To determine the age of the mummy, the scientists tried various chemical tests.

EXERCISE 12. Revising Sentences by Using Introductory Phrase Modifiers. Revise each of the following sentences by placing the modifying phrase at the beginning. (Remember that a modifying phrase used as an adjective should be placed as close as possible to the word it modifies.)

1. We should eat a well-balanced variety of foods, for the sake of our health.
2. The dog, frightened by the storm, cowered under the sofa.
3. The exterminators bored holes through the cement and poured poison beneath the porch to kill the termites.
4. The whole episode, to tell the truth, was a hoax.
5. The fog along the highway looks like ghosts prowling in the darkness, in the Smoky Mountains about midnight.

EXERCISE 13. Writing Sentences That Begin with Modifying Phrases. Use the following phrases to begin sentences of your own. After each sentence, name the kind of phrase with which it begins.

1. After fourteen rainy days
2. Dripping from head to toe
3. To annoy me
4. Sounding like a moose
5. In the middle of the garden

(3) You may begin sentences with subordinate clauses.

EXAMPLES   **After we had explored the dark cave for two hours,** we longed for the return to sunlight.
     While the clerk waited patiently, Sheila and Lynn carefully read the list of ingredients on the cereal package.
     If the cloud cover remains, temperatures over the state will be higher than predicted.

EXERCISE 14. Revising Sentences by Using Introductory Subordinate Clauses. The five simple sentences in this exercise begin with the subject. Using the examples above as a guide, add an introductory subordinate clause that is related to the main idea. Place a comma after each one of your introductory clauses. (You may find the list of subordinating conjunctions on page 324 helpful.)

1. Milton always tried to do the right thing.
2. She could see the finish line ahead of her.
3. He obviously did not remember my name.
4. We could not answer the riddle.
5. The motor ran out of fuel.

REVIEW EXERCISE E. Revising Sentences by Using Introductory Words, Phrases, or Clauses. Revise each of the following sentences, changing the beginning as directed.

Begin these sentences with single-word modifiers.

1. We finally reached the Tennessee River basin.
2. As we drove along the Tennessee River, we often saw dams and large reservoirs.
3. There is less soil erosion in this region nowadays.
4. The Tennessee Valley Authority has certainly made many improvements.
5. Our family, vacationing, saw many other points of interest in the South.

Begin these sentences with modifying phrases.

6. Some Eskimos live in igloos during the winter.
7. They hunt wild game to provide food for themselves.
8. Eskimos need warm clothing for the cold climate.
9. Eskimos use the hide of a walrus for making shoes.
10. The people in the Sahara, unlike the Eskimos, have no difficulty keeping warm.
11. The Arabs wear flowing garments to protect themselves from the hot wind and sun.
12. The Arabian nomads move about from place to place, seeking water and grass for their sheep and camels.
13. They use light, movable tents for shelter.

Begin each of the following sentences with a subordinate clause.

14. There are many coffee plantations in Brazil, because the mild climate is ideal for growing coffee.
15. The coffee thrives when heavy rains fall during the winter months.
16. Harvesting begins when the golden berries fall from the trees in May.
17. The harvest will be a good one if heavy rains have not damaged the blossoms in September.
18. A long process of washing and drying is necessary before the coffee beans are ready to sell.

19. Trains haul tons of coffee to market after the workers have dried the beans for two months.
20. These crops bring prosperity to Brazil because coffee is sold in countries around the world.

REVIEW EXERCISE F. Revising Sentences by Using Introductory Words, Phrases, or Clauses. In the following paragraph, every sentence begins with the subject. Numbering your sentences, revise them to demonstrate what you have learned about varying the beginnings of sentences. Use single-word modifiers, phrases, and clauses.

1. I overheard my parents one night when I was about six years old as they talked about a prowler in our neighborhood. 2. I was awakened later by the crunch of footsteps on the gravel driveway outside my window. 3. Someone was standing in the driveway and looking at our house. 4. My voice failed me completely for a few seconds. 5. My scream, when it finally came, could have been heard a mile away. 6. The person outside, probably startled by my scream, had disappeared. 7. The front door suddenly slammed, and my father dashed into the room. 8. He had remembered, just before going to bed, an important letter that he had forgotten to mail. 9. He had gone out to the mailbox down the block to mail it. 10. My prowler had obviously been my father.

VARYING SENTENCE STRUCTURE

Another cause of sentence dullness is lack of variety in the kinds of sentences in a paragraph. Too many sentences of the same structure can make your style monotonous.

11h. Vary the kinds of sentences you write.

Study the following pairs of sentences. The first sentence in each pair is compound. The second sentence is complex. (See pages 464–65.) Notice that in the second sentence the relationship between ideas is clearer than in the first sentence. (The subordinate clauses are in boldfaced type.)

We visited the Old North Church in Boston, and we went to see the Bunker Hill Monument.

After we had visited the Old North Church in Boston, we went to see the Bunker Hill Monument. [The introductory subordinate clause tells *when* the visit to Bunker Hill was made.]

I saw a woman running across the field, and she later proved to be an Olympic track star.

The woman **whom I saw running across the field** later proved to be an Olympic track star. [The subordinate clause tells *which* woman.]

EXERCISE 15. Revising by Combining Compound Sentences into a Complex Sentence.

Change each of the following compound sentences to a complex sentence. Relate the ideas in each part of the sentence by using the subordinating conjunction or relative pronoun given in parentheses.

EXAMPLE   1. The frightened best man had unexpectedly run out of the church; an altar boy was asked to take his place. (after)

1. *After the frightened best man had unexpectedly run out of the church, an altar boy was asked to take his place.*

1. Louise plays the piano beautifully, and so we will ask her to entertain at our party. (who)
2. The school bus suddenly slowed down, and we saw the roadblock. (when)
3. My cut hand was not healing properly, and so I finally saw a doctor. (because)
4. Charlene had studied the spelling list for thirty minutes, but she continued to examine the words. (although)
5. We harbor ill will, and it usually grows and becomes a troublesome grudge. (if)

6. The neighborhood children play soccer at my house, but they are careful about the lawn and the flowers. (who)
7. We put antifreeze into the radiator of our car, and the first cold wave struck. (before)
8. In the library, Kathryn was reliving joyous events of the summer; she sat with her elbows propped on her open history book. (as)
9. We saw the teacher approaching; we stopped talking and started studying. (as soon as)
10. I enjoy having a room of my own, and I try hard to take care of it. (since)

EXERCISE 16. Revising Sentences for Variety in a Paragraph. Revise the following paragraph, which consists mainly of simple and compound sentences. To vary the style, change or combine some of the sentences into complex sentences using both adjective and adverb clauses. Do not, however, make all of the sentences complex, since your purpose is to achieve variety.

The music and thump of the drums grew louder, and the people lined up along the streets. In another minute, the high-school band would come around the corner. Finally, with a blast of brass, the band emerged from behind the buildings. The drum major raised her feet high and proudly as she marched. She was followed by the musicians. Each of them was wearing a red jacket. The band led the parade of colorful floats. Cheers and applause came from the crowd. Every child stood watching with shining eyes. Each one dreamed of being in the high-school band someday.

PART THREE

TOOLS FOR WRITING AND REVISING:

Grammar ▪ Usage ▪ Mechanics

CHAPTER 12

The Parts of Speech

THE WORK THAT WORDS DO

Every word you speak or write has a definite use in expressing a thought or idea. The way the word is used determines what *part of speech* that word is. There are eight parts of speech:

nouns	verbs	conjunctions
pronouns	adverbs	interjections
adjectives	prepositions	

DIAGNOSTIC TEST

Identifying Parts of Speech. Number your paper 1–20. After each number, write the part of speech of the italicized word that comes after that number in the following paragraph.

EXAMPLE Everyone (1) *has* favorite summer (2) *places*.
1. *verb*
2. *noun*

For (1) *me,* (2) *nothing* is (3) *better* than a trip to the beach. A (4) *hot,* sunny day, when the sand (5) *burns* my feet, is (6) *perfect* (7) *for* acquiring a (8) *tan*. I can run (9) *through* the frothing surf and later sit under a beach umbrella. I (10) *enjoy* being with friends, (11) *but* I also like to be at the beach by (12) *myself*. Even with (13) *people* around me, I (14) *feel* free and able to think my (15) *own* thoughts. At those times I can walk (16) *slowly* at the shore's edge, examining all (17) *that* the sea has washed up. If I accidentally step on a (18) *jellyfish*, I try not to cry (19) *"Ouch!"* as my foot stings. From then on, I walk (20) *more* carefully.

THE NOUN

Perhaps the words most frequently used are those that identify someone or something. These name words are called *nouns*.

12a. A *noun* is a word used to name a person, place, thing, or idea.

Persons	Sharon, Captain Brown, hair stylist, swimmers
Places	Iowa, Mexico City, Mars, Antarctica, library
Things	leaf, cartoon, toothpick, rocket, merry-go-round
Ideas	peace, excellence, truth, justice, equality, honesty

Common and Proper Nouns

There are two classes of nouns, *proper nouns* and *common nouns*. A proper noun names a particular person, place, or thing, and is always capitalized. A common noun names any one of a group of persons, places, or things and is not capitalized.

COMMON NOUNS	PROPER NOUNS
scientist	Madame Curie, Carl Sagan
female	Coretta King, Rita Moreno, Maria Tallchief
city	Cairo, St. Louis, Paris
building	World Trade Center, Buckingham Palace

GRAMMAR

continent	North America, South America, Africa
mountains	Rockies, Alps, Blue Ridge Mountains
day	Monday, Thursday, Sunday

Another way of classifying nouns is to identify them as *concrete* or *abstract*. A concrete noun names an object that can be perceived by the senses: *cloud, thunder, rose.* An abstract noun names an idea, a quality, a characteristic: *freedom, beauty, kindness.*

EXERCISE 1. Identifying and Classifying Nouns. There are twenty-five nouns in the following paragraph. As you write the nouns on your paper, circle all the proper nouns. A name is counted as one noun even if it has more than one part.

1. Many useful and amusing words came into our language during World War II. **2.** Now they are known to most Americans. **3.** One of these odd words is *gremlin.* **4.** During the war, fliers were often troubled by mysterious mechanical failures and malfunctions. **5.** Not knowing what caused these problems, they joked that gremlins—small, mischievous creatures—were in the aircraft. **6.** These gremlins could be helpful as well. **7.** Many fliers claimed they had miraculously escaped danger only because the gremlins had come to their aid. **8.** Artists drew the imps as little men with beards and top hats who played all over the plane.

EXERCISE 2. Classifying Nouns. Write the following nouns. Identify each as a common or a proper noun below. If the noun is proper, name a corresponding common noun. Remember that capitalization is one of the signals of a proper noun.

1. woman	6. city	11. Mt. Fuji	16. airport
2. month	7. park	12. Dallas	17. cousin
3. Peru	8. movie	13. Kansas	18. automobile
4. singer	9. Ohio	14. street	19. river
5. Athena	10. ocean	15. Mrs. Smith	20. team

WRITING APPLICATION A:
Using Proper Nouns to Make Your Writing Specific

When you use proper nouns instead of common nouns, you often give your reader more information. Which sentence below gives more information about what is happening?

He entered the building in that city.
Jeff Hines entered **Carnegie Hall** in **New York City.**

Writing Assignment

You have won an all-expenses-paid vacation to four places you select. Write a daily record of your trip, using at least eight proper nouns to make your writing specific. Underline the proper nouns.

Compound Nouns

Two or more words may be used together as a single noun. In the examples below rule 12a on page 342, you find *hair stylist* and *Captain Brown* in the list of persons, *Mexico City* in the list of places, and *toothpick* and *merry-go-round* in the list of things. These word groups are called *compound nouns.*

The parts of a compound noun may be written as one word, as two or more words, or as a hyphenated word. Here are some other commonly used compound nouns.

EXAMPLES   volleyball, newsstand, news room, cold front,
sister-in-law, push-up, Stratford-on-Avon

If you are in doubt as to how to write a compound noun, you should consult your dictionary. Some dictionaries may give two correct forms for a word; for example, you may find the word *vice-president* written both with and without the hyphen. As a rule, use the form the dictionary lists first.

EXERCISE 3. Identifying Compound Nouns.   Write the compound noun(s) in each of the following sentences. You may use a dictionary.

GRAMMAR

EXAMPLE   1. Our baby sitter is dependable.
           1. *baby sitter*

1. I use a word processor or a typewriter in class.
2. At Jones Beach, we swam in the swimming pool.
3. My brother-in-law lives in Council Bluffs, Iowa.
4. My Old English sheepdog is still a puppy.
5. Please return these books to the bookshelves.
6. I have added computer science to my schedule of courses.
7. Dr. Reilly's waiting room is always crowded.
8. Meet me at the bowling alley near the post office.
9. The fountain pen is now less popular than the ball point.
10. Pat's shoelace came undone during the final race at the meet.

THE PRONOUN

12b. A *pronoun* is a word used in place of a noun or of more than one noun.

One way to refer to something is to use the noun that names it. You usually have to do this to make clear what you mean. However, once you have made clear the identity of the person, place, or thing you are talking about, you can make other references without having to give the name each time.

EXAMPLE   Gloria stepped back from the picture and looked at **it** carefully.

It would be awkward and unnecessary to repeat *the picture* in the last part of this sentence. The pronoun *it* does the job better by simply taking the place of the noun *picture.*

In the following sentences a number of different pronouns are used. Notice that they all take the place of a noun the way *it* does in the example above.

EXAMPLES   Where is Lois? **She** said **she** would be here on time.
            [The pronoun *she,* used twice, takes the place of

Lois in the second sentence.] Our teacher and Mrs. Barnes said **they** would go to the meeting. [The pronoun *they* takes the place of two nouns: *teacher* and *Mrs. Barnes.*]

As these examples show, pronouns almost always refer to a word mentioned earlier. This noun on which the pronoun depends for its meaning is called the *antecedent,* which means "something going before." In the following examples the arrows point from the pronouns to their antecedents.

EXAMPLES   Jill opened her **book** and read from **it.**

The coach showed the **players** how **they** should throw the ball.

Janet took **her** dog to the veterinarian.

Personal Pronouns

The pronouns that have appeared in the examples so far are called *personal* pronouns. In this use, *personal* refers to one of the three possible ways of making statements: The persons speaking can talk about themselves (first person: *I, we*), or they can talk to one person or many (second person: *you*), or they can talk about anyone or anything else (third person: *he, she, it, they*). The few pronouns in English that have different forms to show person are called *personal pronouns.*

Personal Pronouns

	SINGULAR	PLURAL
First person (the person speaking)	I, my,[1] mine, me	we, our, ours, us
Second person (the person spoken to)	you, your, yours	you, your, yours

[1] The possessive forms *my, your, her* etc., are called pronouns in this book. (See page 350.)

Third person
(some other person
or thing spoken
about)

he, his, him,
she, her, hers,
it, its

they, their,
theirs, them

Other Commonly Used Pronouns

Here are other kinds of pronouns you will use in your writing:

REFLEXIVE PRONOUNS (the *-self, -selves* forms of the personal pronouns)

myself

ourselves

yourself

yourselves

himself, herself, itself

themselves

☞ **NOTE** For standard speaking and writing, do not use *hisself* or *theirselves*.

RELATIVE PRONOUNS (used to introduce adjective clauses; see pages 452–53)

who   whom   whose   which   that

INTERROGATIVE PRONOUNS (used in questions)

Who . . .?   Whose . . .?   What . . .?
Whom . . .?   Which . . .?

DEMONSTRATIVE PRONOUNS (used to point out a specific person or thing)

this   that   these   those

INDEFINITE PRONOUNS (not referring to a definite person or thing; frequently used without antecedents)

all	anything	everyone	most
another	both	everything	much
any	each	few	neither
anybody	either	many	nobody
anyone	everybody	more	none

no one	other	some	someone
one	several	somebody	

EXERCISE 4. Identifying Pronouns. Number your paper 1–25. Write in order the twenty-five pronouns in the following paragraph.

Do you remember how you found out there was no Santa Claus? My memory of the scene is as clear as if it happened yesterday. Our holiday tradition included a visit from Santa himself, who joined the family in the living room shortly after midnight. My sisters and I were always cautioned not to leave the living room or even peek out to get an advance view. Santa would be displeased if he met any of us in the hall or in another of the rooms in the apartment. On the night of my discovery, I risked a little snooping. As I stole back to my sisters in the living room, whom did I see in the kitchen but Uncle Jim, adjusting a Santa beard. No one seemed to notice me. A little while later, Santa rushed into the living room, where everyone waited expectantly. Santa greeted each by name, distributed gifts to all, and gave me a knowing wink and a big hug.

EXERCISE 5. Writing Appropriate Pronouns. Write the following paragraph, filling in the twenty blanks with appropriate pronouns. Underline each pronoun you insert.

My main pleasure in reading mystery stories is the effect —— have on —— imagination. What different lives —— live in —— of ——! Sometimes an author chooses to set a story in a genteel English country estate. —— am disguised as a guest. The days are leisurely; servants attend to —— of —— needs. —— of —— companions, also guests, know that —— am stalking the —— of —— —— is a thief. At other times a mystery writer will place —— in an espionage ring. Then, —— is sinister; —— can be trusted; —— can happen. Every move counts in a spy story. Of course, —— always catch the thief, outwit the spies, and live on to enjoy —— next fantasy lifestyle.

GRAMMAR

WRITING APPLICATION B:
Using Pronouns to Make Your Writing Clear

Using pronouns helps you avoid repeating the same nouns over and over. First, however, you must clearly identify the person, place, or thing you are writing about. Otherwise, your story will become thoroughly confusing as in the example below.

> During the discussion of their surprise party for Terry, Marilyn, Jenny, and Andrea decided who would do which jobs. She decided that she would buy the ice cream and the gift. She said she would plan the decorations. Finally, since she could letter neatly, she would make the invitations and a big sign that said "Happy Birthday." The problem was that none of them knew how to bake the cake.

Writing Assignment

A meeting has been called to plan a big Valentine's Day party or dance. You are the secretary. On the committee are class officers, teachers, and the members of the Special Events Committee. Write the minutes of the meeting, imagining that at least four items were discussed: the time and place, the decorations, the food, and the dress. Be sure to tell exactly who made what suggestions without needlessly repeating nouns.

THE ADJECTIVE

You may wish to describe, or make more definite, a noun or pronoun. You then *modify* the word by using an adjective.

12c. An *adjective* modifies a noun or a pronoun.

To *modify* a word means to describe the word or to make its meaning more definite. An adjective modifies a noun or a pronoun by answering one of these questions: *What kind? Which one? How many?* Notice how the boldfaced adjectives that follow answer these questions about the nouns modified.

WHAT KIND?	WHICH ONE?	HOW MANY?
gray sky	**that** girl	**five** fingers
old shoes	**next** day	**many** rivers
clever dog	**either** way	**fewer** hours
low price	**last** chance	**some** problems

Pronoun or Adjective?

Notice that in the phrases above, *that, either, many, fewer,* and *some*—words that may also be used as pronouns—are adjectives, because they modify the nouns in the phrases rather than take the place of the nouns.

The words *my, your, his, her, its, our,* and *their* are called pronouns throughout this book; they are the *possessive* forms of personal pronouns, showing ownership or relationship. Some teachers, however, prefer to think of these words as adjectives because they tell *Which one?* about nouns: *my* sister, *your* book, *our* team, *their* tents.

Nouns Used as Adjectives

Sometimes you will find nouns used as adjectives.

NOUNS	NOUNS USED AS ADJECTIVES
crisp **bacon**	**bacon** sandwich
blinding **snow**	**snow** sculpture
last **December**	**December** sale

Notice in the last example above that a proper noun, *December,* is used as an adjective. Following are some other proper nouns used as adjectives:

Texas chili	**Sioux** warrior
Jackson concert	**Brazil** nut
Maine coast	**Picasso** painting

GRAMMAR

When you find a noun used as an adjective, your teacher may prefer that you call it an adjective. If so, proper nouns used as adjectives will be called *proper adjectives*. Follow your teacher's directions in labeling nouns used as adjectives.

Articles

The most frequently used adjectives are *a, an,* and *the.* These words are usually called *articles*.

A and *an* are indefinite articles; they refer to one of a general group.

EXAMPLES   **A** girl won.
               An elephant escaped.
               This is **an** honor.

A is used before words beginning with a consonant sound; *an* is used before words beginning with a vowel sound. Notice in the third example above that *an* is used before a noun beginning with the consonant *h,* because the *h* in *honor* is not pronounced.

Honor is pronounced as if it began with a vowel. Remember that the *sound* of the noun, not the spelling, determines which indefinite article will be used.

The is a definite article. It indicates that the noun refers to someone or something in particular.

EXAMPLES   **The** girl won.
               The elephant escaped.
               The honor goes to her.

Adjectives in Sentences

In examples you have seen so far, the adjective comes before the noun it modifies. This is its usual position in a sentence.

Ms. Farrell tells **all** students that **good** workers will be given **special** privileges.

A **sweating, exhausted** runner crossed the line.

Sometimes, however, adjectives follow the word they modify.

A dog, **old** and **overweight,** snored in the sun.

Other words may separate an adjective from the noun or pronoun modified.

Beverly was **worried.** She felt **nervous** about the play.

Delighted by the news, he smiled broadly.

EXERCISE 6. Writing Appropriate Adjectives. Write the following sentences, filling in the blanks with adjectives. (Do not use articles.) Use adjectives that answer the questions *What kind? Which one? How many?* Draw an arrow from each adjective to the noun or pronoun it modifies.

1. My family visited the —— zoo on Sunday.
2. —— monkeys were chattering in their —— cages.
3. My sister heard the —— lion roaring and became —— .
4. She laughed, though, when she saw the —— birds with —— feathers on their heads.
5. The —— birds made —— squawks.
6. The seals, —— and —— , performed stunts.
7. The —— elephants appeared —— for our peanuts.
8. The bears were begging for food on their —— feet.
9. By —— afternoon the sky was becoming —— .
10. After a —— day, we arrived home —— and —— .

EXERCISE 7. Revising Sentences by Supplying Interesting Adjectives. The following sentences contain no adjectives, except for articles. Revise each sentence by supplying interesting adjectives to modify some of the nouns or pronouns. Underline the adjectives.

1. Our breakfast consisted of sausage, eggs, toast, and milk.
2. We watched the dancers' steps and movements, and we marveled at their costumes.

3. At Halloween we hear stories of cats, bats, witches, and goblins, all roaming through the night under the moon.
4. At Linda's party, the guests were served sandwiches, meatballs, salad, and, later, fruit and cheese.
5. Everybody at the party received a gift, such as stationery, jewelry, soap, or a book.

WRITING APPLICATION C:
Using Adjectives to Make Your Writing Exact

Your careful use of specific adjectives helps your reader picture what you are describing. You must use just the right adjectives, but not too many. Study the following sentences.

EXAMPLES 1. She wore a pair of jeans.
2. She wore a pair of faded, baggy jeans.
3. She wore a pair of faded, baggy, ugly, wrinkled jeans.

The first sentence does not give many clues. The third sentence rambles on and on. The second sentence seems about right.

Writing Assignment

Write ten sentences. In each sentence describe an item you would like to add to your wardrobe or to your possessions generally; tell why you want it. Carefully select no more than two adjectives for each item. Underline the adjectives. (Articles do not count.)

EXAMPLE I would like a *red, portable* cassette-recorder with earphones to use away from home.

REVIEW EXERCISE A. Identifying Nouns, Pronouns, and Adjectives. Write on your paper the italicized words in the following sentences. Before each word, write the number of its sentence; after the word, write whether it is a noun, a pronoun, or an adjective.

GRAMMAR

EXAMPLE 1. *This* article tells about Shakespeare's *life*.
　　　　　1. *This, adjective*
　　　　　1. *life, noun*

1. Most high-school *students* read at least one *play* by William Shakespeare.
2. *Shakespeare,* the most *famous* playwright of *all* time, was born in Stratford-on-Avon in 1564.
3. He was baptized in the *small* church at Stratford shortly after *his* birth.
4. *He* was buried in the *same* church.
5. On the stone above his grave, *you* can find an *inscription* placing a *curse* on *anyone* who moves his bones from that spot.
6. Out of *respect* for his wish or because of fear of his curse, *nobody* has disturbed the grave.
7. *This* explains why his body was never moved to Westminster Abbey, where many *other* famous *English* writers are buried.
8. Besides seeing the church, the visitor in *Stratford* can see the house in *which* Shakespeare was born.
9. At *one* time visitors could also see the *large* house that Shakespeare bought for *himself* and his *family*.
10. When he retired from the *theater* he lived there, and there he also died.

THE VERB

A noun or a pronoun, no matter how many modifiers it may have, cannot make a sentence. The noun or pronoun must act in some way, or something must be said about it. The part of speech that performs this function is the *verb*. Some verbs express action and some tell something about the subject.

12d. A *verb* is a word that expresses action or otherwise helps to make a statement.

Action Verbs

Words such as *do, come, go,* and *write* are action verbs. Sometimes action verbs express an action that cannot be seen: *believe, remember, know, think,* and *understand.*

EXERCISE 8. Writing Action Verbs. Write twenty action verbs, not including those listed above. Include and underline at least five verbs that express an action that cannot be seen.

There are two large classes of action verbs—transitive and intransitive. A verb is *transitive* when the action it expresses is directed toward a person or thing named in the sentence.

EXAMPLES   Neil **rang** the bell. [The action of the verb *rang* is directed toward *bell*. The verb is transitive.]
Tina **mailed** the package [The action of *mailed* is directed toward *package*. The verb is transitive.]

In these examples the action passes from the doer—the subject—to the receiver of the action. Words that receive the action of a transitive verb are called *objects.*

A verb is *intransitive* when it expresses action (or helps to make a statement) without reference to an object.[1] The following sentences contain intransitive verbs.

EXAMPLES   Last Saturday we **stayed** inside.
The children **laughed.**

The same verb may be transitive in one sentence and intransitive in another.

EXAMPLES   Marcie **studied** her notes. [transitive]
Marcie **studied** very late. [intransitive]
The poet **wrote** a sonnet. [transitive]
The poet **wrote** carefully. [intransitive]

EXERCISE 9. Classifying Verbs as Transitive or Intransitive. Number your paper 1–10. Write the verb of each sentence and label it *v.t.* for transitive or *v.i.* for intransitive.

[1] Like intransitive verbs, linking verbs (*be, seem, appear,* etc.) never take direct objects. (See pages 356–58.)

1. Carl Lewis won four Olympic gold medals.
2. Mr. Ling works for an import company in California.
3. Robert Hayden taught at the University of Michigan.
4. The scouts rescued the stranded campers from the island.
5. Even good friends sometimes disagree.
6. Pablo already went upstairs to study.
7. The architect I. M. Pei came to America from China.
8. April auditioned for the lead role.
9. In all the confusion, John forgot the tickets.
10. At the end of the month, we visited Niagara Falls.

Linking Verbs

Some verbs help to make a statement, not by expressing an action but by serving as a link between two words. These verbs, called *linking verbs* or *state-of-being verbs,* are intransitive verbs.

The most commonly used linking verbs are forms of the verb *be.* Learn the verbs in the following list:

be	shall be	should be
being	will be	would be
am	has been	can be
is	have been	could be
are	had been	should have been
was	shall have been	would have been
were	will have been	could have been

Any verb ending in *be* or *been* is a form of the verb *be.*

Here are some other frequently used linking verbs:

appear	grow	seem	stay
become	look	smell	taste
feel	remain	sound	turn

Notice in the following sentences how each verb is a link between some words on either side of it. The noun, pronoun, or adjective that follows the linking verb fills out or completes the meaning of the verb and refers to a noun or pronoun preceding the verb.

The answer **is** *three*. [answer = *three*]
Rhonda **will be** the captain. [Rhonda = captain]
The casserole **tasted** strange. [strange casserole]
The worker **looked** tired. [tired worker]

☞ **NOTE**   Many of the linking verbs listed can be used as
action (nonlinking) verbs as well.

The wet dog **smelled** horrible. [linking verb—horrible
dog]
The dog **smelled** the thawing roast. [action verb]
The motor **sounded** good. [linking verb—good motor]
The engineer **sounded** the horn. [action verb]

Even *be* is not always a linking verb. It is sometimes followed
by certain adverbs: I was *there*.[1] To be a linking verb, the verb
must be followed by a noun or pronoun that names the subject
or an adjective that describes it.

EXERCISE 10. Writing Appropriate Linking Verbs.   Write a
linking verb for each blank. Use a different verb for each sentence.

1. That building —— the
   new public library.
2. The car —— funny.
3. The moose —— huge.
4. She —— very nervous
   about the driving test.
5. Her garden —— dried
   and brown in the
   drought.
6. Let's hope the evening
   —— cool.
7. We can eat the raspber-
   ries when they —— red.
8. Burt —— grouchy early
   in the morning.
9. The soup —— too salty.
10. She —— healthy and
    full of vigor.

EXERCISE 11. Writing Sentences with Linking Verbs.   Using the linking verb given in italics, change each of the following
word groups to a sentence. Write the sentence on your paper
and underline the linked words.

[1] See pages 360–65 for a discussion of adverbs.

EXAMPLES 1. *grew*   the darker storm clouds
          1. *The storm clouds grew darker.*
          2. *is*   Judge Jennings, a fair person
          2. *Judge Jennings is a fair person.*

1. *became*   the tired players
2. *looked*   Edwin Moses, very relaxed
3. *smelled*   the slightly sour milk
4. *is*   Nell Carter, a good actress
5. *remained*   the unsold property
6. *tasted*   the unripe berries
7. *could be*   real sea serpents
8. *seemed*   the impossible explanation
9. *appeared*   the fully recovered patient
10. *might have been*   the tall woman, the basketball coach

WRITING APPLICATION D:
Using Precise Verbs to Make Your Writing Lively

Giving a little extra thought to the verbs you select gives your writing a special lively interest that it might not otherwise have. Instead of writing the first thing that comes into your mind, look for a particularly appropriate verb. Note the differences that more precise verbs make in the following sentences.

    1. After the kickoff he **ran** down the field.
    1. After the kickoff he **sprinted** down the field.
    2. She **climbed** out of the burning car.
    2. She **clambered** out of the burning car.

Writing Assignment

Picture yourself as your country's only hope for a gold medal in the Olympics. Describe your winning event in detail. Include at least ten especially precise verbs. Underline these verbs.

EXERCISE 12. Writing Sentences with Action Verbs and Linking Verbs. For each noun in the following list, write a sentence in which the noun is followed by an action verb. Then write another sentence, using the same noun with a linking verb.

EXAMPLE 1. saxophone
         1. *The saxophone wailed its sad song.* [action verb]
            The saxophone sounded sad. [linking verb]

1. uncle   2. Rosa   3. meteors   4. farmer   5. actress

Verb Phrases

Parts of the verb *be* may serve another function besides that of linking verb. They may be used as *helping verbs* (sometimes called *auxiliary verbs*) in *verb phrases*. A *phrase* is a group of related words. A verb phrase consists of a main verb preceded by one helping verb or more. Besides all forms of the verb *be*, helping verbs include the following words:

has	shall	may	could	do
have	will	should	might	did
had	can	would	must	does

Helping verbs work together with main verbs as a unit. The helping verbs are in boldfaced type in the following phrases:

is leaving	**may** become	**might have** remained
had seemed	**should** move	**must have** thought
shall be going	**could** jump	**does** sing

Sometimes the parts of a verb phrase are interrupted by other parts of speech.

EXAMPLES She **had** always **been thinking** of her future.
          She **should** not **have borrowed** that necklace.
          We **could** never **have moved** the car alone.

Parts of verb phrases are often separated in questions.

EXAMPLES **Did** you **hear** Jesse Jackson's speech?
          Could your aunt **show** us the slides?
          Has my sister **played** her new album for you?

EXERCISE 13. Identifying Verbs and Verb Phrases. Write on your paper the verbs and verb phrases in the following sentences. Include all helping verbs, even if the parts of a verb phrase are separated by other words. Some sentences contain two verbs or verb phrases.

EXAMPLE 1. We will go to the concert if we can get tickets.
1. *will go, can get*

1. Mr. Jensen always sweeps the floor first.
2. Then he washes the chalkboards.
3. He works slowly but steadily.
4. The weather forecaster had confidently predicted rain.
5. All morning the barometer was dropping rapidly.
6. The storm was slowly moving in.
7. Your dog will become fat if you feed it too much.
8. Dogs will usually eat everything you give them.
9. Cats will stop when they have had enough.
10. After our team has had more practice, we will play better.

THE ADVERB

You know that nouns and pronouns are modified by adjectives. Verbs and adjectives may have modifiers, too, and their modifiers are called *adverbs*. Adverbs also modify other adverbs.

12e. An *adverb* is a word used to modify a verb, an adjective, or another adverb.

Adverbs Modifying Verbs

Sometimes an adverb modifies (makes more definite the meaning of) a verb. Study the following adverbs in boldfaced type. Notice that they answer one of these questions: *Where? When? How? To what extent (how long or how much)?*

WHERE?	WHEN?
We lived **there**.	May we go **tomorrow**?
Please step **up**.	Water the plant **weekly**.
I have the ticket **here**.	We'll see you **later**.

HOW?	TO WHAT EXTENT?
She **quickly** agreed.	I am **completely** happy.
The rain fell **softly**.	He **hardly** moved.
Drive **carefully**.	Did she hesitate **slightly**?

Adverbs may precede or may follow the verbs they modify, and they sometimes interrupt the parts of a verb phrase. Adverbs may also introduce questions.

EXAMPLE   **Where** in the world did you **ever** find that pink and purple necktie? [The adverb *where* modifies the verb phrase *did find*. Notice, too, the adverb *ever,* which interrupts the verb phrase and also modifies it.]

EXERCISE 14. Completing Sentences by Using Appropriate Adverbs.   Number your paper 1–10. Complete each sentence by using an appropriate adverb. Write what the adverb tells: *where* the action was done, *when* the action was done, *how* it was done, or *to what extent* it was done.

 1. Sleep —— .
 2. We can ride —— .
 3. They spoke —— to Mr. Baldwin.
 4. My chow chow snores —— .
 5. They peered around the corner, and then —— went away.
 6. They won —— .
 7. Our neighbors —— say much, but they're —— there when we need them.
 8. Could she listen —— ?
 9. Jan caught the ball —— and threw it —— to first base.
10. He hit his thumb —— with the hammer and yelled —— .

Adverbs Modifying Adjectives

Sometimes an adverb modifies an adjective.

EXAMPLES   Beth did an **exceptionally** fine job. [The adjective *fine* modifies the noun *job*. The adverb *exceptionally* modifies the adjective *fine*, telling *how fine*.]

> The car had a **slightly** damaged fender. [The adverb *slightly* modifies the adjective *damaged,* which in turn modifies the noun *fender.*]

Probably the most frequently used adverbs are *too, so,* and *very.* In fact, these words are overworked. Try to avoid overusing them in speaking and particularly in writing; find more precise adverbs to take their place.

The following adverbs frequently modify adjectives.

extremely	entirely	unusually
dangerously	rather	especially
definitely	completely	surprisingly
quite	terribly	dreadfully

EXERCISE 15. Identifying Adverbs That Modify Adjectives. Write the ten adverbs that modify adjectives in the following sentences. After each adverb, give the adjective modified.

1. Plato, a Greek philosopher, wrote a most interesting book called *The Republic* over two thousand years ago.
2. In *The Republic,* Plato describes the organization of a perfectly just government.
3. Plato's government is for a very small state, such as the city-states that were common in Greece in his time.
4. But his ideas are quite universal and could also apply to large governments.
5. Each citizen of Plato's government belongs in one of three completely distinct classes: workers, the military, or rulers.
6. All citizens study music and athletics, but the most promising students receive additional education.
7. Guardians who protect the laws of Plato's ideal state are trained to be always fair in their decisions.
8. A definitely important concept in *The Republic* is that women and men are equal.
9. Women receive an education exactly equal to men and fight alongside men in wars with neighboring states.

10. Does this quite brief description of Plato's state lead you to accept or reject his ideas of government?

EXERCISE 16. Revising with Adverb Modifiers. Revise the following phrases and sentences by adding one adverb modifier for each of the italicized adjectives. Use a different adverb in each item; do not use *too, so,* or *very.*

1. a *sharp* turn
2. *playful* kittens
3. an *easy* question
4. a *bright* smile
5. a *swept* floor
6. Terri felt *satisfied.*
7. The old mansion was *silent.*
8. Robert became *sick.*
9. Had Clara been *safe*?
10. The test was *difficult.*

Adverbs Modifying Other Adverbs

Sometimes an adverb modifies another adverb. Notice in the first column that each italicized adverb modifies a verb or an adjective. In the second column each added word in boldfaced type is an adverb that modifies the italicized adverb.

EXAMPLES

Calvin was *never* late.   Calvin was **almost** *never* late.

We'll meet *afterward.*   We'll meet **shortly** *afterward.*

She slept *late.*   She slept **too** *late.*

EXERCISE 17. Identifying Adverbs That Modify Other Adverbs. Find and write the ten adverbs that modify other adverbs in the following sentences. After each adverb, write the adverb it modifies.

1. The cat leaped to the windowsill quite agilely.
2. The books were stacked rather haphazardly.
3. Corrie knew she'd have to get up incredibly early to witness the eclipse.
4. The tornado almost completely destroyed the barn.

5. The famous diamond was more heavily guarded than any other exhibit at the museum.
6. My brother is almost always finished with his paper route before I am.
7. She registered too late to be eligible for the first sweepstakes drawing.
8. In the final four minutes of the game Isiah Thomas shot extremely accurately.
9. Usually it seems that each month goes more rapidly than the month before.
10. They walked out on stage most calmly, as if they felt completely relaxed.

WRITING APPLICATION E:
Using Adverbs to Give Focus to Your Writing

Adverbs give precision and focus to what you write. If you have ever performed in a play, you probably know how helpful adverbs can be in stage directions. Read the following directions written by playwrights.

EXAMPLES "The Mother serves **swiftly** from a small bucket of rice. . . ."

The Big Wave, PEARL BUCK

"Bells ringing over city, **gradually** diminishing."

Invasion from Mars, HOWARD KOCH

Writing Assignment

Playwrights do not use adverbs to modify every verb in stage directions. Instead, they use them only to highlight those actions most essential to the scene. Write a paragraph about a competition (sports, music, debating) or other activity you witnessed or participated in recently. Use carefully chosen adverbs to highlight the most essential actions of the competition or other activity.

Forms of Adverbs

You have probably noticed that many adverbs end in -*ly*. You should remember, however, that many adjectives also end in -*ly*: the *daily* newspaper, an *early* train, an *only* child, a *friendly* person. Moreover, words like *now, then, far, already, somewhat, not,* and *right,* which are often used as adverbs, do not end in -*ly*. In order to identify a word as an adverb, do not depend entirely on the ending. Instead, ask yourself: Does this word modify a verb, an adjective, or another adverb? Does it tell *when, where, how,* or *to what extent?*

EXERCISE 18. Identifying Adverbs and the Words They Modify.   Number your paper 1–10, and write the adverbs in each sentence. After each adverb, write the word or expression it modifies. Be able to tell whether the word or expression modified is a verb, an adjective, or another adverb.

1. Tourists in London, England usually visit the Tower of London.
2. A special ceremony called The Ceremony of the Keys is performed there nightly.
3. The three gates of the Tower are securely locked by the Chief Warder, and an escort is especially assigned for the ceremony.
4. The Chief Warder and the escort promptly report to the front of the Tower.
5. The sentry on duty immediately challenges them: "Halt! Who comes there?"
6. The Chief Warder quickly responds, "The Keys."
7. The sentry then asks, "Whose keys?" and the Warder replies distinctly, "Queen Elizabeth's Keys."
8. The Chief Warder then calls solemnly, "God preserve Queen Elizabeth."
9. And all the guards respond together, "Amen."
10. Finally the Chief Warder carries the keys to the Queen's House, and they remain there for the night.

EXERCISE 19. Revising Sentences by Using Appropriate Adverbs. Revise each of the following sentences by adding at least one appropriate adverb. Avoid using the adverbs *too, so,* or *very.*

1. Angelo promised me that he would try to meet the morning train.
2. My coat was torn during the long hike, and Barbara lent me her poncho.
3. Engineering degrees are popular with students because job opportunities are good.
4. The Wallaces are settled into a new house, which they built by themselves.
5. When the baseball season begins, I will be attending games every day.
6. Ronald dribbled to his left and threw the ball into a crowd of defenders.
7. Visits to national monuments and parks remind us that our country has an exciting history.
8. We returned the book to Marcella, but she had planned her report without it.
9. Georgia O'Keeffe displayed her paintings and received the admiration of a large audience.
10. The recipe calls for two or three eggs, but I did not have time to buy any at the store.

REVIEW EXERCISE B. Identifying Nouns, Pronouns, Adjectives, Verbs, and Adverbs. List on your paper the italicized words in the following sentences. Before each word, write the number of its sentence, and after the word, write *noun, pronoun, adjective, verb,* or *adverb.*

EXAMPLE 1. *Early* morning *is* a delightful time of day.
      1. *Early, adjective   is, verb*

1. I *never* used to consider early morning good for *anything* but sleeping.

2. Recently, though, I *have been* on a much *earlier* schedule than usual.
3. The biggest *difference* between early morning and midday lies in the sounds *one* hears.
4. As there are fewer sounds than during the busier *times* of the day, each sound *stands* out.
5. If everyone else in my family is *asleep,* I *hear* even the quiet ticking of my clock.
6. *Every* car that drives *past* can be heard.
7. The drivers in a *hurry* whiz by, while the *more* relaxed drivers roll calmly past.
8. The animals *also* add to the symphony of *morning* sounds.
9. I may hear a dog bark, with several *others* answering in their own *tones.*
10. If I *then* hear a bird singing or calling to others, *I* know that my early-morning concert is complete.

THE PREPOSITION

Certain words in a sentence relate nouns and pronouns to other nouns and pronouns, to verbs, or to modifiers. These words are called *prepositions*.

12f. A *preposition* is a word that shows the relationship of a noun or a pronoun to some other word in the sentence.

The relationship shown by the preposition is an important one. In the following examples, the prepositions in boldfaced type make a great difference in meaning as they relate *St. Bernard* to *bed* and *everything* to *beach*.

The St. Bernard slept **near** my bed.
The St. Bernard slept **under** my bed.
The St. Bernard slept **in** my bed.

Everything **about** the beach was wonderful.
Everything **except** the beach was wonderful.
Everything **from** the beach was wonderful.

The following words are commonly used as prepositions. You should study the list and learn to recognize the words.

Commonly Used Prepositions

aboard	beneath	in	throughout
about	beside	inside	till
above	besides	into	to
across	between	like	toward
after	beyond	near	under
against	but (meaning *except*)	of	underneath
along	by	off	until
among	concerning	on	up
around	down	out	upon
at	during	over	with
before	except	past	within
behind	for	since	without
below	from	through	

> ☞ **NOTE** Many words in this list can also be adverbs. To distinguish between adverbs and prepositions, ask whether the word relates a noun or pronoun following it to a word that comes before it. Compare the following sentences:
>
> Welcome **aboard**. [adverb]
> Welcome **aboard** our boat. [preposition]

There are also compound prepositions, having more than one word. Here are some that are frequently used.

Compound Prepositions

according to	in addition to	next to
as of	in front of	on account of
aside from	in place of	out of
because of	in spite of	owing to
by means of	instead of	prior to

GRAMMAR

The preposition and the noun or pronoun that follows combine to form a *prepositional phrase.* (For a discussion of prepositional phrases, see pages 418–19.)

EXERCISE 20. Revising Sentences by Using Appropriate Prepositions.   Number your paper 1–10. Revise these sentences by using appropriate prepositions or compound prepositions to fill the blanks.

1. Lobsters, the delight of many diners, are large shellfish that live —— the sea.
2. Those who fish —— these creatures are hardy people.
3. They use small, specially constructed boats and a number —— cratelike traps made —— wood.
4. Lobster fishing is not an old industry —— the United States; it has only been practiced —— the last century, because before that time lobster was not thought fit to eat.
5. Farmers used the plentiful lobsters as fertilizer —— their gardens.
6. Traps —— chunks —— fish are lowered —— the sea.
7. The location —— the traps is marked —— colorful floats; the colors, which are registered, identify the owners.
8. The lobster enters the trap —— the part called "the kitchen," tries to escape —— another opening called "the shark's mouth," and then is trapped —— the section called "the parlor."
9. A lobster —— only one claw is called a "cull"; one —— any claws is called a "pistol" or "buffalo."
10. Fishers must return any undersized lobster —— the sea.

THE CONJUNCTION

12g. A *conjunction* joins words or groups of words.

There are three kinds of conjunctions: *coordinating* conjunctions, *correlative* conjunctions, and *subordinating* conjunctions.

Since you will study subordinating conjunctions in connection with subordinate clauses in Chapter 15, at present you need to concern yourself only with the first two kinds, *coordinating* and *correlative* conjunctions.

COORDINATING CONJUNCTIONS	CORRELATIVE CONJUNCTIONS
and	both . . . and
but	not only . . . but also
or	either . . . or
nor	neither . . . nor
for	whether . . . or
yet	
so	

Coordinating conjunctions may join single words, or they may join groups of words. They always connect items of the same kind.

EXAMPLES   guards **and** forwards [two nouns]
on land **or** at sea [two prepositional phrases]
Judy wrote the number down, **but** she lost it. [two complete ideas]

Correlative conjunctions also connect items of the same kind. However, unlike coordinating conjunctions, correlatives are always used in pairs.

EXAMPLES   **Both** Jim Thorpe **and** Roberto Clemente were outstanding athletes. [two proper nouns]
We want to go **not only** to Ontario **but also** to Quebec. [two prepositional phrases]
Either we will buy it now, **or** we will wait for the next sale. [two complete ideas]

EXERCISE 21. Identifying and Classifying Conjunctions.
Number your paper 1–10. Write after the corresponding number all the correlative and coordinating conjunctions from the same sentence. (Separate the conjunctions by commas.) Be prepared to tell whether they are correlative or coordinating conjunctions.

GRAMMAR

EXAMPLE   1. Both she and her sister tried out for the play, but neither got a part.
          1. *both . . . and, but*

1. When we bought a new house, my mother wanted to hire movers, but my father said we could move ourselves more efficiently.
2. He said that we would be not only much faster but also far less expensive than a moving company.
3. Neither my mother nor I was enthusiastic, but Father's mind was made up.
4. Uncle Waldo and his son Fred volunteered to help, for they thought it was a great idea.
5. Both Uncle Waldo and Fred lift weights, and they love to show off their muscles.
6. Father rented a truck, but it wasn't large enough, and we had to make several trips.
7. We could get the sofa through neither the back door nor the front door of the new house; we got it wedged in the front door, and Uncle Waldo strained his back.
8. On the second load, either Fred or my father slipped, and the refrigerator fell on Father's foot.
9. Father's enthusiasm was somewhat dimmed, yet he said his foot didn't hurt much and we were still doing a wonderful job.
10. Whether we saved money or not after paying both Uncle Waldo's and Father's doctor bills and having the doorway of our new home widened is something we don't discuss in our family.

THE INTERJECTION

Sometimes you use a word like *Wow! Hey! Oh!* or *Great!* to show anger, surprise, or some other sudden emotion. These words are called *interjections*.

GRAMMAR

12h. An *interjection* is an exclamatory word that expresses emotion. It has no grammatical relation to the rest of the sentence.

Interjections are not connectives or modifiers. Since they are unrelated to other words in the sentence, they are set off from the rest of the sentence. They are usually followed by an exclamation point. Sometimes, however, when the exclamation is mild, the interjection may be followed by a comma.

EXAMPLES   **Ugh!** There's a skunk somewhere!
               Wonderful! We can go!
               Hey! Be careful of that wire!
               Aw, it wasn't anything.
               Well, I guess that's that.

DETERMINING PARTS OF SPEECH

It is easy to identify a word like *oh* as an interjection. However, the part of speech of a word is not always so simply determined. You must check to see how the word is used in the sentence.

12i. What part of speech a word is depends upon how the word is used in a sentence.

The same word may be used as different parts of speech.

EXAMPLES   The fine feathers of young birds are called **down**. [noun]
               She wore a **down** vest. [adjective]
               The tackle must **down** the runner. [verb]
               Her poster fell **down**. [adverb]
               She lives **down** the street. [preposition]

To determine what part of speech *down* is in each sentence, read the entire sentence. What you are doing is studying the *context* of the word—how the word is used in the sentence. From the context of the word, you can identify the part of speech that *down* is.

EXERCISE 22. Identifying Words as Different Parts of Speech.

Number your paper 1–10. Study the use of each italicized word in the following sentences. Write beside the proper number the part of speech of the italicized word. Be able to justify your answer by giving the *use* of the word in the sentence. Use the following abbreviations:

n.	noun	*adv.*	adverb
pron.	pronoun	*prep.*	preposition
v.	verb	*conj.*	conjunction
adj.	adjective	*interj.*	interjection

1. Did the pond *ice* over?
2. An *ice* storm struck.
3. *Ice* covered the walk.
4. The light flashed *on.*
5. We rode *on* the subway.
6. Her *dive* was perfect.
7. We could *dive* here.
8. He flew a *dive* bomber.
9. We are all here *but* Jo.
10. I slipped, *but* I didn't fall.

CHAPTER 12 REVIEW: POSTTEST 1

Identifying Parts of Speech. Number your paper 1–20. After each number, write the part of speech of the italicized word that comes after that number in the following passage. Be able to explain the use of the word in the sentence.

EXAMPLE   Pioneers (1) *learned* how to recognize (2) *danger.*

1. *verb*
2. *noun*

The (1) *first* pioneers on the Great Plains (2) *encountered* many kinds (3) *of* dangerous animals. (4) *Huge* herds of bison and grizzly bears were a menace to (5) *early* explorers. The (6) *most* ferocious beast of the plains (7) *was* a female (8) *grizzly* protecting her cubs. (9) *Neither* the bison *nor* the grizzly was the most feared animal (10) *on* the frontier. (11) *None* of the creatures, including the fearsome (12) *rattlesnake,* were dreaded so much as the skunk. (13) *Oh,* you may say, that is (14) *ridic-*

ulous. (15) *Yet* it is true. Skunks were not alarming because they (16) *smelled* bad, but because they (17) *so* often carried (18) *rabies*. Since there was no cure for rabies in (19) *those* days, the bite of a rabid skunk was certain to be fatal. The small black and white creatures were carriers of (20) *doom* and struck terror in the stoutest hearts.

CHAPTER 12 REVIEW: POSTTEST 2

Writing Sentences Using the Same Word as Different Parts of Speech. Write twenty short sentences using each of the following words as two different parts of speech. Underline the word, and give its part of speech in parentheses after each sentence.

EXAMPLE   1. up
   1. *We looked up.* (*adverb*)
      We ran up the stairs. (*preposition*)

1. light	5. cook	9. below
2. run	6. ride	10. picture
3. over	7. in	
4. line	8. love	

SUMMARY OF PARTS OF SPEECH

Rule	Part of Speech	Use	Examples
12a	noun	names	**Lydia** reads **novels.**
12b	pronoun	takes the place of a noun	**You** and **they** saw **it.**
12c	adjective	modifies a noun or a pronoun	I got a **new** bike. We were **hungry.**

GRAMMAR

Rule	Part of Speech	Use	Examples
12d	verb	shows action or helps to make a statement	We **swam** and **surfed**. She **was** a candidate.
12e	adverb	modifies a verb, an adjective, or another adverb	They are **here**. We were **quite** surprised. You worked **very** quickly.
12f	preposition	relates a noun or a pronoun to another word	Some **of** the kittens **in** the pet store window had bows **on** their necks.
12g	conjunction	joins words	Carrie **or** Jan will sing.
12h	interjection	expresses strong emotion	**Hey! Hooray! Well**, here we are.

CHAPTER 13

The Parts of a Sentence

SUBJECT, PREDICATE, COMPLEMENT

As you study this chapter, you will become familiar with the structure of a sentence. You will learn to recognize what a sentence is and how its parts fit together to communicate a complete thought. This understanding of sentence structure will help you to speak and to write more effectively.

DIAGNOSTIC TEST

A. Identifying the Parts of a Sentence. Identify the italicized words in the following passage. Use the following abbreviations:

s. subject	*p.a.* predicate adjective
v. verb	*d.o.* direct object
p.n. predicate nominative	*i.o.* indirect object

EXAMPLE   Raising money is hard (1) *work.*
          1. *p.n.*

A carwash can be a good (1) *fund-raiser.* With that thought in mind, the freshman class (2) *planned* a carwash for last Saturday. On Saturday the sky did not look (3) *good.* In fact, the weather report predicted (4) *thunderstorms*. Did (5) *any* of this deter us? No, we (6) *had* our carwash anyway. Our first customer, at 9 A.M., paid (7) *us* a compliment. She said that we were (8) *brave*. The rain began as she was speaking, and she saw our (9) *disappointment*. "Don't worry," she said, "There is (10) *nothing* like a rainwater rinse."

B. Identifying and Punctuating the Kinds of Sentences.

Copy the last word of each of the following sentences, and then give the correct mark of punctuation. Classify each sentence as imperative, declarative, interrogative, or exclamatory.

EXAMPLE   1. The zoo is a fascinating place
           1. *place. declarative*

11. Have you been to the zoo recently
12. I usually go once a year
13. Why don't we go tomorrow
14. Bring your lunch, and be ready to spend the day
15. What a good time we'll have
16. What area do you want to visit first
17. The big cats are awe-inspiring, especially at feeding time
18. What clowns the sea lions are
19. Actually, I enjoy the entire zoo
20. Meet me at the front gate at 9 A.M

THE SENTENCE

Although you often use parts of sentences in casual conversation, you should use complete sentences in your writing.

13a. A *sentence* is a group of words expressing a complete thought.

For your own writing and proofreading, learn to distinguish between sentences and groups of words that are not sentences.

SENTENCE We looked into the room.
NOT A SENTENCE the room with the high ceiling

SENTENCE The clerk was waiting by the door.
NOT A SENTENCE waiting by the door

SENTENCE Who has finished the test?
NOT A SENTENCE after you have finished the test

If a group of words does not express a complete thought, it is a *fragment,* or piece of a sentence, not a sentence.

FRAGMENTS from August to November
the president of our club
doing well in school

These groups of words can become sentences only when the writer adds words to make the thoughts complete.

SENTENCES We play soccer from August to November.
Florence was elected president of our club.
Most of us are doing well in school.

EXERCISE 1. Identifying Sentences and Revising Fragments.
Number your paper 1–10. If the word group is a sentence, write it with correct capitalization and punctuation. If the word group is a fragment, revise it by adding one word or more to make the thought complete, and write the sentence. As you revise, remember to begin the first word with a capital letter and to insert a mark of punctuation after the last word.

1. on Monday or later this week
2. patiently waiting for the mail carrier
3. will you be there tomorrow
4. four people in a small car
5. just yesterday I discovered
6. two strikes and no one on base
7. it runs smoothly
8. leaning far over the railing
9. give me a hand
10. all during the movie and then later at home

SUBJECT AND PREDICATE

13b. A sentence consists of two parts: the *subject* **and the** *predicate*. **The** *subject* **of the sentence is the part about which something is being said. The** *predicate* **is the part which says something about the subject.**

In the following examples, the subjects are separated from the predicates by vertical lines.

> Coyotes | were howling in the distance.
> The telephone in the lobby | rang.
> The woman in the red blouse | is my aunt.

As you see, the subject and the predicate may be only one word each, or they may be more than one word.

In the previous examples, the words to the left of the vertical line make up the *complete subject*. The words to the right of the vertical line make up the *complete predicate*. Often, however, the subject can be in the middle of or at the end of a sentence. Notice the complete subjects, which are in boldfaced type, in the following examples.

> In dim light, will **this camera** take pictures?
> On the table was **a silver vase.**
> Does **Brian's car** have a tape deck?

EXERCISE 2. Identifying the Complete Subject.   Number your paper 1–10. After the corresponding number on your paper, write the complete subject of each sentence.

1. The first repair job in space took place in 1984.
2. The Solar Maximum Mission satellite had made spectacular discoveries about solar flares.
3. Unfortunately, Solar Max blew three fuses.
4. James van Hoften and George Nelson, American astronauts, were assigned to repair the ailing satellite.
5. At first Nelson was unable to dock with the satellite.
6. A docking adapter on the front of his spacesuit failed to latch onto the special pin on the satellite.

7. The two astronauts were able to begin the repair job three days later.
8. Van Hoften removed the panel covering the electronics box.
9. He installed a new unit after removing the damaged box.
10. Is the eighteen-foot-tall satellite still in orbit?

EXERCISE 3. Writing Complete Predicates. Write complete predicates for the following complete subjects to make complete sentences.

1. justice
2. some commercials
3. the store on the corner
4. the woman next door
5. one way to study

The Simple Subject

13c. The *simple subject* is the main word or group of words in the complete subject.

The simple subject is the most important word in the complete subject. This word names the person, place, thing, or idea being talked about.

EXAMPLE   Their scientific discoveries made them famous.
Complete subject   Their scientific discoveries
  Simple subject   discoveries

EXAMPLE   The eloquent Martin Luther King, Jr., made many fine speeches.
Complete subject   The eloquent Martin Luther King, Jr.
  Simple subject   Martin Luther King, Jr.

☞ NOTE   Compound nouns, such as *Martin Luther King, Jr.,* in the example, are considered one noun.

From the examples above, you can see that the complete subject consists of the simple subject and all the words that belong with it. Adjectives and prepositional phrases that modify the simple subject are included in the complete subject.

The term *subject,* when used in connection with the sentence, refers to the simple subject, unless otherwise indicated.

EXERCISE 4. Revising Sentence Fragments. Revise each of the following fragments by adding a complete subject. Underline each simple subject.

1. —— was baying at the moon.
2. —— can make the pizza.
3. —— is needed for this recipe.
4. Was —— the one who won the match?
5. —— rose and soared out over the sea.
6. —— stood on the stage singing.
7. —— were late for their classes.
8. Over in the next town is —— .
9. Buzzing around the room was —— .
10. In the middle of the yard grew —— .

The Simple Predicate

13d. The *simple predicate,* **or** *verb,* **is the main word or group of words within the complete predicate.**

The essential word (or words) in the complete predicate is always the simple predicate, usually referred to as the *verb.* The other words in the complete predicate may affect the meaning of the verb in various ways, often by making it more definite, but it is the verb that is essential in completing the statement.

EXAMPLE   The ambulance raced out of the hospital drive and down the crowded street. [Complete predicate: *raced out of the hospital drive and down the crowded street.* Verb: *raced*]

The simple predicate may consist of a single verb or of a verb phrase. A verb phrase will be more than one word: *will sing, has been broken, may have been trying,* etc.

When you are asked to pick out the simple predicate in a sentence, be sure to include all parts of a verb phrase. In doing so, keep in mind the various helping verbs that are commonly used as parts of verb phrases: *shall, will, has, have, had, do, does, did, may, might, must, can, could, should, would, am, is, are, was, were, be,* and *been.*

Study the following examples, noticing the difference between the complete predicate and the verb.

EXAMPLE   Mark could have accidentally taken my book.
Complete predicate   could have accidentally taken my book.
Verb   could have taken

EXAMPLE   My aunt was sitting on the sofa.
Complete predicate   was sitting on the sofa.
Verb   was sitting

Throughout this book, the word *verb* will be used to refer to the simple predicate, unless otherwise indicated.

EXERCISE 5. Identifying Complete Predicate and Verb.
Make two columns on your paper. Label one of them *Complete predicate* and the other *Verb*. For each of the following sentences, write the complete predicates and the verbs in the appropriate columns. If you find a verb phrase, be sure to include all helping words.

1. Many writers' first novels are autobiographical.
2. *Look Homeward, Angel,* the first novel of Thomas Wolfe, was written about his early life in Asheville, North Carolina.
3. In the novel appear the people and scenes of Wolfe's youth.
4. His mother, father, and brother Ben will always be remembered because of Wolfe's book.
5. The boyhood home of Wolfe is still standing in Asheville.
6. The house and its furnishings are carefully described by Wolfe in *Look Homeward, Angel.*
7. A trip to the Asheville library supplies one with many facts about Wolfe.

GRAMMAR

8. In the library can be found all the newspaper clippings about Wolfe's life and works.
9. At first an outcast in Asheville, Wolfe was later revered by the town's citizens.
10. The whole town mourned the early death of its most famous son.

EXERCISE 6. Writing Complete Sentences by Revising Fragments. A sentence must have a subject and a predicate. Revise the following fragments, making each a complete sentence. Number your paper 1–5, and write each complete sentence after the proper number. Proofread for correct capitalization and end punctuation.

1. the trouble with my lunch period
2. the legs of the table
3. appeared deserted
4. my billionaire aunt from Detroit
5. thousands of screaming fans

REVIEW EXERCISE A. Distinguishing Between Fragments and Sentences; Identifying Subjects and Predicates. Number your paper 1–10. Label each word group *S* for sentence if it contains a subject and a predicate, or *F* for fragment if it does not contain both parts. Then copy the simple subject, underlining it once, and the simple predicate, underlining it twice. (Fragments will lack one or both parts.)

EXAMPLE   1. The talented musicians played well together.
             1. *S* musicians played

1. The jazz sound filled the room.
2. Behind the other instruments was a gently tinkling piano.
3. The saxophonist, with lazy, lingering notes.
4. His friend, the bass player, lent a rich depth to the ensemble's music.
5. A female vocalist with a throaty voice.
6. Charmed the audience with her delivery.

7. Yet, the star of the show was the drummer.
8. For most of the evening she stayed in the background.
9. Until the last half hour.
10. Then she dazzled everyone with her brilliant, high-speed technique.

Finding the Subject

The best way to find the subject of a sentence is to find the verb first. After you have found the verb, ask "Who?" or "What?" in front of the verb.

EXAMPLES Here you can swim year-round. [The verb is *can swim.* Who can swim? The answer is *you,* the subject.]

Over the hill thundered the horses. [The verb is *thundered.* What thundered? The *horses* thundered; therefore, *horses* is the subject.]

The price of those tapes seemed too high to us. [The verb is *seemed.* What seemed? *Price* is the subject.]

EXERCISE 7. Identifying Subject and Verb. Find the subject of each of the following sentences by first finding the verb and then by asking "Who?" or "What?" in front of the verb. After numbering 1–10, write on your paper each verb and its subject. Be sure to include all parts of a verb phrase.

1. Even before the equal rights movement, American women became leaders in their professions.
2. Evangeline Booth was General of the International Salvation Army from 1934 to 1939.
3. The Salvation Army has always treated men and women equally.
4. Have you heard of Nellie Bly, the famous newspaper reporter?
5. In 1890 she traveled alone around the world.
6. Her travels were reported in the *New York World.*

7. Nellie Bly's investigative reporting showed courage and cleverness.
8. In 1876 Melville Bissell invented the carpet sweeper.
9. After the death of her husband in 1888, Anne Bissell managed his company for forty years.
10. Under her management as corporation president, the company sold millions of carpet sweepers.

13e. The *subject* of a verb is never in a prepositional phrase.

You will remember that a prepositional phrase begins with a preposition and ends with a noun or a pronoun: *to the bank, by the door, in the picture, of a book, on the floor, after class, at intermission, for them, except him.* (See pages 418–19.) Since the prepositional phrase contains a noun or a pronoun, and since it often comes before the verb, you may make the mistake of thinking that the noun following a preposition is the subject.

EXAMPLE   Most **of the women** voted.

When you ask "Who voted?" you may be tempted to answer, "Women voted." But on second thought you realize that the sentence does not say the *women voted;* it says *most* of the women *voted.* A word in a prepositional phrase is never the subject. *Women* is in the phrase *of the women.*

Prepositional phrases can be especially misleading when the subject follows the verb.

EXAMPLE   **Around the corner from here** is a store.

Neither *corner* nor *here* is the subject because each word is part of a prepositional phrase. *Store* is the subject of the verb *is.*

EXERCISE 8. Identifying Subject and Verb.   Number your paper 1–10. Write the verb and the simple subject of each sentence.

1. Many regions of America have their own local legends.
2. A pine-forested area of New Jersey is supposedly haunted by the Jersey Devil.

3. This fearsome monster reportedly chases campers and wayward travelers through the woods.
4. The state of Oregon is haunted by legends of the less aggressive Bigfoot.
5. This legendary humanlike creature secludes itself in heavily forested areas.
6. Its shaggy coat of hair looks like a bear's pelt.
7. Bigfoot is gentle and shy by nature, avoiding contact with strangers.
8. Stories around Lake Champlain tell about a monster resembling a sea serpent in the depths of the lake.
9. Many sightings of this beast have been reported to authorities.
10. A number of people have tried to photograph the monster, without success.

The Subject in an Unusual Position

Sentences that ask questions and sentences that begin with *there* or *here* have the subject in an unusual position.

Sentences That Ask Questions

Questions often begin with a verb or with a verb helper. They also frequently begin with words such as *what, when, where, how,* or *why.* Either way, the subject ordinarily *follows* the verb or verb helper.

EXAMPLES How is the **movie** different?
Does **she** have a ride home?
Have **you** eaten dinner?

In questions that begin with a helping verb, like the second example above, the subject always comes between the helper and the main verb. You can also find the subject by turning the question into a statement, finding the verb, and asking "Who?" or "What?" in front of the verb.

EXAMPLES   Was the train late? *becomes* The train was late.
[What was late? *Train*.]
Has she answered the letter? *becomes* She has answered the letter. [Who has answered? *She*.]

Sentences Beginning with *There*

There is never the subject of a sentence except when spoken of as a word, as in this sentence. However, this word often appears in the place before a verb where we would expect to find a subject. *There* can be used to get a sentence started when the real subject comes after the verb. In this use, *there* is called an *expletive*. (The verb and its subject are labeled for you in the following sentences.)

               V   S
EXAMPLES   There is a drawbridge over the river.

                  V   S
         There are insects in our garden.

To find the subject in such a sentence, omit *there* and ask "Who?" or "What?" before the verb.

> There was a clerk at the counter. [*Who* was? *Clerk*. Therefore, *clerk* is the subject.]

With *there* omitted, these sentences read as follows:

> A drawbridge is over the river.
> Insects are in our garden.
> A clerk was at the counter.

EXERCISE 9. Identifying Subjects and Verbs. Number your paper 1–10; write the subjects and verbs in the following sentences after the proper numbers. Write subjects first, verbs second.

1. There are many questions on American history in my book.
2. Naturally, there are answers, too.
3. Under whose flag did Columbus sail?
4. Where is Plymouth Rock?
5. How much do you know about the Lost Colony?

6. What does "squatter's rights" mean?
7. In what area did most of the early Dutch colonists settle?
8. Was there dissension among settlers in Massachusetts?
9. What kinds of schools did the colonists' children attend?
10. How did one travel in colonial America?

WRITING APPLICATION A:
Varying the Position of the Subject to Make Your Writing Interesting

One of the worst things a critic can say to a writer is, "Your writing bores me." If your sentences always start with the subject, your writing will be monotonous; you may bore your reader. Experiment with placing sentence subjects in different positions. Note the following examples:

EXAMPLES   Down the field marched *the band*. [subject at the end]

After the National Anthem, *the band* marched down the field. [subject after an introductory prepositional phrase]

Immediately, *the band* marched down the field. [subject after an introductory adverb]

Writing Assignment

Write a paragraph about your choice of an elective you would like to take next semester. Explain why you are choosing this elective. Add sentence variety by placing at least three of your subjects in a position other than at the beginning.

The Understood Subject

In a request or a command, the subject of a sentence is usually not stated. In such sentences, the person spoken to is understood to be the subject.

GRAMMAR

EXAMPLES   Please answer the phone.
　　　　　　Listen carefully to his question.

In the first sentence, a request, *who* is to answer the phone? *You* are—that is, the person spoken to. In the second sentence, a command, *who* is to listen? Again, *you* are. In each sentence, then, *you* is the understood subject.

Sometimes a request or command will include a name.

EXAMPLES   Ellen, please answer the phone.
　　　　　　Listen carefully to his question, class.

Neither *Ellen* nor *class* is the subject of its sentence. These words are called nouns of *direct address*. They *identify* the person spoken to or addressed. *You,* however, is still the understood subject of each sentence.

Ellen, (you) please answer the phone.

EXERCISE 10. Writing Sentences of Request or Command. Write ten sentences that are requests or commands; include nouns of direct address in five of these sentences. Write the understood subject in parentheses after each sentence, and underline all nouns of direct address.

EXAMPLE   Please turn on the lamp, <u>Carolyn.</u> (*you*)

Compound Subjects

13f. A *compound subject* **consists of two or more subjects joined by a conjunction and having the same verb.**

The conjunctions most commonly used to connect the words of a compound subject are *and* and *or*. Study these sentences:

EXAMPLES   **Antony** baked the bread. [Who baked the bread? Antony baked it. *Antony* is the simple subject.]
　　　　　　Antony and **Mae** baked the bread. [Who baked the bread? Antony baked it. Mae baked it. *Antony* and *Mae,* then, form the compound subject.]

When more than two words are included in the compound subject, the conjunction is generally used only between the last two words. Also, the words are separated by commas.

EXAMPLE Antony, Mae, **and** Pamela baked the bread. [Compound subject: *Antony, Mae, Pamela*]

Correlative conjunctions may be used with compound subjects.

EXAMPLE **Either** Antony **or** Mae baked the bread. [Compound subject: *Antony, Mae*]

EXERCISE 11. Identifying Compound Subjects and Their Verbs. Number your paper 1–10. Write the compound subjects and their verbs in the following sentences.

EXAMPLE 1. Roast turkey and pumpkin pie are often served at Thanksgiving.
1. *Turkey, pie are served*

1. Moles and bats supposedly have very poor eyesight.
2. Kettles of soup and trays of sandwiches were prepared.
3. April, May, and June are related to what famous comic book character?
4. Both you and I should go downtown.
5. Either *Macbeth* or *Othello* features witches in its plot.
6. In that drawer must be her scissors and letter opener.
7. Gerbils and goldfish are popular.
8. There are many often-told jokes and riddles.
9. Where will you and your family vacation this year?
10. There are a dozen eggs and a pound of butter left.

Compound Verbs

13g. A *compound verb* **consists of two or more verbs joined by a conjunction and having the same subject.**

The following sentences show how verbs may be compound.

EXAMPLES   Valerie Brisco-Hooks **entered** and **won** her Olympic events.

They **looked** but **saw** nothing.

The committee **met, voted** on the issue, and **adjourned**.

My sister **will buy** or **lease** a car.

Notice in the last sentence that the helping verb *will* is not repeated before *lease,* though it is understood: My sister *will buy* or *will lease* a car. In compound verbs consisting of verb phrases, the helper may or may not be repeated before the second verb if the helper is the same for both verbs. Often the helper is not repeated when there is a correlative conjunction.

EXAMPLE   They **will** not only **replace** the part but **do** it free of charge.

EXERCISE 12. Identifying Compound Verbs.   Number your paper 1–10; write the compound verbs in the following sentences. Be sure to include verb helpers.

1. Visit, shop, and relax.
2. Pete sings, acts, and dances in the show.
3. At the pie-eating contest, Dan devoured four large apple pies and won the prize of twenty-five dollars.
4. Will you walk home or wait for the four o'clock bus?
5. This kitchen appliance will slice, dice, or chop.
6. Patti will not only bring the salad but also bake a cake for the party.
7. Either pick your socks up and put them in the hamper or go barefoot for the rest of your life.
8. The marching band practiced hard and won the state competition.
9. Jeff rewound the cassette and then pressed the playback button.
10. The newborn calf rose to its feet with a wobbling motion and stood for the first time.

Both the subject and the verb may be compound.

EXAMPLES   The **students** and **teachers** | **wrote** the play and **produced** it.
Either **Jan** or **Beverly** | **will write** the story and **send** it to the paper. [Notice that with the second verb, *send,* the helper *will* is understood.]

REVIEW EXERCISE B. Finding Subjects and Verbs. Write the ten sentences in this exercise. Then, for each sentence, complete the steps that follow:

1. Cross out all prepositional phrases so that you can isolate the verb and the subject.
2. Cross out a *here* or *there* at the beginning of a sentence, thus eliminating these words as possible subjects.
3. Underline all verbs twice; be sure to include all helpers and all parts of a compound verb.
4. Underline all subjects once; be sure to underline all parts of a compound subject.

EXAMPLES   1. ~~At our school,~~ ballads have become very popular.
2. ~~There~~ are individual singers and group singers ~~on the music program~~ tonight.

1. There are ballads for different tastes and occasions.
2. Ballads tell simple stories and create strong moods.
3. In ballads people live, work, love, and die.
4. The words of ballads were written by the common people and therefore relate the concerns of the common people.
5. In one ballad can be heard a jilted lover's complaints.
6. In another is found the lament of a mother for her dead son.
7. The death of a dog and the heroism of a coal miner are related in still other ballads.
8. How can anyone resist the appeal of such simple tales?
9. Everyone at some time or other has felt the emotions of the characters in ballads.

10. Here, then, are some of the reasons for the popularity of ballads since the Middle Ages.

DIAGRAMING SENTENCES

Many students can understand a sentence better when they use a diagram. A diagram is a picture of how the parts of a sentence fit together and how the words in a sentence are related.

Diagraming the Subject and the Verb

A diagram begins with a straight horizontal line. This line is for the main parts of the sentence. Crossing it approximately in the center is a short vertical line that divides the complete subject from the complete predicate. The simple subject is placed to the left of the vertical line, the verb to the right of it.

PATTERN

subject | verb

EXAMPLE   Fish swim.

Fish | swim

If the sentence has an understood subject, place *you* in parentheses on the subject line.

EXAMPLE   Wait!

(you) | Wait

Nouns of direct address are placed on a separate horizontal line above the understood subject.

EXAMPLE   Sit, **Fido.**

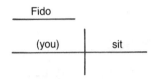

The expletive *there* is also placed on a separate horizontal line. (Modifiers have been omitted from the following diagram.)

EXAMPLE   **There** is a fly in my soup.

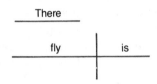

When the sentence has a compound subject, diagram it as in the following example. Notice the position of the coordinating conjunction on the broken line.

EXAMPLE   **Howard** and **Basil** were fishing.

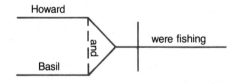

If the verb is compound, it is diagramed in this way:

EXAMPLE   They **went** and **ate.**

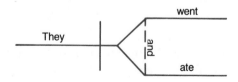

A sentence with both a compound subject and a compound verb is diagramed in this way:

EXAMPLE **Coaches** and **players jumped** and **cheered.**

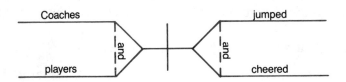

Notice how a compound verb is diagramed when the helping verb is not repeated.

EXAMPLE They are **sitting** and **reading.**

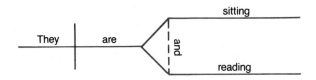

Since *are* is the helper for both *sitting* and *reading,* it is placed on the horizontal line, and the conjunction *and* joins the main verbs *sitting* and *reading.*

Sometimes parts of a compound subject or a compound verb will be joined by correlative conjunctions. Correlatives are diagramed like this:

EXAMPLE **Both** Bob **and** Teri can **not only** draw **but also** paint.

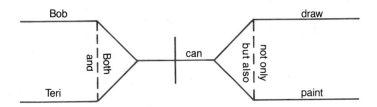

EXERCISE 13. Diagraming Subjects and Verbs. Diagram the following sentences:

1. Hyenas laugh.
2. Listen, Miguel!
3. Chad and he were hiking.
4. Farmers plant and harvest.
5. Both Sally and Beth were nominated and elected.

Diagraming Adjectives and Adverbs

Adjectives modify nouns or pronouns, and adverbs modify verbs, adjectives, or other adverbs. Both adjectives and adverbs are written on slanted lines connected to the words they modify.

PATTERN

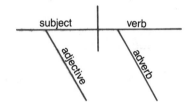

EXAMPLE   **That old** clock has **never** worked.

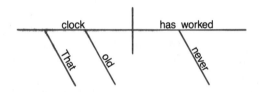

An adverb that modifies an adjective or an adverb is placed on a line connected to the adjective or adverb modified.

EXAMPLE   This **specially** designed glass **very** seldom breaks.

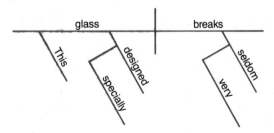

Notice the position of the modifiers in the following example:

EXAMPLE   **Soon** Anne and **her** sister will graduate and will move.

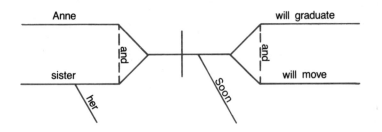

Her modifies only one part of the compound subject: *sister*. *Soon* modifies both parts of the compound verb: *will graduate* and *will move*. Where would *will* have been placed in the diagram if it had not been repeated before *move*?

When a conjunction joins two modifiers, it is diagramed as in this example:

EXAMPLE   The English **and** Australian athletes worked long **and** very hard.

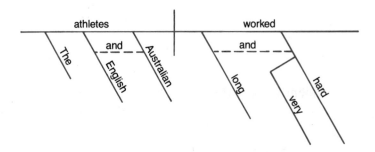

EXERCISE 14. Completing Sentence Diagrams.   Diagrams for the following sentences have been provided for you. Copy them on your paper, and fill them in correctly.

1. Both men spoke convincingly.

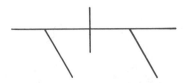

2. Do not swim there.

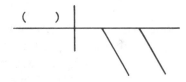

3. A jet travels quite swiftly.

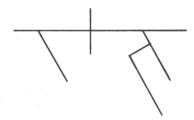

4. A conveniently located store almost always succeeds.

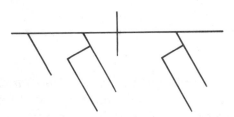

5. The unhappy puppy whined often and very loudly.

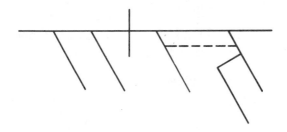

REVIEW EXERCISE C. Diagraming Sentences. Diagram each of the following sentences:

1. Mike and Dan always joke.
2. There is my cat.
3. My brother and Mr. Jones were carefully sorting and filing.
4. Eat well and exercise daily.
5. There lived the wicked witch and her flying monkeys.

REVIEW EXERCISE D. Writing Sentences. Write five separate sentences, using an example of each of the following; underline what is asked for.

EXAMPLE 1. a prepositional phrase
 1. *I peeked* <u>inside the closet</u>.

1. a verb phrase
2. a compound verb
3. a compound subject
4. an understood subject
5. an adverb modifying an adjective

COMPLEMENTS

Every sentence has a *base*. Like the main framework of a building, the base is that part of the sentence on which all other parts are built. A sentence base may consist of only the subject and the verb; for many sentences nothing else is needed.

EXAMPLES Owls <u>hooted</u>.

The <u>ballerina</u> in white <u>was leaping</u>.

Frequently the sentence base will have not only a subject and a verb but also a completer, or *complement*.

13h. A *complement* completes the meaning begun by the subject and the verb.

It is possible for a group of words to have a subject and a verb and not express a complete thought. Notice how the following word groups need other words to complete their meaning.

EXAMPLES This stew tastes
She always was
I told
The car hit

If you add words to complete the meaning, the sentences will make sense.

EXAMPLES This stew tastes **strange.**
She always was **a leader.**
I told **them.**
The car hit **a tree.**

The words *strange, leader, them,* and *tree* are complements; each one completes the thought of the sentence. The complement may be a noun, a pronoun, or an adjective.

Study the structure of these sentences. The base of each sentence—subject, verb, complement—is labeled.

```
                  S       V      C
EXAMPLES   The cat watched us.
                  S              V      C
           The men at that store are courteous.
                        S      V       C
           In our town taxes will be quite high.
           S              V       C
           Marcella might become a chemist.
                     S      V              C
           Those termites caused extensive damage.
```

The complement is never in a prepositional phrase. Look at these sentences:

EXAMPLES   Now she watched the cheering crowd.
Now she watched from the cheering crowd.

In the first sentence, *crowd* is the complement. In the second sentence, *crowd* is the object of the preposition *from;* the prepositional phrase *from the cheering crowd* modifies the verb *watched*.

EXERCISE 15. Writing Sentence Complements.   Write five complete sentences by adding a complement to each of the following listed items.

1. Jim usually seems
2. Tomorrow the class will hear
3. That broiled fish looks
4. Last week our class visited
5. Do you have

EXERCISE 16. Writing Sentences.   Write five sentences using the following verbs and complements. Do not be satisfied with adding only a word or two. Make *interesting* sentences.

Verb	Complement
1. upset	champions
2. shattered	glass
3. feel	responsible
4. desire	peace
5. can become	work

EXERCISE 17. Identifying Subjects, Verbs, and Complements.   Make three columns on your paper. Label the first *subject,* the second *verb,* and the third *complement.* Find the base of each sentence, and write the parts in the appropriate column.

1. The history of the English stage is very interesting.
2. In the beginning churches gave plays for instruction.

3. The stories of early English drama were usually Biblical ones.

4. The plays, however, eventually became too irreverent for religious instruction.

5. The clergy then recommended the abolition of acting within the churches.

6. At the same time, they encouraged the performance of religious drama in courtyards near the churches.

7. The actors presented their plays on wagons in the open air.

8. The top of the wagon soon became a convenient place for "heaven."

9. In Shakespeare's time, the upper stage was an important part of the theater.

10. Shakespeare used the upper stage for the famous balcony scene in *Romeo and Juliet*.

EXERCISE 18. Writing Sentences. Using each word in the list below as a complement, write five sentences. Underline the subject once, the verb twice, and the complement three times.

EXAMPLE   1. popcorn
            1. *Rosie carefully handed the popcorn to John.*

1. pencil
2. bellhop
3. shrewd
4. sluggish
5. clown

The Subject Complement

13i. A *subject complement* **is a noun, pronoun, or adjective that follows a linking verb.[1] It describes or explains the simple subject.**

EXAMPLES   Mark Twain's real name was **Samuel Clemens.**
              The surface felt **sticky.**

[1] Linking verbs are discussed on pages 356–57.

In the first sentence, the complement *Samuel Clemens* explains the subject *name*. In the second, the complement *sticky* describes the subject *surface*.

(1) A *predicate nominative* is one kind of subject complement. It is a noun or pronoun in the predicate that explains or identifies the subject of the sentence.

EXAMPLES   Angela will be our **soloist.**
The astronaut is **she.**
A whale is a **mammal.**

(2) A *predicate adjective* is another kind of subject complement. It is an adjective in the predicate that modifies the subject of the sentence.

EXAMPLES   That soil looks **dry.** [dry soil]
The soup is too **hot.** [hot soup]
She looks **capable.** [capable she]

Subject complements may be compound.

EXAMPLES   The prizewinners are **Jennifer** and **Brad.** [compound predicate nominatives]
The corn tastes **sweet** and **buttery.** [compound predicate adjectives]

EXERCISE 19. Identifying and Classifying Subject Complements. In the sentences of Exercise 17 (page 401) there are five subject complements. List them on your paper. After each noun or pronoun, write *predicate nominative;* after each adjective, *predicate adjective.*

EXERCISE 20. Writing Sentences with Subject Complements. Make sentences of the following groups of words by using nouns, pronouns, or adjectives as subject complements. Use five compound complements. Tell whether each one is a predicate nominative or a predicate adjective.

1. The artist frequently was	6. Are you
2. Those are	7. The weather remained
3. Sara Brown became	8. The test seemed
4. It could be	9. Sol had always felt
5. The house looked	10. That recording sounds

Objects

Objects are complements that do not refer to the subject.

EXAMPLE   Lee Trevino sank the **putt.**

In this sentence, the object *putt* does not explain or describe the subject *Lee Trevino,* and *sank* is an action verb rather than a linking verb.

There are two kinds of objects: the *direct object* and the *indirect object.* Neither is ever in a prepositional phrase.

13j. The *direct object* **of the verb is a noun or pronoun that receives the action of the verb or shows the result of the action. It answers the question "What?" or "Whom?" after an action verb.**

EXAMPLES   Dot asked **Izzy** about the game.
Her poem won an **award.**

In the first sentence, *Izzy* receives the action expressed by the verb *asked* and tells *whom* Dot asked; therefore, Izzy is the direct object. In the second sentence, *award* names the result of the action expressed by the verb *won* and tells *what* her *poem* won; *award* is the direct object.

In the following sentences, observe that each object answers the question "Whom?" or "What?" after an action verb.

S   V   O
Lucy visited me.
S   V   O
Germs cause illness.
S   V   O
They were taking snapshots.

GRAMMAR

```
    S          V           O
```
I will be climbing the mountain.

EXERCISE 21. Identifying Direct Objects. Number your paper 1–10, and write after the appropriate number the direct object for each sentence.

1. This article gives many interesting facts about libraries.
2. Alexandria, in Egypt, had the most famous library of ancient times.
3. This library contained a large collection of ancient plays and works of philosophy.
4. The Roman emperor Augustus founded two public libraries.
5. Fire later destroyed these buildings.
6. Readers could not take books from either the Roman libraries or the library in Alexandria.
7. The monastery library of the Middle Ages first introduced the idea of a circulating library.
8. In the sixth century, everyone in the Benedictine monasteries borrowed a book from the library for daily reading.
9. Today, the United States has thousands of circulating libraries.
10. Readers borrow millions of books from them every year.

13k. The *indirect object* of the verb is a noun or pronoun that precedes the direct object and usually tells "to whom" or "for whom" (or "to what" or "for what") the action of the verb is done.

DIRECT OBJECTS   Sheila told a **story.**
Frank gave a **donation.**

INDIRECT OBJECTS   Sheila told the **children** a story.
Frank gave **Toni** a donation.

In the sentences above, *story* and *donation* are direct objects answering the question "What?" after action verbs. Sheila told a story *to whom? Children,* the answer, is an indirect object. Frank gave a donation *to whom? Toni* is the indirect object.

The indirect objects in the following sentences are boldfaced. Each tells *to whom* or *for whom* something is done.

EXAMPLES   Nataly knit **her friend** a sweater.
My little sister sang **me** a song.
We will give **her** an award.
She often sends **us** a letter.

If the word *to* or *for* is used, the word following it is part of a prepositional phrase, not an indirect object.

PREPOSITIONAL PHRASES   She showed the bird's nest **to me.**
I left some dessert **for you.**

INDIRECT OBJECTS   She showed **me** the bird's nest.
I left **you** some dessert.

Both direct and indirect objects may be compound.

EXAMPLES   Lydia sold **cookies** and **lemonade.** [compound direct object]
Lydia sold **Freddy** *and* **me** lemonade. [compound indirect object]

EXERCISE 22. Identifying and Classifying Complements as Direct Object or Indirect Object.

Number your paper 1–10, and list the indirect and direct objects in the following sentences. After each, write in parentheses *i.o.* (for indirect object) or *d.o.* (for direct object). You will not find an indirect object in every sentence.

1. According to Greek mythology, Daedalus, a famous artist and inventor, built the king of Crete a mysterious building known as the Labyrinth.
2. The complicated passageways of this building give us our word for "a confusing maze of possibilities."
3. After the completion of the Labyrinth, the king imprisoned Daedalus and his son, whose name was Icarus.
4. In order to escape, Daedalus made Icarus and himself wings out of feathers and beeswax.
5. He gave Icarus careful instructions not to fly near the sun.

6. But Icarus soon forgot his father's advice.
7. He flew too high, and the hot sun melted the wax in the wings.
8. Daedalus used his wings wisely and reached Sicily in safety.
9. Mythology tells us many other stories of Daedalus' fabulous inventions.
10. Even today, the name Daedalus suggests genius and inventiveness.

REVIEW EXERCISE E. Identifying and Classifying Complements. Number your paper 1–10, and list the complements in the following sentences. After each, write in parentheses *p.n.* (for predicate nominative), *p.a.* (for predicate adjective), *d.o.* (for direct object), or *i.o.* (for indirect object). Some sentences may have no complements; others may have more than one.

EXAMPLE 1. Last year my brother gave Mom a birthday surprise.
       1. *Mom (i.o.) surprise (d.o.)*

1. My brother Bill made Mom a birthday cake.
2. The project soon became a fiasco.
3. First, Bill cracked the eggs into a bowl.
4. Unfortunately, the shells went in too.
5. Then Bill added the flour and other dry ingredients.
6. The eggbeater whirled them right onto the ceiling.
7. Our ceiling was both powdery and sticky.
8. Bill did not clean the ceiling immediately, and the sticky substance hardened overnight.
9. Mom was not angry, but she did give Bill a suggestion for a gift.
10. "A clean ceiling would be a fine birthday gift," she said.

Diagraming Complements

As part of the sentence base, the subject complement is placed on the horizontal line with the subject and verb. It comes after the verb. A line *slanting toward the subject,* drawn upward from the horizontal line, separates the subject complement from the verb.

PATTERN

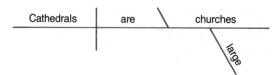

PREDICATE NOMINATIVE   Cathedrals are **large churches.**

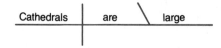

PREDICATE ADJECTIVE   Cathedrals are **large.**

COMPOUND SUBJECT   My sister is **small** and **quiet.**
COMPLEMENT

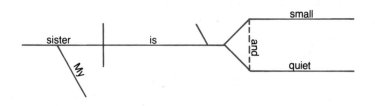

EXERCISE 23. Diagraming Sentences with Complements.

Diagram the following sentences:

1. Dogs remain popular pets.
2. The beautiful collie is an intelligent dog.
3. The amusing dachshund is a good companion.
4. Poodles appear both attractive and clever.
5. The ordinary mutt is often most lovable.

The *direct object* is diagramed in much the same manner as the predicate nominative. The only difference is that the line separating the direct object from the verb is vertical, not slanting.

PATTERN

EXAMPLE   We like **music.**

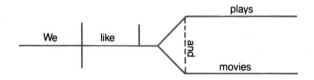

The compound direct object is diagramed as follows:

EXAMPLE   We like **plays** and **movies.**

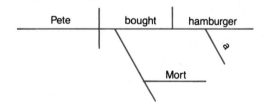

The *indirect object* is diagramed on a horizontal line beneath the verb.

EXAMPLE   Pete bought **Mort** a hamburger.

Note that the slanting line from the verb extends slightly below the horizontal line for the indirect object.

The compound indirect object is diagramed in this way:

EXAMPLE David gave his **family** and **friends** free tickets.

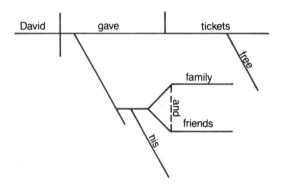

EXERCISE 24. Diagraming Sentences with Modifiers and Complements. Diagram the following sentences.

1. The mistake taught us a costly lesson.
2. Bill Chang told the fans and players the good news.
3. What gave them the chills and the fever?
4. Linda handed me the sealed envelope.
5. The band director issued the other players and me our uniforms and music.

REVIEW EXERCISE F. Identifying the Parts of Sentences.

Identify the italicized words in the passage below. Use the following abbreviations:

s. subject	*p.a.* predicate adjective
v. verb	*d.o.* direct object
p.n. predicate nominative	*i.o.* indirect object

(1) *Many* of Edgar Allan Poe's stories do not deal with horror or terror. Not (2) *all* of his main characters are mad or (3) *evil*. Poe has left (4) *us* many comic (5) *tales*. For instance, "Loss of Breath" (6) *gives* the (7) *reader* a (8) *chance* for hearty laughter.

The (9) *author* saw the (10) *humor* of the expression, "I've lost my breath." He (11) *based* a (12) *story* on it. The main (13) *character* in "Loss of Breath" (14) *is* (15) *Mr. Lackobreath*.

His situation is (16) *amusing*. Angry with his wife, he (17) *argues* furiously and loses his breath. Then the unhappy husband begins a long (18) *search* for his lost breath. Finally he finds it. On the very day of the argument, a (19) *man* by the name of Mr. Windenough had "caught his breath." The end of the story is a happy (20) *one*.

WRITING APPLICATION B:
Using Complements to Make
Your Writing More Concise

Well-chosen complements express your meaning directly and precisely. They enable you to avoid overloading your sentences with explanatory or descriptive modifiers. Notice how longwinded the first example is and how concise the second one is.

EXAMPLES   Whenever our family takes an auto trip, Seth always knows what road we are on, what turns we should make, and what landmarks to look for.
Seth is our family's navigator on auto trips.

Writing Assignment

You are applying for membership in a school or community activity (newspaper staff, sports team, entertainment troupe, etc.) The application form includes space for a brief description of yourself that shows how you are qualified for membership. Choose the group (real or fictitious) to which you are applying. Make a list of at least ten adjectives and nouns that would best describe you to that group. Write the description, using complements that portray you precisely and concisely.

CLASSIFYING SENTENCES BY PURPOSE

Your sentences reflect your purpose as a speaker or writer. You use them to make statements, ask questions, state commands or requests, or express strong feelings. One way of classifying sentences is according to these four purposes.

13l. Sentences may be classified as *declarative*, *imperative*, *interrogative*, or *exclamatory*.

(1) A *declarative* sentence makes a statement.

Declarative sentences make assertions or state ideas without expecting a reply. Most sentences are declarative. All declarative sentences are followed by periods.

EXAMPLE   Dr. Rosalyn Yalow won a Nobel Prize in medicine in 1977.

(2) An *imperative* sentence gives a command or makes a request.

A command or a request has the understood subject *you*. The imperative sentence is usually followed by a period. Very strong commands, however, may take an exclamation point.

EXAMPLES   Open your books to page three.
Be careful of the undertow.
Stop!

(3) An *interrogative* sentence asks a question.

To *interrogate* means to "ask." An interrogative sentence is followed by a question mark.

EXAMPLES   Can she finish in time?
How did she find Irene and Bea?

(4) An *exclamatory* sentence expresses strong feeling. It exclaims.

An exclamatory sentence is always followed by an exclamation point.

EXAMPLES   Oh, no! The battery is dead!
I can't believe this is happening!

EXERCISE 25. Classifying and Punctuating Sentences According to Purpose. Write the last word of each of the following sentences, and then add the correct mark of punctuation. Classify each sentence as imperative, declarative, interrogative, or exclamatory.

EXAMPLE   1. Koji Gushiken is an excellent gymnast
              1. *gymnast. declarative*

1. What a remarkable animal the gorilla is
2. Don't make the mistake of thinking this huge beast is ferocious and destructive
3. The gorilla is the gentle giant of the ape family
4. Do you know that an adult gorilla may weigh over four hundred pounds and stand six feet tall
5. Young gorillas seem to need companionship and affection
6. What happens to a young gorilla that lives in a zoo, far from others of its kind
7. It must have some favorite person to play with and befriend it, or it will pine and refuse to eat
8. Gorillas are as smart as chimpanzees
9. Films and adventure stories often portray this good-natured animal as a savage monster
10. Name the most famous of the fictional film gorillas

CHAPTER 13 REVIEW: POSTTEST 1

A. Identifying the Parts of a Sentence. Number your paper 1–20. Copy each italicized word and identify it, using the following abbreviations:

s. subject	*p.a.* predicate adjective
v. verb	*d.o.* direct object
p.n. predicate nominative	*i.o.* indirect object

EXAMPLE   1. Are you a mystery *fan*?
              1. *fan p.n.*

Sir Arthur Conan Doyle gave his (1) *readers* a wonderful (2) *gift* when he (3) *created* the character of Sherlock Holmes. (4) *Holmes* is the absolute (5) *master* of the science of deduction. He (6) *observes* seemingly insignificant (7) *clues,* applies logical reasoning, and reaches simple yet astounding conclusions.

The Hound of the Baskervilles is an excellent (8) *example* of Holmes in action, for he solves a baffling (9) *mystery.* The (10) *residents* of a rural area believe that a supernatural dog (11) *kills* people at night. Of course, they seek the (12) *aid* of Sherlock Holmes. Using deduction, he solves the mystery and releases the (13) *people* from their fear. The supernatural creature is actually a huge (14) *dog.* It appears (15) *savage* and gruesome because it was painted with phosphorus.

B. Identifying and Punctuating the Kinds of Sentences.
Copy the last word of each of the following sentences, and then give the correct mark of punctuation. Classify each sentence as imperative, declarative, interrogative or exclamatory.

16. How clever Sherlock Holmes is
17. Doyle wrote four novels and fifty-six short stories about Holmes
18. Have you read any of these stories
19. Read just one of these stories and then see whether you can avoid reading more
20. You will see why millions of readers love Sherlock Holmes

---

CHAPTER 13 REVIEW: POSTTEST 2

Writing Sentences. Write your own sentences according to the following guidelines. Underline the specified part or parts.

EXAMPLE 1. A sentence beginning with *There* with a compound subject.
　　　　　1. *There* were *games* and *contests* for the children.

1. A declarative sentence with a compound verb
2. An interrogative sentence with a compound subject
3. An imperative sentence with a noun of direct address
4. A sentence with a direct object
5. A sentence with an indirect object
6. A sentence with a predicate nominative
7. A sentence beginning with an adverb
8. A sentence with an adjective modifying a complement
9. A sentence with a compound complement
10. A sentence ending with the verb

GRAMMAR

CHAPTER 14

The Phrase

PREPOSITIONAL, VERBAL, AND APPOSITIVE PHRASES

In Chapter 12 you learned that two or more words (for example, *will be playing, were laughing, has done*) may be used as a verb. Such a word group is called a *verb phrase*.

Another kind of word group may be used as an adjective, an adverb, or a noun. You have already studied *prepositional phrases*. In this chapter, you will study prepositional phrases in greater detail, and you will learn about other kinds of phrases.

DIAGNOSTIC TEST

A. Identifying and Classifying Prepositional Phrases. The following passage contains ten prepositional phrases. Number your paper 1–10. Write each prepositional phrase in order, the word(s) modified, and the type of phrase (*adj.* for adjective phrase, *adv.* for adverb phrase).

EXAMPLE   1. Our family subscribes to a daily newspaper.
    1. *to a daily newspaper—subscribes—adv.*

A daily newspaper has something for everyone. In its pages we can find news, general information, opinion, and entertainment. Everyone has a favorite part of the paper. Some people begin with the sports pages; others prefer the general news. Comic strips are also offered by many newspapers. Here we can follow characters like Charlie Brown and Snoopy. The opinion pages can be fascinating, especially when a debate between two sides develops. Sometimes the reader discovers the logic behind an argument, while at other times one may wonder why grown people argue about some trivial issue.

B. Identifying Verbals and Appositives. The following sentences contain italicized words and phrases. Number your paper 11–20 and copy each italicized word or phrase. Tell whether each word or phrase is a participle, a gerund, an infinitive, or an appositive.

EXAMPLE 1. The young woman, *an excellent athlete,* wanted *to earn a gold medal* for her *swimming.*
1. *an excellent athlete, appositive*
to earn a gold medal, infinitive
swimming, gerund

11. Amateur athletic competition, *enjoyed* by people throughout history, involves more than *winning an event.*
12. When talented amateurs compete *to test their skills,* much can be gained.
13. The love of a sport, the best *reason* for *entering a competition,* can grow in a wholesome atmosphere.
14. *Sharing hard work* with teammates also helps a person *to appreciate cooperative effort.*
15. Finally, an *exciting* competition is an experience impossible *to forget.*
16. For these reasons, we see competitions *organized* on many levels.
17. We have local competitions with school, town, or club teams, all *concerned* with *trying their best.*
18. District, state, and national competitions, *events* drawn from larger groups, are also popular with amateur athletes around the country.

19. Then we have international competition, the ultimate *dream* for many young people.
20. Both the Olympics and the Special Olympics allow people from *far-removed* areas of the world *to match* themselves against others in their field.

14a. A *phrase* is a group of related words that is used as a single part of speech and does not contain a verb and its subject.

EXAMPLES **has been sitting** [verb phrase; no subject]
about you and me [prepositional phrase; no subject or verb]

A group of words that has a subject *and* a verb is not a phrase.

EXAMPLES **We found** your pen. [a subject and a verb; *we* is the subject of *found*]
if **she will go** [a subject and a verb; *she* is the subject of *will go*]

EXERCISE 1. Identifying Phrases. Number your paper 1–10. Write *p.* if the group of words is a *phrase.* Write *n.p.* if a word group is *not a phrase.*

1. was hoping
2. if she really knows
3. with Alice and me
4. will be writing
5. inside the house
6. since Donna wrote
7. after they leave
8. has been cleaned
9. on Lotte's desk
10. as the plane lands

PREPOSITIONAL PHRASES

14b. A *prepositional phrase* is a group of words beginning with a preposition and ending with a noun or pronoun.

In the following examples of prepositional phrases, the prepositions are boldfaced.

instead of a picnic   **at** our house   **to** the pool

Some prepositions are made up of more than one word, like *instead of* in the first example. Notice that an article or other modifier often appears in the prepositional phrase: the first example contains *a;* the second *our;* the third, *the.*

14c. The noun or pronoun that ends the prepositional phrase is the *object* of the preposition that begins the phrase.

The prepositional phrases in the following sentence are in boldfaced type.

> **In their fight against cancer,** scientists have discovered interferon.

Here *fight* is the object of the preposition *in.* How is *cancer* used? What preposition does it follow?

Objects of prepositions may be compound.

EXAMPLES   Kyoko called **to Nancy and me.** [Both *Nancy* and *me* are objects of the preposition *to.*]
          The marbles were scattered **under the table and chairs.** [The preposition *under* has a compound object, *tables* and *chairs.*]

Do not be misled by a modifier coming after the noun or pronoun in a prepositional phrase; the noun or pronoun is still the object.

EXAMPLE   Mother and Mrs. Braun worked **at the polls** today. [The object of the preposition *at* is *polls;* the adverb *today* tells *when* and modifies the verb *worked.*]

EXERCISE 2. Identifying Prepositions and Their Objects.
In the following sentences there are twenty prepositions. Write each preposition and its object. Indicate the number of the sentence as shown in the example.

EXAMPLE   1. Lady Jane Grey was a most unfortunate queen; she reigned over England for only nine days.
        1. *over—England*
          for—days

1. This bright and lovely young girl was caught up in intrigue and a bloody struggle for power.
2. When Henry VIII died, his young son Edward succeeded him as king.
3. Only a boy, Edward was used by the cunning Duke of Northumberland for his own purposes.
4. Northumberland wanted the power of the throne for himself and his family.
5. Jane had no claim to the throne, for Edward had two sisters, Mary and Elizabeth.
6. Nevertheless, Northumberland forced her into marriage with his own son.
7. The evil duke persuaded the young king that he should name Lady Jane as the heir to the throne.
8. Therefore, when Edward died at fifteen of tuberculosis, Jane Grey was proclaimed queen.
9. After only nine days, the throne was restored to Mary, the rightful heir.
10. Sixteen-year-old Jane was imprisoned and executed on charges of high treason against the crown.

The Adjective Phrase

Prepositional phrases are used in sentences mainly as adjectives and adverbs. Prepositional phrases used as adjectives are called *adjective phrases* and modify nouns or pronouns in much the same way as single-word adjectives.

EXAMPLE   The members **of the club** want sweatshirts **with the club emblem.**

The prepositional phrase *of the club* is used as an adjective modifying the noun *members. With the club emblem* is also used as an adjective because it modifies the noun *sweatshirts.*

Study the following pairs of sentences. Notice that the nouns used as adjectives may easily be converted to objects of prepositions in adjective phrases.

GRAMMAR

NOUNS USED AS ADJECTIVES	ADJECTIVE PHRASES
The **kitchen** light is on.	The light **in the kitchen** is on.
The **Chicago** and **New York** airports are crowded.	The airports **in Chicago and New York** are crowded.

Unlike a one-word adjective, which usually precedes the word it modifies, an adjective phrase always follows the noun or pronoun it modifies.

More than one prepositional phrase may modify the same word.

EXAMPLE   The bottle **of vitamins on the shelf** is mine. [The prepositional phrases *of vitamins* and *on the shelf* modify the noun *bottle*.]

A prepositional phrase may also modify the object of another prepositional phrase.

EXAMPLE   The horse **with the white blaze on its face** broke loose. [The phrase *with the white blaze* modifies the noun *horse*. *Blaze* is the object of the preposition *with*. The phrase *on its face* modifies *blaze*.]

EXERCISE 3. Revising Sentences by Using Adjective Phrases.   Revise the following sentences by using adjective phrases in place of the italicized nouns used as adjectives. Be sure you can tell which word each phrase modifies.

1. Jan Precure has a new *computer* table.
2. We bought a new *porch* swing.
3. The *car* seats were scorching hot.
4. The *St. Louis* arch is a well-known landmark.
5. The *barn* door was left open.
6. We need to get a new *dog* chain.
7. Saturday was a perfect *autumn* day.
8. His music appeals to *rhythm and blues* fans. *(one phrase)*
9. The mayor discussed the *Boston traffic* problem. *(two phrases)*
10. Visitors to the city should have a *subway* map. *(one phrase)*

The Adverb Phrase

When a prepositional phrase is used as an adverb to tell *when, where, how, how much,* or *how far,* it is called an *adverb phrase.*

EXAMPLES   She sailed **across the lake.** [The adverb phrase *across the lake* tells *where* she sailed.]
Tim will finish **by Wednesday.** [The adverb phrase *by Wednesday* tells *when* Tim will finish.]
She answered **with a smile.** [The adverb phrase *with a smile* tells *how* she answered.]
The calculations erred **by two inches.** [*By two inches* is an adverb phrase telling *how far* the calculations erred.]

In the examples above, the adverb phrases modify verbs. An adverb phrase may also modify an adjective or an adverb.

EXAMPLES   Mother is good **at tennis** but better **at volleyball.** [The adverb phrase *at tennis* modifies the adjective *good; at volleyball,* another adverb phrase, modifies the adjective *better.*]
I called Father early **in the morning.** [The adverb phrase *in the morning* modifies the adverb *early.*]

Adjective phrases always follow the words they modify, but an adverb phrase may appear at various places in a sentence.

As is true for adjective phrases, more than one adverb phrase may modify the same word.

EXAMPLE   **During summers,** my older sister works **at the museum.**
[The adverb phrases *during summers* and *at the museum* both modify the verb *works.* The first phrase tells *when* my sister works; the second phrase tells *where* she works. Notice that the first phrase precedes the word it modifies; the second phrase follows it.]

EXERCISE 4. Identifying Adverb Phrases and the Words They Modify.   Number your paper 1–10. Write the preposi-

tional phrases used as adverbs in each sentence. There may be more than one in a sentence. After each adverb phrase, write the word it modifies.

1. Yesterday afternoon, many Chicago residents suffered from the heat.
2. In the morning, my friends and I drove to Lincoln Park.
3. At noon, we ate our big picnic lunch with gusto.
4. Later in the day, we walked around the park.
5. A monument stands near the picnic grounds.
6. This unusual monument shows humanity as it marches through time.
7. In Rockefeller Center I once saw another artist's concept of time.
8. Three figures are painted on the ceiling; they represent Past, Present, and Future.
9. Wherever you stand in the room, Past's eyes are turned away from you; Future's eyes look outward and upward.
10. The eyes of Present, however, look straight at you.

Diagraming Prepositional Phrases

The preposition that begins the prepositional phrase is placed on a slanting line leading down from the word that the phrase modifies. Its object is placed on a horizontal line connected to the slanting line. The slanting line extends slightly below the horizontal line.

EXAMPLES   **By chance,** a peasant uncovered a wall **of ancient Pompeii.** [adverb phrase modifying the verb; adjective phrase modifying the direct object]

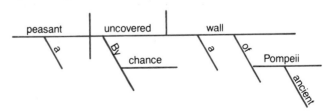

Our team practices late **in the afternoon.** [adverb phrase modifying an adverb]

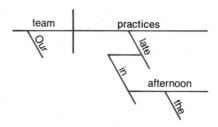

They drove **through the Maine woods** and **into southern Canada.** [two phrases modifying the same word]

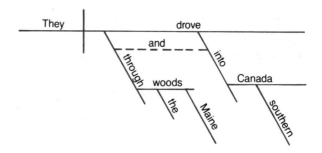

Mother taught the computer game **to my father, my uncles, and me.** [compound object of preposition]

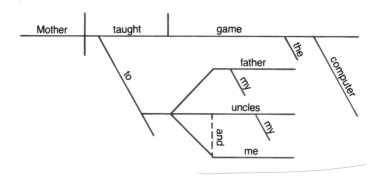

Follow the signs **to Highway 3 in Laconia.** [phrase modifying the object of another preposition]

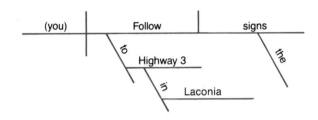

EXERCISE 5. Diagraming Sentences with Prepositional Phrases. Diagram the following sentences.

1. I have read many books by Arthur Conan Doyle about Sherlock Holmes.
2. One story about Holmes and Watson appears in our literature textbook.
3. Dozens of stories about Holmes are available in the school library.
4. The librarian took from his desk a new edition of one of Doyle's books.
5. He placed it in the display case in front of the window.

REVIEW EXERCISE A. Identifying and Classifying Prepositional Phrases.   There are ten prepositional phrases in the following sentences. Number your paper 1–4. List the prepositional phrases in each sentence, and after each, write how the phrase is used—as an adjective or an adverb.

EXAMPLE   1. Theories about the universe have changed over the years.
　　　　　　1. *about the universe—adj.*
　　　　　　over the years—adv.

1. About a half century ago at California's Mount Wilson Observatory, Edwin Hubble discovered that many other galaxies existed outside the Milky Way.

2. Now we know that there are perhaps a million galaxies inside the bowl of the Big Dipper alone.
3. Our galaxy is only one among billions throughout the universe!
4. Would Copernicus be amazed at the extent of space exploration in our time?

WRITING APPLICATION A:
Using Prepositional Phrases
to Add Variety to Your Writing

A few lucky people are skilled in several different areas. They are, for instance, outstanding students, athletes, and musicians. These people are versatile. Prepositional phrases are also versatile. They can explain where (*to the beach*). They can tell when (*in the morning*), and they can tell how long (*for two hours*). They can act as adjectives (the girl *in the third row*) or adverbs (he rested *for a while*).

Writing Assignment

Plan a treasure hunt that includes ten stops for clues. Write a prepositional phrase in each clue. Underline the prepositional phrase and, in parentheses, tell what kind it is. If your clue contains more than one prepositional phrase, be sure to underline all of them.

EXAMPLE   Look *under the west bleacher in the gym.* (adv., adj.)

VERBALS AND VERBAL PHRASES

Verbals are formed from verbs, and like verbs they may be modified by adverbs and may have complements. They are, however, used as other parts of speech.

There are three kinds of verbals: *participles, gerunds,* and *infinitives.*

The Participle

14d. A *participle* is a verb form that can be used as an adjective.

The participle is part verb and part adjective. It might be called a "verbal adjective."

EXAMPLES **Waxed** floors can be dangerously slippery.
Darting suddenly, the cat escaped through the door.

Waxed, formed from the verb *wax,* modifies the noun *floors.* *Darting,* formed from the verb *dart,* modifies the noun *cat.* These verb forms used as adjectives are *participles.*

There are two kinds of participles: *present participles* and *past participles.*

(1) *Present participles* consist of the plain form of the verb plus -*ing*.[1]

EXAMPLES The **pouring** rain drove us inside.
Watching the clock, the coach became worried.

In the first example, *pouring* (formed by adding -*ing* to the verb *pour*) is a present participle modifying the noun *rain.* In the second, the present participle *watching* (consisting of the plain form of the verb *watch* plus -*ing*) modifies the noun *coach*— *watching coach.*

Although participles are formed from verbs, they are not used to stand alone as verbs. A participle may, however, be used with a helping verb to form a verb phrase:

The rain **was pouring.**
The coach **had been watching** the clock.

When a participle is used in a verb phrase, it is considered as part of the verb, not as an adjective.

(2) *Past participles* usually consist of the plain form of the verb plus -*d* or -*ed*. Others are irregularly formed.[2]

[1] The plain form of the verb is the infinitive form. (See pages 497–98.)
[2] See the discussion of irregular verbs on pages 498–500.

EXAMPLES   A **peeled** and **sliced** cucumber can be added to a garden salad. [The past participles *peeled* and *sliced* modify the noun *cucumber*.]
The speaker, **known** for her eloquent speeches, drew applause from the audience. [The past participle *known* modifies the noun *speaker—known speaker*.]

Like a present participle, a past participle can also be part of a verb phrase. When used in a verb phrase it is considered to be part of the verb, not an adjective.

EXAMPLES   She **was told** that tickets were available.
She **has corrected** her homework.

EXERCISE 6. Identifying Participles and the Words They Modify.
Number your paper 1–10. List the participles used as adjectives in the following sentences, and after each participle, write the noun or pronoun modified.

1. The prancing horses were loudly applauded by the delighted audience.
2. The colorful flags, waving in the breeze, brightened the gloomy day.
3. Swaggering and boasting, he made the entire team extremely angry.
4. The game scheduled for tonight has been postponed because of rain.
5. Leaving the field, the happy player rushed to her parents sitting in the bleachers.
6. Rain pattering on the roof made an eerie sound.
7. We thought the banging shutter upstairs was someone walking in the attic.
8. Painfully sunburned, I vowed never again to be so careless at the beach.
9. Terrified by our big dog, the burglar turned and fled.
10. The platoon of soldiers, marching in step, crossed the field to the stirring music of the military band.

EXERCISE 7. Writing Sentences with Participles. Write five sentences, using a different one of the following participles in each. Be careful not to use a participle in a verb phrase.

EXAMPLE 1. latched
            1. *The latched gate will keep trespassers away.*

1. running   3. challenged   5. written
2. scorched   4. missing

EXERCISE 8. Writing Appropriate Participles. Number your paper 1–10. Next to each number, write a participle that fits the meaning of the sentence.

EXAMPLE 1. The —— tide washed over the beach.
            1. *rising*

1. Jan Evers, —— in a recent magazine, describes a tragic forest fire.
2. —— from the point of view of a firefighter, the story is full of accurate detail.
3. A mountain lion, —— by the sweeping flames, is dramatically rescued by the firefighters.
4. —— by the traffic police, the motorist offered an excuse.
5. The tourists —— in the hotel were given a free meal.
6. —— as an excellent place to camp, the park lived up to its reputation.
7. —— by a bee, Candace hurried to the infirmary.
8. The poem describes a spider —— on a thread.
9. We stumbled off the race course, ——.
10. ——, I quickly phoned the hospital.

The Participial Phrase

A participle may be modified by an adverb or by a prepositional phrase, and it may have a complement. These related words combine with the participle in a *participial phrase*.

14e. A *participial phrase* consists of a participle and its related words, such as modifiers and complements, all of which act together as an adjective.

The participial phrase in each of the following sentences is in boldfaced type. An arrow points to the noun or pronoun that the phrase modifies.

EXAMPLES **Switching its tail,** the panther paced. [participle with object *tail*]

She heard me sighing loudly. [participle with the adverb modifier *loudly*]

Living in Nebraska, he learned to respect blizzards. [participle with prepositional phrase modifier *in Nebraska*]

Quickly snatching up the keys, I dashed for the door. [Notice that *quickly,* which precedes the participle and modifies it, is included in the phrase.]

A participial phrase should be placed very close to the word it modifies. Otherwise the phrase may appear to modify another word, and the sentence may not make sense.[1]

MISPLACED He saw a moose riding his motorcycle through the woods. [The placement of the modifier calls up a silly picture. He, not the moose, is riding the motorcycle.]

IMPROVED Riding his motorcycle through the woods, he saw a moose.

EXERCISE 9. Writing Sentences with Participial Phrases.
Write five sentences using a different one of the following parti-

[1] The punctuation of participial phrases is discussed on pages 605–06 and 610–11. The participle as a dangling modifier is discussed on pages 549–51. Combining sentences using participles is discussed on pages 316–17.

cipial phrases in each. Be sure to place each phrase very close to the noun or pronoun it modifies and to punctuate the phrases correctly.

EXAMPLE 1. swirling the beaker of liquid
1. *Swirling the beaker of liquid, Angie watched the solution slowly change color.*

1. decorated with streamers of crepe paper
2. laughing at my silly joke
3. charging like an angry bull
4. kept in a sunny spot
5. speaking as quickly as possible

The Gerund

14f. A *gerund* is a verb form ending in *-ing* that is used as a noun.

A participle is part verb and part adjective. A *gerund* is part verb and part noun. It is formed by adding *-ing* to the plain form of the verb. Like nouns, gerunds are used as subjects, predicate nominatives, direct objects, or objects of prepositions. Study the boldfaced words in the following examples, noting how each is both a verb and a noun.

EXAMPLES **Singing** is fun. [subject]
Their favorite exercise is **running.** [predicate nominative]
Shelly likes **swimming.** [direct object]
Get special shoes for **jogging.** [object of preposition]

Like nouns, gerunds may be modified by adjectives and adjective phrases.

EXAMPLES We listened to the **beautiful** singing **of the cardinal.**
[The adjective *beautiful* and the adjective phrase *of the cardinal* modify the gerund *singing. Singing* is used as the object of the preposition *to*.]

The **loud** ringing **of my alarm** wakes me every morning. [Both the adjective *loud* and the adjective phrase *of my alarm* modify the gerund *ringing*, which is the subject of the sentence.]

Like verbs, gerunds may also be modified by adverbs and adverb phrases.

EXAMPLES Floating **lazily in the pool** is my favorite summer pastime. [The gerund *floating*, used as the subject of the sentence, is modified by the adverb *lazily* and also by the adverb phrase *in the pool*, which tells *where*.]

Brandywine enjoys galloping **briskly on a cold morning.** [The gerund *galloping*, which is a direct object of the sentence, is modified by the adverb *briskly* and also by the adverb phrase *on a cold morning*, which tells *when*.]

Gerunds, like present participles, end in *-ing*. To be a gerund, a verbal must be used as a noun. In the following sentence, three words end in *-ing*, but only one of them is a gerund.

EXAMPLE **Accepting** the coach's advice, she was **planning** to go on with her **training.**

Accepting is a present participle modifying *she*, and *planning* is part of the verb phrase *was planning*. Only *training*, used as object of the preposition *with*, is a gerund.

EXERCISE 10. Identifying and Classifying Gerunds. List each gerund in the following sentences. Then write how each is used: *subject, predicate nominative, direct object,* or *object of preposition.*

1. Her laughing attracted my attention.
2. By studying, you can improve your grades.
3. One requirement is practicing.
4. Yelling violates basic rules of courtesy.

5. Frowning, Dad discouraged our bickering.
6. Yvette's favorite sport is boating.
7. Before leaving, we sat and watched the fading light.
8. Yesterday, Mrs. Jacobs was discussing flying.
9. One of Steve's bad habits is boasting.
10. Without knocking, the hurrying child opened the door.

EXERCISE 11. Identifying and Classifying Gerunds.   List each gerund in the following sentences. Then write how each is used: *subject, predicate nominative, direct object,* or *object of preposition.*

EXAMPLE   1. George's greatest pleasure is fishing.
                 1. *fishing—predicate nominative*

1. Victor's greatest talent is cooking.
2. We never gain anything by wishing for it.
3. Walking is an exercise for everyone, young or old.
4. Do you really enjoy painting?
5. After swimming, the children were ready to go home.
6. Laughing is a healthful exercise.
7. Our planning paid off with an exciting class trip.
8. By taking a hot shower, Adela relaxed her aching muscles.
9. At today's practice we concentrated on passing the ball.
10. The sophomores are enjoying woodworking this semester.

The Gerund Phrase

14g. A *gerund phrase* consists of a gerund together with its complements and modifiers, all of which act together as a noun.

EXAMPLES   **The gentle pattering of the rain** was the only sound. [The gerund phrase is used as the subject of the sentence. The gerund *pattering* is modified by the article *the,* the adjective *gentle,* and the prepositional phrase *of the rain.* Notice that modifiers preceding the gerund are included in the gerund phrase.]

I feared **skiing rapidly down the mountain.** [The gerund phrase is used as the object of the verb *feared*. The gerund *skiing* is modified by the adverb *rapidly* and by the prepositional phrase *down the mountain*.]

His job is **giving the customers their menus.** [The gerund phrase is used as a predicate nominative. The gerund *giving* has a direct object, *menus,* and an indirect object, *customers*.]

Evelyn Ashford won the gold medal for **running the hundred-meter dash.** [The gerund phrase is the object of the preposition *for*. The gerund *running* has a direct object, *dash*.]

☞ **NOTE** Whenever a noun or pronoun comes before a gerund, the possessive form should be used.

EXAMPLES   **Pedro's** constant practicing improved **his** playing.
My playing the radio loudly is a bad habit.

EXERCISE 12. Writing Sentences with Gerund Phrases.

Study the example. Then, following the directions given, write five sentences of your own. Underline the gerund phrase in each of your sentences.

EXAMPLE   1. Use *writing* as the subject of the sentence. Include an adjective modifying the gerund.
1. *Clear writing* is an essential communications skill.

1. Use *cheering* as the subject. Include an adjective phrase modifying the gerund.
2. Use *buying* as the direct object of the sentence. Include a direct object of the gerund.
3. Use *showing* as the object of a preposition. Include in the gerund phrase a direct object and an indirect object of *showing*.

4. Use *talking* as the predicate nominative. Include an adverb and an adverb phrase modifying the gerund.
5. Use *speaking* as a gerund in any way you choose. Include in the gerund phrase a possessive pronoun modifying the gerund.

The Infinitive

14h. An *infinitive* is a verb form, usually preceded by *to*, that can be used as a *noun, adjective,* or *adverb.*

An infinitive consists of the plain form of the verb, usually preceded by *to.* It can be used as a noun, an adjective, or an adverb. Carefully study the following examples.

Infinitives used as nouns: **To love is to care.** [*To love* is the subject of the sentence; *to care* is the predicate nominative.] Cheryl wanted **to work** on the play in any way but **to act.** [*To work* is the object of the verb *wanted; to act* is the object of the preposition *but.*]

Infinitives used as adjectives: The place **to visit** is Williamsburg. [*To visit* modifies *place.*]
That was a record **to beat.** [*To beat* modifies *record.*]

Infinitives used as adverbs: Sabina Miller jumped **to shoot.** [*To shoot* modifies *jumped.*]
Ready **to go,** we loaded the car. [*To go* modifies the adjective *ready.*]

☞ **NOTE** *To* plus a noun or pronoun (*to school, to him, to the beach*) is a prepositional phrase, not an infinitive. An infinitive is always the first principal part of the verb.

EXERCISE 13. Identifying and Classifying Infinitives.
Make a list of the infinitives in the following sentences. Write how each is used: *noun, adjective,* or *adverb.*

EXAMPLE   1. I would like to help you.
            1. *to help—noun*

1. Barbara's ambition is to fly.
2. The road to take is the one on the left.
3. Fred has learned to tap-dance.
4. I am happy to oblige.
5. An easy way to win at tennis does not exist.
6. The grass began to grow after the much-needed rain.
7. The math team went to Coach Norton's house to study.
8. We met at the lake to fish.
9. That is not the correct amount of paper to order.
10. To persist can be a sign of stubbornness.

The Infinitive Phrase

14i. An *infinitive phrase* **consists of an infinitive together with its complements and modifiers.**[1]

Infinitive phrases, like infinitives alone, can be used as adjectives, adverbs, or nouns.

EXAMPLES   **To proofread your writing carefully** is important. [The infinitive phrase is used as a noun, as the subject of the sentence. The infinitive has an object, *writing,* and is modified by the adverb *carefully.*]
They wanted **to vacation in New York.** [The infinitive phrase is used as a noun—the object of *wanted.* The infinitive is modified by the phrase *in New York.*]
She is the player **to watch in the next game.** [The infinitive phrase is used as an adjective modifying the predicate nominative *player.* The infinitive is modified by the adverbial prepositional phrase *in the next game.*]

---

[1] An infinitive may have a subject: I wanted him to help me with my algebra. [*Him* is the subject of the infinitive *to help.* The infinitive, together with its subject, complements, and modifiers, is sometimes called an *infinitive clause.*]

We are eager **to finish this project.** [The infinitive phrase is used as an adverb modifying the predicate adjective *eager*. The infinitive has a direct object, *project*.]

The Infinitive with "to" Omitted

Sometimes the *to* of the infinitive will be omitted in a sentence.

EXAMPLES   I'll help you **pack.**
Marla let the dogs **run** loose in the field.
We watched the dancers **practice** the new routine.

EXERCISE 14. Identifying and Classifying Infinitives and Infinitive Phrases.   Write the infinitives or infinitive phrases in the following sentences. After each one, give its use: *noun, adjective,* or *adverb.*

1. To dance gracefully requires coordination.
2. She wanted to join the chorus.
3. Sandy needs to study.
4. I'm going to the pond to fish.
5. A good way to lose weight is to eat moderately.
6. After our long vacation, we needed to get back in training.
7. The best way to get there is to take the bus.
8. Don't dare open that present before your birthday.
9. Juanita and Matt shopped to find the perfect gift.
10. He lives to swim and to water-ski.

EXERCISE 15. Writing Sentences with Infinitive Phrases. Write five sentences, following the directions given for each. Underline each infinitive phrase on your paper.

1. Use *to succeed* as a direct object.
2. Use *to see* as an adjective, with a phrase modifier.
3. Use *to leave* as an adverb modifying an adjective.
4. Use *to make* as the subject of a sentence. Include a direct object of the infinitive.

5. Use *to catch* in any way you choose. Then write how you used it: *noun, direct object, adverb modifying the verb*, etc.

REVIEW EXERCISE B. Identifying and Classifying Verbals and Verbal Phrases. Number your paper 1–10; after each number, write the verbal or verbal phrase in the sentence. Identify each as *gerund, gerund phrase, infinitive, infinitive phrase, participle,* or *participial phrase.*

EXAMPLE: 1. We heard thunder rumbling in the distance.
   1. *rumbling in the distance—participial phrase*

1. The skillful miming delighted the audience.
2. Several faculty members offered to chaperon the class trip.
3. The luckless hunters passed the time by telling tales of past successes.
4. Squeaking chalk can set people's teeth on edge.
5. Both Cocheta and Sarah love to ride the roller coaster.
6. Playing golf is a popular summertime activity at the resort.
7. The answer to your question can be found in the book lying on this desk.
8. Even those who never write letters enjoy receiving them.
9. If you were to review a recent movie, which would you select?
10. Jody was proud of his worn-out catcher's mitt, but his teammates thought it was too old.

Diagraming Verbals and Verbal Phrases

Participial phrases are diagramed as follows:

EXAMPLE **Wagging its tail,** the large dog leaped at me.

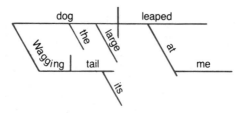

Gerunds and gerund phrases are diagramed as follows:

EXAMPLE **Being tired of the constant cold is a good reason for taking a vacation in the winter.** [Gerund phrases used as subject and as object of preposition. The first gerund has a subject complement (*tired*); the second one has a direct object (*vacation*) and an adverb prepositional phrase modifier (*in the winter*).]

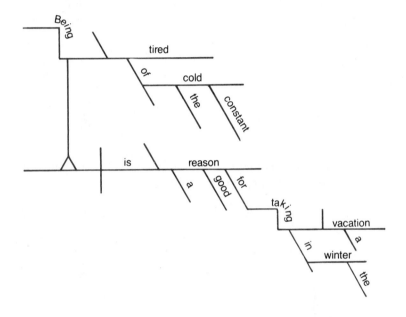

Infinitives and infinitive phrases used as modifiers are diagramed like prepositional phrases.

EXAMPLE I am leaving early **to get the tickets.** [Infinitive phrase used as adverb. The infinitive has an object, *tickets*.]

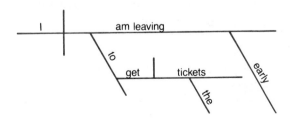

Infinitives used as nouns are diagramed as follows:

EXAMPLE **To join the Air Force** is his longtime ambition.

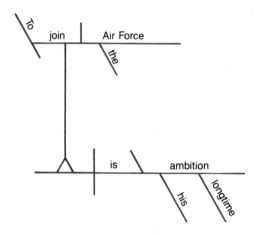

Notice how the subject of an infinitive is diagramed and how the infinitive is diagramed when *to* is omitted:

EXAMPLE Our brother helped us **play** the game.

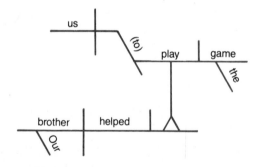

EXERCISE 16. Diagraming Sentences with Verbal Phrases.
Diagram the following sentences:

1. Riding our horses in the field will be fun.
2. Knowing the danger, I waved to warn them.
3. To make good tacos, use fresh tortillas.
4. Until reading that article, I wanted to be a distance runner.

5. The camp counselor working in the stables made us clean the stalls.

WRITING APPLICATION B:
Using Verbals to Enliven Your Writing

Have you heard of a little lizard called a chameleon? It has the ability to change its color according to its background. Verbs are similarly variable. They can change into participles, gerunds, or infinitives, according to how they are used in sentences. Using verbals gives your writing liveliness and movement that it might not otherwise have.

EXAMPLES The Eiffel Tower is 984 feet high and is a popular tourist attraction in Paris.
Soaring 984 feet into the Paris sky, the Eiffel Tower is a popular tourist attraction.

The second example, using a participial phrase, has more life and movement.

Writing Assignment

You plan to enter a triathlon. This is a race in which you ride your bicycle, run, and swim—one right after the other. Think of various kinds of exercises you should do to get in shape for this race. Write about your training program. Use at least five verbals to bring more life and movement to your explanation of the different exercises your training includes. Underline and classify the verbals.

EXAMPLE <u>Lifting weights</u> makes my arms stronger. (gerund)

APPOSITIVES AND APPOSITIVE PHRASES

Sometimes a noun or pronoun will be followed immediately by another noun or pronoun that identifies or explains it.

EXAMPLE The sculptor **Noguchi** has designed sculpture gardens.

In this sentence, the noun *Noguchi* tells *which* sculptor. *Noguchi* is said to be *in apposition with* the word *sculptor*. *Noguchi* in this sentence is called an *appositive*.

14j. An *appositive* is a noun or pronoun that follows another noun or pronoun to identify or explain it.

EXAMPLE Eric, a talented **musician,** plans to study in Europe.

Like any noun or pronoun, an appositive may have adjective and adjective phrase modifiers. If it does, it is called an *appositive phrase*.

14k. An *appositive phrase* is made up of the appositive and its modifiers.

In the following sentences the appositives and appositive phrases are in boldfaced type.

EXAMPLES My neighbor, **Dr. Welber,** got her degree in entomology, **the scientific study of insects.**
Lucy Babcock, **my longtime friend,** has a new Scotch terrier, **MacTavish.**

☞ **NOTE** Occasionally the appositive phrase precedes the noun or pronoun explained.

EXAMPLES **An accomplished gardener,** Mr. Bostwick could grow vegetables in Antarctica.
The terror of our block, little Alison, was on the warpath.

Appositives and appositive phrases are usually set off by commas, unless the appositive is a single word closely related to the preceding word. The comma is always used when the word to which the appositive refers is a proper noun.

EXAMPLES   Judge Randolph, **the woman running for Congress,** is our guest speaker.
My brother **Richard** goes to college.
Linda, **the editor,** assigned the story.
Maria is from Madison, **a town on the Ohio River.**

In diagraming, place the appositive in parentheses after the word with which it is in apposition.

EXAMPLE   The next show, **a musical comedy about high school,** was written by Mike Williams, **a talented young playwright.**

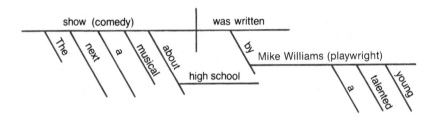

EXERCISE 17. Identifying Appositive Phrases.

Write the appositive phrases in each of the following sentences. Underline the appositive in each phrase, and be sure that you know the word to which each appositive refers.

1. Our community has a new organization, a writers' club called Writers, Inc.
2. Marquita Wiley, a college instructor, started the organization at the request of several of her former English students.
3. Ms. Wiley, a published author, conducts the meetings as workshops.
4. The writers meet to read their works in progress, fiction or poetry, and to discuss suggestions for improving their writing.
5. The members, people from all walks of life, have varied interests.

WRITING APPLICATION C:
Using Appositives to Add Clarity to Your Writing

Sometimes electric lights use three-way bulbs. Each time you turn the switch, a little more light fills the room. Appositives work similarly. Located next to their nouns, they add information that helps to clarify what you are talking about.

EXAMPLE   A machine records changes in heartbeat, blood pressure, and respiration.

A machine, *the polygraph*, records changes in heartbeat, blood pressure, and respiration.

Writing Assignment

You have been asked by your principal to chair a fundraising committee to build a new auditorium for your school. Make two different lists of people. On the first list include five students and faculty members who would be good committee members. On the second list include five people you intend to ask for donations. Use an appositive phrase to identify each of the ten people. Underline these phrases.

EXAMPLE   Maria Townsend, mayor of Topeka

REVIEW EXERCISE C. Identifying Verbals and Appositives. List the verbals and appositives in each sentence. After each, write in parentheses whether the word is *appositive, gerund, infinitive,* or *participle.*

EXAMPLE   1. Lucky, a performing seal, was able to attract the audience's attention by slapping the surface of the water.

1. *performing (participle)*
   seal (appositive)
   attract (infinitive)
   slapping (gerund)

1. Jumbo, the largest bush elephant ever held in captivity, was bought by the London Zoological Gardens in 1865.
2. Children enjoyed the thrill of riding on a seat strapped to its back.
3. Sold to P. T. Barnum in 1882, Jumbo was sent to the United States.
4. A star circus attraction until its death, Jumbo was tragically killed in a railroad accident in 1885.
5. Performing in Barnum's circus made the acrobat rich and famous.
6. Bobbie, a sheep dog from Oregon, accompanied its master on a trip to Indiana.
7. Its master stopped at a garage to make repairs one day.
8. As a result of fighting with a big bull terrier, Bobbie was chased away from the garage.
9. Having lost its master, the dog headed back to Oregon.
10. Crossing rivers, deserts, and mountains, the dog managed to complete the long journey in only six months.

CHAPTER 14 REVIEW: POSTTEST 1

A. Identifying and Classifying Prepositional Phrases. The following passage contains ten prepositional phrases. Number your paper 1–10, and write each prepositional phrase in order. After each phrase write the word(s) it modifies, and the type of phrase it is (*adj.* for adjective phrase, *adv.* for adverb phrase).

EXAMPLE   1. The museums of different cities are fascinating to tourists.
  1. *of different cities—museums—adj.*
  to tourists—fascinating—adv.

New York City has a wealth of museums, both large and small. The first that comes to mind is the American Museum of Natural History, which has exhibits about almost everything. Human history and customs are shown, and the world's many animals are presented in their natural settings. Exhibits about both earth and space round out the offerings. This museum is also special because of the Hayden Planetarium, which features shows about the heavens. The entire complex is popular because it offers something for everyone. The city's other museums, while also fascinating, are more specific in their purposes.

B. Identifying Verbals and Appositives. The following sentences contain italicized verbals and appositives. Number your paper 11–20 and copy each italicized word, telling whether it is a participle, a gerund, an infinitive, or an appositive.

EXAMPLE 1. For some reason, *cleaning* a room, that *dreaded project,* always seems *to create* new projects.
    1. *cleaning—gerund*   *project—appositive*
       dreaded—participle   *to create—infinitive*

11. First, John tackled the pile of records and tapes *lying* near his *unused* stereo system.
12. John's first discovery, a real *shock,* was that the albums were *outdated.*
13. The tapes were worse; *left* by *visiting* friends, most did not even belong to John.
14. John realized that his *broken* stereo system was the culprit.
15. By *repairing* the stereo, John could give himself a reason *to update* his music collection.
16. *Trained* in electronics, John began *to work* and soon saw the problem.
17. After a *satisfying* morning, John had a *working* stereo system but a room no cleaner than before.
18. His sister didn't help by *crying* out, ''Mom's coming *to see* how your room looks!''
19. Quickly *picking* the scraps of wire off the floor, John greeted his mother by *playing* a record on the stereo.
20. Although *pleased* that John had done such a fine job with the stereo, Mom nevertheless insisted on his *cleaning* the room before he did anything else.

CHAPTER 14 REVIEW: POSTTEST 2

Writing Sentences with Phrases. Write ten sentences, following the directions given for each. Underline the specified phrase in each sentence.

1. Use an *adjective phrase* modifying the object of a preposition.
2. Use an *adverb phrase* modifying an adjective.
3. Use an *adverb phrase* modifying a verb.
4. Use a *participial phrase* modifying a subject.
5. Use a *participial phrase* modifying a direct object.
6. Use a *gerund phrase* as a subject.
7. Use a *gerund phrase* as a predicate nominative.
8. Use an *infinitive phrase* as a noun.
9. Use an *infinitive phrase* as an adverb.
10. Use an *appositive phrase* in the subject.

GRAMMAR

The Clause

INDEPENDENT AND SUBORDINATE CLAUSES

Like a phrase, a clause is a word group used as a part of a sentence. The difference is that a clause contains a verb and its subject, while a phrase does not.

DIAGNOSTIC TEST

A. Identifying and Classifying Subordinate Clauses. Number your paper 1–10. Write the subordinate clause in each of the following sentences. Identify the clause as *adj.* (adjective), *adv.* (adverb), or *n.* (noun). If the clause is used as an adjective or adverb, write the word or words it modifies. If the clause is used as a noun, write *subj.* for subject, *d.o.* for direct object, *i.o.* for indirect object, *p.n.* for predicate nominative, or *o.p.* for object of a preposition.

EXAMPLES   1. Emily Dickinson, who was a great American poet, was born in 1830.
        1. *who was a great American poet, adj., Emily Dickinson*
        2. I have noticed that her poems do not have titles.
        2. *that her poems do not have titles, n., d.o.*

1. Emily visited with her friends until she became a recluse in her father's house.
2. There she wrote the poetry that critics now acclaim as "great American poetry."
3. Unfortunately, only seven of Emily's poems were published while she was alive.
4. After she died in 1886, her other poems were published.
5. My teacher, Mrs. Brooks, has read whatever poems Dickinson had written.
6. Emily Dickinson is a poet whose poetry I read often.
7. The poems I have just finished reading are "A Narrow Fellow in the Grass" and "Apparently with No Surprise."
8. Dickinson's imagery in "Apparently with No Surprise" is what impresses me most.
9. I read her poems aloud so that I can listen to their rhythms.
10. Whatever I read by Emily Dickinson inspires me.

B. Classifying Sentences According to Structure.   Number your paper 11–20. Classify each of the following sentences according to its structure. Next to each number, write *simple, compound, complex,* or *compound-complex.* Be sure that you can identify all subordinate and independent clauses.

EXAMPLES   1. My history class and I visited the Senate chamber of the United States Capitol last week.
   1. *simple*
   2. Before we went, though, we read about the United States Senate.
   2. *complex*

11. Originally state legislatures voted for United States senators, but today voters elect the senators.
12. In 1913 Congress passed the Seventeenth Amendment, which gave voters the right to elect senators.
13. Today, voters elect a senator to a six-year term, and they can reelect a senator any number of times, if they wish.

14. Voters elect two senators from each state.
15. To be elected a senator, a person must have been a United States citizen for at least nine years.
16. In addition, she or he must by at least thirty years old and live in the state that she or he would like to represent.
17. Do you know what a United States senator does?
18. One very important job of a United States senator is to introduce bills into the Senate.
19. Another important job of a senator is to approve or reject certain presidential appointments, such as those of federal judges, ambassadors, and Cabinet members.
20. As I watched the Senate in session last week, I thought that I might like to become a United States senator someday.

15a. A *clause* is a group of words that contains a verb and its subject and is used as part of a sentence.

Although every clause has a subject and verb, not all clauses express a complete thought. Those that do are called *independent clauses*. Such clauses could be written as separate sentences. We think of them as clauses when they are joined with one additional clause or more in a single larger sentence. Clauses that do not make complete sense by themselves are called *subordinate clauses*. Subordinate clauses do the job of nouns, adjectives, or adverbs just as phrases do.

KINDS OF CLAUSES

15b. An *independent* (or *main*) *clause* expresses a complete thought and can stand by itself.

To see how independent clauses can be written as separate sentences, consider the following example (independent clauses are underlined).

EXAMPLES   <u>Ms. Santana works in one of the law offices in downtown Concord,</u> and <u>she has a successful practice.</u>

Each clause has its own subject and verb and expresses a complete thought. In this example, the clauses are joined by a comma and the coordinating conjunction *and*. They could also be written with a semicolon between them:

Ms. Santana works in one of the law offices in downtown Concord; she has a successful practice.

or as separate sentences:

Ms. Santana works in one of the law offices in downtown Concord. She has a successful practice.

15c. A *subordinate* (or *dependent*) *clause* does not express a complete thought and cannot stand alone.

Subordinate means "lesser in rank or importance." Subordinate clauses (also called *dependent* clauses) are so described because they need an independent clause to complete their meaning.

SUBORDINATE CLAUSES   before you know it
because I told him
after the show is over

Most subordinate clauses are introduced by a word like *when, if, until,* or *because* that makes them subordinate. When we hear a clause that starts with one of these words, we know that there has to be at least one more clause in the sentence, and that at least one of the other clauses must be an independent clause.

EXERCISE 1. Identifying Independent and Subordinate Clauses.   Number your paper 1–10. Identify each clause in italics by writing either *independent* or *subordinate* after the corresponding number.

1. *When my family went to New York last summer,* we visited the Theodore Roosevelt museum.

GRAMMAR

2. *The museum has been established in the house* where Roosevelt was born.
3. It is located on the basement floor of Roosevelt's birthplace, *which is on East Twentieth Street.*
4. *The museum contains books, letters, and documents* that pertain to Roosevelt's public life.
5. There are mounted heads of animals, a stuffed lion, and zebra skins from the days *when Roosevelt was hunting big game in Africa.*
6. *Because Roosevelt was once a cowboy,* there are also branding irons and chaps.
7. Before Theodore Roosevelt became President, *he gained fame in the Spanish-American War.*
8. During that war he led the Rough Riders, *who made the famous charge up San Juan Hill.*
9. Trophies *that Roosevelt received during his life* are on exhibit in the museum.
10. *The Roosevelt Memorial Association,* which established the museum, *charges a nominal admission fee to visitors.*

THE USES OF SUBORDINATE CLAUSES

Subordinate clauses, like phrases, function in sentences as single parts of speech. A subordinate clause can be used as an adjective, an adverb, or a noun, thus enabling us to express ideas that are difficult or impossible to state with single-word nouns and modifiers alone.

The Adjective Clause

15d. An *adjective clause* is a subordinate clause used as an adjective to modify a noun or pronoun.

In the following sentences the arrow points to the noun or pronoun that each adjective clause modifies.

EXAMPLES   This is the new music video **that I like best.**

Griffins, **which are mythological beasts,** are seen on many coats of arms.

The adjective clause follows the word it modifies, and it is sometimes set off by commas and sometimes not. Commas should be used unless the clause answers the question *Which one?* in which case no commas are used. In the first example, the clause *that I like best* tells *which* video; no comma is used. In the second example, the clause *which are mythological beasts* does not tell *which* griffins. It merely describes griffins. The clause is therefore set off by commas. (See pages 605–07.)

Relative Pronouns

Adjective clauses are generally introduced by *relative pronouns.* The relative pronouns are *who, whom, whose, which,* and *that.* They are called *relative* because they *relate* the adjective clause to the word that the clause modifies. In Chapter 1, you learned that the noun to which a pronoun refers is the *antecedent* of the pronoun. The noun or pronoun modified by the adjective clause, then, is the antecedent of the relative pronoun that introduces the clause. Besides introducing the adjective clause, the relative pronoun has a function in the clause.

EXAMPLES   Lois, **who enjoys running,** has decided to enter the marathon. [The relative pronoun *who* relates the adjective clause to *Lois. Who* is used as the subject of the adjective clause.]

Donna suggested the science project **that I exhibited at the fair.** [*Project,* the word that the clause modifies, is the antecedent of the relative pronoun *that.* The pronoun is used as the direct object in the adjective clause.]

The students questioned the data **on which the theory was based.** [The relative pronoun *which* is the object of the preposition *on* and relates the adjective clause to the pronoun's antecedent, *data.*]

We met the singer **whose record was released this week.** [The relative pronoun *whose* shows the relationship of the clause to *singer. Singer* is the antecedent of *whose.*]

Frequently the relative pronoun in the clause is omitted. The pronoun is understood and still has a function in the clause.

EXAMPLE   Here is the cheeseburger **you ordered.** [The relative pronoun *that* is understood. Here is the cheeseburger *that* you ordered. The pronoun relates the adjective clause to cheeseburger and is used as the direct object in the adjective clause.]

Occasionally an adjective clause will be introduced by the words *where* or *when.*

EXAMPLES   They showed us the stadium **where the game would be held.**
Summer is the season **when I feel happiest.**

EXERCISE 2. Identifying Adjective Clauses.   After the proper number on your paper, write the adjective clause from the corresponding sentence, underlining the relative pronoun that introduces the clause. Then write the antecedent of the relative pronoun after the clause.

EXAMPLE   1. The students who published the yearbook felt proud.
1. *who published the yearbook—students*

1. The people who tape television commercials are called production workers.
2. At the aquarium we saw a frog that is highly poisonous.
3. John Keats, who was one of the most promising of English poets, died in Rome.
4. The theater where we saw the play is being renovated.
5. Is this the captain whose quick thinking saved so many lives?
6. Lord Byron is the poet who was called "the most interesting personality in history."

7. Byron had a rebellious nature that often got him into trouble, but he also had a sense of humor.
8. The young Byron attended a university that would not let him keep his dog in his rooms.
9. He then found a pet for which the university had no rules.
10. Soon the authorities had to decide how to deal with a young poet who kept a tame bear in his rooms.

EXERCISE 3. Revising Sentences by Supplying Adjective Clauses. Revise each of the following sentences by substituting an adjective clause for each italicized adjective. Underline the adjective clause in your sentence.

EXAMPLES
1 The *angry* citizens gathered in front of City Hall.
   1. *The citizens, <u>who were furious over the recent tax increase</u>, gathered in front of City Hall.*
   2. The *old* history books lay on the shelf.
   2. *The history books, <u>which were yellow and tattered from many years of use</u>, lay on the shelf.*

1. The *colorful* painting caught our attention at the gallery.
2. The *patient* photographer sat on a small ledge all day.
3. The two parties argued all week over the *important* contract.
4. We decided on an expedition to the top of the *high* peak.
5. At the assembly, Ms. Leon made a *surprising* announcement.
6. Edgar and his friends cautiously entered the *dark* cave.
7. *Competent* Edna Jackson easily won her first political campaign.
8. The trainer used a tight leash for the *disobedient* dog.
9. Dodging to his left, Manuel scored the *winning* goal.
10. Near the stable, Pamela walked sadly with her *lame* horse.

The Adverb Clause

15e. An *adverb clause* is a subordinate clause that modifies a verb, an adjective, or an adverb.

An adverb clause tells *how, when, where, why, how much, to what extent,* or *under what condition* the action of the main verb takes place.

EXAMPLES   **After I revised my paper,** I typed it. [The adverb clause *After I revised my paper* tells when I typed it.]
Because manicotti takes so long to prepare, Joy makes it only on special occasions. [*Because manicotti takes so long to prepare* tells why Joy makes it only on special occasions.]
You may come along **if you want to.** [*If you want to* tells under what condition you may come along.]

The adverb clauses in the examples above modify verbs. Adverb clauses may also modify adjectives or adverbs.

EXAMPLES   His pitching arm is stronger today **than it ever was.** [The adverb clause modifies the adjective *stronger,* telling to what *extent* his arm is stronger.]
My cousin Adele reads faster **than I do.** [The adverb clause modifies the adverb *faster,* telling how much faster my cousin Adele reads.]

Subordinating Conjunctions

Adverb clauses are introduced by *subordinating conjunctions.*

Subordinating Conjunctions

after	before	unless
although	if	until
as	in order that	when
as if	since	whenever
as long as	so that	where
as soon as	than	wherever
because	though	while

☞ **NOTE** Remember that *after, before, since, until,* and *as* may also be used as prepositions.

GRAMMAR

EXERCISE 4. Identifying and Classifying Adverb Clauses.

After numbering your paper 1–10, write the subordinating conjunction and the last word of each adverb clause in the following sentences; then write what the clause tells: *when, where, how, why, how much, under what condition?* A sentence may have more than one adverb clause. (Notice that introductory adverb clauses are usually set off by commas.)

EXAMPLES 1. Though we didn't read much of Robert Frost's poetry in my class, he is still my favorite poet.
        1. *Though—class, under what condition*
        2. We will read "Mending Wall" as soon as we finish "At Woodward's Gardens."
        2. *as soon as—Gardens, when*

1. If you have never read any of Frost's poetry, you might like to read about him first.
2. Robert Frost and his family moved to New England when Frost was ten years old.
3. While Frost was growing up, he held many different jobs.
4. After he had taught awhile, he attended Harvard University.
5. Frost decided to move to England after he had studied at Harvard for two years.
6. While Frost was in England, he published two books of poetry.
7. After the public in England read his poetry, they acclaimed Frost as a great poet.
8. When Frost returned to the United States, he continued writing poetry.
9. Though Frost describes New England landscapes in his poems, the meanings of the poems themselves are much deeper.
10. You might like to keep some of Frost's books of poetry so that you will have them when you want them.

EXERCISE 5. Writing Sentences with Adverb Clauses.

Write five sentences of your own, using the following subordinate clauses as adverbs.

EXAMPLE 1. When the mail arrived
           1. *When the mail arrived, I was glad to find a letter from my cousin.*

1. if you read Emily Dickinson's poetry
2. although he liked pizza
3. whenever we play our record albums
4. while she was studying for her history exam
5. after your sister finishes her tennis game

The Noun Clause

15f. A *noun clause* is a subordinate clause used as a noun.

A noun clause may be used as a subject, a complement (predicate nominative, direct object, indirect object), or the object of a preposition.

Study the structure of the following sentences:

Subject	**What she did** was brave.
Predicate nominative	The winner will be **whoever runs fastest.**
Direct object	She learned **what the answer was.**
Indirect object	We tell **whoever calls** the sales prices.
Object of preposition	He checks the ID cards of **whoever visits.**

Noun clauses are usually introduced by *that, what, whatever, who, whoever, whom,* and *whomever.*

EXAMPLES They did not know **who it could be.** [The introductory word *who* is the predicate nominative of the noun clause—*it could be who.*]
        Show us **what you bought.** [The introductory word *what* is the direct object of the noun clause—*you bought what.*]
        She wished **that she were older.** [The introductory word *that* has no other function in the sentence.]

Noun clauses are sometimes used without the introductory word. Compare the noun clauses in the following sentences:

His mother said **that he could go.**
His mother said **he could go.** [The introductory word *that* is understood.]

EXERCISE 6. Identifying and Classifying Noun Clauses.

Write the first and the last word of each noun clause in these sentences. Then tell how the noun clause is used: *subject, predicate nominative, direct object, indirect object*, or *object of a preposition*. (You will not find noun clauses in every sentence.)

EXAMPLE 1. We moved to New England and did not know what we would find there.

    1. *what—there direct object*

1. What surprised me first were the yellowish green fire engines.
2. I had thought that fire engines were always red.
3. Our neighbors explained that the odd color kept the fire engines from being confused with other large red trucks.
4. My sister Patti was surprised by what she saw at the bowling alley.
5. The small grapefruit-sized bowling balls with no holes were not what she was used to!
6. Whoever can knock down the pins with one of those bowling balls must be an expert.
7. We learned that this sport is called "candlepin bowling."
8. I was pleasantly surprised by the delicious ice cream.
9. They should give an award to whoever invented New England ice cream.
10. Now after one year in New England, both Patti and I are happy in our new home.

Diagraming Subordinate Clauses

In a diagram, an adjective clause is joined to the word it modifies by a broken line leading from the relative pronoun to the modified word—that is, to the antecedent of the relative pronoun.

EXAMPLE   The restaurant **that we like best** serves excellent
          seafood.

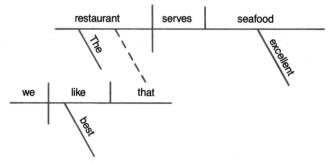

EXAMPLE   He is the teacher **from whom I take lessons.**

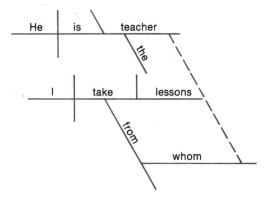

In diagraming an adverb clause, place the subordinating conjunction that introduces the clause on a broken line leading from
the verb in the adverb clause to the word the clause modifies.

EXAMPLE   **If you visit Texas,** you should see the Alamo.

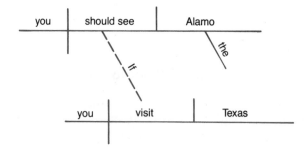

GRAMMAR

How a noun clause is diagramed depends upon its use in the sentence. It also depends on whether or not the introductory word has a specific function in the noun clause. Study the following examples.

EXAMPLES **What you eat** affects your health. [The noun clause is used as the subject of the independent clause. The introductory word *what* is the direct object in the noun clause.]

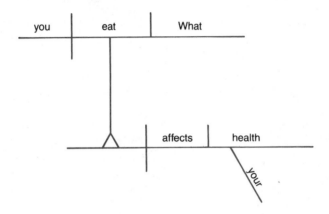

We strongly suspected **that the cat was the thief.** [The noun clause is the direct object of the independent clause. The word *that* has no function in the noun clause except as an introductory word.]

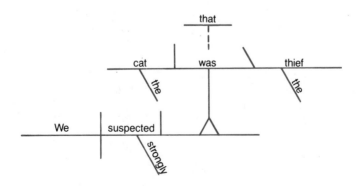

WRITING APPLICATION A:
Using Subordination to
Highlight Important Points in Your Writing

When you write, some of your details or ideas are more important than others. You can help your readers know what you consider important by using subordination. Use independent clauses to express more important points; use dependent or subordinate clauses for less important ones.

EXAMPLES 1. I received my project paper back from Mr. Di Carlo, and I was delighted with my grade. [Coordination makes the writer's getting the paper back and being delighted with the grade seem equal in importance.]
2. When I received my project paper back from Mr. Di Carlo, I was delighted with my grade. [By using subordination, the writer emphasizes delight with the grade; to the writer, this is more important than merely getting the paper back.]

Writing Assignment

Write a paragraph telling in detail how you go about getting organized to study for a big test. Where do you study? How do you keep from being distracted? Do you take notes or make an outline? Include these and other details. Not everything you do is equally important. Show this by putting some of your details into subordinate clauses. Use at least five subordinate clauses. Underline each one.

EXERCISE 7. Diagraming Sentences with Subordinate Clauses. Diagram the following sentences.

1. What Catherine saw at Monticello was extremely interesting to all of us.
2. Monticello, which was the home of Thomas Jefferson, is located near Charlottesville, Virginia.

3. If you visit Monticello, you will see many fascinating devices that Jefferson invented.
4. The inventions that particularly interested Catherine were two dumbwaiters that ran between the dining room and the cellar.
5. If I ever visit my cousin who lives in Virginia, I know that we will go to Monticello.

SENTENCES CLASSIFIED ACCORDING TO STRUCTURE

In Chapter 2 you learned that sentences are classified according to *purpose* as declarative, imperative, interrogative, or exclamatory. Sentences may also be classified according to *structure*.

15g. Classified according to structure, there are four kinds of sentences: *simple, compound, complex,* **and** *compound-complex.*

(1) A *simple sentence* **has one independent clause and no subordinate clauses. It has only one subject and one verb, although both may be compound.**

EXAMPLE   George Vancouver was exploring the Northwest.

(2) A *compound sentence* **has two or more independent clauses but no subordinate clauses.**

In effect, a compound sentence consists of two or more simple sentences joined by a semicolon or by a comma and a coordinating conjunction.

EXAMPLE   In 1792 Vancouver discovered a channel, and he gave it an unusual name.

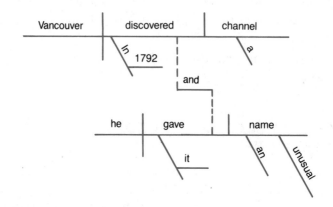

> ☞ **NOTE**   If the compound sentence has a semicolon and no conjunction, place a straight broken line between the two verbs.

(3) A *complex sentence* has one independent clause and at least one subordinate clause.

EXAMPLE   He originally thought that the channel was a harbor. [Here the subordinate clause is the direct object of the independent clause.]

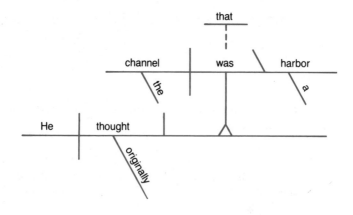

(4) A *compound-complex sentence* contains two or more independent clauses and *at least* one subordinate clause.

EXAMPLE   Since it was not a harbor, Vancouver had been deceived, and Deception Pass became its name.

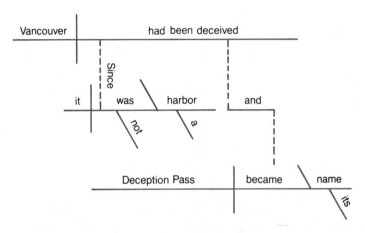

EXERCISE 8. Classifying Sentences According to Structure.

Number your paper 1–10. Classify each of the following sentences according to its structure. Next to each number, write *simple, compound, complex,* or *compound-complex.* Be sure that you can identify all subordinate and independent clauses.

1. American women have held positions of responsible political leadership in the development of our nation.
2. As we study the history of our government, we become aware that many women have been appointed or elected to high government positions.
3. President Franklin Roosevelt appointed Frances Perkins Secretary of Labor in 1933; since then, several other women have been Cabinet members.
4. In 1953, Oveta Culp Hobby was named Secretary of Health, Education, and Welfare, a newly created Cabinet post.
5. In 1977 President Carter appointed Patricia Roberts Harris Secretary of Housing and Urban Development, and thus the United States had its first black woman Cabinet member.

6. President Ronald Reagan, who was elected in 1980, appointed three women to key posts: these were Elizabeth Dole, Secretary of Transportation; Margaret Heckler, Secretary of Health and Human Services; and Jeanne J. Kirkpatrick, Ambassador to the United Nations.
7. Several states have elected women to public office.
8. Kentucky and Vermont have governors who are women.
9. In 1984, Geraldine Ferraro became the first woman nominated for vice-president by a major party.
10. We know that women will continue to hold high positions in government, but when will a woman win the presidency?

WRITING APPLICATION B:
Using a Variety of Sentence Structures in Writing

In most neighborhoods each house has a slightly different look. The reason for this is that humans like variety. That is why you as a writer should build your sentences with variety in mind. Some can be simple, some compound, some complex, and some even compound-complex. Notice the sentence variety in the following paragraph.

EXAMPLES   Last spring some of us wanted a baseball diamond. [simple] We looked around the neighborhood, and we found an empty lot. [compound] After we had discussed our plan with the owner, we asked our parents about fixing it up. [complex] When the cleanup day came, some of us cleared trash, and the rest of us worked on smoothing the turf. [compound-complex] The project took three full weekends. [simple]

Writing Assignment

Write a similar paragraph about an important project. Include at least one of each kind of sentence. Write the kind of sentence in parentheses after the sentence.

EXERCISE 9. Diagraming Sentences with Subordinate Clauses. Diagram the following sentences:

1. Tonight I am going to a concert with my parents, but I would prefer to play chess with you.
2. When she saw the accident, she looked for help and then telephoned the police.
3. Twenty seniors in the graduating class will be attending college, and twelve of them have received scholarships.
4. Leaving for school, I knew that it would rain today, yet I did not carry my umbrella.
5. When my sister practices her singing lessons, Muff curls up on the piano bench and purrs, but when I play my trumpet, that cat yowls and hides under the sofa.

REVIEW EXERCISE A. Classifying Subordinate Clauses. Number your paper 1–10. Decide whether each of the following numbered and italicized clauses functions as an adjective, an adverb, or a noun, and write *adjective, adverb,* or *noun* after the proper number. Be prepared to explain your answers.

(1) *As we left the courtroom,* we did not feel very sorry for the men (2) *who had been on trial.* (3) *Although they had not committed a serious crime,* they had broken the law. The law says (4) *that removing sand from a beach is illegal.* They were caught (5) *because they could not move their truck,* (6) *which had become stuck in the sand.* (7) *After the judge had read the law to them,* the men claimed (8) *that they had never heard of it.* The judge, (9) *who did not believe this,* fined each man twenty-five dollars. The men promised (10) *that they would not steal any more beach sand.*

REVIEW EXERCISE B. Classifying Subordinate Clauses. Number your paper 1–10. If the subordinate clause in each of the following sentences is used as an adjective or an adverb, write the word(s) the clause modifies. If the clause is used as a noun, write *subj.* for subject, *d.o.* for direct object, *i.o.* for indirect object, *p.n.* for predicate nominative, or *o.p.* for object of a preposition.

EXAMPLE 1. When our science book described insect-eating plants, we listened with amazement.
1. *listened*

1. Plants that eat insects usually live in swampy areas.
2. Because the soil in these regions lacks nitrogen, these plants do not get enough nitrogen through their roots.
3. The nitrogen that these plants need must come from the protein in insects.
4. How these plants catch their food makes them interesting.
5. A pitcher plant's sweet scent attracts whatever insect is nearby.
6. The insect thinks that it will find food inside the plant.
7. What happens instead is the insect's drowning in the plant's digestive juices.
8. The Venus' flytrap has what looks like small bear traps at the ends of its stalks.
9. When a trap is open, an insect can easily fit inside it.
10. An insect is digested by the plant in a slow process that takes several days.

CHAPTER 15 REVIEW: POSTTEST 1

A. Identifying and Classifying Subordinate Clauses. Number your paper 1–10. Write the subordinate clause in each of the following sentences. Identify the clause as *adj.* (adjective), *adv.* (adverb), or *n.* (noun). If the clause is used as an adjective or adverb, write the word or words it modifies. If the clause is used as a noun, write *subj.* for subject, *d.o.* for direct object, *i.o.* for indirect object, *p.n.* for predicate nominative, or *o.p.* for object of a preposition.

EXAMPLE 1. After our last class Elena, Freda, and I decided that we would go bicycling in the park.

1. *that we would go bicycling in the park, n., d.o.*
2. As we set out for the park, we had no idea of the difficulties ahead.
2. *As we set out for the park, adv., had*

1. Since we all lived far from the park, we decided to rent bikes at the park.
2. The man from whom we rented bikes was most helpful.
3. The three of us had bicycled six miles when Sandy's bike got a flat tire.
4. What we found was a nail in the tire.
5. We decided to take the bike to whatever bike shop was the nearest.
6. The woman at the bike shop knew that she could fix the tire quickly.
7. After we paid for the repair, we rode back to the park and bicycled for an hour.
8. The three of us were worried, though, that the man at the rental shop might not pay us back.
9. When we returned our bikes, we showed the man the bike with the repaired tire.
10. He reimbursed us for the money we had spent to fix the tire.

B. Classifying Sentences According to Structure. Number your paper 11–25. Classify each of the following sentences according to its structure. Next to each number, write *simple, compound, complex, or compound-complex.* Be sure that you can identify all subordinate and independent clauses.

EXAMPLE 1. Amanda now plays the violin because of a winter concert that she heard back in the third grade.
1. *complex*

11. Amanda loved the sound of the orchestra at her school's winter concert, and she decided then to study the violin.
12. Children's violins come in various sizes so that children of different ages can play them comfortably.

13. When she was in the sixth grade, Amanda played a full-sized violin.
14. Amanda did not always enjoy the many hours of practice, but they were necessary because the instrument is so complicated.
15. Just playing the proper notes, without being too sharp or too flat, can be difficult on a violin.
16. On a keyboard instrument, one presses a key and can hear the note for that key.
17. On a violin, however, the placement of a finger on the string can affect the pitch of the note.
18. If the pitch of each note is not exactly correct, the result can be a barely recognizable tune.
19. Once a student has mastered pitch to some extent, he or she still has a great deal to think about, for posture, hand position, and bowing technique all require great concentration.
20. Why would anyone want to play an instrument requiring so much concentration and dedication?
21. The students themselves may offer many reasons, but pride of accomplishment is always one.
22. When students can actually create music with this stubborn instrument, they have reason to be proud.
23. Playing music with others adds another dimension, and the excitement of concerts and recitals is something that these young musicians might want to experience.
24. For whatever reasons, children continue to select difficult instruments and to work hard at playing them.
25. Music, like sports and other activities that demand practice, will always have its enthusiasts.

CHAPTER 15 REVIEW: POSTTEST 2

Writing a Variety of Sentence Structures. Write your own sentences according to the following guidelines:

1. A simple sentence with a compound verb
2. A complex sentence with an adjective clause
3. A compound-complex sentence
4. A compound sentence with two independent clauses joined by the conjunction *but*
5. A complex sentence with a noun clause used as a subject
6. A simple sentence with a compound subject
7. A complex sentence with an adverb clause placed at the end of the sentence
8. A complex sentence with a noun clause used as a direct object
9. A compound sentence with two independent clauses joined by the conjunction *or*
10. A complex sentence with a noun clause used as an object of a preposition

Agreement

SUBJECT AND VERB, PRONOUN AND ANTECEDENT

Certain words that are closely related in sentences have matching forms. Subjects and verbs have this kind of close relationship, as do pronouns and their antecedents. When such words are correctly matched, they *agree* grammatically.

DIAGNOSTIC TEST

Identifying and Correcting Errors in Subject-Verb and Pronoun-Antecedent Agreement. In most of the following sentences, a verb does not agree with its subject, or a pronoun does not agree with its antecedent. For each sentence write the incorrect verb or pronoun, followed by the correct form. If the sentence is correct, write *C*.

EXAMPLE 1. Peter and Mark likes to play baseball.
         1. *likes—like*

1. Computer science, in addition to foreign languages, are offered at our junior high school.
2. Since either Janet or Brian always bring a camera, we are sure to have pictures of this occasion.

3. The faculty at our school want to give the student body more privileges.
4. *Romeo and Juliet* are required reading in our English class, and many of the students are eager to begin this play.
5. Each of the children completed their project, which was a set of woven baskets.
6. The brook between the two hills are filled with trout.
7. Either Edna or the other girls is going to plan the party.
8. Geraldo knows what to expect at camp, but Ines don't have any idea.
9. Everyone in the French classes wants to go to the French restaurant, but not all of them can go.
10. Neither of the dogs are vicious, but they both bark fiercely at strangers.
11. Three weeks was not enough time for the class project.
12. Because athletics are good for people, everyone in school is asked to participate in some sport.
13. Neither Charlotte nor Thelma want to be the first to jump into the cold water.
14. The public want more information about the candidates in this election.
15. A line of angry thunderclouds loomed over the horizon.
16. While Mr. Cheung and his students don't agree on this problem, the answer key agrees with Mr. Cheung.
17. Every flower along the pathways is blooming right now.
18. I can't read Steven's poem because there is too many smudges on the paper.
19. Few of the people here for vacation wants to live here year-round.
20. Philip and Barbara sang their duet so beautifully that everyone in the audience was impressed.

USAGE

One way in which two words can agree with each other grammatically is in *number*. Number indicates whether the word refers to one person or thing, or to more than one.

16a. When a word refers to one person or thing, it is *singular* in number. When a word refers to more than one, it is *plural* in number.

Nouns and pronouns have number. The following nouns and pronouns are singular because they name only one person or thing: *student, child, it, berry*. The following are plural because they refer to more than one: *students, children, they, berries*.

EXERCISE 1. Classifying Nouns and Pronouns by Number. Number your paper 1–10. After each number, write whether the word is *singular* or *plural*.

1. lawyer	4. woman	7. ours	9. sound
2. bag	5. feet	8. weeks	10. those
3. my	6. books		

AGREEMENT OF SUBJECT AND VERB

Verbs have number, too. In order to speak and write standard English, you must make verbs agree with their subjects.

☞ **NOTE** To understand the chapters on usage, you should know the meaning of the term *standard English*. The word *standard* suggests a model with which things can be compared. In this case, the model—standard English— is the English generally used in well-edited newspapers, magazines, and books; by broadcasters; and by educated people of the English-speaking community.

Nonstandard English is the term used in this book to describe variations in usage that are limited to a particular region, group, or situation. Examples of nonstandard English are local speech dialects and slang words that do not become widely used.

USAGE

STANDARD	NONSTANDARD

<table>
<tr><td>He doesn't care.</td><td>He don't care.</td></tr>
<tr><td>They played well.</td><td>They played good.</td></tr>
<tr><td>Can you teach me the rules?</td><td>Can you learn me the rules?</td></tr>
<tr><td>Hilda and she won easily.</td><td>Hilda and her won easily.</td></tr>
</table>

16b. A verb agrees with its subject in number.

(1) Singular subjects take singular verbs.

EXAMPLES My **friend likes** algebra. [The singular verb *likes* agrees with the singular subject *friend*.]
A **girl** in my neighborhood **plays** in the school band. [The singular verb *plays* agrees with the singular subject *girl*.]

(2) Plural subjects take plural verbs.

EXAMPLES My **friends like** algebra.
Several **girls** in my class **play** in the school band.

Generally, nouns ending in -*s* are plural (*friends*, *girls*), but verbs ending in -*s* are singular (*likes*, *plays*). Since the form of the verb used with the singular pronouns *I* and *you* is regularly the same as the plural form, agreement in number presents problems mainly in the third person forms.

	SINGULAR	PLURAL
First person	I help	We help
Second person	You help	You help
Third person	He, she, *or* it helps	They help

EXERCISE 2. Identify the Correct Number of Verbs. Number your paper 1–10. Write the verb in parentheses that agrees with the subject.

1. he (was, were) 3. children (hurries, hurry)
2. they (comes, come) 4. you (has, have)

USAGE

5. she (is, are)
6. teachers (does, do)
7. neighbor (says, say)

8. it (flies, fly)
9. players (goes, go)
10. they (looks, look)

16c. The number of the subject is not changed by a phrase following the subject.

Remember that a verb agrees in number with its subject, not with the object of a preposition. *The subject is never part of a prepositional phrase.*

EXAMPLES   The **sign** near the glass doors **explains** the exhibit.
The **paintings** of Emilio Sanchez **were hanging** in the gallery.

Compound prepositions such as *together with, in addition to,* and *along with* following the subject do not affect the number of the subject.

EXAMPLES   **Anne,** together with her cousins, **is** backpacking in Nevada this summer.
Robert, along with Jean and Tom, **has** been nominated for class president.

EXERCISE 3. *Oral Drill.* **Using the Correct Number of Verbs in Sentences with Phrases Following the Subjects.** Repeat each sentence, stressing the italicized words.

1. The *rules* in this textbook *are* guidelines for using standard English.
2. *Mastery* of these rules *leads* to improvement in speaking and writing.
3. The correct *use* of verbs *is* especially important.
4. Correct *spelling,* in addition to correct usage of verbs, *is* an essential writing skill.
5. *People* in the business world *look* carefully at letters of application.
6. *Letters* with nonstandard English *do* not make a good impression.

EXERCISE 4. Identifying Subjects and the Correct Number of Verbs in Sentences with Phrases Following the Subjects. Number your paper 1–10. Write the subject of each sentence, then the verb in parentheses that agrees with it.

EXAMPLE   1. Units of measure sometimes (causes, cause) confusion.

　　　　　　1. *Units—cause*

1. The confusion among shoppers (is, are) certainly understandable.
2. The traditional system of indicating quantities (makes, make) shopping a guessing game.
3. For example, the quantity printed on yogurt containers (tells, tell) the number of ounces in a container.
4. A shopper on the lookout for bargains (does not, do not) know whether liquid or solid measure is indicated.
5. Different brands of juice (shows, show) the same quantity in different ways.
6. One can with a label showing twenty-four ounces (contains, contain) the same quantity as a can with a label showing one pint eight ounces.
7. Shoppers' confusion, along with rising prices, (is, are) a matter of concern to consumer groups.
8. The metric system, in use in European countries, (solves, solve) most of the confusion.
9. The units in this system (has, have) a relationship to one another.
10. Consumer groups in this country (continues, continue) to advocate a uniform system of measurement.

16d. The following pronouns are singular: *each, either, neither, one, everyone, everybody, no one, nobody, anyone, anybody, someone, somebody.*

Read the following sentences aloud, stressing the subjects and verbs in boldfaced type.

EXAMPLES **Each** of the athletes **runs** effortlessly. [each one runs]
Neither of the women **is** ready to start. [neither one is]
Everyone in my family **has** enjoyed the games.
Someone in the audience **was** waving a large flag.

Note that the first word in each of the example sentences is followed by a phrase. The object of the preposition in each of the first two sentences is plural: *athletes, women.* However, since each of the four sentences has a singular pronoun as subject, each verb is also singular.

16e. The following pronouns are plural: *several, few, both, many.*

Study the use of subjects and verbs in these sentences. Read the sentences aloud.

EXAMPLES **Few** of the athletes **have** qualified.
Several of the runners **are** exercising.
Many on the team **practice** daily.
Were both of the games postponed?

16f. The pronouns *some, all, most, any,* **and** *none* **may be either singular or plural.**

These pronouns are singular when they refer to a singular word and plural when they refer to a plural word.

EXAMPLES **Some** of the show **is** funny. [*Some* refers to singular *show.*]

Some of the entertainers **are** funny. [*Some* refers to plural *entertainers.*]

All of the cast **looks** young.

All of the performers **look** young.

Most of his routine **sounds** familiar.

Most of his jokes **sound** familiar.

Was any of the criticism positive?

Were any of the reviews positive?

None of the music **is** catchy.

None of the tunes **are** catchy.

The words *any* and *none* may be singular even when they refer to a plural word if the speaker is thinking of each item individually, and plural if the speaker is thinking of several things as a group.

EXAMPLES **Any** of these books **is** worth reading. [*Any one book* is worth reading.]

Any of these books **are** worth reading. [*All* are worth reading.]

None of the books **was** overdue. [*Not one* was overdue.]

None of the books **were** overdue. [*No books* were overdue.]

EXERCISE 5. Identifying Subjects and the Correct Number of Verbs. This exercise covers rules 16d, 16e, and 16f. Number your paper 1–10. Write the subject of each sentence, then write the correct verb.

1. Each of the comedians (tries, try) to outdo the other.
2. Somebody on the bus (was, were) whistling.
3. All of the apples (is, are) spoiled.
4. Neither of these books (has, have) an index.
5. Everybody in my class (plans, plan) to attend the rally.
6. Few of these jobs (sounds, sound) challenging.
7. Several of those plants (grows, grow) well indoors.
8. No one in his office (leaves, leave) early.
9. Both of her parents (has, have) offered us a ride.
10. Most of those songs (is, are) from the sixties.

USAGE

REVIEW EXERCISE A. Proofreading Sentences for Subject-Verb Agreement. Number your paper 1–10. Proofread each sentence. If the verb agrees with the subject, write a plus (+) on your paper after the corresponding number. If the verb does not agree with the subject, correct it.

1. One of the most popular booths display Victorian dollhouses.
2. Each of the players are in position.
3. The uniforms for the baseball team include hats.
4. A news leak to reporters is a common occurrence during a political campaign.
5. Both bridges on the highway was swept away.
6. Someone said you was first in line.
7. My cousin, along with my best friend, is taking trumpet lessons.
8. Every one of the guards have to sign in.
9. One of my friends have a motorized wheelchair.
10. Our projects in science includes a model of the lower jaw.

WRITING APPLICATION A:
Using Correct Verb Forms to Make Your Writing Clear

When you write, you may concentrate so hard on getting your ideas down on paper that you make an error in subject-verb agreement. The time to catch such errors is when you read what you have written. As you read, look carefully at each verb to make sure that it agrees with its subject in number.

Writing Assignment

Write a paragraph about a field trip you took last year. Tell where you went, what you saw and did, and how you and your classmates reacted to the trip. Read your paragraph carefully to make sure that every verb agrees with its subject.

The Compound Subject

16g. Subjects joined by *and* take a plural verb.

The following compound subjects joined by *and* name more than one person or thing and must take plural verbs.

EXAMPLES   **Leslie Silko** and **Mari Evans are** poets. [Two persons are.]

            Imagery and **metaphor help** poets express their feelings. [Two things help.]

If a compound subject names only one person or thing, then the verb must be singular.

EXAMPLES   My **pen pal and best friend is** my cousin. [One person is.]

            Pumpkin seeds and raisins makes a tasty snack. [The one combination makes.]

In the sentences above, the compound subjects are thought of as units (one person, one snack) and are therefore singular.

16h. Singular subjects joined by *or* or *nor* take a singular verb.

EXAMPLES   After dinner, either **Anne** or **Tony loads** the dishwasher. [Either Anne *or* Tony loads the dishwasher, not both.]

            Neither the **coach** nor the **principal is** happy with the team's performance. [Neither *one* is happy.]

EXERCISE 6. Revising Sentences with Compound Subjects. If the sentence has a compound subject joined by *and*, change the conjunction to *or*, and make the necessary change in the number of the verb. If the sentence has a compound subject joined by *or*, change the conjunction to *and*, and make the necessary change in the number of the verb.

EXAMPLES   1. Anne and Carl are providing the entertainment.

            1. *Anne or Carl is providing the entertainment.*

            2. Rain or snow has been predicted for today.

            2. *Rain and snow have been predicted for today.*

USAGE

1. The dog or the cat has torn up the evening newspaper.
2. My father and his friend are rewiring our house.
3. A mature woman or man is wanted for gardening chores.
4. A cartoon and an essay appear on the editorial page every day.
5. The car and the bus were to blame for the five-car pile-up on State Street.

16i. When a singular subject and a plural subject are joined by *or* **or** *nor,* **the verb agrees with the subject nearer the verb.**

ACCEPTABLE   Neither the losers nor the **winner was** happy with the outcome of the match.

ACCEPTABLE   Neither the winner nor the **losers were** happy with the outcome of the match.

Try to avoid such awkward constructions.

BETTER   The winner was not happy with the outcome of the match, and neither were the losers.

REVIEW EXERCISE B. *Oral Drill.* **Using the Correct Number of Verbs with Singular and Plural Subjects.** Read the following sentences aloud, stressing the italicized words.

1. The *books* on that shelf *need* dusting.
2. A *carton* of duck eggs *is* in the refrigerator.
3. *Tina* and *Betty are* first cousins once removed.
4. *Playing* games or *listening* to old records *is* an enjoyable way to spend a rainy Saturday.
5. *Several* of these insects *eat* through wood.
6. Every *one* of you *has* met my friend Phil.
7. Neither *Eileen* nor *Greg cares* for country music.

REVIEW EXERCISE C. Revising Sentences and Proofreading Them for Subject-Verb Agreement. Revise each of the following sentences, (1) following the directions in parentheses and (2) changing the number of the verb to agree with the subject if necessary.

USAGE

EXAMPLE 1. The teachers have finished grading the tests. (Change *The teachers* to *Each of the teachers*.)
    1. *Each of the teachers has finished grading the tests.*

1. My aunt is planning to tour Nairobi National Park. (Change *aunt* to *aunts*.)
2. Jan and Vi have already seen that movie. (Change *and* to *or*.)
3. Nobody on the team plans to attend the opening ceremonies. (Change *Nobody* to *Many*.)
4. My grandmother, as well as my mother, is working on the quilt. (Change *grandmother* to *grandparents*.)
5. Most of the food for the party is in the cafeteria refrigerator. (Change *food* to *salads*.)
6. Neither the librarian nor the aides have found the missing card. (Change *Neither the librarian nor the aides* to *Neither the aides nor the librarian*.)
7. Cereal, toast, and milk are my usual breakfast. (Change *Cereal, toast, and milk* to *Ham and eggs*.)
8. Some of my classmates take the bus to school. (Change *Some* to *One*.)
9. The puppy playing with the children is only two months old. (Change *puppy* to *puppies* and *children* to *child*.)
10. Few of the reporters' questions were answered in detail. (Change *Few* to *Neither*.)

Other Problems in Agreement

16j. *Don't* and *doesn't* must agree with their subjects.

Contractions are two words combined into one, with one or more letters omitted. *Don't* is the contraction for *do not*, *doesn't* for *does not*.

With the subjects *I* and *you* and with plural subjects, use *don't* (*do not*).

EXAMPLES   I **don't** know.   They **don't** give up.
               You **don't** say.   These **don't** shrink.
               We **don't** want to.   Apathetic people **don't** care.

With other subjects, use the singular *doesn't* (*does not*).

EXAMPLES   He **doesn't** know.   One **doesn't** give up.
               She **doesn't** say.   This **doesn't** shrink.
               It **doesn't** want to.   Donna **doesn't** care.

The errors in the use of *don't* and *doesn't* are usually made when *don't* is incorrectly used with *it, he,* or *she.* Remember always to use *doesn't* with these singular subjects.

EXERCISE 7. *Oral Drill.* Using *Doesn't* with Singular Subjects.   Read the following sentences aloud.

1. It doesn't amuse me.
2. That doesn't solve my problem.
3. My mother doesn't know you.
4. One doesn't criticize others.
5. He doesn't have a summer job.

EXERCISE 8. Writing *Doesn't* or *Don't* with Subjects.   After numbering your paper 1–10, write the correct form (*doesn't* or *don't*) for each sentence.

1. She —— influence me.
2. This —— taste sweet.
3. He says he —— want to play.
4. These —— impress me.
5. It —— look like snow.
6. One of them —— plan to go.
7. They —— want to help.
8. Harold —— know about the party.
9. One of you —— have the right answer.
10. Dorothy and Elise —— like the new band uniforms.

16k. Collective nouns may be either singular or plural.

USAGE

Collective nouns are singular in form, but they name a *group* of persons or things.

EXAMPLES
group	committee	club	family
flock	herd	swarm	public
jury	army	audience	assembly
class	team	faculty	fleet

Collective nouns are used with plural verbs when the speaker or writer is referring to the individual parts or members of the group acting separately. They are used with singular verbs when the statement refers to the group acting together as a unit.

EXAMPLES   The class **has** elected its officers.
[*Class* is thought of as a unit.]
The class **have** completed their projects.
[*Class* is thought of as individuals.]

☞ **USAGE NOTE**   Be sure that any pronoun referring to the collective noun has the same number as the noun (*its* in the first example above, *their* in the second).

EXERCISE 9. Writing Sentences with Collective Nouns. Select five collective nouns and write five pairs of sentences showing clearly how the nouns you choose may be either singular or plural.

EXAMPLE   1. *The jury is ready.*
The jury are still arguing among themselves.

16l. A verb agrees with its subject, not with its predicate nominative.

When the subject and the predicate nominative are of different numbers, you should always remember that *the verb agrees with the subject*.

STANDARD   The marching **bands are** the main attraction.

STANDARD   The main **attraction is** the marching bands.

16m. When the subject follows the verb, as in sentences beginning with *there* and *here* and in questions, be careful to determine the subject and make sure that the verb agrees with it.

Each of the following subjects agrees with its verb.

EXAMPLES   Here **is** a **list** of addresses.
Here **are** two **lists** of addresses.
There **is** my **notebook.**
There **are** my **notebooks.**
Where **is Helen**? Where **is Walter**?
Where **are Helen** and **Walter**?

Contractions such as *here's, where's, how's,* and *what's,* include the contracted form of *is.* Do not use one of these contractions unless a singular subject follows it.

NONSTANDARD   There's some important announcements on the bulletin board.

STANDARD   There **are** some important **announcements** on the bulletin board.

STANDARD   There**'s** a **bulletin board** covered with important announcements.

16n. Words stating amount are usually singular.

A word or group of words stating a weight, a measurement, or an amount of money or time is usually considered as one item and takes a singular verb.

EXAMPLES   **Twenty dollars is** too much for concert tickets.
Two hours is a long time to wait.
Three fourths of the show **is** over.

Sometimes, however, the amount is thought of as individual pieces or parts. If so, a plural verb is used.

EXAMPLES   **Five** of the dollars **were** borrowed.
Two of the hours **were** spent in line.
Three fourths of the songs **are** new.

16o. The title of a work of art, literature, or music, even when plural in form, takes a singular verb.

In the following sentences, notice that each title takes a singular verb, since it is only one work of art.

EXAMPLES *Great Expectations* **is** one of my favorite novels. [one book]
Blue Lines **is** an early painting by Georgia O'Keeffe. [one work of art]

16p. *Every* or *many a* before a subject calls for a singular verb.

EXAMPLES **Every** homeowner and storekeeper **has** joined the clean-up drive.
Many a litterbug **was** surprised by the stiff fines.

16q. A few nouns, although plural in form, take a singular verb.

Some nouns end in *s* yet are considered singular in meaning. The word *news,* for example, takes a singular verb.

The **news** of the nominee for Vice-President **was** a surprise to many observers.

Names of certain diseases also end in *s* but are singular nouns: *measles, mumps, rickets.*

Rickets is a serious problem in some countries.

Words ending in *-ics* are generally used with a singular verb: *athletics, mathematics, physics, civics, economics, politics.*

Politics is a controversial topic.

EXERCISE 10. Identifying Subjects and the Correct Number of Verbs. This exercise covers rules 16k through 16q. Number your paper 1–10. Write the subject of each sentence on your paper. Select the correct verb, and write it after the subject.

EXAMPLE 1. Many a book (has, have) been written about the beauties of our country.
1. *Many a book—has*

1. The class (has, have) chosen titles for their original plays.
2. First prize (was, were) two tickets to Hawaii.
3. Three quarters of the movie (was, were) over when we arrived.
4. Rattlesnakes (was, were) the topic of last week's meeting of the hiking club.
5. Every student in the class (has, have) memorized a poem.
6. *War and Peace* (is, are) a world-famous novel.
7. Two thirds of the missing books (was, were) returned.
8. Mathematics (is, are) an important part of many everyday activities.
9. Where (is, are) the paragraphs you wrote?
10. Four weeks (is, are) enough time to rehearse the play.

REVIEW EXERCISE D. *Oral Drill.* **Using Subject-Verb and Pronoun-Antecedent Agreement.** Repeat each of the following sentences, stressing the italicized words.

1. His main *concern is* his two horses.
2. *Many a* man and woman in our cities *doesn't* have a car.
3. *Is economics* taught at your high school?
4. My *family is* planning to hold *its* reunion in October.
5. My *family are* planning *their* schedules now.
6. *Are* there any green *apples* in that basket?
7. *Romeo and Juliet has* been made into a ballet, a Broadway musical, and at least two movies.
8. *Two weeks is* more than enough time to write a report.

REVIEW EXERCISE E. **Identifying the Correct Number of Verbs.** Number your paper 1–10. Choose the correct verb in parentheses, and write it after the appropriate number.

1. Mumps (is, are) a common childhood disease.
2. Taxes (is, are) always a main issue during an election year.
3. Not one of the ushers (knows, know) where the lounge is.
4. The team (is, are) on a winning streak.
5. Carol, as well as Irene, (writes, write) a column for the *East High Record*.

6. "Beauty and the Beast" (is, are) a folk tale that exists in many different cultures.
7. Ten pounds (is, are) far too much weight for a young child to carry in a backpack.
8. It is difficult to concentrate when there (is, are) radios and stereos blasting away.
9. (Has, Have) either of you read *To Kill a Mockingbird*?
10. In most situation comedies, there (is, are) very wise characters, very foolish characters, and very lovable characters.

AGREEMENT OF PRONOUN AND ANTECEDENT

You learned in Chapter 12 that the word to which a pronoun refers is called its *antecedent*. (For example, in the preceding sentence, *pronoun* is the antecedent of *its*.) There should always be agreement between the pronoun and its antecedent.

16r. A pronoun agrees with its antecedent in number and gender.

A few singular personal pronouns have forms that indicate the gender of the antecedent. *He, his,* and *him* are used if the antecedent is masculine. *She, her,* and *hers* are used if the antecedent is feminine. *It* and *its* are used if the antecedent is neither masculine nor feminine.

EXAMPLES   **Colette** performs **her** solo today.
James makes **his** debut tomorrow.
The **show** has the Old West as **its** theme.

When the antecedent of a personal pronoun is another kind of pronoun, it is often necessary to look in a phrase following the antecedent to determine gender.

EXAMPLES   **One** of the **women** in the acting class designs **her** own costumes.
Each of the **boys** rode **his** bicycle to school.

USAGE

Sometimes the antecedent may be either masculine or feminine; sometimes it may be both. Some writers use the masculine form of the personal pronoun to refer to such antecedents. Other writers, however, prefer to use both the masculine and the feminine forms in such cases.

EXAMPLES **Every one** of the students shouted **his** approval.
or
Every one of the students shouted **his or her** approval.
A **person** must always choose **his** friends carefully.
or
A **person** must always choose **his or her** friends carefully.

You can often avoid the awkward *his or her* construction by rephrasing the sentence, using the plural form of the pronoun.

EXAMPLES **All** of the students shouted **their** approval.
Persons must always chose **their** friends carefully.

In conversation, you may find it more convenient to use a plural personal pronoun when referring to singular antecedents that can be either masculine or feminine. This form is becoming increasingly popular in writing as well and may someday become acceptable as standard written English.

EXAMPLES **Everybody** packed **their** lunch in insulated bags.
Each member of the Senior Citizen Club received **their** tickets in advance.

(1) Use a singular pronoun to refer to *each, either, neither, one, everyone, everybody, no one, nobody, anyone, anybody, someone,* **or** *somebody.*

EXAMPLES **Someone** left **his** (*or* **his or her**) hat on the field.

One of the parakeets escaped from **its** cage.

Notice in these sentences that a prepositional phrase does not alter the number of the antecedent. Each antecedent is singular, and a singular pronoun must be used for agreement.

Exception: Sometimes the meaning of the antecedents *everyone* and *everybody* is clearly plural. In such cases the plural pronoun should be used.

ABSURD   Everyone laughed when he saw the clowns.

BETTER   **Everyone** laughed when **they** saw the clowns.

(2) Two or more singular antecedents joined by *or* or *nor* should be referred to by a singular pronoun.

EXAMPLES   Neither **Richard nor Bob** distinguished **himself** in the finals.
              Paula or Janet will present **her** views on the subject.

> ☞ **NOTE**   Rules (1) and (2) are often ignored in conversation; nevertheless, they should be followed in writing.

(3) Two or more antecedents joined by *and* should be referred to by a plural pronoun.

EXAMPLES   **Mona and Janet** left early because **they** had to be home before ten o'clock.
              Mother and Dad celebrated **their** anniversary yesterday.

EXERCISE 11. Identifying Antecedents and Writing Pronouns That Agree with Them.   Number your paper 1–10. Copy the antecedent for each blank in the following sentences; then, for each blank, write a pronoun that will agree with its antecedent. Follow the rules for standard written English.

1. A person should always try ⸺ best.
2. The uniform company finally sent Bert and Ken the shirts that ⸺ had ordered.

3. Claire or Ida will go to the nursing home early so that —— can help the residents into the lounge.
4. Several of the volunteers contributed —— own money.
5. Each of the contestants answered —— questions correctly.
6. Both of the girls packed —— bags carefully.
7. Everyone wore a name tag on —— jacket.
8. Neither of the women withdrew —— job application.
9. Anyone can belong if —— is interested.
10. Neither the coaches nor the players blamed —— for the loss.

EXERCISE 12. Proofreading Sentences for Pronoun-Antecedent Agreement.   Most of the following sentences contain errors in agreement of pronoun and antecedent. Number your paper 1–10. If the sentence is correct, write *C*. If there is an error in agreement, write the corrrect form of the pronoun so that it will agree with its antecedent.

1. George has chosen Walt Disney as the subject of his report.
2. Someone else in our class has also submitted their topic.
3. Dominic, one of the Perrone twins, has chosen Alfred Hitchcock as their subject.
4. Neither George nor Dominic will have difficulty finding material for their report.
5. Each of these moviemakers' films has left their mark on the entertainment world.
6. Both Audrey and Sue offered their help with proofreading to George and Dominic.
7. Each boy refused politely, saying that they would proofread the report on their own.
8. Does everyone, including George and Dominic, know that they must assemble facts, not opinions?
9. Neither George nor Dominic should forget to include anecdotes about their subject.
10. Nobody likes to discover that they just read a list of dull facts about an interesting subject.

WRITING APPLICATION B:
Using Pronouns Correctly to Make Your Writing Clear

In your writing, make sure that every pronoun agrees with its antecedent in number. If you write, "Each of the girls took their turn at bat," for example, your reader has to pause and mentally correct the sentence to: "Each of the girls took her turn at bat." Such errors are distracting and may make your reader put aside your writing.

Writing Assignment

Write a paragraph explaining how two of your friends, teachers, or neighbors are alike and how they are different. Read the paragraph carefully, making sure that every pronoun agrees with its antecedent in number.

CHAPTER 16 REVIEW: POSTTEST

Proofreading Sentences for Subject-Verb and Pronoun-Antecedent Agreement. In most of the following sentences, a verb does not agree with its subject, or a pronoun does not agree with its antecedent. Number your paper 1–25, and for each sentence write the incorrect verb or pronoun, followed by the correct form. If the sentence is correct, write *C*. Follow the rules for standard written English.

EXAMPLE   1. Making well-balanced meals are easy if you plan your shopping.
      1. *are—is*

1. Although the inn welcomed tourists, cars and buses was seldom seen parked there.
2. Every attempt Gary made to ford the streams were unsuccessful.
3. After graduation everybody in the group went their own way.

4. When the truck overturned, a herd of cattle were set free on the expressway.
5. Few of the new styles appeal to me.
6. Either Joyce or Eugene have been chosen as freshman editor of the school paper.
7. Our club is a tightly knit group, and every member has an equal voice.
8. A major concern among students are their grades.
9. Two weeks were not enough time to prepare for our trip.
10. Not one of our tomato plants are producing any fruit, but the green beans seem to be thriving.
11. Everyone brought their own records to the party, but no one wanted to sort out the records at the end of the evening.
12. Each of the six-week-old kittens was finally given away.
13. Neither of your stories sound believable, but the second one is at least interesting.
14. Most of the stew have been eaten by now.
15. Many of their experiments have failed, but Dr. Jenkins and his assistant never gives up hope.
16. Richard, along with many others, don't always concentrate hard enough on math problems.
17. There is a brush, a comb, and a mirror on the dresser top.
18. ''Birches'' are a beautiful poem by Robert Frost.
19. Many a sailor have perished on this coast, crashing on its partly submerged rocks.
20. Measles have been almost completely conquered by a vaccine.

CHAPTER 17

The Correct Use of Verbs

PRINCIPAL PARTS, REGULAR AND IRREGULAR VERBS

People sometimes use verbs in a nonstandard way. For example, you may hear someone say, "I have went," "She brung it," "The TV is broke," or "Set down." Such usage is very noticeable in a conversation or in a composition and indicates to others a lack of knowledge of the rules of standard English.

DIAGNOSTIC TEST

A. Writing the Past and Past Participle Forms of Irregular Verbs. Number your paper 1–10. After each number, write the correct form (past or past participle) of the verb given at the beginning of the sentence.

EXAMPLE   1. *write* I have ⎯⎯ a story about the big snowstorm last winter.
    1. *written*

1. *blow* The wind ⎯⎯ all night long during the snowstorm.
2. *fall* When we looked out in the morning, at least a foot of snow had ⎯⎯ .

3. *see* Alana was overjoyed when she —— the snow.
4. *eat* We have never —— breakfast as quickly as we did then.
5. *run* Dressed warmly, we —— outside to enjoy the snow.
6. *come* Later, a few of the neighbors —— over to join us.
7. *know* We should have —— , though, that we would soon feel too cold to play.
8. *go* Soon almost everyone had —— home to warm up.
9. *freeze* We went inside, certain that we were —— through.
10. *bring* Fortunately, Father had —— in a load of firewood.

B. Revising Verb Tense or Voice. Number your paper 11–15. Revise each sentence that uses a verb in the wrong tense or that uses an awkward passive voice, correcting the error(s). If a sentence is correct, write *C*.

11. The football was kicked perfectly by Josh, so that it spirals between the goal posts.
12. The coach paced restlessly on the sidelines while the team executes a difficult play for a first down.
13. The long hours of practice pay off; the team is ready.
14. The bitter cold was forgotten by the cheering fans.
15. The third quarter had begun before the band gets back to the stands.

C. Determining Correct or Incorrect Use of Lie–Lay, Sit–Set, and Rise–Raise in Sentences. Number your paper 16–20. If a sentence is correct, write a + after its number; if it is incorrect, write a 0.

16. Moira loves to set by the sunny window on winter afternoons.
17. I will sit in the deck chair; you may lay in the hammock.
18. Set the bread dough over a pan of warm water, and it will rise faster.
19. They raised the flag just as the sun was raising.
20. Prices of raw materials have risen sharply, forcing manufacturers to rise the price of manufactured goods.

THE PRINCIPAL PARTS OF VERBS

The four basic forms of a verb are called the *principal parts*.

17a. The four principal parts of a verb are the *infinitive*, the *present participle*, the *past*, and the *past participle*.

The four principal parts of the verb *ring*, for example, are *ring* (infinitive), *ringing* (present participle), *rang* (past), and *rung* (past participle).

EXAMPLE   The bells **ring** every day.
The bells are **ringing** now.
The bells **rang** at noon.
The bells have **rung** for the last time today.

Notice that the forms of the present participle and past participle are used with helping verbs—*am, is, are, has, have,* etc.

Regular Verbs

17b. A verb that forms its past and past participle forms by adding -d or -ed to the first principal part (infinitive) is a *regular verb*.[1]

INFINITIVE	PRESENT PARTICIPLE	PAST	PAST PARTICIPLE
use	using	used	(have) used
suppose	supposing	supposed	(have) supposed
risk	risking	risked	(have) risked

You will observe that the present participle of many regular verbs ending in *-e* drops the *-e* before adding *-ing*.

Usage errors sometimes occur in the choice of the past and the past participle forms of regular verbs. Do not carelessly omit the *-d* or *-ed* of the past or past participle of regular verbs like those listed above.

NONSTANDARD   We use to play soccer.
STANDARD   We **used** to play soccer.

[1] A few regular verbs have an alternate past form ending in *-t;* for example, the past form of *burn* may be *burned* or *burnt*.

NONSTANDARD	She was suppose to come early.
STANDARD	She was **supposed** to come early.

You can avoid other mistakes by correcting faulty spelling and pronunciation of words like *attacked* and *drowned*.

NONSTANDARD	We were attackted by mosquitoes.
STANDARD	We were **attacked** by mosquitoes.

NONSTANDARD	Someone has drownded.
STANDARD	Someone has **drowned.**

EXERCISE 1. *Oral Drill.* Pronouncing the Past and Past Participle Forms of Regular Verbs Correctly. Read each sentence aloud, stressing the italicized verb.

1. Rosie *used* to do needlepoint.
2. What has *happened* to your bicycle?
3. Several people were *drowned* in the flood.
4. The agents *risked* their lives.
5. Aren't you *supposed* to sing?
6. The game was well *advertised*.
7. The article unfairly *attacked* the mayor.
8. He *carried* the suitcases to the car.

Irregular Verbs

17c. A verb that forms its past and past participle in some other way than a regular verb is an *irregular verb*.

Irregular verbs form their past and past participle in various ways: by changing the vowel, by changing consonants, by adding *-en,* or by making no change at all.

INFINITIVE	PAST	PAST PARTICIPLE
begin	began	(have) begun
bring	brought	(have) brought
put	put	(have) put

Irregular Verbs Frequently Misused

INFINITIVE	PRESENT PARTICIPLE	PAST	PAST PARTICIPLE
begin	beginning	began	(have) begun
blow	blowing	blew	(have) blown
break	breaking	broke	(have) broken
bring	bringing	brought	(have) brought
burst	bursting	burst	(have) burst
choose	choosing	chose	(have) chosen
come	coming	came	(have) come
do	doing	did	(have) done
drink	drinking	drank	(have) drunk
drive	driving	drove	(have) driven
eat	eating	ate	(have) eaten
fall	falling	fell	(have) fallen
freeze	freezing	froze	(have) frozen
give	giving	gave	(have) given
go	going	went	(have) gone
know	knowing	knew	(have) known
ride	riding	rode	(have) ridden
ring	ringing	rang	(have) rung
run	running	ran	(have) run
see	seeing	saw	(have) seen
shrink	shrinking	shrank	(have) shrunk
speak	speaking	spoke	(have) spoken
steal	stealing	stole	(have) stolen
swim	swimming	swam	(have) swum
take	taking	took	(have) taken
throw	throwing	threw	(have) thrown
write	writing	wrote	(have) written

USAGE

Since so many English verbs are regular, you may tend to make some irregular verbs follow the same pattern. However, you should avoid such forms as *throwed, knowed, bursted,* or *blowed,* which are considered nonstandard. If you are in doubt about the parts of a verb, consult your dictionary, which lists the principal parts of irregular verbs.

Remember that the present participle and past participle

forms, when used as main verbs (simple predicates) in sentences, always require helping verbs. The present participle is used with forms of the verb *be: am taking, was throwing.* The past participle is used with *have, has,* or *had: have broken, had chosen;* or with a form of *be: was chosen.* When you memorize the principal parts of a verb, you will help yourself if you always include *have* with the past participle. As you repeat principal parts, say, for example: *do, did, have done* or *see, saw, have seen.*

NONSTANDARD   We already seen that program.
STANDARD   We **have** already **seen** that program.

EXERCISE 2. Writing the Principal Parts of Irregular Verbs.
Your teacher may dictate to you the first principal part of the irregular verbs listed on page 499. Study the list so that you can write from memory the other principal parts of each verb. Place *have* before the past participle.

EXERCISE 3. Writing the Past and Past Participle Forms of Irregular Verbs.
Number your paper 1–20. If the first principal part is given, change it to the past form. If the past form is given, change it to the past participle. Write *have* before the past participle form.

EXAMPLES   1. eat   2. took
           1. *ate*   2. *have taken*

1. do	6. know	11. choose	16. shrank
2. began	7. spoke	12. broke	17. ran
3. see	8. stole	13. drink	18. ring
4. rode	9. blew	14. drove	19. fell
5. went	10. bring	15. froze	20. swim

EXERCISE 4. Identifying the Correct Forms of Irregular Verbs.
Number your paper 1–10. Write the correct one of the two verbs in parentheses. When your paper has been corrected, read each sentence aloud several times, stressing the correct verb.

USAGE

1. A huge manta ray had (came, come) to the surface.
2. Maureen (did, done) her best to find a job.
3. Our water pipes have (froze, frozen) again.
4. The last bell had already (rang, rung).
5. The balloon (bursted, burst) with a loud pop.
6. Jesse Jackson (give, gave) the reporters a copy of the speech he was to deliver that evening.
7. I have never (rode, ridden) on a roller coaster.
8. Have you ever (saw, seen) the gigantic trees in Redwood National Park?
9. Someone (drank, drunk) all the fruit juice.
10. The sound of the wind (began, begun) to grow louder.

EXERCISE 5. Identifying the Correct Forms of Irregular Verbs. Follow the instructions for Exercise 4.

1. This morning I (swam, swum) ten laps.
2. We have never (drove, driven) out to the lake.
3. These jeans must have (shrunk, shrank) two sizes.
4. Have the roads (began, begun) to ice over?
5. Nina (brought, brung) her Frisbee to the picnic.
6. Julia Fields has (gave, given) several readings of her poetry.
7. Has everyone (went, gone) to the park?
8. My shopping bag suddenly (bursted, burst) open on the bus.
9. Have you (wrote, written) to your cousin yet?
10. Yesterday I (drank, drunk) a glass of buttermilk for the first time.

EXERCISE 6. *Oral Drill.* Using the Past and Past Participle Forms of Verbs. Read each of the following sentences *aloud* three times, stressing the correct verbs.

1. *Have* you *begun* the research for your report?
2. Last week we *saw* two classic movies.
3. The bell *rang* and the door *burst* open.
4. She *has written* a poem for the school newspaper.
5. He *brought* his rock collection to school.
6. They *risked* their lives for adventure.

USAGE

7. I *have known* her since the first grade.
8. The relay team *has broken* the world record.
9. He *has brought* sandwiches for everybody.
10. She *has given* us her permission.

WRITING APPLICATION A:
Using Verb Forms Correctly to Make Your Writing Clear

Although most English verbs are regular, some of the words you may use frequently in your writing are irregular. Think how often you use forms of *do, go,* and *see,* for example. Until you are certain that you can write the forms of verbs correctly, it is important to check them in a dictionary. Otherwise, your reader may have trouble understanding your writing.

Writing Assignment

Write a paragraph about an imaginary trip you took to another place in another time (past or future). Read your paragraph carefully, and use a dictionary to check any verb forms you are not sure you have used correctly.

REVIEW EXERCISE A. Writing the Past and Past Participle Forms of Verbs. Number your paper 1–20. Write the correct form of the verb given at the beginning of each sentence.

1. *steal* Someone has —— our TV set.
2. *burst* The car suddenly —— into flames.
3. *drink* They —— juice with their sandwiches.
4. *use* He —— to camp out every summer.
5. *do* They —— their best to repair the damage.
6. *give* Grandmother has —— us some old photos.
7. *know* We have —— about the change in coaches since May.
8. *risk* The detective —— her life.
9. *ring* The alarm —— at six o'clock.

USAGE

10. *run*   Ella Grasso —— for governor and won.
11. *break*   Someone has —— the lock on my bike.
12. *speak*   Has he —— to you yet?
13. *drive*   I had never —— on that road before.
14. *choose*   What topic have you ——?
15. *fall*   A tree has —— across the highway.
16. *go*   He has —— to the supermarket.
17. *speak*   Has anyone —— to you about the test?
18. *swim*   I have —— out to the float every day.
19. *go*   Where has everyone ——?
20. *run*   Everyone —— around the lake.

REVIEW EXERCISE B. Writing the Past and Past Participle Forms of Verbs. Number your paper 1–20, and follow the instructions for Review Exercise A.

1. *throw*   The catcher should have —— the ball to first base.
2. *freeze*   Has the pond —— yet?
3. *throw*   I —— the old clippings away.
4. *write*   Bernice has —— me a long letter.
5. *see*   Have you —— that actor in person?
6. *swim*   I —— in that pond yesterday.
7. *shrink*   The curtains have —— two inches.
8. *choose*   They have —— the nominees.
9. *blow*   The wind —— all night.
10. *take*   She hasn't —— her road test yet.
11. *give*   He —— me a ride to the store.
12. *ride*   Have you ever —— a horse?
13. *drown*   No one has —— at that beach.
14. *come*   He —— home in time for supper.
15. *ring*   Have you —— the bell?
16. *happen*   This has —— too often to be a coincidence.
17. *see*   I —— him at the concert.
18. *take*   I have already —— six rolls of film.
19. *fall*   A sparrow had —— from its nest.
20. *climb*   How far has he ——?

USAGE

REVIEW EXERCISE C. Proofreading Sentences for Correct Verb Forms. Number your paper 1–20. Read each of the following sentences aloud. If a sentence is correct, write *C* after the proper number. If the form of a verb is wrong, write the correct verb form after the appropriate number.

1. The plane suddenly bursted into flames.
2. Gettysburg was chose as the site of the famous battle because the town was important to both sides.
3. Ironically, the Confederate Army attackted the town from the north, and the Union Army defended it from the south.
4. In medieval times a person could be drowned for a crime.
5. Hank Aaron had broke Babe Ruth's home-run record.
6. Eudora Welty has wrote appealing stories about the South.
7. At the end of the war, General Robert E. Lee ask that the Confederate soldiers be allowed to keep their horses.
8. Carl Lewis run the relay in record time to win his fourth gold medal at the 1984 Summer Olympics.
9. According to legend, many knights risked their lives searching for the Holy Grail, the cup used at the Last Supper.
10. No single incident begun the French Revolution of 1789.
11. Alice's amazing adventures began after she had fell down the rabbit hole.
12. On its first voyage, the *Titanic* struck an iceberg in the Atlantic and sunk.
13. In recent years, the U.S. dollar has shrunk in value.
14. When the death bell rung for her lover, Barbara Allen knew that it also rung for her.
15. After defeating Grendel, Beowulf drunk the cup of mead.
16. According to legend, the unicorn is suppose to be able to detect poison with its horn.
17. The Green Knight come to King Arthur's court and dared someone to cut off his head.
18. Gertrude Ederle swum the English Channel in fourteen hours and thirty-one minutes.
19. By nightfall the English army had drove two hundred miles.

20. The news that the Alamo had fell was greeted with tears.

Tense

The time expressed by a verb is called the *tense* of the verb. Every verb has six tenses: the *present tense,* the *past tense,* the *future tense,* the *present perfect tense,* the *past perfect tense,* and the *future perfect tense.* The tenses are formed from the principal parts.

Study the following list of the six tense forms of *go.* Giving all the forms of a verb in this way is called *conjugating* the verb; the list is called a *conjugation.*

Conjugation of Go

Present Tense

Singular	*Plural*
I go	we go
you go	you go
he, she, *or* it goes	they go

Past Tense

Singular	*Plural*
I went	we went
you went	you went
he, she, *or* it went	they went

Future Tense

Singular	*Plural*
I will (shall) go	we will (shall) go
you will go	you will go
he, she, *or* it will go	they will go

Present Perfect Tense

Singular	*Plural*
I have gone	we have gone
you have gone	you have gone
he, she, *or* it has gone	they have gone

USAGE

Past Perfect Tense

Singular	*Plural*
I had gone	we had gone
you had gone	you had gone
he, she, *or* it had gone	they had gone

Future Perfect Tense

Singular	*Plural*
I will (shall) have gone	we will (shall) have gone
you will have gone	you will have gone
he, she, *or* it will have gone	they will have gone

Each of the six tenses has an additional form called the *progressive form,* which expresses continuing action. It consists of a form of the verb *be* plus the present participle of the verb. The progressive is not a separate tense but an additional form of each of the six tenses in the conjugation.

Present Progressive	am, are, is going
Past Progressive	was, were going
Future Progressive	will (shall) be going
Present Perfect Progressive	has, have been going
Past Perfect Progressive	had been going
Future Perfect Progressive	will (shall) have been going

Consistency of Tense

17d. Do not change needlessly from one tense to another.

When writing about events that occurred in the past, choose verbs in the past tense. Do not suddenly shift, without reason, to the present tense. Similarly, when writing about an action that takes place in the present, do not use verbs in the past tense unnecessarily.

NONSTANDARD	Cara fielded the ball and throws the runner out. [*Fielded* is past tense; *throws* is present tense.]
STANDARD	Cara **fielded** the ball and **threw** the runner out. [Both *fielded* and *threw* are past tense.]
NONSTANDARD	He stands on the mound and stared at the batter. [*Stands* is present tense, *stared* is past tense.]
STANDARD	He **stands** on the mound and **stares** at the batter. [*Stands* and *stares* are both present tense.]

The perfect tenses are mainly used in expressing action that has been completed, or finished.

| NONSTANDARD | I regretted that I chose such a broad topic for my report. [Since the action of choosing was completed before the action of regretting, the verb should be *had chosen,* not *chose.*] |
| STANDARD | I regretted that I **had chosen** such a broad topic for my report. |

EXERCISE 7. Proofreading a Paragraph to Make the Tenses of the Verbs Consistent. Proofread the following paragraph looking for needless changes of tense. Decide whether the following paragraph should be told in the present or past tense. Then change verb tenses to achieve consistency.

It all started as soon as I came home from school. I am in my room, and I have planned to study for two hours. It was about 5 o'clock. To my surprise, Nancy Chang decided to drop by. She dashes into the house, slams the door behind her, and yells for me. What she wanted is a fishing companion. She has been thinking about going fishing all week. Getting my gear together, I become excited and can almost see the fish fighting over which one is to be my first catch. On our way out to the lake, we see clouds begin to form, and we knew we are in for trouble. It rains all right, for the whole weekend. Once again the fish had been granted a week's reprieve.

WRITING APPLICATION B:
Using Verb Tenses Consistently to Make Your Writing Clear

Keeping verb tenses consistent in your writing helps your reader understand which events took place when. If you move from past to present and back to past again, for example, your reader may become confused about the order in which the events occurred. To make your writing clear and easy to follow, be sure to use verb tenses consistently.

Writing Assignment

Write a paragraph about a time when you learned how to play a game or a sport. Read your paragraph carefully to make sure that all your verb tenses are consistent.

ACTIVE AND PASSIVE VOICE

A verb is said to be in the *active* voice when it expresses an action performed *by* its subject. A verb is in the *passive* voice when the action it expresses is performed *upon* its subject.

ACTIVE VOICE   The coach instructed us. [The subject performs the action.]

PASSIVE VOICE   We were instructed by the coach. [The subject receives the action.]

Only transitive verbs—those that can take objects—can be used in the active voice. Compare the subjects of the following related sentences:

                    S   O
ACTIVE   The author provides helpful diagrams.

                    S
PASSIVE   Helpful diagrams are provided by the author.

The object of the active sentence has become the subject of the passive one. The subject of the active sentence is expressed in the passive sentence only in a prepositional phrase. In fact, it can be omitted from the passive sentence.

PASSIVE   Helpful diagrams are provided.

The verb in a passive sentence is always a verb phrase that includes a form of the verb *be* and the past participle of the main verb. If other helping verbs appear in the active sentence, they must also be included in the passive. For example:

s   o
ACTIVE   Willa Cather **wrote** *My Ántonia*.

s
PASSIVE   *My Ántonia* **was written** by Willa Cather.

s   o
ACTIVE   Someone **has erased** the tapes.

s
PASSIVE   The tapes **have been erased.**

The passive voice puts the emphasis on the person or thing receiving the action rather than upon the one performing it. It may be used in situations in which the speaker does not know or does not wish to say who performed the action (as in the last example above). However, you should avoid a succession of passive sentences, which sounds weak and awkward.

EXERCISE 8. Classifying Sentences by Voice. Number your paper 1–5. After the appropriate number, indicate whether each of the following sentences is active or passive.

1. The album was reviewed unfavorably by most critics.
2. The student body elects the council president.
3. Angelo's courageous act averted a tragedy.
4. W. C. Handy composed the blues classic "St. Louis Blues."
5. Handy's contributions to jazz music are appreciated by modern musicians.

EXERCISE 9. Revising Sentences with Verbs in the Active and Passive Voice. Revise the sentences in Exercise 8, changing the active voice to passive, and the passive voice to active.

USAGE

EXAMPLE 1. Mary addressed the envelopes.
          1. *The envelopes were addressed by Mary.*

WRITING APPLICATION C:
Using the Active Voice to Make Your Writing Direct and Forceful

Using the active voice helps make your writing direct and forceful. Notice how the following sentence carries the reader through the action from beginning to end .

ACTIVE Jody lofted the volleyball over the net to the other team.

When you use the passive voice, your reader does not know who performed the action until the end of the sentence.

PASSIVE The volleyball was lofted over the net to the other team by Jody.

Although the passive voice does have certain uses, you should generally avoid it in your writing.

Writing Assignment

Write a paragraph about a hobby or pastime you enjoy. Read your paragraph carefully, making sure that you have avoided using the passive voice unless you have a sound reason for doing so.

SPECIAL PROBLEMS WITH VERBS

Lie and Lay

The verb *lie* means "to rest" or "to recline," "to remain in a lying position." Its principal parts are *lie, lying, lay, (have) lain.* The verb *lie* never takes an object.

The verb *lay* means "to put" or "to place" (something). Its principal parts are *lay, laying, laid, (have) laid.* These forms may have objects (receivers of the action).

INFINITIVE	PRESENT PARTICIPLE	PAST	PAST PARTICIPLE
lie (to rest)	lying	lay	(have) lain
lay (to put)	laying	laid	(have) laid

Study these examples of the use of the verb *lie*.

I sometimes **lie** on the floor.
The bills **are lying** on the table.
Yesterday Lambert **lay** on the grass.
How long **have** the bills **lain** there?

Notice how the following examples of the use of the verb *lay* differ from those above.

Lay those books down.
I **am laying** the clean towels on this chair.
Yesterday Lambert **laid** the bricks on the patio.
Have you **laid** your report aside?

By taking time to think through each form of these verbs, you can establish the habit of using them correctly. When faced with a *lie-lay* problem, ask yourself two questions:

1. What is the meaning I intend? Is it "to be in a lying position," or is it "to put something down"?

2. What is the time expressed by the verb, and which principal part is required to express this time?

Remember that the verb *lie* may be used to describe the lying position of inanimate objects as well as people and animals. Regardless of its having once been put down, the object *lies* (not *lays*) there.

PROBLEM   When I heard about the blizzard, I (lay, laid) in bed for an extra hour.

Question 1   Meaning? The meaning here is "to remain in a lying position." The verb that means "to remain in a lying position" is *lie*.

Question 2   Principal part? The time is past and requires the past form, which is *lay*. [lie, *lay*, lain]

SOLUTION   When I heard about the blizzard, I **lay** in bed for an extra hour.

USAGE

PROBLEM	Calvin (lay, laid) the jacket on the bed.
Question 1	Meaning? The meaning here is "to put." The verb that means "to put" is *lay*.
Question 2	Principal part? The time is past and therefore requires the past form, which is *laid*. [lay, *laid*, laid]
SOLUTION	Calvin **laid** the jacket on the bed.

PROBLEM	How long have you (lain, laid) there?
Question 1	Meaning? The meaning here is "to be in a lying position." The verb that means "to be in a lying position" is *lie*.
Question 2	Principal part? The time requires the past participle with *have*. The past participle of *lie* is *lain*. [lie, lay, *lain*]
SOLUTION	How long **have** you **lain** there?

EXERCISE 10. *Oral Drill.* **Using the Forms of *Lie* and *Lay* Correctly.** Read each of the following sentences aloud several times. Be able to explain why the verb is correct.

1. We carefully *laid* the old map on the table.
2. Yesterday afternoon all the cows *lay* under a shade tree.
3. A wet towel is *lying* on the sand.
4. Enid was carefully *laying* the tiles on the floor.
5. The best route *lay* to the west.
6. That box has *lain* in your closet for weeks.
7. His thoughts *lie* miles away.
8. Yesterday I *laid* the pliers on the bench, and they should still be *lying* there.

EXERCISE 11. Writing the Forms of *Lie* and *Lay*. After numbering your paper 1–10, write the correct form of the proper verb (*lie-lay*) for each of these sentences.

1. He —— the report aside and called for order.
2. I shall —— down for a while.
3. She has —— on the couch all morning.

4. The baby was —— quietly in the nurse's arms.
5. Is that today's paper —— in the mud?
6. I have —— the shoes near the fire to dry.
7. —— down, Rags.
8. The lace had —— in the trunk for years.
9. Our cat —— in the sun whenever it can.
10. I —— back and rested my head on the cushions.

Sit and Set

The verb *sit* means "to rest in an upright, seated position." The principal parts of *sit* are *sit, sitting, sat, (have) sat. Sit* almost never has an object.

The verb *set* means "to put," "to place" (something).[1] The principal parts of *set* are *set, setting, set, (have) set. Like *lay,* set* may take an object. Notice, also, that *set* does not change to form the past or past participle.

INFINITIVE	PRESENT PARTICIPLE	PAST	PAST PARTICIPLE
sit (to rest)	sitting	sat	(have) sat
set (to put)	setting	set	(have) set

Study the following examples:

Sit down.	Cups **sit** on the tray.
Set it down here.	I **set** the cups there.

EXERCISE 12. Oral Drill. Using the Forms of Sit and Set Correctly. Read the following sentences aloud several times. Think of the *meaning* of the verbs until you feel that you know the right uses of *sit* and *set*.

1. I *set* the chairs on the lawn.
2. The campers *were sitting* around the fire.

---

[1] There are several uses of the verb *set* that do not mean "to put" or "to place"; for example: "The sun *sets*," "Hens *set* on eggs," "*set* one's watch," "*set* a speed record," "*set* out to do something."

3. Fern *sat* next to Scott.
4. Please *set* the table.
5. Please *sit* still.
6. The car *sat* there all week.
7. Have we really *sat* here that long?
8. Dolores *sat* down and *set* the teapot in front of me.

EXERCISE 13. Writing the Forms of *Sit* and *Set*. Number your paper 1–10. For each of the blanks in the following sentences, write the correct form of *sit* or *set*.

1. Please —— here, Mrs. Brown.
2. Have you —— the seedlings in the sun?
3. We were —— in the park during the fireworks.
4. Someone has already —— the kettle on the stove.
5. Grandfather is busily —— tomato plants in the garden.
6. At the concert, Keith —— near Isabelle.
7. My cat rarely —— on my lap.
8. They were —— on the rocks, watching the surf.
9. We had —— still for almost an hour.
10. Have you ever —— on the beach at sundown?

Rise and Raise

The verb *rise* means "to go in an upward direction." Its principal parts are *rise, rising, rose, (have) risen.* Like *lie,* the verb *rise* never has an object.

The verb *raise* means "to move something in an upward direction." Its principal parts are *raise, raising, raised, (have) raised.* Like *lay* and *set, raise* may take an object.

INFINITIVE	PRESENT PARTICIPLE	PAST	PAST PARTICIPLE
rise (to go up)	rising	rose	(have) risen
raise (to move something up)	raising	raised	(have) raised

I always **rise** early.
Someone **will raise** that question.
The price index **rose** sharply.
The publisher **raised** the price of the paper.

EXERCISE 14. *Oral Drill.* **Using the Forms of** *Rise* **and** *Raise* **Correctly.** Repeat each of the following sentences aloud three times, stressing the italicized verbs.

1. The tide *rises* early this weekend.
2. We *raised* our voices in song.
3. A woman *rose* from her seat and *raised* an objection.
4. The teacher *raised* his eyebrows.
5. Everyone in my house *rises* early except me.
6. Has the sun *risen* yet?
7. Everyone *rose* when the judge entered the room.
8. The builders had *raised* the barn in just a day.

EXERCISE 15. **Writing the Forms of** *Rise* **and** *Raise*. Number your paper 1–10, and write the correct form of *rise* or *raise* for each of the following blanks.

1. Please —— and face the class.
2. After the speech, the reporters —— several questions.
3. Will the governor —— the sales tax again?
4. The price of fuel has —— steadily.
5. Let's get there before the curtain —— .
6. Jerry, one of the stagehands, will —— the curtain.
7. The bread has —— beautifully.
8. The moon —— and slipped behind a cloud.
9. The candidate —— to address her supporters.
10. The children —— when the bell rang.

REVIEW EXERCISE D. **Writing Sentences Using the Forms of** *Lie* **and** *Lay,* *Sit* **and** *Set,* **and** *Rise* **and** *Raise*. Write ten sentences, using each of the following verbs.

USAGE

1. rise	5. was lying	9. has been rising
2. raised	6. was laying	10. had lain
3. have sat	7. will sit	
4. have set	8. has been setting	

REVIEW EXERCISE E. Identifying the Correct Forms of *Lie* and *Lay, Sit* and *Set,* and *Rise* and *Raise.* Number your paper 1–10. Choose the correct verb in parentheses, and write it after the proper number.

1. (Sit, Set) the bird cage on some newspapers.
2. The cage is (sitting, setting) on some papers.
3. Please (lie, lay) these blankets on the bed.
4. The blankets are (lying, laying) on the bed.
5. Bea (rose, raised) from the couch and answered the door.
6. Has Susie (lain, laid) down for her nap?
7. The wiring (lies, lays) behind the walls.
8. The plumber (lay, laid) the pipes under the floor.
9. Get up, the sun is (rising, raising)!
10. Someone (sat, set) on my lunchbag.

REVIEW EXERCISE F. Writing Sentences Using the Correct Forms of Verbs. Write ten sentences, using each of the following verbs. Supply appropriate helping verbs if needed.

1. set	4. drunk	7. chose	9. lain
2. laid	5. laying	8. sat	10. lying
3. rose	6. raised		

CHAPTER 17 REVIEW: POSTTEST

Proofreading Sentences for Correct Verb Forms and Sound Use of Tense or Voice. Number your paper 1–25 in a column. Read each of the following sentences. If the verb is correct, write *C* after the corresponding number. If it is incorrect or awkward, write the correct verb form or revise the sentence. Some sentences may have more than one incorrect verb.

1. I use to want a pet ferret, but I ask my parents, and they said, "No, not in an apartment." 2. One day last year, I was setting on the front steps reading the newspaper when I spot an ad for, of all things, a ferret. 3. Deciding to investigate, I fold the paper, hop on my bike, and rode to the pet shop that had placed the ad.

4. When I arrived at the store, I seen the ferret right away. 5. She was laying in a box on top of the counter. 6. I told the owner of my interest, and she reaches into the box. 7. When she withdrew her hand, the ferret was holding onto her finger with what looked like very sharp teeth.

8. I cautiously reached out and takes the ferret's hindquarters in my cupped hands. 9. The rest of her long body poured slowly into my hands until she was sitting on her haunches. 10. She looked up at me and suddenly clamps her teeth on my thumb. 11. The ferret done it to show me who was boss. 12. I should have knowed then that my troubles had just began.

13. I ran all the way home and persuaded my parents to let me keep the ferret on a trial basis. 14. I had already give her a name—Ferris the Ferret—and I lose no time rushing back to the pet shop. 15. When I come home with Ferris, I sit a dish of cat food in front of her. 16. She stuck her snout into the dish and ate greedily. 17. After she had went into each room in the apartment, she choosed the top of the TV as her special place. 18. When my parents objected, I made a cardboard house with two entry holes and set it in a corner of my bedroom. 19. Ferris sniffed around her new home; then she goes in and laid down for a nap.

20. For the next few days, Ferris spent her time either napping or nipping. 21. She always attackted me when I least expected it. 22. Once, as she lies on my desk while I am studying, she suddenly locked her teeth in my earlobe. 23. I was so startled that I jump up quickly, and Ferris wound up laying on the floor with a look that makes me feel guilty. 24. The next day the bad news was gave to me by my parents: Ferris had to go back to the pet shop. 25. I no longer want a pet ferret, but I have wrote to the local zookeeper to ask about snakes.

The Correct Use of Pronouns

NOMINATIVE AND OBJECTIVE USES

Nouns and pronouns have *case*. The case of a noun or pronoun depends upon the word's use in the sentence. In English, there are three cases: *nominative, objective,* and *possessive.*

DIAGNOSTIC TEST

Identifying Correct Forms of Pronouns.   Number your paper 1–20. After each number, write the correct form of the pronoun in parentheses. Be able to give reasons for your answers.

EXAMPLE   1. (We, Us) girls have built a picnic table.
             1. *We*

1. Mr. Nickerson thanked Odessa and (I, me) for shoveling the snow off his walk.
2. Wenona couldn't remember (who, whom) had borrowed her pencil.
3. The last two people to arrive, Susan and (I, me), had had trouble finding the skating rink.
4. Because Gloria complained about her teammates, the coach lectured Gloria and (they, them) on team spirit.

5. (We, Us) boys went on an all-day hike.
6. Was the winner of the race (he, him) or Aaron?
7. No one except Bill and (she, her) went to the fair.
8. The pictures of the Grand Canyon impressed them more than (we, us), for we had seen the real thing.
9. Diane and (I, me) painted the room together.
10. Everyone at the dance contest applauded the winning couple, Marco and (she, her).
11. Alan, (who, whom) I did the typing for, said that he will pay me on Friday.
12. Tom, like you and (I, me), enjoys playing tennis.
13. At the top of the steep hill stood Tammy and (he, him).
14. Ellis was worried about his project, but Mrs. Asato gave (he, him) an A.
15. We went horseback riding with the two guides, Ed and (he, him).
16. Elisha was as excited as (they, them) about their vacation plans.
17. Can you give Teresa and (I, me) directions to State Street?
18. Hector wrote this song for you and (I, me).
19. Carolyn has been playing the guitar longer than (he, him).
20. The sewing was done by Akela and (he, him).

Choosing the correct case form for a noun is no problem, since the form remains the same in the nominative and objective cases.

EXAMPLE The **woman** [nominative] went into business with another **woman** [objective].

Only in the possessive case does a noun change its form, usually by adding an apostrophe and an *s*.

EXAMPLE That **woman's** business is thriving and may expand.

Personal pronouns, however, have various case forms. In the following sentence, for example, the pronouns in boldfaced type all refer to the same person. They have three different forms because of their different uses.

EXAMPLE **I** [nominative] forgot to bring **my** [possessive] notebook with **me** [objective].

You can avoid using pronouns incorrectly by learning the case forms of pronouns and their use in sentences.

THE CASE FORMS OF PERSONAL PRONOUNS

Study the following list of personal pronouns, noticing the changes in form.

Personal Pronouns

NOMINATIVE CASE	OBJECTIVE CASE	POSSESSIVE CASE
Singular		
I	me	my, mine
you	you	your, yours
he, she, it	him, her, it	his, her, hers, its
Plural		
we	us	our, ours
you	you	your, yours
they	them	their, theirs

You and *it* have the same form in the nominative and the objective case. Only the following pronouns have different nominative and objective forms. Memorize both lists.

NOMINATIVE CASE	OBJECTIVE CASE
I	me
he	him
she	her
we	us
they	them

EXERCISE 1. Classifying Pronouns.   Number your paper 1–10. If the pronoun is in the nominative case, write the corre-

sponding objective case pronoun; if it is in the objective case, write the corresponding nominative case pronoun.

1. they   3. me   5. she   7. I   9. us
2. him   4. we   6. he   8. them   10. her

THE NOMINATIVE CASE

18a. The subject of a verb is in the nominative case.

EXAMPLES   **He** and **I** joined a book club.
            We students are planning a field trip.
            She was glad that **they** were elected.

In the first sentence, *He* and *I* are subjects of the verb *joined.* In the second, *We* is the subject of *are planning.* In the third, *She* is the subject of *was; they* is the subject of *were elected,* the verb in the subordinate clause.

Most errors in the use of pronouns as subjects are made when the subject is compound, particularly when both parts of the compound subject are pronouns.

COMPOUND SUBJECT   **She** and **they** answered the ad.

You can often avoid using the incorrect form by trying each pronoun separately with the verb. Of course you would never say *Her answered the ad* or *Them answered the ad.*

She answered the ad. **They** answered the ad.
She and **they** answered the ad.

Sometimes a pronoun will have a noun appositive.[1]

We students are going on a trip.

You can arrive at the correct form for the pronoun in such sentences by reading the sentence without the noun appositive: *We are going on a trip.*

Sometimes the pronouns *we* and *they* sound awkward when used as parts of a compound subject. In such instances, it is often advisable to revise the sentence.

[1] For the definition of an appositive, see page 442.

AWKWARD We and they hope to sit together at the game.
 BETTER We hope to sit with them at the game.

EXERCISE 2. *Oral Drill*. Using Pronouns as Subjects.
Read each sentence aloud, stressing the italicized pronouns.

1. *We* girls made a sand sculpture.
2. It was apparent that *he* and *I* had won the debate.
3. My brother and *I* are painting the inside of the garage.
4. *We* boys heard that Tim and *she* were disappointed.
5. *He* and *she* said that *we* volunteers were responsible for counting the ballots.
6. Where are my parents and *they*?
7. Will you and *he* help us with the book sale?
8. *She* and her sister have made posters for the party at the Senior Citizens' Center.

EXERCISE 3. Identifying Pronouns Used as Subjects.
Number your paper 1–5. Write the pronouns that are used as subjects in the following sentences. Do not include *you*.

1. I certainly hope that you and I can agree.
2. Why don't you and she try out for track?
3. We said that you and they would come.
4. No one knows where she and I have been.
5. We two have been friends since kindergarten.

EXERCISE 4. Writing Sentences Using Compound Subjects.
Write five sentences, using the following as subjects.

1. he and I
2. Warren and we
3. Doris and she
4. they and their friends
5. you boys and we girls

18b. A predicate nominative is in the nominative case.

A predicate nominative is a noun or pronoun that follows a linking verb and explains or identifies the subject of the

USAGE

sentence (see pages 402–403). A pronoun used as a predicate nominative always follows a form of the verb *be* or verb phrases ending in *be* or *been.*

EXAMPLES This is **he.**
It may be **she.**
It should have been **they.**

☞ **USAGE NOTE** Listening to conversations, you will often hear people say, "it's me." Although *I,* not *me,* is the nominative case pronoun, widespread usage has made *It's me* acceptable spoken English. Either *It's me* or *It's I* is acceptable. Similar expressions such as *That's him* or *Could it have been her?* (in which the rule calls for *he* and *she*) may be considered as acceptable in speaking, but you should avoid them in writing.

As you do the following exercises, follow the rule for written English: *A predicate nominative is in the nominative case.*

EXERCISE 5. Writing Pronouns Used as Predicate Nominatives. Complete the following sentences by adding pronouns in the nominative case used as predicate nominatives. Use *I, he, she, we,* and *they.*

1. Was it —— ?
2. I thought it was —— .
3. The winner is —— .
4. That was —— .
5. Can it be —— ?

THE OBJECTIVE CASE

The following pronouns are in the objective case:

> him, her   me   us   them

These pronouns are used as direct objects, indirect objects, and objects of prepositions. (Review pages 404–407 and 419–20.)

18c. The direct object of a verb is in the objective case.

STANDARD   Clem called **her.** [*Clem* is the subject of the verb *called*. Clem called *whom*? The answer is *her.*]

NONSTANDARD   Clem's call surprised Dad and I. [*I* is a nominative case pronoun and should not be used as direct object of the verb.]

STANDARD   Clem's call surprised Dad and **me.**

When the object is compound, try each pronoun object separately. "Clem's call surprised I" is obviously incorrect. Hence, "Clem's call surprised Dad and I" is also incorrect.

NONSTANDARD   He paid we helpers generously for our work.

STANDARD   He paid **us** helpers generously for our work.

EXERCISE 6. *Oral Drill.* **Using Pronouns as Direct Objects.** Recite each of the following sentences, stressing the italicized pronouns.

1. They saw Hilda and *me* at the fair.
2. Julia said that she recognized *him* and *me* at once.
3. Has anyone called *her* or *him* lately?
4. Thelma often visits Charlene and *her.*
5. They drove *us* girls to the bus station.
6. A dog chased *her* and *me* out of the yard.
7. The search party found Duane and *him* in the woods.
8. Did you ask *them* or *us*?

EXERCISE 7. Writing Pronouns Used as Direct Objects. Number your paper 1–10. Write appropriate pronouns for the blanks in these sentences. Use a variety of pronouns. (Do not use *you* or *it*.)

1. I found Nina and ―― in the library.
2. Will you help ―― or ―― ?
3. The sudden noise frightened Alex and ―― .
4. Jimmy Santos called both Maria and ―― .

5. You must trust Anita and —— .
6. I need you and —— right now.
7. Sylvia Chu drove Candy and —— to the movies.
8. We all watched Gene and —— .
9. These gloves fit both Carl and —— .
10. We saw Carol and —— in a canoe.

18d. The indirect object of the verb is in the objective case.

As you have already learned, an indirect object tells *to whom* or *for whom* something is done. Pronouns used as indirect objects are in the objective case: *me, him, her, us, them.*

EXAMPLES   The librarian gave **her** a pass.
Molly lent **me** two books.
Chip loaned **him** the skateboard.

EXERCISE 8. *Oral Drill.* **Using Pronouns as Indirect Objects.**   Recite each of the following sentences, stressing the italicized pronouns.

1. Someone handed *him* and *me* several pamphlets.
2. Show Esther and *her* your snapshots of the wedding.
3. Sara made Dad and *me* mittens and matching scarves.
4. Our teacher gave *us* students an oral quiz.
5. Send Tom and *me* your new address.
6. My parents told *her* and *me* the news.
7. Mrs. Bashar gave *him* and *her* applications.
8. Tell Bill and *me* the story that you told the principal and *him*.

EXERCISE 9. Writing Pronouns Used as Indirect Objects.
Number your paper 1–10. Supply appropriate pronouns for the blanks in the following sentences. Use a variety of pronouns. (Do not use *you* or *it*.)

1. Sal asked —— the most difficult question.
2. Alex baked —— a loaf of banana bread.

3. The teacher handed —— and —— the homework assignments.
4. Linda threw —— the ball.
5. Mr. Young has never told —— and —— the real story.
6. Writing stories gives —— great pleasure.
7. We brought —— T-shirts from California.
8. Mr. Cruz gave —— a pen as a graduation gift.
9. Ruth carved —— an animal out of soap.
10. Iris bought —— a sweater.

REVIEW EXERCISE A. Identifying Correct Forms of Pronouns. Number your paper 1–20. Write the correct pronoun in parentheses for each sentence. Be prepared to give the use of each pronoun in the sentence.

1. Sean and (I, me) visited the computer fair.
2. (We, Us) two spent hours looking at the different displays.
3. A guide showed (we, us) boys the latest models.
4. She told Sean and (I, me) some interesting facts about computer technology.
5. Another guide and (she, her) turned on the computer.
6. After (they, them) had pushed a few buttons, a cathode-ray tube lit up and several words appeared on the screen.
7. One of the guides asked Sean and (I, me) if (we, us) boys wanted to operate the computer.
8. (He, Him) and (I, me) quickly agreed, and she gave (we, us) boys instructions.
9. In a short time, we had surprised (she, her) and several bystanders with our ability.
10. Sean and (I, me) soon found another fascinating display.
11. A guide named Judith showed Sean and (I, me) all kinds of walking machines.
12. (She, Her) and her twin sister were demonstrating the machines.
13. Judith and (she, her) introduced Sean and (I, me) to one of the robots.

USAGE

14. It reached out and touched (he, him) and (I, me) with a plastic "hand."
15. Then Sean and (I, me) watched as Judith and her sister took turns dancing with the robot.
16. Judith and (she, her) gave (we, us) boys a chance to dance with the robot, too.
17. (They, Them) and the crowd around the display seemed to enjoy our performance.
18. When the dance was over, the robot escorted Sean and (I, me) back to the display area.
19. Sean and (I, me) asked Judith how the robot worked.
20. (She, Her) patiently explained the control panel.

18e. The object of a preposition is in the objective case.

A prepositional phrase begins with a preposition (see the list on page 368) and ends with a noun or pronoun. The final word in a prepositional phrase is the *object of the preposition* that begins the phrase. A pronoun used as an object of a preposition must be in the objective case.

| with **me** | before **her** | without **them** |
| for **us** | behind **him** | |

Errors in usage often occur when the object of a preposition is compound. Again, you can usually tell the correct pronouns by trying each one separately in the prepositional phrase.

to Elizabeth and **me**   about you and **them**
except Jeanne and **her**   by Jim and **him**

EXERCISE 10. *Oral Drill.* Using Pronouns as Objects of Prepositions. Read each of the following sentences aloud, stressing the italicized words.

1. Talk over your problems *with her* and *them.*
2. I addressed cards *to* my mother and *her.*
3. *Between* you and *me,* I am worried *about them.*

4. She is always very polite *to him* and *me*.
5. The coaches rode in a bus *in front of us* players.
6. A stray dog was running *toward* Luke and *her*.
7. First prize was shared *by* Jen and *me*.
8. May I go camping *with* you and *them*?

EXERCISE 11. Revising Prepositional Phrases by Correcting Pronoun Forms. Number your paper 1–10. If the sentence is correct, write *C*. If there are pronoun errors, revise the prepositional phrase, correcting the pronoun forms.

EXAMPLES 1. Are you leaving with Kara and them?
     1. *C*
     2. Nobody but Tricia and I volunteered to serve on the committee.
     2. *but Tricia and me*

1. Just between you and I, this dessert is too sweet.
2. Everyone but you and he solved the puzzle.
3. The principal came toward we students.
4. Shall we stand in front of Donna and him?
5. We discussed the project with everyone except you and she.
6. Celeste, like you and me, prefers tennis to squash.
7. Next to Anna and I sat Mr. Kelsch, the music teacher.
8. Sit here between him and me.
9. For Carolyn and I, that assignment is easy.
10. Everyone except you and she is wearing a costume.

☞ **USAGE NOTE** Pronouns used in apposition are in the same case as the word to which they refer.

EXAMPLES The winners, **he, she,** and **I,** thanked the committee.
[Since *winners* is the subject of the sentence, the pronouns in apposition with it (*he, she, I*) must be in the nominative case.]

Every volunteer except two, **him** and **her,** received an award. [Since *two* is the object of the preposition *except,* the appositives must be in the objective case.]

The teacher introduced the speakers, Laura and **me.** [Since *speakers* is the direct object of *introduced,* the pronoun *me,* which is in apposition to *speakers,* must be in the objective case.]

WRITING APPLICATION A:
Using Pronoun Forms to Make Your Writing Correct

Using pronoun forms correctly can make a difference in the way your readers react to your writing. If you mistakenly write, "Linda toured the art show with Frances and I," for example, your readers may think that you are careless or that you do not know any better. Such errors may result in negative reactions to your writing as a whole.

Writing Assignment

Write a paragraph about an event, such as a concert or a neighborhood festival, that you went to with two of your friends or family members. Read your writing carefully to make sure that you have used pronoun forms correctly.

REVIEW EXERCISE B. Identifying Correct Pronoun Forms.

Number your paper 1–20. Write the correct pronoun in parentheses. Two sentences have two sets of parentheses.

1. This conversation is between Lou and (I, me).
2. I'm positive it was (they, them).
3. Did Alva or (she, her) leave a message?
4. Mrs. Lopez hired (we, us) boys for the summer.
5. (He, Him) and (I, me) are working on a special project.
6. Is that package for Mother or (I, me)?

USAGE

7. No one told Otto or (I, me) about the game.
8. I play *Scrabble* with my aunt and (she, her).
9. (We, Us) girls are expert players.
10. I hope you and (she, her) will be on time.
11. When are your parents and (they, them) coming home?
12. I don't know (he, him) or his friends very well.
13. Everyone except (he, him) and (I, me) heard the news first-hand.
14. I don't believe you or (he, him).
15. I think the girl up front is (she, her).
16. Between you and (I, me), I like your plan better.
17. (We, Us) two have tickets for the concert.
18. The teacher gave James and (I, me) extra math homework.
19. That's (he, him) on the red bicycle.
20. Come to the game with (we, us) girls.

SPECIAL PRONOUN PROBLEMS

There are two kinds of problems you will frequently run across. One is the choice between *who* and *whom;* the other is which pronoun to use in an incomplete construction.

Who and Whom

The pronoun *who* also has different forms in the nominative and the objective cases. *Who* is the nominative form; the objective form is *whom.* Similarly, *whoever* is nominative; *whomever* is objective.

☞ **USAGE NOTE** In spoken English, the use of *whom* is becoming less common. In fact, when you are speaking, you may correctly begin any question with *who* regardless of the grammar of the sentence.

In written English, however, you should distinguish between *who* and *whom*. *Who* is used as subject or predicate nominative, and *whom* is used as an object.

Often *who* or *whom* will appear in subordinate clauses.

18f. The use of *who* or *whom* in a subordinate clause is determined by the function of the pronoun in the clause.

When you are deciding whether to use *who* or *whom* in a subordinate clause, follow these steps:

1. Find the subordinate clause.
2. Decide how the pronoun is used in the clause—as subject, predicate nominative, object of the verb, or object of a preposition.
3. Determine the case of the pronoun according to the rules of standard English.
4. Select the correct form of the pronoun.

EXAMPLES

PROBLEM Do you know (who, whom) she is?

Step 1 The subordinate clause is (*who, whom*) *she is.*

Step 2 In this clause, the subject is *she,* the verb is *is,* and the pronoun is the predicate nominative: *she is* (*who, whom*).

Step 3 As predicate nominative, the pronoun is in the nominative case.

Step 4 The nominative form is *who.*

SOLUTION Do you know **who** she is?

PROBLEM Margaret Mead, (who, whom) I read about in several articles, wrote interesting books.

Step 1 The subordinate clause is (*who, whom*) *I read about in several articles.*

Step 2 In this clause, the subject is *I;* the verb is *read.* The pronoun is the object of the preposition *about: I read about* (*who, whom*).

Step 3 The object of a preposition is in the objective case.

Step 4 The objective form is *whom.*

USAGE

SOLUTION Margaret Mead, **whom** I read about in several articles, wrote interesting books.

The sentence, of course, would also be correct with the preposition before the pronoun: *Margaret Mead, about whom I read in several articles, wrote interesting books.*

Remember that no words outside the clause affect the case of the pronoun. In the second problem, the entire clause was used as a direct object of the verb *do know,* but the pronoun was used as a predicate nominative (nominative case).

EXAMPLE Do you know who she is?

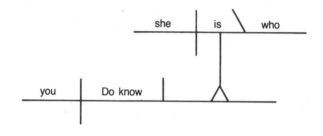

> ☞ **USAGE NOTE** Frequently, *whom* in subordinate clauses is omitted (understood).

EXAMPLES The woman (whom) I admire is Dr. Mead.
The woman (whom) I read about is a well-known anthropologist.

EXERCISE 12. Classifying Pronouns Used in Subordinate Clauses.

On your paper, write each subordinate clause in the sentences that follow. Then tell how the pronoun (*who* or *whom*) is used in its own clause—as subject, predicate nominative, object of the verb, or object of a preposition.

EXAMPLE 1. Take this book to Eric, whom you met yesterday.
1. *whom you met yesterday, object of verb*

1. Mr. Cohen is the man who lives next door to us.
2. Mr. Cohen, whom we saw yesterday, lives next door to us.
3. The woman who was speaking to me is conducting a survey.
4. The woman to whom I was speaking is conducting a survey.
5. Can you tell me who that teacher is?
6. She is a substitute teacher whom we all like.
7. Anyone who misses the bus will be penalized by the coach.
8. I wonder who that can be.
9. Whom Mona finally voted for is a secret.
10. Is there anyone who can help me?

EXERCISE 13. Classifying Pronouns Used in Subordinate Clauses and Identifying Correct Forms.

Number your paper 1–10. After the proper number, give the use of the pronoun in parentheses. Then write the correct pronoun.

EXAMPLE   1. I know (who, whom) you are.
1. *predicate nominative, who*

1. Mrs. James, (who, whom) I work for, owns a pet shop.
2. Is there anyone here (who, whom) needs a bus pass?
3. She is the only one (who, whom) everybody trusts.
4. Her grandmother, to (who, whom) she sent the flowers, won the over-fifty marathon.
5. I helped Mr. Thompson, (who, whom) was shingling his porch roof.
6. Eileen couldn't guess (who, whom) it was.
7. It was John Adams (who, whom) founded the American Society of Arts and Letters.
8. Both of the women (who, whom) ran for election to the city council were elected.
9. That author (who, whom) you admire is scheduled to visit the local bookstore next Tuesday.
10. Edgar Degas, (who, whom) we are studying in art class, is well known for his painting of Parisian theater scenes.

USAGE

WRITING APPLICATION B:
Using *Who* and *Whom* to Make Your Writing Correct

Most people overlook mistakes in the use of *who* and *whom* in speech, but they expect writers to be more careful. Using *who* and *whom* incorrectly in writing may give the impression that you are careless or do not know how to use the two forms.

Writing Assignment

To practice using *who* and *whom* correctly, write a paragraph about a group of people you know. You may use one of the following sentence beginnings or one of your own.

1. Most of my friends . . .
2. Many of my relatives . . .
3. Many of the teen-agers in my town . . .

EXAMPLE   Most of my neighbors work. The woman who lives next door manages a shoe store. The man whom everyone on the block calls "Chief," who lives two houses down the street from us, sells real estate. In back of us is a couple, both of whom work for the school board. He works in maintenance, and she is in charge of the switchboard. I don't know the people who just moved in across the street, but I see them leave for work each day.

REVIEW EXERCISE C. Correcting Pronoun Forms. If all of the pronouns in a sentence are correct, write *C*. If a pronoun has been used incorrectly, write the correct case form.

1. Estelle and me are the editors of a magazine published by our school. 2. Students who want to submit their stories give them to either Estelle or I. 3. After us two have read the stories,

we call a general staff meeting. 4. Then all of us students who make up the staff choose the best stories.

5. When the stories have been selected by us staff members, they are sent to the printer along with a page layout. 6. Both Estelle and me go to the print shop to discuss the magazine with the printer. 7. One printer who we spoke to complimented us on the magazine. 8. Sometimes, however, someone will question she or I about the layout of a page or the length of a story.

9. Rick and Emily, who the art teacher highly recommended, work on the cover design. 10. All of us students who work on the magazine are relieved when the latest issue is finally published and distributed.

11. Last month a prize was offered to the student whom, in our judgment, submitted the best story. 12. The judges, Estelle, Rick, and me, read each entry carefully. 13. None of us knew who had written which story. 14. When Estelle had finished reading one story, she burst out laughing and handed it to Rick and I. 15. "Here, read this," she said. "You'll wonder who wrote this one."

16. The story was about a girl who took her dog, Rags, to see a movie about horses. 17. The woman who Rags sat next to kept staring at him, but Rags' full attention was on the screen. 18. When the movie was over, the woman lost no time approaching the girl, whom, with Rags in her arms, was headed for the nearest exit.

19. The woman said, "Your dog's interest in the movie was certainly a surprise to all of we people who sat near him."

20. The girl, who nothing seemed to bother, replied politely, "I was surprised, too; neither him nor me liked the book."

The Pronoun in an Incomplete Construction

Notice the difference in meaning that the choice of pronouns can make in sentences with incomplete constructions.

EXAMPLES   Everyone knows that you like Jo better than **I.**
Everyone knows that you like Jo better than **me.**

In the first sentence the choice of the pronoun *I* indicates that it is the subject of an understood verb: *Everyone knows that you like Jo better than I like Jo.* In the second sentence, the choice of the pronoun *me,* which is in the objective case, indicates that it is the object of the understood verb *like: Everyone knows that you like Jo better than you like me.*

The case of the pronoun depends upon how the omitted part of the sentence would be completed.

18g. After *than* and *as* introducing an incomplete construction, use the form of the pronoun that you would use if the construction were completed.

The following sentences are correct because they clearly express the meaning intended by the writer. The words in the brackets show how each could be completed.

EXAMPLES   I wrote you more often than **he** [wrote you].
                I wrote you more often than [I wrote] **him.**

                Did you help Ada as much as **I** [helped Ada]?
                Did you help Ada as much as [you helped] **me**?

EXERCISE 14. Completing Incomplete Constructions and Classifying Pronoun Forms.   Beginning with the *than* or *as,* complete each sentence, using the correct form of the pronoun. After the sentence, write the use of the pronoun in the completed clause, telling whether it is a subject or an object.

EXAMPLE   1. Kim was as surprised as (I, me).
            1. *as I was—subject*

1. Justin plays the guitar better than (I, me).
2. The story mystified him as well as (we, us).
3. Is your sister older than (he, him)?
4. Have they studied as long as (we, us)?
5. We have known him longer than (she, her).
6. Are you more conservative than (he, him)?
7. Did you enjoy the book as much as (I, me)?
8. I like Mark better than (they, them).

9. Many people are less fortunate than (we, us).
10. Are you as optimistic as (she, her)?

EXERCISE 15. Writing Sentences with Pronouns. Write ten sentences, correctly using the following words and phrases.

1. who
2. whom
3. we members
4. us members
5. you and I
6. you and me
7. as much as he
8. as well as him
9. more than I
10. more than me

CHAPTER 18 REVIEW: POSTTEST

Correcting Pronoun Forms. Number your paper 1–20. If a sentence is correct, write *C*. If a pronoun is used incorrectly, write the correct form of the pronoun.

1. The politician spoke to us members of the Debate Society.
2. During the Olympic trials, every diver except she received a low score from the judges.
3. The children who Inez brought home from the fair were sleeping in the car.
4. My instructor, who had been stunned by my quick recovery after a fall from the high bar, gave me a good score.
5. I wrote a beautiful poem about my grandfather and he.
6. I hope that you and them can manage the fruit stand.
7. Sometimes it was difficult to tell who was having a better time, them or us.
8. Many people wanted to know whom the winners were.
9. It is unlikely that Betty and me can make enough money

this summer to pay for a trip to the Canadian Rockies.

10. The Steins and us watched the trapeze artist swinging in the air.
11. If it is she who is supposed to be in charge, please notify us.
12. This letter is strictly between you and I.
13. Why can't you and her cooperate?
14. Tyrone and he are playing backgammon at Regina's house.
15. We girls were happy with the results of the election for class president.
16. Him and his father are taking a class in microwave cooking at a local appliance store.
17. It couldn't have been her.
18. He is more energetic than me.
19. Our neighbors, Mrs. Brandt and he, helped us move.
20. Rick couldn't spot Maura and I in the crowd at the fair.

USAGE

The Correct Use of Modifiers

COMPARISON AND PLACEMENT

A modifier describes or limits the meaning of another word. There are two kinds of modifiers: adjectives and adverbs. Besides one-word modifiers, you have studied several other kinds of modifiers—prepositional phrases, verbal phrases, and subordinate clauses—all of which may be used as adjectives or adverbs.

DIAGNOSTIC TEST

A. Correcting Forms of Modifiers. Number your paper 1–10. For each sentence, write the error in comparison followed by the correct form. If the sentence is correct, write *C*.

EXAMPLES 1. His problem is more worse than yours.
       1. *more worse—worse*
      2. Her cat is larger than any cat I've ever seen.
      2. *any—any other*

1. Which did you like best, the book or the movie?
2. The sun is brighter than anything in our solar system.
3. The tomatoes from our garden taste sweeter than those from the store.

4. This is the most nicest surprise I've ever had!
5. Raymond has always been courteouser than his brother.
6. The Nile is longer than any river in the world.
7. Which is the most difficult part of writing for you, finding an idea or expressing it in words?
8. Don't you feel more better now that you've had a rest?
9. Trees growing near the ocean are often much smaller than those growing in more protected areas.
10. Which is the best course to take, upstream or downstream?

B. Correcting Dangling or Misplaced Modifiers. The following sentences contain dangling or misplaced modifiers. Rewrite each sentence so that it is clear and correct.

EXAMPLES   1. The young girl walked her dog in the plaid dress.
           1. *The young girl in the plaid dress walked her dog.*
           2. Running across the field, my ankle was sprained.
           2. *Running across the field, I sprained my ankle.*

11. Enjoying their lunch, the rainclouds loomed menacingly over the picnickers.
12. I gave a book to my young cousin containing many pictures of dinosaurs.
13. We hung the pictures when we had finished arranging the furniture on the walls.
14. In different parts of the world, we have read about unusual customs.
15. A tree was destroyed by a bulldozer that was eighty years old.
16. Sharon relaxed in the sun and watched her fishing line happily whistling a tune.
17. A lawn mower was used to cut the lawn that spluttered, smoked, and finally stalled.
18. He placed a tray on the table of fresh raw vegetables.
19. The new books were displayed so that students would notice them and read them on the circulation desk.

20. The mayor pledged that he would build more parks at the political rally.

COMPARISON OF MODIFIERS

Adjectives state qualities of nouns or pronouns.

hot day   **sandy** beach   **low** tide   **last** one

You can show the degree to which one noun has a quality by comparing it with another noun that has the same quality.

This beach is **sandier** than that one.

Similarly, you can show degree or extent by using adverbs to make comparisons.

I changed into my bathing suit **quickly**, but Lois changed into hers even **more quickly.**

19a. The forms of modifiers change when they are used to show comparison.

There are three degrees of comparison: *positive, comparative,* and *superlative.* Notice in the following examples how the forms of modifiers change to show comparison.

POSITIVE	COMPARATIVE	SUPERLATIVE
short	shorter	shortest
young	younger	youngest
fearful	more fearful	most fearful
rapidly	more rapidly	most rapidly
bad	worse	worst
good	better	best

Regular Comparison

(1) A modifier of one syllable regularly forms its comparative and superlative by adding -*er* and -*est.*

POSITIVE	COMPARATIVE	SUPERLATIVE
low	lower	lowest
large	larger	largest
deep	deeper	deepest

(2) Some modifiers of two syllables form their comparative and superlative degrees by adding -er and -est; other modifiers of two syllables form their comparative and superlative degrees by means of *more* and *most*.

In general, the *-er, -est* forms are used with two-syllable modifiers unless they make the word sound awkward. The *more, most* forms are used with adverbs ending in *-ly*.

POSITIVE	COMPARATIVE	SUPERLATIVE
gentle	gentler	gentlest
lovely	lovelier	loveliest
careful	more careful	most careful
famous	more famous	most famous
slowly	more slowly	most slowly

☞ **USAGE NOTE** Some two-syllable modifiers may take either *-er, -est* or *more, most: common, commoner, commonest* or *common, more common, most common.*

When in doubt about which way a two-syllable modifier is compared, consult an unabridged dictionary.

EXERCISE 1. Writing Comparative and Superlative Forms. Write the forms for the comparative and superlative degrees of the following words:

| 1. fast | 3. happy | 5. simple | 7. safe | 9. anxious |
| 2. soon | 4. careful | 6. hazy | 8. wisely | 10. pretty |

(3) Modifiers having more than two syllables form their comparative and superlative degrees by means of *more* and *most*.

POSITIVE	COMPARATIVE	SUPERLATIVE
energetic	more energetic	most energetic
significantly	more significantly	most significantly

EXERCISE 2. *Oral Drill.* Using Comparative and Superlative Forms. Give the comparative and superlative degrees of (1) *original,* (2) *reasonably,* (3) *important,* (4) *appropriately,* and (5) *pessimistic.*

(4) Comparison to indicate less or least of a quality is accomplished by using the word *less* or *least* before the modifier.

POSITIVE	COMPARATIVE	SUPERLATIVE
helpful	less helpful	least helpful
frequent	less frequent	least frequent

EXERCISE 3. *Oral Drill.* Using Comparisons to Indicate Less or Least of a Quality. Give the comparisons to indicate less and least of the five words listed in Exercise 2.

Irregular Comparison

Adjectives and adverbs that do not follow the regular methods of forming their comparative and superlative degrees are said to be compared *irregularly.*

POSITIVE	COMPARATIVE	SUPERLATIVE
bad	worse	worst
good well	better	best
many much	more	most

Caution: Do not add the *-er, -est* or *more, most* forms to irregularly compared forms: *worse,* not *worser* or *more worse.*

EXERCISE 4. Using Comparative and Superlative Forms. Number your paper 1–10. For the blank in each sentence, write the correct form of the word in italics before that sentence.

USAGE

EXAMPLE   1. *bad* My notebook looks —— than Joshua's.
                1. *worse*

1. *well* I can skate —— now than I could last year.
2. *many* She caught the —— fish of anyone in our group.
3. *bad* That is the —— movie I have ever seen.
4. *much* We have —— homework than we had last week.
5. *good* Ella has the —— attendance record of anyone.
6. *many* Are there —— plays or short stories in your literature book?
7. *good* Lloyd is the —— pitcher on our baseball team this year.
8. *much* Of the three groups of volunteers, our group cleaned up the —— litter.
9. *good* Both of the poems were good, but I thought that Sarah's was —— than his.
10. *bad* My cold is —— than hers.

REVIEW EXERCISE A. Writing Comparative and Superlative Forms.   Write the comparative and superlative forms of the following modifiers. If you are in doubt about the forms of two-syllable modifiers, consult an unabridged dictionary.

1. bad	6. fuzzy	11. noisy	16. patiently
2. good	7. rough	12. safely	17. intelligent
3. tall	8. strong	13. quick	18. graceful
4. early	9. loose	14. funny	19. important
5. many	10. well	15. poorly	20. lonely

Use of Comparative and Superlative Forms

19b. Use the comparative degree when comparing two things; use the superlative degree when comparing more than two.

The comparative form of a modifier is used for comparing two things, as the following examples indicate:

EXAMPLES   In my opinion, "The Adventure of the Three Garridebs" is **better** than "The Red-headed League."
Writing mysteries seems **more challenging** than writing nonfiction.

The superlative form of a modifier is used for comparing three or more items.

EXAMPLES   This is the **best** Sherlock Holmes story that I have ever read.
Writing a mystery story is the **most challenging** assignment I've had so far.

☞ **USAGE NOTE**   In everyday conversation, it is acceptable in some cases to use the superlative degree in comparing two things: *Put your best foot forward.*

EXERCISE 5. Writing Sentences with Comparative and Superlative Forms.   Using the correct forms of adjectives or adverbs, write five sentences comparing two things and five comparing more than two.

19c. Do not omit the words *other* or *else* when comparing one thing with a group of which it is a part.

It is illogical to say, "Ruth is more agile than any member of her gymnastics team." Obviously, Ruth is a member of her team, and she cannot be more agile than herself. The word *other* should be used in such comparisons: "Ruth is more agile than any *other* member of her gymnastics team."

ILLOGICAL   Our dentist, Dr. Greene, is gentler than any dentist.
CORRECTED   Our dentist, Dr. Greene, is gentler than any **other** dentist.

Similarly, "That pitcher has struck out more batters than anyone on the team" is illogical, since the pitcher is a member of the team. Here, *else* should be added: "That pitcher has struck out more batters than anyone else on the team."

ILLOGICAL   Cicely ran faster than anyone.
CORRECTED   Cicely ran faster than anyone **else.**

EXERCISE 6. *Oral Drill.* **Using Comparisons Logically.** The comparisons in this exercise are illogical because of the omission of the words *other* or *else*. As you read the sentences, supply the needed word so that each sentence is logical.

1. My grandmother is wiser than anyone I know.
2. My sister has more cassettes and records than anyone in the family.
3. Your report is more imaginative than any report submitted so far.
4. Brent can pass better than anyone on the team.
5. This ring is more precious to me than anything I own.

EXERCISE 7. Revising Sentences by Making Comparisons Logical. Number your paper 1–5 and revise each sentence, adding *other* or *else* to make it logical.

EXAMPLE   1. Rodney spells better than anyone in his class.
            1. *Rodney spells better than anyone else in his class.*

1. Today has been colder than any day this year.
2. Alice eats more slowly than anybody in this cafeteria.
3. Flying is faster than any type of travel.
4. My sunflowers grew taller than any flowers in my garden.
5. Luis enjoys swimming more than anything.

19d. Avoid double comparisons.

A double comparison is incorrect because it contains both *-er* and *more* or *-est* and *most*.

NONSTANDARD   She is more funnier than he.
   STANDARD   She is **funnier** than he.

NONSTANDARD   This is the most costliest bicycle in the store.
   STANDARD   This is the **costliest** bicycle in the store.

EXERCISE 8. Revising Modifiers by Eliminating Double Comparisons.

Number your paper 1–5. Copy each incorrect modifier, and revise it by crossing out the unnecessary part to eliminate the double comparison.

EXAMPLES   1. Today is more colder than yesterday.
   1. ~~more~~ colder
   2. Today is the most beautifulest day we've had in a long time.
   2. most beautiful~~est~~

1. That is the most elegantest sweater that I have ever seen.
2. You seem to be trying more harder in school this year.
3. She is more quicker at figures than Rita.
4. The illustrations help make the explanations more clearer to the readers.
5. Georgia is more larger in area than any other state east of the Mississippi.

19e. Be sure your comparisons are clear.

Your sentences should state clearly what things are being compared: For example, in the sentence "The average temperature in Dallas is higher than Spokane," the comparison is not clear. *The average temperature in Dallas* is not being compared to *Spokane,* but rather to *the average temperature* in Spokane. The sentence should read: *The average temperature in Dallas is higher than the average temperature in Spokane (or . . . than that in Spokane).*

UNCLEAR   The hide of the rhinoceros is harder than the alligator.
   BETTER   The hide of the rhinoceros is harder than the hide of the alligator.

Often an incomplete construction is used in a comparison: *You are luckier than she.* Both parts of the comparison should be stated if there is any chance of misunderstanding.

USAGE

USAGE

UNCLEAR	I visited her more than Elise.
BETTER	I visited her more than I visited Elise.
BETTER	I visited her more than Elise visited her.

WRITING APPLICATION A:
Using Comparative and Superlative Forms of
Modifiers Correctly to Make Your Writing Clear

Using the comparative and superlative forms of modifiers correctly helps your readers understand how two or more items of the same kind are different from one another. If you write, "Our new apartment is larger than our old one," for example, your reader understands one way in which the two apartments are different from each other. Similarly, if you write, "Ernesto is the best math student in the ninth grade," your readers understand one way in which Ernesto is different from all the other ninth-graders.

Writing Assignment

Write a paragraph comparing two or more teams, such as sports, debating, or cheerleading teams. Read your paragraph carefully to make sure that you have used comparative and superlative forms of modifiers correctly.

REVIEW EXERCISE B. Revising Sentences by Correcting Modifiers. Number your paper 1–10. If all the modifiers in a sentence are correct, write *C*. If a modifier is incorrect, revise the sentence, making whatever correction is needed.

1. The monkeys were noisier than any animals at the zoo.
2. The hare was faster, but the tortoise was more persistent.
3. Which do you think is the most ferocious—the lion or the tiger?
4. Her hair is longer than any girl in school.
5. According to some statistics, traveling in an airplane is safer than an automobile.

6. Earth is nearer to the sun than Mars.
7. In ''The Road Not Taken,'' the narrator considers two paths and chooses the least traveled one.
8. Tantalus was more cruelly punished than any mythic figure.
9. After hearing all three auditions, the director decided that Jim was the best singer.
10. The wings of the female mosquito beat more faster than the wings of the male.

DANGLING MODIFIERS

19f. A modifying phrase or clause that does not clearly and sensibly modify a word in a sentence is a *dangling modifier*.

When a modifying phrase containing a verbal comes at the beginning of a sentence, the phrase is followed by a comma. Immediately after that comma should come the word that the phrase modifies.

Strolling through the park, I saw a brown rabbit in the underbrush. [*I* was strolling.]

To understand poetry, the reader needs some knowledge of figurative language. [The *reader* needs some knowledge to understand poetry.]

Posted on the bulletin board, the flier announced the date and place of the cleanup campaign. [The *flier* was posted on the bulletin board.]

Each of the following sentences contains a dangling modifier—a modifier that either appears to modify a word other than the one it is meant to modify or does not modify any word at all.

Strolling through the park, a rabbit peered out at me from the underbrush. [The sentence implies that the rabbit was strolling.]

To understand poetry, a knowledge of figurative language is necessary. [The sentence implies that knowledge understands.]

Posted on the bulletin board, Dotty saw a flier announcing the date and place of the cleanup campaign. [Was Dotty posted on the bulletin board?]

EXERCISE 9. Writing Sentences with Introductory Modifiers. Write ten complete sentences, using the following introductory modifiers. Follow each modifier by a word it can *clearly* and *sensibly* modify.

EXAMPLE   1. Having solved one problem,

          1. *Having solved one problem, Joe Harris found that another awaited him.*

1. Leaping from branch to branch,
2. Feared and hunted,
3. Nodding her head,
4. To avoid the rain,
5. Hiding behind the couch,
6. To answer that question,
7. While eating our lunch,
8. Cuffing each other playfully,
9. Diving suddenly into the pool,
10. Gazing out the window,

Correcting Dangling Modifiers

To correct a dangling modifier, you should either rearrange the words in the sentence or add words to make the meaning logical and clear.

DANGLING   To become a physicist, years of study and research are required.

CORRECTED   To become a physicist, you (*or* one) must spend years studying and doing research.

      or   If you want to become a physicist, you must spend years studying and doing research.

DANGLING   While lighting the birthday candles, the cake started to crumble.

CORRECTED   While I was lighting the birthday candles, the cake started to crumble.

or   While lighting the birthday candles, I noticed the cake starting to crumble.

EXERCISE 10. Revising Sentences by Eliminating Dangling Modifiers.   Most of the following sentences contain dangling modifiers. Number your paper 1–20. If a sentence is correct, write *C* after the corresponding number. If it is incorrect, revise the sentence to eliminate the dangling modifier.

1. After cleaning up the vacant lot, refreshments were served.
2. Walking through the main gate, the swimming pool lies to your right.
3. Rumbling loudly, no one seemed to hear the oncoming storm but me.
4. To earn spending money, Mother gave me a job addressing envelopes.
5. While riding my bicycle, my safari hat kept blowing off my head.
6. To succeed in that career, you must be ambitious.
7. After studying hard for an exam, a long walk can be refreshing.
8. Standing at the intersection, we watched a chartered bus speed by.
9. To prepare adequately for a test, a thorough review is usually advisable.
10. Before leaving the camping grounds, be sure to extinguish the fire.
11. To be well informed, you should read a daily newspaper and a weekly news magazine regularly.
12. While walking in the woods, the sound of singing birds is an enjoyable experience.
13. To understand the meaning of a sentence, even the little words can be important.

USAGE

14. Running across the open field, I felt my knee buckle.
15. To become a great athlete, dedication and self-discipline are needed.
16. Standing on the beach, a school of dolphins suddenly appeared.
17. After winning the last game of the season, the fans gave the players a standing ovation.
18. While mopping the kitchen, my baby brother woke up from his nap.
19. Turning the corner, the library lies straight ahead.
20. Sitting up on its hind legs, the dog begged for a treat.

MISPLACED MODIFIERS

A dangling modifier makes the meaning of a sentence absurd. Just as damaging to the clear expression of ideas are misplaced modifiers.

19g. Modifying phrases and clauses should be placed as near as possible to the words they modify.

Misplaced Phrase Modifiers

The following examples of misplaced phrases show the importance of placing phrase modifiers as near as possible to the words they modify.

MISPLACED   I read about the bank robbers who were captured in this morning's paper. [Here, *in this morning's paper* seems to indicate where the bank robbers were captured.]

CORRECTED   In this morning's paper, I read about the bank robbers who were captured.

MISPLACED   At the age of eight, my parents sent me to camp.
CORRECTED   At the age of eight, I was sent to camp by my parents.
or   When I was eight, my parents sent me to camp.

MISPLACED   On the bottom shelf of the refrigerator, I could not find the fruit juice.

CORRECTED   I could not find the fruit juice on the bottom shelf of the refrigerator.

EXERCISE 11. Revising Sentences by Placing Modifiers Near the Words They Modify.   Revise the following sentences so that they make sense. Either place phrase modifiers as near as possible to the words they modify or turn a phrase into a clause. Be sure that you do not misplace another modifier in revising a sentence.

1. Grazing peacefully, we saw a herd of buffalo in the distance.
2. We gave the boxes of cereal to the children with prizes inside.
3. At five years of age, my grandfather taught me to make tortillas.
4. One advertiser handed out roses to customers with dollar bills pinned to them.
5. I borrowed a radio from my sister with a weather band.
6. There should be a collection of hats worn by your grandmother in the attic.
7. Our cat enjoys pieces of food slipped to it by the family under the table.
8. She ate two peaches and a plate of strawberries with relish.
9. In a tank at the aquarium, we watched the seals playing.
10. I could see the scouts marching over the hill with my binoculars.

Misplaced Clause Modifiers

Place an adjective or adverb clause as near as possible to the word it modifies. Notice how the meaning of the following sentence is distorted by a misplaced clause modifier.

MISPLACED   I bought a seat for my bicycle that is made of fur.

USAGE

Since the modifying clause *that is made of fur* seems to modify *bicycle,* the sentence is ridiculous. The clause should be close to the word it modifies, as follows:

CORRECTED   I bought a seat that is made of fur for my bicycle.

To correct misplaced clauses, place the modifying clause as close as possible to the word it modifies.

MISPLACED   The money is still in my wallet that I meant to return to you.
CORRECTED   The money that I meant to return to you is still in my wallet.

MISPLACED   There is a car in the garage that has only one door and no windshield.
CORRECTED   In the garage there is a car that has only one door and no windshield.

EXERCISE 12. Revising Sentences by Placing Clauses Near the Words They Modify.   Revise each sentence, placing the misplaced clause near the word it modifies.

1. Birds are kept away by scarecrows, which like to eat seeds.
2. The disabled truck is now blocking the overpass that suddenly went out of control.
3. There was a bird in the tree that had a strange-looking beak.
4. A huge dog chased my bicycle that was growling.
5. An old log sat on the table that was covered with dark green moss.
6. We thanked the clerk at the post office that had helped us with our overseas packages.
7. There are several books on our shelves that were written by Jessamyn West.
8. A boy was standing at the bus stop that looked remarkably like my cousin.
9. She crossed the river on a ferry, which was a mile wide.
10. There is a flower garden behind the shed that is planted with prize-winning dahlias.

WRITING APPLICATION B:
Placing Modifiers Correctly to Make Your Writing Clear

Placing modifiers near the words they modify makes your writing clear and easy to follow. If you mistakenly write, "Waking up in the middle of the night, the roar of the wind startled me," for example, your readers have difficulty in knowing who or what is waking up; it clearly cannot be the roar of the wind. Similarly, if you write, "Inside the oven, I suddenly noticed that the casserole was burning," readers get a mental picture of you inside the oven. To avoid confusing—or losing—your readers, be sure not to misplace modifiers in your writing.

Writing Assignment

Write a paragraph describing a crowd that you were part of recently, such as a crowd at a play or a sports event. Read your paragraph carefully, making sure that you have not misplaced any modifiers.

USAGE

CHAPTER 19 REVIEW: POSTTEST

Revising Sentences by Correcting Modifiers. All of the following sentences contain errors in the use of modifiers or appositives: mistakes in comparisons or dangling or misplaced modifiers. Revise each sentence so that it is clear and correct.

1. When traveling through Scotland, I discovered that stories about monsters were more popular than any kind of story.
2. Having received a great deal of publicity, I already knew about the so-called Loch Ness monster.
3. The first person to sight the monster, a veterinary student from Edinburgh, was Arthur Grant.
4. One day Grant came upon a strange creature cycling on a road near the shore of Loch Ness.

5. On cycling closer, the monster took two great leaps and plunged into the lake.

6. As you might expect, numerous theories were presented about the identity of the monster in the local paper.

7. Some people thought the monster must be a freshwater species of sea serpent, and others believed the whole story was a hoax; of these two theories, the first is obviously the most fascinating.

8. Having found a huge, dead creature on the shore of the lake in 1942, the mystery of the monster was believed finally to be solved.

9. The scientists called it a large shark who examined the specimen.

10. Though having supposedly gone from the lake, many new sightings of the monster have been reported.

11. Supplying heat from the sun's rays, many people know about solar energy.

12. Windmills help to convert wind into electricity, which blows freely across the earth.

13. To create electricity, moving water can also be employed.

14. Geothermal energy, less well known than any power source, comes from the heat stored in the earth's crust.

15. Geothermal energy is brought to the earth's surface, consisting of steam and hot water, by geysers and fumaroles.

16. Having heard of geysers, springs that throw out heated water and steam, something about this form of energy is known to some people.

17. Geysers are often visited by tourists, which send up jets of hot water and steam.

18. Fumaroles, holes in volcanic regions that send up only steam, are considered the best source of geothermal energy.

19. Simpler equipment can be used with pure steam than a steam-and-water mixture.

20. In several countries, people have been making use of geothermal energy for years, such as Iceland and Japan.

A Glossary of Usage

COMMON USAGE PROBLEMS

This chapter contains a short glossary of English usage, treating several kinds of usage problems. Some require the writer or speaker to choose between two words, according to the meaning intended. Others involve a choice between two words, in which one word is less acceptable than the other. A few of the words and expressions discussed here should be avoided altogether.

DIAGNOSTIC TEST

Correcting Errors in Usage.   In each of the following sets of expressions, one expression contains an error in usage. Number your paper 1–20. Copy each incorrect expression, and write the correct expression after it.

EXAMPLE   1. as far as we can see, between the two of us, not going anywheres, the woman whom I saw
1. *not going anywheres—not going anywhere*

1. learned his lesson, where it's at, wait outside the office, heard that she left

2. will affect her health, a short way to go, set it down, reads less books
3. had ought to wait his turn, among the three puppies, played the drums well, they don't like it
4. discovered a new star, picked fewer apples, should have known, the situation changed some
5. between lunch and dinner, they will join us, the girl which I met, except for him
6. the bus that arrived, the girl who sings, having little or no affect, Walter cooked the dinner
7. grows beside the brook, bring the lantern when you go, unless it rains, a person that I trust
8. these type of hats, leave the chair there, it is no problem, that shirt looks good
9. the weather has improved somewhat, that kind of wrench, the effect was terrible, see them stars
10. a broken window, not available anywhere, car runs good, more effort than that
11. she and I went, left it somewheres, inside the ski lodge, sit near me
12. fell off of the branch, sounds as though he has a cold, if she had heard, between those two trees
13. fewer planes took off, has asked for nothing, accepted the trophy, just a little ways
14. let her sleep, between the four of us, to whom I mailed the package, those tapes
15. two others besides her went, could of gone, had scarcely enough seating, he thinks as I do
16. ought to help, might have won, sounds like it's coming closer, brought me the news
17. brighter then daylight, have but one hour, saw fireflies everywhere, nowhere else to go
18. take the script to her, the man whom we helped, that there car, as fast as we can
19. seemed like a good idea, can hardly wait, change this tire, she don't know

20. balloon burst yesterday, learned him how to swim, let the kite go, invented a new gadget

---

a, an These *indefinite articles* refer to one of a general group.

EXAMPLES **A** student walked into the library.
Our town needs **a** hospital.
May I please have **an** apple?
Martha worked for **an** hour.

Use *a* before words beginning with a consonant sound; use *an* before words beginning with a vowel sound. In the examples above, *a* is used before *hospital* because *hospital* begins with a consonant sound. *An* is used before *hour* because *hour* begins with a vowel sound.

accept, except *Accept* is a verb; it means "to receive." *Except* may be either a verb or a preposition. As a verb, it means "to leave out" or "to omit"; it is usually used in the passive voice. (See pages 508–509.) As a preposition, *except* means "excluding."

EXAMPLES We **accept** your apology.
Senior citizens will be **excepted** from the fee.
Everyone **except** me has seen the exhibit.

affect, effect *Affect* is a verb meaning "to influence." *Effect* used as a verb means "to accomplish." Used as a noun, *effect* means "the result of some action."

EXAMPLES The bright colors **affect** the patients beneficially.
The doctors hope the treatment will **effect** a cure for the disease.
The bright colors have a beneficial **effect** on the patients.

ain't Avoid this word in speaking or writing; it is nonstandard English.

all the farther, all the faster Used in some parts of the country to mean "as far as" or "as fast as."

USAGE

DIALECT   This is all the faster I can go.
STANDARD   This is **as fast as** I can go.

among   See **between, among.**

and etc.   *Etc.* is an abbreviation of the Latin phrase *et cetera,* meaning "and other things." Thus, *and etc.* means "and and other things." Do not use *and* with *etc.*

EXAMPLE   My younger sister collects string, bottle caps, stickers, **etc.** [not *and etc.*]

anywheres, everywheres, nowheres, somewheres   Use these words without the final *s.*

EXAMPLE   That bird is described **somewhere** [not *somewheres*] in this book.
I searched **everywhere** [not *everywheres*] for a blouse to match that skirt.

as   See **like, as.**

as if   See **like, as if.**

at   Do not use *at* after *where.*

NONSTANDARD   This is where I live at.
STANDARD   This is where I live.

beside, besides   *Beside* means "by the side of" someone or something; it is always a preposition. *Besides* as a preposition means "in addition to." As an adverb, *besides* means "moreover."

EXAMPLES   Sit **beside** me on the couch.
Besides songs and dances, the show featured several comedy sketches.
I have a long walk home. **Besides,** it's starting to snow.

between, among   Use *between* when you are thinking of two things at a time, even though they may be part of a group consisting of more than two.

EXAMPLES   Stand **between** Alice and Noreen in the third row.
The Civil War is sometimes called the War **Between** the States. [Although thirty-five states were involved, the war was *between* two sides.] The manager could not decide which of the four players to select, as there was not much difference **between** them. [Although there are more than two players, each one is being thought of and compared with the others separately.]

Use *among* when you are thinking of a group rather than of separate individuals.

EXAMPLES   There was some confusion **among** the jurors about one part of the defendant's testimony. [The jurors are thought of as a group.]
We collected only ten dollars **among** the four of us.

bring, take   *Bring* means "to come carrying something." *Take* means "to go carrying something." Think of *bring* as related to *come, take* as related to *go.*

EXAMPLES   **Bring** that box over here.
Now **take** it down to the basement.

bust, busted   Avoid using these words as verbs. Use a form of either *burst* or *break.*

EXAMPLES   The balloon **burst** [not *busted*] loudly.
The firefighters **broke** [not *busted*] a window.

EXERCISE 1. Identifying Correct Usage.

This exercise covers the usage problems discussed on pages 557–61. Number your paper 1–20. After each number, write the correct word from the parentheses in the corresponding sentence.

1. Is that (all the farther, as far as) you were able to hike?
2. (Beside, Besides) my aunts and uncles, all my cousins are coming to our family reunion.

3. Please (accept, except) this gift as an expression of our thanks.
4. There was complete agreement (between, among) the members of the council.
5. Please (bring, take) this package to the main post office.
6. I (busted, broke) my arm when I fell.
7. I can't find that brand of paint (anywhere, anywheres).
8. (Beside, Besides) all this clothing, we also collected several boxes of canned goods.
9. Everyone seemed greatly (affected, effected) by her gracious thank-you note.
10. The boiler (busted, burst), but fortunately no one was in the basement at the time.
11. I have to (bring, take) these supplies to the cafeteria.
12. Ms. Yu (accepted, excepted) my excuse for being absent.
13. The (affects, effects) of an earthquake can be devastating.
14. I've spent all my money. (Beside, Besides), I've already seen that movie.
15. Please (bring, take) this bill to Copy Service for copying.
16. Their parents distributed the gifts equally (between, among) the four children.
17. The (affects, effects) of lasers on surgical procedures have been remarkable.
18. My schedule this year includes English, social studies, science, (etc., and etc.)
19. He generously divided the prize money (among, between) his three brothers.
20. I took some home-grown tomatoes to my grandmother, who lives in (a, an) high-rise.

can't hardly, can't scarcely   See **The Double Negative** (page 572).

could of   *Could have* sounds like *could of* when spoken. Do not write *of* with the helping verb *could*. Write *could have*. Also avoid *ought to of, should of, would of, might of,* and *must of.*

EXAMPLE   Diane could **have** [not *of*] telephoned us.

discover, invent   *Discover* means "to be the first to find, see, or learn about something that already exists." *Invent* means "to be the first to do or make something."

EXAMPLES   Marguerite Perey **discovered** the element francium.
The zipper was **invented** in 1925.

don't, doesn't   *Don't* is the contraction of *do not: doesn't* is the contraction of *does not.* Use *doesn't,* not *don't,* with *he, she, it, this,* and singular nouns.

EXAMPLES   It **doesn't** [not *don't*] matter.
This **doesn't** [not *don't*] make sense.

effect   See **affect, effect.**

everywheres   See **anywheres,** etc.

fewer, less   *Fewer* is used with plural words; *less* with singular words. *Fewer* tells "how many"; *less,* "how much."

EXAMPLES   There are **fewer** gypsy moths this year.
They have done **less** damage to the trees.

good, well   *Good* is always an adjective. Never use *good* to modify a verb; use *well,* which is an adverb.

NONSTANDARD   Pancho Gonzales played good.
STANDARD   Pancho Gonzales played **well.**

Although it is usually an adverb, *well* is used as an adjective to mean "healthy."

EXAMPLE   She does not feel **well.** [predicate adjective meaning "healthy"]

☞ **USAGE NOTE**   *Feel good* and *feel well* mean different things. *Feel good* means "to feel happy or pleased." *Feel well* simply means "to feel healthy."

EXAMPLES The news made her feel **good.**
I didn't feel **well,** so I went home.

The use of *good* as an adverb is increasing in conversational English, but it should not be so used in writing.

EXERCISE 2. Identifying Correct Usage. This exercise covers the usage problems discussed on pages 562–64. Write the correct word in parentheses for each sentence.

1. You should (of, have) written sooner.
2. Who (discovered, invented) what makes fireflies glow?
3. (Don't, Doesn't) Sidney know that we're leaving in five minutes?
4. I usually do (good, well) on that kind of test.
5. Some doctors advise their patients to eat (fewer, less) eggs.
6. He (don't, doesn't) look especially healthy to me.
7. If I had known, I might (of, have) helped you with your problem.
8. We had (fewer, less) snowstorms this year.
9. Our teacher (doesn't, don't) require us to type our reports.
10. Whoever (discovered, invented) the escalator must have been ingenious.

REVIEW EXERCISE A. Correcting Errors in Usage. This exercise covers the most important usage problems discussed in the glossary so far. If a sentence is correct, write *C*. If a sentence contains an error in usage, write the correct form.

1. Beside you and Janet, no one knows about my vacation plans.
2. The tire on my bicycle burst.
3. Did you bring flowers to your aunt when you visited her in her new home?
4. That box contains less cookies than this one.
5. Why won't you except my help?

6. The beautiful spring weather is effecting my powers of concentration.
7. In the salad, I put tomatoes, celery, onions, lettuce, green pepper, etc.
8. You should of given us your new phone number.
9. Don't anyone know when this game will start?
10. We felt good because the practice sessions went so well.
11. Is that all the faster you can read?
12. We're trying to decide between this movie and that one.
13. Everywheres we went there were long lines.
14. My motion to adjourn the meeting was not excepted by the president.
15. Who discovered the cordless telephone?
16. What affect did the investigation have on the congressional candidate?
17. We lay beside the lake and watched the swans.
18. Between the four of us, we managed to move the piano without breaking anything.
19. The girl waving the banner don't go to our school.
20. Perhaps I should of called before coming to see you at your home.

had of   See **of.**

had ought, hadn't ought   Unlike other verbs, *ought* is not used with *had*.

> NONSTANDARD   Lee had ought to plan better; he hadn't ought to have left his packing until the last minute.
>
> STANDARD   Lee **ought** to plan better; he **ought not** to have left his packing until the last minute.
>
> *or*   Lee **should** plan better; he **shouldn't** have left his packing until the last minute.

haven't but, haven't only   See **The Double Negative** (page 572).

he, she, they   Do not use an unnecessary pronoun after a noun. This error is called the *double subject.*

NONSTANDARD   My mother she grows all her own herbs.
STANDARD   My mother grows all her own herbs.

kind, sort, type   The demonstrative words *this, that, these,* and *those* must agree in number with the words *kind, sort, type: this type, these types.*

EXAMPLE   I like **this kind** of jeans better than any of **those** other **kinds.**

learn, teach   *Learn* means "to acquire knowledge." *Teach* means "to instruct" or "to show how."

EXAMPLE   Some coaches **teach** classes in gymnastics, where young gymnasts can **learn** many techniques.

leave, let   *Leave* means "to go away" or "to depart from." *Let* means "to allow" or "to permit."

NONSTANDARD   Leave her speak if she insists.
STANDARD   **Let** [allow] her speak if she insists.
STANDARD   Let's **leave** on time for a change.

less   See **fewer, less.**

like, as   *Like* is a preposition. In informal English, *like* is often used as a conjunction meaning "as"; but in formal English, *as* is always preferable.

EXAMPLES   She looks **like** her sister. [The preposition *like* introduces the phrase *like her sister.*]
We should do **as** our coach recommends. [*As our coach recommends* is a clause and needs the conjunction *as* (not the preposition *like*) to introduce it.]

like, as if   In formal written English, *like* should not be used for the compound conjunctions *as if* or *as though.*

EXAMPLE   Scamp looks **as though** [not *like*] he has been in the swamp again.

might of, must of   See **could of.**

no, none, nothing   See **The Double Negative** (page 572).

USAGE

nowheres   See **anywheres,** etc.

of   Do not use *of* with prepositions such as *inside, off, outside, beneath,* etc.

> EXAMPLE   He fell **off** [not *off of*] the ladder **outside** [not *outside of*] the garage.
> What's **inside** [not *inside of*] that box?

Of is also unnecessary with *had.*

> EXAMPLE   If I **had** [not *had of*] seen you, I would have waved.

ought to of   See **could of.**

EXERCISE 3. Identifying Correct Usage.   This exercise covers the most important usage problems discussed on pages 565–67. Number your paper 1–10. Write the correct choice or choices from the parentheses in each sentence.

1. (Leave, Let) me tell you about Shakespeare's story of *Romeo and Juliet.*
2. Perhaps Romeo, a Montague, (hadn't ought, ought not) to have gone to the Capulets' party, for the (Montagues they, Montagues) were rivals of the Capulets.
3. However, if he (hadn't, hadn't of), he would not have met Juliet.
4. After the Capulets' party, Romeo stood in the garden (outside, outside of) Juliet's room; they declared their love for one another.
5. Shakespeare writes (these kind, these kinds) of scenes very well.
6. Perhaps the young couple (hadn't ought, ought not) to have married at all.
7. In a fight, (Romeo he, Romeo) killed Juliet's cousin Tybalt; because of this, Romeo was banished from Verona.
8. Juliet could hardly bear to (leave, let) Romeo go; nevertheless, she (hadn't ought to, shouldn't) have taken the sleeping potion.

9. Believing Juliet dead, Romeo returned to Verona and killed Paris (outside of, outside) Juliet's tomb. Then he killed himself.
10. The death of Romeo and Juliet (learned, taught) the Montagues and the Capulets a bitter lesson and finally ended the feud.

rise, raise   See pages 514–15.

said, same, such   Avoid artificial uses of these words.

> EXAMPLES   I wrote to the editor and kept a copy of **the letter.** [not *said letter*]
> She earned ten dollars and deposited **it** [not *same*] in her savings account.
> Mrs. Lopez wanted a special kind of wood, but **it** [not *such*] was not available.

shall, will   Some people prefer to use *shall* with first person pronouns and *will* with second and third person pronouns in the future and future perfect tenses. Nowadays, most Americans do not make this distinction. *Will* is acceptable in the first person as well as in the other two.

sit, set   See pages 513–14.

so   This word is usually overworked. In writing, avoid using it whenever you can.

> NOT GOOD   The basketball tryouts lasted all day, so the coach could not post the results by noon.
> BETTER   Because the basketball tryouts lasted all day, the coach could not post the results by noon.
> *or*   The basketball tryouts lasted all day; therefore, the coach could not post the results by noon.

some, somewhat   In writing, do not use *some* for *somewhat* as an adverb.

> NONSTANDARD   My grammar has improved some.
> STANDARD   My grammar has improved **somewhat.**

than, then   Do not confuse these words. *Than* is a conjunction; *then* is an adverb.

> EXAMPLES   This box is heavier **than** that one.
> We wrapped the presents. **Then** we hid them in the closet.

them   *Them* should not be used as an adjective. Use *these* or *those*.

> EXAMPLE   I like **these** [not *them*] sneakers, don't you?

this here, that there   The *here* and the *there* are unnecessary.

> EXAMPLE   I'm buying **this** [not *this here*] cassette instead of **that** [not *that there*] one.

this kind, sort, type   See **kind**, etc.

way, ways   Use *way*, not *ways*, in referring to a distance.

> EXAMPLE   We hiked a long **way** [not *ways*].

when, where   Do not use *when* or *where* incorrectly in writing a definition.

> NONSTANDARD   A "bomb" in football is when a quarterback throws a long pass.
> STANDARD   A "bomb" in football is a long pass thrown by the quarterback.

where   Do not use *where* for *that*.

> EXAMPLE   I read in this magazine **that** [not *where*] Marie Ledbetter is a champion parachutist.

which, that, who   Remember that the relative pronoun *who* refers to people only; *which* refers to things only; *that* refers to either people or things.

> EXAMPLES   Here is the man **who** will install the new carpet. [person]
> That is the color **which** we selected. [thing]
> It is the kind of carpet **that** will wear well. [thing]

USAGE

The dealer is a person **that** stands behind a product. [person]

who, whom See pages 530–31.

without, unless Do not use the preposition *without* in place of the conjunction *unless*.

EXAMPLE will not be able to sing **unless** [not *without*] my cold gets better.

would of See **could of.**

EXERCISE 4. Identifying Correct Usage. The sentences in this exercise cover the most important usage problems presented on pages 568–70. Number your paper 1–20. Write the correct one of the two expressions in parentheses in each sentence.

1. Do not use more paper (than, then) you need.
2. The doctor said that Aunt Etta is starting to get her strength back (some, somewhat).
3. (Without, Unless) it stops snowing, we'll have to call off the hike.
4. (That, That there) motorbike belongs to my grandfather.
5. (Them, Those) dogs have impressive pedigrees.
6. Athena was one of the goddesses (who, which) lived on Olympus.
7. Someone hand me (them, those) nails and (that, that there) hammer.
8. I am saving money to buy (that, that there) typewriter.
9. Judge Constance Baker Motley is the daughter of a cook (who, which) emigrated from the West Indies.
10. It is only a short (way, ways) to the bus stop.
11. The directions are a lot less complicated (than, then) they first seemed.
12. I read (where, that) Roanoke Island isn't (anywhere, anywheres) near Roanoke, Virginia.

13. (Them, Those) jars of homemade preserves should be stored in a cool place.
14. Tricia relaxed (some, somewhat) after she began to speak.
15. We plan to visit (that, that there) exhibit before it closes.
16. On the news, I heard (where, that) the game was called off because of rain.
17. Please set (them, those) books on the desk.
18. (This, This here) pot and (those, those there) dishes should be soaked before you wash them.
19. Is she the player (who, which) is favored to win at Wimbledon this year?
20. He would not have released the report (without, unless) he had first verified his sources.

REVIEW EXERCISE B. Revising Sentences by Correcting Errors in Usage. This exercise covers the most important usage problems on pages 565–70. Revise each of the following sentences, correcting the errors in usage.

1. Optimism is when a person always looks on the bright side.
2. Elsie she is a better contestant than George is.
3. Take this here rake and them seedlings to Mrs. Murphy like I asked.
4. If I had of started my report sooner, I might of finished it on time.
5. I heard where people will not be allowed near the concert hall without they show their tickets.
6. The tire came off of the truck and rolled a long ways down the turnpike.
7. Alice Cunningham has promised to learn us karate.
8. The people which witnessed the crime hadn't ought to have left before the police arrived.
9. My parents they refuse to leave me stay out past ten o'clock.
10. Them sailors welcomed the children aboard the *Intrepid*.

USAGE

THE DOUBLE NEGATIVE

In a *double negative*, two negative words are used when one is sufficient. Avoid such double negatives as those listed here.

can't hardly, can't scarcely   The words *hardly* and *scarcely* convey a negative meaning. They should never be used with another negative word.

> EXAMPLES   I **can** [not *can't*] **hardly** turn the key in the lock.
> We **have** [not *haven't*] **scarcely** enough money for a snack.

haven't but, haven't only   In certain uses, *but* and *only* convey a negative meaning and should not be used with *not*.

> EXAMPLE   We **had** [not *hadn't*] **but** five minutes to catch our train.

no, nothing, none   Do not use these words with another negative word.

> NONSTANDARD   That answer doesn't make no sense.
> STANDARD   That answer **makes no** sense.
> STANDARD   That answer **doesn't make any** sense.

> NONSTANDARD   The field trip won't cost nothing but carfare.
> STANDARD   The field trip **won't cost anything** but carfare.
> STANDARD   The field trip **will cost nothing** but carfare.

> NONSTANDARD   We searched for ripe berries, but there weren't none.
> STANDARD   We searched for ripe berries, but there **weren't any.**
> STANDARD   We searched for ripe berries, but there **were none.**

EXERCISE 5. Revising Sentences by Correcting Errors in Usage.   Revise each of the following sentences, correcting the usage errors.

1. Rachel didn't say nothing to him.

2. There isn't hardly anything left to eat.
3. I haven't borrowed but one book from the library this week.
4. Laura couldn't hardly make herself heard.
5. What you're saying doesn't make no sense to me.
6. By the time we wrote for tickets, there weren't none left.
7. Hasn't no one in the class read *And Now Miguel*?
8. There aren't but three eggs in the refrigerator.
9. Didn't you never say nothing about the noise?
10. I haven't never told no one about our discovery.

USAGE

WRITING APPLICATION:
Using Standard English to Make Your Writing Correct

Your readers are used to reading standard English in books, newspapers, and magazines. If you use nonstandard English in your writing, they may think that you do not know or do not care about standard English. The correct use of the words and expressions in this Glossary will help your writing conform to standard English.

Writing Assignment

Using the examples in this chapter as models, write ten sentences to illustrate the following usage rules. Proofread carefully, making sure that you have applied each rule correctly.

1. *Good* is always an adjective.
2. Do not use *of* with *had*.
3. *Let* means "to allow" or "to permit."
4. Do not use double subjects.
5. *Them* is not an adjective.
6. Do not use *where* for *that*.
7. *Who* refers to people only.
8. Do not use another negative word with *hardly*.
9. Do not use *haven't only*.
10. Do not use another negative word with *none*.

CHAPTER 20 REVIEW: POSTTEST

Revising a Passage by Correcting Errors in Usage. Each of the sentences in the following passage contains at least one usage error. Revise the passage, correcting all usage errors.

EXAMPLE 1. Everyone accept him joined the club.
1. *Everyone except him joined the club.*

1. Our school has a hiking club that learns us how to appreciate nature. 2. We usually go to parks that we might not of discovered by ourselves. 3. We'll go anywheres that can be reached by bus in three hours. 4. First we learn what to bring with us when we go. 5. The less things we have to carry, the better off we are. 6. Beside water, a hat, and a jacket, little else is needed. 7. Those which pack too much soon wish they hadn't of. 8. After all, a ten-mile hike effects you differently when you are weighted down then when you are not.

9. Our adviser, Mr. Graham, he knows where all the best hiking areas are at. 10. He always tells us that we can't see nothing interesting without we're willing to exert ourselves. 11. But we can't hardly keep up with him once he starts walking.

12. We go on these sort of walks because we enjoy them. 13. Although we sometimes think our lungs will bust, everyone wants to keep up with the others. 14. The real reward is when we see an unusual sight, like a fawn, a family of otters, a panoramic view, and etc. 15. Than we know that this here hiking is worthwhile. 16. We also can except nature like it is and not try to change it none. 17. We get upset with people who can't go anywheres without leaving some mark in said place.

18. Everyone in the club feels the same way, so we're going to start a campaign. 19. We want people to enjoy being inside of a park without busting or changing nothing there. 20. We'd all rather have more hikers and less people destroying nature.

CHAPTER 21

Capital Letters

THE RULES FOR CAPITALIZATION

In written or printed English, a capital letter at the beginning of a word not only serves as a signal to the reader (indicating, say, the beginning of a sentence) but also may mark a significant difference in meaning (for example, the difference between *may* and *May*). In your writing, then, you should use necessary capitals and avoid unneeded capitals. Learning the rules of capitalization will help you develop this writing skill.

MECHANICS

DIAGNOSTIC TEST

Correcting Sentences by Capitalizing Words. Number your paper 1–20. Write the word or words that should be capitalized in the following sentences. If a sentence is correct, write *C*.

EXAMPLE 1. Bike riding is prohibited on Main street.
1. *Street*

1. The park is two blocks west of the methodist church.
2. Last august, Ms. Johnson drove from New York City to the rocky mountains.

3. When the Saint Lawrence Seaway opened in 1959, large ships from the Atlantic ocean were able to reach ports on the Great Lakes for the first time.

4. Grandpa Henry and aunt Frances discussed politics at our yearly family reunion.

5. Many of the roman myths are filled with violence.

6. During world war II, Gloria's grandmother was a volunteer for the red cross.

7. After the movie, we went out for italian food.

8. The Industrial Revolution drastically changed American life in the 1800's.

9. Sandra Day O'Connor was the first woman to be appointed to the United States supreme court.

10. Mr. Lewis' house is on the corner of Fifty-third Street and Maple Boulevard.

11. Frank and Ellen will take chemistry II next year, but I will take latin instead.

12. I visited a large museum in Mexico city that has hundreds of indian artifacts.

13. Our boat, *misty cloud,* came in third in the race sponsored by the Lakeview sailing club.

14. The drama critic of the *State journal* gave our production of *Carousel* a good review.

15. The freshmen at Adams high school have planned their spring field trip.

16. At the concert, the captain of the wrestling team recited a poem while the school choir hummed.

17. The class saw a film about the limestone caves in Carlsbad Caverns national park.

18. The network will televise today's game at Wrigley field between the Cubs and the Astros.

19. My parents donated our hoover vacuum cleaner to the Salvation army.

20. After hurricane allen struck, the governor declared the region a disaster area.

MECHANICS

21a. Capitalize the first word in every sentence.

INCORRECT   the world of computers has its own language. a complete list of instructions for the computer is a *program*. the person who figures out the program is called the *programmer*. the equipment is called *hardware,* and the programs are called *software*.

CORRECT   The world of computers has its own language. A complete list of instructions for the computer is a *program*. The person who figures out the program is called the *programmer*. The equipment is called *hardware,* and the programs are called *software*.

Traditionally, the first word of a line of poetry is capitalized.

EXAMPLE   There was an old man of Tralee
　　　　　　Who was bitten so much by a flea
　　　　　　　　That he put out the light,
　　　　　　　　Saying, "Now he can't bite,
　　　　　　For he'll never be able to see."

Some modern poets (E. E. Cummings, for example) do not follow this practice. They may capitalize only the first word or sometimes not even that. When you are quoting, use capital letters exactly as they are used in the poem.

EXERCISE 1. Correcting Sentences by Capitalizing Words. Make a list of the ten words that should be capitalized in the following paragraph. Capitalize the words you list.

　　　work has begun on developing a new kind of laser radar this instrument would be especially useful for blind people how does the radar work a laser device, which is small enough to fit onto an eyeglass frame, emits invisible infrared light beams when the light strikes an object, it bounces back to a receiver placed in the blind person's ear the receiver, in turn, sounds a small tone with this sort of device, the blind person can "hear" any object nearby the device is very promising in fact it may one day replace the cane or the

Seeing Eye dog as an aid for the blind there are few better examples of how beneficial laser research can be.

21b. Capitalize the pronoun *I* and the interjection *O.*

Although it is rarely used, *O* is always capitalized. Generally, it is reserved for invocations and is followed by the name of the person or thing being addressed. You will more often use the interjection *oh,* which is not capitalized unless it is the first word in a sentence.

EXAMPLES   The play was a hit, but **oh**, how frightened **I** was!
               "Exult **O** shores! and ring **O** bells!" is a line from
               Walt Whitman's poem "**O** Captain! My Captain!"

EXERCISE 2. Correcting Sentences by Capitalizing Words.
Number your paper 1–5. If an item is correct, write *C.* If there are errors in the use of capitals, copy the item, inserting capitals where needed and omitting unnecessary capitals.

1. yesterday i learned the psalm that begins, "Bless the Lord, o my soul."
2. I haven't really decided about my future, but Oh, how I'd like to be an astronaut!
3. In the poem "The Fool's Prayer," the jester pleads, "O Lord, be merciful to me, a fool!"
4. The car had to stop suddenly, and Oh, was i glad my seat belt was fastened!
5. My favorite lines from the play are
    "see how she leans her cheek upon her hand.
    oh, that i were a glove upon that hand,
    that i might touch that cheek!"

21c. Capitalize proper nouns and proper adjectives.

As you study the following words, observe (1) the difference between a common noun and a proper noun and (2) the ways proper adjectives are formed from proper nouns.

COMMON NOUNS	PROPER NOUNS	PROPER ADJECTIVES
a **poet**	**Homer**	Homeric simile
a **country**	**Turkey**	Turkish border
a **queen**	**Queen Elizabeth**	Elizabethan drama

Common nouns name a class or group. For example, *city* and *state* are common nouns because they name one of a group of places. Common nouns are not capitalized unless they begin a sentence or a direct quotation or are included in a title (see page 593). Proper nouns, such as *Denver* and *Colorado,* name *particular* people, places, or things. They are always capitalized.

Some proper names consist of more than one word. In these names, short prepositions (generally, fewer than five letters) and articles are not capitalized.

EXAMPLES Tomb **of** the Unknown Soldier
Society **for** the Prevention **of** Cruelty **to** Animals
Ivan the Terrible

Proper adjectives usually modify common nouns: *Chinese checkers.* Sometimes, however, the proper adjective modifies a proper name (for example, *Victorian England*) or is part of a proper name (for example, *Arctic Circle*).

☞ **NOTE** Proper nouns and adjectives sometimes lose their capitals through frequent usage; examples are *watt* and *titanic*.

EXERCISE 3. Writing Proper Adjectives and Proper Nouns.

For each proper noun listed, give its proper adjective. You may use your dictionary. After the proper adjective, write an appropriate noun for the adjective to modify. For each common noun, give two proper nouns.

EXAMPLES 1. Canada   2. continent
1. *Canadian bacon*   2. *Europe, Australia*

1. Mexico   3. river   5. lake
2. Spain   4. holiday

(1) Capitalize the names of persons.

EXAMPLES   GIVEN NAMES   SURNAMES

           Alana   Diaz

           Mark   Collins

(2) Capitalize geographical names.

Towns, Cities: **Portland, Detroit, Annapolis**
Counties, Townships: **Kane County, Sheffield Township**
States: **Alaska, Georgia, Missouri, Vermont**
Sections: **the East, the North, the Southwest, the Middle West, New England**

> ☞ **NOTE** The words *north, west, southeast,* etc., are not capitalized when they indicate direction: *traveling southeast* but *driving through the Southeast; states in the North* but *north of town.*

Countries: **the United States of America, Canada, New Zealand**
Continents: **North America, Asia, Europe, Africa**
Islands: **Long Island, the West Indies, the Isle of Palms**
Mountains: **Rocky Mountains, Mount McKinley, the Alps, the Mount of Olives**
Bodies of Water: **Pacific Ocean, Adriatic Sea, Red River, Lake of the Woods**
Roads, Highways, Streets: **Route 66, Interstate 78, Pennsylvania Turnpike, Seneca Avenue, West Twenty-first Street**
Parks: **Yellowstone National Park, Cleburne State Park**

> ☞ **NOTE** In a hyphenated number, the second word begins with a small letter.

Notice that words like *City, Island, River, Street,* and *Park* are capitalized because they are part of the name. If words like these are not part of a proper name, they are common nouns and therefore are not capitalized. Compare the following lists.

PROPER NOUNS	COMMON NOUNS
life in New York City	life in a big city
Liberty Island	a faraway island
crossing the Spokane River	across the river
on State Street	on a narrow street

EXERCISE 4. Recognizing the Correct Use of Capital Letters. Number your paper 1–20. After the proper number, write the letter of the correct form (*a* or *b*).

1. a. Her shop is on Union Street in San Francisco.
   b. Her shop is on union street in San Francisco.
2. a. We went canoeing on the Ohio river.
   b. We went canoeing on the Ohio River.
3. a. He now lives in Texas.
   b. He now lives in texas.
4. a. I read the article on south America.
   b. I read the article on South America.
5. a. She took a snapshot of the Grand canyon.
   b. She took a snapshot of the Grand Canyon.
6. a. Summers in the southeast are often humid.
   b. Summers in the Southeast are often humid.
7. a. Yellowstone National Park is in Wyoming.
   b. Yellowstone National park is in Wyoming.
8. a. The City of Richmond is the capital of Virginia.
   b. The city of Richmond is the capital of Virginia.
9. a. Pensacola is on the gulf of Mexico.
   b. Pensacola is on the Gulf of Mexico.
10. a. Her address is 1614 Peachtree Street.
    b. Her address is 1614 Peachtree street.
11. a. We must protect our State parks.
    b. We must protect our state parks.
12. a. I will be at Forty-Second Street and Park Avenue.
    b. I will be at Forty-second Street and Park Avenue.

MECHANICS

13. a. Louisville is in Jefferson County.
    b. Louisville is in Jefferson county.
14. a. The North sea is East of Great britain.
    b. The North Sea is east of Great Britain.
15. a. Atlanta is a fast-growing city in the south.
    b. Atlanta is a fast-growing city in the South.
16. a. Does an interstate highway link Cleveland and Buffalo?
    b. Does an Interstate Highway link Cleveland and Buffalo?
17. a. The Hawaiian Islands are southwest of California.
    b. The Hawaiian islands are Southwest of California.
18. a. Drive Northeast until you get to New Haven.
    b. Drive northeast until you get to New Haven.
19. a. Like Salt Lake City, Provo borders a lake.
    b. Like Salt Lake City, Provo borders a Lake.
20. a. Laredo is on the Mexican Border.
    b. Laredo is on the Mexican border.

WRITING APPLICATION A:
Using Capital Letters Correctly to Make Your Writing Clear

The correct use of capital letters helps your readers understand your meaning. If you write "The great Salt Lake is near the Nevada border" instead of "The Great Salt Lake is near the Nevada border," for example, readers may not understand that the word *Great* is actually part of the name of the lake. Instead, they may wonder what is great about the lake.

Writing Assignment

Write a short paragraph telling about a town or city that you know well. Give its exact location (the county, state, section of the country), and name some of its streets. Also tell about the points of interest—parks, dams, lakes, mountains—that your state is proud of. Be sure to capitalize all of the geographical names that you use.

MECHANICS

(3) Capitalize names of organizations, business firms, institutions, and government bodies.

Organizations: United Fund, National Basketball Association, Air National Guard

---

☞ **NOTE** The word *party* is usually written without a capital letter when it follows a proper adjective: *Republican party, Democratic party, Federalist party.*

Business firms: Quaker Oats Company, Southern Bell, J. C. Penney Company
Institutions: United States Naval Academy, Tufts University, Radcliffe College, North High School, Bellevue Hospital

---

☞ **NOTE** Do *not* capitalize words like *hotel, theater, college,* and *high school* unless they are part of a proper name.

EXAMPLES   Jackson High School   a high school principal
             Copley Square Hotel   a hotel in Boston
             Fox Theater   a theater in Atlanta

Government bodies: Congress, Federal Bureau of Investigation, House of Representatives, State Department [Usage is divided on the capitalization of such words as *post office* and *courthouse.* You may write them either way unless the full name is given, when they must be capitalized: *Kearny Post Office, Victoria County Courthouse.*]

(4) Capitalize the names of historical events and periods, special events, and calendar items.

Historical events and periods: French Revolution, Boston Tea Party, Middle Ages, World War II

MECHANICS

Special events: Interscholastic Debate Tournament, Gulf Coast
  Track and Field Championship, Parents' Day
Calendar items: Saturday, December, Labor Day, Mother's Day

☞ **NOTE** Do not capitalize the names of seasons unless
personified: *summer, winter, spring, autumn,* or *fall,* but
"Here is Spring in her green dress."

  Names of seasons are also capitalized when they are part of
the names of special events: Winter Carnival, Spring Festival.

(5) Capitalize the names of nationalities, races, and religions.

Nationalities: Canadians, an American, a Greek
Races: Oriental, Caucasian
Religions: Christianity, a Baptist, Moslems, Buddhists

(6) Capitalize the brand names of business products.

EXAMPLES Formica, Ford, Teflon

☞ **NOTE** Do not capitalize the noun that often follows a
brand name: *Teflon pan.*

**(7) Capitalize the names of ships, planets, monuments, awards,
and any other particular places, things, or events.**

Ships, Trains: the *Mayflower,* the *Discovery,* the *Yankee Clipper,*
  the *Silver Meteor*
*Aircraft, Spacecraft, Missiles: Pioneer 10, Solar Maximum Mis-
  sion Satellite, Columbia*
Planets, Stars: Mars, Jupiter, the Milky Way, the Dog Star

MECHANICS

☞ **NOTE** Planets, constellations, asteroids, stars, and groups of stars are capitalized; however, unless they are listed with other heavenly bodies, *sun, moon,* and *earth* are not capitalized.

Monuments, Memorials: Washington Monument, Lincoln Memorial

Buildings: Chrysler Building, Rockefeller Center Tower

Awards: Purple Heart, Distinguished Service Cross, Masquers' Dramatic Medal, Key Club Achievement Award

EXERCISE 5. Correcting Words and Phrases by Capitalizing Words. Copy the following items, using capitals correctly.

1. venus and mercury
2. a shopping center on north twenty-third street
3. lafayette park in tallahassee, florida
4. some wheaties cereal
5. jefferson racquet club
6. harvard university
7. nike tennis shoes
8. on memorial day
9. a methodist
10. the sinking of the *lusitania*

EXERCISE 6. Writing Sentences Using Capital Letters Correctly. Correctly use each of the following words in a sentence of your own.

1. river
2. River
3. motel
4. Motel
5. street
6. Street
7. march
8. March
9. west
10. West

21d. Do *not* capitalize names of school subjects, except for languages and for course names followed by a number.

EXAMPLES This year I am taking algebra, English, civics, Typing I, and a foreign language. Sophomore year I plan to take American government, English, geometry, Biology I, and Spanish.

MECHANICS

> ☞ **NOTE** Do *not* capitalize the members of a class (*freshman, sophomore, junior, senior*) unless part of a proper noun: All *freshmen* should meet after school to discuss the *Freshman-Sophomore Banquet*.

REVIEW EXERCISE A. Correcting Sentences by Capitalizing Words. Copy the following sentences, using capitals as needed.

1. in tuesday's class, mrs. garcia explained that the diameter of earth is only 226 miles more than that of venus.
2. this year's freshmen will be required to take more english, science, and mathematics than did previous classes at briarwood county high school.
3. last summer in chicago we visited wrigley field and the museum of science and industry, which is known all over the world.
4. the episcopal rector, the baptist minister, and the jewish rabbi organized the group discussion.
5. are german, latin, and science the most helpful courses for someone planning to go into medicine?
6. after i went to the mall and the hardware store, i stopped at quick mart on twenty-second street for some milk and dog food.
7. we vacationed in the west, stopping to see pike's peak and going camping and fishing in colorado.
8. in kentucky, one of the border states between the north and the south, you can visit mammoth cave; churchill downs, the site of the kentucky derby; and the lincoln birthplace national historic site, in hodgenville.
9. after labor day last fall, the presbyterian youth fellowship sponsored a softball tournament at maxwell field.
10. augustus saint-gaudens, a great sculptor who came to the united states from ireland as a child, showed abraham lincoln as a tall, serious man standing with his head bowed.

21e. Capitalize titles.

(1) Capitalize the title of a person when it comes before a name.

EXAMPLES   President Kennedy   Mrs. Chin
            Dr. Dooley   Miss Acosta
            Professor Simmons   Principal Phillips

(2) Capitalize a title used alone or following a person's name only if it refers to a high official or to someone to whom you wish to show special respect.

EXAMPLES   As the Queen of England's oldest son, Charles, the
            Prince of Wales, is in line to be King of England.
            The Reverend spoke at the graduation.
            I saw the President addressing the press outside the
            White House.
            Paul Jacobs, president of our debating club, met
            with two of the speakers before the debate.
            My brother Philip, a lieutenant in the Marine Corps,
            served in Beirut.

☞ **NOTE**   When a title is used alone in direct address, it
is usually capitalized.

EXAMPLES   Well, Doctor, what is your diagnosis?
            May I speak now, Sir?
            I think, Senator, the issue is critical.

(3) Capitalize words showing family relationship when used with a person's name but *not* when preceded by a possessive.

EXAMPLES   Aunt Ellen, Cousin Frances, Grandfather, my
            mother, your father, Harold's grandmother

Exception: When family-relationship words like *grandmother*
    and *uncle* are customarily thought of as part of a name,
    capitalize them even after a possessive noun or pronoun.

EXAMPLE   My Uncle Ted is coming for Christmas.

☞ **NOTE**   Words of family relationship may be capitalized or not when used in place of a person's name: I called *Mother* or I called *mother.*

---

(4) Capitalize the first and last words and all important words in titles of books, periodicals, poems, stories, movies, television programs, paintings, and other works of art.

Unimportant words in a title are *a, an, the,* and short prepositions (fewer than five letters) and coordinating conjunctions.

The words *a, an,* and *the* written before a title are capitalized only when they are part of a title: the *Saturday Review, The Education of Henry Adams.*

Before the names of magazines and newspapers, *a, an,* and *the* are usually not capitalized: I read the *Miami Herald.*

The Bible and the books of the Bible are always capitalized.

EXAMPLES   *I Know Why the Caged Bird Sings, The Sea Around Us, Ordinary People* [books]
the *Atlantic,* the *Riverton Gazette* [periodicals]
"The Charge of the Light Brigade" [poem]
"The Pit and the Pendulum" [story]
Gone with the Wind, Return of the Jedi [movies]
Mona Lisa, The Thinker [works of art]
Treaty of Paris, Declaration of Independence, Bill of Rights [historical documents]
Meet the Press, Sixty Minutes, Wild Kingdom [television programs]
"Tennessee Waltz," *The Marriage of Figaro,* "The Flight of the Bumblebee," Beethoven's *Ninth Symphony* [musical compositions]

(5) Capitalize words referring to the Deity.

EXAMPLE   God and His universe

☞ **NOTE**   The word *god* is not capitalized when it refers to the gods of ancient mythology: *The Greek poet paid tribute to the god Zeus.*

EXERCISE 7. Correcting Phrases and Sentences by Capitalizing Words.   Number your paper 1–10. If the capitalization in a phrase or sentence is correct, write *C*. If the capitalization is incorrect, write the correct form.

1. mayor Feinstein
2. "Home on The Range"
3. the *Reader's Digest*
4. elected president
5. the president of the United States
6. was a Roman God
7. my mom looks like my grandmother higgins.
8. my Cousin's parents
9. N. Scott Momaday won the Pulitzer Prize.
10. *the Mystery of Edwin Drood*

WRITING APPLICATION B:
Using Capital Letters Correctly to Make Your Writing Clear

Using necessary capital letters in your writing helps your readers follow your meaning. Just as important as using necessary capitals is avoiding unnecessary ones.

EXAMPLES   The states in the Midwest are referred to as the nation's breadbasket.
The States in the Midwest are referred to as the Nation's Breadbasket.

As these examples show, the unnecessary capitals in the second sentence are not only distracting, they also tend to give equal emphasis to all of the capitalized words.

Writing Assignment

Write two sentences of your own to illustrate each of the five rules for capitalizing titles. (ten sentences in all)

MECHANICS

REVIEW EXERCISE B. Correcting Sentences by Capitalizing Words. Copy the following sentences, and use capitals wherever needed. In this exercise, apply all the rules you have learned in this chapter.

1. speaking to the seniors of berea high school, mrs. carter praised *losing battles,* a well-known novel by eudora welty.
2. on the friday before memorial day, we drove 150 miles south of washington to williamsburg; after dinner we talked with mr. smith, the manager of the williamsburg inn.
3. since we were running late, we hailed a taxi instead of waiting for a city bus to take us to the ritz theater.
4. in london, my mom and her sister, aunt sarah, went to the british museum, saw trafalgar square, and toured the Tower of London.
5. professor massey studied at the library of congress and the folger shakespeare library during july and august.
6. althea gibson's autobiography, *i always wanted to be somebody,* was published by harper & row.
7. i took photographs of independence hall, which stands on chestnut street in philadelphia, pennsylvania.
8. as a freshman, will you be able to take art and band in addition to english, math, history I, and spanish?
9. Ms. Walker contrasted the belief in many gods with the belief in one god when we studied ancient greek culture.
10. after the soldiers bravely fought against the forces of general santa anna in 1836, the alamo became famous as a symbol of american freedom, like the statue of liberty.

CHAPTER 21 REVIEW: POSTTEST

Correcting Sentences by Capitalizing Words. Number your paper 1–25. Write the word or words that should be capitalized in each sentence. If a sentence is correct, write *C.*

EXAMPLE   1. We visited the White house in Washington.

           1. *House*

1. Val's new schwinn bike had a flat tire.
2. My father is taking a course in public speaking.
3. Bilingual people in Quebec speak french and english.
4. The atmosphere on venus is one hundred times denser than the atmosphere on earth.
5. The Appalachian trail passes through fourteen states.
6. The opossum can be found as far south as Argentina and as far north as Canada.
7. We watch Macy's Thanksgiving day parade on television.
8. Our group raised money for the American heart association.
9. We saw miniature sculpture in jade and ivory at the exhibit of chinese art.
10. Lisa trained to be in the wheelchair races at the university.
11. The highest point in Kansas is mount Sunflower, in Wallace county.
12. On Saturdays, the Browns listen to their favorite radio show, *A Prairie home Companion*.
13. My sister works at Martha's Ace hardware store.
14. In drama 101 we read excerpts from *Life on the Mississippi*.
15. The solar telescope on *skylab* took spectacular photographs.
16. The U.S. congress is made up of the senate and the house of representatives.
17. Bill spends all his free time at Brookfield zoo.
18. Both rabbi Frankel and reverend Stone organized aid for the victims of the fire.
19. We went to Disney World over easter vacation.
20. The summer games of the 1984 olympics were held in los angeles, California.
21. Cindy and Tom go to choir practice every Thursday.
22. Mr. Williams is a reporter for United Press international.
23. Wheat was first cultivated along the nile river.
24. My brother goes to Whitman junior college.
25. Janet received the durant award for her essay.

MECHANICS

SUMMARY STYLE SHEET

Names of Persons

Malvina Hoffman	a **s**culptor
Mr. Jeff Rosenwald	a **f**riend of the family
Dr. Marjorie Hempel	our family **d**octor

Geographical Names

Mexico City	a **c**ity in Mexico
Shetland County	a **c**ounty in North Carolina
the **Canary Islands**	some **i**slands in the Atlantic
Great Smoky Mountains	climbing **m**ountains
Pacific Ocean	across the **o**cean
Sixth Street	a narrow **s**treet
Abilene State Park	a **s**tate **p**ark
in the **East, North, Midwest**	traveling **e**ast, **n**orth, **w**est

Organizations, Business Firms, Institutions, Government Bodies

Oakdale Garden Club	a **c**lub for gardeners
Your Move Van Lines	a moving **c**ompany
Vernon High School	a small **h**igh **s**chool
Supreme Court	a traffic **c**ourt
Department of Commerce	a **d**epartment of government

Historical Events and Periods, Special Events, Calendar Items

the **Civil War**	a bitter **w**ar
Atomic Age	an **a**ge of progress
National Open Golf Tournament	a **g**olf tournament
Labor Day	a national **h**oliday
April, July, October, January	**s**pring, **s**ummer, **a**utumn, **w**inter

Nationalities, Races, Religions

British	a **n**ationality
Caucasian	a **r**ace
Roman Catholic	a **r**eligion
God and His universe	the **g**ods of ancient **R**ome and myths about them

Brand Names

Ford Fairmont	an automobile
Magnavox	a tape player

Other Particular Places, Things, Events, Awards

Great Republic	a clipper ship
City of New Orleans	a train
Apollo	a spacecraft
Nobel Prize	a prize
North Star	a bright star
Earth, Mars, Jupiter, Saturn, Pluto	on the earth
Jefferson Memorial	a memorial to Jefferson
Washington Monument	a monument in Washington
Senior Class Picnic	a senior in high school
Congressional Medal of Honor	a medal for bravery

Specific Courses, Languages

Biology I	my biology class
French	a foreign language
United States History II	the history book

Titles

Mayor Bradley	a mayor
Good morning, Mayor.	
the President of the United States	the president of the class
the Senator from New Hampshire	a senator's decision
the Queen of England	a queen's duties
Uncle John	my uncle
her Aunt Marie	her aunt
A Wrinkle in Time	a novel
the New York Times	a daily newspaper
Holy Bible	a religious book

CHAPTER 22

Punctuation

END MARKS AND COMMAS

In speaking, voice inflections and pauses help make your meaning clear. In writing, marks of punctuation such as end marks and commas substitute for these inflections and pauses.

Be sure to use proper marks of punctuation when you write or revise your compositions. Correct punctuation makes your writing easier to understand.

DIAGNOSTIC TEST

Correcting Sentences by Adding End Marks and Commas.
Write the following sentences, adding end marks and commas where necessary.

EXAMPLE   1. After our hike in the woods we rested
            1. *After our hike in the woods, we rested.*

1. Where were you at 10:00 A.M. on February 14 1984
2. Joe asked me who was bringing the plastic forks paper plates and Styrofoam cups to the picnic
3. Reva look out for that pothole in the road

4. Bits of paper which were thrown out of office windows showered the crowds that lined the parade route

5. Working in pairs the researchers studied acorn woodpeckers in New Mexico and Arizona and California

6. In answer to your question I plan to leave on Monday July 2 and return on Wednesday August 15

7. However Dr Shirley M Richards our guest speaker needs no introduction

8. Use light colors by the way to make a small room seem larger

9. Well that's the last time I ever ride in a car with my brother Ted

10. A radiator hose that is cracked or brittle should be replaced immediately

11. We used our emergency candles during the power failure but Carlton used his lantern

12. No Sue didn't know that Michael had found the car keys which had fallen into the laundry basket

13. The reporter asked Melba Moore who starred in *Purlie* how she feels about her success as a singer a dancer and an actress

14. We used to live in Lansing but now we live at 457 Cleveland Rd Huntsville Alabama

15. The sun danced over the cool dark water and shone through the branches of the tall pine trees

16. Everyone who goes to the construction site should wear a hard hat for protection

17. After we had complained to Mrs Finch about the assignment we had to write letters of apology

18. Is the card addressed to Robert Daniels or to Robert Daniels Jr

19. Christy says that Tae Kwon Do a Korean martial art improved her concentration and gave her self-confidence

20. The batter hoping to advance the runners laid down a perfect bunt

MECHANICS

END MARKS

End marks—periods, question marks, and exclamation points—indicate your purpose. For instance, if you intend to state a fact, you use a period to end your statement. (For a classification of sentences according to purpose, see Chapter 13, pages 411–12.)

22a. A statement is followed by a period.

Periods follow declarative sentences, sentences that make statements. Notice in the second example that a declarative sentence containing an indirect question is followed by a period.

EXAMPLES   Nancy Lopez won the tournament. [declarative sentence]
Flora wondered who had already gone.

22b. A question is followed by a question mark.

Use a question mark after an interrogative sentence.

EXAMPLES   Can a cat see color?
Was the plane late?
Who wrote this note? You?

A direct question may have the same word order as a declarative sentence. Since it *is* a question, however, it is followed by a question mark.

EXAMPLES   A cat can see color?
The plane was late?

Be sure to distinguish between a declarative sentence that contains an indirect question and an interrogative sentence, which asks a direct question.

INDIRECT QUESTION   He asked me **what worries her.** [declarative]

DIRECT QUESTION   What worries her? [interrogative]

22c. An exclamation is followed by an exclamation point.

EXAMPLES Hurrah! What a great play!
Be careful!

Sometimes declarative and interrogative sentences show such strong feeling that they are more like exclamations than statements or questions. If so, an exclamation point should be used instead of a period or question mark.

EXAMPLES Here comes the bus!
Can't you speak up!

22d. An imperative sentence is followed by either a period or an exclamation point.

Imperative sentences, particularly commands, may also show strong feeling. In such cases, an exclamation point should be used. When an imperative sentence makes a request, it is generally followed by a period.

EXAMPLES Be quiet!
Please be quiet.
Turn off your radio.

Sometimes, to be courteous, a writer will state a command or request in the form of a question. Because of the purpose, however, the sentence is really an imperative sentence and is therefore followed by a period or an exclamation point.

EXAMPLES May I say a few words now.
Will you stop that!

22e. An abbreviation is followed by a period.

EXAMPLES A. E. Housman [Alfred Edward Housman]
Mr., Jr., Dr. [Mister, Junior, Doctor]
Calif., Mass. [California, Massachusetts]
A.M., P.M. [*ante meridiem, post meridiem*]
B.C., A.D. [before Christ, *Anno Domini*]
Ave., St., Rd. [Avenue, Street, Road]
lb., oz., in., ft. [pound or pounds, ounce or ounces, inch or inches, foot or feet]

MECHANICS

If an abbreviation comes at the end of a statement, do not use an additional period as an end mark.

EXAMPLE   Mrs. Tavares visited her relatives in Newark, N.J.

BUT   How long did she stay in Newark, N.J.?

Abbreviations for government agencies and international organizations and some frequently used abbreviations are correctly written without periods. Abbreviations in the metric system are often written without periods, especially in science books.

EXAMPLES   TV, IQ, FM, UFO, ROTC, USAF, UN, rpm, km, cm, ml, kg

---

☞ **NOTE** The two-letter state abbreviations without periods are used only when the ZIP code number is included.

When in doubt about whether to use periods with abbreviations, consult a dictionary.

EXERCISE 1. Correcting Sentences by Adding End Marks.
Write the following sentences, adding periods, question marks, or exclamation points.

1. What a car
2. Whose car is that
3. We asked who owned that car
4. Roman troops invaded Britain in 54 BC
5. By AD 800 Baghdad was already an important city
6. Dr Edward Jenner gave the first vaccination against smallpox in 1796
7. Why do children enjoy using computers
8. Please explain why so many children enjoy using computers
9. Will you show me how I can program the computer
10. Hurrah Another coin for my collection

WRITING APPLICATION A:
Using End Marks to Make Your Purpose Clear

End marks let your readers know whether you are making a statement, asking a question, or expressing strong feelings. Notice how the purpose of the sentence "I won first prize" changes according to the end mark used:

EXAMPLES I won first prize. (a statement of fact)
I won first prize? (a question)
I won first prize! (an exclamation)

To make the purposes of your sentences clear, be sure to use appropriate end marks.

Writing Assignment

Correctly using periods, question marks, and exclamation points, write ten sentences as directed.

1. One sentence stating a fact
2. One sentence making a request
3. One exclamation
4. Two direct questions
5. Two declarative sentences containing indirect questions
6. One imperative sentence that shows strong feeling
7. One imperative sentence that does not show strong feeling
8. One courteous command in the form of a question

MECHANICS

COMMAS

Commas are necessary for clear expression of ideas. As you read the following sentences aloud, notice how the placement of the comma affects the meaning of each sentence.

EXAMPLES When someone calls you, answer immediately.
When someone calls, you answer immediately.

Failing to use necessary commas may confuse your reader.

CONFUSING   The friends I have invited are Ruth Ann Jerry Lee Derrick Martha and Julie. [How many friends?]

CLEAR   The friends I have invited are Ruth Ann, Jerry Lee, Derrick, Martha, and Julie. [five friends]

22f. Use commas to separate items in a series.

Notice in the following examples that the number of commas in a series is only one less than the number of items in the series.

EXAMPLES   All of my cousins, aunts, and uncles came to our family reunion. [nouns]
My grandparents were excited, happy, and proud that so many came. [adjectives]
The adults talked, laughed, took photographs, and shared memories. [verbs]
The children played in the yard, at the playground, and by the pond. [prepositional phrases]
I shall always remember that weekend of feasting, telling stories, and playing games. [gerund and gerund phrases]
Those who had flown to the reunion, who had driven many miles, or who had even taken time off from their jobs were glad that they had come. [subordinate clauses]

When the last two items in a series are joined by *and,* you may omit the comma before the *and* if the comma is not necessary to make the meaning clear.

CLEAR WITH COMMA OMITTED   The salad contained lettuce, tomatoes, cucumbers, carrots and radishes.

NOT CLEAR WITH COMMA OMITTED   Our school newspaper has editors for news, sports, humor, features and art. [How many editors are there, four or five? Does one person serve as feature *and* art editor, or is an editor needed for each job?]

CLEAR WITH COMMA INCLUDED   Our school newspaper has editors for news, sports, humor, features, and art. [five editors]

Some writers prefer always to use the comma before the *and*, whether or not it is necessary for clarity. Follow your teacher's instructions on this point.

> ☞ NOTE Some words—such as *bread and butter, rod and reel, table and chairs*—are used in pairs and may be set off as one item in a series: *My favorite breakfast is milk, bacon and eggs, and fruit.*

(1) If all items in a series are joined by *and* or *or*, do not use commas to separate them.

EXAMPLES   I need tacks and nails and a hammer.
Sam or Carlos or Yolanda can baby-sit tonight.

(2) Independent clauses in a series are usually separated by semicolons. Short independent clauses, however, may be separated by commas.

EXAMPLES   The sky grew dark; tree branches swayed in the wind; the cold deepened; the first snowflakes fell.
The sky darkened, branches swayed, the cold deepened, and the first snowflakes fell.

22g. Use commas to separate two or more adjectives preceding a noun.

EXAMPLE   Are you going to that hot, crowded, noisy mall?

When the last adjective in a series is thought of as part of the noun, the comma before the adjective is omitted.

EXAMPLES   I study in our small dining room.
I'll drink cool, refreshing orange juice.

Compound nouns like *dining room, orange juice,* and *post office* are considered single units—as though the two words were one word. In the previous sentences, *small* modifies the unit *dining room; cool* and *refreshing* modify *orange juice.*

A good test to determine whether the adjective and noun form a unit is to insert the word *and* between the adjectives. In the first sentence, *and* cannot be logically inserted: *small and dining room*. In the second sentence, *and* would be logical between the first two adjectives (*cool and refreshing*) but not between the second and third (*refreshing and orange*). If *and* fits sensibly between the adjectives, use a comma.

Another test is to change the order of the adjectives. *Refreshing, cool orange juice* would be correct, but not *orange refreshing juice* or *dining small room*. If the order of the adjectives cannot be reversed sensibly, no comma should be used.

EXERCISE 2. Correcting Sentences by Adding Commas. Number your paper 1–10. Write each series in the following sentences, adding commas where needed.

EXAMPLE   1. Rita plays soccer volleyball and softball.
 1. *soccer, volleyball, and softball*
or
 1. *soccer, volleyball and softball*

1. Dr. Charles Drew worked as a surgeon developed new ways of storing blood and was the first director of the Red Cross blood bank program.
2. I am going to take English science social studies algebra and Spanish.
3. The loud insistent school bell woke us from our dreams.
4. Please pass those delicious blueberry pancakes the butter and the syrup.
5. My twin sister can run faster jump higher and do more push-ups than I can.
6. That store sells newspapers magazines and paperbacks.
7. Horns tooted tires screeched a whistle blew and fire sirens moaned.
8. Steel is made from iron other metals and small amounts of carbon.
9. The clown wore a long navy blue coat with big red plastic gloves and floppy yellow tennis shoes.

MECHANICS

10. Robert Browning says that youth is good that middle age is better and that old age is best.

EXERCISE 3. Writing Series Using Commas Correctly.

Think of an appropriate series of words, phrases, or clauses for each blank below; then write each series, properly punctuated, after the appropriate number.

1. My doctor said that ——— .
2. You can win the election by ——— .
3. A ——— woman won the marathon.
4. The qualities I admire most in a person are ——— .
5. On my street you can see ——— .

22h. Use commas before *and, but, or, nor, for, so,* **and** *yet* **when they join independent clauses.**

A comma is used before a coordinating conjunction when the words on *each side* of the conjunction can stand alone as a complete thought. Do not be misled by compound verbs, which often make a sentence look as though it contains two independent clauses. Compare the structures of the two sentences in the following diagrams:

COMPOUND SENTENCE   (two independent clauses)
  Mara cleared the table, and Roland did the dishes.

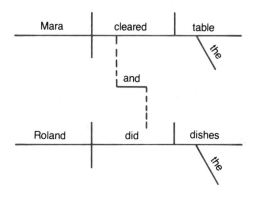

SIMPLE SENTENCE   (one subject with a compound verb)
Roland cleared the table and did the dishes.

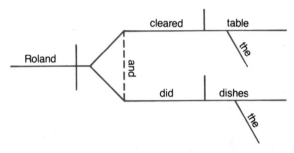

Study the following correctly punctuated compound sentences, noticing that independent clauses (with a subject *and* a verb) appear on both sides of *and, but, or, nor, for,* and *yet.*

Hector pressed the button**, and** the engine started up.
She doesn't have much money**, but** she wants to help you.
He will take karate lessons**, or** he will study judo.
She would never argue**, nor** would she complain to anyone.
We wanted to see the new movie**, for** it had received excellent reviews.
Naomi Carter has her own telephone**, yet** she still gets calls on her parents' line.

☞ **NOTE**   A comma is always used before *for* and *yet* joining two independent clauses. The comma may be omitted, however, before *and, but, or,* or *nor* when the independent clauses are very short and when there is no possibility of misunderstanding.

EXAMPLE   I read that book and I liked it.

EXERCISE 4) Correcting Compound Sentences by Adding Commas. Number your paper 1–10. Where commas should be used, write the word preceding each comma, the comma, and the conjunction following it. If a sentence is correct as it is written, write *C*.

EXAMPLES 1. New York led in the first inning by two runs but Houston was leading in the third inning by a score of six to two.
          1. *runs, but*
          2. Patrick finished his letter and took it to the post office.
          2. *C*

1. It is important to know first aid for an accident can happen at any time.
2. More than 100,000 people in the United States die in accidents each year and many millions are injured.
3. Many household products can cause illness or even death yet they are often kept where small children can reach them.
4. Biking accidents are common wherever cars and bicycles share the same road but bicycle lanes are provided in many communities.
5. Car accidents are the leading cause of childhood fatalities but seat belts have saved many lives.
6. Everyone should know what to do in case of fire and different escape routes should be tested beforehand.
7. To escape a fire, stay close to the floor, and be very cautious about opening doors.
8. Hold your breath and keep low and protected behind a door as you open it for a blast of superheated air from an adjoining room or hallway can be fatal.
9. An injured person should not be allowed to get up nor should liquid be given to an unconscious victim.
10. Always have someone with you when you swim or you may find yourself without help when you need it.

22i. Use commas to set off nonessential clauses and nonessential participial phrases.

A nonessential (or nonrestrictive) clause or participial phrase adds information that is not necessary to the main idea in the sentence.

MECHANICS

As you read the following sentences aloud, pause and lower your voice to indicate that each boldfaced clause or participial phrase is not essential to the basic meaning of the sentence.

NONESSENTIAL CLAUSES   Eileen Murray**, who is at the top of her class,** wants to go to medical school.
Texas**, which has the most farms in the United States,** produces one fourth of the country's oil.

NONESSENTIAL PHRASES   Tim Ricardo**, hoping to make the swim team,** practiced every day.
*The Lord of the Rings***, written by J. R. R. Tolkien,** is a fantasy that has been translated into many different languages.

Each boldfaced clause or phrase above can be omitted because it is not essential to identify the word it modifies. For example, the first clause, *who is at the top of her class,* does not identify Eileen Murray; neither does the first phrase, *hoping to make the swim team,* identify Tim Ricardo. Each clause or phrase may be omitted without changing the meaning of the sentence: *Eileen Murray wants to go to medical school. Tim Ricardo practiced every day.*

However, when a clause or phrase is necessary to the meaning of a sentence, or when it tells *which one,* the clause or phrase is *essential* (or *restrictive*), and commas are *not* used.

Notice how the meaning of each sentence below changes when the essential clause or phrase is omitted.

ESSENTIAL CLAUSES   All students **whose names are on that list** must report here.
A contest **that I might be able to win** is described in that newspaper.

☞ **NOTE**   An adjective clause beginning with *that* is usually essential.

ESSENTIAL PHRASES   Swimmers **hoping to make the swim team** must practice extra hours. [Not all swimmers; just those hoping to make the swim team.]

A book **written by J. R. R. Tolkien** has been widely translated. [Not any book, but one by J. R. R. Tolkien.]

EXERCISE 5 Correcting Sentences with Nonessential Clauses by Adding Commas.   Seven of the following sentences contain nonessential clauses; write and properly punctuate these sentences. For the three sentences that are correct as written, write *C*.

1. *Doonesbury* which is my favorite comic strip makes me think as well as laugh.
2. Our math teacher who also teaches gym will leave at the end of the year.
3. The amusement rides that are most exciting may be the most dangerous.
4. My grandfather who likes to work on old cars just bought a 1960 convertible.
5. People who carry credit cards should keep a record of their account numbers at home.
6. Sally Yamoto who is class president plans to go to Yale.
7. A town like Cottonwood which has a population of five thousand seems ideal to me.
8. All dogs that pass this obedience test will get a reward.
9. Creosote which is made from coal tar is one of the chemicals that may cause cancer.
10. In "The Gift of the Magi" which is a very beautiful short story, the two main characters who are deeply in love make sacrifices in order to buy gifts for each other.

EXERCISE 6 Correcting Sentences with Participial Phrases by Adding or Removing Commas.   If a sentence is

MECHANICS

correctly punctuated, write *C* after the proper number. Write the other sentences, punctuating them correctly.

1. People, visiting the reservation, will be barred from burial sites, which are considered holy by Native Americans.
2. Players breaking training will be dismissed from the team.
3. Students, planning to go on the field trip, should bring their lunches.
4. The ants swarming onto the tablecloth made straight for the picnic basket.
5. An owl hooting in the distance sounded as lonely as I felt.
6. Elizabeth Blackwell completing her medical studies in 1849 became the first female doctor in the United States.
7. Pressure and heat acting on the remains of plants and animals turn them into gas or oil or coal.
8. Every child, registering for school for the first time, must present evidence of certain vaccinations.
9. The astronauts living in space for several days studied the effects of weightlessness.
10. The castle built as a fortress in the sixteenth century is now famous as a tourist attraction.

EXERCISE 7. Correcting Sentences with Nonessential Clauses and Participial Phrases by Adding Commas. Number your paper 1–10. If a sentence is correctly punctuated, write *C*. If a sentence is incorrect, copy on your paper each word that should be followed by a comma, and place a comma after it.

EXAMPLES 1. A novelist whose latest book is a best seller gave a talk at our school.
　　　　　1. *C*
　　　　　2. The velocity of a tornado which is the fastest wind on earth may reach 700 miles an hour.
　　　　　2. *tornado, earth,*

1. Ellen Barnes who is captain of the basketball team is an honor student.

2. Players who are late for practice will be sent back to the locker room.
3. We are looking for high-school students who are interested in a Saturday job.
4. My friends knowing how much I like funny sweat shirts gave me several of them for my birthday last month.
5. Some members of the audience thinking the show was over left their seats.
6. The new library which is in the center of the campus is easy to get to.
7. Anyone looking for some good detective novels should consult Barry who collects them.
8. Last night's concert reviewed in this morning's newspaper was the best I have ever heard.
9. A telephone directory that lists phone numbers by address rather than by name is used by telephone operators.
10. The luxurious dirigible *Hindenburg* which was built in Germany in the 1930's exploded as it arrived in New Jersey killing thirty-six people.

REVIEW EXERCISE A. Correcting Sentences by Adding Commas. Most of the following sentences require commas. Write the sentences, adding commas where necessary. If a sentence does not require any commas, write *C*.

EXAMPLE 1. The emu is a large flightless bird from Australia.
1. *The emu is a large, flightless bird from Australia.*

1. The students sold crafts art and baked goods at the bazaar.
2. John Wayne whose real name was Marion Morrison won an Academy Award for *True Grit*.
3. Add flour mix the ingredients and stir the batter.
4. People who come to the game early will be allowed to take pictures of the players.
5. A *Raisin in the Sun* written by Lorraine Hansberry will be performed by the Grantville Community Players and will run for three weeks.

MECHANICS

6. The float in the homecoming parade was covered with delicate pink rose petals and small white sunflower seeds.
7. Members of the planning committee met for three hours but they still have not chosen a theme for the dance.
8. Helium which is used in balloons and airships which is mixed with oxygen for deep-sea divers and which is used for arc welding is an inert gas.
9. An eclipse that occurs when the earth blocks the sun's light from the moon is called a lunar eclipse.
10. In one month our little town was besieged by a tornado and a flood and a fire yet we managed to survive.

22j. Use commas after certain introductory elements.

(1) Use a comma after words such as *well, yes, no, why,* etc., when they begin a sentence.

EXAMPLES **Yes,** she's going to the cafeteria.
Ah, there's nothing like cold water on a hot day!

(2) Use a comma after an introductory participial phrase.

EXAMPLES **Switching on a flashlight,** the ranger led the way down the path.
Disappointed by the high prices, we made up a new gift list.

(3) Use a comma after a succession of introductory prepositional phrases.

EXAMPLES **Inside the fence at the far end of her property,** she built a potting shed.
By the end of the train ride, the children were exhausted.

A short introductory prepositional phrase does not require a comma unless the comma is necessary to make the meaning clear.

EXAMPLES   **At our house** we share all the work.
            At our house, work is shared by everyone. [The comma is necessary to avoid reading *house work*.]

(4) Use a comma after an introductory adverb clause.

EXAMPLES   **After Andrés Segovia had played his last guitar concert,** the audience applauded for more than fifteen minutes.
            When you see smoke, you know there is a fire.

EXERCISE 8. Correcting Sentences with Introductory Elements by Adding Commas.   Number your paper 1–10. If a sentence lacks a comma, write the word that should be followed by a comma, and place a comma after it. If a sentence is correct, write *C*.

EXAMPLES   1. When Marco Polo visited China in the thirteenth century he found an advanced civilization.
            1. *century,*
            2. In China the Europeans saw silk, paper money, and porcelain for the first time.
            2. *C*

1. Although there was a great deal of poverty in China the ruling classes lived in splendor.
2. Valuing cleanliness Chinese rulers took baths every day.
3. Instead of using coins the Chinese used paper money.
4. After marrying a Chinese woman lived in her mother-in-law's home.
5. After one Chinese emperor had died he was buried with more than eight thousand statues of servants and horses.
6. Respected by all their descendants old people were highly honored.
7. Built around 200 B.C. the Great Wall is 2,400 miles long.
8. Until modern freeways were built the Great Wall was the world's longest construction.
9. In Chinese art people are very small and are usually shown in harmony with nature.

10. Yes Chinese landscapes are a marked contrast to Western painting.

22k. Use commas to set off elements that interrupt the sentence.

Two commas are used around an interrupting element—one before and one after.

EXAMPLES   That boy, in fact, worked very hard.
               Linda, by the way, sends her regards.

Sometimes an "interrupter" comes at the beginning or at the end of a sentence. In these cases, only one comma is needed.

EXAMPLES   Nevertheless, you must go with me.
               I need the money, however.
               Therefore, the answer is wrong.

(1) Appositives and appositive phrases are usually set off by commas.

EXAMPLES   Everyone, **even his parents,** thinks he is making a mistake.
               Rita Moreno, **my favorite actress,** stars in the movie I rented.
               My dog, **a collie,** is very gentle.

Sometimes an appositive is so closely related to the word preceding it that it should not be set off by commas. Such an appositive usually has no modifiers; that is, there is no appositive phrase.

EXAMPLES   my cousin **Betty**   we **women**
               the writer **Ralph Ellison**   us **students**

EXERCISE 9. Correcting Sentences with Appositives and Appositive Phrases by Adding Commas. Write (1) the word preceding the appositive (if any), (2) the appositive or appositive phrase, and (3) the word following the appositive or appositive phrase (if any) in each sentence. Correctly punctuate the appositives. If a sentence does not require commas, write *C*.

EXAMPLE   1. My cousin Claudia a college student consulted Dr.
Moniz an allergy specialist about the harmful
effects of pollution.

  1. *cousin Claudia, a*
      Claudia, a college student, consulted
      Moniz, an allergy specialist, about

1. "Ecology" an obscure word not many years ago has become a popular term today.
2. The word's origin is *oikos* the Greek word for "house."
3. Ecology is the study of an enormous house the world of all living things.
4. Ecologists study the bond of a living organism to its environment the place in which it lives.
5. Humans one kind of living organism affect their environment in both beneficial and harmful ways.
6. My cousin Claudia is worried about the environment.
7. She and many of her friends attended Earth Day a festival devoted to ecology.
8. An amateur photographer my cousin prepared a slide show on soil erosion in Grant Park.
9. One of many displays at the Earth Day Festival my cousin's presentation attracted wide attention.
10. The mayor a member of the audience soon promised to appoint a committee to correct the problem.

EXERCISE 10. Writing Sentences with Appositives Using Commas Correctly.   Use each of the following items as an appositive in a sentence of your own. Be sure to use commas if necessary.

1. the cheerleaders
2. a West Point cadet
3. the cashier at the movie
4. my gym teacher
5. my favorite book

(2) Words used in direct address are set off by commas.

EXAMPLES **Linda,** you know the rules.
           I did that exercise last night, **Miss Ryan.**
           Your room, **Bernice,** needs cleaning.

EXERCISE 11. Correcting Sentences with Words in Direct Address by Adding Commas. Write and correctly punctuate the sentences that follow.

1. Dad why can't I go to the movies tonight?
2. As soon as you're ready Virginia we'll leave.
3. Yes Mother I washed the dishes.
4. What we need Mayor Wilson are more playgrounds.
5. Will you answer the last question James?

(3) Parenthetical expressions are set off by commas.

Parenthetical expressions are side remarks that add information or relate ideas. In writing, you should ordinarily use commas to set off parenthetical matter.[1]

The following expressions are commonly used parenthetically: *consequently, however, moreover, nevertheless, therefore, after all, as a matter of fact, at any rate, for example, for instance, in fact, in my opinion, in the first place, of course, on the contrary, on the other hand, generally speaking, I believe* (*guess, know, hope, think, suppose*), *to tell the truth.*

EXAMPLES **On the contrary,** I am glad that you told me about
           the error.
           She is, **in fact,** a dentist.
           You should try out for quarterback, **in my opinion.**

Some expressions may be used both parenthetically and not parenthetically. Compare the following pairs of correctly punctuated sentences; read the sentences aloud.

PARENTHETICAL

Sandra will, **I think,** enjoy the program.
However, did you finish your report on time?
To tell the truth, he tries.

[1] For the use of parentheses and dashes to set off parenthetical matter, refer to pages 675–79.

NOT PARENTHETICAL

I think Sandra will enjoy the program.
However did you finish your report on time?
He tries **to tell the truth.**

☞ **NOTE** A contrasting expression introduced by *not* is parenthetical and must be set off by commas.

EXAMPLE   It is the spirit of the giver**, not the gift,** that counts.

EXERCISE 12. Correcting Sentences with Parenthetical Elements by Adding Commas.   Number your paper 1–10. Write the following: (1) the word (if any) preceding each parenthetical element, (2) the parenthetical element itself, and (3) the word (if any) following it. Supply the necessary punctuation.

EXAMPLE   1. Nevertheless no one of course can predict the future.

        1. *Nevertheless, no one, of course, can*

1. Some changes can be predicted from current trends however.
2. A towering skyscraper would in theory be a good place to live.
3. In fact tall apartment buildings are far from ideal.
4. Elevators break down for instance and children generally speaking must play outside.
5. In the future I believe there will be many types of cities.
6. One kind of city I think will have plastic trees and flowers where real ones can no longer grow.
7. In another kind of city however cars and trucks that emit pollutants will be outlawed.
8. Consequently people will exercise by walking or by riding bicycles.
9. Moreover people may even grow most of their own food.
10. Some cities I suppose might orbit the earth; other cities might float on oceans.

22l. Use commas in certain conventional situations.

(1) Use a comma to separate items in dates and addresses.

EXAMPLES My parents moved to Oakland, California, on Wednesday, December 5, 1984.

On December 5, 1984, their address became 25 Peralta Road, Oakland, CA 94611.

Notice that no comma divides *December 5* (month and day) or *25 Peralta Road* (house number and street name) because each is considered one item. The ZIP code is not separated from the name of the state by a comma: New Bedford, MA 02740.

(2) Use a comma after the salutation of a friendly letter and after the closing of any letter.

EXAMPLES Dear Mrs. Chin,   Sincerely yours,
My dear Anna,   Yours very truly,

(3) Use a comma after a name followed by *Jr., Sr., M.D.*, etc.

EXAMPLES Allen Davis, Jr.   Ens. Charles Jay, U.S.N.
Carol Ferrara, M.D.   Martin Luther King, Jr.

EXERCISE 13. Correcting Sentences by Adding Commas. Write and correctly punctuate any of the following sentences that need commas. If a sentence is correct as it stands, write *C* next to the number.

1. Please send this letter to Ms. Marybeth Correio 1255 S.E. 56th Street Belleview WA 98006.
2. On April 6 1909 Matthew Henson, assistant to Commander Robert E. Peary, reached the North Pole.
3. I glanced quickly at the end of the letter, which read, "Very sincerely yours Alice Ems Ph.D."
4. The Constitution of the United States was signed on September 17 1787 eleven years after the adoption of the Declaration

of Independence on July 4 1776.
5. Did you go to the desert in March or April in 1985?

22m. **Do not use unnecessary commas.**

Too much punctuation is just as confusing as not enough punctuation. This is especially true of commas.

CONFUSING   My friend, Jessica, said she would feed my cat and my dog, while I'm away, but now, she tells me, she is too busy.

CLEAR   My friend Jessica said she would feed my cat and my dog while I'm away, but now she tells me she is too busy.

Have a *reason* (either a definite rule or a matter of meaning) for every comma or other mark of punctuation that you use. When there is no rule requiring punctuation and when the meaning of the sentence is clear without it, do not insert any punctuation mark.

REVIEW EXERCISE B. Correcting Sentences by Adding Commas. Number your paper 1–10. For each sentence write all words that should be followed by a comma. Place a comma after each one.

EXAMPLE   1. Yes Phyllis I know that you want to transfer to Bayside the high school with a volleyball team.
            1. *Yes, Phyllis, Bayside,*

1. Scuttling across the dirt road the large hairy spider terrified Steve Ellen and me.
2. Whitney not Don won first prize.
3. Although German shepherds are most often trained as guide dogs other breeds that have been used are Labrador retrievers golden retrievers and Doberman pinschers.
4. According to her birth certificate she was born July 7 1971 in Juneau Alaska.
5. Angela and Jennifer are you both planning to write poems?

MECHANICS

6. All poetry entries should be sent to Poetry Contest 716 North Cliff Drive Salt Lake City UT 84103.
7. The best time to plant flower seeds of course is just before a rainy season not in the middle of a hot dry summer.
8. Our neighbor Miss Allen manages two apartment houses.
9. As a matter of fact most horses can run four miles without having to stop.
10. The Comanches like many nomadic tribes once traveled throughout Kansas New Mexico Texas and Oklahoma.

REVIEW EXERCISE C. Correcting Sentences by Adding End Marks and Commas. Number your paper 1–10. Write the following sentences, adding end marks and commas where necessary.

1. Kathleen you did well on the last algebra test but you don't seem to be concentrating now
2. Did you know that this lovely flower is a bluebonnet a variety of wild lupine
3. Last week I met Mr Ted Griffin the teacher I had for fourth grade at my first school Highland Park
4. Well my father was transferred from Portland Oregon to Denver Colorado on March 1 1980 and then from Denver Colorado to Pocatello Idaho on September 10 1983
5. After breakfast Mom I am going to call Della write to my pen pal and put flea powder on the cat
6. Until January 1 please forward my mail to 1208 North Lakeview Drive Tampa FL 33618
7. I don't like camping out generally speaking but the camping we did in Yosemite National Park which is in northern California was great fun
8. The baby who lives next door cries all night and fire trucks drive down our street from dusk to dawn
9. Ouch Who left these roller skates on the steps
10. Turn off the TV pick up your shoes and socks and go to your room right now young man

WRITING APPLICATION B:
Using Commas to Make Your Writing Clear

Commas used correctly help your readers follow your meaning. Consider the following two examples:

INCORRECT   You dust Joe, and Kathy will vacuum.
  CORRECT   You dust, Joe, and Kathy will vacuum.

As you can see, just one comma can make a great deal of difference in the meaning of a sentence.

Writing Assignment

Using the Summary of Uses of the Comma (page 621), write twenty sentences to illustrate the rules, as directed. Before each sentence, write the number of the rule it illustrates.

1. Three sentences illustrating rule 22f (illustrating both subrules)
2. Two sentences illustrating rule 22g
3. Three sentences illustrating rule 22h
4. Two sentences illustrating rule 22i, one with a nonessential clause; the other with a nonessential participial phrase
5. Four sentences illustrating rule 22j (one for each subrule)
6. Three sentences illustrating rule 22k (one for each subrule)
7. Three sentences illustrating rule 22l (one for each subrule)

MECHANICS

CHAPTER 22 REVIEW: POSTTEST

Correcting Sentences by Adding End Marks and Commas.
Write the following paragraphs, adding end marks and commas where necessary.

EXAMPLE 1. Computers therefore are not my cup of tea
           1. *Computers, therefore, are not my cup of tea.*

1. Although TV commercials will tell you otherwise computers are not for everyone 2. One day in the showroom of a computer store I stared at a terminal for more than half an hour but I was still unable to locate the on-off switch 3. The demonstrator Ms Pearl Rangely PhD tried her hardest to be helpful 4. A computer consultant she pointed unhesitatingly to switches buttons and boxes 5. She pressed keys she flashed words on the screen and she pushed around a device called a "mouse" 6. I was confused and puzzled and frustrated yet I was also fascinated

7. Dr Rangely who had encountered confused consumers before told me that I had "terminal" phobia 8. With a frown I asked her what that meant 9. She replied grinning broadly that it was the fear that bits and bytes can actually bite 10. What a comedian 11. Totally disenchanted I left the store

12. I headed for the library to check out everything that I could find about computers: books magazines catalogs and pamphlets 13. For example I read *The Soul of a New Machine* a fascinating book written by Tracy Kidder 14. When I had finished the book I knew about input output high-level languages and debugging 15. Armed with this knowledge I returned to the store on Friday March 13 16. Well the same demonstrator was there smiling like a Cheshire cat 17. I rattled off several questions which I think must have startled her 18. In one afternoon Dr Rangely taught me something about every computer in the store 19. I left however without asking one simple embarrassing question 20. To tell the truth I still don't know where the on-off switch is

SUMMARY OF USES OF THE COMMA

22f. Use commas to separate items in a series.
- (1) If all items in a series are joined by *and* or *or,* do not use commas to separate them.
- (2) Independent clauses in a series are usually separated by semicolons. Short independent clauses are sometimes separated by commas.

22g. Use commas to separate two or more adjectives preceding a noun.

22h. Use commas before *and, but, or, nor, for,* and *yet* when they join independent clauses.

22i. Use commas to set off nonessential clauses and nonessential participial phrases.

22j. Use commas after certain introductory elements.
- (1) Use a comma after words such as *well, yes, no, why,* etc., when they begin a sentence.
- (2) Use a comma after an introductory participial phrase.
- (3) Use a comma after a succession of introductory prepositional phrases.
- (4) Use a comma after an introductory adverb clause.

22k. Use commas to set off sentence interrupters.
- (1) Appositives and appositive phrases are usually set off by commas.
- (2) Words used in direct address are set off by commas.
- (3) Parenthetical expressions are set off by commas.

22l. Use commas in certain conventional situations.
- (1) Use a comma to separate items in dates and addresses.
- (2) Use a comma after the salutation of a friendly letter and after the closing of any letter.
- (3) Use a comma after a name followed by *Jr., Sr., Ph.D.,* etc.

22m. Do not use unnecessary commas.

MECHANICS

CHAPTER 23

Punctuation

SEMICOLONS AND COLONS

Although semicolons and colons are used less often than end marks and commas, they are important. In this chapter you will learn how to use these two marks of punctuation correctly.

DIAGNOSTIC TEST

Correcting Sentences by Using Semicolons and Colons.
Number your paper 1–20. Most of the following sentences use a comma or no punctuation mark at all where there should be a semicolon or a colon. Write the word preceding each error; then add the needed mark. If the sentence is correct, write *C*.

EXAMPLE 1. In the morning I scrubbed the floor, washed the car, and did the laundry, in the afternoon I read a mystery novel.
   1. *laundry;*

1. Leon finished his model of the *Apollo 7,* now he is working on a model of the *Eagle.*
2. My sister has records by the following jazz artists, Sarah Vaughan, Buddy Rich, Oscar Peterson, and Ella Fitzgerald.

3. Heating a home can be very expensive, however, people can cut these costs by installing insulation and storm windows.

4. The most abundant minerals in the human body are calcium, phosphorus, and iron.

5. Nearsightedness is called myopia, farsightedness is called hyperopia.

6. I wrote to my senator on Thursday, September 20, 1984, and on September 27, just a week later, I received a reply.

7. For the opinion survey, Billie will call the Grays, the Mitchells, and the Millers, and Jesse will call the Chuns, the Van Horns, and the Schmidts.

8. I keep the following quotation, from a letter written by Martin Luther King, Jr., on the wall over my desk at home, "Injustice anywhere is a threat to justice everywhere."

9. Ms. Larussa leaves for work at 7 30 every morning and returns promptly at 5 35 every evening.

10. For your report on photographers, you may write about Margaret Bourke-White, Dorothea Lange, Alfred Stieglitz, or Edward Weston.

11. The manual alphabet originated in France in the eighteenth century, it was first taught in the United States by Thomas Hopkins Gallaudet.

12. When you deliver a speech, you should always have good eye contact, use visual aids, and move around, otherwise, you will put your audience to sleep.

13. We met many people on the plane to Hawaii, two from Albany, New York, one from San Diego, California, three from Austin, Texas, and five from Pittsburgh, Pennsylvania.

14. Dr. Martha Loomis cited Proverbs 29 11 and 29 22 as warnings against letting anger get the best of you.

15. Cora Mae hurt her ankle when she slid into second base, nevertheless, she bandaged it and finished the game.

16. In class today we discussed the contributions of Gutenberg, the inventor of movable type, Galileo, the inventor of the first complete astronomical telescope, and Newton, the discoverer of the laws of gravity.

MECHANICS

17. On her trip to Europe, Stephanie toured Italy, Spain, France, and Belgium.
18. Arnie was really surprised to see Jill, Margie, and me, we had managed to keep his birthday party a secret.
19. We can always go to the museum, the exhibit this month features Alaskan Eskimo art.
20. Channel 34 is going to broadcast some classic movies next week, *The African Queen, Gone with the Wind, Mrs. Miniver,* and *Casablanca.*

SEMICOLONS

A semicolon looks like what it is: part period and part comma. It says to the reader, "Stop here a little longer than you stop for a comma but not so long as you stop for a period."

Semicolons are used primarily in compound sentences. Since most writers depend largely upon simple and complex sentences to express ideas, the semicolon is not often used. As you study the uses of semicolons, follow the lead of professional writers; use the semicolon correctly and effectively but sparingly.

23a. Use a semicolon between independent clauses in a sentence if they are not joined by *and, but, or, nor, for,* or *yet*.

Notice in the examples that the semicolon takes the place of the comma and the conjunction joining the independent clauses.

EXAMPLES First I had a sandwich and a glass of milk**, and** then I called you for the homework assignment.
First I had a sandwich and a glass of milk**;** then I called you for the homework assignment.
Patty likes to act**, but** her sister gets stage fright.
Patty likes to act**;** her sister gets stage fright.

Similarly, a semicolon can take the place of a period between two independent clauses that are closely related.

EXAMPLE   Sarah looked out at the downpour. Then she put on
her raincoat and boots. [two simple sentences]
Sarah looked out at the downpour; then she put on
her raincoat and boots.

As you study the following sentences (taken from the works
of professional writers), observe that a complete thought appears on *both* sides of each semicolon and that the two independent clauses are not joined by *and, but, or, nor, for,* or *yet.*
Since the thoughts in the independent clauses in each sentence
are closely related, a semicolon is better than a period.

EXAMPLES   Echoes of the anthem shivered in the air; the tears
that slipped down many faces were not wiped away
in shame.

MAYA ANGELOU

The late pears mellow on a sunny shelf; smoked
hams hang to the warped barn rafters; the pantry
shelves are loaded with 300 jars of fruit.

THOMAS WOLFE

Knowledge without commitment is wasteful;
commitment without knowledge is dangerous.

HUBERT H. HUMPHREY

EXERCISE 1. Correcting Sentences by Adding Semicolons Between Independent Clauses.   Number your paper
1–10. For each sentence, write the word before each needed
semicolon, the semicolon, and the word that comes after it. In
some instances, you may prefer to use a period. If so, write the
word before the needed period, the period, and the word (capitalized) following it.

EXAMPLES   1. Great earthquakes usually begin gently only one
or two slight shocks move the earth.
1. *gently; only*
2. In minutes, however, violent shocks begin to
tear the earth apart there are few natural forces
with the destructive potential of earthquakes.
2. *apart. There*

1. Pressure often builds along faults, or cracks, in the earth's crust the weight of this pressure causes earthquakes.
2. The San Andreas fault extends the entire length of California earthquakes often occur at various points along this fault.
3. During an earthquake, huge chunks of the earth's crust begin to move the San Francisco earthquake of 1906 was one of the most destructive earthquakes recorded in history.
4. Energy released during an earthquake is tremendous it can equal the explosive force of 180 metric tons of TNT.
5. Scientists study the force of earthquakes they measure this force on a scale of numbers called the Richter scale.
6. An earthquake measuring less than 5 on the Richter scale is not serious more than 1,000 earthquakes measuring 2 or less occur daily.
7. In 1906 one of the most powerful earthquakes in history occurred in the Pacific Ocean near Ecuador its Richter measurement was 8.9.
8. Tidal waves are a dangerous result of earthquakes geologists use the Japanese word *tsunami* for these destructive waves.
9. Predicting when earthquakes will occur is not yet possible predicting where they will occur is somewhat more certain.
10. Earthquakes seem to strike in a regular time sequence in California, for example, a major earthquake usually occurs every fifty to one hundred years.

23b. Use a semicolon between independent clauses joined by such words as *for example, for instance, that is, besides, accordingly, moreover, nevertheless, furthermore, otherwise, therefore, however, consequently, instead, hence.*

These words are often transitional expressions linking independent clauses. When used in this way, they are preceded by a semicolon. They are, however, usually followed by a comma.

INCORRECT	Emma felt shy, however, she soon made some friends.
CORRECT	Emma felt shy**;** **however,** she soon made some friends.

INCORRECT   My parents are strict, for example, I can watch
            TV only on weekends.

CORRECT   My parents are strict**; for example,** I can watch
            TV only on weekends.

Caution: When the expressions listed in the rule appear *within* one of the clauses, not as a transition *between* clauses, they are usually punctuated as interrupters (set off by commas). The two clauses are still separated by a semicolon: *Our student council voted to have a Crazy Clothes Day; the principal,* **however,** *vetoed the idea.*

23c. A semicolon (rather than a comma) may be needed to separate independent clauses joined by a coordinating conjunction when there are commas within the clauses.

This use of the semicolon often helps to make a sentence clear.

CONFUSING   Alan, Eric, and Kim voted for her, and Scott and
            Vanessa voted for Jason.

CLEAR   Alan, Eric, and Kim voted for her**;** and Scott and
            Vanessa voted for Jason.

CONFUSING   Scanning the horizon for the source of the whirring
            sound, Leo saw a huge, green cloud traveling in
            his direction, and, suddenly recognizing what it
            was, he knew that the crops would soon be eaten
            by a horde of grasshoppers.

CLEAR   Scanning the horizon for the source of the whirring
            sound, Leo saw a huge, green cloud traveling in
            his direction**;** and, suddenly recognizing what it
            was, he knew that the crops would soon be eaten
            by a horde of grasshoppers.

EXERCISE 2. Correcting Sentences by Adding Semicolons Between Independent Clauses. Follow the directions for Exercise 1 (page 625) as you show where to use semicolons in the following sentences.

MECHANICS

1. My mother and I usually fly to Massachusetts just before school starts, however, last year we flew there in July.
2. My grandparents live near Cape Cod, that is why we go there so often.
3. I miss my friends and sometimes find the yearly trip to Cape Cod boring, besides, my cousins in Massachusetts are all older than I am.
4. To my great surprise, we had a good time last year, we even did some sightseeing in Boston, Plymouth, and Marblehead.
5. One hot day my mother, grandparents, and I went to the beach, and my grandfather immediately went down to the water for a swim.
6. My grandfather, who is sixty-seven, loves the water and is a strong swimmer, nevertheless, we worried when we saw that he was swimming out farther and farther.
7. Grandpa, to our great relief, finally turned around and swam back to shore, he was astonished that we had been worried about him.
8. While he was in the water, Mother had gathered driftwood, dug a shallow pit in the sand, and built a fire in it, and Grandma had put lobster, corn, and potatoes on the coals to roast.
9. By the time we had finished eating, it was quite late, consequently, everyone else on the beach had gone home.
10. We didn't leave for home right away, instead, we spent the evening watching the darkening ocean, listening to the whispering waves, and watching the stars come out.

23d. Use a semicolon between items in a series if the items contain commas.

EXAMPLES   I have post cards from Paris, France; Rome, Italy; Lisbon, Portugal; and London, England.

The Photography Club will meet on Wednesday, September 12; Wednesday, September 19; Tuesday, September 25; and Tuesday, October 2.

EXERCISE 3. Correcting Sentences by Adding Semi-colons Between Items in a Series. All of the following sentences contain items in a series. Copy each incorrectly punctuated sentence, adding the needed semicolons. If a sentence needs no semicolons, write *C* after the corresponding number on your paper.

1. In the fifteenth century, the kings of France, England, and Spain grew stronger as they unified their power.
2. Africa's then-powerful kingdoms included Mali, on the Niger River, Benin, in Nigeria, and Karanga, in southern Africa.
3. The Incas in Peru planted crops, such as corn, domesticated animals, such as the llama, and developed crafts, such as weaving.
4. The Mohawks, Senecas, Oneidas, Onondagas, and Cayugas banded together in about 1400 to advance peace, civil authority, and righteousness.
5. Mrs. Gillis said that we could choose to write about Dekanawidah, the Huron founder of the Iroquois League, Mansa Musa, the great Muslim emperor of Mali, Tamerlane, the cruel Mongol conquerer of the Ottoman Turks, or Alexander the Great, the Macedonian conquerer of Greece and the Persian Empire.

REVIEW EXERCISE A. Correcting Sentences by Adding Semicolons. Number your paper 1–10. Then read the following sentences and decide where semicolons should be used. For each incorrectly punctuated sentence, write the word preceding the needed semicolon, the semicolon, and the word following. If a sentence needs no semicolon, write *C* after the appropriate number on your paper.

EXAMPLE   1. The largest animal in the world today is the blue whale the largest blue whale ever caught measured slightly more than 113.5 feet and weighed about 170 tons.
　　　　　1. *whale; the*

1. The largest toothed whale, the sperm whale, hunts giant squid along the bottom of the ocean after taking a deep breath of air, the whale dives more than half a mile below the surface of the ocean.
2. Some whale species exhibit remarkable social behavior for example, members of a group may stay with a wounded animal or even support it in the water.
3. Dolphins speak to one another by means of whistles, squeaks, clicks, barks, and grunts, they also effectively communicate by ultrasonic sounds reflected from objects that are nearby.
4. Since it has a large brain and lives for about thirty years, a dolphin may be trained for long periods, in fact, some scientists believe that one day dolphins will be able to communicate with humans.
5. Dolphins play by pushing objects, such as small logs, balancing floating objects, such as seaweed or feathers, on their fins, and doing complicated swimming maneuvers, such as riding swells, diving in formation, and synchronized leaping into the air.
6. Whale meat is used as food for animals in some countries whale oil is, of course, an essential ingredient in many soaps and cosmetics.
7. Ambergris, a dark, sticky material found in the intestines of the sperm whale, is used to make expensive perfumes accordingly, an ounce of ambergris is extremely valuable.
8. In the past 250 years, whalers have nearly wiped out one species of whale after another, and they continue to threaten those species that have managed to survive despite the whalers' disregard.
9. Although several countries have, in recent years, banned the killing of certain whale species, the blue whale remains an endangered species, and it is perilously close to extinction.
10. Whale-watching cruises originated with the public's growing concern over the survival of whales today whale-watching continues to attract as many as 350,000 people a year.

MECHANICS

WRITING APPLICATION A:
Using Commas and Semicolons to Make Your Writing Clear

By using commas and semicolons correctly, you let your readers know whether to separate or connect the ideas in your writing. In general, commas are used to separate or set off items. Semicolons are most often used to join closely related ideas.

Writing Assignment

Using semicolons and commas where appropriate, write two sentences to illustrate each of the following patterns of punctuation (ten sentences in all).

1. PATTERN Independent clause; independent clause.
   EXAMPLE Camilla is a marathon runner; she has participated in five marathons.
2. PATTERN Independent clause, coordinating conjunction and independent clause.
   EXAMPLE Camilla is a marathon runner, and she has participated in five marathons.
3. PATTERN Introductory element, independent clause; independent clause.
   EXAMPLE A marathon runner, Camilla has participated in five marathons; the last one was in Chicago.
4. PATTERN Independent clause; transitional word, independent clause.
   EXAMPLE Camilla is a dedicated marathon runner; therefore, she is always in training for her next race.
5. PATTERN Independent clause with commas; coordinating conjunction and independent clause.
   EXAMPLE Camilla is training for the marathon, playing soccer, and taking art class; and Jack is playing ice hockey and taking French lessons.

MECHANICS

COLONS

Generally, the colon is used to call the reader's attention to what comes next.

23e. Use a colon to mean "note what follows."

(1) Use a colon before a list of items, especially after expressions like *as follows* **and** *the following*.

EXAMPLES You will need to bring **the following equipment:** a sleeping bag, a warm sweater, and extra socks.
Additional supplies are **as follows:** a toothbrush, toothpaste, a change of clothes, and a pillow.
At the crossroads we saw three signs: To Norway, To Paris, and To Lisbon.
You need to shop for several items: brown shoelaces, a quart of milk, and five or six carrots.

In the last two examples, the items that follow the colon are used as appositives. If a word is followed by a list of appositives, the colon is used to make the sentence clear.

> ☞ NOTE   When a list follows immediately after a verb or a preposition, do not use a colon.

INCORRECT You need to shop for: brown shoelaces, a quart of milk, and five or six carrots.

CORRECT You need to shop for brown shoelaces, a quart of milk, and five or six carrots.

INCORRECT Additional supplies are: a toothbrush and toothpaste, a change of clothes, a towel, a pillow, and an air mattress.

CORRECT Additional supplies are a toothbrush and toothpaste, a change of clothes, a towel, a pillow, and an air mattress.

(2) Use a colon before a long, formal statement or quotation.

MECHANICS

EXAMPLE   Horace Mann had this to say: "Do not think of
knocking out another person's brains because he
differs in opinion from you. It would be as rational
to knock yourself on the head because you differ
from yourself ten years ago."

23f. Use a colon in certain conventional situations.

(1) Use a colon between the hour and the minute.

EXAMPLES   9:30 P.M.   8:00 A.M.

(2) Use a colon between chapter and verse in referring to passages from the Bible.

EXAMPLES   Esther 3:5   Exodus 1:6–14

(3) Use a colon after the salutation of a business letter.

EXAMPLES   Dear Ms. Luiz: Dear Dr. Fenton:
            Dear Sir: To Whom It May Concern:

EXERCISE 4. Correcting Sentences by Adding Colons.
Number your paper 1–10. If a sentence does not need a colon,
write *C*. If a colon is required, copy the word the colon should
follow and write a colon after it. If a colon is needed to divide
numbers, copy the numbers and add the needed colon.

EXAMPLE   1. When I came into class at 9 15 A.M., everyone
              was writing a theme based on the West African
              proverb that was written on the board "To know
              nothing is bad; to learn nothing is worse."
            1. *9:15 board:*

1. Last month I read the following novels *Going to the Sun* by
   Jean George and *The Secret of Blue Beach* by Scott O'Dell.
2. The desk was littered with papers, a mug, and dirty socks. C
3. At the festival we bought tacos and refried beans. C
4. The qualities she likes most in a person are as follows reliability, a good sense of humor, and a willingness to work.

MECHANICS

5. You must learn to spell the following new words:*aneurysm, fluoroscope, peregrination,* and *serendipity.*

6. An enduring statement of loyalty, found in Ruth 1:16, begins as follows:"Entreat me not to leave thee or to return from following after thee, for whither thou goest, I will go."

7. Mrs. Hughes named the three students who had completed extra projects:Marshall, Helena, and Regina.

8. From 8:00 A.M. until 6:00 P.M., Mr. Brooks sells brushes, brooms, and cleaning products.

9. Alone in the house at night, I heard some scary sounds the creaking of a board, the scratching of tree branches against a window, and the hissing of steam in the radiator.

10. Tomorrow's test will include the marks of punctuation that we have studied so far:commas, semicolons, and colons.

WRITING APPLICATION B:
Using Colons to Make Your Writing Clear

A colon signals your readers to "stay tuned" because something else is coming along. Colons introduce the second part of a sentence, which is usually not a complete thought.

Writing Assignment

You have volunteered to order items that the members of your club can sell to raise money for club activities. First, decide what kind of items you will sell (ball point pens, dried fruit, book covers, etc.) and how many you will order. Then make up a name and address for a company and write an order letter to the company's customer service department.

REVIEW EXERCISE B. Correcting Sentences by Adding Semicolons and Colons. Using semicolons and colons, write and correctly punctuate the following sentences.

1. A small, windowless log cabin stood against the rail fence directly behind it ran a muddy stream.
2. Because the club has run out of funds, the following supplies must be brought from home pencils, erasers, paper, and envelopes.
3. I will consider only the following part-time jobs gardening, baby-sitting, and walking dogs.
4. Other jobs take too much time for example, if I worked in a store, I would probably have to work most nights.
5. American cowhands used the ten-gallon hat as protection from the sun and as a dipper for water the leather chaps they wore served as protection from thorny bushes.
6. A rabbi, a minister, and a priest discussed their interpretations of Isaiah 2 2 and 5 26.
7. In his speech Dr. Hayakawa quoted from several poets Rudyard Kipling, David McCord, and Nikki Giovanni.
8. Sojourner Truth, a former slave, could neither read nor write however, this accomplished woman spoke eloquently against slavery and for women's rights.
9. From 1853 to 1865 the United States had three presidents Franklin Pierce, a Democrat from New Hampshire James Buchanan, a Democrat from Pennsylvania and Abraham Lincoln, a Republican from Illinois.
10. From 12 30 to 1 00 P.M., I was so nervous that I could not sit still I paced up and down, swinging my arms and taking deep breaths, while I rehearsed each play over and over in my mind.

MECHANICS

CHAPTER 23 REVIEW: POSTTEST

Correcting Sentences by Adding Semicolons and Colons.
Write the word preceding each punctuation error, and write after it the needed semicolon or colon. If the sentence is correct, write *C*.

EXAMPLE 1. Someday, robots may do many things for us, wash windows, answer the telephone, make repairs, and serve dinner.
   1. *us:*

1. I didn't go to the game last night, instead, I took care of my baby brother.
2. The band members will perform at the civic center on Tuesday, January 15, at the Kiwanis Club on Saturday, January 19, and at the Oak Nursing Home on Friday, January 25.
3. For the lesson on figures of speech, we had to find examples of simile, metaphor, personification, and hyperbole.
4. My cousin, who is extremely shy, never asks to join an activity consequently, he stays at home a great deal.
5. Lowell has traveled to rain forests in many parts of the world, Borneo, Brazil, Costa Rica, and Sri Lanka.
6. The Constitutional Convention opened on May 25, 1787, however, the Constitution, which is the foundation of our country, was not declared in effect until 1789.
7. Cape Porpoise, Maine, Nameless, Tennessee, and Liberty Bond, Washington, are among the many little towns described by William Least Heat Moon in *Blue Highways: A Journey into America.*
8. The endurance events for the one-day Ironman Triathlon, which is held annually in Hawaii and is open to both men and women, are as follows, swimming, 2.4 miles in the ocean, bicycling, 112 miles, and running, 26.2 miles.
9. For this soup, I need lentils, a hambone, an onion, and butter or margarine.
10. The others were upset about the flat tire, I, however, was glad to get out of the car and stretch my legs.
11. The Kentucky Derby, at Churchill Downs in Louisville, is a gala event, people come from all over the world to see the race.
12. The Tower of Babel, as described in Genesis 11 1–9, closely resembled a ziggurat, or terraced pyramid.

13. The singers, who were on a one-month tour, performed their most popular songs for the fans, and everywhere they went, they were greeted with cheers and applause.
14. Mary Cassatt, an American impressionist painter, often painted her subjects from above, her bird's-eye perspective can be seen in *The Bath* and *The Fitting*.
15. Tornado warnings have been issued for Lake County, Kane County, parts of Cook County, including Chicago, and parts of Northern Indiana.
16. Seeing the carnival brought back memories of the county fairs she had attended as a child, barkers hawking tickets, sweet smells, and multicolored lights blinking on the rides.
17. The Spaniards who first settled in America built forts, mission churches, and pueblos, evidence of their influence on American architecture can be found in the Southwest.
18. The REM (which stands for "rapid eye movement") stage of sleep was first discovered in the 1950's, during the REM stage, the sleeper has dreams and is quite active.
19. My brother does not like violence on television, in the movies, or in books, nor does he play violent games like hockey and football.
20. Erica never misses a football game on TV, last Saturday, for example, she watched football from 12 00 P.M. to 10 00 P.M.

MECHANICS

CHAPTER 24

Punctuation

ITALICS AND QUOTATION MARKS

DIAGNOSTIC TEST

A. Correcting Sentences by Adding Underlining (Italics) and Quotation Marks. Number your paper 1–10. Write each letter, word, or title that should be either underlined or put in quotation marks. Then supply underlining or quotation marks, whichever is needed. Some sentences require more than one answer.

EXAMPLE 1. According to The Book of Word Histories, there is a close connection between the words lettuce and galaxy.

        1. *The Book of Word Histories*
           lettuce
           galaxy

1. The concert ended with a stirring rendition of The Stars and Stripes Forever.
2. There's Still Gold in Them Thar Hills, an article in Discovery, describes attempts to mine low-grade gold deposits on Quartz Mountain in California.
3. The first chapter in Introduction to Poetry is titled Rhythm in Nature.

4. The overture to Mozart's opera The Magic Flute is often played as a concert piece.

5. Beowulf, a long epic poem, is an Anglo-Saxon tale of vengeance and death.

6. As a baby sitter I have read the children's book The Pokey Little Puppy at least a dozen times.

7. Horace Greeley founded the Tribune, a successful and influential New York newspaper; in it he published his famous antislavery essay The Prayer of Twenty Millions.

8. Although the poem When You Are Old has three stanzas, it contains only one sentence.

9. The word recommend has two m's but only one c.

10. Robert Fulton's steamboat, Clermont, was the first one that could be operated without losing money.

B. Correcting Sentences by Adding Quotation Marks for Dialogue.

Write the following sentences, correctly punctuating the dialogue. Be sure the quotation marks are in the correct position relative to other marks of punctuation.

EXAMPLE   Listen carefully! ordered Mrs. Garcia. Every student who plans to go on the field trip must have a note from home.

"Listen carefully!" ordered Mrs. Garcia. "Every student who plans to go on the field trip must have a note from home."

11. Before our field trip begins, said Mrs. Garcia, be sure that you have a notebook and a collection kit.

12. Will we need binoculars? asked Melvin.

13. Leave your binoculars at home, suggested Mrs. Garcia. Your ears will be more helpful than your eyes on this trip.

14. What will we be able to hear so far out in the country? asked Arnold.

15. What a question! exclaimed Felicia. On a nature walk in the springtime, you can hear all sorts of sounds.

MECHANICS

16. I hope that we hear and see some birds, said Koko. Didn't someone once say, The birds warble sweet in the springtime?
17. What, asked James, are we doing about lunch? My mother promised to pack my favorite kinds of sandwiches.
18. Don't worry, said Mrs. Garcia. Most birds are quiet at midday. We can have our lunch then.
19. Marcia said, Mrs. Garcia, would you believe that I don't know one birdcall from another?
20. That's all right, Marcia, laughed Mrs. Garcia. Some birds obligingly call out their names for you. For example, the bobolink repeats its name: Bob-o-link! Bob-o-link!

ITALICS

Italics are printed letters that lean to the right, *like this*. When you write or type, you indicate italics by underlining the words you want italicized. If your composition were to be printed, the typesetter would set the underlined words in italics. For example, if you type

Daniel Defoe wrote <u>Robinson Crusoe</u>.

the sentence would be printed like this:

Daniel Defoe wrote *Robinson Crusoe*.

24a. Use underlining (italics) for titles of books, plays, films, periodicals, works of art, long musical compositions, television programs, book-length poems, ships, and so on.

EXAMPLES   *Great Expectations* [a novel]
Our Town [a book-length play]
St. Louis Post-Dispatch [a newspaper]
Seventeen [a magazine]
Madama Butterfly [an opera]
Haydn's *Surprise Symphony* [a long musical composition]

Venus de Milo [a statue]
Titanic [a ship]
Spirit of St. Louis [a plane]

The words *a, an,* and *the,* written before a title, are italicized only when they are part of the title. Before the names of newspapers and magazines, however, they are not italicized, even if they are capitalized on the front page of the newspaper or on the cover of the magazine.

EXAMPLES   I am reading Pearl Buck's *The Good Earth.*
In the museum we saw Edmonia Lewis' statue *The Death of Cleopatra.*
My parents subscribe to the *Wall Street Journal* and the *Atlantic.*

Magazine articles, chapter headings, and titles of short poems, short stories, and short musical compositions, when referred to in a composition, should be placed in quotation marks, not italicized. See page 648 for this rule.

24b. Use underlining (italics) for words, letters, and figures referred to as such and for foreign words.

EXAMPLES   The word *Mississippi* has four *s*'s and four *i*'s.
The *3* on that license plate looks like an *8.*
The only French expression I know is *à la carte.*

EXERCISE 1. Correcting Sentences by Adding Underlining (Italics).   Write all the words and word groups in the following sentences that should be italicized; underline each. Before each word or word group, write the number of its sentence.

1. Jason named his ship Argo because Argus had built it.
2. Mr. Butler likes to use foreign words and phrases such as modus operandi, alors, and au revoir.
3. Have you read the novel Dragonsong by Anne McCaffrey?
4. When I spelled occurrence with one r, I was eliminated from the spelling contest.

MECHANICS

5. The Gilbert and Sullivan comic opera The Mikado and the Puccini opera Madama Butterfly are both set in Japan.

6. Shani asked if she could borrow my copy of Sports Illustrated.

7. Mrs. Hopkins said that if she had to describe me in one word, the word would be loquacious.

8. My mother, who grew up in Chicago, still subscribes to the Chicago Tribune.

9. My favorite painting is Georgia O'Keeffe's Black Iris; my favorite sculpture is Constantin Brancusi's Bird in Space.

10. My parents own a set of the Encyclopaedia Britannica, and my aunt, who lives within walking distance of us, just bought a set of The World Book Encyclopedia.

QUOTATION MARKS

24c. Use quotation marks to enclose a direct quotation—a person's exact words.

EXAMPLES   Melanie said, **"**This car is making a very strange noise.**"**
"Maybe we should pull over,**"** suggested Amy.

Do not use quotation marks for *indirect* quotations.

DIRECT QUOTATION   Stephanie said, **"**I am going to wash the car.**"** [the speaker's exact words]

INDIRECT QUOTATION   Stephanie said that she was going to wash the car. [not the speaker's exact words]

Caution: Be sure to place quotation marks at both the beginning and the end of a direct quotation.

INCORRECT   She shouted, ''We can win, team!

CORRECT   She shouted, **"**We can win, team!**"**

24d. A direct quotation begins with a capital letter.

EXAMPLE   Explaining the lever, Archimedes said, "Give me a place to stand, and I can move the world."
Miss Perez said, "The rest of the chapter, of course." [Although this quotation is not a sentence, it is apparently Miss Perez' complete remark.]

Exception: If the direct quotation is obviously a fragment, it may begin with a small letter.

EXAMPLE   Are our ideals, as Scott says, mere "statues of snow" that soon melt? [The quotation is obviously only a part of Scott's remark.]

24e. When a quoted sentence is divided into two parts by an interrupting expression such as *he said* or *Mother asked,* the second part begins with a small letter.

EXAMPLES   "I wish," she said, "that you were here."
"I know," I answered, "and I will be soon."

If the second part of the quotation is a new sentence, a period (not a comma) follows the interrupting expression; and the second part begins with a capital letter.

EXAMPLE   "I tried to schedule an interview," the reporter said. "She told me she was too busy."

Caution: An interrupting expression is not a part of a quotation and therefore should not be inside quotation marks.

INCORRECT   "Let's sit here, I whispered, not way down there."

CORRECT   "Let's sit here," I whispered, "not way down there." [Two pairs of quotation marks are needed for the broken quotation.]

When two or more sentences are quoted together, use only one set of quotation marks.

INCORRECT   Brennan said, "I like to sit close to the screen." The sound is better there."

CORRECT   Brennan said, "I like to sit close to the screen. The sound is better there."

MECHANICS

24f. A direct quotation is set off from the rest of the sentence by commas or by a question mark or an exclamation point.

EXAMPLES Delores explained, "You know how much I like chicken," as she passed her plate for more.
The plumber shouted, "Turn off that faucet!" as water gushed out of the pipe.

24g. Other marks of punctuation when used with quotation marks are placed according to the following rules:

(1) Commas and periods are always placed inside closing quotation marks.

EXAMPLES "I haven't seen the movie," remarked Jeannette, "but I understand it's excellent."
As I had feared, Mr. Watkins announced, "Close your books for a pop quiz."
He read aloud "Ode to the End of Summer," a poem by Phyllis McGinley.

(2) Colons and semicolons are always placed outside closing quotation marks.

EXAMPLES Socrates once said, "As for me, all I know is that I know nothing"; I wonder why everyone thinks he was such a wise man.
The following actresses were cited for "best performance in a leading role": Sally Field, Bette Midler, Marsha Mason, and Jane Fonda.

(3) Question marks and exclamation points are placed inside the closing quotation marks if the quotation is a question or an exclamation; otherwise, they are placed outside.

EXAMPLES "Is it too cold in here?" the manager asked as I shivered.
"Yes!" I answered. "Please turn down the air conditioner!"

Can you explain the saying, "Penny wise, but pound foolish"?

Stop singing "London Bridge"!

EXERCISE 2. Writing Sentences with Direct and Indirect Quotations. If a sentence contains an indirect quotation, change it to a direct quotation, correctly punctuated. If a sentence contains a direct quotation, change it to an indirect quotation, correctly punctuated. Check your answers carefully.

EXAMPLES
1. Our social studies teacher said, "Allen Wright, a Choctaw Indian, gave the name Oklahoma to the area then known as Indian Territory."
   1. *Our social studies teacher said that Allen Wright, a Choctaw Indian, gave the name Oklahoma to the area then known as Indian Territory.*
2. He explained that Oklahoma became a state in 1907.
   2. *He explained, "Oklahoma became a state in 1907."*

1. When we planned our trip to Europe, Mother said, "Our stops should include some castles."
2. Our tour book says that Colchester Castle, built in 1080, is a good place to start.
3. My little brother Mark asked whether the castles were haunted.
4. "No," said Mother, "but we'll stay close together so that you won't be afraid."
5. In England, Mark told Mother that he wanted to swim in a moat.
6. "Warwick Castle," said our guide, "is one of the most beautiful in England."
7. "One of its towers," he went on to say, "was built in 1066."
8. "Is it still the home of the Earls of Warwick?" I asked.
9. The guide said that the castle contains many works of art.
10. "I like the collection of suits of armor best," said Mark.

MECHANICS

24h. When you write dialogue (a conversation), begin a new paragraph every time the speaker changes.

EXAMPLE

"You have just come down?" said Mr. Drummle, edging me a little away with his shoulder.

"Yes," said I, edging *him* a little away with *my* shoulder.

"Beastly place," said Drummle. "Your part of the country, I think?"

"Yes," I assented. "I am told it's very like your Shropshire."

"Not in the least like it," said Drummle.

CHARLES DICKENS

WRITING APPLICATION A:
Using Quotation Marks for Dialogue to Make Your Writing Clear

Dialogue adds interest to your writing by making your readers feel as if they can actually hear your characters talking. If you fail to use quotation marks correctly, however, readers may decide that it is too much trouble to figure out who is saying what and put your writing aside. To make your writing clear, always read your paper carefully to make sure that you have used quotation marks correctly for dialogue.

Writing Assignment

Write a page of dialogue that will show your ability to use quotation marks correctly. You could retell a favorite anecdote in your own words, letting the dialogue of the speakers carry the action forward, or report the exact words of a conversation that will entertain your classmates. You can get ideas for interesting dialogues by remembering definite situations—for example, arguing about a play on the baseball diamond, apologizing for a social blunder, trying to escape from a determined sales person, or mistaking a stranger for an old friend.

MECHANICS

24i. When a quoted passage consists of more than one paragraph, put quotation marks at the beginning of each paragraph and at the end of the entire passage. Do not put quotation marks after any paragraph but the last.

EXAMPLE   "At nine o'clock this morning," read the news story, "someone entered the Mill Bank by the back entrance, broke through two thick steel doors guarding the bank's vault, and escaped with sixteen bars of gold.

"No arrests have been made, but state police are confident the case will be solved within a few days."

☞ NOTE   A long passage (not dialogue) from a book or other printed source is often set off from the rest of the text so as to be easily recognizable as quoted matter. The entire passage may be indented; in printed matter it may be set in small type; and in typewritten copy it may be single-spaced instead of double-spaced. When a passage taken from another source has been identified by one of these devices, no quotation marks are necessary.

24j. Use single quotation marks to enclose a quotation within a quotation.

EXAMPLES   Annoyed, Becky snapped, "Don't tell me, 'That's not the way to do it.'"

Mrs. Wright said, "In a letter to a schoolgirl, W. E. B. Du Bois wrote, 'Get the very best training possible, and the doors of opportunity will fly open before you.'"

I asked, "How dare you say 'yuck!'?"

REVIEW EXERCISE A. Correcting Sentences by Adding Quotation Marks for Dialogue.   Write each of the following short passages, adding quotation marks where necessary. Remember to begin a new paragraph each time the speaker changes.

MECHANICS

1

Race-car driver Janet Guthrie, said Chet, reading from his notes, is a trained physicist who has spent many years working in an important job for an aircraft corporation.

2

Who shot that ball? Coach Larsen wanted to know. I did, came the reply from the small, frail-looking player. Good shot, the coach informed him, but always remember to follow your shot to the basket. I tried but I was screened, said the player.

3

The *Brownsville Beacon,* the editorial began, will never support a candidate who tells the taxpayers, Vote for me and I will cut taxes.

The reason is simple. Taxes, just like everything else in this inflationary society, must increase. Any candidate who thinks otherwise is either a fool or a liar.

4

In the interview the candidate said I am a very hospitable person. Yes her husband agreed, Ralph Waldo Emerson must have been thinking of you when he said Happy is the house that shelters a friend.

24k. Use quotation marks to enclose titles of short works such as articles, short stories, essays, poems, songs and individual episodes of television programs; and of chapters and other parts of books.

EXAMPLES   The title of the chapter you are now studying is "Punctuation."

The article "What Teen-agers Need to Know About Diets" should be required reading.

The poem "On Aging" by Maya Angelou is one of my grandmother's favorites.

EXERCISE 3. Correcting Sentences by Adding Quotation Marks for Titles.   After the proper number on your paper, write the following sentences, correctly using quotation marks.

EXAMPLE   1. Did O. Henry write The Last Leaf?
　　　　　　　 1. *Did O. Henry write "The Last Leaf"?*

1. One of the titles on our required reading list is Lincoln's Gettysburg Address.
2. It can be found in our literature book, in the chapter titled Essays and Speeches.
3. A Start in Life by Ruth Suckow is a realistic story.
4. A popular Old English riddle song is Scarborough Fair.
5. Have you read Split Cherry Tree by Jesse Stuart?
6. Which Eve Merriam poem is your favorite, Cheers or How to Eat a Poem?
7. The Celebrated Jumping Frog of Calaveras County was the first of Mark Twain's stories to bring him recognition as a humorist.
8. Have you read Fran Lebowitz's essay Tips for Teens?
9. Lowlands, Shenandoah, and Yo, Heave Ho! are three popular sea chanteys.
10. Emily Dickinson's poem I'm Nobody! Who Are You? sums up her attitude toward fame.

Remember that long poems and long musical compositions are italicized, not quoted. (See page 640.) As a rule of thumb, you italicize the title of any poem long enough to be published in a separate volume. Such poems are usually divided into titled or numbered sections—cantos, parts, books, etc. Examples are Milton's *Paradise Lost,* Tennyson's *Idylls of the King,* and Lowell's *Life Studies.* Long musical compositions include operas, symphonies, ballets, oratorios, and concertos.

EXAMPLES   In my report on Coleridge, I plan to quote from Part VII of *The Rime of the Ancient Mariner* and from the second stanza of "Kubla Khan."

At her recital, she will play "Valse" from Tchaikovsky's *Swan Lake.*

Mr. Kelleher sang "Summertime" from *Porgy and Bess.*

MECHANICS

WRITING APPLICATION B:
Using Underlining (Italics) and
Quotation Marks to Make Your Writing Clear

Underlining (italics) and quotation marks are important signals for your readers. When you underline the title of a book, for example, your readers understand that you are discussing a full-length work, not a short story. Similarly, quotation marks around a chapter title signal that you are referring to a specific chapter, not to the entire book. Quotation marks are especially important for dialogue, of course, because they signal the exact words characters say to one another.

Writing Assignment

Write ten sentences of your own, as instructed. Read your sentences carefully to make sure that underlining (italics) and quotation marks are correctly placed.

1. Two sentences, each containing the title of a book, play, movie, or periodical and the title of an article, poem, short story, or song
2. Two quoted sentences, each interrupted by an expression such as *she said*
3. Two sentences, each containing an indirect quotation
4. Two sentences, each containing a quoted question
5. One interrogatory sentence ending with a quotation that is not a question
6. One sentence containing a quotation within a quotation

REVIEW EXERCISE B. Correcting Sentences by Adding Underlining (Italics) and Quotation Marks. Write the following sentences, adding underlining (italics) and quotation marks.

1. The Bay Area Youth Theater is presenting Lorraine Hansberry's play A Raisin in the Sun.

2. Hilda announced that she is going to sing Some Enchanted Evening from the musical South Pacific.
3. I have tickets to the opera Carmen, said Karen, and I would like you to be my guest.
4. The Spanish word for goodbye is adiós; the Swahili word is kwaheri.
5. My favorite story by Arthur Conan Doyle is The Adventure of the Dying Detective, which is included in the anthology The Complete Sherlock Holmes.
6. Mrs. Loudon said, I like your report on Ernest Hemingway. Remember, however, that *Ernest* is spelled without an *a*.
7. In her review of The King and I, the drama critic for the Los Angeles Times commented, This production is an excellent revival of a play that never seems to wear thin.
8. The paper I wrote on Shakespeare's play Julius Caesar is titled The Noblest Roman.
9. Mrs. Howard asked, In Julius Caesar, who said, This was the noblest Roman of them all? Which Roman was being described?
10. Have you read Hannah Armstrong, one of the poems in Spoon River Anthology by Edgar Lee Masters?

REVIEW EXERCISE C. Correcting Sentences by Adding Underlining (Italics) and Quotation Marks. Write the following sentences, adding underlining (italics) and quotation marks where necessary.

1. Today, Mr. Reyes announced, we are going to talk about an early American genius, Benjamin Franklin.
2. Didn't someone write a book about Franklin and a mouse? asked Veronica. I think it's called Ben and Me.
3. Yes, Veronica, Mr. Reyes answered. That biography was written from the point of view of Amos, Franklin's pet mouse.
4. Wasn't the author Robert Lawson? asked Bonnie Lou.
5. That's correct! exclaimed Mr. Reyes. Now, who can tell me some of Franklin's achievements?

6. He invented electricity, didn't he? asked Kelley.

7. Well, he didn't exactly invent electricity, corrected Mr. Reyes, but his experiment proved that lightning is a form of electricity.

8. Didn't he help draft some of our important historical documents? asked Veronica.

9. Yes, said Mr. Reyes, and Franklin was also a printer, a publisher, an inventor, and a diplomat. For your homework I want you to read from Franklin's Autobiography. I'd also like a volunteer to read from Poor Richard's Almanack.

10. I read some of that book in the Girl Scouts, said Kelley. It includes sayings such as If you would know the value of money, try to borrow some.

CHAPTER 24 REVIEW: POSTTEST

Correcting Sentences by Adding Underlining (Italics) and Quotation Marks. Write the following sentences, correctly using underlining (italics) and quotation marks.

EXAMPLES
1. Don't forget your umbrella, said Jody. The weather report calls for rain.

1. *"Don't forget your umbrella,"* said Jody. *"The weather report calls for rain."*

2. Laura has just read two books by the Cleavers: Dust of the Earth and Queen of Hearts.

2. *Laura has just read two books by the Cleavers:* Dust of the Earth *and* Queen of Hearts.

1. An Introduction to Haiku includes examples of early haiku, the seventeen-syllable Japanese verse form; two of my favorites are New Year's Day and Seen from Horseback.

2. Every time I meet Mrs. Gilley, said Paco, she says, Remember me to your mother.

3. Be careful not to confuse allusion with illusion, warned Mrs.

Bunnell. When you use either word, remember to spell it with two l's.

4. My grandmother asked what I wanted for my birthday, a subscription to Time or to Popular Mechanics.

5. I'm glad that you enjoyed The Ransom of Red Chief, said Joan. Do you plan to read more of O. Henry's short stories?

6. In his book The Medusa and the Snail, Dr. Lewis Thomas includes an essay titled Notes on Punctuation.

7. Quotation marks, says Dr. Thomas, should be used honestly and sparingly.

8. Dr. Thomas continues, Above all, quotation marks should not be used for ideas that you'd like to disown. Nor should they be put in place around clichés.

9. Were you and Sue at the concert? I asked. I didn't see you come in.

10. Dad said, I heard you say, I'll be home before ten o'clock.

11. Have you read the poems In Memoriam and Elegy for J.F.K.?

12. The movie A Night to Remember is based on the sinking of the luxury ocean liner Titanic.

13. Reprints of the article Fill Your Senses, Light Your Life, which was condensed from the magazine Sports Afield, are available from Reader's Digest.

14. We'll be back from Miami, Mother told our neighbors, in two weeks or when our money runs out, whichever comes first.

15. Forget it! Wally shouted. The last time you said, I have a great idea for making money, I wound up without a cent.

16. The operas The Barber of Seville and The Marriage of Figaro met with royal opposition because both poked fun at the aristocracy.

17. I'm from San Juan, the newcomer said. Does anyone here know anything about San Juan?

18. Yes, I replied. My parents grew up in San Juan, and I was born there.

MECHANICS

19. Welcome aboard the Molly B., said the skipper. It may look a bit rusty, but it's still a seaworthy ship.
20. Go out there and fight, ordered the coach. The other team is just as tired as you are.

CHAPTER 25

Punctuation

APOSTROPHES

Apostrophes are necessary for expressing meaning clearly in written English. For instance, the difference in meaning between *shell* and *she'll* or *shed* and *she'd* is indicated in writing by the apostrophe (and, of course, the context).

If you sometimes forget to use apostrophes, or if you use them incorrectly, the rules in this chapter will prove helpful.

DIAGNOSTIC TEST

Correcting Sentences by Using Apostrophes Correctly. Number your paper 1–20. In the following sentences, apostrophes are either missing or incorrectly used. After the proper number, write the correct form of each incorrect word.

EXAMPLE 1. The Greeks alphabet derived from Semitic alphabet's.
  1. *Greeks', alphabets*

1. The discovery that the spoken word could be represented by written marks is probably one of humankinds greatest imaginative feats'.

2. Many ancient peoples, who's awe of the written word was based on ignorance, felt that writing had a magic power of it's own.
3. Writing was practiced by the elders' of a tribe to preserve the tribes lore as well as its laws.
4. Were not sure when or how writing began, but we do know that it existed several century's before 3000 B.C.
5. Theres plenty of evidence that people communicated through they're drawings long before they could write.
6. Spain and France's wonderful cave drawings were painted 30,000 or more year's ago.
7. The Peruvians message system was a complicated arrangement of knots.
8. The Sumerians cuneiforms and the Egyptians hieroglyphics are the earliest complete systems' of writing known to us.
9. After many years work, scholars were still unable to decipher the hieroglyphics.
10. Then one of Napoleons soldiers found a tablet that provided the key.
11. It's surface was inscribed with identical texts' in Greek and in hieroglyphics.
12. They're search over, the scholars were able to unlock the meaning of the hieroglyphics.
13. Hardwick Book Stores window features a display of early systems of writing.
14. For Nancy and my report on the history of writing, we asked one of Mr. Hardwicks clerks for permission to examine the display.
15. We found out that Us, Ws, and Js werent used in English writing until the Middle Ages.
16. The Chinese, who's written language at one time included 50,000–80,000 characters, still use about 8,000 of those characters.
17. In China, ones mastery of basic reading depends on learning at least one eighth of those characters'.

18. Did you know that the most widely used alphabet is our's?
19. My sister-in-laws interest in writing includes calligraphy.
20. According to her, the practice of calligraphy is like childs play.

Possessive Case

The possessive of a noun or pronoun shows ownership or relationship. The nouns and pronouns printed in boldfaced type in the following sentences are in the possessive case.

OWNERSHIP   She is a teacher in **Maria's** school.

Can I count on **your** vote?

RELATIONSHIP   **Anne's** friend uses a wheelchair.

You need a good **night's** sleep.

I appreciate **your** coming so soon.

25a. **To form the possessive case of a singular noun, add an apostrophe and an** *s*.

EXAMPLES   Kia's problem   a night's work
the mayor's desk   this evening's paper
Mrs. Ross's job   a dollar's worth

Exception: A proper name ending in *s* may add only an apostrophe if the name consists of two or more syllables or if the addition of *'s* would make the name awkward to pronounce. Examples: *Ulysses'* (not *Ulysses's*) *plan; Mrs. Rawlings'* (not *Rawlings's*) *car.*

EXERCISE 1. Using Apostrophes to Form the Possessive Case of Singular Nouns.   Form the possessive case of each of the following singular words. After each possessive word, write an appropriate noun.

MECHANICS

EXAMPLE 1. Theresa
1. *Theresa's pencil*

1. baby	5. car	9. Mr. Chan
2. uncle	6. Terry	10. Miss Joyce
3. year	7. Ellen	
4. cent	8. mouse	

25b. To form the possessive case of a plural noun ending in *s*, add only the apostrophe.

EXAMPLES both aunts' husbands   cousins' visit

Although most plural nouns end in *s*, some are irregular. (See page 692. To form the possessive case of a plural noun that does not end in *s*, add an apostrophe and an *s*.

EXAMPLES children's shoes   deer's crossing

EXERCISE 2. Forming the Possessive Case of Plural Nouns. Write the possessive case of each of the following plural nouns:

1. women	5. princesses	9. mice
2. cats	6. dollars	10. parents
3. teachers	7. elves	
4. enemies	8. oxen	

Caution: Do not use an apostrophe to form the *plural* of a noun. Remember that the apostrophe shows ownership or relationship; it is nearly always followed by a noun.

INCORRECT Two players' left their gym suits in the locker room.

CORRECT Two players left their gym suits in the locker room. [simple plural]

CORRECT Two **players'** gym suits were left in the locker room. [The apostrophe shows that the gym suits belong to the two players.]

EXERCISE 3. Correcting Phrases by Forming the Possessive Case of Nouns. Revise the following phrases by using the possessive case.

EXAMPLE   1. parties for seniors
               1. *the seniors' parties*

1. prizes for winners
2. manners for teen-agers
3. yokes of oxen
4. duties of nurses
5. names of players
6. suits for women
7. organization for principals
8. medals for veterans
9. routines for dancers
10. roles for actresses

EXERCISE 4. Recognizing Correct Forms of Nouns. Number your paper 1–10. After the proper number, write the correct form of the noun in parentheses.

EXAMPLE   1. Two (candidates, candidates') spoke at the (voters, voters') forum.
               1. *candidates, voters'*

1. Two (friends, friends') and I asked the (mayor's, mayors) committee to set aside Lake Palmer as a wildlife sanctuary.
2. On a recent hike along the lake, we saw several (birds, birds') nests.
3. A flock of (ducks, ducks') paddled in the shallow water.
4. A (ducks, duck's) bill sieves out tiny water (plants, plants') and (animals, animals').
5. At this time of year, the (mallard's, mallards) plumage is especially colorful.
6. We tried not to disturb some (grebes, grebes') that were swimming with their young on their (backs, backs').
7. Pilar pointed out how the young (birds, birds') held onto their (parents, parents') feathers with their (bills, bills').
8. Two meetings have been scheduled to hear opposing (views, views') on the proposal.
9. (Citizens, Citizens') rights as well as environmental concerns must be considered.

10. The (children's, childrens') point of view will be presented by my sister (Karen's, Karens) friend.

SUMMARY

The following examples illustrate rules 25a and 25b.

Singular	Singular Possessive	Plural	Plural Possessive
cousin	cousin's letter	cousins	cousins' letters
student	student's paper	students	students' papers
week	week's salary	weeks	two weeks' salary
dime	dime's worth	dimes	two dimes' worth
hostess	hostess's idea	hostesses	hostesses' ideas
pony	pony's harness	ponies	ponies' harnesses
lynx	lynx's roar	lynxes	lynxes' roar
wife	wife's career	wives	wives' careers
man	man's shirt	men	men's shirts
child	child's toy	children	children's toys
hero	hero's medal	heroes	heroes' medals

25c. Possessive personal pronouns do not require an apostrophe.

Possessive personal pronouns are

my, mine   our, ours
your, yours   their, theirs
his, her, hers, its

Caution: The possessive form of *who* is *whose,* not *who's* (meaning "who is"). Similarly, do not write *it's* (meaning "it is") for *its,* or *they're* (meaning "they are") for *their.*

My, your, her, its, our, and *their* are used before a noun. *Mine, yours, hers, ours,* and *theirs,* on the other hand, are never used before a noun; they are used as subjects, complements, or objects in sentences. *His* may be used in either way.

EXAMPLES   That is **your** watch. That watch is **yours. Her** idea was wonderful. **Hers** was the best idea.

> Samantha has **your** sweater. Samantha has a sweater of **yours**.
>
> Renell has **our** plant; Ariel has **theirs**.
>
> There is **his** record. There is a record of **his**.

EXERCISE 5. Recognizing Correct Forms of Possessive Personal Pronouns. Number your paper 1–10. After the proper number, write the correct form of the pronoun in parentheses.

EXAMPLE 1. Ralph Ellison, (who's, whose) book *Invisible Man* won a National Book Award, studied music at Tuskegee Institute.
1. *whose*

1. You will be pleased to hear, Sumi, that two poems of (yours, yours') have been selected for the literary magazine.
2. When I first read this book, I was surprised by the quality of (its, it's) artwork.
3. (Hers, Hers') is the bicycle with the reflectors on (its, it's) fenders.
4. Eudora Welty, (who's, whose) short stories involve eccentric characters, is my favorite writer.
5. "The trophy is (ours, ours')!" shouted the captain as the *Flying S* crossed the finish line.
6. (Theirs, Theirs') is the only house with blue shutters, so you should have no difficulty finding it.
7. Penny and Arline worked as gardeners this summer and saved (their, they're) money for a ski trip.
8. The students (who's, whose) names are called are to report backstage.
9. (Their, They're) schedule calls for a math test on Tuesday.
10. (Who's, Whose) signature is this?

25d. Indefinite pronouns in the possessive case require an apostrophe and *s*.

EXAMPLES   nobody's wish   another's viewpoint
           someone's license   neither's school

EXERCISE 6. Recognizing Correct Forms of Possessive Pronouns. Number your paper 1–10. Choose the correct word in parentheses, and write it after the corresponding number.

1. The reward is (yours, your's).
2. (Ours, Our's) works better than (theirs, their's).
3. (Who's, Whose) game is that?
4. (Theirs, Their's) is not to reason why; (theirs, their's) is but to do and die.
5. My family is pleased with (its, it's) vacations.
6. It wasn't (anyone's, anyones') fault that we missed the bus.
7. (Eithers, Either's) project may win first prize at the Science Fair.
8. (Ones, One's, Ones') teeth should be checked regularly.
9. (Everybodys, Everybody's, Everybodys') trees must be irrigated.
10. That dog of (their's, theirs) should be on a leash.

REVIEW EXERCISE A. Writing the Singular, Plural, and Possessive Forms of Nouns. Make four columns on your paper headed *Singular, Singular Possessive, Plural,* and *Plural Possessive.* Write those forms of each of the following words. Add a suitable noun to follow each word in the possessive case. If you do not know how to spell a plural form, use your dictionary.

1. parent
2. typist
3. bicycle
4. referee
5. baby
6. woman
7. penny
8. hardware store
9. musician
10. lioness

REVIEW EXERCISE B. Correcting the Forms of Nouns and Pronouns. Number your paper 1–10. Write correctly the incorrect word or words in each of the following sentences.

EXAMPLE 1. Tanya's sister is one of the finalist's in the leagues' contest.
1. *finalists, league's*

MECHANICS

1. My teachers sister, Mrs. Taylor, is an attorney.
2. Lorena, don't buy more than fifty cent's worth of peanuts.
3. The drivers heroism during the accident was impressive.
4. The principal studied the childrens' attendance records.
5. We are reading Emily Dickinsons' poetry.
6. The doctor wants me to come back in six week's time.
7. Who's turn is it to summarize the President's speech?
8. The planes' rudder may have jammed during the descent.
9. One of Hercules labors was to capture the Creton bull.
10. My sister Janets friends say that the new teacher is a favorite of their's.

25e. In compound words, names of organizations and business firms, and words showing joint possession, only the last word is possessive in form.

COMPOUND WORDS   everyone **else's** worry
community **board's** meeting
vice-**president's** contract
brother-in-**law's** gift

ORGANIZATIONS   United **Fund's** drive

BUSINESS FIRMS   Berkeley Milk **Company's** trucks

JOINT POSSESSION   Peggy and **Madeline's** bookcase
children and **parents'** concerns
Rodgers and **Hart's** musical *Pal Joey*

Exceptions: When one of the words showing joint possession is a pronoun, both words should be possessive in form: **Peggy's and my bookcase** [*not Peggy and my bookcase*].

> ☞ **NOTE**   Use the *of* phrase to avoid awkward possessive forms.

AWKWARD   the director of the Cazadero Music Festival's daughter

BETTER   the daughter of the director of the Cazadero Music Festival

MECHANICS

AWKWARD   the Society for the Prevention of Cruelty to Animals' advertisement

BETTER   the advertisement of the Society for the Prevention of Cruelty to Animals

25f. When two or more persons possess something individually, each of their names is possessive in form.

EXAMPLES   **Mrs. Martin's** and **Mrs. Blair's** cars [the cars of two different women]

Asha's and **Daniella's** tennis rackets [individual, not joint, possession]

EXERCISE 7. Revising Phrases by Using the Possessive Case. Revise the following phrases by using the possessive case.

EXAMPLE   1. The book owned by Natalie and Stan

1. *Natalie and Stan's book*

1. the carpet of Sylvia and Mary
2. the customers of Lenihan Moving Company
3. the duet of Gwen and Kiana
4. letters written by the editor in chief
5. the history of the Alamo
6. the job shared by Isabel and me
7. the representatives of the Beneficial Life Insurance Company
8. one tractor belonging to my uncle and one to us
9. the expensive farewell dinner given by the Accounting Department
10. the business of her mother-in-law

REVIEW EXERCISE C. Correcting Sentences by Using Apostrophes. From the following sentences, list in order on your paper all words requiring apostrophes, and insert the apostrophes. After each word, write the thing possessed or related. One sentence does not need an apostrophe.

MECHANICS

1. For months Hillcrest High Schools student council had been trying to raise money for the schools clubs and activities.

2. The student councils presidents name was Ruth Ann, and the vice-presidents name was Don. 3. The sophomores representative, Elaine, liked the idea of doing car washes at Garcias gas station. 4. Don proposed that students ask for donations from stores like Browns School Supply Center and Ortegas Sporting Equipment Company.

5. "After all," Don said, "Mr. Browns store is the towns only school supply store. 6. If it weren't for our schools business, neither stores profits would be as high as they are."

7. "Well, we always get our moneys worth at both stores," said Elaine, who happened to be Dons cousin. 8. "Remember, too, that Ortegas Sporting Equipment Company outfits the schools soccer team, my brothers Little League team, and my sisters volleyball team."

9. "Both companies reputations are excellent," said Ruth Ann. 10. "Mr. Browns and Mr. Ortegas profits are well deserved."

11. Lucy, the juniors representative, made the next suggestion. 12. "Instead of asking for money, why don't we earn the money by buying magazines at wholesale prices and then selling them to our parents, to our parents friends, and to friends of ours?"

13. After listening to Lucys idea, Ruth Ann said, "We wouldn't make more than a few cents worth of profit on each months magazine sales. 14. Besides, I doubt that we could get our parents cooperation. 15. Many parents may already subscribe to the magazines we offer."

16. Elaine, whose turn it was to speak next, had an idea that caught everyones attention. 17. "A walkathon," she said, "could be Aprils major fund-raising activity. 18. The towns merchants could donate prizes, and the students could walk to raise money for the schools activities."

19. The student councils vote to sponsor a walkathon was unanimous. 20. The council members hopes were high as they left the meeting, determined to arouse their classmates interest in Hillcrest High Schools First Annual Walkathon.

Contractions

25g. Use an apostrophe to show where letters or numbers have been omitted in a contraction.

A contraction is a shortened form of a word or figure (*can't* for *cannot*, *'81* for *1981*) or of a group of words (*she'll* for *she will*, *let's* for *let us*, *o'clock* for *of the clock*). Contractions are used chiefly in conversation and in informal writing. The apostrophes in contractions indicate where letters have been left out.

EXAMPLES   I am not going.   I'm not going.
You are early.   You're early.
Betty is studying.   Betty's studying.
She has left already.   She's left already.
I had made a mistake.   I'd made a mistake.

Ordinarily, the word *not* is shortened to *n't* and added to a verb without any change in the spelling of the verb.

is not	isn't	were not	weren't
are not	aren't	has not	hasn't
does not	doesn't	have not	haven't
do not	don't	had not	hadn't
did not	didn't	would not	wouldn't
was not	wasn't	should not	shouldn't

Exceptions: will not   won't
cannot   can't

Remember: do not confuse contractions with possessive pronouns. Study the following lists:

CONTRACTIONS	POSSESSIVE PRONOUNS
Who's at bat? [*Who is*]	**Whose** bat is that?
It's roaring. [*It is*]	Listen to **its** roar.
You're too busy. [*You are*]	**Your** friend is busy.
There's a kite. [*There is*]	That kite is **theirs.**
They're tall trees. [*They are*]	**Their** trees are tall.

MECHANICS

WRITING APPLICATION:
Using Apostrophes Correctly
to Make Your Writing Clear

Using apostrophes correctly helps make your meaning clear to your readers. Compare the following two sentences:

EXAMPLES   There's is the best exhibit.
            Theirs is the best exhibit.

In reading the first sentence, you probably thought that the writer was simply pointing out the best exhibit and that he or she had mistakenly repeated the verb (*'s* and *is*). In the second sentence, however, it is clear that the writer is telling whose exhibit he or she thinks is the best one. Read your writing carefully to make sure that you have used apostrophes correctly.

Writing Assignment

Write ten sentences of your own, using correctly each of the following words:

1. it's   6. there
2. you're   7. whose
3. their   8. its
4. who's   9. they're
5. your   10. theirs

EXERCISE 8. Correcting Sentences by Using Apostrophes for Contractions.   Number your paper 1–10. If any of the following sentences has a contraction without an apostrophe, copy the contraction and add a correctly placed apostrophe. If a sentence is correct as it stands, write *C*.

1. "Youve changed," she said.
2. World War II ended in 45.
3. Whos coming to the party?
4. "The stores about to close," said the clerk.

MECHANICS

5. Several stores were closed because of the storm.
6. Well try to make it.
7. Well, try to make it.
8. She gets up at 6 o clock.
9. Im very glad to meet you.
10. Dont you play chess?

EXERCISE 9. Recognizing the Correct Use of Apostrophes.
Number your paper 1–10. Choose the correct word in parentheses, and write it after the proper number.

1. I think (your, you're) the best.
2. (Who's, Whose) going my way?
3. (It's, Its) your turn.
4. *Who is* and *who has* may be shortened to (*who's, whose*).
5. (There, Their, They're) washing the windows.
6. (*It's, Its*) is a contraction.
7. (*It's, Its*) is a possessive pronoun.
8. (Who's, Whose) that masked man?
9. (Who's, Whose) sneakers are these?
10. (Theirs, There's) no end in sight.

Plurals

25h. Use the apostrophe and *s* to form the plural of letters, numbers, and signs, and of words referred to as words.

EXAMPLES   Grandma always tells me to mind my *p*'s and *q*'s.
You received three *80*'s and two *90*'s.
Do not use *&*'s for *and* 's.

EXERCISE 10. Forming the Plurals of Items by Using Apostrophes.   Number your paper 1–10. Correctly form the plural of each of the following italicized items:

1. *q* look like *g*
2. the late *1960*
3. put *X* at the end
4. *+* and *−*

5. all *A* and *B*
6. pronounce your *t*
7. no *but,* please
8. their *oh* and *ah*
9. rows of *Z*
10. dot your *i*

CHAPTER 25 REVIEW: POSTTEST

Correcting Sentences by Using Apostrophes Correctly.
Number your paper 1–20. In the following sentences, apostrophes are either missing or used incorrectly. After the proper number, write the correct form of each incorrect word.

EXAMPLE   1. Im still working on todays assignment.
        1. *I'm, today's*

1. Ive just finished tonights homework. 2. Writing a composition is usually two hours hard work for me, but Im pleased with this one. 3. Ill read it over carefully to make sure that my handwritings legible. 4. My teacher has trouble with my *d*s, *t*s, and *o*s. 5. He also objects to my overuse of *and*s and *so*s. 6. If theres an error, Ill have to rewrite the composition. 7. Thats one good reason for being careful, isnt it?

8. My compositions title is "A Reign of Animals." 9. Mothers friend suggested that I call it "Whose in Charge Here?" 10. My familys love for animals is well known in the neighborhood and among our friends'. 11. At the moment were owned by two inside cats, three outside cats, one resident dog, and one visiting dog.

12. During our dog Peppers walks, Im usually followed by at least one other dog. 13. Some owners care of their dogs never seems to go beyond grooming and feeding them. 14. The City Councils decision to fine owners' who let they're dogs run loose makes sense to me. 15. Theres one huge dog who's nightly wanderings are the talk of the neighborhood. 16. His names Hugo, and weve taken him in several times after hes

MECHANICS

narrowly escaped being hit by a car. 17. As a matter of fact, Hugo and Peppers feeding dishes sit side by side in our kitchen.

18. Peter, our senior cat, who was once one of our neighborhoods strays, isnt about to run from anyones dog. 19. At times weve seen him safeguarding other cats of ours' by running in front of them and staring down an approaching dog and it's owner. 20. Our dogs and cats different personalities never cease to fascinate me.

CHAPTER 26

Punctuation

HYPHENS, DASHES, PARENTHESES

DIAGNOSTIC TEST

Writing Sentences with Correct Use of Hyphens, Dashes, and Parentheses. Write the following sentences, using hyphens, dashes, and parentheses where they are needed. (Do not add commas in these sentences.)

EXAMPLE 1. Nancy Wing she is the ex champion will award the golf trophies.
1. *Nancy Wing—she is the ex-champion—will award the golf trophies.*

1. I will be twenty one on the twenty first of September.
2. A dog I think it was a poodle jumped into the lake.
3. Many voters thought that the candidate's remarks were un American.
4. He claimed and no one denied it that the money was misplaced when the office was relocated.
5. In *The House of Mirth* 1905, Edith Wharton criticizes urban life.
6. At the auction someone bid one thousand dollars for a pre Revolutionary desk.

7. The Historical Society the local members, that is will conduct a tour of the harbor.
8. If she wins the marathon we're all rooting for her the trophy will still be ours.
9. "Operator, please call" Then the phone went dead.
10. Next month of course, I'll write you before then we're going on an overnight hike.
11. My sister Patricia her nickname is "Peachy" wants to be a marine biologist.
12. I have never or at least, *almost* never forgotten a name after an introduction.
13. Bake the meat at 450° F 232° C for about forty minutes.
14. The mayor elect hoped that the proposal would pass by a two thirds majority.
15. A former all state quarterback, our coach insists that there is no such thing as a self made star.
16. "It sounds like" gasped Jeff as he dashed for the window.
17. Destroyed by Rome 146 B.C., Corinth was later rebuilt by Julius Caesar 44 B.C.
18. Neither contestant could spell the word both tried twice, so the emcee declared a tie.
19. Thirty six teen-agers or maybe it was thirty seven helped clean up the park after the concert.
20. "What What shall I do now?" Laura asked.

HYPHENS

As you know, some compound words are hyphenated (*self-confidence*); some are written as one word (*firefighter*); some are written as two or more words (*post office*). In recent years, the trend has been to spell most compound words without hyphens, either as two words (*open compounds*) or as one word (*solid compounds*). Whenever you need to know whether a word is hyphenated, consult your dictionary. In addition, learn the uses of the hyphen that are explained in this chapter.

26a. Use a hyphen to divide a word at the end of a line.

If you will look at the right margins of pages in this book, you will see that hyphens are often used to divide words at the ends of lines. *A word must always be divided between syllables.*

INCORRECT

The mayor's campaign dinner was organized by the co-mmunity alliance members.

CORRECT

The mayor's campaign dinner was organized by the com-munity alliance members.

If you need to divide a word and are not sure about its syllables, look it up in your dictionary. Keep in mind these rules for word division:

1. Do not divide one-syllable words.

INCORRECT

The line of people waiting to buy tickets stret-ched halfway down the block.

CORRECT

The line of people waiting to buy tickets stretched halfway down the block.

CORRECT

The line of people waiting to buy tickets stretched halfway down the block.

2. Try to avoid dividing capitalized words.

INCORRECT

Marian's mother works at the Lawrence Hall of Sci-ence.

CORRECT

Marian's mother works at the Lawrence Hall of Science.

MECHANICS

3. Divide an already hyphenated word *only* at a hyphen.

INCORRECT

The conference speaker this morning is my mother-in-law.

CORRECT

The conference speaker this morning is my mother-
in-law.

4. Do not divide a word so that one letter stands alone.

INCORRECT

The utility company built a dam to generate e-
lectricity.

CORRECT

The utility company built a dam to generate electricity.

EXERCISE 1. Using Hyphens to Divide Words at the Ends of Lines. Copy each word, and use a hyphen to indicate where you would divide it at the end of a line. If necessary, check your dictionary for the proper syllabication. If a word should *not* be divided, write *carry forward* after its number.

EXAMPLES   1. thoroughly
               1. *thor-oughly* (or *thorough-ly*)
               2. cooked
               2. *carry forward*

1. original
2. library
3. fourth
4. unprecedented
5. parentheses
6. tomorrow
7. breathe
8. business
9. among
10. son-in-law

26b. Use a hyphen with compound numbers from twenty-one to ninety-nine and with fractions used as adjectives.

EXAMPLES   twenty-four eggs
               one-half cup [but *one half* of the flour]

26c. Use a hyphen with the prefixes *ex-*, *self-*, *all-*, and with the suffix *-elect*, and with all prefixes before a proper noun or proper adjective.

EXAMPLES   ex-coach   mid-July
            self-made   pro-American
            all-star   anti-Communist
            President-elect   pre-Revolutionary

EXERCISE 2. Writing Hyphenated Words. In the following sentences, ten hyphens are needed. Write the words that should be hyphenated, correctly punctuated, on your paper.

1. The exgovernor presented the all American trophy at the competition.
2. Until 1959, the United States flag had forty eight stars; soon it may have fifty one.
3. In twenty five days my grandparents will celebrate their forty fifth wedding anniversary; about three fourths of the family will attend the celebration.
4. The exambassador's lecture focused on the post Andean era.
5. He added one half teaspoon of vanilla to the mixture and set the timer for thirty five minutes.

DASHES

As you have learned, many words and phrases are used *parenthetically;* that is, they break into the main thought. They are explanations, qualifications, or just "side remarks." They do not affect the grammatical construction of the sentences in which they occur.

Most parenthetical elements are set off by commas (see page 614) or parentheses (see page 677). Sometimes, however, words or phrases or clauses used parenthetically may demand a stronger separation. In such instances, a dash is used.

26d. Use a dash to indicate an abrupt break in thought or speech or an unfinished statement or question.

MECHANICS

EXAMPLES   Judy—Ms. Lane, I mean—will be your new supervisor.
Our dog—he's a long-haired dachshund—is too affectionate to be a good watchdog.
"Why—Why can't I come, too?" Janet asked hesitatingly.
"You're being—," Tina began and then stopped.

EXERCISE 3. Writing Sentences with Appropriate Use of Dashes.   Write the following sentences and insert dashes where they are appropriate.

1. "I'd like to thank" and then Tom blushed and quickly sat down.
2. We were surprised in fact, amazed to learn that the game had been called off.
3. The valedictorian that is, the student with the highest average will be given a special award.
4. "I I just don't know," she murmured.
5. My brother's engagement it's a secret, by the way will be announced Sunday.

REVIEW EXERCISE A. Writing Sentences with Appropriate Use of Hyphens and Dashes.   Write the following sentences, inserting hyphens and dashes where they are needed.

EXAMPLE   1. My grandmother's beautiful quilts all of them handmade will someday be priceless.
1. *My grandmother's beautiful quilts—all of them handmade—will someday be priceless.*

1. That man he seemed very suspicious to me walked quickly to his car and drove away.
2. This year the allstar team will be chosen by popular vote.
3. Her music brought her the self fulfillment that she had sought.
4. "I guess I guess I was mistaken," he apologized.
5. Be sure to enclose a self addressed envelope.

MECHANICS

6. In the recent class election, thirty five votes constituted a two thirds majority.
7. Some people unfortunately too many tried to push ahead in line.
8. They greeted the visitors with a twenty one-gun salute.
9. Allie Morgan I've known her all my life is teaching me woodworking.
10. My cousin, a self confessed cat-lover, talked about his cats the entire evening.

PARENTHESES

Parentheses set off elements that serve as explanations or qualifications. Parentheses are *enclosing* marks, used in pairs.

26e. Use parentheses to enclose material that is added to a sentence but is not considered of major importance.

EXAMPLES   During the Middle Ages (from about A.D. 500 to A.D. 1500), Moslems and Vikings invaded Europe. Aunt Constance (Mother's aunt and my great-aunt) will meet us at the airport.

Material enclosed in parentheses may range from a single word to a short sentence. The short sentence in parentheses may be one that stands by itself or one that is part of the sentence as a whole.

Punctuation marks are used within parentheses when they belong with the parenthetical matter, as in the following example about a pen. However, a punctuation mark is not placed within parentheses if it belongs to the sentence as a whole.

EXAMPLES   Fill in the application carefully. (Use a pen.)
That old house (it was built at the turn of the century) may soon become a landmark.

In general, follow these two rules for using parentheses:

1. Any material within parentheses may be omitted without changing the basic meaning and construction of the sentence.

MECHANICS

2. Note that commas, dashes, and parentheses are frequently interchangeable, especially for setting off incidental words or phrases. Commas are more common than dashes; dashes are more common than parentheses.

EXERCISE 4. Writing Sentences with Appropriate Use of Parentheses. Write each sentence, adding needed parentheses and punctuating the parenthetical elements correctly.

EXAMPLE 1. A fly-specked calendar five years out of date hung on the kitchen wall.

1. *A fly-specked calendar (five years out of date) hung on the kitchen wall.*

1. I reread all the *Oz* books that I own a considerable number.
2. Edna St. Vincent Millay 1892–1950 began writing poetry as a child.
3. In 1850 California entered the Union as a free state. You will read more about this in a later chapter.
4. Gwendolyn Brooks *A Street in Bronzeville* was her first book has received high praise from critics.
5. Killer whales that's what Shamu is can be trained to perform tricks.

REVIEW EXERCISE B. Writing Sentences with Appropriate Use of Hyphens, Dashes, and Parentheses. Write the following sentences, inserting hyphens, dashes, and parentheses where they are needed.

EXAMPLE 1. The biographies of several outstanding athletes Cheryl Toussaint, Cathy Rigby, Micki King are included in *Women Who Win.*

1. *The biographies of several outstanding athletes (Cheryl Toussaint, Cathy Rigby, Micki King) are included in* Women Who Win.

1. We are definitely going to Honolulu probably in mid August and I can hardly wait.
2. The author Stephen Crane 1871–1900 borrowed money to pay for the publication of his first novel.

3. During Crane's brief career he died at twenty nine of tuberculosis he wrote five novels, several short stories, and two volumes of poetry.
4. "Let me say" the candidate began before he was interrupted by hecklers.
5. I am in favor completely in favor of your proposal.
6. Information about the budget for women's sports see Supplement B is included in this report.
7. My father he prides himself on always being prompt wears a self winding watch.
8. There are only twenty one days count them before vacation.
9. "But But what happened?" Sylvia asked nervously.
10. I think but I could be wrong that it costs two dollars.

WRITING APPLICATION:
Using Dashes and Parentheses Sparingly to Keep Your Writing Clear

Think of the dash and parentheses as punctuation marks that signal an interruption. Whether the interruption is an abrupt break in your thought pattern or an insertion of information that is not of major importance, it turns your readers away from your main message. If you interrupt yourself frequently, you will confuse your readers and make it difficult for them to follow your main point. Use the dash and parentheses sparingly.

Writing Assignment

Write a paragraph to a pen pal telling about some custom or tradition that is unique to your family, school, or community. Read your completed paragraph carefully, underlining each dash and set of parentheses you have used. If your paragraph contains more than one of each, you have probably used these punctuation marks too freely. Revise the paragraph, using no more than one dash (or set of dashes) and one set of parentheses.

MECHANICS

CHAPTER 26 REVIEW: POSTTEST

Writing Sentences with Appropriate Use of Hyphens, Dashes, and Parentheses. Write the following sentences, using hyphens, dashes, and parentheses where they are needed. (Do not add commas in these sentences.)

EXAMPLE 1. This morning I counted twenty one birds most of them songbirds at our backyard feeder.
1. *This morning I counted twenty-one birds—most of them songbirds—at our backyard feeder.*

1. The Mayas an unusually artistic and intelligent people contributed to the culture of the Aztecs.
2. James Fenimore Cooper 1789–1851 attended Yale but did not graduate he was expelled because of a prank.
3. If you have ever dreamed of finding buried treasure and who hasn't? your search could begin on Padre Island.
4. The pictures in my mother's 1956 yearbook it's called *Images* remind me of the TV show *Happy Days*.
5. Because of renewed interest in track and field, Ms. Acosta she's our coach expects the team to attract new members.
6. George Grinnel, who founded the National Audubon Society, was a self taught expert on the American West and helped negotiate treaties with three Indian tribes the Blackfoot, Cheyenne, and Pawnee.
7. Twenty six students most of them from the advanced math class represented our school at the all state chess match.
8. Henry Viscardi he founded Abilities, Inc. dedicated his life to creating opportunities for the handicapped.
9. Rachel Carson was working for the U.S. Fish and Wildlife Service created in 1956 when she first noticed the destruction of plant and animal life by pesticides.
10. Her book *Silent Spring* copyright 1962 first alerted the public to the dangers of environmental pollution.

11. The Battle of Bunker Hill June 17, 1775 damaged the confidence of the British.
12. Grandmother whispered, "Please turn" and then fell asleep.
13. The Egyptian and Indian cobras they are the traditional snake charmers' snakes are deaf.
14. The soup was three fourths water and one fourth vegetables.
15. The symptoms of the common cold sneezing, cough, sore throat, and headache are rarely accompanied by a fever.
16. The ex treasurer of our club he's an extremely self confident person is now running for class president.
17. Our representative Democrat voted against the proposal; however, it received the required two thirds majority.
18. My sister she lives in Boston now is studying pre Columbian art.
19. The trunk it had belonged to my great aunt makes an interesting coffee table.
20. Our dads were in the same graduating class at MIT 1960.

MECHANICS

CHAPTER 27

Spelling

IMPROVING YOUR SPELLING

No one is a born speller. Everybody must work to learn to spell words correctly. The suggestions and rules in this chapter are designed to help you help yourself to learn to spell better.

GOOD SPELLING HABITS

The following italicized rules are suggestions for forming good habits that will help you spell words now and in the future, in school and out of school.

1. *Keep a list of your spelling errors.* One way to record your words is to prepare a spelling page with four columns. In the first column, correctly spell the word you missed. (Never enter a misspelled word on your spelling page.) In the second column, write the word again, this time divided into syllables and accented. In the third column, write the word once more, circling the spot that gives you trouble. In the fourth column, give the reason for your mistake, or set down any comment that will help you to learn the word.

EXAMPLES

probably	prob′a·bly	prob(a)bly	Pronounce correctly.
usually	u′su·al·ly	usua(ll)y	*usual* + *ly* (Study rule 27d.)

MECHANICS

2. *Use the dictionary as a spelling aid.* In order to keep an accurate word list (the only kind of any value), you will need to look up your misspelled words in the dictionary. Don't guess about the correct spelling.

3. *Learn to spell by syllables.* A syllable is a word part that can be pronounced by itself. For instance, the word *thor'ough* has two syllables; the word *sep'a·rate* has three syllables. When you divide a long word into its syllables, you make a number of shorter parts out of it. Since short parts of words, or groups of letters, are easy to spell, you make spelling easier.

EXERCISE 1. Spelling Words by Dividing Them into Syllables. Look up the following words in your dictionary, and divide each one into syllables. Pronounce each syllable correctly, and learn to spell the word by syllables.

1. representative
2. fascinate
3. candidate
4. temperature
5. apparent
6. similar
7. benefit
8. definition
9. acquaintance
10. awkward

4. *Avoid mispronunciations that lead to spelling errors.* Since you often spell words according to the way you pronounce them, mispronunciation causes misspelling. For instance, if you say *mis·chie'vi·ous* instead of *mis'chie·vous,* you will spell the word incorrectly by adding an extra syllable.

EXERCISE 2. *Oral Drill.* Stressing Correct Pronunciation of Spelling Words. After carefully studying the correct pronunciations in parentheses below, read each word aloud three times, stressing the correct pronunciation of the italicized letters.

1. at*hl*ete (ath'lēt)
2. chil*dren* (chil'drən)
3. drow*ned* (dround)
4. *es*cape (ə·scāp', e·scāp')
5. lib*ra*ry (lī'brer·ē, -brə·rē)
6. light*n*ing (līt'ning)
7. *per*haps (pər·haps')
8. pro*bab*ly (prob'ə·blē)
9. qui*et* (kwī'ət)
10. rec*og*nize (rek'əg·nīz)

MECHANICS

5. *Revise your papers to avoid careless spelling errors.* Although rereading takes only a few minutes, it makes a great difference in the correctness of your work. As you find and revise your spelling errors, be sure to eliminate all botchy handwriting. When you carelessly dot closed *e*'s, make your *o*'s look like *a*'s and your *g*'s like *q*'s, or hurriedly write over letters, you will make twice as many spelling errors as you would if you were more careful about your handwriting. Remember, too, that careless mistakes in handwriting can distort your meaning. For instance, an undotted *i* looks like an *e,* and an uncrossed *t* may be interpreted as an *l.*

6. *To master the spelling of a word, pronounce it, study it, and write it.* When you are trying to learn how to spell a word, first *pronounce the word,* noting its syllables.

Second, *study the word,* noticing especially any letters which might make the spelling hard. Notice, for example, that *doctor* has two *o*'s, that *where* has *here* in it, and that *across* has only one *c,* being composed of two little words: *a + cross.*

Third, *write the word.* This will help to fix the spelling in your mind.

EXERCISE 3. Spelling Commonly Misspelled Words from Dictation. Copy each of the following words. Carefully observe the italicized silent letters as you write. Then have a friend dictate the words to you. (Your teacher may do this in class).

1. ans*w*er	6. *k*now*le*dge	11. r*h*ythm	16. tonig*h*t
2. a*w*kward	7. *w*rit*t*en	12. use*d* to	17. sur*e*ly
3. *wh*ole	8. of*t*en	13. instead	18. thoug*h*
4. toward	9. condem*n*	14. me*a*nt	19. throu*gh*
5. *k*now, *k*new	10. colum*n*	15. *a*isle	20. nin*e*ty

7. *Learn lists of commonly misspelled words.* Most spelling errors made by students are made in relatively few frequently written words. Lists of such words appear on pages 705–708.

EXERCISE 4. Studying More Commonly Misspelled Words. Study each word carefully. If you misspell any word, put it on your spelling list.

across	busy	friend	minute	surely
again	buy	grammar	none	tear
all right	can't	guess	off	thing
almost	color	half	once	think
always	coming	having	paid	through
among	country	heard	raise	tired
any	dear	hoping	really	together
began	doesn't	laid	safety	truly
belief	eager	later	shoes	Tuesday
bigger	early	likely	speak	very
built	February	making	speech	wear
business	forty	many	straight	Wednesday

8. *Learn to spell by making associations.* Make any kind of association that will help you to remember a difficult word. For example, the word *earnest* has two words in it, *ear* and *nest; delivery* has *liver.* You can link rhyming words, putting an easy word with a hard one: *ear, hear; truly, unruly; loose, noose.*

EXERCISE 5. Spelling Words by Making Associations. Find the words within words in each of the following.

EXAMPLE 1. laboratory
     1. *Laboratory has both labor and orator.*

1. bulletin
2. ninety
3. meant
4. copies
5. courteous
6. explanation
7. immediately
8. excellent
9. apparent
10. handkerchief

SPELLING RULES

Although most spelling is learned by memorizing words, you can "figure out" the correct spelling of many words after you have mastered the rules given on the following pages.

ie and *ei*

27a. Write *ie* when the sound is long *e*, except after *c*.

MECHANICS

EXAMPLES   achieve   ceiling   field   piece   shield
            believe   chief   grief   receive   thief
            brief   deceit   niece   relief   yield

EXCEPTIONS   either, leisure, neither, seize, weird

Write *ei* when the sound is not long *e,* especially when the sound is long *a.*

EXAMPLES   neighbor   weigh   forfeit
            rein   counterfeit   height
            reign   foreign   heir
            veil

EXCEPTIONS   friend, mischief, kerchief

EXERCISE 6. Spelling *ie* and *ei* Words.   Write the following words, supplying the missing letters (*e* and *i*) in the correct order.

1. p . . . ce   5. conc . . . ve   8. n . . . ther
2. f . . . nd   6. fr . . . ght   9. s . . . ze
3. ch . . . f   7. h . . . ght   10. r . . . gn
4. c . . . ling

-cede, -ceed, and *-sede*

27b. Only one English word ends in *-sede: supersede;* only three words end in *-ceed: exceed, proceed,* and *succeed;* all other words of similar sound end in *-cede.*

EXAMPLES   precede   recede   secede
            intercede   concede   accede

Adding Prefixes and Suffixes

A *prefix* is one, or more than one, letter or syllable added to the beginning of a word to change its meaning.

27c. When a prefix is added to a word, the spelling of the word itself remains the same.

Take, for example, the word *do*. By adding the prefixes *un-* or *over-*, you have the words *undo* and *overdo*. The spelling of the word *do* does not change. Study the following examples:

im + mortal = **im**mortal	mis + step = **mis**step
un + certain = **un**certain	over + rule = **over**rule

A *suffix* is one, or more than one, letter or syllable added to the end of a word to change its meaning.

27d. When the suffixes *-ness* and *-ly* are added to a word, the spelling of the word itself is not changed.

EXAMPLES   sure + ly = sure**ly**
real + ly = real**ly**
useful + ness = useful**ness**
polite + ness = polite**ness**

EXCEPTIONS   Words ending in *y* usually change the *y* to *i* before *-ness* and *-ly:* empty—emptiness; easy—easily. One-syllable adjectives ending in *y*, however, generally follow rule 27d: *dry—dryness; sly—slyly. True* and *due* drop the final *e* before *-ly: truly, duly.*

EXERCISE 7. Spelling Words with Prefixes and Suffixes.
Number your paper 1–10. Correctly spell each of the following words as you add the prefix or suffix indicated.

1. un + necessary	6. occasional + ly
2. re + commend	7. keen + ness
3. il + legal	8. cleanly + ness
4. im + mature	9. mean + ness
5. dis + appear	10. sure + ly

EXERCISE 8. Spelling Words with Suffixes.
Number your paper 1–10. First, correctly add the suffix *-ly* to these words: *hungry, true, necessary, noisy, sleepy.* Then add the suffix *-ness* to *tardy, happy, saucy, flighty, heavy.*

27e. Drop the final *e* before a suffix beginning with a vowel.

EXAMPLES

    hope + ing = hoping   imagine + ary = imaginary

    fame + ous = famous   admire + ation = admiration

EXCEPTIONS 1. mile + age = mileage

             2. The final *e* is kept in some words to avoid confusion with other words: *dyeing* and *dying*, *singeing* and *singing*.

             3. The final *e* is kept in words ending in *ce* or *ge* to retain the soft sound when adding suffixes beginning with *a* or *o: peaceable, advantageous, courageous.*

EXERCISE 9. Spelling Words with Suffixes. Apply rule 27e as you add each designated suffix, and decide whether or not to keep or drop the final *e*. (Keep in mind the exceptions to the rule.)

1. become + ing
2. guide + ance
3. continue + ous
4. surprise + ed
5. shine + ing
6. ridicule + ous
7. please + ant
8. believe + ing
9. courage + ous
10. determine + ation

27f. Keep the final *e* before a suffix beginning with a consonant.

EXAMPLES nine + ty = ninety   awe + some =

             hope + ful = hopeful   awesome

             entire + ly = entirely   pave + ment =

             care + less = careless   pavement

EXCEPTIONS due + ly = duly   nine + th = ninth

              true + ly = truly   awe + ful = awful

              whole + ly = wholly   argue + ment =

                                    argument

              acknowledge + ment =   judge + ment =

              acknowledgment   judgment

EXERCISE 10. Spelling Words with Suffixes. Apply rules 27e and 27f as you add each designated suffix, and decide whether to keep or drop the final *e*. (In this exercise there are no exceptions to the rules.)

1. announce + ment
2. use + age
3. imagine + ary
4. care + ful

5. sincere + ly
6. write + ing
7. virtue + ous
8. desire + able

9. hope + less
10. safe + ty

27g. With words ending in _y_ preceded by a consonant, change the _y_ to _i_ before any suffix not beginning with _i_.

EXAMPLES

fifty + eth = fiftieth
lazy + ness = laziness
worry + ed = worried
mystery + ous = mysterious
hasty + ly = hastily

beautify + ing = beautifying
terrify + ing = terrifying
worry + ing = worrying
verify + ing = verifying
imply + ing = implying

EXCEPTIONS   1. Some one-syllable words:
                    shy + ness = shyness
                    spry + ly = spryly
                    sky + ward = skyward
             2. _lady_ and _baby_ with suffixes: _ladylike, ladyship; babyhood_

Observe that words ending in y preceded by a vowel usually do not change their spelling before a suffix:

joy + ful = joyful
array + ed = arrayed

boy + hood = boyhood
gay + est = gayest

EXERCISE 11. Spelling Words with Suffixes.   Apply rule 27g as you add each designated suffix and decide whether or not to change the final _y_ to _i_. (In this exercise, there are no exceptions to the rule.)

1. extraordinary + ly
2. try + ing
3. deny + al
4. carry + ed

5. apply + cation
6. defy + ant
7. satisfy + ed

8. rely + able
9. amplify + er
10. certify + cate

27h. Double the final consonant before a suffix that begins with a vowel if _both_ of the following conditions exist:

MECHANICS

(1) the word has only one syllable or is accented on the last syllable.

(2) the word ends in a single consonant preceded by a single vowel.

EXAMPLES

drop + ing = dropping   occur + ence = occurrence
plan + ed = planned   propel + er = propeller
sit + ing = sitting   control + ed = controlled

If both of these conditions do not exist, the final consonant is not doubled before a suffix.

jump + ed = jumped   tunnel + ing = tunneling
appear + ance = appearance   sprint + er = sprinter

EXERCISE 12. Spelling Words with Suffixes. Apply rule 27h as you add each designated suffix.

1. swim + ing
2. begin + er
3. control + ed
4. hot + est
5. expect + ation
6. inform + ed
7. number + ing
8. sprint + ing
9. riot + ous
10. stop + age

The Plural of Nouns

Changing a singular noun to a plural noun sometimes presents problems. The rules on the following pages will help you solve these problems.

27i. Observe the rules for spelling the plural of nouns.

(1) The regular way to form the plural of nouns is to add an *s*.

SINGULAR	boat	nickel	teacher	house
PLURAL	boats	nickels	teachers	houses

(2) The plural of nouns ending in *s, x, z, ch,* or *sh* is formed by adding *es*.

The addition of *es* to the following words makes them pronounceable because of the extra syllable *es* creates.

SINGULAR	PLURAL	SINGULAR	PLURAL
glass	glasses	waltz	waltzes
Mrs. Jones	the Joneses	beach	beaches
box	boxes	dish	dishes

EXERCISE 13. Spelling the Plurals of Nouns.   Correctly write the plural of each of the following nouns:

1. guess
2. ax
3. tongue
4. wall
5. dollar
6. cafeteria
7. watch
8. branch
9. speech
10. amateur

(3) The plural of nouns ending in *y* preceded by a consonant is formed by changing the *y* to *i* and adding *es*.

SINGULAR	sky	army	story	baby
PLURAL	skies	armies	stories	babies

EXCEPTION   The plural of proper nouns: *the Hardys, the Carys.*

(4) The plural of nouns ending in *y* preceded by a *vowel* is formed by adding an *s*.

SINGULAR	delay	key	boy	guy
PLURAL	delays	keys	boys	guys

EXERCISE 14. Spelling the Plural of Nouns.   Write the plural of each of the following nouns:

1. lady
2. relay
3. donkey
4. copy
5. butterfly
6. ally
7. lullaby
8. quantity
9. day
10. jalopy

(5) The plural of some nouns ending in *f* or *fe* is formed by changing the *f* to *v* and adding *s* or *es*.

MECHANICS

As you study the formation of the plural of the following nouns, notice the way the nouns are pronounced.

SINGULAR	roof	belief	leaf	wife	calf
PLURAL	roofs	beliefs	leaves	wives	calves

EXERCISE 15. Spelling the Plural of Nouns. Write the plural of each of these nouns:

1. thief   2. chef   3. life   4. knife   5. giraffe

(6) The plural of nouns ending in _o_ preceded by a vowel is formed by adding _s;_ the plural of nouns ending in _o_ preceded by a consonant is formed by adding _es_.

SINGULAR	radio	rodeo	echo	hero	tomato
PLURAL	radios	rodeos	echoes	heroes	tomatoes

EXCEPTIONS   Nouns ending in _o_ preceded by a consonant and _referring to music_ form the plural by adding _s_.

SINGULAR	alto	solo	piano
PLURAL	altos	solos	pianos

EXERCISE 16. Spelling the Plural of Nouns. Write the plural of the following nouns:

1. shampoo   3. hobo   5. torpedo
2. soprano   4. veto

(7) The plural of a few nouns is formed in irregular ways.

SINGULAR	foot	man	ox	mouse	child	tooth
PLURAL	feet	men	oxen	mice	children	teeth

(8) The plural of compound nouns written as one word is formed by adding _s_ or _es_.

SINGULAR	spoonful	smashup	icebox
PLURAL	spoonfuls	smashups	iceboxes

MECHANICS

(9) The plural of compound nouns consisting of a noun plus a modifier is formed by making the noun plural.

SINGULAR	PLURAL
sister-in-law	sisters-in-law
notary public	notaries public
attorney-at-law	attorneys-at-law

(10) Some nouns are the same in the singular and the plural.

SINGULAR AND PLURAL   deer, trout, Japanese, sheep

EXERCISE 17. Spelling the Plural of Nouns. Write the plural form of each of the following nouns:

1. woman   5. maid of honor   9. deer
2. ox   6. armful   10. Chinese
3. foot   7. mouse
4. son-in-law 8. man-of-war

(11) The plural of some foreign words is formed as in the original language.

SINGULAR	crisis	datum	analysis	alumnus
PLURAL	crises	data	analyses	alumni

☞ **NOTE** A few words taken from the foreign languages have an alternate plural form, regularly formed as in English: *appendix: appendices* or *appendixes*. Sometimes the English plural is the preferred one; the plural of *formula* is preferably *formulas,* not *formulae.* Consult your dictionary to determine the preferred spelling of the plural of such words.

(12) The plural of numbers, letters, signs, and words used as words is formed by adding an apostrophe and *s*.

EXAMPLES   Put the *g*'s and the *6*'s in the second column.
            Change the *&*'s to *and*'s.

MECHANICS

WORDS OFTEN CONFUSED

If you will master each word in the lists on the following pages, you can eliminate many errors in your compositions. Some of these words are confusing because they are homonyms—their pronunciation is the same. Others are confusing because their spelling is the same or similar.

advice	[noun] *counsel* He gave me some excellent *advice*.
advise	[verb] *to give advice* She *advised* me to finish high school.
affect	[verb] *to influence* What he said did not *affect* my final decision.
effect	[verb] *to accomplish;* [noun] *consequence* or *result* The mayor has *effected* many changes during her administration. The *effect* of these changes has been most beneficial.
all ready	[pronoun plus adjective] *everyone ready* When he arrived, we were *all ready* to go.
already	[adverb] *previously* Sharon has *already* gone.
all right	[This is the only acceptable spelling. Although it is in the dictionary, the spelling *alright* has not yet come into standard usage.]
all together	*everyone in the same place* When we were *all together,* we opened the gifts.
altogether	*entirely* He was *altogether* wrong.

brake
stopping device
The *brakes* on our car are good.

break
shatter, sever
The last straw *breaks* a camel's back.

capital
[noun] *city* or *money used by business*; [adjective] *punishable by death* or *of major importance* or *excellent*
Raleigh is the *capital* of North Carolina.
Mrs. Dawson will need more *capital* to modernize her equipment.
Killing a police officer is a *capital* crime.
She made a *capital* error in preparing that important report.
This is a *capital* detective story.

capitol
[noun] *building; statehouse*
In Raleigh, the *capitol* is located on Fayetteville Street.

choose
[used for present and future tense] *select*
You may *choose* your own partner.

chose
[past tense—rhymes with *hose*]
Yesterday she *chose* to postpone the meeting.

coarse
rough, crude
The *coarse* material is very durable.
He never uses *coarse* language.

course
path of action or progress; unit of study; track or way; also used with *of* to mean *as was to be expected*
The airplane lost its *course* in the storm.
I am taking a *course* in algebra.
She is at the golf *course*.
Of *course*, you have met Ellen.

MECHANICS

EXERCISE 18. Selecting Correct Spelling Words to Complete Sentences. Number your paper 1–20. After the proper number write the correct one of the words in parentheses.

1. Betty has (all ready, already) handed in her paper.
2. (All right, Alright), I'll wrap the package now.
3. What was the coach's (advice, advise) to you players?
4. Are you taking a (coarse, course) in sewing?
5. This poison is supposed to have a deadly (affect, effect).
6. Last night we (choose, chose) our leader.
7. She did not, of (coarse, course), remember me.
8. The mechanic adjusted the (brakes, breaks).
9. You should know the (capital, capitol) of your state.
10. You can (choose, chose) your own music.
11. They were (all together, altogether) at dinner.
12. The newspaper strike seriously (affected, effected) sales in department stores.
13. I'm sure that the baby will be (all right, alright).
14. His (coarse, course) manners offended everyone.
15. A fragile piece of china (brakes, breaks) easily.
16. Our state (capital, capitol) is built of limestone and marble.
17. May we (choose, chose) between a dance and a picnic?
18. She was not (all together, altogether) satisfied.
19. Are they (all ready, already) to go now?
20. In *Hamlet,* Polonius gives (advice, advise) to his son.

EXERCISE 19. Writing Sentences with Words Often Confused. Write twenty original sentences correctly using all the words you have just studied. Use each word at least once.

---

complement   *something that completes or makes perfect; to complete or make perfect*
Linking verbs are followed by subject *complements.*
The office has a full *complement* of personnel.
The yellow rug *complemented* the warm-looking room.

compliment   *a remark that says something flattering about a person; to say something flattering*
I was not impressed by her flowery *compliments*.
I must *compliment* you on that lovely flower arrangement.

---

consul   *the representative of a foreign country*
The French *consul* was guest of honor.

council   *a group called together to accomplish a job*
The city *council* will debate the proposed bond issue tonight.

councilor   *a member of a council*
At the council meeting Mother plans to introduce Dr. Watkins, the new *councilor*.

counsel   *advice; the giving of advice*
I am deeply grateful for your *counsel*.

counselor   *one who gives advice*
I do not think I am qualified to be your *counselor*.

---

des'ert   *a dry region*
Be sure to fill the gas tank before you start across the *desert*.

desert'   *to leave*
She *deserted* her comrades.

dessert'   *the final course of a meal*
What do you plan to have for *dessert* tonight?

EXERCISE 20. Selecting Correct Spelling Words to Complete Sentences.   Number your paper 1–10. After the proper number write the correct one of the words in parentheses.

1. The funds are for a (desert, dessert) irrigation project.
2. The Security (Consul, Council, Counsel) of the United Nations consists of fifteen members.

MECHANICS

3. The new hat will (complement, compliment) my suit.
4. Miss Patton is my guidance (councilor, counselor).
5. The house looks (deserted, desserted).
6. Listen to your parents' (consul, council, counsel).
7. I passed on your charming (complement, compliment) to Isabel.
8. At their meeting, all the members of the city (council, counsel) agreed that the tax proposal was unworkable.
9. Baked Alaska is my favorite (desert, dessert).
10. In the opera *Madama Butterfly*, Sharpless is the American (consul, counsel) in Japan.

EXERCISE 21. Writing Sentences with Words Often Confused. Write ten original sentences, each with one of the words you have just studied.

formally	*properly, according to strict rules* Should he be *formally* introduced?
formerly	*previously, in the past* The new consul was *formerly* a Senator.

hear	*to receive sounds through the ears* Did you *hear* the President's speech?
here	*this place* Come *here*, Rover.

its	[possessive of *it*] The bird stopped *its* singing.
it's	*it is* *It's* an easy problem.

lead	[present tense, pronounced lēd] *to go first* I'll *lead* the way.
led	[past tense of *lead*] Last week she *led* us to victory.

lead [pronounced led] *a heavy metal;* also *graphite* in a pencil
The *lead* on my line was too heavy for the cork.

---

loose [rhymes with *noose*] *free, not close together*
The string on the package is too *loose*.
The car swerved out of the *loose* gravel.

lose [pronounced l͞oz] *to suffer loss*
Do not *lose* our lunch money.

---

moral having to do with *good* or *right;* also *a lesson of conduct*
It is a *moral* question.
These fables all have a *moral*.

morale *mental condition, spirit*
The *morale* of the citizens is low.

---

passed [verb, past tense of *pass*]
He *passed* us in the corridor.

past [noun] the history of a person; also [adjective] former; also [preposition] farther on than
I didn't inquire about his *past*.
Her *past* experience got her the job.
I went *past* the house.

---

peace opposite of *strife*
After the long war, *peace* was welcome.

piece *a part of something*
Do you care for a *piece* of pie?

MECHANICS

EXERCISE 22. Selecting Correct Spelling Words to Complete Sentences.   Number your paper 1–20. After the proper number write the correct one of the words in parentheses.

1. We could hardly (here, hear) the speaker.
2. The class is proud of (its, it's) progress.
3. The commander praised the division's high (morale, moral).
4. It is already (passed, past) nine o'clock.
5. Facing defeat, he did not (lose, loose) courage.
6. The searchers hoped that the dog would (lead, led) them to the lost skier.
7. Mother told us to stay (hear, here).
8. The hard-driving fullback (led, lead) the team to victory.
9. I have more interest in it than I (formally, formerly) had.
10. Molly (passed, past) all her examinations.
11. We asked what the (moral, morale) of the story was.
12. I like a pencil that has soft (led, lead).
13. Everyone was (formally, formerly) dressed at the dance.
14. (It's, Its) too late to catch the early train.
15. There Benito found true (peace, piece) of mind.
16. June shouted, "I'll give you a (peace, piece) of my mind!"
17. When my shoelace came (lose, loose), I tripped and fell.
18. Mrs. Hogan just (past, passed) me in the hall.
19. This (peace, piece) of chicken is bony.
20. Clara never seems to (lose, loose) her temper.

EXERCISE 23. Writing Sentences with Words Often Confused. Write twenty original sentences correctly using the words you have just studied. Use each word at least once.

plain	*not fancy; also a flat area of land; also clear* Steven wears very *plain* clothes. The storm lashed the western *plains*. She made her point of view *plain*.
plane	*a flat surface, a level; also a tool; also an airplane* Are you taking *plane* geometry? The debate was conducted on a high *plane*. Martin made the wood smooth by using a *plane*. The *plane* arrived at the airport on time.

principal	*head of a school;* also, as an adjective, *main* or *most important* Ted had a long talk with the *principal.* Winning is not our *principal* goal.
principle	*a rule of conduct;* also *a law* or *a main fact* We live by certain *principles.* They don't know the first *principles* of physics.
quiet	*silent, still* The library should be a *quiet* place.
quite	*to a great extent or degree; completely* My little brother is *quite* clever for his age. I *quite* understand your reasons for not attending.
shone	[past tense of *shine*] The sun *shone* this morning.
shown	*revealed* Laurie has not *shown* me her scrapbook.
stationary	*in a fixed position* The chairs were not *stationary.*
stationery	*writing paper* Use white *stationery* for business letters.
than	[a conjunction, used for comparisons] Jimmy enjoys swimming more *than* golfing.
then	[an adverb or conjunction indicating *at that time* or *next*] Did you know Barbara *then*? I polished my shoes; *then* I combed my hair.
their	[possessive of *they*] The girls gave *their* opinions.

MECHANICS

there   *a place* [also used to begin a sentence (see page 387)]
I'll be *there* on time.
There aren't any cookies left.

they're   *they are*
They're at the station now.

EXERCISE 24. Selecting Correct Spelling Words to Complete Sentences. Number your paper 1–20. Write the correct one of the words in parentheses after the proper number.

1. Please be as (quiet, quite) as possible in the school corridors.
2. Mrs. Carver is the (principal, principle) of our school.
3. The last reel of the movie was not (shone, shown).
4. The deer remained (stationary, stationery) for nearly a minute.
5. Not paying debts is against his (principals, principles).
6. Dr. Palmer was (quiet, quite) pleased with the results of the experiment.
7. That night the big moon (shone, shown) brightly.
8. Did you buy a box of blue (stationary, stationery)?
9. (Than, Then) he erased the board and started over.
10. Melissa knows how to use a (plain, plane) in shop class.
11. Your (principal, principle) problem is learning to spell.
12. What did you do (than, then)?
13. A coyote was crossing the (plain, plane).
14. Do you still live (their, they're, there)?
15. Al has mastered the basic (principals, principles) of chess.
16. Do you drink your coffee (plain, plane) or with milk?
17. I can work much faster (than, then) he can.
18. All of the freshmen invited (their, there, they're) parents to the party.
19. (Their, There, They're) coming here tomorrow.
20. (Their, There) are two *s*'s in *omission* and in *possible*.

MECHANICS

EXERCISE 25. Writing Sentences Using Words Often Confused. Write twenty original sentences correctly using the words you have just studied. Use each word at least once.

threw	*hurled* Freddy *threw* three strikes.
through	*in one side and out the opposite side* The fire truck raced *through* the heavy traffic.

to	*[a preposition; also part of the infinitive form of a verb]* She told us *to clean* the windows. [infinitive] They have gone *to the store.* [prepositional phrase]
too	*[adverb] also; more than enough* I like soccer, and Ted does, *too.* He was *too* tired to think clearly.
two	*one + one* I noticed *two* packages on the sofa.

waist	*the middle part of the body* This dress is too large in the *waist.*
waste	*unused material;* also, *to squander* During the war, children collected *waste* fats. Please do not *waste* money on that.

weak	*feeble; lacking force; opposite of strong* The fawn is too *weak* to walk yet. We could not hear his *weak* voice.
week	*seven days* Carol has been gone a *week.*

weather	*conditions outdoors [no h sound]* The *weather* suddenly changed.

MECHANICS

whether	indicates alternative or doubt [pronounce the *h*] She didn't know *whether* or not to enter.

---

who's	*who is, who has* I can't imagine *who's* at the door now. *Who's* been marking in my book?
whose	[possessive of *who*] *Whose* bicycle is this?

---

your	[possessive of *you*] What is *your* idea?
you're	*you are* Joe, *you're* the best friend I have.

EXERCISE 26. Selecting Correct Spelling Words to Complete Sentences. Number your paper 1–20. Write after the proper number the correct one of the words given in parentheses in the following sentences:

1. The (weather, whether) in Mexico City was pleasant.
2. Dad (threw, through) the skates into my closet.
3. Sally is going to the concert. Are you going (to, too, two)?
4. Next (weak, week) the Bears will play the Packers.
5. We were in Boston a (weak, week).
6. The ball crashed (threw, through) the window.
7. Those children are (to, too, two) tired to study.
8. (Your, You're) trying too hard, Tommy.
9. (To, Too, Two) of the puppies are brown.
10. I don't remember (weather, whether) I signed the check.
11. I became (weak, week) in the knees when she announced my entrance.
12. (Your, You're) sleeve is torn.
13. Each majorette wore a gold sash around her (waist, waste).
14. (Whose, Who's) bat is it?
15. Tell me (weather, whether) or not we won.

16. The water seeped (threw, through) the basement window.
17. (Whose, Who's) going to be first?
18. I forgot (to, too, two) address the envelope.
19. You should not consider this a (waist, waste) of time.
20. I couldn't decide (weather, whether) or not to agree.

REVIEW EXERCISE. Selecting Correctly Spelled Words.
Number your paper 1–10. After the appropriate number, write the correctly spelled word in parentheses in the following phrases:

1. a (brief, breif) talk
2. (neither, niether) one
3. (course, coarse) cloth
4. some good (advice, advise)
5. chocolate cake for (desert, dessert)
6. many (heros, heroes)
7. on the (cieling, ceiling)
8. two (copies, copys)
9. driving (passed, past) the theater
10. (weather, whether) or not to stay

50 Spelling Demons

Here are fifty simple words that cause many people trouble. It is wise to be aware of them. You will learn them most easily if you study them five at a time.

ache	cough	guess	once	tired
again	could	half	ready	tonight
always	country	hour	said	trouble
answer	doctor	instead	says	wear
blue	does	knew	shoes	where
built	don't	know	since	which
busy	early	laid	sugar	whole
buy	easy	meant	sure	women
can't	every	minute	tear	won't
color	friend	often	though	write

300 Spelling Words

The list that follows contains words that you should learn this year if you do not already know them. They are grouped by tens so that you may conveniently study them ten at a time.

absence
absolutely
acceptance
accidentally
accommodate
accompany
accomplish
accurate
accustomed
achievement

acquaintance
actually
administration
affectionate
agriculture
amateur
ambassador
analysis
analyze
anticipate

apology
apparent
appearance
approach
approval
arguing
argument
assurance
attendance
authority

available
basically
beginning
believe
benefit

benefited
boundary
Britain
calendar
campaign

capital
category
certificate
characteristic
chief
circuit
circumstance
civilization
column
commissioner

committees
comparison
competent
competition
conceivable
conception
confidential
conscience
conscious
consistency

constitution
continuous
control
cooperate
corporation
correspondence
criticism
criticize
cylinder
debtor

decision
definite
definition
deny
description
despise
diameter
disappearance
disappointment
discipline

disgusted
distinction
distinguished
dominant
duplicate
economic
efficiency
eighth
elaborate
eligible

embarrass
emergency
employee
encouraging
environment
equipped
essential
evidently
exaggerate
exceedingly

excellent
excessive
excitable
exercise
existence

expense
extraordinary
fascinating
fatal
favorably

fictitious
financier
flourish
fraternity
frequent
further
glimpse
glorious
grabbed
gracious

graduating
grammar
gross
gymnasium
happiness
hasten
heavily
hindrance
humorous
hungrily

hypocrisy
hypocrite
icy
ignorance
imagination
immediately
immense
incidentally
indicate
indispensable

inevitable
innocence
inquiry
insurance
intelligence
interfere
interpretation
interrupt
investigation
judgment

knowledge
leisure
lengthen
lieutenant
likelihood
liveliness
loneliness
magazine
maneuver
marriage

marvelous
mechanical
medieval
merchandise
minimum
mortgage
multitude
muscle
mutual
narrative

naturally
necessary
negligible
niece
noticeable

obligation
obstacle
occasionally
occurrence
offense

official
omit
operations
opportunity
oppose
optimism
orchestra
organization
originally
paid

paradise
parallel
particularly
peasant
peculiar
percentage
performance
personal
personality
perspiration

persuade
petition
philosopher
picnic
planning
pleasant
policies
politician
possess
possibility

MECHANICS

practically	renewal	sponsor
precede	repetition	straighten
precisely	representative	substantial
preferred	requirement	substitute
prejudice	residence	subtle
preparation	resistance	succeed
pressure	responsibility	successful
primitive	restaurant	sufficient
privilege	rhythm	summary
probably	ridiculous	superior
procedure	sacrifice	suppress
proceed	satire	surprise
professor	satisfied	survey
proportion	scarcely	suspense
psychology	scheme	suspicion
publicity	scholarship	temperament
pursuit	scissors	tendency
qualities	senate	thorough
quantities	sensibility	transferring
readily	separate	tremendous
reasonably	sergeant	truly
receipt	several	unanimous
recognize	shepherd	unfortunately
recommendation	sheriff	unnecessary
referring	similar	urgent
regretting	skis	useful
reign	solemn	using
relieve	sophomore	vacancies
remembrance	source	vacuum
removal	specific	varies

PART FOUR

RESOURCES FOR WRITING AND STUDYING

CHAPTER 28

The Library

LOCATION AND
ARRANGEMENT OF FACILITIES

Your school or community library is a center of media resources. It is a storehouse of knowledge and enjoyment. All you need do to use it and enjoy it is make yourself familiar with its resources and tools.

ARRANGEMENT OF BOOKS

Library books are arranged in two ways, depending on whether the book is fiction or nonfiction. These two kinds of books are kept in different parts of the library.

Fiction

28a. Books of fiction are arranged in alphabetical order according to the author's last name.

Books of fiction are placed together in one section and are arranged in alphabetical order according to the last name of the author. If there are several books by the same author, these are further arranged alphabetically by the first word of the title (not counting *A, An,* or *The*).

For example, suppose you want to find Robert Louis Stevenson's *The Master of Ballantrae.* Having located the fiction section, you move to the *S*'s, to find authors whose last names begin with *S*. You may see books by Sayers, Shippen, and Stevens before you come to Stevenson. You may then find books by Dorothy Stevenson and Janet Stevenson before you come to Robert Louis Stevenson. When you find his name, you will see titles such as *The Black Arrow* and *Kidnapped* before you find *The Master of Ballantrae; Treasure Island* may follow your book.

☞ **NOTE** Authors' names that begin with *Mc* are alphabetized as though the name were spelled *Mac*; *St.* is alphabetized as though spelled out (*Saint*).

Nonfiction

28b. Nonfiction books are arranged according to the Dewey decimal system.

Many school libraries use the Dewey decimal system. This system was developed by Melvil Dewey, an American librarian.[1] Under this system, all nonfiction books are numbered and grouped according to ten subject classes. The classifications with the numbers that stand for them are

[1] The Library of Congress system of cataloging, used in many public libraries and high-school libraries, classifies all books, both fiction and nonfiction. Each general subject category (Philosophy, Science, etc.) is assigned a code letter. For example, the letter *H* at the beginning of a call number designates Social Science. In addition, whole categories are often subdivided by adding a second code letter to the first. Thus letter *P* (which designates Literature) may be followed by the letter *S* to specify American literature. Call numbers include the letter codes, followed by a series of numbers that identify specific books within a category. For example, the book *Responses: Prose Pieces 1953–1976*, by Richard Wilbur, an American author, has the Library of Congress call number PS 3545. A complete schedule of Library of Congress categories and their letter codes is usually available in the reference section of any library using this system.

000–099 General Works (encyclopedias, periodicals, book lists, books about the library). Since many of these are reference books, some libraries use the letter *R* before the number.

100–199 Philosophy (psychology, conduct, personality)

200–299 Religion (bibles, theology, mythology)

300–399 Social Sciences (communication, economics, education, etiquette, folklore, government, law)

400–499 Philology or Language (grammars, dictionaries, foreign languages)

500–599 Science (animals, astronomy, biology, botany, chemistry, geology, general science, mathematics, physics)

600–699 Technology (agriculture, aviation, business management, engineering, health, home economics, medical science, pollution control)

700–799 The Arts (motion pictures, music, painting, photography, sculpture, recreation, sports)

800–899 Literature (poetry, drama, essays, criticism, history of literature)

900–999 History (archaeology, geography, travel)

Biographical works dealing with the lives of several persons (collective biography) are marked 920. However, individual biographies (the life of one person) are generally kept in a separate section. In most libraries they are marked **B,** but in some they are given the number 92. Under the **B** (or the 92) comes the initial of the last name of the subject of the biography. A biography of Franklin D. Roosevelt would be marked in this way:

B (or **92**)
R (or **Roosevelt**)

All the books about Roosevelt are arranged alphabetically by author's last name.

Nonfiction books other than individual biographies are marked on the spine of the book with their proper number. Each of the main subject groups is divided into ten subgroups, and each of the subgroups is further divided. Still more specific subdivisions are made by using decimals. For example, if you are looking for a play by Shakespeare, the general subject is Literature, which is numbered 800–899. The exact number for English drama is 822, and the number for Shakespeare is 822.3. Though at first glance this may appear quite complicated, in practice it makes it possible for you as a library user to find any book you are looking for—once you know its number.

This does not mean that you have to memorize the Dewey decimal system; it simply means that you should understand how it works.

THE CARD CATALOG

Every nonfiction book in the library has a Dewey decimal system number of its own. The number appears on any one of several cards arranged in a cabinet called the *card catalog*. This number is called the *call number.*

28c. **Every nonfiction book has a call number that appears on its catalog card.**

The call number appears in the upper left-hand corner of the catalog card. For example, a nonfiction travel book on Germany may have the number 941.3. Fiction books may be marked **F** or may have no number at all.

28d. **The card catalog lists books by title, author, and subject.**

For each book in the library's collection, the card catalog contains a *title card,* an *author card,* and, if the book is nonfiction, a *subject card.* The cards are filed in alphabetical order in the catalog drawers. The drawers are labeled like the volumes of an encyclopedia, for example **A—AMY, AN—AZ, B—BIO, BIP—BUL,** and so on.

The Title Card

The simplest way to find a particular book is to look for the title card. At the top of the title card is the title of the book.

Its position in the alphabetical order is determined by the first word of the title, unless the first word is *A*, *An*, or *The*, in which case the book will be listed under the second word of the title. For example, *The Last of the Mohicans* will be listed under **L**.

The Author Card

On the author card, the author's name appears at the top with the title of the book appearing directly below it. For each title by the same author, there will be a separate author card. The author cards will be arranged according to the alphabetical order of the titles. For example, the author card for *The Master of Ballantrae* will precede the card for *Treasure Island,* also by Stevenson, in the card catalog; "Stevenson, Robert Louis" will be printed at the top of each card.

The Subject Card

Nonfiction books are also cataloged according to the subject with which they deal. If, for example, you are an amateur photographer and want to learn how prints are developed, you look for cards under "Photography." Under this large subject classification there may be further divisions, such as "Photography—Print Developing."

Often books may be listed under more than one subject heading. A book about baseball may be listed under "Sports," "Athletics," "Baseball," and even "Games."

"See" and "See Also" Cards

A "see" or "see also" card refers you to another section of the catalog; it is a cross-reference card. Suppose you want to find some books by Mark Twain. You might look for the author card under **T**. Instead of finding cards for his books there, you possibly would find under "Twain, Mark" a card saying, "See Clemens, Samuel Langhorne" (Twain's real name). The "see" card, then, directs you to a different part of the catalog, in this case the **C** file.

"See also" cards refer you to other subjects closely related to the one in which you are interested. If you are looking under "Newspapers," you may find a card saying "See also Journalism." Looking up "Journalism," you will find more books on your subject.

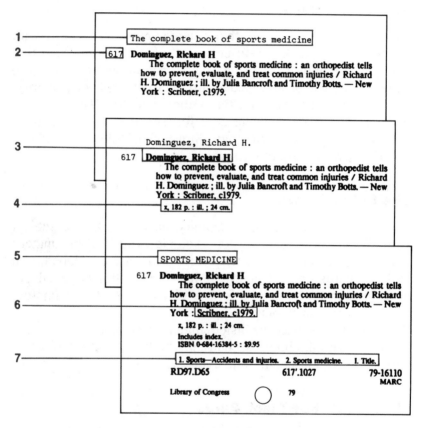

Top to bottom: title, author, and subject cards

The title, author, and subject cards above contain the following information, as indicated by the keyed numbers:

1. Title heading
2. Call Number
3. Author

4. Physical description of the book
5. Subject heading
6. Publisher and date of publication

7. Other headings under which the book is listed (This book can be listed under sports accidents and injuries.)

In addition to the title, author, and subject, the catalog card also tells you the publisher of the book, the place and date of publication, the number of pages, and whether the book has illustrations or maps; and occasionally it gives a brief statement about the contents of the book.

SUMMARY OF INFORMATION IN THE CARD CATALOG

1. The **call number,** showing the location of the book on the library shelves
2. The **author,** full name, date of birth, and—if no longer alive—date of death (Many libraries omit the dates.)
3. The **title**
4. The **subject**
5. **Cross references** to other books or subjects, where appropriate
6. **Publisher,** place and date of publication, number of pages, illustrations

EXERCISE 1. Finding Information Using the Card Catalog. Number your paper 1–10. Using the card catalog in your library, find the following information:

A. Find the author cards for the following writers and list one book for each. If there is no card, put "not in our library" after the proper number.
   1. Robert Frost
   2. James Thurber

B. Look up these title cards to see if these books are in your library. If they are, list the author and biographical dates; if not, write "not in our library."
   3. *Anne Frank: The Diary of a Young Girl*
   4. *Shane*

C. Find a book in your library on each of these subjects. List
   one title and author for each.
   5. Nuclear energy
   6. Exploration of space

D. List the title, author, call number, and date of publication
   for the following books:
   7. A book on careers
   8. A book of poetry

E. List the title and author of a book *about* the following people:
   9. John F. Kennedy
   10. Golda Meir

REFERENCE TOOLS

Your library may have a special reference room where reference
books are kept. In any case, all reference books will be kept in
one section of the library. Some may be on closed shelves, and
you must ask the librarian for them. Others are usually on open
shelves or on tables. Reference books are in constant demand.
They must be readily available at all times. For this reason they
must be used only in the library.

When you use any book as a study or reference tool, you
will save time by familiarizing yourself with the parts of that
book. Knowing the following parts of a book will enable you to
use the book effectively.

1. The table of contents. A list at the beginning of the book
that includes chapter titles and subdivisions and the page number where each begins.

2. Index. An alphabetical list at the end of the book that
includes the specific topics treated in the book and the exact
page or pages where the topic is treated.

3. Glossary. An alphabetical list of technical and difficult
words and terms used in the book with definitions and explanations for each.

Every library has several main types of reference books:

(1) dictionaries, (2) encyclopedias, (3) biographical dictionaries, (4) atlases, (5) almanacs, (6) books on specific subjects such as literature, authors, etc., and (7) reference guides showing where information may be found.

The *Readers' Guide*

28e. To find a magazine article, use the *Readers' Guide*.

The *Readers' Guide to Periodical Literature* may be regarded as the card catalog for magazines. It indexes all the articles, poems, and stories in more than a hundred magazines; the magazines are listed in the front of each volume.

The *Readers' Guide* appears in a paperback edition monthly six months a year and semimonthly six months. Each issue lists articles published two to four weeks previously. From time to time these issues are combined into single volumes covering periods of several months. Clothbound cumulations appear at one-year intervals. Notice the following sample entries:

SOLOTAROFF, Theodore — author entry
Rukeyser: poet of plenitude. Nation 230:277-8
Mr 8 '80

SOLOVIOFF, Nicholas — title of article
Monumental relics of abandoned technology
[reproductions of paintings] Fortune 101:88-
95 Ja 28 '80

SOLOWEY, E. M.
Land reclamation in the Arava: Kibbutz — date of magazine
Ketura. il BioScience 30:112-14 F '80

SOLUBILITY
How electric fields modify alkane solubility in — author's name
lipid bilayers. S. H. White. bibl f il Science
207:1075-7 Mr 7 '80

SOLVENTS — subject entry
Printmaking: solvents. J. A. Waller and L.
Whitehead. Am Craft 40:81 F/Mr '80

SOLZHENITSYN, Aleksandr Isaevich
Nobeliana. [excerpt from The oak and the calf: — volume number
tr by H. Willetts] il por New Repub 182:23-5
Mr 22 '80
Solzhenitsyn on Communism [tr by A. Klimoff] — magazine
por Time 115:48-9 F 18 '80
Writer underground [excerpt from The oak and — page reference
the calf; tr by H. Willetts] N Y Times Bk R
85:3+ F 10 '80

SOMALIA
Defenses
See also
United States—Navy—Forces in Somalia — division of
main subject
Foreign relations
Ethiopia
See Ethiopia—Foreign relations—Somalia

As you can see from the sample entries on the previous page, magazine articles are listed by subjects (SOLVENTS) and by authors (SOLOWEY, E. M.). Except for stories, magazine articles are not listed by title in the *Readers' Guide*. The subject and author entries appear in a single alphabetical list; the subject SOLVENTS is followed by the author entry SOLZHENITSYN, Aleksandr. The first word of the subject entry and the author's last name in the author entry are printed in capital letters. Each entry lists the title of the article, the name of the magazine, and the publication date. The subject entry also lists the author of the article. The *Readers' Guide* employs in its entries a system of abbreviations; a key to these abbreviations appears in the front of the *Readers' Guide*. Most names of magazines are also abbreviated (*Bsns W* for *Business Week*); these are noted in the list of magazines that also appears at the front.

You will observe that "see" and "see also" references are also given in the *Readers' Guide*—for example, under SOMALIA, "*See also* U.S. Navy in Somalia."

Usually you will find posted near the *Readers' Guide* a list of the magazines to which your library subscribes and a notation on which back issues are available. If there is no list, the librarian can supply the information.

EXERCISE 2. Interpreting Abbreviations in the *Readers' Guide*. Referring to the "Key to Abbreviations" and to the "List of Periodicals Indexed" at the front of the *Readers' Guide,* give the meaning of each of the following:

1. Sci N L	5. v	9. +
2. cond	6. Je	10. por
3. 54:320–56	7. Sch & Soc	
4. Atlan	8. abr	

EXERCISE 3. Finding Articles in the Readers' Guide. Find in the *Readers' Guide* one article listed under each of the following subjects. For each article, give the title, author (if given), magazine, date, and page numbers.

EXAMPLE   1. National parks
          (Looking in the *Readers' Guide*, you might find
          the following entry: A guide to national parks. S.
          Birnbaum. il Good Housekeep 198:192+ Je '84)
     1. *"A Guide to National Parks," by S. Birnbaum,
        illustrated. Good Housekeeping, Volume 198,
        page 192 and continued on later pages, June 1984*

1. Lasers   4. Astrology
2. Television   5. Boats
3. Education

The Vertical File

28f. To find a pamphlet, use the vertical file.

Much valuable information is published in pamphlet form. The
Division of Public Documents of the U.S. Government Printing
Office alone publishes hundreds of pamphlets each year; many
industrial concerns and educational organizations also issue
pamphlets regularly. Your librarian files these materials in a
vertical file. Sometimes newspaper clippings of special interest
will also be included. Each pamphlet or clipping is placed in a
folder and filed away in a cabinet. For up-to-the-minute material,
you will find the vertical file very useful.

Microfilm and Microfiche

28g. Use microfilm and microfiche to find information.

To save space, many libraries store some publications (newspapers, magazines, and books) or documents on microfilm or
microfiche. *Microfilm* is a roll or reel of film containing photographically reduced publications. You view the film through a
projector that enlarges each microscopic image to a size suitable
for reading. *Microfiche* is a sheet of film, rather than a roll or
reel, containing photographically reduced publications. To read

the microfiche, you use a machine that, like the microfilm projector, enlarges the microscopic images to a readable size. The librarian can help you to use microfilm or microfiche.

Computers

28h. Use computers to find information.

Many libraries are replacing their present book lists, catalogs, and periodical lists with a computerized system. When using a computerized system, you type the information you need into the computer—for example, *subject: automobile design*. Then the computer searches for the titles and locations of the publications on that subject and prints a list. Depending on the type of computer, you might have to read the list from the screen, or you might be able to get a printout, or printed copy, of the list of books or periodicals. The librarian can help you to use the computers.

Dictionaries of Synonyms

A dictionary of synonyms can be of great help to you in your writing. The most famous of these is *Roget's Thesaurus of English Words & Phrases*. *Thesaurus* means "treasury," in this instance a treasury of words. If, for example, you have over used the adjective "good" in the first draft of a composition, you can find in the *Thesaurus* over a hundred synonyms for "good," as well as many antonyms and cross-references to related words. However, be careful to select the word that expresses the meaning that you wish to convey. Check the word's meaning in the dictionary.

There is now an edition called *Roget's Thesaurus in Dictionary Form*. All entries are arranged in alphabetical order, with synonyms grouped according to meaning. If you know how to use the dictionary, you can use this edition of the *Thesaurus*.

Similar to the *Thesaurus* is *Webster's New Dictionary of Synonyms*. Either book will help you to avoid needless repetition and, incidentally, to enlarge your vocabulary.

Encyclopedias

Encyclopedias are made up of a collection of articles, often illustrated, alphabetically arranged by subject. It is usually the first source you use in obtaining information on a subject. If you are writing a long paper or giving a report, you will turn to the encyclopedia for general information and an overall view of your subject before proceeding to books and periodicals.

To find information on a particular subject in the encyclopedia, you may use first the guide letters on the spine of each volume and then the guide words at the top of the pages. It is better though to look in the index, usually the last volume of the set. Here you may find that your subject is discussed in several different articles that appear in different volumes.

You may find (by looking on the title page) that the encyclopedias in your library were published several years ago. For up-to-date information, you should check the annual or yearbook that many encyclopedia companies publish every year. These yearbooks will give the most recent events and latest developments in your subject field.

The following well-known encyclopedias are usually available in most libraries.

Collier's Encyclopedia   *Encyclopaedia Britannica*
Compton's Encyclopedia   *World Book Encyclopedia*
Encyclopedia Americana

Compton's Encyclopedia and *World Book Encyclopedia* are written for younger readers.

Shorter encyclopedias of one or two volumes include *The New Columbia Encyclopedia, The Random House Encyclopedia,* and the *Lincoln Library of Essential Information.*

Biographical Reference Books

Although encyclopedias include biographical articles, there are several special books devoted to accounts of the lives of famous people. Several of these special books will be helpful to you when you search for biographical data for class reports.

Current Biography (currently prominent people)
Dictionary of American Biography (famous deceased Americans)
Dictionary of National Biography (distinguished deceased English persons)
Who's Who (famous living international figures)
Who's Who in America (distinguished living Americans)

A valuable series of reference works by Stanley Kunitz is composed of biographies of authors. Unlike the two *Who's Who* books, Kunitz's works give much "human-interest" information and also include photographs.

Stanley J. Kunitz and Howard Haycraft:
    British Authors of the Nineteenth Century
    American Authors 1600–1900
    Twentieth Century Authors
Stanley J. Kunitz and Vineta Colby:
    European Authors 1000–1900

Information about world authors (1950–1975) is contained in *World Authors.*

Interesting profiles of modern writers appear in *Contemporary Authors* and *Contemporary Authors: First Revision.*

Other biographical reference books are *Webster's Biographical Dictionary, World Biography, American Men of Science, American Men and Women of Science,* and *American Women Writers.*

Atlases

An atlas is much more than just a book of maps. It contains a vast amount of information about the cities and countries of the world—including facts about population, resources, industries, natural wonders, climate, exports and imports, history. Especially useful are the following atlases:

    National Geographic Atlas of the World
    Goode's World Atlas
    Hammond Ambassador World Atlas
    The New York Times Atlas of the World

Almanacs

Almanacs are full of information on current events. They also contain much of historical interest: facts, dates, statistics, sports records, etc. The two most useful almanacs are *The World Almanac and Book of Facts* and the *Information Please Almanac*. Both are published annually. Remember to use the index to find information quickly; it is found in the front of *The World Almanac* and in the back of the *Information Please Almanac*.

Reference Books About Literature

There are several collections of quotations, the most famous of which is Bartlett's *Familiar Quotations*. Bartlett's book is useful when you want to know the following information:

1. The author of a quotation
2. The literary work in which the quotation appeared
3. The complete quotation when you know only a part
4. A few famous lines by any author
5. Quotations by various authors on a particular subject

Bartlett's is arranged chronologically by author. Under each author's name, the quotations are further arranged chronologically according to the date on which they were said or written. Two separate indexes are included in the back of the book. One lists the authors alphabetically; the other is an alphabetical listing of subjects or key words from the quotations. You can use the author index to find the number of the page that contains quotations from a particular author's works. If you know the quotation or a part of it, you can use the index to find its author or the full quotation. Suppose, for instance, that you want to find out who wrote

> Ring out the thousand wars of old,
> Ring in the thousand years of peace.

If you look under either *ring* or *peace,* both key words in the quotation, you will find the page given where the quotation appears, along with references to other quotations containing the same key words.

In addition to Bartlett's, Stevenson's *Home Book of Quotations* is especially useful if you want a quotation on a certain subject. The quotations in Stevenson's book are arranged alphabetically by subject. There are also many cross-references. If, for example, you are looking under *Freedom,* you will find several entries there and also a note, *see also Liberty,* with five subheads.

Other good indexes of quotations include the following ones:

Flesch's *New Book of Unusual Quotations*
Mencken's *A New Dictionary of Quotations*
Oxford Dictionary of Quotations

A book of quotations that gives the quotations in their contexts is *McGill's Quotations in Context.*

Granger's *Index to Poetry* tells you *where* to find a poem or popular prose passage. Granger's book lists poems and prose passages according to subject, title (or first line), and author. You can use it to learn where you can find a certain literary work, who wrote a certain work, and what poems and passages have been written on a particular subject. You will not find the poem or passage itself in Granger's *Index.*

If you are looking for a poem, however, you will probably find it in Stevenson's *Home Book of Verse* or *Home Book of Modern Verse.* These large collections contain many well-known poems, classified under general headings such as "Love Poems" or "Familiar Verse." Three additional excellent poetry anthologies are Van Doren's *An Anthology of World Poetry* (arranged by countries) and Untermeyer's *Modern American Poetry* and *Modern British Poetry* (arranged in chronological order; also available in a single volume). All five books have indexes by title, author, and first line.

There are many other useful reference books on literature. They include

Oxford Companion to American Literature
Cambridge History of American Literature (3 volumes)
Burke & Howe's *American Authors and Books*
Oxford Companion to English Literature
Cambridge History of English Literature (15 volumes)

Harper's Dictionary of Classical Literature
Brewer's Dictionary of Phrase and Fable
Benét's *Reader's Encyclopedia*
Book Review Digest
Short Story Index
Essay & General Literature Index (7 volumes)
Oxford Companion to the Theatre
Logasa's *Index to One-Act Plays*
Play Index

Other Special Reference Books

You might find the following reference books of interest, according to the subject that you are researching.

Dictionary of American History (companion to the *Dictionary of American Biography*)
Encyclopedia of American Facts and Dates
Encyclopedia of the Social Sciences
Encyclopedia of Sports
Encyclopedia of Religion
The International Cyclopedia of Music and Musicians, ed. Oscar Thompson
Grove's *Dictionary of Music and Musicians*
McGraw-Hill *Encyclopedia of Science and Technology*
Murphy's How and Where to Look It Up
Webster's New Geographical Dictionary (companion to *Webster's Biographical Dictionary*)

EXERCISE 4. Selecting Encyclopedias, Atlases, or Almanacs. Go to the library and locate the encyclopedias, atlases, and almanacs. After you have looked up each of the following items, write after the appropriate number on your paper the name of the reference work you used. Do not use the same book twice.

1. A list of national parks
2. A portrait of Margaret Bourke-White, and reproductions of her photographs

3. A chart of Archimedes' principle of specific gravity
4. A list of points of interest in Kansas
5. Types of cosmetic makeup used for motion pictures
6. The origin and development of polo
7. A discussion and illustrations of three kinds of mosquitoes
8. Last year's major league baseball statistics
9. The population of Vermont
10. A map of Sweden

EXERCISE 5. Selecting Reference Books. Number your paper 1–10. After the corresponding number, write the title of the reference book that would be best to use for researching that item. Do not include dictionaries or encyclopedias.

1. A picture and biography of Jim Rice, a baseball player
2. The names of the five states that border Nevada
3. A list of quotations about science and beauty
4. A quotation from the works of Emily Dickinson
5. A biography of the American author Sinclair Lewis
6. A book listing synonyms for *creative*
7. A brief list of facts about Lorraine Hansberry, the American playwright.
8. A list of facts about Martha Graham, the American dancer
9. The complete poem "Song of the Open Road"
10. A book containing the limerick by Edward Lear beginning "There was an Old Man in a boat"

EXERCISE 6. Finding Information in Reference Books. Referring to the proper reference book, answer the following questions. Give your sources.

1. What is the Pulitzer Prize? Name the most recent Pulitzer Prize-winning (a) novelist, (b) poet, (c) playwright. Cite the work for which each won the award.
2. What is the Nobel Prize? Who was the first American to win the Nobel Prize for literature? What other Americans have won it?

3. Identify each of the following and give the most recent winner of each: Walker Cup, Stanley Cup, Davis Cup.
4. Who won the Academy Awards for best actor and best actress last year?
5. What television show won the Emmy award for best comedy series last year?

EXERCISE 7. Using Books of Quotations.   Find the author of the following quotations. Remember to look under a key word. A short quotation like "leave no stone unturned" (Euripides), for example, may be cited under *leave, stone,* and *unturned.*

1. I'll tell the world.
2. As good as gold.
3. What fools these mortals be!
4. Beauty is in the eye of the beholder.
5. All that glisters is not gold.
6. After great pain, a formal feeling comes.
7. Uneasy lies the head that wears a crown.
8. No one can make you feel inferior without your consent.
9. To thine own self be true.
10. To strive, to seek, to find, and not to yield.
11. The fault . . . is not in our stars, but in ourselves . . . .
12. For there is no friend like a sister in calm or stormy weather.
13. A little learning is a dangerous thing.
14. With malice toward none, with charity for all.
15. The only thing we have to fear is fear itself.

CHAPTER 29

The Dictionary

ARRANGEMENT AND CONTENT OF DICTIONARIES

The most frequently used reference book is the dictionary. There are in fact many different kinds of dictionaries, each with its special uses. This chapter will show you the differences between kinds of dictionaries and suggest in a general way what you may expect to find in each of them.

KINDS OF DICTIONARIES

There are so many special kinds of dictionaries. Here we will consider and give examples from the three kinds of dictionaries that you will be making most use of right now: the unabridged dictionary, the abridged or "college-size" dictionary, and the school dictionary.

The Unabridged Dictionary

An unabridged dictionary of the English language lists most of the English words in daily use. Because new words come into the language every day, no dictionary can be completely up-to-date. The word "unabridged" merely means that a dictionary is not a shorter version of some larger dictionary.

There are several unabridged dictionaries in print. Undoubtedly the best known is *Webster's New International Dictionary,* which has been kept up-to-date through succeeding editions. The word *international* means that this dictionary contains information about words as they are used throughout the English-speaking world. It therefore has some entries and spellings that are mainly used in Scotland, Australia, Canada, and so on. It is, however, mainly an American dictionary, and the great majority of its entries deal with meanings, pronunciations, and usages that are current in the United States.

Following are three entries for the word *funnel,* reproduced from *Webster's Third New International Dictionary.*

funnel 1a

¹fun·nel \'fən²l\ *n* -s *often attrib* [ME *fonel, funel,* fr. OProv *fonilh,* fr. ML *fundibulum,* short for L *infundibulum,* fr. *infundere* to pour in, fr. *in* + *fundere* to pour — more at IN, FOUND] **1 a :** a utensil that has typically the shape of a hollow cone with a tube extending from the point, is designed to catch and direct a downward flow of liquid or some other substance, and is sometimes fitted or combined with a strainer or filter — see SEPARATORY FUNNEL **b :** something shaped like a funnel (as a conical part, passage, or hole); *specif* **:** the swimming funnel of a cephalopod **c :** one that serves as a constricted channel or central agent or organization through which something passes or is transmitted **2 :** a stack or flue for the escape of smoke or for ventilation; *specif* **:** the stack of a ship **3 :** a cylindrical band of metal; *esp* **:** one around the top of an upper mast around which the rigging fits **4 :** RUNNING GATE **5 :** FUNNEL CLOUD **6 :** a black usu. cylindrical metal hood attached to a spotlight to prevent the spill of light outside the illuminated area of a stage

²funnel \"\ *vb* **funneled** *also* **funnelled; funneled** *also* **funnelled; funneling** *also* **funnelling; funnels** *vi* **1 :** to have or take the shape of a funnel **:** NARROW, WIDEN (a shallow, rounded valley bottom ∼s into a miniature gorge with steep bluffs —*Jour. of Geol.*) **2 :** to move to or from a focal point or into a central channel (the gang . . . ∼ed onto the end of the jetty off the slope —R.O.Bowen) (orders were ∼ing out to the ships from the flagship —Alexander Griffin) **3 :** to pass through or as if through a funnel; *specif* **:** to move through a constricted passage or central medium (the fierce winds which ∼ed up the valley center —John Steinbeck) (through the great port ∼s much of the overseas commerce —*Newsweek*) (thousands of pictures . . . ∼ed back to the press and public through the public-relations division —Robert Moora) ∼ *vt* **1 :** to cause to funnel: **a :** to form into the shape of a funnel (∼s his hands and shouts through them) **b :** to cause to move to or from a focal point or into a central channel (traffic is ∼ed into consolidation stations . . . and fanned out to destinations —*Distribution Age*) (airlift's traffic pattern ∼s planes from widely separated . . . bases into two 20-mile-wide corridors —*Nat'l Geographic*) **c :** to direct to a single recipient or distribute from a single source (impurities ∼ed into the air by automobiles, backyard bonfires, and factory chimneys —*N.Y. Times*) (∼ the kerosine into the tank) **d :** to send or direct through a narrow passage or central medium (pass . . . through which were ∼ed troops and supplies —F.T.Chapman) (cupped her hands over the lens of the flashlight, ∼ing the light through a small opening —E.S. Gardner) (if a bank ∼s its news through a public-relations firm —*Banking*) **2 :** to serve as a means for the transmission or direction of (accused the press of ∼ing secret military information to Soviet Russia —*Newsweek*) (∼ . . . high-caliber young people to the agency business —*Printers' Ink*)

³fun·nel \'fün²l, 'fan-\ *n* -s [origin unknown] *dial Eng* **:** HINNY

Notice the many examples of actual uses included in the entry in the unabridged dictionary. These illustrative quotations are set off in angle brackets (‹ ›).

The College Dictionary

A "college-size" dictionary is an abridged dictionary: it is shorter and less detailed than an unabridged dictionary. It may contain from 125,000 to 160,000 words, but less is likely to be said about each of these words than in an unabridged dictionary. One college dictionary differs from another in its methods of presenting information.

The sample column below reproduces a number of entries from a college dictionary. Notice how the treatment of the word *funnel* differs from that in the sample from the unabridged dictionary on page 731.

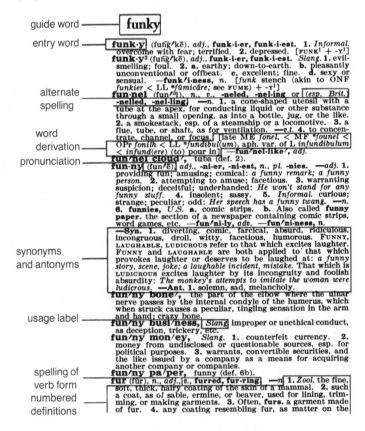

guide word — **funky**

entry word — **funk·y** (fuṅg′kē), *adj.*, **funk·i·er, funk·i·est. 1.** *Informal.* overcome with fear; terrified. **2.** depressed. [FUNK¹ + -Y¹]
funk·y² (fuṅg′kē), *adj.*, **funk·i·er, funk·i·est.** *Slang.* **1.** evil-smelling; foul. **2. a.** earthy; down-to-earth. **b.** pleasantly unconventional or offbeat. **c.** excellent; fine. **d.** sexy or sensual. **—funk′i·ness,** *n.* [funk stench (akin to ONF *funkier* < LL *fūmicāre*; see FUME) + -Y¹]

alternate spelling — **fun·nel** (fun′ⁿl), *n., v.,* **-neled, -nel·ing** or (*esp. Brit.*) **-nelled, -nel·ling** **—***n.* **1.** a cone-shaped utensil with a tube at the apex, for conducting liquid or other substance through a small opening, as into a bottle, jug, or the like. **2.** a smokestack, esp. of a steamship or a locomotive. **3.** a flue, tube, or shaft, as for ventilation. **—***v.t.* **4.** to concentrate, channel, or focus.

word derivation — [late ME *fonel,* < MF *founel* < OPr *fonilh* < LL *fundibul(um),* aph. var. of L *infundibulum* < *infund(ere)* (to) pour in] **—fun′nel·like′,** *adj.*

pronunciation — **fun′nel cloud′,** tuba (def. 2).

fun·ny (fun′ē), *adj.,* **-ni·er, -ni·est,** *n., pl.* **-nies. —***adj.* **1.** providing fun; amusing; comical: *a funny remark; a funny person.* **2.** attempting to amuse; facetious. **3.** warranting suspicion; deceitful; underhanded: *He won't stand for any funny stuff.* **4.** insolent; sassy. **5.** *Informal.* curious; strange; peculiar; odd: *Her speech has a funny twang.* **—***n.* **6. funnies,** *U.S.* comic strips. **b.** Also called **funny paper.** the section of a newspaper containing comic strips, word games, etc. **—fun′ni·ly,** *adv.* **—fun′ni·ness,** *n.*

synonyms and antonyms — **—Syn. 1.** diverting, comic, farcical, absurd, ridiculous, incongruous, droll, witty, facetious, humorous. FUNNY, LAUGHABLE, LUDICROUS refer to that which excites laughter. FUNNY and LAUGHABLE are both applied to´that which provokes laughter or deserves to be laughed at: *a funny story, scene, joke; a laughable incident, mistake.* That which is LUDICROUS excites laughter by its incongruity and foolish absurdity: *The monkey's attempts to imitate the woman were ludicrous.* **—Ant. 1.** solemn, sad, melancholy.

fun′ny bone′, the part of the elbow where the ulnar nerve passes by the internal condyle of the humerus, which when struck causes a peculiar, tingling sensation in the arm and hand; crazy bone.

usage label — **fun′ny busi′ness,** *Slang* improper or unethical conduct, as deception, trickery, etc.

fun′ny mon′ey, *Slang.* **1.** counterfeit currency. **2.** money from undisclosed or questionable sources, esp. for political purposes. **3.** warrants, convertible securities, and the like issued by a company as a means for acquiring another company or companies.

spelling of — **fun′ny pa′per,** funny (def. 6b).

verb form — **fur** (fûr), *n., adj., v.,* **furred, fur·ring** **—***n.* **1.** *Zool.* the fine,

numbered definitions — soft, thick, hairy coating of the skin of a mammal. **2.** such a coat, as of sable, ermine, or beaver, used for lining, trimming, or making garments. **3.** Often, **furs.** a garment made of fur. **4.** any coating resembling fur, as matter on the

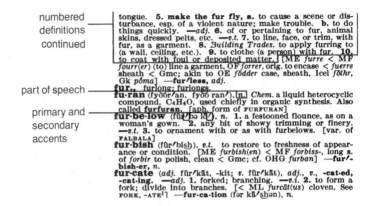

numbered definitions continued — tongue. **5. make the fur fly, a.** to cause a scene or disturbance, esp. of a violent nature; make trouble. **b.** to do things quickly. —*adj.* **6.** of or pertaining to fur, animal skins, dressed pelts, etc. —*v.t.* **7.** to line, face, or trim, with fur, as a garment. **8.** *Building Trades.* to apply furring to (a wall, ceiling, etc.). **9.** to clothe (a person) with fur. **10.** to coat with foul or deposited matter. [ME *furre* < MF *fourr(er)* (to) line a garment, OF *forrer,* orig. to encase < *fuerre* sheath < Gmc; akin to OE *fōdder* case, sheath, Icel *fōthr,* Gk *pōma*] —**fur′less,** *adj.*

part of speech — **fur., furlong; furlongs.**

primary and secondary accents — **fu·ran** (fyŏŏr′an, fyŏŏ ran′), *n.* *Chem.* a liquid heterocyclic compound, C₄H₄O, used chiefly in organic synthesis. Also called **furfuran.** [aph. form of FURFURAN]

fur·be·low (fûr′bə lō′), *n.* **1.** a festooned flounce, as on a woman's gown. **2.** any bit of showy trimming or finery. —*v.t.* **3.** to ornament with or as with furbelows. [var. of FALBALA]

fur·bish (fûr′bish), *v.t.* to restore to freshness of appearance or condition. [ME *furbish(en)* < MF *forbiss-,* long s. of *forbir* to polish, clean < Gmc; cf. OHG *furban*] —**fur′bish·er,** *n.*

fur·cate (*adj.* fûr′kāt, -kit; *v.* fûr′kāt), *adj., v.,* **-cat·ed, -cat·ing.** —*adj.* **1.** forked; branching. —*v.i.* **2.** to form a fork; divide into branches. [< ML *furcāt(us)* cloven. See FORK, -ATE¹] —**fur·ca·tion** (fər kā′shən), *n.*

The School Dictionary

The dictionary that you probably know best is the *school dictionary*—one designed with students of your age and background specifically in mind. The school dictionary contains fewer words than college dictionaries, and these are defined with a younger student's experience in mind. The following will give you an idea of the treatment of words in a school dictionary.

Oneida • open

Onei·da \ō-'nīd-ə\ *n* : a member of an Iroquoian people originally of what is now central New York [Iroquois *Onē yóde',* literally, "standing rock"]

onei·ric \ō-'nīr-ik\ *adj* : of or relating to dreams : DREAMY [Greek *oneiros* "dream"]

one·ness \'wən-nes\ *n* **1** : the quality, state, or fact of being one (as in thought, spirit, or purpose) **2** : IDENTITY 1

oner·ous \'än-ə-rəs, 'ō-nə-\ *adj* : being difficult or burdensome ⟨an *onerous* task⟩ [Middle French *onereus,* from Latin *onerosus,* from *oner-, onus* "burden"] — **oner·ous·ly** *adv* — **oner·ous·ness** *n*

one·self \wən-'self, ,wən-\ *also* **one's self** \wən-, ,wən-, ,wenz-\ *pron* **1** : a person's self : one's own self — used reflexively as object of a preposition or verb or for emphasis in various constructions **2** : one's normal, healthy, or sane condition or self

one-sid·ed \'wən-'sīd-əd\ *adj* **1** : lacking in objectivity : BIASED ⟨take a *one-sided* view of a problem⟩ **2** : decided or differing by a wide margin ⟨a *one-sided* game⟩ ⟨a *one-sided* score⟩

one-step \'wən-,step\ *n* : a ballroom dance marked by quick walking steps backward and forward in 2/4 time — **one-step** *vi*

one·time \'wən-,tīm\ *adj* : FORMER ⟨a *onetime* teacher⟩

one-to-one \,wən-tə-'wən, -də-\ *adj* : pairing each element of a set with one and only one element of another set ⟨a *one-to-one* correspondence⟩

It is essential that you find out for yourself how the material is presented and arranged in the college or school dictionary that you are using. All dictionaries have introductory notes that explain such matters.

EXERCISE 1. Finding Information in Your Dictionary. Study the table of contents at the front of your dictionary. Notice where the introductory notes are to be found, where the definitions start, and where special tables, charts, or other features may be found. Then write on your paper the part of your dictionary in which you think each of the following items of information can be found. Use *front matter* for anything that comes before the actual definitions, *main part* for the alphabetical listing of entries, and *back matter* for anything that comes later. If you think an item might be in two places, give both.

EXAMPLE   1. The pronunciation of the word *naïve*
           1. *main part*

1. An explanation of the way syllables are divided in the dictionary entries
2. The meaning of the abbreviation *Brit.*
3. The population of Tokyo
4. The capital of Alaska
5. The life dates (birth and death) of George Washington
6. The number of centimeters in a cubic inch
7. The meaning of the abbreviations *n., adj.,* and *v.t.*
8. The meaning of *prism*
9. An explanation of the meaning of *vowel* and *consonant*
10. An explanation of the treatment of prefixes in the dictionary

KINDS OF INFORMATION IN DICTIONARIES

29a. Learn what your dictionary tells you about words.

As you study the following kinds of information that dictionaries contain, examine both the sample entries on pages 731–733 and the ones in the following sections.

Spelling

The dictionary is the authority on correct spelling. If a word may be spelled two ways, the dictionary usually gives the more common spelling first.

If there is a spelling problem connected with forming the plural of a word or with adding a suffix (like *-ed, -ing, -ness*), the dictionary shows you how to spell these words. Examples are *fur, furred,* and *funnier, funniest.*

EXERCISE 2. Finding the Spelling of Words. Number your paper 1–10. Find the answers to the following questions in your dictionary.

A. Which is the preferred spelling for the following words?
 1. neighbor, neighbour
 2. tranquillity, tranquility
 3. lodestar, loadstar
 4. draught, draft
 5. catalogue, catalog
B. Correctly add the suffix listed on the right to the word on the left. If a word has two spellings, list the preferred spelling.
 6. lonely est   9. happy ness
 7. refer ed   10. travel ing
 8. usual ly

Capital Letters

If you are not sure about capitalizing a word, the dictionary will help you. Some words may or may not have a capital, depending upon how you use the word. For example, *democratic* is usually listed as an uncapitalized common adjective; however, when the particular party is designated in the list of definitions, then a capital is used—*Democratic party.*

EXERCISE 3. Checking the Capitalization of Words. Check your dictionary to find out whether (or when) the following words are capitalized. If the words may be used both ways, write sentences illustrating both uses.

1. arab	5. mercury	9. scot
2. bible	6. mumbo jumbo	10. state
3. escalator	7. president	
4. god	8. republican	

Syllables

The dictionary divides all words into syllables: for instance, *ac cu rate* is divided into three syllables. If your dictionary should use a small dot or dash to show the breaks between syllables, *do not confuse this dash or dot with the hyphen.* Be sure that you know what the hyphen looks like in your dictionary by looking up such words as *mother-in-law* or *ack-ack.*

EXERCISE 4. Checking the Syllabication of Words. Divide the following words into syllables. Check your work in the dictionary.

1. forevermore	3. old-fashioned	5. recognize
2. impractical	4. preliminary	

Pronunciation

To show how a word is pronounced, the dictionary uses *diacritical marks,* which indicate the sounds of vowels, and it respells the word using certain consonants to mean certain sounds. Dictionaries differ somewhat in the marking systems they use. As you learn to master your dictionary's method of showing the correct pronunciation of a word, you will need to refer to the pronunciation key (usually given at the bottom or the top of each page). On pages 740–43, you will find further explanation and exercises on pronunciation.

Part of Speech

A part-of-speech label is given for every word listed in your dictionary. The label is likely to be one of the following abbreviations:

n.	noun	*pron.*	pronoun
v. or *vb.*	verb	*prep.*	preposition
adv.	adverb	*conj.*	conjunction
adj.	adjective	*interj.*	interjection

In addition, most dictionaries label those verbs that take objects *v.t.* (for *transitive verb*) and those that do not *v.i.* (for *intransitive verb*). Many verbs that can be used with or without an object have some of their meanings labeled *v.i.* and some labeled *v.t.* The distinction between transitive and intransitive verbs is discussed on pages 508–09 of this book.

EXERCISE 5. Classifying Words According to Their Part(s) of Speech. Look up these words in your dictionary, and classify each one according to its part of speech. (If a word may be used as three or four parts of speech, write each use after the proper number on your paper.)

1. base
2. beside
3. court
4. forward
5. jerk

Etymology

Your dictionary also explains the etymology or the origin and history of a word. To indicate the languages from which a word has come, abbreviations such as *L.* (Latin) and *F.* (French) are used. The meanings of these and other abbreviations are given in the key to the symbols and abbreviations at the front of the dictionary. Look on page 731 and notice the origin of *funnel.*

EXERCISE 6. Writing the Etymologies of Words. After the proper number on your paper, write the etymology of each of the following words. If your student dictionary does not give the etymologies, go to an unabridged or college dictionary. If a word is unfamiliar to you, learn its meaning when you look up its etymology.

1. chlorophyll
2. exorbitant
3. kaleidoscope
4. phosphorus
5. pince-nez

Meaning

A dictionary defines words. When a word has many different meanings, seek out the particular definition that you are looking for. Notice on page 731 the different meanings for *funnel* as a noun. There is a difference between a *funnel* for liquid and a stage *funnel*.

Some dictionaries place the oldest meaning first; others list the meanings in the order of their use, the most common meaning being given first. Either way, you will need to look over the many definitions until you find the one that fits the sentence in which you have found the word.

EXERCISE 7. Finding the Exact Meaning of a Word. Number your paper 1–5. Look up the exact meaning of each italicized word in these sentences, and write the meaning after the corresponding number.

1. Now I will *pose* for a snapshot.
2. His attitude seems to be a *pose*.
3. On the counter was a novelty key *ring*.
4. The *rings* indicated that the tree was twenty years old.
5. I was late because I did not hear the bell *ring*.

Usage Labels

Most dictionaries give some indication as to levels of usage. Words or meanings may be labeled *Slang, Colloq.* (colloquial), *Obs.* (obsolete, no longer in common use), etc. Not all dictionaries use the same labels, and even when they do, the labels may not mean the same thing. Read the introductory section of your dictionary to find out what the usage labels mean. Words and meanings that are not labeled are considered standard English.

EXERCISE 8. Finding the Usage Labels of Words. Look up the following words in your dictionary to see whether or not they are considered standard English. If you find no label anywhere in the definitions of a word, write *standard* on your paper after the proper number. If you find a usage label indicating a special classification, write the label on your paper, using the abbreviation found in your dictionary.

1. blob   3. glitch   5. pep
2. bug   4. hydrogen

Synonyms and Antonyms

A synonym is a word having almost the same meaning as the word being defined: *calm, serene.* An antonym is a word having the opposite meaning: *hot, cold.* Frequently, you will find not only a listing of synonyms but also the distinctions of meanings. When you want to choose the exact word for your meaning, your dictionary, with its listing of synonyms and its cross references, will help you find the word.

EXERCISE 9. Finding Synonyms for Words.   Look up the following words in your dictionary, and make a list of the synonyms given for each word.

1. freedom   3. shrewd   5. loud
2. laughable   4. rough

Illustrations

If the meaning of a word can best be shown by a picture, the dictionary may give an illustration. For example, the sample entries on page 731 include an illustration of a funnel.

29b. Find out what your dictionary tells you about people and places.

In your dictionary the names of people and places are either listed in a special biographical, geographical, or "proper names" section, or listed in the main body along with all other words. You can easily discover which method your dictionary uses.

In an entry about a person, the dictionary will give the spelling and pronunciation of the person's name, the dates of the person's birth and death, information about nationality, and finally the reason for the person's fame. For a U.S. Presdent, the entry includes the dates of his presidency. The dictionary will tell you how to spell and pronounce the name of a place; what it is (river, island, city); where it is; how big it is; and why it is important. Very frequently, information about history and government is given.

EXERCISE 10. Finding Information About People and Places. Use your dictionary to help you write answers to the following questions.

1. Where is Madagascar?
2. How high is Mount Everest?
3. When was Ralph Bunche born?
4. What was the Hydra?
5. What was the nationality of Nellie Melba?

REVIEW EXERCISE. Finding Information in the Dictionary. Number your paper 1–10. By using your dictionary, correctly answer each of the following questions.

1. What is the correct syllable division of *hypochondriac*?
2. Which is the preferred spelling—*pretence* or *pretense*?
3. When, if ever, is the word *army* capitalized?
4. What part of speech is *please*?
5. Can *bread* be used as a slang word?
6. What is the etymology of the word *jujitsu*?
7. What is the meaning of the word *ossify*?
8. What is the meaning of *NCO*?
9. Who was Alfred Bernhard Nobel?
10. Is it correct to use the word *swell* as an adjective in formal writing?

PRONUNCIATION

29c. Use your dictionary for pronunciation.

Because the actual spelling of many English words does not clearly indicate how they are pronounced, dictionaries use simplified respellings and special symbols called diacritical marks to show pronunciation. For example, the *HBJ School Dictionary* shows the word *bite* respelled without the final, silent *e* and the *i* is written with a straight line above it. The pronunciation is shown as [bīt].

What you will need to know is how to interpret the pronunciation given in your dictionary. To do this you must familiarize yourself with the explanatory notes dealing with pronunciation and with the pronunciation key. Most dictionaries explain the system they use in the introductory pages. A full key is usually given inside the front cover. Many dictionaries print a shorter key on each page or set of facing pages. The key illustrates the use of each letter and symbol used by means of simple examples that everyone knows how to pronounce. For example, the pronunciation key printed below tells you that the letter *a* with the diacritical mark – above it is pronounced like the letter *a* in the word *ace*.

PRONUNCIATION KEY: add, āce, câre, pälm; end, ēven; it, īce; odd, ōpen, ôrder; tŏŏk, pōōl; up, bûrn; ə = a in *above*, e in *sicken*, i in *flexible*, o in *melon*, u in *focus*; yōō = u in *fuse*; oil; pout; check; go; ring; thin; **t**his; zh, vision.

"Pronunciation Key" from *Funk and Wagnall's Standard College Dictionary*. Copyright © 1977 by Harper & Row, Publishers, Inc. Reprinted by permission of Harper & Row, Publishers, Inc.

The Schwa

If your dictionary is a recent one, you are probably already familiar with the symbol (ə), called the *schwa* (shwä). This upside-down *e* is used to represent the blurred, unclear sound of "uh" in such words as

alone	(ə·lōn′)
nickel	(nik′əl)
Hannibal	(han′ə·bəl)
collect	(kə·lect′)
support	(sə·pôrt′)

Some dictionaries use this symbol in respelling one-syllable words and other words in which the schwa appears in an accented syllable. Other dictionaries use the schwa only for unaccented syllables.

EXERCISE 11. Finding the Pronunciation of Words. Using
the pronunciation key of your dictionary, pronounce each of the
following words.

1. acknowledge
2. aghast
3. athletic
4. pressure

5. suppose
6. choir
7. generous
8. phonograph

9. these
10. thought

Accent Marks

In words of more than one syllable, one syllable is always
spoken louder than the others. The syllable stressed in this way
is said to be accented, and it is marked in the pronunciation in
one of several ways, depending again on the dictionary you are
looking at.

	WSD[1]	WNNCD	T-B	SCD
battery	ˈbat ə-rē	ˈbat ər-ē	batʹər i	batʹər ē

In some words, the placing of the accent makes a great deal
of difference. For example, if we accent the first syllable of
rebel, we have a noun meaning "a rebellious person," while if
we accent the second, we have a verb meaning "to rise up or
battle against authority."

For certain words of three or more syllables, the dictionary
gives two accents. The first, as shown above, is called the
primary accent; the second is called the *secondary accent.* Dictionaries handle accent marks in different ways. Some put accent marks before the syllable being stressed; some after. Some
use a light mark for the secondary accent; some place the secondary accent to the left and below the stressed syllable. Notice
how it is done in four dictionaries for the word *elevator.*

	WSD[1]	WNNCD
elevator	ˈel-ə-ˌvāt-ər	ˈel-ə-ˌvāt-ər

	T-B	SCD
	elʹə vātʹər	elʹə·vātʹər

[1] The abbreviations stand for *Webster's School Dictionary, Webster's Ninth New Col-
legiate Dictionary, Thorndike-Barnhart High School Dictionary,* and *Standard College
Dictionary,* respectively.

EXERCISE 12. Finding the Pronunciation, Stress, and Syllabication of Words. Look up the pronunciation of each of the following words in your dictionary and copy it after the appropriate number. Be sure to include accent marks and diacritical marks. Indicate syllable division in whatever way your dictionary does.

1. appropriate (adjective)
2. appropriate (verb)
3. establish
4. instrumental
5. promote

EXERCISE 13. Finding the Stress and Part(s) of Speech of Words. Find the exact meaning of each italicized word in the following sentences. Then rewrite the italicized word, its pronunciation (showing the accented syllable), and its part of speech.

EXAMPLE 1. What can his *object* be?
I don't know, but I *object* to his method.
1. (*ob'ject*), *n.*
(*ob·ject'*), *v.*

1. What is your favorite *subject*?
You should not *subject* him to ridicule.
2. Many people *protest* against war.
Their *protest* is objected to by others.
3. No one is *perfect,* but people do try to *perfect* themselves.
4. I do not *suspect* her of malice, but her attitude is *suspect*.
5. All young people *rebel,* but she remained a *rebel* all her life.

CHAPTER 30

Vocabulary

CONTEXT CLUES, SYNONYMS, WORD ANALYSIS

The best way to increase your vocabulary is to read widely and to remember a good deal of what you have read. There are, however, ways of improving your efficiency in learning the new words that you encounter in your reading.

This chapter is intended to help you develop skills that will be useful in building a better vocabulary.

DIAGNOSTIC TEST

A. Number your paper 1–5. After the proper number, write the letter of the meaning for the italicized word in the sentence. Use context clues to find the most appropriate definition.

a. clever
b. deadly
c. betray
d. difference
e. to show off
f. to move from one position to another
g. to clear or acquit

1. The defendant hoped that the jury would *absolve* him of the accusation.
2. Asking local restaurants to donate the food for the dance was Pat's *ingenious* idea.
3. When the chemical truck overturned, residents were evacuated because of the *lethal* fumes.
4. While everyone appreciates success, not everyone admires those who *flaunt* it.
5. A typing error caused the *discrepancy* between the original report and the printed version.

B. Number your paper 1–5. After the proper number, write the synonym for the italicized word. Use context clues to find the best synonym.

1. We thought that her immediate, intense dislike for the music was rather *bizarre*.
   a. frightening   b. strange   c. common   d. careful
2. Although the dog appeared *docile*, we noticed that its eyes followed us around the room.
   a. easily managed   b. stupid   c. dishonest   d. nervous
3. *Ominous* black clouds caused us to quickly pack up the picnic.
   a. hungry   b. threatening   c. boring   d. tired
4. Selling candy door to door for ten hours makes a *grueling* day.
   a. frightening   b. capable   c. startling   d. exhausting
5. We hope to have room for several *candid* photographs in the yearbook.
   a. unposed   b. hidden   c. rude   d. doubting

WAYS TO LEARN NEW WORDS

Context

The total situation in which a word is used is called its *context*. The words that surround a particular word are one part of the context; the circumstances in which the word is used are another part.

30a. Learn new words from their contexts.

If you find a new word in your reading, examine the context for clues to the word's meaning. The most common context clues are *definition, synonym, example,* and *comparison or contrast.*

Definition

A writer often will define a word by restating it in a different way. For example, the dictionary definition of *superfluous* is "beyond what is required or sufficient." In the following sentence notice that "more than minimal" defines *superfluous.*

> The candidate's costly campaign was superfluous since he was unopposed and did not need more than minimal advertising.

Synonym

Sometimes a writer will use a synonym for a new word in the same sentence. For example, if you did not know the meaning of the word *rostrum,* the writer's use of the synonym *platform* in the following sentence would help you understand its meaning.

> As the speaker approached the rostrum, a disturbance made the students divert their attention from the platform.

Example

You may be able to guess the meaning of a word from examples in the context. Read the following sentence.

> The Queen of England and the King of Denmark were among the sovereigns who attended the royal wedding.

If the Queen of England and the King of Denmark are examples of *sovereigns,* you should be able to guess that *sovereigns* are the "heads of state in a monarchy."

Comparison or Contrast

A writer may compare or contrast an unfamiliar word with a more common word or phrase. In the following sentence the word *fallacy* is compared with the word *mistake*.

> It is a fallacy to believe that ant bites are harmless, and disregarding wasp bites is also a mistake.

In the following sentence you can tell by the context that *demoralized* is contrasted with *encouraged*, By contrasting the two words, the writer shows that they are opposite in meaning.

> Although the other team outweighed them, the players were encouraged rather than demoralized.

EXERCISE 1. Using Context Clues to Define Words. Number your paper 1–10. Using context clues, determine the meaning of the italicized word from the following list of definitions. Write the correct letter beside the proper number.

a. qualified
b. refuge or shelter
c. safe or unthreatened by
d. able to speak effortlessly
e. floatable
f. good-natured
g. average
h. cautious
i. an agreement to perform an illegal act
j. political disorder and confusion
k. sentimental
l. to wander aimlessly

1. If someone falls from a boat, throw him a life vest or another *buoyant* object.
2. The lively conversation made up for the rather *mediocre* meal.
3. An old tree house in the back yard was his *haven* from the rest of the world.

4. The lack of laws and leadership brought the country to a state of *anarchy*.
5. Be sure to get a *competent* electrician, for one who is un- skilled will not be able to fix the wiring.
6. Children can be protected from measles if they get a shot which makes them *immune* to the disease.
7. Be *wary* in situations such as walking alone on dark streets and swimming alone at night.
8. The tourists were upset when the cab driver *meandered* around the park, for they had a plane to catch and they did not want to miss it.
9. The *conspiracy* to kill President Lincoln was a plot that involved several people.
10. Although Jenny is *fluent* in French and Spanish, she is very hesitant in German.

EXERCISE 2. Using Context Clues to Define Words.
Number your paper 1–10. Copy each italicized word in the following passage, and write next to it either a definition or a *synonym*. When you have completed the exercise, check the dictionary meanings, rewrite those you had wrong, and restudy the context that you missed. Add new words to your notebook list.

Although our team had played a good game, the second half of the ninth inning found our (1) *adversaries* holding a three-run lead, and this seemed too big for us to (2) *surmount*. Our hope (3) *diminished* further when our first batter flied out to center, but it revived a little when Frank, our pitcher, hit a double. Our opponents decided to use (4) *strategy,* and they gave an (5) *intentional* base on balls to George, our third batter. Excitement reached a (6) *climax* when Eddie, the fourth man up, hit a sharp grounder that the second baseman was unable to (7) *intercept*. (8) *Subsequent* events were almost too quick to follow. With the bases full, Joe, our catcher, hit a home run, and the (9) *frenzied* spectators rushed out on the field and carried him with wild (10) *acclaim* to the clubhouse.

30b. Learn to find the meaning that fits the context.

Some words in English, like *carbon dioxide,* have only one meaning; some have only a few very closely related meanings; most common words have many. The word *point,* for example, may mean "a place," "the tip of a pencil," "a unit of scoring in a game," "the main idea that someone is trying to express," and many other things as well. Since dictionaries define all of the important uses of a word, it is important when looking for a word's meaning not to settle for the very first definition that is listed for an entry word.

You must keep in mind the context in which you read or heard the word. You can then try the various meanings until you find the one that fits. Take this sentence, for example:

The general **dispatched** the captive quickly and painlessly.

The meaning of the sentence depends upon the meaning of *dispatched.* Of the three definitions your dictionary is certain to give—(1) to send away, (2) to put to death, (3) to dispose of quickly, as business—only the second really fits. The sentence means that the general put the captive to death in a quick and painless way.

To make the differences between the word's various meanings clear, dictionary makers often provide sample contexts as part of the definition. The context for the first meaning of *dispatch* might be "to dispatch a messenger." When such examples are given, you can easily compare your context with them to make sure you have found the meaning you want.

EXERCISE 3. Finding the Correct Meaning in the Dictionary. The italicized words in the following sentences all have a number of different meanings. Using your dictionary, find the meaning that fits the context best and write it on your paper.

1. Both of the candidates appeared to tire in the last *hectic* days of the campaign.
2. The courts of the dictator made a *farce* of justice.
3. Occasionally one of Judy's friends would *impose* on her generosity.

4. It was like Harry never to think of the *orthodox* solution to a problem.
5. It was soon evident that the ruthless leader's civilized manners were only a *veneer*.

Using the Right Word

30c. Select the right synonym, the word that conveys the precise meaning and impression you want to give.

The English language is rich in synonyms—words that have the same general meaning but that have subtle shades of difference between them. Choosing the right synonym can mean a great deal when you are trying to write clearly and effectively. For example, *opponent* and *enemy* are both synonyms for the word *adversary*. However, the three words are not always interchangeable because of the subtle differences in meaning. Read the following examples.

The basketball teams were *adversaries* on the court.
During a war, it is sometimes difficult to know who is your friend and who is your *adversary*.

From the context, you can tell that *enemies* is too strong to be a good synonym for *adversaries* in the first sentence. The teams were *opponents*. In the second sentence, however, enemy would be a good substitute for *adversary*.

EXERCISE 4. Selecting Synonyms to Complete Sentences. Number your paper 1–10. Next to each number write the synonym for *walk* that would be appropriate to the sentence context.

amble	pace	promenade	stroll	tread
march	plod	stride	tramp	wander

1. The referee picked up the ball, —— back five yards, and put it on our thirty-yard line.

2. Over a thousand veterans —— in the Memorial Day parade.
3. —— the deck of a large ocean liner is an exhilarating experience.
4. The tall man —— ahead of his companions.
5. The horse —— slowly along the path as its rider enjoyed the scenery.
6. Unaware of the surroundings, the blissful couple —— slowly, arm in arm.
7. The cows had —— a path to the stream.
8. The happy boy on his vacation —— idly beside the brook.
9. Hoping to make up the lost time, the hikers —— resolutely through the underbrush.
10. The weary hiker, lifting each foot with obvious effort, —— up the hill.

EXERCISE 5. Selecting Appropriate Adverbs.   Number your paper 1–10. Refer to the dictionary for the exact meaning of each adverb. Write the adverb that best answers the question.

barbarously	genially	ungraciously
comprehensively	grotesquely	reluctantly
defiantly	nocturnally	reverently
ferociously		

1. How did the tiger bare its teeth at the visitors in the zoo?
2. How did the tourists stand at the Tomb of the Unknown Soldier?
3. How did the Goths and Vandals act when they sacked and burned the city of Rome?
4. How did the nervous patient approach the dentist's chair?
5. How did the captured heroine stare at her enemy?
6. How did the announcer smile as she greeted the contestant?
7. How was the unnatural-looking clown dressed?
8. How did the weary couple greet the unexpected guests?
9. How did the well-prepared student answer the examination questions?
10. When do owls hunt for prey?

30d. Learn to understand and use literary terms.

As you continue to study and write about literature, you will need to learn and use specific literary terms. You may be asked to classify a reading assignment as a *comedy* (a humorous story or play with a happy ending) or a *tragedy* (a serious story or play with an unhappy ending). Perhaps you want to explain how the *atmosphere* (the feeling pervading a work) relates to the *setting* (place and time). If you were asked to describe the characters in a story, you might say that the *protagonist* (main character) was either interesting or a *stereotype* (an unchanging, unconventional character). Another assignment might be to illustrate how an author uses *foreshadowing* (a hint of something to come) in the *plot* (the main story). Whether you are taking a test, participating in classroom discussion, or writing an assignment, you will find that using proper literary terms will be a great asset to you.

EXERCISE 6. Defining Literary Terms. Number your paper 1–10. Write the letter from column B that is appropriate for the numbered word in column A. Use your dictionary as needed.

A	B
1. biographical	a. painfully moving or touching
2. didactic	b. idealistic and fanciful
3. farcical	c. appealing to emotion by sensationalism and exaggeration
4. fictitious	
5. hackneyed	d. marked by broad or boisterous humor
6. melodramatic	e. ornate in style
7. poignant	f. ridiculing a custom, habit, or idea
8. realistic	g. of a person's life
9. romantic	h. overused, commonplace, stale
10. satirical	i. clear and simple
	j. in literature, representing life as it actually is
	k. intended to instruct, teacherlike
	l. not real, imaginary, made up

PREFIXES AND ROOTS

English has borrowed words from almost all languages, but particularly from Latin and Greek. Knowing the meaning of a Greek or Latin word element gives you an understanding of a great many English words.

These word elements may be the part of a word that comes first, called the *prefix;* they may be the main part, called the *root;* they may be the part added at the end, called the *suffix.* Many words have only one or two of these parts, but some have three. Consider the word *semiannual.* This word is composed of the prefix *semi-,* meaning "half" in Latin; the root *-annu-,* meaning "year" in Latin; and the suffix *-al,* from a Latin suffix meaning "pertaining to." The word *semiannual* means "pertaining to an event that occurs every half year." (The same root may show a vowel change in different words. In *biennial,* for example, *-enni-* is actually the same root as *-annu-.*

30e. **Learn some of the common Latin prefixes and roots.**

LATIN PREFIX	MEANING	LATIN ROOT	MEANING
ad-	to, toward	-cis-	cut
bi-	two	-fid-	faith
con-	with	-ped-	foot
in-	into	-spec-	look
intro-	within	-voc-	call

The word parts from Latin listed above are commonly used in English words. If you learn the meaning of these prefixes and roots, you will be able to figure out the meaning of a great many words in which they occur.

EXERCISE 7. Using Latin Prefixes and Roots to Define Words. Number your paper 1–5. Write the prefix and its meaning and the root and its meaning for each word in the following numbered list. Then write the meaning of the whole word. Use your dictionary if necessary.

EXAMPLE 1. submarine
 1. *sub (under) + mare (sea) = underwater boat*

1. biped   3. confide   5. introspect
2. incise   4. advocate

    Here are some other commonly used Latin prefixes and roots. Before you do the exercise that follows them, try to think of words in which these parts appear. Can you see a relationship between the meaning of the part and the meaning of the whole word?

LATIN PREFIX	MEANING	LATIN ROOT	MEANING
ab-, abs-	off	-cid-	kill
re-	back, again	-cogn-	know
sub-	below, under	-dic-, -dict-	say, speak
		-hom-	man
		-pond-	a weight
		-prob-	prove
		-sed-	seat
		-ten-, -tens-	stretch
		-tract-	draw
		-vert-, -vers-	turn

EXERCISE 8. Using Latin Prefixes and Roots to Define Words.
Number your paper 1–10. For each italicized word, write the part or parts derived from Latin and their meanings. Then write the meaning of the word as it is used in the phrase. Use the lists on pages 753–54 and your dictionary.

EXAMPLES   1. *dictate* letters
       1. *dict (speak) = speak a message for someone to write down*
       2. *subtract* the balance
       2. *sub (below) + tract (draw) = withdraw or take away the balance*

1. to *recognize* a friend
2. a detective from the *homicide* division
3. faultless *diction*
4. act of *subversion*
5. a *ponderous* elephant
6. on *probation*
7. *retract* the statement
8. a *tenuous* conclusion
9. a *versatile* musician
10. a *sedentary* job

30f. Learn some of the common Greek prefixes and roots.

There are many words in English that are derived from Greek words. Study the following list of common prefixes and roots.

GREEK PREFIX	MEANING
auto-	self
di-, dia-	between, across
eu-	good
hydro-	water
micro-	small
ortho-	right, straight
sym-	together
tri-	three

GREEK ROOT	MEANING
-astr-, -aster-	star
-chiro-	hand
-dox-	opinion
-geo-	earth
-graph-	write
-log-	speech, science of something
-nomy-	law
-phobia-	dread of
-phon-	sound
-pod-	foot

EXERCISE 9. Using Greek Prefixes and Roots to Define Words. Number your paper 1–10, skipping a line after each number. Copy the italicized words that follow. After referring to the list above and your dictionary, write the part or parts derived from Greek and their meaning. Then write the meaning of the word as it is used in the phrase.

EXAMPLE 1. a case of *hydrophobia*
1. *hydro (water)* + *phobia (dread)* = *a case involving a dread of water*

1. marked by an *asterisk*
2. an *autograph* collector
3. studying *geology*
4. examining a *microphone*

5. granted *autonomy*   8. an *orthodox* believer
6. treated by a *chiropodist*   9. a flutist in the *symphony*
7. a flattering *eulogy*   10. standing on a *tripod*

EXERCISE 10. Understanding the Meanings of Latin and Greek Prefixes. Write the meaning of each of the following Latin and Greek prefixes. Then write a word in which the prefix appears. Be prepared to explain the relationship between the meaning of the prefix and the meaning of the word.

1. ad-	4. di-, dia-	7. intro-	9. re-
2. auto-	5. bi-	8. anti-	10. sub-
3. con-	6. in-		

EXERCISE 11. Understanding the Meanings of Latin and Greek Roots. Write the meaning of each of the following Latin and Greek roots. Then write a word in which the root appears. Be prepared to explain the relationship between the meaning of the root and the meaning of the word.

1. -astr-	4. -dox-	7. -ped-	9. -ten-, -tens-
2. -chiro-	5. -graph-	8. -prob-	10. -vers-
3. -cis-	6. -log-		

30g. Learn the origins of words as an aid to developing vocabulary.

Words with Interesting Histories

Study the origin of each word when you look it up in the dictionary. For example, in the entry for the word *candidate* you will find the following: [*L. candidatus,* clothed in white]. *L.* means "Latin," and *candidatus* is the Latin word from which *candidate* comes. The explanation of this word origin tells you that in ancient Rome candidates wore white robes. Many other words have interesting stories connected with them.

EXERCISE 12. Writing the Definitions and Origins of Words. Number your paper 1–5. Next to the appropriate number, write the italicized word. By referring to the dictionary, write the definition of each word, the language of its origin, and the background of its meaning.

1. Digital computers now do in a few seconds *calculations* that would take mathematicians months or years to complete.
2. The engineer *detonated* the explosive, and the rock split.
3. The disloyal citizen was *ostracized* by his fellow towns-people.
4. *Tantalizing* odors from the kitchen made us hungry.
5. The fortuneteller wore heavy, *tawdry* jewelry.

Foreign Words in English

Many foreign words and phrases have become part of the English language. Sometimes their pronunciation becomes "An-glicized," while their spelling remains as it was in the original language. Examples of such expressions are *en masse,* meaning "in a group," *joie de vivre,* meaning "joy in living," and *tête-à-tête,* meaning "a private conversation between two people."

EXERCISE 13. Defining Foreign Expressions. Number your paper 1–10. For each expression, write the letter of its meaning from column *B* and the language from which it comes.

A	B
1. cliché	a. the best people
2. deluxe	b. the masses
3. elite	c. witty replies
4. hoi polloi	d. a midday rest
5. incognito	e. a meal at a fixed price
6. patio	f. a marble floor
7. repartee	g. with name concealed
8. siesta	h. timeworn expression
9. table d'hôte	i. never satisfied
10. terra firma	j. a terrace
	k. solid earth
	l. elegant

REVIEW EXERCISE. Defining Words With Synonyms. The words in this exercise have been chosen from all those you have studied in this chapter. Number your paper 1–20, and write the correct answer choice next to each number.

1. The news of the team victory was greeted with *acclaim.*
   a. acquisition   b. applause   c. desire   d. land
2. Charles knew that he could outrun any *biped.*
   a. animal with two feet   b. bison   c. pedigree
   d. three-footed stool
3. Her *didactic* attitude in the meeting was resented by the other students.
   a. tightened   b. knocking   c. teacherlike
   d. flowerlike
4. The *frenzied* crowd pulled down the goal posts.
   a. wearied   b. carried   c. excited   d. carved
5. The day before the wedding was *hectic* for the bride's mother.
   a. colorful   b. frantic   c. emphatic   d. humorous
6. We felt that he was unfairly *ostracized* from the group.
   a. banished   b. enrolled   c. combined
   d. distracted
7. Until Kirk has a chance to raise his grades, the coach has him on *probation.*
   a. connection   b. decision   c. courage
   d. trial period
8. After announcing her candidacy for class president, Lou Ann explained her campaign *strategy.*
   a. leveling   b. planning   c. excelling
   d. participating
9. At the carnival the children bought *tawdry* hats and wore them all day.
   a. haughty   b. small   c. showy   d. inconspicuous
10. Furniture with an oak *veneer* is less expensive than that made of the solid wood.
    a. terrace   b. metal   c. coloring   d. thin surface

11. The plot of the movie was so *hackneyed* that we could easily guess the outcome.
    a. overused   b. careful   c. successful   d. unusual
12. A carpenter comes across so many different projects that he must indeed be *versatile*.
    a. many-skilled   b. cautious   c. timely
    d. portable
13. We were not surprised when the boring movie received *mediocre* reviews.
    a. loud   b. wonderful   c. average   d. delightful
14. Our shop teacher is actually a very *competent* craftsman.
    a. preferable   b. late   c. inferior   d. skilled
15. Because of his past poor performances, we were *wary* of Joe's offer to be chairman of the dance.
    a. elated   b. suspicious   c. distracted   d. honored
16. As a publicity stunt, the movie star was asked to *detonate* the old theater that had to be torn down.
    a. annoy   b. honor   c. cause to explode   d. buy
17. The new center is a *haven* for abused children.
    a. shelter   b. leader   c. physician   d. tent
18. The doctor in the operating room hesitated as though he couldn't remember where to *incise* his patient.
    a. take   b. speak   c. visit   d. cut into
19. Although his voice was pleasant, his meaning was *ominous*.
    a. threatening   b. disappearing   c. hungry   d. nice
20. Few people today take time to *meander* through the woods.
    a. examine   b. donate   c. wander   d. run

Word List

The following list of 300 words has been selected from books generally read by students your age. It should form the basis of your vocabulary study for the year. Make it a regular practice to learn new words from the list. Add them to the list in your notebook, giving the pronunciation and meaning as you find them in the dictionary. Ten words a week will be as many as you can handle efficiently.

abhor
abrasive
accessible
acclaim
acknowledge
adage
addicted
adversary
advocate
affected

agility
agitation
alleged
allusion
aloof
alteration
amends
amity
animated
annals

apathy
apparition
applicable
arrogance
assassin
assess
asterisk
attribute
autonomous
belligerent

benefactor
benign
bibliography
bilingual
biographical

bisect
bizarre
bland
brochure
buoyant

cadence
carnivorous
cascade
centrifugal
chivalry
chronic
chronological
circumscribe
citadel
clamber

collaborate
collateral
comply
condolence
congeniality
congruent
connive
conspiracy
contaminate
contemptible

cope
credentials
culmination
cumbersome
cynic
deficient
defile
defraud
demoralize
denote

denounce
depict
depreciate
devout
dexterity
diligent
discreet
discretion
discriminate
disperse

disrupt
dissuade
docile
drastic
dubious
dupe
dwindle
elapse
elude
emerge

emissary
encore
entice
epic
equation
eradicate
essence
evict
exasperate
expend

exploit
extremity
extrovert
fallacy
fatality

fauna
fervent
figurative
flora
fluent

formidable
fraternize
frenzied
frivolous
functional
galvanize
garb
gaudy
genealogy
genial

granular
grueling
haphazard
havoc
hectic
herald
hereditary
hideous
hindrance
hoax

homage
horde
humanitarian
humanoid
hygiene
ideally
illiterate
immaterial
immunity
impertinent

inaudible
incalculable
incandescent
incessant
incompatible
incompre-
hensible
inconspi-
cuous
inconvenient
indivisible
induction

infamous
infest
inflammation
influential
initiative
instigate
intact
intensive
intervention
intimate

intimidate
intonation
inventory
inverse
invigorating
irksome
irony
irreducible
irretrievable
jaunt

jovial
jurisdiction
kindle

landlocked
larceny
lavish
lax
lethal
liability
maintenance

malicious
manifest
manipulate
meander
medieval
meditate
medley
metamorphosis
metaphor
mimic

misconstrue
moor
morbid
murky
nauseate
necessitate
negotiate
nimble
nominal
nonchalant

obsession
obtuse
omen
ominous
opaque
oppressive
optimistic
oratory

orthodox
ostracize

ovation
palatial
panorama
paramount
passive
patio
perceptible
perennial
perspective
pessimistic

plaintiff
plaintive
poach
ponderous
potency
potion
precedent
predatory
premature
preposterous

priority
promenade
prominence
prospective
prowess
pungent
quest
quorum
quota

rapture

raucous
ravenous
recede
recession
reconcile
relevant
reluctant
repast
replenish
replica

reprimand
resourceful
retract
retrieve
rostrum
satirical
sector
seethe
simile
sinister

skeptical
smug
soliloquy
solvent
somber
sovereign
spurn
stagnant
statute
subsequent

superfluous
surmount
surpass
susceptible
tantalizing
tentative
tolerate
transcribe
transpire
tripod

trivial
turbulent
tycoon
ultimate
uncanny
undergo
unkempt
unscrupulous
upheaval
utilize

vanity
veneer
venerable
virtual
volatile
wary
wrangle
wry
yearn
zodiac

CHAPTER 31

Studying and Test-Taking Skills

PURPOSES AND TECHNIQUES

In each of your subjects, you are expected to complete different kinds of homework assignments, prepare for oral and written class projects, and study for tests. There are skills and procedures that can make your studying more effective and your test taking more successful.

STUDY SKILLS

All of your studying has two basic purposes. You study to learn information about some particular subject or topic. You study to evaluate, to interpret, and to apply the information you have learned.

Following the SQ3R Method

31a. Use the SQ3R Method.

An educational psychologist, Francis Robinson, developed a method of study called *SQ3R*. The SQ3R Study Method is made up of five simple parts:

1. *S—Survey* the entire study assignment, whether it is a chapter, a section, or a complete book. Look at the headings, the material in boldface and italics, the charts, outlines, and summaries. Get a general sense of the scope of the material.

2. *Q*—Make a list of *questions* to be answered after completing your reading. Sometimes the writer will have included questions; sometimes your teacher will provide them. At other times you will have to develop your own questions.

3. *R—Read* the material section by section; think of answers to your questions as you read.

4. *R—Recite* in your own words answers to each question in your list.

5. *R—Review* the material by re-reading quickly, looking over the questions, recalling the answers.

EXERCISE 1. Applying the SQ3R Study Method to a Homework Assignment. Select an assignment in any one of your subjects. Follow the five steps of the SQ3R Study Method to complete the assignment.

Understanding the Assignment

31b. Be sure you understand the assignment.

Many students waste time because they do not have a clear idea of what is expected of them. To avoid this kind of frustration, always follow these steps:

(1) Write down all assignments.

Be precise. Note exactly what you have to do: "English lit. book: read 103–116, write out answers for 3, 5, and 7—p. 117: due Monday." Also, use some kind of system to indicate papers, reports, or other tasks that must be finished at a certain time.

(2) Review the assignment as a whole before beginning work.

Glance through the assigned reading to see what the focus of the selection is. Look over study questions; they alert you to what you should concentrate on as you read.

(3) Be sure you know what is expected of you.

Check whether the teacher expects you to use a particular format or follow a schedule. Does the assignment require that you use an outline, write a summary, or prepare an oral report?

Adjusting Your Reading Rate

31c. Learn to adjust your reading rate to the content of the material and the purpose for which you are reading.

Vary your reading pace depending on what you are reading and why you are reading. For example, you are likely to *scan* a passage, that is, glance through the material very quickly, if you are looking only for certain points or particular details.

However, when you want to get a general idea of what the work is about, or when you are doing a quick review just before a test, you *skim* through it; that is, you go through it quite quickly, looking for the main points and paying little attention to details.

When you are reading a newspaper or are doing recreational reading, it is likely you will use a *fast* rate; that is, take more time than for skimming yet still read quite rapidly.

However, you are likely to slow down even more—to an *average* rate—when reading material that is more serious or that is written in a somewhat unfamiliar way.

Finally, when you are having trouble understanding the ideas or the vocabulary of a selection, when you are reading very technical material, or when you are attempting to remember many details, you should expect to read slowly and at a *thoughtful* rate.

EXERCISE 2. Analyzing Reading Rates. As you answer the following questions, use the hints indicated in the previous section on understanding your assignment.

1. Read rapidly through all the questions in this exercise before writing any answers.
2. What kind of reading rate would you use to go over a chapter in your history textbook five minutes before taking a test?
3. Skim through the previous five pages and copy down all the sentences beginning with the word *But*.
4. What kind of reading rate are you likely to use to find a detail you must know to answer a study question?
5. Determine your actual thoughtful reading rate by timing how long it takes you to read a three- to five-page section from a textbook you find difficult.
6. List two items that you are likely to read at a fast rate.
7. Write down the author, title, and publisher of ten items you would expect to read at an average rate.
8. What kind of reading rate would you expect to use when preparing a chapter that has just been assigned in your science class?
9. List and define the five major reading rates along with five examples of when you might expect to use each.
10. Do only the even-numbered questions in this exercise, beginning with item 2. At the end, look back over your answer sheet to see how well you followed the directions in item 1.

Using Graphics and Illustrations

31d. Make good use of graphics and illustrations.

Many textbooks and informational articles include diagrams, maps, graphs, and illustrations. Do not skip over these visual aids—study them. They have been carefully selected and designed to make information clearer and more understandable. For example, the circle graph shown here clearly illustrates the comparative numbers of people emigrating from different countries between the years 1820 and 1859.

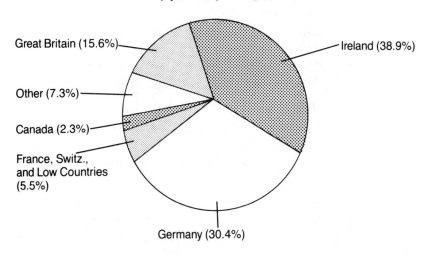

IMMIGRATION TO THE UNITED STATES 1820 – 1859
(by country of origin)

Great Britain (15.6%)

Ireland (38.9%)

Other (7.3%)

Canada (2.3%)

France, Switz.,
and Low Countries
(5.5%)

Germany (30.4%)

Total Number of Immigrants

1820 – 24	38,689
1825 – 29	89,813
1830 – 34	230,442
1835 – 39	307,939
1840 – 44	400,031
1845 – 49	1,027,306
1850 – 54	1,917,527
1855 – 59	897,027
total	4,908,774

Source: *Statistical Abstract of the United States*

Understanding Terms

31e. Be able to recognize and define the terms used in the subject you are studying.

Every subject has its own special terminology or vocabulary, that is, words that refer to specific materials, ideas, actions, or processes in that field. For example, in English class, you are expected to understand and use terms like *noun, verb, predicate* or to know what to do when you are told to *scan the meter of a poem.* In your science class, you may be asked to *prepare a suspension* or *calibrate your microscope.*

Look for *typographical clues* that an important term is being used. Many textbooks make it easy to find important terms by setting them off in boldfaced type, printing them in a second color, or using *italics* when they are introduced.

EXAMPLE   The small amount a person pays for [insurance] protection is called the *premium.* The large loss against which a person is insured is the *principal sum.* The contract that gives this kind of protection is an *insurance policy.*

Also look for key terms in (1) headings within a chapter, (2) words defined in footnotes or sidenotes, (3) study questions that ask you to define terms, and (4) listings in the glossary or index of a book.

You will not always find typographical clues. However, you should be able to identify important terms from the *context.* Look both for technical words and for words that are clearly being used in a special sense.

Notice how the five *basic elements* listed in the following example are clearly meant to be understood in the way they are used in literary criticism, even though they are not set off in italics or boldfaced type.

EXAMPLE   The novel and the short story make use of the same basic elements: plot, character, setting, point of view, and theme.

Understanding terms is essential to effective study. When you come across an unfamiliar term, look it up in the glossary or use the index to find where it was introduced and defined. Use the dictionary as well. Dictionary entries for words which have a technical as well as a common meaning may be labeled with a particular subject heading, such as *Law, Med.,* etc.

EXERCISE 3. Identifying Important Information.   Write complete answers for each of the following items.

1. List the words in the following sentence that you think are part of the terminology a student in a biology class would be expected to know.

   Mitotic division of chromosomes always results in daughter cells with chromosomes identical in both numbers and kind to each other and to the parent cell.

2. Look up the following terms in your dictionary, and copy the definition that explains how the term is used in the field given in parentheses.

   a. suspension (auto mechanics)   d. will (law)
   b. run (politics)   e. capital (accounting)
   c. dressing (medicine)

Recognizing Main Ideas

31f. Find the main ideas of the material being studied.

The main idea of a piece of writing is the most important point that the author wants to make. Sometimes the main idea is stated. Sometimes it is implied, or suggested.

(1) Main ideas may be stated.

The main idea of a piece of writing is usually stated as a complete sentence. For example, the main idea of a paragraph about toys may be: "People have played with toys since ancient times."

The following paragraph is from "The Ageless Appeal of Annie" by Bill Blackbeard. The topic is *Little Orphan Annie*. The main idea is "*Little Orphan Annie* was a popular comic strip when it began, and, under its new name, *Annie,* it remains popular today."

Cartoonist Harold Gray's "Little Orphan Annie" was a dynamic hit right from its shy beginning in just one newspaper, the *New York Daily News,* in 1924. During the comic's hey-day, it reached tens of millions of readers from the pages of over 500 American dailies from coast to coast. The strip survived Gray's death in 1968, a succession of other artists, and several years of reruns, only to emerge as popular as ever in its latest incarnation, "Annie," penned by veteran strip designer Leonard Starr and currently running in the nation's Sunday funnies.

(2) Main ideas may be implied.

Sometimes the main idea is implied, or suggested. You have to read closely, add up all the details, and state the main idea in your own words.

For example, in the following paragraph from "Tales About Tubs" by Eugene W. Dunlop, the main idea is implied.

Tomb pictures show that the ancient Egyptians preferred bathing in privacy to a plunge in the crocodile-infested Nile. In the *Odyssey* Homer tells of Grecian heroes enjoying hot baths. The Romans also enjoyed the bath, and their engineers built the largest bathing facilities in history. The Emperor Caracalla's establishment was six times the size of London's St. Paul's Cathedral and could serve almost 2,000 people at once. The baths of Diocletian had a capacity of over 3,000.

The topic of this paragraph is "baths." What does this paragraph tell you about baths? First, it tells you that the ancient Egyptians preferred baths. Second, it tells you that the ancient Greek heroes enjoyed baths. Third, it tells you that the Romans enjoyed baths so much that they built the largest baths in history. From these details the main idea is "People enjoyed baths thousands of years ago."

EXERCISE 4. Finding the Main Idea. Write the stated or implied main idea for each of the following paragraphs.

1

Codes and ciphers have changed the course of history. Many a famous battle has been won or lost through ciphers and codes. They have both caused and prevented wars. They have carried across frontiers many dangerous secrets. When broken, they have brought ruin to men and nations. They are used daily by every government in the world and are in more frequent use than most people realize.

JOHN LAFFIN

2

Your quiet breathing when you are sitting still makes 10 decibels of sound. Doctors are listening for the faint heart and lung sounds when they put a stethoscope to a patient's chest. In the wilderness the rustling leaves, the chirping birds, and scurrying animals make noise of 20 to 30 decibels. Two students who are sitting at opposite ends of a table in the school cafeteria will be unable to hear each other very well; the dishes banging, the talk and shouts and movements, make a background sound level of at least 63 decibels.

LUCY KAVALER

Recognizing and Remembering Details

31g. Be able to recognize and remember specific details.

In addition to main ideas, you will often be required to learn specific details such as dates, events, names of persons or works. At times, you will be expected to know exact details— the date on which the Declaration of Independence was signed or the name of the author of *Great Expectations*.

In other cases, you will be expected to show that you know the general context into which a detail fits. For example, you might have to show you know that the Declaration of Independence was signed at the beginning of the Revolutionary War instead of during the French and Indian War or that Dickens wrote novels, not poetry or music.

When you study, consider whether you will be asked about very specific details or whether you should concentrate on learning the more general, approximate facts that have to do with the way isolated details are related to one another. Of course, you often have to know both, but it is part of the job of studying and of answering to figure out which kind of specific information is important in a given situation.

EXERCISE 5. Classifying Specific Information. Number your paper 1–5. Read through the following questions that you might find in a textbook or test. For each, write *detail* if you feel the answer should provide very specific details and *approximate* if the answer draws on your memory of more generalized knowledge.

1. From what books did Indian children learn to read? What subjects were studied at Nalanda?
2. Put each of the following names or ideals in one of these six categories: literature, mathematics, science, philosophy, religion, or government.

Ajanata caves	*Bhagavad-Gita*
monism	civil service examinations

3. What reason does Madame Loisel give for needing a jewel to go with her dress?
4. Are all antibiotics made from mold?
5. Classify these artists as novelists, poets, or painters: Picasso, Steinbeck, Milton, Hemingway, Degas, Yeats.

Distinguishing Between Fact and Opinion

31h. Be able to tell the difference between fact and opinion.

Most of what you read and study contains both facts and opinions. You will find it necessary to distinguish between these two types of statements.

(1) A statement of fact contains information that can be proved true or false.

A statement of fact contains information about things that have happened in the past or are happening in the present. For example, here are three statements of fact.

John McEnroe is a tennis player.
Many people came to watch McEnroe play in the U.S. Open.
John McEnroe was born in 1959.

(2) A statement of opinion expresses a personal belief or attitude. It contains information that cannot be proved true or false.

Some statements of opinion predict the future; they contain information that cannot be proved true or false at the present. Others are about the past or present.

Bill Cosby is our best comedian.
There will never be a singer as magnificent as Beverly Sills.
Everyone knows that it is lovely to sit outside on a cool summer evening and listen to a Beethoven symphony.

Sometimes a statement of opinion contains words like "Everyone knows that" or "The truth is that" or "It's a fact that." Don't let these words mislead you into thinking that a statement of opinion is a statement of fact.

Remember also that not everything presented as a statement of fact is true or accurate. Be prepared to go to some reliable source to establish that a given statement is true. Among the common sources you might refer to are direct experience, an expert, a properly done experiment, well-established data or statistics, an encyclopedia, a dictionary, an almanac, or some other reliable reference work.

EXERCISE 6. Evaluating Facts and Opinions. Number your paper 1–5. After the proper number, write whether each of the following items is a fact or an opinion. If it is a fact, write some kind of evidence or source you could use to establish it (direct experience, encyclopedia, textbook, almanac, etc.).

1. The Great Pyramid of Giza consists of more than two million blocks of stone and is 450 feet (148 meters) high.
2. The many difficulties involved in its construction indicate that the Egyptian builders of the pyramid must have been skillful engineers.

3. Egypt was one of the world's greatest civilizations.
4. The Egyptians developed a number system based on *ten*.
5. Many Egyptians were buried with a copy of *The Book of the Dead*, a collection of hymns, prayers and magic chants.

Interpreting Nonliteral Statements

31i. Learn to recognize and interpret nonliteral statements.

What weapon would you use to kill an hour? How can the President take a complex issue such as tax policy into his own hands? How much gold was there, and where was it stored in the Golden Age of Greece?

Most people would recognize that all these questions are ridiculous. They know that to "kill an hour," "to take something into your own hands," and "Golden Age" are all figurative expressions in which one thing is expressed in terms of another.

Understanding figurative language involves a two-part process in which you first identify exactly what the two terms are and then figure out the meaning or the impression that is suggested by the relationship between them. To test whether or not you really do understand the expression, *paraphrase* it, that is, put it in your own words.

The comparison can be *explicit*. Clauses that begin with *like, as, such as, reminding one of* often signal a figurative expression. You are given the two elements being compared. But you must figure out for yourself exactly what the comparison suggests about the person, experience, or idea.

EXAMPLE   Tom answered all my questions quickly and easily, but even so I was *reminded of a well-trained dog* in a circus act. [The comparison makes it clear the speaker feels Tom was not giving sincere and spontaneous answers but had been told what to reply.]

In other cases, the comparison will be *implicit*. You will have to analyze the context. If the standard dictionary meaning, or denotation, of a word or phrase doesn't fit the context, see if there is a commonly accepted figurative meaning that would be suitable. Here are some common forms of figurative language and the questions that will help you to interpret each form.

1. *Extension of a specialized definition.* Ask yourself: What is the literal meaning and in what sense is it being generalized?

EXAMPLE   The governor's support from big business has eroded in the past year. [*Erode* is a geological term meaning "to wear away gradually by the forces of nature." It is often used figuratively to indicate a gradual loss.]

2. *Metaphorical expressions.* Ask the same question you ask about explicit comparisons: In what way can the two elements be understood as being alike?

EXAMPLE   Mrs. McCarty was the mortar that held the family together. [Comparing Mrs. McCarty to the cement that holds bricks together suggests that the family members though individual like bricks, are closely connected with each other.]

3. *Allusion.* Ask yourself: What is notable about the person, item, or event that is referred to and what kind of image does the association suggest?

EXAMPLE   I respect Mrs. Jones as a teacher because she never gives Mickey Mouse assignments. [Since Mickey Mouse cartoons are predictable and associated with young children, you should recognize that Mickey Mouse assignments make no serious demands on your intelligence or creativity.]

EXERCISE 7. Comprehending Nonliteral Statements.
Number your paper 1–5. After each number, identify the use of the italicized word or phrase as literal or figurative. Briefly paraphrase the sentences that have figurative expressions.

1. Kent *exploded* when he heard the money was lost.
2. Fortunately no one was hurt when the gas tank *exploded*.
3. Lil always *kept a tight rein* on her emotions.

4. Mona *mapped out* a strategy for getting Ben to the party.

5. The man decided *to take the injured bird in his own hands.*

Paraphrasing Poetry

31j. Learn to test whether or not you understand a poem by trying to paraphrase it in prose.

We have said that paraphrasing is an excellent strategy for testing your understanding of what you read in general. However, you may need practice to use this skill with poetry.

In a poem the main idea is almost always implied rather than stated directly so that you must repeatedly call on your ability to interpret figurative language. Follow this process.

1. *Identify the subject.* Read the poem, trying to identify the subject of the poem. Remember that the subject may be implied rather than stated outright. Often, the title offers some clue about the author's main theme.

2. *Identify central images and figurative language.* Read the poem several more times. Look for the central images and examples of figurative language. What do the images and expressions imply?

3. *Paraphrase the main point.* In your own words briefly state the main point of the poem, including an explanation of all central images.

Remember a paraphrase is a *restatement*—not an extended explanation or an expression of your reaction. Stick to what the poem says. However, since so much is implied in poetry, a paraphrase might end up slightly longer than the original poem.

EXAMPLE   WITH THE DOOR OPEN

Something I want to communicate to you,
I keep my door open between us.
I am unable to say it,
I am happy only
with the door open between us.

DAVID IGNATOW

1. The first line indicates the subject of the poem is communication.

2. The central image of the poem is an open door. The phrase *open door* suggests that there are no barriers; it is often used figuratively to indicate the willingness to talk freely, negotiate, or accept rather than to insist on scheduled, formal arrangements. However, the phrase *I am unable to say it* suggests that the speaker has trouble putting his feelings into words.

3. Paraphrase of "With the Door Open": The speaker wants the person to whom the poem is addressed to know that he is receptive to that person; even though the speaker has difficulty putting it in words, he is happy only when there are no barriers between them.

EXERCISE 8. Paraphrasing a Poem.   Read the following short poems and choose one you find interesting. Identify the subject and the central images or figurative expressions, and then write a paraphrase.

SEPARATION

Your absence has gone through me
Like a thread through a needle.
Everything I do is stitched with its color.

W. S. MERWIN

FIRE AND ICE

Some say the world will end in fire,
Some say in ice.
From what I've tasted of desire
I hold with those who favor fire.
But if it had to perish twice,
I think I know enough of hate
To say that for destruction ice
Is also great
And would suffice.

ROBERT FROST

Taking Notes

31k. Take clear, concise study notes.

The study notes that you take in class and for assigned reading are useful in reviewing what you have learned. The following tips will help you take good study notes.

1. Use sheets of paper, rather than note cards.
2. Set off the main subjects as headings. In a lecture, listen for an introductory sentence to a main topic. For example, "I am going to talk about three major themes we find in Wordsworth's poetry." In a textbook the headings are usually reliable subject indicators.
3. Do not go into great detail in your study notes. Outline what was said. Use single words or phrases to take down key ideas. Indent supporting points under these headings. Then indent each of the points discussed. If you do make note of some detail, paraphrase rather than quote word for word.
4. Take notes as you listen to a lecture. Make it a habit to review those notes sometime later the same day. Doing so helps fix the material in your mind. At the same time, you should still be able to remember and fill in points that you did not record adequately.
5. When you read through material for the first time, discipline yourself to read a section through and then note down the important points. Try to do so from memory rather than by looking back at the book. This practice will focus your attention.

Summarizing Study Material

31l. Be able to write a précis of reading material.

At times your teacher may ask you to do a *précis*, that is, a written summary of a reading assignment. In effect, the précis involves writing out the kind of information that your study notes should include. Thus, you may find that the process of writing a précis helps you digest and remember what you read better than study notes alone do. Writing a précis includes the following steps:

1. Read thoughtfully through the selection you are going to summarize.

2. Read the passage a second time; then list the major points of the selection in your own words. As a general rule, include one point for each full paragraph. (See information on main ideas on pages 42–45.) Do not mention supporting details or examples; also leave out introductory or concluding details that are not critical to the main point. Take advantage of the typographical clues in your textbooks—points included in headings or in boldfaced type should show up in the précis.

3. Write the précis. Use your own words and write full sentences. While your summary should be complete, it should also be brief. The usual rule is that a précis should be no more than one third the length of the original. Remember that a good précis summarizes what the passage said. It does not include your reaction.

Summarizing, or précis writing, involves critical thinking skills. You must analyze the material to decide what is important. You must decide if a detail is an essential supporting point or one that can be left out. It is challenging to write a précis that is complete and yet concise. Always check your précis against the original for accuracy, and be prepared to revise it.

Study the following précis of the material following rule 31k (page 778). Compare it with the original.

EXAMPLE PRÉCIS   Five points to keep in mind when taking study notes are (1) use sheets of paper rather than notecards; (2) include headings to indicate main points; (3) keep notes brief and in outline format; (4) take lecture notes while listening but review them later; (5) do reading notes after reading through the section once.

EXERCISE 9. Applying Study Skills. Use the following diagram and reading passage to complete this exercise.

MAYOR – COUNCIL PLAN OF CITY GOVERNMENT

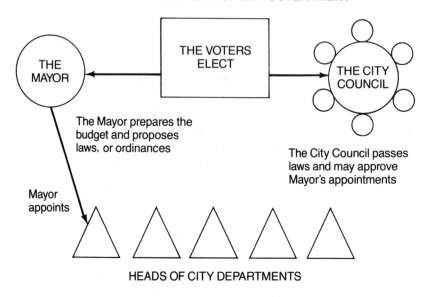

HEADS OF CITY DEPARTMENTS

MAYOR–COUNCIL GOVERNMENT

The oldest and most common form of city government is the **mayor-council plan.** The diagram shows the organization of this form of government. In this kind of government, the lawmaking body is called the **city council.** The chief executive of the city government is the **mayor,** who sees that city laws, or ordinances, are enforced. The mayor and members of the city council are elected by the voters of the city. Their term of office varies, but in most cases it is either two years or four years.

Under the mayor-council government, the city is divided in districts called **wards.** Each ward elects one member of the council. In some cities, though, the people elect several **council members-at-large.** That is, they are chosen by all the voters in the city. Almost all city councils have just one house.

City voters also elect other officials, including a treasurer, judges of the municipal courts, a city attorney, or solicitor, and tax assessors. Other officials, either elected or appointed, are the heads of departments for police, firefighting, traffic, water, welfare, parks and playgrounds, civil defense, housing, licenses, and purchasing.

1. How does the diagram show who is elected and who is appointed in the mayor-council plan of city government?
2. How does the diagram indicate that the mayor is one person while the city council has a number of members?
3. Write study notes for this passage.
4. Write a précis of the selection. It should be no more than sixty words.

Writing in Other Courses

31m. Use writing to explore topics and concepts in history or social studies.

Writing about topics and concepts from a content-area subject, such as social studies or history, can help you to understand the class better. The most common forms of writing in these subjects are research papers and reports (see pages 229–250). Sometimes, however, you can explore topics or illustrate concepts in social studies or history through other forms of writing.

One way to use writing in history or social studies is to keep a journal in which you record your reactions to concepts, events, and people you are studying. Using writing in this way enables you to discover your own thoughts and feelings about the course material. The reactions you record in your journal can also be a source of subjects to write about—a writer's notebook you develop in history or social studies, just as you might do in an English class (see pages 16–18). You can also use a journal to respond to specific questions your teacher gives you. Such questions will also enable you to explore the topics, concepts, events, and historical figures you are studying. For example, your history or social studies teacher might ask you to write about one of the following questions:

1. Compare the role of citizens in Athenian democracy with that of citizens in the Roman republic.

2. Describe three contributions of Roman culture to Western civilization.
3. Identify the significant causes of the French Revolution.
4. Trace the stages in the development of towns and cities during the middle ages.

By writing about questions like these, you will explore and think about the material you are studying—but from your own perspective, or point of view. This should enable you to develop a deeper understanding of the subject.

Another way to learn through writing in history or social studies is to use fictional forms, such as dialogues and personal narratives, but based on historical figures. In these cases, you will adopt the perspective, or point of view, of the particular historical figure; you will also apply your knowledge of the historical period in which the person lived.

You might, for example, write a dialogue between George Washington and Thomas Jefferson in which they discuss the ideals that the new American government should meet. You might also use the dialogue format for an interview with a historical figure. Here you can act as the interviewer, or you can have one historical figure interview another. For example, Eleanor Roosevelt could interview Mary Todd Lincoln about being a president's wife during wartime. (For more on writing dialogue, see pages 197–200.) You might also write a personal narrative in which you are a historical figure telling about a significant experience, such as President Harry S. Truman explaining his decision to drop the H-bomb on Hiroshima, Japan, in 1945. In each case, you will take a more personal look at history or social studies.

You can also "write to learn" in history or social studies by writing book reviews about literary works that deal with historical events, periods, or figures. For example, you might review *The Crucible,* Arthur Miller's play about the Salem witch trials, or Jim Bishop's retelling of Abraham Lincoln's assassination, *The Day Lincoln Was Shot.* This kind of writing combines two things: your knowledge of history and your evaluation of the writer's treatment of it. To write this kind of book review, you should begin by reviewing the facts about the event or figure in encyclopedias and other reference books. Then you should do a close reading of the literary work. Take careful notes about the sequence of events, the author's attitude about the work's topic, and any details that you find striking or interesting.

Your book review should answer any one of the following questions: How accurately does the literary work portray the historical figure, period, or event? How does this literary work add to your historical understanding? Does the author of the literary work present a biased view of the topic—and if so, how is the bias justified, or explained? When you write your book review, you should include supporting details from reference books and from the literary work to develop your ideas. (See also pages 250–255, on writing a book report on a novel.)

No matter what kind of writing you do in history or social studies, or in any other course, remember to apply your knowledge of description, narration, exposition, and persuasion (Chapters 3, 4, 5, and 6), as well as your knowledge of the structure and development of paragraphs and compositions (Chapters 2, 4, and 5). In addition, remember to apply your knowledge of the writing process (Chapter 1) to improve your writing in all your content-area classes.

EXERCISE 10. Writing in History or Social Studies. Following the steps in the writing process, prepare any one of the writing activities listed below.

1. Using any one of the questions on pages 781–782, or a question your teacher provides, prepare a journal entry about a topic you are currently studying in history or social studies.
2. Write a dialogue, an interview, or a personal narrative about at least one historical figure you are studying now.
3. Write a book review of a literary work about an historical period, figure, or event. In your review, answer any one of the questions on pages 781–782.

PREPARING FOR AND TAKING TESTS

Not all tests are the same. Some test memory; others involve critical thinking skills. In some tests, you must write exact, brief answers; in others you must write detailed answers. Learn the strategies that will help you study and perform well on each type.

Studying for Objective Tests

31n. Study for objective tests by identifying and reviewing the specific information that will be included.

When you study for objective tests, look through the study questions in your textbook, and review class notes to identify important terms or facts. Test yourself to see if you can remember the information in more than one form. For example, you may be responsible for knowing a number of important terms. List these terms. Then test yourself on how well you can define each one without looking at your book or notes. Next, ask someone to read the definitions to you, and see if you can remember the correct terms. Note which items you have difficulty with, and go over them again. If possible, review all the terms once more shortly before the actual test.

If your test will include labeling diagrams or a map, test yourself beforehand either by labeling a practice diagram that you have drawn or by covering over the labels and seeing if you can remember what they say. If problems of some sort will be included, do practice problems and then check your answers with the book.

Completing Objective Tests

31o. Learn the strategies that improve performance on the different kinds of objective tests.

Whether the test is multiple-choice, true-false, fill-in-the-blank, or short-answer identification, take time to preview the test. Skim rapidly through the test as soon as you get it. Note how many questions there are, and look for sections that seem especially easy or especially difficult. Then use that information to budget your time, that is, to figure out how much time you should spend on each part of the test.

Read each question carefully so you know exactly what is being asked, but do not spend too much time on any one question. If you have studied well, you will find that the first answer you think of is usually correct. If you are not at all sure about a question, make some kind of mark and go on to answer the items you do know. Go back to the difficult ones later. In addition, keep in mind these points about the different kinds of objective test questions.

1. *Multiple-choice questions.* In this kind of test you are asked to pick which of three or four choices best answers the question.

EXAMPLE   In the mayor-council plan of government, the voters do not elect (a) the president; (b) heads of the city departments; (c) the mayor; (d) members of the city council. [Usually one item will clearly be wrong. For example, *a* is clearly not correct since the president is not part of a city government. One or two choices will be *related* to the subject; at least one of these may seem possible, but it will not actually fit the question as it is asked. (Such choices might be too general, too specific, or related to another part of the subject.) For example, *c* and *d* are both part of the mayor-council plan and are related to voting. However, notice that the question is worded to ask which is *not* elected—look back at the diagram in Exercise 9 to confirm that *b* is the only correct answer.]

2. *True/false questions.* Pay close attention to the wording of true-false questions. Mark the statement false if any part of it is not true. Check yourself by mentally identifying these ways in which a true-false statement can be incorrect: (a) A true-false statement may identify one term or date with the wrong definition or fact. (b) A true-false statement may contain something that is wrong. (c) A true-false statement may join two terms that are not related as stated.

EXAMPLES   a. A noun is the part of speech that tells the action in a sentence. [While there is a part of speech that tells the action, it is a verb, not a noun.]

             b. An inch equals 3.14 centimeters. [Since an inch is equal to 2.54 centimeters, this statement is false.]

             c. All adverbs modify verbs and end in -*ly*. [It is true that all words that modify a verb and most that end in -*ly* are adverbs. However, words that modify an adjective can be adverbs as well; so too, words that do not end in -*ly* can act as adverbs. When a statement contains words like *all, never, always, only,* be sure there are no exceptions before you mark the statement true.]

3. *Fill-in-the-blank or short answer identifications.* If you are asked to fill in a term or to give an identification or definition of a given term, expect to use the terminology or facts that have been stressed in the textbook and in classroom discussion.

For example, if *cycle* was included in a list of items you are supposed to identify in a biology test, provide the definition that deals with life cycles, not the one related to two-wheeled motor vehicles.

Try to make your short answer specific rather than vague. For example, do not just identify *chlorophyll* as "a substance found in a plant"; show that you know its importance and function by answering, "a plant substance that makes photo-synthesis possible." However, if you are unsure of details, do put down a general answer rather than nothing at all.

EXERCISE 11. Applying Strategies For Taking Objective Tests.   Answer the following questions as study preparation for an objective test based on the material in this chapter.

1. Prepare a list of twelve key terms on which you might be tested.
2. Write two of each of the following kinds of objective test questions using the key terms you listed for item 1: multiple-choice; true-false; fill-in-the-blank; short-answer identification.

Preparing for Essay Tests

Essay Questions

Essay tests require you to think critically about material you have learned and to express your understanding of that material in an organized way.

The best way to prepare for such a test is to read your text or notes carefully; memorize main points and important details. Figure out a few possible questions on your own and write out the answers. Then check your answers against the material that has been presented in class and in the readings.

Writing answers to essay questions involves critical thinking. There is no single right answer, as there is in an objective test. However, the teacher may expect to see certain facts or points included in the answer. If, in studying, you gathered main points and significant details, you will be ready to write complete, well-supported answers.

Planning and Writing Essay Answers

31p. Plan your time and your answer for an essay question.

When you are handed an essay test, scan all of the questions. Note how many answers you are expected to write; if you can choose from several items, decide which one or ones you can best answer. Then plan how much time to spend on each answer, and follow your schedule.

In your schedule include three phases: prewriting, writing, and revising. Do not skip any of the stages.

As you begin, read the question carefully. Be certain about what is being asked. Remember, the question may include several tasks. For example, look at this essay question:

Define figurative language. Use examples from at least three poems included in this unit to illustrate some of the major kinds of figurative language.

You are being asked here to do three things: (1) to define figurative language; (2) to give examples of major types of figurative language; (3) to draw those examples from at least three different poems. An answer that fails to do any of these things will be an incomplete answer.

Make a few notes on scrap paper as you develop a thesis statement and briefly outline the main points to support it. This kind of planning allows you to concentrate on the *thinking* part of the process without having to worry about the *expression* at the same time.

Next, write your answer. Use your thesis statement as the introduction. Refer to your notes; make sure your answer follows the directions.

Often you do not have time to completely rewrite your answer, but do allow a minute or two to read over what you have written. Make sure you have a thesis statement and proofread for your spelling and punctuation.

If you do run out of time, it is often worthwhile to hand in your rough outline or notes. With these the teacher can see your answer is incomplete because you didn't have enough time, not because you didn't know the material.

Answering Varied Kinds of Essay Questions

31q. Be familiar with the common forms of essay questions and know what is expected in the answer for each type.

Essay questions on tests generally ask you to complete one of several tasks. Each of these tasks is expressed in a verb. Each task requires a special technique. The following list shows key verbs and the task each verb signals.

Essay Test Questions

TYPE OF TEST	KEY VERB(S)	TASK AND TECHNIQUE
Analysis	analyze	Take something apart to see how each part works
Comparison	compare	Point out likenesses *or* differences
Contrast	contrast	Point out differences

TYPE OF TEST	KEY VERB(S)	TASK AND TECHNIQUE
Comparison and contrast	compare and contrast	Point out similarities *and* differences
Description	describe	Give a picture in words
Development	develop, list, outline, present trace	List events, show development
Discussion	discuss	Examine in detail
Explanation	explain	Give reasons for something being the way it is
Illustration	demonstrate, illustrate, present, show	Provide examples to support a point
Interpretation	interpret	Give the meaning or significance of something

An essay answer contains a thesis statement that makes clear the task to be completed and the content and purpose of the answer. The answer develops the thesis statement by using details that do what the essay task requires. Some details will give a picture; some will give reasons; others will give the meaning or significance, etc.

EXAMPLE   Development question:
Show how events in his life influenced the development of Mr. Rochester's character.

Thesis statement:
We can understand the kind of man Mr. Rochester was when we trace the events in his life.

Developing details:
Your answer must include details about Mr. Rochester's character, the kind of man he was. For each character detail, you should include at least one event from his life that contributed to the development of that trait.

EXERCISE 12. Analyzing Essay Questions. For each of the following sample essay questions, identify the key words that state the specific task in the question. State briefly what you must do to answer the question. Also tell what points should be included in the thesis statement.

1. Compare the scoring system used in three different sports.

2. Show how the use of a third-person narrator helps create the sense of suspense in the short story "The Most Dangerous Game."

3. While many people consider comic books a waste of time, others claim that they are valuable in getting some poor readers involved, that they represent a legitimate popular art form, and that a collection can be a worthwhile economic investment. Present and defend your personal opinion about the value of comics, using specific examples.

4. List the BASIC commands that will program the computer to print your name on the screen five times; explain what each command tells the computer to do.

5. Both "Loveliest of Trees" and "I Wandered Lonely as a Cloud" express delight in nature. How are the speakers' attitudes toward nature similar? Are their attitudes different in any way? If so, how?

6. Trace the changes in the U.S. Constitution that affect the selection of the President.

7. Analyze the economic conditions that helped cause the Civil War. Include at least three factors.

8. Give the steps involved in making a bill become a law.

9. Compare the military ability of Alexander the Great and Julius Caesar. Refer to at least three specific battles.

10. There have been cockroaches since the days of the dinosaurs. Describe some of the characteristics that make this insect such a good survivor.

PART FIVE

SPEAKING AND LISTENING

CHAPTER 32

Speaking Before Groups

PRESENTING VARIOUS KINDS OF SPEECHES

Speaking before groups is easy if you have some training and experience. In this chapter you will learn how to handle some of the most common speech situations you will meet in school.

PREPARING A SPEECH

A good speech requires careful preparation. This section will guide you through the necessary steps in preparing a speech for delivery. Note that preparing a speech is in many ways like preparing a paragraph or a composition. Be sure to refer to the detailed suggestions for selecting and limiting a subject and organizing content in Chapter 1, pages 8–24.

32a. Choose an appropriate subject.

Sometimes the subject of your speech will be given to you, or you may be given a choice among several subjects. If the choice of subject is left to you, you should be guided by two principles, each similar to considerations affecting your choice of subjects for a paragraph or composition.

(1) Choose a subject that you know well and that you find interesting.

When you talk from firsthand experience, from observation, or from research, you are not at a loss for ideas, you speak fluently, and you convey enthusiasm. Your listeners will be attentive because they are aware that you know what you are talking about and that you are interested in the subject. For example, if you have gone on an overnight hike, tell about your experiences. Suppose you volunteer at a local hospital. Your experience has helped you decide to become a doctor. Preparing a talk about medical careers will certainly be interesting to you.

(2) Choose a subject that is interesting to you and your audience.

Be sure to consider the needs, background, and interests of your audience when you chose a subject. For example, medical careers can be interesting to students because students are often concerned about choosing an occupation. If your audience is made up of adults, you might change your focus—emphasizing, for example, your local hospital's need for new doctors.

EXERCISE 1. Choosing a Subject for a Speech. List five subjects that you feel able to speak about because of your experience. In a sentence or two for each, write what your experience is.

EXAMPLE How to Collect Stamps. My grandmother has taught me how to sort, identify, and store stamps.

32b. Limit your subject so that it can be adequately treated in your speech and so that it reflects a definite purpose.

When preparing a speech, as in preparing a composition or paragraph, you should also be concerned with limiting your subject. For example, it would be difficult to prepare a speech on a broad subject like "automobiles," because there is a world of ideas to discuss on this subject. Instead, you must limit, or narrow, this broad subject to one aspect—perhaps "my experiences with an antique car club" or "simple directions for changing a flat tire." The same principles writers use for analyzing a subject, or dividing it into its smaller parts, can help you to narrow a subject into a *topic* for your speech. Refer to pages 8–14 of Chapter 1 for ideas on developing topics.

Another way in which you should limit your subject is by determining a definite purpose for your speech. Know beforehand *why* you are speaking. Your purpose may be to inform, to convince, to entertain, or to move to action.

Once you determine your purpose, always keep it in mind when preparing your talk. Suppose, for example, that you are going to speak to your English class about automobiles. What you say depends largely on your purpose—that is, your purpose determines how you will limit the subject to a topic. For example, if your purpose is *to inform,* you may discuss what a buyer should keep in mind before purchasing a secondhand car. On the other hand, if your purpose is *to entertain,* you may talk about a travel adventure you have had. If your purpose is *to move to action,* you may suggest ways to conserve gasoline.

EXERCISE 2. Developing a Topic for Your Speech.   Suppose you were asked to speak to your classmates on one of the following subjects. Decide on a purpose for your talk, then limit the subject to three topics. For each topic you develop, also list three points your talk will cover.

1. Baseball
2. Biking
3. School regulations
4. Earning money
5. My neighborhood

32c. Gather material for your speech.

After you have settled on your topic and purpose, your next step is to gather material. Follow these steps:

1. *Explore your own background.* You may know more about your subject than you think. Examine your information and ideas. What do they suggest for further exploration? The infor-

mation-gathering strategies used in the writing process will also be helpful here. (See pages 14–21 of Chapter 1.)

2. *Observe.* Watch and listen for ideas or material related to your topic. You may learn from conversations, newspapers, or television programs.

3. *Interview.* Ask someone who knows a great deal about your topic to give you additional information.

4. *Read.* When you have completed the preceding three steps, it is time to use the library. Consult encyclopedia articles, books, and magazines. Take notes for easy reference.[1]

5. *Reflect.* Allow ample time to think about your speech, adding and discarding ideas. Jot down new thoughts as they occur to you. This kind of preparation is a slow process, but it results in thorough knowledge of your subject and will contribute to self-confidence as you talk.

EXERCISE 3. Gathering Material for Your Speech. Select a topic for a three-minute talk to your class. List the sources of information you will consult, using the following headings:

1. Your own experience (describe it)
2. Situations you may observe for information
3. People you are going to interview, and questions you will ask them
4. Books and periodicals (name of the book, magazine, or newspaper, title of chapter or article, page number)

Use one of the following topics, or choose one of your own.

1. How to earn money
2. Why study history?
3. The man or woman I most admire
4. The best vacation in the world
5. Protect the whales!

32d. Prepare an outline for your talk.

---

[1] See instructions on taking notes in Chapter 7, pages 221–222.

Your final step is to arrange the material you have gathered for your speech. If you have jotted down your notes on index cards with each idea on a separate card, you can easily put them in sequence. Lay aside those that do not seem to fit logically into your plan. If it seems that your speech will be too long for the time allowed, decide which sections could be excluded. Remove those cards and review your organization.

Do not try to write out your speech word for word. Instead, prepare an outline—just as you might do in writing a composition or paragraph—to help you arrive at the best arrangement of main and supporting ideas. Preparing an outline can also help to fix these ideas in your memory. Later you can develop the wording of your speech from this outline.[1]

An outline for a short speech should usually cover only one side of a page and should include only your main points. The following outline is a good example.

Model Outline

TRAINING A DOG

Purpose: To inform
 I. The importance of training
   A. Value to dog
   B. Value to owner
 II. Basic training
   A. Housebreaking
   B. Walking on a leash
   C. Responding to owner's call
 III. Advanced training
   A. Further training in obedience
   B. Training for hunting
 IV. Things to avoid
   A. Coddling
   B. Overfeeding

EXERCISE 4. Preparing an Outline for Your Speech. Using the topic and the sources you chose for Exercise 3, prepare an outline for a three-minute speech.

[1] For a full discussion of outlining, see pages 128–130.

32e. Make a strong introduction and conclusion.

Prepare your introduction carefully. A good speaker catches the audience's attention at the very beginning with something that will pique their interest. Begin with an unusual fact or observation, a question, or even an exaggeration; then develop your topic. For specific suggestions about writing introductory paragraphs, see pages 134–135 of Chapter 4.

EXAMPLES State champions! Is that too wild a dream for our baseball team this year?
Boxing, button collecting, bookbinding, and beetles—all these are hobbies that people enjoy. But I'm here to speak in praise of bowling.

A common problem for speakers is knowing how to stop. They often drift to a halt weakly like a motorboat that has run out of gas. The conclusion is your last chance to drive home main ideas, so you should conclude by summarizing your major points. For further help, see pages 139–140 of Chapter 4.

EXAMPLES Our baseball team should have a good season. Most of last year's players are back; we have some promising newcomers; the pitching staff is strong; and we have the best coach in Staunton County.
If you're looking for a hobby, take up bowling. It's fun because you can join the bowling club. It's inexpensive because the local alley has a low rate for students. You may even become a champion!

DELIVERING A SPEECH

If you have gone through the preparatory steps, you are almost ready to deliver your speech.

32f. Prepare for delivering a speech.

Probably you feel nervous before speaking to a group. Nervousness is only a sign that your body is keyed for action. Experienced performers often admit that they are tense before stepping on the stage, but once they begin, the nervousness disappears. Just guard against *excessive* nervousness.

Here are some practical suggestions for delivering a speech.

1. *Know your topic and audience thoroughly.* Begin your preparation well in advance. Mull over your topic, talk about it with your parents and friends, and read as much as you can about it. Also think about the needs and interests of your particular audience. When you know your material and audience thoroughly, you will gain self-confidence.

2. *Practice.* Rehearse your talk aloud, preferably before a full-length mirror. Do not try to memorize the speech. (You may, however, memorize the first and last sentences so that you can start smoothly and finish gracefully.)

3. *Keep your purpose in mind.* Think of what you want your listeners to believe, feel, or do. Concentrate on *why* you are speaking.

4. *Relax.* Yawn, breathe deeply, and let yourself go limp for a moment or two before you face your audience. These actions reduce tension.

Nonverbal Communication

Body movements and gestures are types of nonverbal communication. They are often used during a speech. For example, if you are expressing doubt, you might shrug your shoulders.

32g. Use nonverbal communication effectively.

When speaking, look at your audience. Eye contact can do two important things: (1) It can hold your audience's attention and (2) it can tell you the audience's reaction to your talk.

Keep your gestures under control. A good speaker uses gestures to emphasize words. Gestures can show anger, surprise, disgust, and many other feelings. Exaggerated gestures, however, only distract an audience. A nervous speaker might gesture uncontrollably. Since audiences read gestures as they listen to words, choose gestures with care.

Pause between parts of your speech. Short pauses during your talk can relieve tension and signal your audience that a new topic is about to begin.

EXERCISE 5. Delivering Your Speech. Deliver the three-minute speech for which you prepared in Exercises 3 and 4.

Pronunciation and Enunciation

Learn to use standard pronunciation and to enunciate words correctly. These skills will be an asset in all your speaking.

32h. Learn to pronounce words correctly.

(1) Listen to good speakers.

Radio and television announcers, public speakers, actors and actresses, and teachers are generally good models to imitate in pronunciation.

(2) Refer to the dictionary.

Always use a dictionary to check the pronunciation of unfamiliar words.

EXERCISE 6. Using the Dictionary to Learn the Pronunciation of Words. With the aid of a dictionary, learn the pronunciation of the following words.

admirable	corps	finale	laboratory
ally	coupon	finance	particular
alternate	decade	formerly	penalize
champion	faucet	hospitable	recipe
column	February	influence	secretive
comfortable	final	interesting	usually

EXERCISE 7. Using Standard Pronunciation in Sentences. Write ten sentences using words in Exercise 6. Try saying the sentences casually as you would in conversation, but be sure you use standard pronunciation.

EXAMPLE   Did the official penalize the champion?

(3) Do not omit sounds or syllables.

Speakers sometimes omit essential sounds. Pronounce each of the following words with particular attention to the sound represented by the boldfaced letter:

accept	length	probably
asked	library	recognize
exactly	picture	strength

Be sure to pronounce the sound of *h* in these words:

huge	humane	humid
human	humble	humor

Be careful not to leave out a syllable when you use these words in public speaking.

accidentally	electric	history
actually	family	jewel
average	finally	mathematics
champion	generally	memory
chocolate	geography	mystery
company	giant	poetry
cruel	grocery	suppose

EXERCISE 8. *Oral Drill*. Pronouncing Words in Sentences Correctly. Read the following sentences aloud, making sure you pronounce each word correctly.

1. Poetry is no longer a mystery to me.
2. History and geography are both concerned with humanity.
3. I finally went to the library on Saturday.
4. Bill generally whistles while he does mathematics.
5. This electric cord is exactly nine feet in length.
6. That giant dog has great strength.
7. The champion did not see the humorous picture.
8. Thank you; I shall accept your offer of chocolate.

9. I suppose Mel upset the vase accidentally.
10. What is the average length of your swims?

(4) Do not add sounds or syllables.

Study the following words to be sure you do not add a syllable or a sound when you pronounce them.

athlete	grievous	lightning
burglar	hindrance	translate
chimney	laundry	umbrella

(5) Do not transpose sounds.

There are some words in which sounds are often transposed. Speakers may say, for example, *calvary* for *cavalry, modren* for *modern*. Be careful of the following:

cavalry	performance	poinsettia
hundred	perspiration	prescription
irrelevant	modern	tragedy

EXERCISE 9. *Oral Drill.* Pronouncing Words in Sentences Correctly.
Read the following sentences aloud, making sure you pronounce each word correctly.

1. That elm tree must have been blown down in the gale.
2. The lightning seemed to touch the chimney.
3. The Colemans have four modern paintings for sale.
4. Paula hopes to make a name for herself in the realm of music.
5. Slight stature is no hindrance to some athletes.
6. These hundred bales of cotton came from Mississippi.
7. The burglar must have come down the fire escape.
8. Can you draw any ideas from Shakespeare's tragedy?
9. Maggie's performance makes her a prodigy.
10. The horse cavalry has grown irrelevant in warfare.

32i. Improve your enunciation by sounding your words clearly.

To enunciate means to speak clearly and distinctly. To enunciate clearly, you must move your lips, tongue, and jaw. Practice nonsense phrases and sentences such as the following ones to develop clear enunciation.

Betty Botta bought a bit of butter.
"But," said Bet, "this butter's bitter.
If I put it in my batter,
It will make my batter bitter."

Prunes and prisms, prunes and prisms.

The big black bug bit the big black bear.

Truly rural, truly rural.

When speaking, be careful not to link each sentence with the one before by saying *and*. At the end of each sentence, stop! Begin each new sentence cleanly.

Another common fault is the use of *uh* between words or sentences. Avoid asking *you know?* at the ends of sentences.

EXERCISE 10. Pronouncing Words Ending in -ng. People often substitute *n'* for *ng*, as, for example, *swimmin'* for *swimming*. List twenty words ending in *-ng*, and check your pronunciation of each word.

EXERCISE 11. *Oral Drill.* Pronouncing Final Consonant Combinations. The final consonant combinations in the following words are difficult to pronounce. Practice until you can say each word clearly and easily.

1. width	7. lengths	13. twelfths	19. myths
2. hundredth	8. respects	14. folds	20. accepts
3. lifts	9. acts	15. builds	21. depths
4. shifts	10. facts	16. adjusts	22. precincts
5. crafts	11. mists	17. desks	23. asks
6. hyacinths	12. fifths	18. youths	24. tenths

EXERCISE 12. *Oral Drill.* Pronouncing Words Correctly. Practice saying the following pairs of words, being careful not to substitute *d* for *t,* or *t* for *th*.

1. riding	writing	6. true	through
2. medal	metal	7. taught	thought
3. pedal	petal	8. boat	both
4. madder	matter	9. tent	tenth
5. biding	biting	10. tree	three

KINDS OF SPEAKING SITUATIONS

The pages that follow describe three kinds of speaking assignments you should be prepared to fulfill.

Talking About an Experience or Telling a Story

Beginning speakers are often asked to speak about a personal experience or tell an interesting story. You should learn to do this smoothly and entertainingly. Preparing to tell a story is similar to preparing to write a story. Refer to the detailed suggestions for planning and developing a story in Chapter 6.

32j. Relate experiences and stories by using dramatic effects.

(1) Begin with action.

Arouse the interest and curiosity of your audience. Start in the middle of things and let your listeners fill in the background. Read the following examples of openings.

1

When I awoke one night in camp and found a snake coiled at the foot of my bed, I was a bit upset.

2

I did not stop to think when I saw smoke pouring out of the window of my neighbor's house. I rushed to the phone and shouted, "I want to report a fire!"

(2) Use direct conversation.

The exact words of a speaker are more interesting and lively than an indirect statement. Compare these two versions of the same incident.

In March 1775, Patrick Henry stood before the Virginia Legislature. He said he would rather die than live under British rule. His speech is one of the most famous in American history.

In March 1775, Patrick Henry stood before the Virginia Legislature and delivered these ringing words: "Is life so dear, or peace so sweet, as to be purchased at the price of chains and slavery? . . . I know not what course others may take, but as for me, give me liberty or give me death!" Patrick Henry's call to battle is one of the most famous speeches in American history.

(3) Maintain suspense.

Include details and episodes that keep your listeners in suspense. Lead to a climax. Do not reveal the ending too soon. See pages 204–207 in Chapter 6 for additional information on developing action and conflict.

(4) Use action-packed verbs.

A good storyteller chooses specific verbs that help a listener to see, feel, and hear.

GENERAL   Alice walked into the room.
SPECIFIC   Alice strolled [limped, dashed] into the room.

EXERCISE 13. Relating an Unusual Experience. Briefly relate an unusual experience you have had or have heard about. It may be exciting, amusing, or both, but the incident or its outcome should be unusual. Be sure you begin with action, use conversation and specific verbs, and maintain suspense.

EXERCISE 14. Relating an Incident in the Life of a Famous Person. Relate an unusual incident in the life of a famous man or woman. Use the library to get your facts; then retell the incident in your own words. Remember to arouse the interest and curiosity of your audience. The following are suggestions.

1. Barbara Jordan
2. Amelia Earhart
3. Martin Luther King, Jr.
4. Chris Evert Lloyd
5. Thomas Edison
6. N. Scott Momaday
7. Marie Curie
8. Muhammad Ali
9. John F. Kennedy
10. Sen. John Glenn

Talking About Current Events

Current happenings of local, state, national, or international significance are suitable subjects for talks before groups. So, too, are events in the fields of business, science, music, art, sports, education, and literature.

32k. Choose current events to talk about that are important to you and your audience.

Your talk should be more than a restatement of a news item. It should express a fresh and original viewpoint—your own. A current-events talk may be divided into two parts: (1) a statement of the facts and (2) an interpretation of the facts.

Where can you obtain the facts? Accounts in reputable newspapers or news magazines provide a source of material. So do radio and television broadcasts. For background information, consult histories, encyclopedias, and atlases.

You cannot expect, of course, to interpret fully all of the complex events of our complex world. When you select a current event to talk about, keep the following principles in mind.

(1) Limit your topic.

Choose a limited topic that has some significance for you and your listeners and can be covered well in a short speech.

TOO BROAD	The energy crisis
SUITABLE	How a midwestern town used solar energy
TOO BROAD	Forest conservation
SUITABLE	Congress votes for six new national parks

(2) Choose a topic about which you can talk intelligently.

Many current happenings are so involved and so puzzling that there are honest differences of opinion about them. Thorough study often leaves one uncertain about what to think of an event. Do not feel that you *must* express an original opinion about your topic if you do not have one. Instead, show that you have thought about the event—and share some of your thoughts.

For example, a student may report on a speech in favor of preserving a local wilderness area. Without giving an opinion, the student can raise some questions about the issue: Is it valuable for use by the public? How would it be protected? The report will be a stimulating one even though personal "interpretation" has been in the form of questions. For further help about discussing an opinion, see pages 168–170 and pages 772–773.

EXERCISE 15. Delivering a Talk on a Current Event. Deliver a three-minute talk on an important current event. Prepare an outline to guide you when speaking.

Talking About Books, Movies, and Television Shows

Reporting on books and dramatic programs helps to sharpen your own appreciation of them and gives your listeners ideas and suggestions for their own entertainment.

32l. Make a report on a book, movie, or television program by describing and evaluating your subject.

Your purpose in a book report is to tell enough about the book so that your listeners may decide whether they want to read it. A book report includes at least two elements: (1) a description of the plot or contents and (2) your evaluation.

Always remember to begin a report or review by giving the title and author.

When discussing fiction or drama, do not reveal the entire plot, because you may give away the ending for your audience. Tell just enough to build interest. For example, you may describe an exciting or amusing incident or scene.

Also describe the appearance and the personality traits of the main characters. Show how they act under certain circumstances and how they change during the story. Include some of the following topics in your report. Do not try to discuss them all.

1. Setting (time and place)
2. Climax
3. Style (language, tone or attitude, narrative or descriptive detail)
4. Humor (Illustrate by reading a few paragraphs aloud.)
5. An incident that reveals character
6. A brief account of the author's life
7. The theme

Your listeners will want to hear your opinion of the book, movie, or television show. Do not be satisfied with a statement such as, "I enjoyed it immensely." Explain why you found it interesting. Was it because of the style, plot, language, or setting?

In reporting on nonfiction, include the title and author and consider topics such as the following:

1. Scope (What are the main topics?)
2. Style (Are the explanations interesting? Clear?)
3. Usefulness (What useful information have you learned from reading it? Discuss an event, discovery, problem, or topic in detail.)

EXERCISE 16. Delivering a Report on a Book. Read and report orally to your class on a novel, biography, drama, or work of nonfiction that your teacher has approved in advance. Prepare an outline to guide you when speaking.

EXERCISE 17. Delivering a Review of a Movie or a Television Play. Orally review a good movie or television play that you have recently seen. Prepare an outline to guide you when speaking.

CHAPTER 33

Listening

SHARPENING LISTENING SKILLS

If you are an average student, you spend about 65 percent of your day listening. You listen more than you speak, you speak more than you read, and you read more than you write. By learning to listen more effectively, you can improve your performance at school and in a career.

PURPOSEFUL LISTENING

Know why you are listening and always keep your purpose in mind. Are you listening to become informed, to understand and follow directions, or to form a judgment?

33a. Keep in mind your purpose for listening.

(1) Listen to gain information.

Forgetting sets in immediately after learning. To retain the important parts of what you hear, pay close attention to what is said and review it immediately.

EXERCISE 1. Listening to Gain Information. Compose five questions similar to those that follow. Read them aloud, pausing about five seconds after each question to allow your classmates time to jot down their answers. Have your classmates check their answers to determine how accurately they listened.

1. In the series of numbers *7—2—5—4—3*, the fourth number is ——— .
2. In this list, *in—on—up—at—of,* the third word is ——— .
3. In the list of words *and—off—but—for—how,* the word beginning with *o* is ——— .
4. In the announcement "Send your entries together with 25¢ to Music Contest, Post Office Box 119, New York, N.Y. 10006," the post office box number is ——— .
5. In the statement "Ed and Linda will make the campfire, Bea and Paula will set up the tent, and Charlie will cook the food," what is Bea's job?

(2) Listen carefully to instructions.

As you listen to instructions, follow these guidelines:

    a. Ask questions if you do not understand something.
    b. Take notes if the instructions are long or complicated or if they are to be carried out at some later time.
    c. Do not let your attention wander; you may miss an essential detail.

EXERCISE 2. Listening Carefully to Instructions. Explain how to do or make something, taking care that each step of the process is in correct order. Give your classmates a chance to ask questions before calling on them to repeat your instructions.

33b. Listen carefully during discussions.

Give each speaker in a discussion your full attention. If someone asks you a question, be sure you understand the question exactly before giving an answer. Rephrase the question in your own words or ask the speaker to repeat the question if you are not sure you understand it.

Sometimes during a discussion a question may come into your mind as you listen. Be sure the speaker has not already answered your question or is not about to answer it.

EXERCISE 3. Listening Carefully During Discussions. Invite one of your classmates to lead a group discussion. This leader will begin the discussion by giving a short oral report. (See page 796 for a list of possible topics.) Each member of the class will then ask the leader one question. Be careful not to repeat questions or to ask something not related to the talk.

LISTENING TO SPEECHES

During speeches, a good listener uses special skills to remember and evaluate the speech.

33c. Listen accurately to speeches.

There is no point in listening if you fail to understand the speaker's message. Listen for important clues in a speech.

(1) Notice the structure of a speech or lecture.

A good speaker prepares an outline of a formal speech and sticks to this plan. A good listener can discern the structure of a speech by asking such questions as these:

    a. What is the speaker's topic?
    b. What are the main points?
    c. What facts are offered as proof?
    d. What does the speaker want me to feel, believe, or do?

Make a mental outline as you listen, or jot down notes in the form of an outline to help you follow the speaker's main points and details.

(2) Listen for transitional words, phrases, and sentences.

A speaker will sometimes give an audience clues by telling in the introduction what the main points will be, by signaling them with transitional devices, and by summarizing them.

MAIN POINTS   I want to speak to you about George Washington as a surveyor, soldier, and President.
There are three reasons why I am opposed to increasing our membership dues this year.

TRANSITIONAL   Next . . .
DEVICES   In the second place . . .
In conclusion . . .
Finally . . .

SUMMARIES   A high-school education, therefore, is necessary if you want to lead a satisfying and useful life.
Consequently, I was thankful that I had been trained to help heart attack victims.

(3) Pay attention to nonverbal clues.

A speaker may communicate with unspoken, or nonverbal, messages such as posture, gestures, and facial expressions. Do gestures mark the main points? Does a shrug indicate details that can be forgotten?

EXERCISE 4. Understanding the Structure of Speeches.

Borrow a book of speeches from the library. Ask a teacher or a classmate to read a short speech from it. The rest of the class should note the structure of the speech, making a rough outline as they listen. When the outlines are compared, how closely do they resemble one another? Analyze the ways in which students were guided (or perhaps misled) to perceive the structure of the speech.

33d. Evaluate what you hear in speeches.

As a listener, always think carefully about what you are hearing.

(1) Distinguish main ideas from facts and other details.

Facts and other details are important as a foundation for ideas. If you try to recall all the facts a speaker mentions, however, you may miss the main point.

What is the main idea in the following paragraph?

> Cigarette smoking produces many harmful effects and shortens life. For almost four years the American Cancer Society studied approximately 200,000 men between the ages of fifty and sixty-nine. In that time 7,316 of the regular cigarette smokers died. During the same time 4,651 nonsmokers of the same age died. The difference of 2,665 can be regarded as the number of excess deaths associated with smoking. Most of the excess deaths resulted from coronary-artery disease. Some were caused by lung cancer and others by diseases of the arteries, bladder, and liver. The death rate from all causes was higher among smokers than nonsmokers.

EXERCISE 5. Listening for the Main Idea of a Paragraph.
Compose a paragraph that states facts and other details to prove a point. (See Chapter 3 for help in writing this type of paragraph.) Read your paragraph aloud and ask your classmates to recall the main idea.

(2) Distinguish facts from opinions.

A fact is a statement about something that actually happened or that exists. Facts can be proved to be true by making personal observations, referring to experts, or using reference books. An opinion cannot be proved true; it represents someone's belief or judgment. Of the following statements, which are facts and which are opinions?

> Water boils at 100° Celsius.
> Everyone should study a foreign language.
> To find the area of a rectangle, multiply the length by the width.
> The opening of the Panama Canal was the most important event in history.
> My political party has the better candidate.

EXERCISE 6. Distinguishing Between Facts and Opinions in a Paragraph. Analyze the following paragraph. On a separate piece of paper, list which ideas are facts and which are opinions.

1. The 1920's were the years of the "Harlem Renaissance," when black writers, poets, and performers captured the mood and imagination of the entire nation. 2. The best poet of this age was Langston Hughes, who wrote of the joys, sorrows, and hopes of black Americans. 3. The most famous performer was Bessie Smith, the blues singer, who recorded hundreds of memorable songs.

(3) Listen for propaganda devices.

Sometimes speakers attempt to persuade listeners by using propaganda devices such as the following:

Name-calling. When a speaker attempts to defeat an opponent by unfair personal attacks, do not believe what you hear until the person under attack has had a full opportunity to reply or until you have examined the evidence.

Slogans. Slogans are catchy and easily remembered; however, they oversimplify by reducing a chain of arguments to a few words. Sometimes slogans can be dangerous. Accept a slogan only after you have thought about it carefully.

EXAMPLES   "Ask not what your country can do for you, but what you can do for your country."
                                              —JOHN F. KENNEDY
                America, the beautiful.
                Peace at any price.

The testimonial. Well-known personalities are often used to persuade you to vote a certain way, buy a certain product, or adopt a certain belief. Ask yourself: Is the speaker an authority in the field? Is the speaker unbiased? Knowing something about the speaker's background and reputation will help you judge the value of any testimonial.

The bandwagon. Most people like to do what others do and believe as others believe. Propagandists know and capitalize on this human characteristic. You need willpower and the ability to think for yourself to resist hopping on the bandwagon.

EXERCISE 7. Evaluating Propaganda Devices in the Media. Find an example of each of the preceding propaganda devices. You may use radio and television commercials. For each example, tell how an alert listener should respond.

INDEX

Index

INDEX

819

with intervening phrase, 476
words stating amount, 486
Ain't, 559
All, any, most, none, some, 478–79
All ready, already, 694
All right, 694
All the farther, all the faster, 559
All together, altogether, 694
Allusion, 775
Almanacs, 725
Alternating method of comparison or
contrast, 89
Among, between, 560–61
An, a, 559
And etc., 560
Anglo-Saxon, 279–80
Antonyms in dictionaries, 739
Any, all, most, none, some, 478–79
Anywheres, 560
Apostrophe, 655–70
diagnostic test, 655–57
plurals of letters, numbers, signs,
words, 668
possessive case, 657–65
rules for using, 655–70
summary chart of possessives, 660
to form plural possessives, 658
to form singular possessives, 657
unnecessary with personal pronouns,
660–61
with contractions, 666
Appositive
defined, 442
diagraming, 443
punctuating with commas, 442, 612
Appositive phrase
as sentence fragment, 307
combining sentences by using, 318
defined, 442
diagnostic test, 416–18
punctuating with commas, 442, 612
Argument
in a persuasive composition, 171–74
in a persuasive paragraph, 96–97
Article
defined, 351
indefinite, 559
As, like, 566
As if, like, as though, 566
At, 560
Atlases, 724
Attitude, writer's toward subject, 11–12
Audience
choosing an appropriate subject for,
10

for a book report, 250
for a letter to the editor, 156
for a paragraph, 63–64
for a persuasive composition, 169
for a short story, 188
for a summary, 225–26
for an expository composition, 122
how audience affects writing, 63–64
identifying, 5–7
Author card, 715
Auxiliary verb = Helping verb

B

Bad, comparison of, 543
Bandwagon appeal, 98
Bartlett's *Familiar Quotations*, 725
Be, forms of, 356
Begin, principal parts, 499
Beside, besides, 560
Between, among, 560–61
Biblical chapter and verse, using colons
to separate, 633
Bibliography (Works Cited)
MLA style, 240–42, 244–45
model, for research report, 249
working bibliography, 233–34
Biographical information in dictionar-
ies, 739–40
Biographical reference books, 723–24
Biography, classification of in library,
713
Block method of comparison or con-
trast, 89
Blow, principal parts, 499
Body of a business letter, 260
Book report, 250–55
audience and purpose, 250
developing a working plan, 251–52
evaluating, 252–53
guidelines for evaluating, 253
model book report, 253–55
prewriting steps, 250–52
reading the novel, 251
revising, 252–53
taking notes, 251
writing a first draft, 252
Books, speaking about, 807–808
Books. *See* Library
Both, few, many, several, 478
Brainstorming
for expository composition, 117
to gather information for writing,
18–19

D

INDEX

F

G

Q

INDEX

Y